THE COMP SOLUTION

Every 4LTR Press solution includes:

Visually Engaging Textbook + **Online Study Tools** + **Tear-Out Resource Cards** + **Interactive eBook**

STUDENT RESOURCES:

- Interactive eBook
- Online Handbook
- Auto-Graded Quizzes
- Flashcards
- Writing Tutorials
- Grammar Podcasts
- Sample Papers
- Videos
- Portable Resource Cards

Students sign in at **www.cengagebrain.com**

INSTRUCTOR RESOURCES:

- All Student Resources
- Engagement Tracker
- First Day of Class Instructions
- LMS Integration
- Instructor's Manual
- Test Bank
- PowerPoint® Slides
- Instructor Prep Cards

Instructors sign in at **www.cengage.com/login**

"I really like how the book is set up...I love the Resource Cards, they are a concise way to reference important information."

– Kristen Keesee, student, *Boston University*

Engagement Tracker launches, giving faculty a window into student usage of digital tools.

4LTR Press adds eBooks in response to a 10% uptick in digital learning preferences.

AUGUST 2010

NOVEMBER 2010

1 out of every 3 (1,400) schools has adopted a 4LTR Press solution.

750,000 students are IN.

Third party research confirms that 4LTR Press digital solutions improve retention and outcomes.

IN 2011

60 unique solutions across multiple course areas validates the 4LTR Press concept.

CourseMate

Students access the 4LTR Press Web site at 4x's the industry average.

APRIL 2011

1 out of every 2 (2,000) schools has a 4LTR Press adoption.

IN 2011

2,000

AUGUST 2011

Over 1 million students are IN.

We're always evolving. Join the 4LTR Press In-Crowd on Facebook at www.facebook.com/4ltrpress

2012 AND BEYOND

WADSWORTH
CENGAGE Learning

***COMP*, Second Edition**
Randall VanderMey, Verne Meyer, John Van Rys,
Pat Sebranek

Senior Publisher: Lyn Uhl

Publisher: Monica Eckman

Acquiring Sponsoring Editor: Margaret Leslie

Senior Development Editors: Leslie Taggart, Joanne Butler

Assistant Editor: Amy Haines

Editorial Assistant: Danielle Warchol

Media Editor: Janine Tangney

Executive Marketing Manager: Stacey Purviance

Marketing Manager: Melissa Holt

Marketing Coordinator: Brittany Blais

Marketing Communications Manager: Linda Yip

Content Project Manager: Rosemary Winfield

Art Director: Marissa Falco

Manufacturing Planner: Betsy Donaghey

Rights Acquisition Specialist: Timothy Sisler

Production Service: Sebranek, Inc.

Senior Photo Permissions Account Manager: Deanna Ettinger

Design Assistant: Hannah Wellman

Cover Image: ©shutterstock.com

Compositor: Sebranek, Inc.

Sebranek, Inc.: Steven J. Augustyn, April Lindau, Colleen Belmont, Chris Erickson, Mariellen Hanrahan, Dave Kemper, Tim Kemper, Rob King, Chris Krenzke, Lois Krenzke, Mark Lalumondier, Jason C. Reynolds, Janae Sebranek, Lester Smith, Jean Varley

For product information and technology assistance, contact us at
Cengage Learning Customer & Sales Support, 1-800-354-9706
For permission to use material from this text or product,
submit all requests online at **www.cengage.com/permissions**
Further permissions questions can be e-mailed to
permissionrequest@cengage.com

Library of Congress Control Number: 2011942002

ISBN-13: 978-1-133-30774-7
ISBN-10: 1-133-30774-4

Wadsworth
20 Channel Center Street
Boston, MA 02210-1202
USA

Cengage Learning is a leading provider of customized learning solutions with office locations around the globe, including Singapore, the United Kingdom, Australia, Mexico, Brazil, and Japan. Locate your local office at:
international.cengage.com/region

Cengage Learning products are represented in Canada by Nelson Education, Ltd.

For your course and learning solutions, visit **www.cengage.com**

Purchase any of our products at your local college store or at our preferred online store **www.cengagebrain.com**.
Instructors: Please visit **login.cengage.com** and log in to access instructor-specific resources.

Printed in the United States of America
3 4 5 6 7 15 14 13

Brief Contents

wavebreakmedia ltd, 2011 / Used under license from Shutterstock.com

Part Two — Forms of Writing

GrandeDuc, 2011 / Used under license from Shutterstock.com

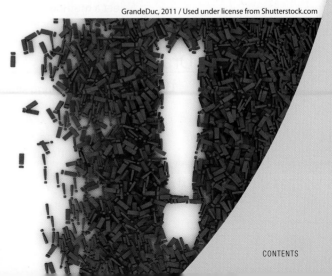

Part Three — Handbook

Contents

Part One Writing Process

What are LOs?
LOs are Learning Outcomes—what students will gain as they work through each chapter.

Part Two Forms of Writing

Narrative, Descriptive, and Reflective Writing

Peter Waters, 2011 / Used under license from Shutterstock.com

Analytical Writing

Quang Ho, 2011 / Used under license from Shutterstock.com

Part Three Handbook

Thematic Contents

PART 1
WRITE

"Literacy is not a luxury, it is a right and a responsibility. If our world is to meet the challenges of the twenty-first century, we must harness the energy and creativity of all our citizens."

—Bill Clinton

1

Understanding the Reading-Writing Connection

When you write, you are sending a message into the world. But here's the thing: before you could write, you needed to read. And your writing needs a reader, if it is to be something more than static words on a page or a screen. Whether it's a poem or a novel, a tweet or an essay, a blog or a lab report, reading and writing work symbiotically—in a close relationship where one depends on the other.

In your college work (and even beyond), you'll do plenty of reading and writing, and *COMP: Write* aims to help you improve both of these abilities in its attention to the writing process, its presentation of student and professional essays, its instruction in different forms of writing, its attention to research, and its focus on grammar. However, this first chapter looks directly at the reading-writing connection so that you can begin to strengthen those ties in your own work.

Now more than ever, reading and writing involve not only words but also visual images. For that reason, this chapter also asks you to pull visuals into view as part of the reading-writing connection.

Learning Outcomes

LO1 Use the SQ3R reading strategy.

LO2 Read actively.

LO3 Respond to a text.

LO4 Summarize a text.

LO5 Effectively analyze images.

LO6 Think critically through writing.

Use the SQ3R reading strategy. LO1

Obviously, reading a novel, a textbook, and a Web page are all different activities. Nevertheless, all college reading assignments can be approached systematically, especially when your goal is to absorb and engage the text. One strategy for critical reading, especially of information-rich texts, is called **SQ3R: Survey, Question, Read, Recite,** and **Review**. Here is how SQ3R works.

Survey

The first step in SQ3R is to preview the material. Check for clues to each part of the rhetorical situation:

Rhetorical Situation

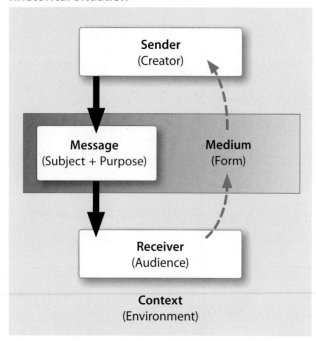

Read about the author. Then read the title and the opening and closing paragraphs to get a sense of the main points. Glance at all other pages, noting headings, topic sentences in paragraphs, boldface type, illustrations, charts, maps, and other cues to the content and organization.

Benefits: Surveying helps you (1) focus on the writer's message, (2) identify its organization, and (3) anticipate how the text will develop.

Question

As you survey, begin to ask questions that you hope to answer as you read.

- **Read any questions that accompany the reading.** Look at the end of the reading or in a study guide.

- **Turn headings into questions.** If a subhead says, "The Study," ask, "How was the study conducted?"

- **Imagine test questions for major points.** If the reading draws conclusions about self-control, ask, "What conclusions does the author draw about self-control?"

- **Ask the journalist's questions:** Ask *who, what, where, when, why,* and *how*? Whose attitudes are changing? What are their attitudes? Where is the change strongest? When is it occurring? Why is it happening? How?

Benefits: Asking questions keeps you actively thinking about what you are reading and helps you absorb information.

Read

As you encounter facts and ideas, ask these questions: What does this mean? How do the ideas relate to each other and to what I know? What's coming next?

Keep track of your answers by taking notes, annotating the text, mapping, or outlining. (See pages 5–7 for more on these active-reading techniques.) Read difficult parts slowly; reread them if necessary. Look up unfamiliar words or ideas, and use your senses to imagine the events, people, places, or things you are

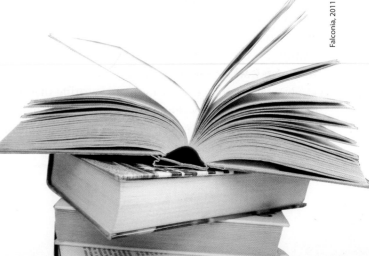

reading about. Imagine talking with the writer. Express agreement, lodge complaints, ask for proof—and imagine the writer's response or look for it in the text.

Benefits: Engaging actively with the text in this way will draw you deeper into the world of the writing. You'll trigger memories and make surprising connections.

Recite

After finishing a page, section, or chapter, recite the key points aloud. Answering *Who? What? When? Where? Why?* and *How?* questions is a quick way of testing yourself on how well you understood what you read. You can also recite the key points by listing them or writing a summary (see pages 8–9).

Benefits: Reciting tests your comprehension, drives the material deeper into your long-term memory, and helps you connect the content with what you already know.

Review

As soon as you finish reading the material, double-check the questions you posed in the "question" stage of SQ3R. Can you answer them? Glance over any notes you made as well. But don't stop there if the reading is especially important. You will remember the material much better by spacing out your reviews; spend a few minutes reviewing each text over the next few days. Consider the following helpful memory techniques:

- **Visualize the concepts in concrete ways.**
  Example: If a text discusses a study about self-control, imagine a television panel discussing the topic.
- **Draw diagrams or develop clusters.**
  Example: See the cluster on page 7.
- **Put the material in your own words.**
  Example: See the summary on page 9.
- **Teach it to someone.**
  Example: For a study about self-control, explain the main points to a friend or relative—in person, on the phone, or by e-mail.
- **Use acronyms or rhymes.**
  Example: "*i* before *e* except after *c*."

Benefits: Research shows that reviewing within 24 hours helps considerably to move information from your short-term memory to your long-term memory. You will also improve your memory if you create a network of associations with the information you want to remember, if you link the memory to two or more senses, or if you reorganize the material while still retaining the substance with accuracy.

Read actively.

Truly active reading is a kind of mental dialogue with the writer. Use these strategies to read actively:

- **Pace yourself.** Read in stretches of thirty to forty-five minutes, followed by short breaks.
- **Anticipate.** When you break, think about what is coming next and why.
- **Read difficult parts aloud.** Or take turns reading aloud with a partner.
- **Take thoughtful notes.** Find a note-taking system that works for you. (See pages 347–348). This is especially true for research projects.
- **Annotate the text.** Mark up the text (if you own it) or a photocopy. Underline or highlight key points. Write a "?" beside puzzling parts. Write key words in the margin and add personal observations.

Read, annotate, and respond to a text.

The following article first appeared in June 2, 2010, in a monthly column in the *Fast Company* newsletter. The author, Dan Heath, is also coauthor (with his brother) of the best-selling business books *Made to Stick* and *Switch*. He is currently a consultant to the Policy Programs at the Aspen Institute. Read the following article, using SQ3R and active-reading strategies.

Why Change Is So Hard: Self-Control Is Exhaustible

1   You hear something a lot about change: People won't change because they're too lazy. Well, I'm here to stick up for the lazy people. In fact, I want to argue that what looks like laziness is actually exhaustion. The proof comes from a psychology study that is absolutely fascinating.

The Study

2   So picture this: Students come into a lab. It smells amazing—someone has just baked chocolate-chip cookies. On a table in front of them, there are two bowls. One has the fresh-baked cookies. The other has a bunch of radishes. Some of the students are asked to eat some cookies but no radishes. Others are told to eat radishes but no cookies, and while they sit there, nibbling on rabbit food, the researchers leave the room—which is intended to tempt them and is frankly kind of sadistic. But in the study none of the radish-eaters slipped—they showed admirable self-control. And meanwhile, it probably goes without saying that the people gorging on cookies didn't experience much temptation.

3   Then, the two groups are asked to do a second, seemingly unrelated task—basically a kind of logic puzzle where they have to trace out a complicated geometric pattern without raising their pencil. Unbeknownst to them, the puzzle can't be solved. The scientists are curious how long they'll persist at a difficult task. So the cookie-eaters try again and again, for an average of 19 minutes, before they give up. But the radish-eaters—they only last an average of 8 minutes. What gives?

The Results

4   The answer may surprise you: They ran out of self-control. Psychologists have discovered that self-control is an exhaustible resource. And I don't mean self-control only in the sense of turning down cookies or alcohol; I mean a broader sense of self-supervision—any time you're paying close attention to your actions, like when you're having a tough conversation or trying to stay focused on a paper you're writing. This helps to explain why, after a long hard day at the office, we're more likely to snap at our spouses or have one drink too many—we've depleted our self-control.

5   And here's why this matters for change: In almost all change situations, you're substituting new, unfamiliar behaviors for old, comfortable ones, and that burns self-control. Let's say I present a new morning routine to you that specifies how you'll shower and brush your teeth. You'll understand it and you might even agree with my process. But to pull it off, you'll have to supervise yourself very carefully. Every fiber of your being will want to go back to the old way of doing things. Inevitably, you'll slip. And if I were uncharitable, I'd see you going back to the old way and I'd say, You're so lazy. Why can't you just change?

6   This brings us back to the point I promised I'd make: That what looks like laziness is often exhaustion. Change wears people out—even well-intentioned people will simply run out of fuel.

Reading for Better Writing

Working by yourself or with a group, answer these questions:

1. In a single sentence, state the thesis of the essay.

2. In a few sentences, tell how the findings of the study help explain why change is difficult.

3. Compare your notes and annotations with a partner. Which parts of your notes and annotations are the same? Which parts are different? How does discussing the content of the essay reinforce or otherwise alter your understanding of the essay?

4. Think about your own life. What sorts of activities require you to exert a great deal of self-control? What sort of activities do you find too tempting to resist when you have "run out" of self-control? How could this information help you avoid temptation?

Note: Reading actively also involves evaluating texts. For help, see pages 344–345, where you'll find instruction on evaluating resources for research projects.

Map the text.

If you are visually oriented, you may understand a text best by mapping out its important parts. One way to do so is by "clustering." Start by naming the main topic in an oval at the center of the page. Then branch out using lines and "balloons," where each balloon contains a word or phrase for one major subtopic. Branch out in further layers of balloons to show even more subpoints. If you wish, add graphics, arrows, drawings—anything that helps you visualize the relationships among ideas.

Outline the text.

Outlining is the traditional way of showing all the major parts, points, and subpoints in a text. An outline uses parallel structure to show main points and subordinate points. See pages 46–48 for more on outlines.

Sample Outline for "Why Change Is So Hard: Self-Control Is Exhaustible"

1. Introduction: Change is hard not because of laziness but because of exhaustion.
2. A study tests self-control.
   a. Some students must eat only cookies—using little self-control.
   b. Some students must eat only radishes—using much self-control.
   c. Both sets of students have to trace a pattern without lifting the pencil—an unsolvable puzzle.
      ▪ Cookie-only students last an average of 19 minutes before quitting.
      ▪ Radish-only students last an average of 8 minutes before quitting.
3. Results show that self-control is exhaustible.
   a. Avoiding temptation and working in a hard, focused way require self-control.
   b. Change requires self-control.
   c. Failure to change often results from exhaustion of self-control.

Respond to a text.

In a sense, when you read a text, you enter into a dialogue with it. Your response expresses your turn in the dialogue. Such a response can take varied forms, from a journal entry to a blog to a discussion-group posting.

Follow these guidelines for response writing.

On the surface, responding to a text seems perfectly natural—just let it happen. But it can be a bit more complicated. A written response typically is not the same as a private diary entry but is instead shared with other readers, whether your instructor or a class. You develop your response keeping in mind your instructor's requirements and the response's role in the course. Therefore, follow these guidelines:

1. **Be honest.** Although you want to remain sensitive to the context in which you will share your response, be bold enough to be honest about your reaction to the text—what it makes you think, feel, and question. To that end, a response usually allows you to express yourself directly using the pronoun "I."

2. **Be fluid.** Let the flow of your thoughts guide you in what you write. Don't stop to worry about grammar, punctuation, mechanics, and spelling. These can be quickly cleaned up before you share or submit your response.

3. **Be reflective.** Generally, the goal of a response is to offer thoughtful reflection as opposed to knee-jerk reaction. Show, then, that you are engaging the text's ideas, relating them to your own experience, looking both inward and outward. Avoid a shallow reaction that comes from skimming the text or misreading it.

4. **Be selective.** By nature, a response must limit its focus; it cannot exhaust all your reactions to the text. So zero in on one or two elements of your response, and run with those to see where they take you in your dialogue with the text.

Sample Response

Here is part of a student's response to Dan Heath's "Why Change Is So Hard" on page 6. Note the informality and explanatory tone.

> Heath's report of the psychological experiment is very vivid, referring to the smell of chocolate-chip cookies and hungry students "gorging" on them. He uses the term "sadistic" to refer to making the radish-eaters sit and watch this go on. I wonder if this mild torment plays into the student's readiness to give up on the later test. If I'd been rewarded with cookies, I'd feel indebted to the testers and would stick with it longer. If I'd been punished with radishes, I might give up sooner just to spite the testers.
>
> Now that I think of it, the digestion of all that sugar and fat in the cookies, as opposed to the digestion of roughage from the radishes, might also affect concentration and performance. Maybe the sugar "high" gives students the focus to keep going?

Summarize a text.

Writing a summary disciplines you by making you pull only essentials from a reading—the main points, the thread of the argument. By doing so, you create a brief record of the text's contents and exercise your ability to comprehend, analyze, and synthesize.

Use these guidelines for summary writing.

Writing a summary requires sifting out the least important points, sorting the essential ones to show their relationships, and stating those points in your own words. Follow these guidelines:

1. **Skim first; then read closely.** First, get a sense of the whole, including the main idea and strategies for support. Then read carefully, taking notes as you do.

2. **Capture the text's argument.** Review your notes and annotations, looking for main points and clear connections. State these

briefly and clearly, in your own words. Include only what is essential, excluding most examples and details. Don't say simply that the text talks about its subject; tell what it says about that subject.

3. **Test your summary.** Aim to objectively provide the heart of the text; avoid interjecting your own opinions and presence as a writer. Don't confuse an objective summary of a text with a response to it (shown on the previous page). Check your summary against the original text for accuracy and consistency.

Sample Summary

Below is a student's summary of Dan Heath's "Why Change Is So Hard," on page 6. Note how the summary writer includes only main points and phrases them in her own words. She departs from the precise order of details, but records them accurately.

> In the article "Why Change Is So Hard," Dan Heath argues that people who have trouble changing are not lazy, but have simply exhausted their self-control. Heath refers to a study in which one group of students was asked to eat cookies and not radishes while another group in the same room was asked to eat radishes and not cookies. Afterward, both groups of students were asked to trace an endless geometric design without lifting their pencils. The cookie-only group traced on average 19 minutes before giving up, but the radish-only group traced on average only 8 minutes. They had already used up their self-control. Heath says that any behavioral change requires self-control, an exhaustible resource. Reverting to old behavior is what happens due not to laziness but to exhaustion.

Insight: Writing formal summaries—whether as part of literature reviews or as abstracts—is an important skill, especially in the social and natural sciences. For a sample abstract, see page 390.

Effectively analyze images. LO5

Images communicate, just as words do. Most images in everyday life are made to communicate quickly—magazine covers, ads, signs, movie trailers, social-media photos, and so on. Other images require contemplation, such as the *Mona Lisa*. When you view an image, analyze it effectively through careful viewing and interpreting.

Actively view images.

When you look at an image, take it all in by doing the following:

- **Survey the image.** See it as a whole, but also study the focal point, the background-foreground relationship, left and right content, and colors.
- **Inspect the image.** Examine all the details and the relationships between parts.
- **Question the image.** Who created the image, and why? What is the image's subject and message? Who is the intended viewer? In what medium and context does the image appear (e.g., magazine, academic report, Web page)?
- **Understand the purpose.** What is this image meant to do? Arouse curiosity? Entertain? Inform? Illustrate a concept? Persuade?

Actively interpret images.

Interpreting an image follows naturally from viewing or "reading" the image. Interpreting means figuring out what the image or design is meant to do, say, or show. Interpreting requires you to think more deeply about each element of the rhetorical situation, and complications with each element.

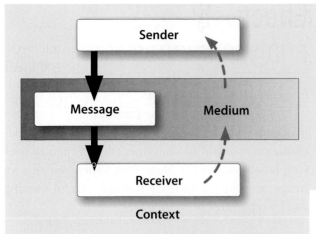

Sender

Message   Medium

Receiver

Context

- **Sender:** Who created the image—a photographer, a painter, a Web designer? Why did the person create it? What other people might have been involved—editors, patrons?

  Complications: The sender might be unknown or a group.

- **Message:** What is the subject of the image? How is the subject portrayed? What is the main purpose of the image—to entertain, to inform, to persuade, to entice, to shock?

  Complications: The message might be mixed, implied, ironic, unwelcome, or distorted. The subject might be vague, unfamiliar, complex, or disturbing.

- **Medium:** What is the image—a painting, a cartoon panel, a photo? How might the image have been modified over time? What visual language has the sender used?

  Complications: The medium might be unusual, unfamiliar, or multiple. The visual languages might be literal, stylized, numeric, symbolic, and so on.

- **Receiver:** Whom was the image made for? Are you part of the intended audience? What is your relationship with the sender? Do you agree with the message? How comfortable are you with the medium? What is your overall response to the image?

  Complications: You might be uninterested in, unfamiliar with, or biased toward the message.

- **Context:** What was the context in which the image was first presented? What context surrounds the image now? Does the image fit its context or fight it?

  Complications: The context might be disconnected, ironic, changing, or multilayered.

Insight: Like words, visuals can be cliches—trite, misleading, or worn-out expressions of concepts or ideas. For example, TV ads for weight-loss drugs commonly picture scantily clad, fit young people, deceptively linking use of the drug to beauty, youth, and sex.

Interpret an image.

© Bazuki Muhammad/REUTERS

Discussion

This color photograph shows a multireligious commemoration of the 229,000 victims of the Indian Ocean tsunami of December 26, 2004.

The symbolism is clearly rooted in the points of light created by the candle balloons, where light itself is a cross-cultural symbol of hope, endurance, the human spirit, and God's presence. The skyward angle of the photograph, with the clusters of candle balloons floating up and the people in the lower right of the frame, creates this sense of vertical longing and release, emphasizing perhaps humanity's longing to solve life's mysteries, including death and disaster.

Although the large, just-released candle balloons are most prominent, the viewer's eyes are also drawn upward, where clusters of far-off candles become constellations of starlike lights. The mourners in the right of the frame, forming a loose circle, are all gazing skyward, like the viewer. Ordinary people in ordinary clothes, they appear to be clapping and, for some, the clapping shows their hands virtually in a posture of prayer. In this way, the image both mourns the dead and celebrates life.

Sender:	Photographer Bazuki Muhammad; authors of *COMP: Write*
Message:	Thais release candle balloons during a mass prayer for victims of the Indian Ocean tsunami. The message is to remember those who died, but move forward with hope.
Medium:	Digital color photograph
Receiver:	The intended viewer was anyone reading a newspaper, magazine, or Web article. The current viewer is likely a student or an instructor in a composition course.
Context:	This photograph was part of a series provided by Reuters for global newspapers. It now is part of a composition text.

Think critically through writing.

LO6

Reading, viewing, and writing can all be means of critical thinking. In college, you often need to show your ability to think critically about topics and issues by analyzing complex processes, synthesizing concepts, weighing the value of opposing perspectives, and applying principles. To think critically through your writing, practice the strategies that follow.

Ask probing questions.

Every field uses questions to trigger critical thinking. For example, scientific questions generate hypotheses, sociological questions lead to studies, mathematical questions call for proofs, and literary criticism questions call for interpretations. A good question opens up a problem and guides you all the way to its solution. But not all questions are created equal. Consider the differences:

- **"Rhetorical" questions** aren't meant to be answered. They're asked for effect.
  Example: Who would want to be caught in an earthquake?
- **Closed questions** seek a limited response and can be answered with "yes," "no," or a simple fact.
  Example: Would I feel an earthquake measuring 3.0 on the Richter scale?
- **Open questions** invite brainstorming and discussion.
  Example: How might a major earthquake affect this urban area?
- **Theoretical questions** call for organization and explanation of an entire field of knowledge.
  Example: What might cause a sudden fracturing of Earth's crust along fault lines?

To improve the critical thinking in your writing, ask better questions. The strategies on the next page will help you think freely, respond to reading, study for a test, or collect your thoughts for an essay.

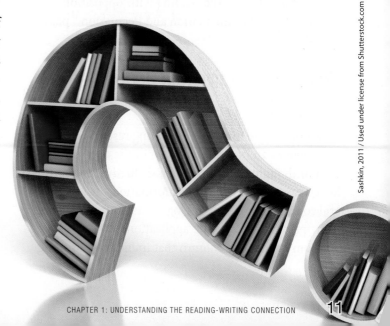

Sashkin, 2011 / Used under license from Shutterstock.com

Ask open questions. Closed questions sometimes choke off thinking. Use open questions to trigger a flow of ideas.

Ask "educated" questions. Compare these questions: (A) What's wrong with television? (B) Does the 16.3 percent rise in televised acts of violence during the past three years signal a rising tolerance for violence in the viewing audience? You have a better chance of expanding the "educated" question—question B—into an essay because the question is clearer and suggests debatable issues.

Keep a question journal. Divide a blank notebook page or split a computer screen. On one side, write down any questions that come to mind regarding the topic that you want to explore. On the other side, write down answers and any thoughts that flow from them.

Write Q & A drafts. To write a thoughtful first draft, write quickly, then look it over. Turn the main idea into a question and write again, answering your question. For example, if your main idea is that TV viewers watch far more violence than they did ten years ago, ask *Which viewers? Why?* and *What's the result?* Go on that way until you find a key idea to serve as the main point of your next draft.

fyi For more help with critical-thinking skills such as making and supporting claims, recognizing logical fallacies, and dealing with opposition, see "Strategies for Argumentation and Persuasion," pages 176–187.

Practice inductive and deductive logic.

Questions invite thinking; reasoning responds to that challenge in an organized way. Will the organization of your thoughts be inductive or deductive? Inductive logic reasons from specific information toward general conclusions. Deductive logic reasons from general principles toward specific applications. Notice in the diagram in the next column that inductive reasoning

starts with specific details or observations (as shown at the base) and then moves "up" to broader ideas and eventually to a concluding generalization. In contrast, deduction starts with general principles at the top and works down, applying the principles to explain particular instances.

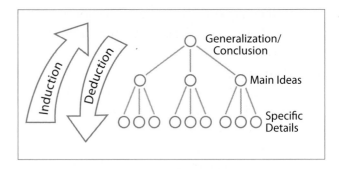

Example: Read through the paragraphs below from a student essay, "If We Are What We Wear, What Are We?" by Allison Young. The first paragraph works deductively, the second paragraph inductively. Note how each approach affects the message.

The American excuse for owning multiples is that (A) clothing styles change so rapidly. At the end of the '80s, trends in high fashion changed every two and a half months (During 95). Even for those of us who don't keep up with high fashion, styles change often enough that our clothing itself lasts much longer than the current trend. Perhaps this is one of the reasons the average American spent $997 on clothing in 1996 (U.S. Department of Commerce).

While Americans are spending a thousand dollars (B) on clothing a year, people in Ethiopia make an average of only $96 a year, those in Bangladesh $280, and the average Filipino worker makes $1,052 (United Nations Statistics Division). I, on the other hand, made over $5,000 last year, and that job was only part-time. When an American college student can earn more money at her part-time job than three billion people each make for a living, it's time to question our culture and ask, as Alan During did, "How much is enough?"

(A) **Deduction:** generalization to specific details
(B) **Induction:** specific details to generalization

Critical-Thinking and Writing Activities

As directed by your instructor, complete the following critical-thinking and writing activities.

1. Northrop Frye has argued that "[n]obody is capable of free speech unless he [or she] knows how to use language, and such knowledge is not a gift: It has to be learned and worked at." How does Frye's claim relate to the discussions of reading, viewing, and writing in this chapter?

2. In a newspaper or magazine (print or online), find a brief article that discusses a recent scientific study (similar to Dan Heath's article on page 6). Read your selected article by practicing the SQ3R method. Then do the following: map the text, write a response to it, and summarize it. If the article has visual content, view and interpret any images. Finally, generate a list of probing questions and speculative answers related to the article's topic.

3. In a print or digital publication, find an image that is striking. Using the instruction on effectively analyzing images, draft an interpretation of the image.

4. Read three or four articles on a current issue that interests you. Using what you've learned, draft two paragraphs on the issue—one patterned deductively and the other inductively.

Checklist: Learning Outcomes

Use the checklist below to assess how well you are practicing the reading-writing connection.

____ I effectively use the SQ3R method for reading texts.

____ I read texts actively through annotation, mapping, outlining, and evaluating.

____ I can write a meaningful response to a text.

____ I can effectively summarize a text so as to get at the core argument.

____ I effectively analyze images through active viewing and interpreting strategies.

____ I practice effective critical thinking through writing that asks probing questions and that works logically through induction and/or deduction.

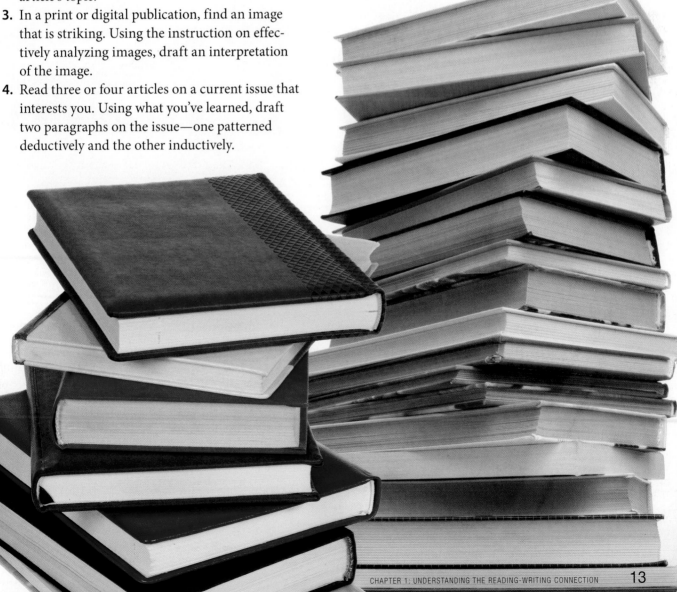

PART **1**
WRITE

"Essays are experiments in making sense of things."
—Scott Russell Sanders

2

One Writer's Process

An essay is an attempt to understand a topic more deeply and clearly. That's one of the reasons this basic form of writing is essential in many college courses. It's a tool for both discovering and communicating.

How do you move from an assignment to a finished, polished essay? The best strategy is to take matters one step at a time, from understanding the assignment to submitting the final draft. Don't try to churn out the essay the night before it's due.

This chapter shows how student writer Angela Franco followed the writing process outlined in chapters 3 through 8.

Learning Outcomes

LO1 Understand the assignment.

LO2 Focus your topic and plan the writing.

LO3 Write a first draft.

LO4 Revise the draft.

LO5 Seek a reviewer's response.

LO6 Edit the writing for style.

LO7 Edit the writing for correctness.

LO8 Check for documentation and page-design problems.

Understand the assignment. LO1

In this chapter, you will follow student Angela Franco as she writes an assigned essay for her Environmental Policies class. Start by carefully reading the assignment and discussion below, noting how she thinks through the rhetorical situation.

Angela examined the assignment.

Angela carefully read her assignment and responded with the notes below.

> "Explain in a two- to three-page essay how a local environmental issue is relevant to the world community. Using *COMP: Write* as your guide, format the paper and document sources in APA style, but omit the title page and abstract. You may seek revising help from a classmate or from the writing center."

■ **Role**
• I'm writing as a student in Environmental Policies, and as a resident of Ontario.

■ **Subject**
• The subject is a recent environmental issue.

■ **Purpose**
• My purpose is to explain how the issue is relevant to all people. That means I must show how this issue affects my audience—both positively and negatively.

■ **Form**
• I need to write a two- to three-page essay—that sounds formal.
• I'll need to include a thesis statement, as well as references to my sources using APA style.

■ **Audience**
• My audience will be people like me—neighbors, classmates, and community members.
• I'll need to keep in mind what they already know and what they need to know.

■ **Context**
• I'll use the guidelines and checklists in *COMP: Write* to evaluate and revise my writing.
• I'll get editing feedback from Jeanie and from the writing center.

Tip For each step in the writing process, choose strategies that fit your writing situation. For example, a personal essay in an English class might require significant time getting started, whereas a lab report in a chemistry class might require little or none.

Angela explored and narrowed her assignment.

Angela explored her assignment and narrowed its focus by clustering and freewriting.

Cluster — When she considered environmental issues, Angela first thought of water pollution as a possible topic for her essay. After writing the phrase in the center of her page, she drew from memories, experiences, and readings to list related ideas and details. Notice how she used three different-colored inks to distinguish the topic (blue) from ideas (red) and details (green).

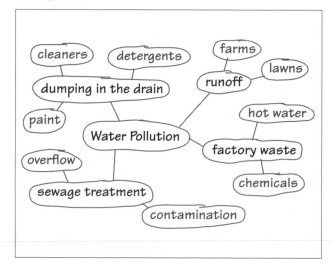

Freewriting — Angela decided to freewrite about the water pollution caused a few years earlier by improper sewage treatment in a small Canadian town.

> I remember reading an article about problems in a small Canadian town. People actually died. The water they drank was contaminated. This is becoming a problem in developed countries like ours. I thought for a long time this was a problem only in developing countries. So who

is responsible for sewage treatment? Who guarantees the safety of our drinking water? How does water get contaminated? Are there solutions for every kind of contamination: mercury, PCBs, sewage?

Narrowed Assignment — Based on her freewriting, Angela rephrased her assignment to narrow its focus.

Explain in a two- to three-page essay how a recent water pollution problem in a small Canadian town is relevant to the world community.

Focus your topic and plan the writing. — LO2

Angela reviewed her narrowed assignment and reassessed her topic.

Narrowed Writing Assignment

Explain in a two- to three-page essay how a recent water pollution problem in a small Canadian town is relevant to the world community.

Angela focused her topic.

To focus her topic, Angela answered the journalistic questions (five Ws and H).

Topic: Water pollution in a small Canadian town

Who? - Farm operators, wastewater officials, Walkerton residents
What? - Water supply contaminated
- Spread bacteria (E. coli)
- Caused disease
- Clean, fresh water depleted
Where? - Walkerton, Ontario
When? - May 2000
Why? - Improper regulation; human error
How? - Groundwater from irrigation, untreated sewage, and runoff

Angela researched the topic.

Angela then did some research to check her information and collect more details for her paper. She recorded all the essential data on each source and then listed the specific details related to her topic. Here's one source:

CBC News. (2010, May 17) "Inside Walkerton: Canada's worst ever E. coli contamination." CBC News.
- May 15—water sampled
- May 17—first patients with flu-like symptoms
- May 18—Lab confirms E. coli contamination in water, but Public Utilities Commission (PUC) does not report information.
- May 19—Medical Health Office (MHO) discovers E. coli outbreak, but is assured by the PUC that the water is safe.
- May 20—At least 40 people treated at hospital with bloody diarrhea, but PUC says twice that water is safe.
- May 21—MHO tells people not to drink water, runs their own test.
- May 23—MHO finds E. coli, learns of May 18 memo, and that chlorinator not working for some time.
- May 24—Three adults and a baby die of E. coli.

Angela decided how to organize her writing.

With a focus selected, Angela used the three guide-lines below to choose the best organizational pattern for her writing.

Quick Guide: Organization Pattern

1. Review your assignment and record your response.

Assignment:
Explain in a two- to three-page essay how a recent environmental issue is relevant to the world community.

Response:
My assignment clearly states that I need to explain my topic, so I have a general idea of how my paper will be organized.

2. Decide on your thesis statement and think about your essay's possible content and organization.

Thesis Statement:
The water pollution incident in Walkerton, Ontario, had a devastating effect that every town should learn from.

Response:
After reading my thesis statement, it's obvious that I'm going to be writing about a problem and its causes.

3. Choose an overall method and reflect on its potential effectiveness.

Response:
Looking at the list of methods, I see that I can use cause/effect or problem/solution. After making two quick lists of my main points using both approaches, I decided to use a problem/ solution approach. I will still talk about causes and effects in my essay—they just won't be front and center. With problem/solution, I need to first present the problem clearly so that readers can fully understand it and see why it's important. Then I need to explore solutions to the problem—maybe what they did in Walkerton and what we all need to do to make water safe.

Tip Many essays you write will be organized according to one basic method or approach. However, within that basic structure you may want to include other methods. For example, while developing a comparison essay you may do some describing or classifying. In other words, you should choose methods of development that (1) help you understand the topic and (2) help your readers understand your message.

Write a first draft. LO3

After composing her opening, middle, and closing paragraphs, Angela put together her first draft. She then added a working title.

The writer uses a series of images to get the reader's attention.

The thesis statement (red) introduces the subject.

The writer describes the cause of the problem.

The writer indicates some of her source material with a citation.

The writer covers the solutions that were used to resolve the problem.

Water Woes

It's a hot day. Several people just finished mowing their lawns. A group of bicyclists—more than 3,000—have been passing through your picturesque town all afternoon. Dozens of Little Leaguers are batting, running, and sweating. What do all these people have in common? They all drinks lots of tap water, especially on hot summer days. They also take for granted that the water is clean and safe. But in reality, the water they drink could be contaminated and pose a serious health risk. That's just what happened in Walkerton, Ontario, where a water pollution incident had a devastating effect that every town can learn from.

What happened in Walkerton Ontario? Heavy rains fell on May 12. It wasn't until May 21 that the townspeople were advised to boil their drinking water. The rains washed cattle manure into the town well. The manure contained E coli, a type of bacteria. E coli is harmless to cattle. It can make people sick. Seven days after the heavy rains, people began calling public health officials. The warning came too late. Two people had already died (Wickens, 2000).

Once Walkerton's problem was identified, the solutions were known. The government acted quickly to help the community and to clean the water supply. One Canadian newspaper reported that a $100,000 emergency fund was set up to help families with expenses. Bottled water for drinking and containers of bleach for sanitizing and cleaning were donated by local businesses.

So what messed up Walkerton? Basically, people screwed up! According to one news story, a flaw in the water treatment system allowed the bacteria-infested water to enter the well. The manure washed into the well, but the chlorine should have killed the deadly bacteria. In Walkerton, the PUC group fell asleep at the wheel.

At last, the Provincial Clean Water Agency restored the main water and sewage systems by flushing out all of the town's pipes and wells. The ban on drinking Walkerton's water was finally lifted seven months after the water became contaminated.

Could any good come from Walkerton's tragedy? Does it have a silver lining? It is possible that more people are aware that water may be contaminated. Today people are beginning to take responsibility for the purity of the water they and their families drink. In the end, more and more people will know about the dangers of contaminated water—without learning it the hard way.

The concluding paragraph stresses the importance of public awareness.

Angela kept a working bibliography.

As she researched her topic, Angela kept a working bibliography—a list of resources that she thought might offer information helpful to her essay. During the writing process, she deleted some resources, added others, and edited the document that became the references page on page 29.

Working References

CBC News. (2010, May 17). "Inside Walkerton: Canada's worst ever E.coli contamination." CBC News.

Phone interview with Alex Johnson, Walkerton Police Department, 23 September 2007.

Blackwell, Thomas (2001, January 9). Walkerton doctor defends response. The Edmonton Journal. http://edmontonjournal.com.

Rudchenko Liliia, 2011 / Used under license from Shutterstock.com

Revise the draft. ___ L◯4

After finishing the first draft, Angela set it aside. When she was ready to revise it, she looked carefully at global issues—ideas, organization, and voice. She wrote notes to herself to help keep her thoughts together.

Angela's Comments

> I need to give my opening more energy.

> Does my thesis still fit the paper?—Yes.

> Using time sequence, put this paragraph in better order.

> Move this paragraph —it interrupts the discussion of causes.

Water Woes

It's ~~a~~ *an unusually* hot ~~day.~~ *Saturday afternoon.* Several people just finished mowing their lawns. A group of bicyclists—more than 3,000—have been *pedal up the street.* ~~passing through your picturesque town all afternoon.~~ Dozens of Little Leaguers are batting, running, and sweating. What do all these people have in common? They all drinks lots of tap water, especially on hot summer days. They also take for granted that the water is clean and safe. But in reality, the water they drink could be contaminated and pose a serious health risk. That's just what happened in Walkerton, Ontario, where a water pollution incident had a devastating effect that every town can learn from.

What happened in Walkerton Ontario? Heavy rains fell on May 12. It wasn't until May 21 that the townspeople were advised to boil their drinking water. The rains washed cattle manure into the town well. The manure contained E coli, a type of bacteria. E coli is harmless to cattle. It can make people sick. Seven days after the heavy rains, people began calling public health officials. The warning came too late. Two people had already died (Wickens, 2000).

Once Walkerton's problem was identified, the solutions were known. The government acted quickly to help the community and to clean the water supply. One Canadian newspaper reported that a $100,000 emergency fund was set up to help families with expenses. Bottled water for drinking and containers of bleach for sanitizing and cleaning were donated by local businesses.

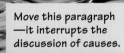

went wrong in   Human error was a critical factor.
So what ∧messed up Walkerton? ∧Basically, people screwed up!
First,
∧According to one news story, a flaw in the water treatment system
allowed the bacteria-infested water to enter the well. Even after ∧The manure
washed into the well, ~~but~~ the chlorine should have killed the deadly
bacteria. In Walkerton, the ~~PUC group fell asleep at the wheel.~~ ←
In addition
→ ~~At last,~~ ∧the Provincial Clean Water Agency restored the main
water and sewage systems by flushing out all of the town's pipes
and wells. The ban on drinking Walkerton's water was finally lifted
seven months after the water became contaminated.

Could any good come from Walkerton's tragedy? ~~Does it have
a silver lining?~~ It is possible that more people are aware that
water may be contaminated. Today people are beginning to take
responsibility for the purity of the water they and their families
drink. In the end, more and more people will know about the
dangers of contaminated water—without learning it the hard way.

Public Utilities Commission was responsible for overseeing
the testing and treating of the town's water, but they failed
to monitor it properly. Apparently, shortcuts were taken when
tracking the water's chlorine level, and as a result, some of the
water samples were mislabeled. There was also a significant
delay between the time that the contamination was identified
and the time it was reported.

Seek a reviewer's response.

Next, Angela asked a peer to review her work. His comments are in the margin. Angela used them to make additional changes, including writing a new opening and closing.

Reviewer's Comments

Angela's Changes

Could you make the opening more relevant and urgent?

Could you clarify your focus on the topic?

Add the year and other specific details.

Make sure you document all source material—you have just one citation in your draft.

Water Woes

WARNING: City tap water is polluted with animal waste. Using the water for drinking, cooking, or bathing could cause sickness or death.

According to the Seirra Club, run-off pollutants from farm cites are steadily seeping into our streams, lakes, reservoirs and wells. Because much of our drinking water comes from these resources, warnings like the one above are already posted in a number of U.S. and Canadian communities, and many more postings will be needed (Sierra Club, 2005). As the Seirra Club argues, the pollution and related warnings are serious, and failure to take them seriously could be deadly. For example, a few years ago the citizens of Walkerton Ontario learned that the water that they believed to be clean was actually poisoned.

The events began
~~What happened~~ in Walkerton, ~~Ontario? Heavy rains fell~~ on May 12, 2000, when heavey rains ~~The rains~~ washed cattle manure into the town well. The manure contained E coli, a type of bacteria. E coli is harmless to cattle. It can make people sick. Seven days after the heavy rains, people began calling public health officials to complain of nausea and diarrhea. It wasn't until May 21 that the townspeople were advised to boil their drinking water. The warning came too late. Two people had already died, and more than 2,000 were ill (Wickens, 2000).

Several factors contributed to the terrible tragedy in Walkerton, including human error.
~~So what went wrong in Walkerton? Human error was a~~ The Edmonton Journal ~~critical factor.~~ First, according to ~~one news story,~~ a flaw in the water treatment system allowed the bacteria-infested water to (Blackwell, 2001) enter the well. Even after the manure washed into the well, the chlorine should have killed the deadly bacteria. In Walkerton,

the Public Utilities Commission was responsible for overseeing the testing and treating of the town's water, but it failed to monitor it properly. Apparently, shortcuts were taken when tracking the water's chlorine level, and as a result, some of the water samples were mislabeled. There was also a significant delay between the time that the contamination was identified and the time it was reported.

Use active voice.

Once Walkerton's problem was identified, ~~the solutions were known.~~ The government acted quickly to help the community and to clean the water supply. One Canadian newspaper *The Edmonton Journal* reported a $100,000 emergency fund was set up to help families with expenses. Bottled water for drinking and containers of bleach for basic sanitizing and cleaning ~~were donated by local businesses.~~ In addition, the Provincial Clean Water Agency restored the main water and sewage systems by flushing out all of the town's pipes and wells. The ban on drinking Walkerton's water was finally lifted seven months after the water became contaminated.

Consider adding details—maybe an entire paragraph— calling readers to action, and stating your thesis clearly.

As the Sierra Club warned and the citizens of Walkerton learned, water purity is a life-and-death issue. Fortunately, both the United States and Canada have been addressing the problem. For example, since 2001, more states and provinces are tightening their clean-water standards, more communities have begun monitoring their water quality, and more individuals have been using water-filtration systems, bottled water, or boiled tap water. However, a tragedy like that in Walkerton could happen again. To avoid such horror, all of us must get involved by demanding clean tap water in our communities and by promoting the polices and procedures needed to achieve that goal.

Edit the writing for style. LO6

When Angela began editing, she read each of her sentences aloud to check for clarity and smoothness. The first page of Angela's edited copy is shown below.

The writer revises the title.

Water Woes_in Walkerton_

> Warning: City tap water is polluted with animal waste. Using the water for drinking, cooking, or bathing could cause sickness or death.

According to the Seirra Club, run-off pollutants from farm cites are steadily seeping into our streams, lakes, reservoirs, and wells. Because much of our drinking water comes from these resources, warnings like the one above are already posted in a number of

She qualifies her statement, replacing "will" with "might."

U.S. and Canadian communities, and many more postings ~~will~~ _might_ be needed _in the future_ (Sierra Club, 2005). As the Seirra Club argues, the pollution and related warnings are serious, and failure to take them seriously could be deadly. For example, a few years ago the citizens of Walkerton Ontario learned that the water that they believed to be clean was ~~actually~~ _tragically_ poisoned.

The events in Walkerton began on May 12, 2000, when heavy rains washed cattle manure into the town well. The manure

She rewrites and combines several choppy sentences.

contained ~~E. coli. a~~ bacteria, _commonly called_ ~~E coli~~ _While E coli_ is harmless to cattle, _It_ can make people sick. Seven days after the heavy rains, people began calling public health officials to complain of nausea and diarrhea. It wasn't until May 21 that the townspeople were advised to boil their drinking water. The warning came too late. Two people had already died, and more than 2,000 were ill (Wickens, 2000).

Several factors contributed to the ~~terrible~~ tragedy in Walkerton, including human error. First, according to The Edmonton Journal,

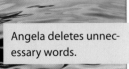

Angela deletes unnecessary words.

a flaw in the water treatment system allowed the ~~bacteria~~ infested water to enter the well (Blackwell, 2001). Even after the manure washed into the well, the chlorine . . .

Edit the writing for correctness.

LO7

Angela reviewed her edited copy for punctuation, agreement issues, and spelling. The first page of Angela's proofread essay is shown below.

Water Woes in Walkerton

> Warning: City tap water is polluted with animal waste. Using the water for drinking, cooking, or bathing could cause sickness or death.

The writer corrects errors that the spell checker did not pick up.

According to the Sierra Club, run-off pollutants from farm sites are steadily seeping into our streams, lakes, reservoirs, and wells. Because much of our drinking water comes from these resources, warnings like the one above are already posted in a number of U.S. and Canadian communities, and many more postings might be needed in the future (Sierra Club, 2005). As the Sierra Club argues, the pollution and related warnings are serious, and failure to take them seriously could be deadly. For example, a few years ago the citizens of Walkerton, Ontario, learned that the water that they believed to be clean was tragically poisoned.

She adds a comma between the city and province.

The events in Walkerton began on May 12, 2000, when heavy rains washed cattle manure into the town well. The manure contained bacteria commonly called *E. coli*. While *E. coli* is harmless to cattle, it can make people sick. Seven days after the heavy rains, people began calling public health officials to complain of nausea and diarrhea. It wasn't until May 21 that the townspeople were advised to boil their drinking water. The warning came too late. Two people had already died, and more than 2,000 were ill (Wickens, 2000).

She adds periods and italicizes "E. coli" to show that it is a scientific term.

Several factors contributed to the tragedy in Walkerton, including human error. First, according to The Edmonton Journal, a flaw in the water treatment system allowed the infested water to enter Walkerton's well (Blackwell, 2001). Even after the manure washed into Walkterton's well, the chlorine should have . . .

She adds a word for clarity.

Check for documentation and page-design problems. LO8

After proofreading and formatting her essay, Angela added a heading and page numbers. She also added more documentation and a references page at the end. As assigned, she omitted the title page and abstract.

The writer revises the title.

The title is changed. The warning is emphasized with red print.

An appropriate font and type size are used.

Running Head: Clean Water Is Everyone's Business   1

Angela Franco

Professor Kim Van Es

English 101

October 18, 2011

Clean Water Is Everyone's Business

> Warning: City tap water is polluted with animal waste. Using the water for drinking, cooking, or bathing could cause sickness or death.

According to the Sierra Club, run-off pollutants from farm sites are steadily seeping into our streams, lakes, reservoirs, and wells. Because much of our drinking water comes from these resources, warnings like the one above are already posted in a number of U.S. and Canadian communities, and many more postings might be needed in the future (Sierra Club, 2005). As the Sierra Club argues, the pollution and related warnings are serious, and failure to take them seriously could be deadly. For example, a few years ago the citizens of Walkerton, Ontario, learned that the water that they believed to be clean was tragically poisoned.

The events in Walkerton began on May 12, 2000, when heavy rains washed cattle manure into the town well. The manure contained the bacteria commonly called *E. coli*. While *E. coli* is harmless to cattle, it can make people sick. Seven days after the heavy rains, people began calling public health officials to complain of nausea and diarrhea. It wasn't until May 21 that the townspeople were advised to boil their drinking water. The warning came too late. Two people had already died, and more than 2,000 were ill (Wickens, 2000).

Title and page number are used on each page.

Each claim or supporting point is backed up with reasoning and evidence.

Several factors contributed to the tragedy in Walkerton, including human error. First, according to the *Edmonton Journal*, a flaw in the water treatment system allowed the infested water to enter Walkerton's well (Blackwell, 2001). Even after the manure washed into Walkerton's well, the chlorine should have killed the deadly bacteria. In Walkerton, the Public Utilities Commission was responsible for overseeing the testing and treating of the town's water, but it failed to monitor the procedure properly ("Walkerton's water-safety," 2000). Apparently, shortcuts were taken when tracking the water's chlorine level, and as a result, some of the water samples were mislabeled. There was also a significant delay between the time that the contamination was identified and the time it was reported.

The writer continues to give credit throughout the essay.

Once Walkerton's problem was identified, the government acted quickly to help the community. In its December 7, 2000, edition, the *Edmonton Journal* reported that a $100,000 emergency fund was set up to help families with expenses. Local businesses donated bottled water for drinking and containers of bleach for basic sanitizing and cleaning. In addition, the Provincial Clean Water Agency restored the main water and sewage systems by flushing out all of the town's pipes and wells. Seven months after the water became contaminated, the ban on drinking Walkerton's water was finally lifted.

The writer restates her thesis in the last sentence.

As the Sierra Club warns and the citizens of Walkerton learned, water purity is a life-and-death issue. Fortunately, both the United States and Canada have been addressing the problem. For example, since 2001, more states and provinces have been tightening their clean-water standards, more communities have been monitoring their water quality, and more individuals have been using water-filtration systems, bottled water, or boiled tap water. However, a tragedy like that in Walkerton could happen again. To avoid such horror, all of us must get involved by demanding clean tap water in our communities and by promoting the policies and procedures needed to achieve that goal.

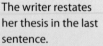

Rudchenko Liliia, 2011 / Used under license from Shutterstock.com

References

Blackwell, T. (2001, January 9). Walkerton doctor defends response. *The Edmonton Journal*. Retrieved September 22, 2010, from <http://edmontonjournal.com>.

Sierra Club. (2005) Water sentinels: Keeping it clean around the U.S.A. Retrieved September 24, 2008, from <http://sierraclub.org/watersentinels/>.

Walkerton's water-safety tests falsified regularly, utility official admits. (2000, December 7). *The Edmonton Journal*. Retrieved April 2, 2005, from <http://edmontonjournal.com>.

Wickens, B. (2000, June 5). Tragedy in Walkerton. *Maclean's*, 113(23), 34–36.

Sources used are listed correctly, in alphabetical order.

Each entry follows APA rules for content, format, and punctuation.

Critical-Thinking and Writing Activities

Complete these activities by yourself or with classmates.

1. Scott Russell Sanders suggests that "essays are experiments in making sense of things." Does Sanders' statement ring true? What makes such experiments flop or succeed? What kinds of "sense" do essays create?

2. Review Angela's writing process. How does it compare with your own writing process on a recent assignment?

3. Review the peer-editing instructions in "Revising Collaboratively" (pages 77–78). Then reread the reviewer's comments in the margins of Angela's second revision (pages 23–24). Do the comments reflect the instructions? Explain.

Cross-Curricular Connections

Angela used APA style, which is standard for the social sciences: psychology, sociology, political science, and education. MLA style is standard for English and humanities. Make sure to find out what documentation style your instructor requires.

Checklist: Learning Outcomes

_____ I can analyze an assignment, select a topic, and assess my rhetorical situation.

_____ I can research my topic, plan my writing, and gather/organize information.

_____ I can write a first draft with an engaging opening, an informative middle, and a unifying closing.

_____ I can revise my writing for strong ideas, logical organization, and an informed voice.

_____ I can use a peer response to complete a second revision.

_____ I can edit for style (e.g., precise words and smooth sentences).

_____ I can proofread for correct spelling, mechanics, usage, and grammar.

"I think I did pretty well, considering I started out
with nothing but a bunch of blank paper."
—Steve Martin

3

Starting

The blank page or screen can be daunting for any writer. That's because writing doesn't go from nothing to a masterpiece in one step. Writing is a process, much like painting.

This chapter focuses on beginning that process. It provides numerous concrete strategies for understanding writing assignments, deciding on a topic, and exploring it. The very act of writing generates ideas and creates new connections that will make it easy to fill the blank page.

Learning Outcomes

LO1 Discover your process.

LO2 Understand the rhetorical situation.

LO3 Understand the assignment.

LO4 Select, limit, and explore your topic.

LO5 Collect information and track your sources.

Discover your process. LO1

It's easy to feel overwhelmed by a writing project—especially if the form of writing is new to you, the topic is complex, or the paper must be long. However, using the writing process will relieve some of that pressure by breaking down the task into manageable steps. An overview of those steps is shown below, and key principles are addressed in the right column and on the next page.

Consider the writing process.

The following flowchart maps out the basic steps in the writing process. As you work on your writing project, periodically review this diagram to keep yourself on task.

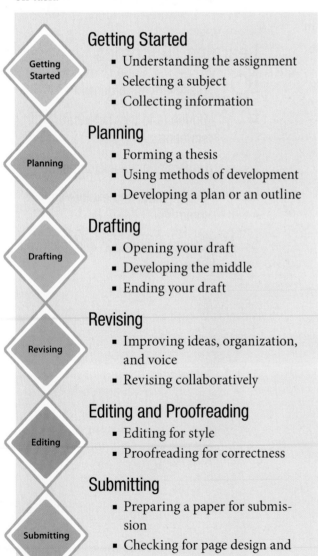

Getting Started
- Understanding the assignment
- Selecting a subject
- Collecting information

Planning
- Forming a thesis
- Using methods of development
- Developing a plan or an outline

Drafting
- Opening your draft
- Developing the middle
- Ending your draft

Revising
- Improving ideas, organization, and voice
- Revising collaboratively

Editing and Proofreading
- Editing for style
- Proofreading for correctness

Submitting
- Preparing a paper for submission
- Checking for page design and documentation

Adapt the process to your project.

The writing process shown in the previous column is flexible, not rigid. As a writer, you need to adapt the process to your situation and assignment. To do so, consider these essential principles.

Writing tends not to follow a straight path. While writing begins with an assignment or a need and ends with a reader, the journey in between is often indirect. The steps in the writing process are recursive, meaning you will sometimes move back and forth between them. For example, during the revision phase, you may discover that you need to draft a new paragraph or do more research.

Each assignment presents distinct challenges. A personal essay may develop best through clustering or freewriting; a literary analysis through close reading of a story; a lab report through the experimental method; and a position paper through reading of books and journal articles, as well as through careful and balanced reasoning.

Writing can involve collaboration. From using your roommate as a sounding board for your topic choice to working with a group to produce a major report, college writing is not solitary writing. In fact, many colleges have a writing center to help you refine your writing assignments. (See page 79 for more.)

Each writer works differently. Some writers do extensive prewriting before drafting, while others do not. You might develop a detailed outline, whereas someone else might draft a brief list of topics. Experiment with the strategies introduced in chapters 2–7, adopting those that help you.

Good writing can't be rushed. Although some students regard pulling an all-nighter as a badge of honor, good writing takes time. A steady, disciplined approach will generally produce the best results. For example, by brainstorming or reading early in a project, you stimulate your subconscious mind to mull over issues, identify problems, and project solutions—even while your conscious mind is working on other things. Similarly, completing a first draft early enough gives you time to revise objectively.

Different steps call for attention to different writing issues. As you use the writing process, at each stage keep your focus where it belongs:

1. While getting started, planning, and drafting, focus on global issues: ideas, structure, voice, format, and design.
2. During revising, fix big content problems by cutting, adding, and thoroughly reworking material. (Our experience is that students benefit the most from revising—but spend the least time doing it!)
3. While editing and proofreading, pay attention to small, local issues—word choice, sentence smoothness, and grammatical correctness. Worrying about these issues early in the writing process interrupts the flow of drafting and wastes time on material that later is deleted.

Understand the rhetorical situation.

Rhetoric is the art of using language effectively. As Aristotle, Quintilian, and others have explained, your language is effective when all aspects of your message fit the rhetorical situation:

Rhetorical Situation

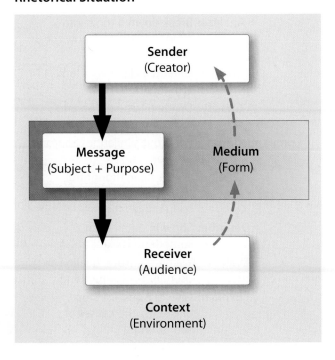

Think of your role as the writer.

Are you writing as a concerned citizen, as a student in a class, as a friend relating a story, as a reporter providing news, as a blogger giving an opinion? Your role in writing and otherwise communicating affects the level of language you use, the voice you use, the types of details you include, and so on.

Understand your subject.

To truly understand your subject, you need to gather and assimilate all relevant details about it, including its history, makeup, function, and impact on people and culture. Knowing those details will help you narrow your focus to a specific thesis and support it well.

> **Writing with Sources:** As you search for information, think about which types of sources are recommended or expected for the assignment. Which should be avoided?

Understand your purpose.

Key words in an assignment—such as *analyze, explain, defend,* or *describe*—tell you what the purpose of the writing is supposed to be. Understanding why you are writing helps you choose an organizational strategy, such as classification, definition, or process. (See pages 34–35.)

> **Writing with Sources:** Think of the sources that will most help you with your purpose, whether to entertain, compare, inspire, enlighten, and so on.

Understand your audience.

For any writing task, you must understand your audience in order to develop writing that meets their needs. To assess your audience, answer questions like these:

- Who are my readers: instructor? classmates? Web users?
- What do they know about my topic, and what do they need to know?
- How well do they understand the terminology involved?
- What are their attitudes toward the topic and toward me?

- How well do they read written English—or visuals such as graphs and charts?
- How will they use my writing (as entertainment or to complete a task)?

Note: Answers to such questions will help you develop meaningful sentences (pages 82–87), choose appropriate words (pages 87–90), and select relevant visuals.

> **Writing with Sources:** Ask yourself what sources your reader will best understand and most respect. What sources will add to your credibility and authority?

Understand the medium (form).

Many communication options are available for every message. Academic forms include essays, analyses, reports, proposals, research papers, reviews, and so on. It is important to understand the form of the assignment. What works well in a narrative about a past experience would not work as well in a lab report. Also, each of these forms can contain multiple media: written elements, graphics, photos, drawings, videos, audios, links, and so on. Understanding the overall medium and the media within it will help you succeed.

> **Writing with Sources:** Make sure you understand the way that sources are to be cited in the form of communication you are using. (See 270–297 for MLA and APA styles.)

Think about the context.

Think about how this assignment relates to others in the course. Consider these issues:

- **Weight:** Is this an everyday assignment, a weekly or biweekly one, or the big one?
- **Assessment:** Find out how the assignment will be graded. What rubric will be used?
- **Intent:** Make certain that you understand the goals of the assignment and understand what your instructor wants you to get out of it.

Note: If the writing you are doing is not in response to an assignment, think about the environment in which the message will be read. What is the history of this issue? What is the current climate like? What might the future be?

> **Writing with Sources:** If you are writing material that will be reviewed and debated by others in your field, think about what sources you would most want your writing to appear in. Make certain you understand the submission guidelines for the source.

Understand the assignment. LO3

Each college instructor has a way of personalizing a writing assignment, but most assignments will spell out (1) the objective, (2) the task, (3) the formal requirements, and (4) suggested approaches and topics. Your first step, therefore, is to read the assignment carefully, noting the options and restrictions that are part of it. The suggestions below will help you do that. (Also see pages 14–29 for one writer's approach.)

Read the assignment.

Certain words in the assignment explain what main action you must perform. Here are some words that signal what you are to do:

Key Words

Analyze:	Break down a topic into subparts, showing how those parts relate.
Argue:	Defend a claim with logical arguments.
Classify:	Divide a large group into well-defined subgroups.
Compare/contrast:	Point out similarities and/or differences.
Define:	Give a clear, thoughtful definition or meaning of something.
Describe:	Show in detail what something is like.
Evaluate:	Weigh the truth, quality, or usefulness of something.
Explain:	Give reasons, list steps, or discuss the causes of something.
Interpret:	Tell in your own words what something means.

Olexiy Bayev, 2011 / Used under license from Shutterstock.com

Reflect: Share your well-considered thoughts about a subject.

Summarize: Restate someone else's ideas very briefly in your own words.

Synthesize: Connect facts or ideas to create something new.

Options and Restrictions — The assignment often gives you some choice of your topic or approach but may restrict your options to suit the instructor's purpose. Note the options and restrictions in the following short sample assignment:

> Reflect on the way a natural disaster or major historical event has altered your understanding of the past, the present, or the future.

Options:
1. You may choose any natural disaster or historical event.
2. You may focus on the past, present, or future.
3. You may examine any kind of alteration.

Restrictions:
1. You must reflect on a change in your understanding.
2. The disaster must be natural.
3. The historical event must be major.

Relate the assignment to the goals of the course.

1. How much value does the instructor give the assignment? (The value is often expressed as a percentage of the course grade.)
2. What benefit does your instructor want you to receive?
   - Strengthen your comprehension?
   - Improve your research skills?
   - Deepen your ability to explain, prove, or persuade?
   - Expand your style?
   - Increase your creativity?
3. How will this assignment contribute to your overall performance in the course? What course goals (often listed in the syllabus) does it address?

Relate the assignment to other assignments.

1. Does it build on previous assignments?
2. Does it prepare you for the next assignment?

Relate the assignment to your own interests.

1. Does it connect with a topic that already interests you?
2. Does it connect with work in your other courses?
3. Does it connect with the work you may do in your chosen field?
4. Does it connect with life outside school?

Reflect on the assignment.

1. **First impulses:** How did you feel when you first read the assignment?
2. **Approaches:** What's the usual approach for an assignment like this? What's a better way of tackling it?
3. **Quality of performance:** What would it take to produce an excellent piece of writing?
4. **Benefits:** What are the benefits to your education? to you personally? to the class? to society?
5. **Features:** Reflect further on four key features of any writing assignment.
   Purpose: What is the overall purpose of the assignment—to inform, to explain, to analyze, to entertain? What is the desired outcome?
   Audience: Should you address your instructor? your classmates? a general reader? How much does the reader already know about the topic? What type of language should you use?
   Form: What are the requirements concerning length, format, and due date?
   Assessment: How will the assignment be evaluated? How can you be sure that you are completing the assignment correctly?

Select, limit, and explore your topic.

For some assignments, finding a suitable subject (or topic) may require little thinking on your part. If an instructor asks you to summarize an article in a professional journal, you know what you will write about—the article in question. But suppose the instructor asks you to analyze a feature of popular culture in terms of its impact on society. You won't be sure of a specific writing topic until you explore the possibilities. Keep the following points in mind when you conduct a topic search. Your topic must . . .

- meet the requirements of the assignment.
- be limited in scope.
- seem reasonable (that is, be within your means to research).
- genuinely interest you.

Limit the subject area.

Many of your writing assignments may relate to general subject areas you are currently studying. Your task, then, is to select a specific topic related to the general area of study—a topic limited enough that you can treat it with some depth in the length allowed for the assignment. The following examples show the difference between general subjects and limited topics:

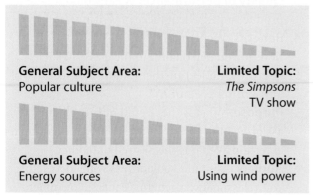

General Subject Area:
Popular culture

Limited Topic:
The Simpsons
TV show

General Subject Area:
Energy sources

Limited Topic:
Using wind power

Conduct your search.

Finding a writing idea that meets the requirements of the assignment should not be difficult, if you know how and where to look. Follow these steps:

1. Check your class notes and handouts for ideas related to the assignment.

2. Search the Internet. Type in a keyword or phrase (the general subject stated in the assignment) and see what you can find. You could also follow a subject tree to narrow a subject. (See pages 332–334.)
3. Consult indexes, guides, and other library references. *The Readers' Guide to Periodical Literature*, for example, lists current articles published on specific topics and where to find them. (See page 327.)
4. Discuss the assignment with your instructor or an information specialist.
5. Use one or more of the prewriting strategies described on the following pages to generate possible writing ideas.

Explore for possible topics.

You can generate possible writing ideas by using the following strategies. These same strategies can be used when you've chosen a topic and want to develop it further.

Journal Writing — Write in a journal on a regular basis. Reflect on your personal feelings, develop your thoughts, and record the happenings of each day. Periodically go back and underline ideas that you would like to explore in writing assignments. In the following journal-writing sample, the writer came up with an idea for a writing assignment about the societal impacts of popular culture.

> I read a really disturbing news story this morning. I've been thinking about it all day. In California a little girl was killed when she was struck by a car driven by a man distracted by a billboard ad for lingerie featuring a scantily clothed woman. Not only is it a horrifying thing to happen, but it also seems to me all too symbolic of the way that sexually charged images in the media are putting children, and especially girls, in danger. That reminds me of another news story I read this week about preteen girls wanting to wear the kinds of revealing outfits that they see in music videos, TV shows, and magazines aimed at teenagers. Too many of today's media images give young people the impression that sexuality should begin at an early age. This is definitely a dangerous message.

shooarts, 2011 / Used under license from Shutterstock.com

Freewriting — Write nonstop for ten minutes or longer to discover possible writing ideas. Use a key concept related to the assignment as a starting point. You'll soon discover potential writing ideas that might otherwise have never entered your mind. Note in the following example that the writer doesn't stop writing even when he can't think of anything to say. Note also that he doesn't stop to correct typos and other mistakes.

Popular culture. What does that include? Television obviously but that's a pretty boring subject. What else? Movies, pop music, video games. Is there a connection between playing violent video games and acting out violent behavior? Most video players I know would say no but sometimes news reports suggest a connection. Is this something I'd want to write about? Not really. What then? Maybe I could think about this a different way and focus on the positive effects of playing video games. They release tension for one thing and they can really be challenging. Other benefits? They help to kill time, that's for sure, but maybe that's not such a good thing. I would definitely read more if it weren't for video games, tv, etc. Maybe I could write about how all the electronic entertainment that surrounds us today is creating a generation of nonreaders. Or maybe I could focus on whether people aren't getting much physical exercise because of the time they spend with electronic media. Maybe both. At least I have some possibilities to work with.

zirconicusso, 2011 / Used under license from Shutterstock.com

Quick Guide: Freewriting

Freewriting is the writing you do without having a specific outcome in mind. You simply write down whatever pops into your head as you explore your topic. Freewriting can serve as a starting point for your writing, or it can be combined with any of the other prewriting strategies to help you select, explore, focus, or organize your writing. If you get stuck at any point during the composing process, you can return to freewriting as a way of generating new ideas.

Reminders

- **Freewriting helps you get your thoughts down on paper.** (Thoughts are constantly passing through your mind.)
- **Freewriting helps you develop and organize these thoughts.**
- **Freewriting helps you make sense out of things** that you may be studying or researching.
- **Freewriting may seem awkward at times,** but just stick with it.

The Process

- **Write nonstop and record whatever comes into your mind.** Follow your thoughts instead of trying to direct them.
- **If you have a particular topic or assignment to complete, use it as a starting point.** Otherwise, begin with anything that comes to mind.
- **Don't stop to judge, edit, or correct your writing;** that will come later.
- **Keep writing even when you think you have exhausted all of your ideas.** Switch to another angle or voice, but keep writing.
- **Watch for a promising writing idea to emerge.** Learn to recognize the beginnings of a good idea, and then expand that idea by recording as many specific details as possible.

The Result

- **Review your writing and underline the ideas you like.** These ideas will often serve as the basis for future writings.
- **Determine exactly what you need to write about.** Once you've figured out what you are required to do, you may then decide to do a second freewriting exercise.
- **Listen to and read the freewriting of others;** learn from your peers.

Listing
— Freely list ideas as they come to mind, beginning with a key concept related to the assignment. (Brainstorming—listing ideas in conjunction with members of a group—is often an effective way to extend your lists.) The following is an example of a student's list of ideas for possible topics on the subject of news reporting:

Aspect of popular culture: News reporting

Sensationalism

Sound bites rather than in-depth analysis

Focus on the negative

Shock radio

Shouting matches pretending to be debates

Press leaks that damage national security, etc.

Lack of observation of people's privacy

Bias

Contradictory health news confusing to readers

Little focus on "unappealing" issues like poverty

Celebration of "celebrity"

zirconicusso, 2011 / Used under license from Shutterstock.com

Clustering
— To begin the clustering process, write a key word or phrase related to the assignment in the center of your paper. Circle it, and then cluster ideas around it. Circle each idea as you record it, and draw a line connecting it to the closest related idea. Keep going until you run out of ideas and connections. The following is a student's cluster on the subject of sports:

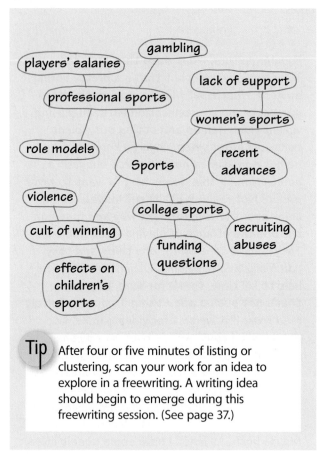

Tip After four or five minutes of listing or clustering, scan your work for an idea to explore in a freewriting. A writing idea should begin to emerge during this freewriting session. (See page 37.)

Collect information and track your sources. LO5

Writer and instructor Donald Murray said that "writers write with information. If there is no information, there will be no effective writing." How true! Before you can develop a thoughtful piece of writing, you must gain a thorough understanding of your topic; to do so, you must carry out the necessary reading, reflecting, and researching. Writing becomes a satisfying experience once you can speak with authority about your topic. Use the following guidelines when you start collecting information. (Also see "Research and Writing" in this book.)

- Determine what you already know about your topic. (Use the strategies below this bulleted list.)
- Consider listing questions you would like to answer during your research.
- Identify and explore possible sources of information. (See page 40.)
- Carry out your research following a logical plan. (See pages 40–41.)

Find out what you already know.

Use one or more of the following strategies to determine what you already know about a writing topic.

1. **Focused freewriting:** At this point, you can focus your freewriting by (1) exploring your limited topic from different angles or (2) approaching your freewriting as if it were a quick draft of the actual paper. A quick version will tell you how much you know about your topic and what you need to find out.

2. **Clustering:** Try clustering with your topic serving as the nucleus word. Your clustering should focus on what you already know. (See page 38.)

3. **Five W's of writing:** Answer the five W's—Who? What? When? Where? and Why?—to identify basic information on your subject. Add How? to the list for better coverage.

4. **Directed writing:** Write whatever comes to mind about your topic, using one of the modes listed below. (Repeat the process as often as you need to, selecting a different mode each time.)

Describe it: What do you see, hear, feel, smell, and taste?

Compare it: What is it similar to? What is it different from?

Associate it: What connections between this topic and others come to mind?

Analyze it: What parts does it have? How do they work together?

Argue it: What do you like about the topic? What do you not like about it? What are its strengths and weaknesses?

Apply it: What can you do with it? How can you use it?

Ask questions.

To guide your collecting and researching, you may find it helpful to list questions about your topic that you would like to answer. Alternatively, you can refer to the questions below. These questions address problems, policies, and concepts. Most topics will fall under one of these categories. Use those questions that seem helpful as a guide to your research.

	Problems	Policies	Concepts
Description	What is the problem? What type of problem is it? What are its parts? What are the signs of the problem?	What is the policy? How broad is it? What are its parts? What are its most important features?	What is the concept? What are its parts? What is its main feature? Whom or what is it related to?
Function	Who or what is affected by it? What new problems might it cause in the future?	What is the policy designed to do? What is needed to make it work? What are or will be its effects?	Who has been influenced by this concept? Why is it important? How does it work?
History	What is the current status of the problem? What or who caused it? What or who contributed to it?	What brought about this policy? What are the alternatives?	When did it originate? How has it changed over the years? How might it change in the future?
Value	What is its significance? Why? Why is it more (or less) important than other problems? What does it symbolize or illustrate?	Is the policy workable? What are its advantages and disadvantages? Is it practical? Is it a good policy? Why or why not?	What practical value does it have? Why is it superior (or inferior) to similar concepts? What is its social worth?

Identify possible sources.

Finding meaningful sources is one of the most important steps you will take as you prepare to write. Listed below are tips that will help you identify good sources:

1. **Give yourself enough time.** Finding good sources of information may be time-consuming. Books and periodicals you need may be checked out, your computer service may be down, and so on.
2. **Be aware of the limits of your resources.** Print material may be out-of-date. Online information may be more current, but it may not always be reliable. (See pages 337–340 for ways to help you evaluate information.)
3. **Use your existing resources to find additional sources of information.** Pay attention to books, articles, and individuals mentioned in reliable initial sources of information.
4. **Ask for help.** The specialists in your school library can help you find information that is reliable and relevant. These people are trained to find information; don't hesitate to ask for their help. (See page 324.)
5. **Bookmark useful Web sites.** Include reference works and academic resources related to your major.

Explore different sources of information. — Of course, books and Web sites are not the only possible sources of information. Primary sources such as interviews, observations, and surveys may lead you to a more thorough and meaningful understanding of a topic. (See pages 337–340.)

Primary Sources	Secondary Sources
Interviews	Articles
Observations	Reference book entries
Participation	Books
Surveys	Web sites

Carry out your research. — As you conduct your research, try to use a variety of reliable sources. It's also a good idea to choose an efficient note-taking method before you start. You will want to take good notes on the information you find and record all the publishing information necessary for citing your sources. (See pages 347–348.)

Reserve a special part of a notebook to question, evaluate, and reflect on your research as it develops. The record of your thoughts and actions created during this process will mean a great deal to you—as much as or more than the actual information you uncover. Reflection helps you make sense of new ideas, refocus your thinking, and evaluate your progress.

Track sources.

Follow these strategies for tracking sources and taking notes.

Track resources in a working bibliography. — Once you find a useful book, journal article, news story, or Web page, record identifying information for the source. For more help, see page 346.

Use a note-taking system that respects sources. — Essentially, your note-taking system should help you keep an accurate record of useful information and ideas from sources while also allowing you to engage those sources with your own thinking. For a discussion of possible systems, see pages 347–348.

Distinguish summaries, paraphrases, and quotations. — As you read sources, you will find material that answers your questions and helps you achieve your writing purpose. At that point, decide whether to summarize, paraphrase, or quote the material:

A summary pulls just the main points out of a passage and puts them in your own words: Summarize source material when it contains relevant ideas and information that you can boil down.

A paraphrase rewrites a passage point by point in your own words: Paraphrase source material when all the information is important but the actual phrasing isn't especially important or memorable.

A quotation records a passage from the source word for word: Quote when the source states something crucial and says it well. Note: In your notes, always identify quoted material by putting quotation marks around it.

Summarizing, paraphrasing, and quoting are treated more fully on pages 349–351. Here is a brief example, with the original passage coming from Coral Ann Howells' *Alice Munro*, published in 1998 by Manchester University Press as part of its Contemporary World Writers series.

Original:
"To read Munro's stories is to discover the delights of seeing two worlds at once: an ordinary everyday world and the shadowy map of another imaginary or secret world laid over the real one, so that in reading we slip from one world into the other in an unassuming domestic sort of way."

Summary:
Munro's fiction moves readers from recognizable reality into a hidden world.

Paraphrase:
Reading Munro's fiction gives readers the enjoyment of experiencing a double world: day-to-day reality and on top of that a more mysterious, fantastic world, with the result that readers move smoothly between the worlds in a seamless, ordinary way.

Quotation:
Munro's fiction takes us into "the shadowy map of another imaginary or secret world laid over the real one."

Critical-Thinking and Writing Activities

As directed by your instructor, complete the following critical-thinking and writing activities by yourself or with classmates.

1. Writer Ralph Fletcher shares, "When I write, I am always struck at how magical and unexpected the process turns out to be." Would you describe the writing process you follow as "magical" and "unexpected"? Why or why not?

2. Reread one of your recent essays. Does the writing show that you thoroughly understood your subject, met the needs of your audience, and achieved your purpose?

3. Below is a list of general subject areas. Select one that interests you and do the following: Using the strategies on pages 36–38, brainstorm possible topics and select one. Then use the strategies on pages 38–41 to explore what you know about that topic and what you need to learn.

Arts/music	Environment
Health/medicine	Work/occupation

Cross-Curricular Connections
Different academic disciplines require different methods of research note taking. Investigate the styles of research note taking used in your discipline.

Checklist: Learning Outcomes

Use this checklist as a guide to help you plan your writing.

_____ I understand the writing process—getting started, planning, drafting, revising, editing and proofreading, and submitting—and I adapt it to fit each project and my own individual style.

_____ I know how to analyze the rhetorical situation:
- **My role**—my position and my goals
- **The subject**—the general area of inquiry
- **The purpose**—to inform, explain, analyze, persuade
- **The form**—essay, narrative, editorial, research paper
- **The audience**—who they are, what they know, what they need
- **The context**—weight, assessment, positioning of the project.

_____ I know how to analyze an assignment, watching for options and restrictions.

_____ I know how to select a subject and explore it through journal writing, freewriting, listing, clustering, and dialogue. I know how to focus the topic to fit the assignment and my interests.

_____ I know how to collect information and track it through note-taking and research strategies.

"Have a vision. Be demanding."
—Colin Powell

4

Planning

Some of us are meticulous planners. We organize our lives in advance and formulate strategies for completing every task. Others of us live more in the moment, believing that whatever needs to get done will get done, with or without a plan.

In writing, author and instructor Ken Macrorie calls for a blend of these two approaches: "Good writing," says Macrorie, "is formed partly through plan and partly through accident." In other words, too much early planning can get in the way of the discovery aspect of writing, while not enough planning can harm the focus and coherence of your writing.

Learning Outcomes

LO1 Revisit the rhetorical situation.

LO2 Form your thesis statement.

LO3 Select a method of development.

LO4 Develop a plan or an outline.

Revisit the rhetorical situation.

LO1

Use the following planning checklist to help you decide whether to move ahead with your planning or reconsider your topic.

Rhetorical Checklist

Writer
____ Am I interested in this topic?
____ How much do I know about this topic, and how much do I need to learn?

Subject
____ Does the topic fit with the subject requirements of the assignment?
____ Is the topic the right size—not too general or too specific—for the assignment?
____ What sources can I use to find out more about this topic?

Purpose
____ What are the specific goals of the assignment?
____ Am I writing to entertain, inform, explain, analyze, persuade, reflect?

Form
____ What form should I create: essay, proposal, report, review?

Audience
____ Will my readers be interested in this topic? How can I interest them?
____ What do they know and need to know about it? What opinions do they have?

Context
____ What weight does this assignment have in terms of my grade?
____ How will the assignment be assessed?

Working with Sources: For projects that involve research, consider how the rhetorical situation can guide your use of sources:

1. For your **subject**, which sources offer reliable information and analysis that has shaped your thinking and pointed toward a working thesis?

2. To achieve your **purpose** (to entertain, inform, analyze, and/or persuade), which resources/sources should be featured in your writing?

3. Given your **audience**, which resources will help you create credibility with the audience and clarify the topic for them?

Form your thesis statement.

LO2

As you gain knowledge about your topic, you should concurrently develop a more focused interest in it. If all goes well, this narrowed focus will bring to mind a thesis. A **thesis statement** identifies the central idea for your writing. It usually highlights a special condition or feature of the topic, expresses a specific claim about it, or takes a stand.

State your thesis in a sentence that effectively expresses what you want to explore or explain in your essay. Sometimes a thesis statement develops early and easily; at other times, the true focus of your writing will emerge only after you've done some initial writing.

Find a focus.

A general subject area is typically built into your writing assignments. Your task, then, is to find a limited writing topic and examine it from a particular angle or perspective. (You will use this focus to form your thesis statement.)

General Subject ··········	Alternative energy sources
Limited Topic ··········	Wind power
Specific Focus ··········	Wind power as a viable energy source in certain settings.

Serhiy Shullye, 2011 / Used under license from Shutterstock.com

State your thesis.

You can use the following formula to write a thesis statement for your essay. A thesis statement sets the tone and direction for your writing. Keep in mind that at this point you're *writing a working* thesis statement—a statement in progress, so to speak. You may change it as your thinking on the topic evolves.

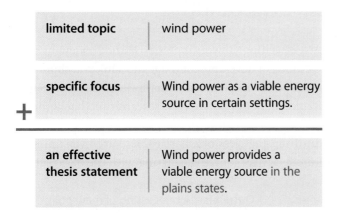

limited topic	wind power
specific focus	Wind power as a viable energy source in certain settings.

+

an effective thesis statement	Wind power provides a viable energy source in the plains states.

Working with Sources: Sometimes your writing can take direction specifically from your sources. You may consider making your thesis a response to a specific source. For example, if one source is especially strong or especially contrary to your own thinking, you could shape your thesis as an affirmation of the strong source's authority or as a rebuttal to the contrary source's claims.

Select a method of development.

LO3

In his classic book *On Writing Well,* William Zinsser identifies "striving for order" as one of the keys to effective writing. For some assignments, this is not a problem because an **organizing pattern** is built right into the assignment. For example, you might be asked to develop a process paper, which you would organize chronologically. When a pattern is not apparent, one might still evolve naturally as you gather information. If this doesn't happen, examine your thesis statement to see what method of development it suggests.

Let your thesis guide you.

An effective thesis will often suggest an organizing pattern. Notice how the thesis statements below direct and shape the writing to follow. (Also see page 46.)

Thesis (Focus) for a Personal Narrative

Writers of personal narratives do not always state a thesis directly, but they will generally have in mind an implied theme or main idea that governs the way they develop their writing. The thesis below focuses the reader's attention on a less-than-perfect day in the life of a perfect flight attendant. (See pages 105–106.)

> From the first day Northwest hired me in Minneapolis in 1969, I tried to be a model flight attendant, to develop the qualities my operations manual demanded: poise, good judgment, initiative, adaptability and a spotless appearance. But one time I slipped up: I fell asleep.

Thesis for a Cause-and-Effect Essay

A cause-and-effect essay usually begins with one or more causes followed by an explanation of the effects, or with a primary effect followed by an explanation of the causes. In the thesis below, the writer credits team sports with helping to advance women into leadership roles in major corporations. (See pages 162–175.)

> While most of America's corporations are still commanded by male chief executives, women are gaining ground, winning vice-presidential and top management slots and, in a few cases, the highest leadership roles. Many of these young female executives say playing team sports helped them get ahead.

Thesis for an Essay of Comparison

Some comparisons treat one subject before the other (subject by subject), others discuss the subjects point by point, and some treat similarities and then differences. The writer of the thesis below introduces her comparison and contrast of two different views of Islamic dress—both of which she holds. (See pages 155–156.)

> To wear hijab—Islamic covering—is to invite contradiction. Sometimes I hate it. Sometimes I value it.

Thesis for an Essay of Classification

An essay of classification identifies the main parts or categories of a topic and then examines each one. In the thesis below, the writer identifies four ways to discuss literature, and he examines each one in turn. (See pages 134–135.)

> There are four main perspectives, or approaches, that readers can use to converse about literature.

Thesis for a Process Essay

Process essays are organized chronologically. As indicated in the thesis below, the writer of this essay will explain how cancer cells multiply and affect the body. (See pages 141–142.)

> When a cell begins to function abnormally, it can initiate a process that results in cancer.

Thesis for a Position Essay

A position paper first introduces a topic and then states a position in its thesis. The thesis statement below defines the writer's position on nuclear energy. (See pages 194–196.)

> However, the risks of nuclear power far outweigh its benefits, making fossil fuels the safer and more environmentally responsible option.

Thesis for an Essay of Definition

An essay of definition explores the denotation, connotation, and history of a term. In the following thesis statement, the writer names the two words he will explore—*deft* and *daft*—and provides an overview of the definition essay. (See page 118.)

> Let me see if I can explain the original meaning and also how daft and deft came to part company.

Thesis for an Essay Proposing a Solution

A problem-solution essay usually begins with a discussion of the problem and its causes and then examines possible solutions. In the following thesis statement, the writer points to a problem in the supposedly gender-equal society of the United States. After explaining the problem, she offers and argues for a specific solution. (See pages 229–232.)

> Fatherlessness is the most harmful demographic trend of this generation. Yet, despite its scale and social consequences, fatherlessness is a problem that is frequently ignored or denied.

Develop a plan or an outline.
LO4

After writing a working thesis and reviewing the methods of development (pages 45–46), you should be ready to organize the information you have collected. Remember, organizing your research and background information before you start writing can make the drafting stage less of a hassle. Here are five strategies for effective organizing, starting with the basic list.

Quick List	A brief listing of main points (See below.)
Topic Outline	A more formal plan, including main points and essential details (See page 47.)
Sentence Outline	A formal plan, including main points and essential details, written as complete sentences (See page 48.)
Writing Blueprints	Basic organizational strategies preferred for different forms of writing (See pages 48–49.)
Graphic Organizer	An arrangement of main points and essential details in an appropriate chart or diagram (See pages 50–51.)

Quick Lists

Though listing is the simplest of all the methods of organization, it can help you take stock of your main ideas and get a sense of what further research or planning needs to be done. There is no right or wrong way to go about listing. The key is to come up with a system that works best for you. Here are two examples that you may consider: the basic bulleted list, which briefly lists the main points you will discuss, and a T Chart, which lists the main points on one side and a supporting detail on the other side.

Sample Basic List

Topic: Different ways to discuss literature —— Topic

- Focus on the text itself
- Focus on the text and the reader
- Focus on the author of the text
- Focus on ideas outside of literature

Main Points

Sample T Chart

Topic: Different ways to discuss literature —— Topic

Main Points	Supporting Details
Text-centered approach	Emphasizes structure and rules
Audience-centered approach	Relationship between reader and text
Author-centered approach	Emphasizes the writer's life

Insight: Planning is adaptable. Some writers prefer to generate an outline before they begin writing, while others prefer to make a more detailed outline after having written a draft. In the latter strategy, an outline can serve as a tool for evaluating the logic and completeness of the paper's organization.

ollirg, 2011 / Used under license from Shutterstock.com

Topic Outline

If you have a good deal of information to sort and arrange, you may want to use a topic outline for your planning. In a topic outline, you state each main point and essential detail as a word or phrase. Before you start constructing your outline, write your working thesis statement at the top of your paper to help keep you focused on the subject. (Do not attempt to outline your opening and closing paragraphs unless you are specifically asked to do so.)

An effective topic outline is parallel in structure, meaning the main points (I, II, III) and essential details (A, B, C) are stated in the same way. Notice how the sample outline below uses a parallel structure, making it easy to follow.

Thesis: There are four main —— Thesis
perspectives, or approaches, that
readers can use to converse about
literature.

   I. Text-centered approaches —— Main Point
     A. Also called formalist criticism
     B. Emphasis on structure of text and rules of genre
     C. Importance placed on key literary elements

Supporting Details

  II. Audience-centered approaches
     A. Also called rhetorical or reader-response criticism
     B. Emphasis on interaction between reader and text

 III. Author-centered approaches
     A. Emphasis on writer's life
     B. Importance placed on historical perspective
     C. Connections made between texts

 IV. Ideological approaches
     A. Psychological analysis of text
     B. Myth or archetype criticism
     C. Moral criticism

Insight: The text-filled outlines on pages 48–49 all display the organization of "Four Ways to Talk About Literature," (pages 132–133).

Sentence Outline — A **sentence outline** is a more formal method of arrangement in which you state each main point and essential detail as a sentence. Writing a sentence outline helps you determine how you will express your ideas in the actual writing. Here is an example.

Sentence Outline

Thesis: There are four main perspectives, or approaches, that readers can use to converse about literature. ———— Thesis

   I. A text-centered approach focuses on the literary piece itself. ——— Main Point

      A. This approach is often called formalist criticism.

      B. This method of criticism examines text structure and the genre's rules.

      C. A formalist critic determines how key literary elements reinforce meaning.
          — Supporting Details

  II. An audience-centered approach focuses on the "transaction" between text and reader.

      A. This approach is often called rhetorical or reader-response criticism.

      B. Each reader's interaction with a text is unique.

 III. An author-centered approach focuses on the origin of a text.

      A. An author-centered critic examines the writer's life.

      B. This method of criticism may include a historical look at a text.

      C. Connections may be made between the text and related works.

Working with Sources: When your writing project involves sources, the planning phase will include a great deal of sorting through material. Outlining can help you organize your primary and secondary sources to best support your thesis. As you organize your research in your outline, ask these questions:

- Where and how should I work with primary sources—interviews, surveys, analyses, observations, experiments, and other data I have collected?
- Where and how should I bring in secondary sources—scholarly books, journal articles, and the like?

Writing Blueprints

The writing blueprints on this page and the next lay out basic organizational strategies for different forms of writing. The blueprints may help you arrange the details of your essay or even find holes in your research.

Classification Blueprint

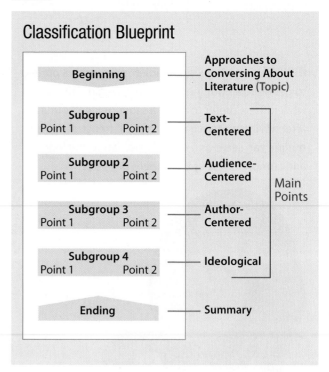

Comparison – Contrast Blueprint

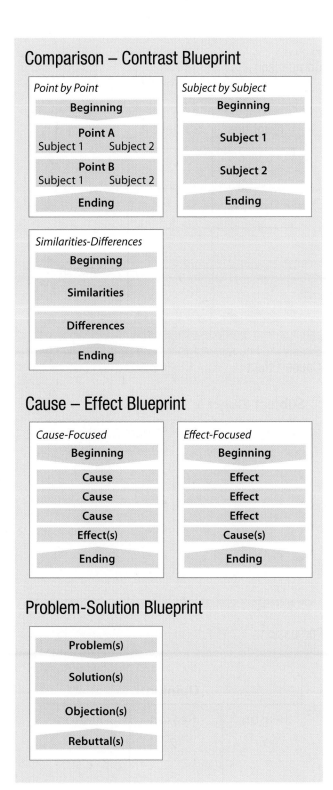

Point by Point

Beginning

Point A
Subject 1   Subject 2

Point B
Subject 1   Subject 2

Ending

Subject by Subject

Beginning
Subject 1
Subject 2
Ending

Similarities-Differences

Beginning
Similarities
Differences
Ending

Cause – Effect Blueprint

Cause-Focused

Beginning
Cause
Cause
Cause
Effect(s)
Ending

Effect-Focused

Beginning
Effect
Effect
Effect
Cause(s)
Ending

Problem-Solution Blueprint

Problem(s)
Solution(s)
Objection(s)
Rebuttal(s)

Graphic Organizers — If you are a visual learner, you may prefer using a graphic organizer to arrange your ideas for writing. A **graphic organizer** allows you to arrange main points and essential details in an appropriate chart or diagram. Graphic organizers can help you map out your ideas and illustrate relation-

ships between them. Here is a **line diagram** that was used to organize some of the same ideas that were outlined previously.

Line Diagram

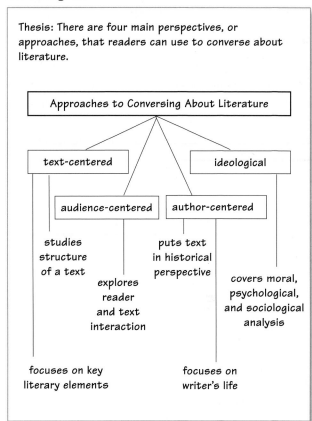

Thesis: There are four main perspectives, or approaches, that readers can use to converse about literature.

Approaches to Conversing About Literature

- text-centered
  - studies structure of a text
  - focuses on key literary elements
  - audience-centered
    - explores reader and text interaction
- ideological
  - author-centered
    - puts text in historical perspective
    - focuses on writer's life
  - covers moral, psychological, and sociological analysis

Graphic Organizers:
Quick Guide

The following graphic organizers relate to the methods of development discussed on pages 45–46. Each one will help you collect and organize information for expository or persuasive writing. Adapt the organizers as necessary to fit your particular needs or personal style.

Comparison

Qualities	Subject A	Subject B

Comparison/Contrast (Venn Diagram)

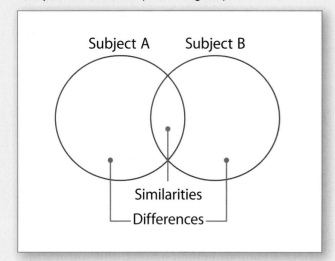

Cause-Effect

Subject (Object of Study)

Causes (Because of . . .)	**Effects** (. . . these conditions resulted)
•	•
•	•
•	•
•	•

Process Analysis

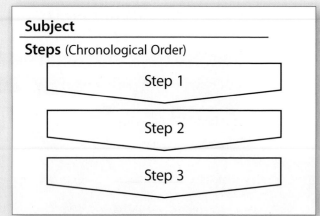

Persuasion

Opinion

Reason 1	Reason 2	Reason 3

Definition

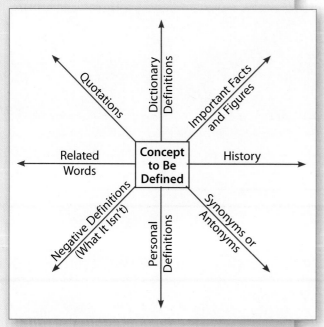

Classification

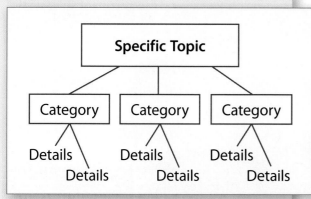

Problem/Solution

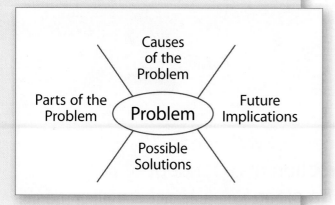

Critical-Thinking and Writing Activities

As directed by your instructor, complete the following activities.

1. Author Ken Macrorie claims that "good writing is formed partly through plan and partly through accident." Do you agree? Why or why not? Relate Macrorie's idea to your own writing experiences. How carefully do you plan? How much do you leave to accident?

2. A number of organizational patterns are discussed on pages 45–46. Choose one of these patterns and select a model essay from chapters 9–18 that follows the pattern. Read the essay, note the thesis, and explain how the writer develops it.

Cross-Curricular Connections

In most disciplines, it is common practice early in the paper to "survey the literature" on the topic. In a literary analysis, you might survey common interpretations of a key concept before you relay your view.

1. Identify the studies that should be included in the review.

2. Categorize studies by approach or arrange them chronologically.

Checklist: Learning Outcomes

Use this checklist as a guide to help you plan your writing.

_____ I have taken stock of the rhetorical situation.
- I have reviewed the information I have collected so far.
- My planning and research fully address my subject, purpose, and audience.

_____ I have developed a focused thesis statement.
- My thesis statement reflects a limited topic.
- My thesis statement clearly states the specific idea I plan to develop.
- The thesis is supported by the information I have gathered.

_____ I have patterned my writing from my thesis.
- The thesis suggests a pattern of organization for my essay.

_____ I have organized my research.
- I have organized my support in a list, an outline, or a graphic organizer.
- I have arranged my source material under my main supporting points.

"First drafts are concerned with ideas,
with getting the direction and concept of
the piece of writing clear."

—Toby Fulwiler

5

Drafting

French novelist Anatole France once said that his first drafts could have been written by a schoolboy, his next draft by a bright college student, his third draft by a superior graduate, and his final draft "only by Anatole France." Think in those terms as you write your first draft. Your main objective is to get ideas down; you'll have a chance later to improve your writing.

This chapter provides information and advice about drafting a college-level essay. You'll find specific advice for creating the three main parts and arranging information.

Learning Outcomes

LO1 Review your writing situation.

LO2 Opening: Introduce your topic and line of thinking.

LO3 Middle: Develop and support your main points.

LO4 Closing: Complete, clarify, and unify your message.

LO5 Use sources effectively.

Review your writing situation.

As you prepare to write, think about the parts of the rhetorical situation:

Think about your role.

Are you writing as a student, a citizen, a friend, a member of a scholarly community or discipline? Use a voice that represents you well.

Focus on your subject.

As you develop your first draft, these strategies can help you keep your subject in focus.

- Use your outline or writing plan as a general guide. Try to develop your main points, but allow new ideas to emerge naturally.
- Write freely without being too concerned about neatness and correctness. Concentrate on developing your ideas, not on producing a final copy.
- Include as much detail as possible, continuing until you reach a logical stopping point.
- Use your writing plan or any charts, lists, or diagrams you've produced, but don't feel absolutely bound by them.
- Complete your first draft in one or two sittings.
- Use the most natural voice you can so that the writing will flow smoothly. If your voice is too formal during drafting, you'll be tempted to stop and edit your words.

Reconsider your purpose.

Briefly review (1) what you want your writing to do (your task), (2) what you want it to say (your thesis), and (3) how you want to say it.

Reconsider your audience.

Review who your readers are, including their knowledge of and attitude toward your topic. Then get ready to talk with them, person to person.

Review the form and context.

Make sure you understand the type of writing you should do, the weight of the assignment, and any assessment issues.

Basic Essay Structure: Major Moves

The following chart lists the main writing moves that occur during the development of a piece of writing. Use it as a general guide for all of your drafting. Remember to keep your purpose and audience in mind throughout the drafting process.

Opening

Engage your reader.
Stimulate and direct the reader's attention.
Establish your direction.
Identify the topic and put it in perspective.
Get to the point.
Narrow your focus and state your thesis.

Middle

Advance your thesis.
Provide background information and cover your main points.
Test your ideas.
Raise questions and consider alternatives.
Support your main points.
Add substance and build interest.
Build a coherent structure.
Start new paragraphs and arrange the support.
Use different levels of detail.
Clarify and complete each main point.

Ending

Reassert the main point.
Remind the reader of the purpose and rephrase the thesis.
Urge the reader.
Gain the reader's acceptance and look ahead.

Opening: Introduce your topic and line of thinking.

LO2

The opening paragraph is one of the most important elements in any composition. It should accomplish at least three essential things: (1) engage the reader; (2) establish your direction, tone, and level of language; and (3) introduce your line of thought.

Advice:	The conventional way of approaching the first paragraph is to view it as a kind of "funnel" that draws a reader in and narrows to a main point. Often, the final sentence explicitly states your thesis.
Cautions:	Don't feel bound by the conventional pattern, which may sound stale if not handled well.
	Don't let the importance of the first paragraph paralyze you. Relax and write.

The information on the next two pages will help you develop your opening. You can refer to the sample essays in the handbook for ideas.

Engage your reader.

Your reader will be preoccupied with other thoughts until you seize, stimulate, and direct his or her attention. Here are some effective ways to "hook" the reader:

- Mention little-known facts about the topic.

  Beads may have been what separated human ancestors from their Neanderthal cousins. Yes, beads.

- Pose a challenging question.

  Why would human ancestors spend days carving something as frivolous as beads while Neanderthals spent days hunting mammoths?

- Offer a thought-provoking quotation.

  "The key thing in human evolution is when people start devoting just ridiculous amounts of time to making these [beads]," says archeologist John Shea of Stonybrook University.

- Tell a brief, illuminating story.

  When I walked into the room, I had only to show my hand to be accepted in the group of strangers there. The Phi Delta Kappa ring on my finger—and on all of our fingers—bound us across space and time as a group. Our ancestors discovered the power of such ornamentation forty thousand years ago.

Establish your direction.

The direction of your line of thought should become clear in the opening part of your writing. Here are some moves you might make to set the right course:

- Identify the topic (issue). Show a problem, a need, or an opportunity.
- Deepen the issue. Connect the topic, showing its importance.
- Acknowledge other views. Tell what others say or think about the topic.

Get to the point.

You may choose to state your main point up front, or you may wait until later to introduce your thesis. For example, you could work inductively by establishing an issue, a problem, or a question in your opening and then build toward the answer—your thesis—in your conclusion. (See page 12 for more on inductive reasoning.) Sometimes, in fact, your thesis may simply be implied. In any case, the opening should at least hint at the central issue or thesis of your paper. Here are three ways to get to the point:

1. **Narrow your focus.** Point to what interests you about the topic.

2. **Raise a question.** Answer the question in the rest of the essay.

3. **State your thesis.** If appropriate, craft a sentence that boils down your thinking to a central claim. You can use the thesis sentence as a "map" for the organization of the rest of the essay. (See pages 45–46, 58–61, and 312–314.)

Weak Opening

Although the opening below introduces the topic, the writing lacks interesting details and establishes no clear focus for the essay.

> I would like to tell you about the TV show *The Simpsons*. It's about this weird family of five people who look kind of strange and act even stranger. In fact, the characters aren't even real—they're just cartoons.

Strong Opening

In the essay opener below, the writer uses his first paragraph to get his readers' attention and describe his subject. He uses the second paragraph to raise a question that leads him to a statement of his thesis (underlined).

> The Simpsons, stars of the TV show by the same name, are a typical American family, or at least a parody of one. Homer, Marge, Bart, Lisa, and Maggie Simpson live in Springfield, U.S.A. Homer, the father, is a boorish, obese oaf who works in a nuclear power plant. Marge is an overprotective, nagging mother with an outrageous blue hairdo. Ten-year-old Bart is an obnoxious, "spiky-haired demon." Lisa is eight and

a prodigy on the tenor saxophone and in class. The infant Maggie never speaks but only sucks on her pacifier.

> What is the attraction of this yellow-skinned family that stars on a show in which all of the characters have pronounced overbites and only four fingers on each hand? Viewers see a little bit of themselves in everything the Simpsons do. <u>The world of Springfield is a parody of the viewer's world, and Americans can't get enough of it.</u> Viewers experience this parody in the show's explanations of family, education, workplace, and politics.

Insight: Note how, after stating the thesis, the writer forecasts the method of developing that thesis.

Middle: Develop and support your main points. LO3

The middle of the essay is where you do the "heavy lifting." In this part you develop the main points that support your thesis statement.

Advice:	As you write, you will likely make choices that were unforeseen when you began. Use "scratch outlines" (temporary jottings) along the way to show where your new ideas may take you.
Cautions:	Writing that lacks effective detail gives only a vague image of the writer's intent.
	Writing that wanders loses its hold on the essay's purpose.

For both of these reasons, always keep your thesis in mind when you develop the main part of your writing. For help, refer to the guidelines and models on the next five pages. You can refer to the sample essays in this book for additional ideas.

Advance your thesis.

If you stated a thesis in the opening, you can advance it in the middle paragraphs by covering your main points and supporting them in these ways.

Explain:	Provide important facts, details, and examples.
Narrate:	Share a brief story or re-create an experience to illustrate an idea.
Describe:	Tell in detail how someone appears or how something works.
Define:	Identify or clarify the meaning of a specific term or idea.
Analyze:	Examine the parts of something to better understand the whole.
Compare:	Provide examples to show how two things are alike or different.
Argue:	Use logic and evidence to prove that something is true.
Reflect:	Express your thoughts or feelings about something.
Cite authorities:	Add expert analysis or personal commentary.

Test your ideas.

When you write a first draft, you're testing your initial thinking about your topic. You're determining whether your thesis is valid and whether you have enough compelling information to support it. Here are ways to test your line of thinking as you write:

Raise questions. Try to anticipate your readers' questions.

Consider alternatives. Look at your ideas from different angles; weigh various options; reevaluate your thesis.

Answer objections. Directly or indirectly deal with possible problems that a skeptical reader might point out.

Build a coherent structure.

Design paragraphs as units of thought that develop and advance your thesis clearly and logically. For example, look at the brief essay that follows, noting how each body paragraph presents ideas with supporting details that build on and deepen the main idea.

Seeing the Light

All lightbulbs make light, so they're all the same, right? Not quite. You have many choices regarding how to light up your life. Two types of bulbs are the traditional incandescent and the newer, more compact fluorescent. By checking out how they're different, you can better choose which one to buy. [1] [A]

While either incandescent or compact fluorescent bulbs can help you read or find the bathroom at night, each bulb makes light differently. In an incandescent bulb, electricity heats up a tungsten filament (thin wire) to 450 degrees, causing it to glow with a warm, yellow light. A compact fluorescent is a glass tube filled with mercury vapor and argon gas. Electricity causes the mercury to give off ultraviolet radiation. That radiation then causes phosphors coating the inside of the tube to give off light. [2] [B]

Both types of bulbs come in many shapes, sizes, and brightnesses, but compacts have some restrictions. Because of their odd shape, compacts may not fit in a lamp well. Compacts also may not work well in very cold temperatures, and they can't be used with a dimmer switch. [3] [C]

On the other hand, while compact fluorescents are less flexible than incandescents, compacts are four times more efficient. For example, a 15-watt compact [4] [D]

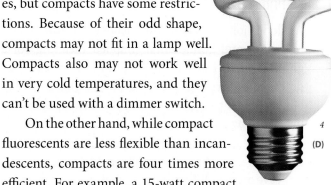

(A) The writer introduces the topic and states his thesis.
(B) The writer starts with a basic explanation of how the two types of lightbulbs function differently.
(C) The writer shifts his attention to weaknesses of compact bulbs.
(D) He next explains the strengths of compacts.

produces as many lumens of light as a 60-watt incandescent! Why? Incandescents turn only about 5 percent of electricity into light and give off the other 95 percent as heat.

5
(E) But are compacts less expensive than incandescents? In the short run, no. A compact costs about $15 while an incandescent costs only a dollar. However, because compacts burn less electricity—and last 7 to 10 times longer—in the long run, compacts are less expensive.

6
(F) Now that you're no longer in the dark about lightbulbs, take a look at the lamp you're using to read this essay. Think about the watts (electricity used), lumens (light produced), efficiency, purchase price, and lamplife. Then decide how to light up your life in the future.

(E) He acknowledges that compacts cost more, but he justifies the cost.
(F) The writer rephrases his thesis as a challenge.

Arrange supporting details.

Organizing information in a logical pattern within a paragraph strengthens its coherence. The following pages explain and illustrate organizational strategies, providing suggested transitions to go with them. (See also pages 75–76.)

Definition

A definition provides the denotation (dictionary meaning) and connotation (implied meaning) of a given term. It often provides examples, gives anecdotes, and offers negative definitions—what the thing is not. In the paragraph below, the writer begins his definition by posing a question.

First of all, what is the grotesque—in visual art and in literature? A term originally applied to Roman cave art that distorted the normal, the grotesque presents the body and mind so that they appear abnormal— different from the bodies and minds that we think belong in our world. Both spiritual and physical, bizarre and familiar, ugly and alluring, the grotesque shocks us, and we respond with laughter and fear. We laugh because the grotesque seems bizarre enough to belong only outside our world; we fear because it feels familiar

enough to be part of it. Seeing the grotesque version of life as it is portrayed in art stretches our vision of reality. As Bernard McElroy argues, "The grotesque transforms the world from what we 'know' it to be to what we fear it might be. It distorts and exaggerates the surface of reality in order to tell a qualitative truth about it."

—John Van Rys

Illustration

An illustration supports a general idea with specific reasons, facts, and details.

As the years passed, my obsession grew. Every fiber and cell of my body was obsessed with the number on the scale and how much fat I could pinch on my thigh. No matter how thin I was, I thought I could never be thin enough. I fought my sisters for control of the TV and VCR to do my exercise programs and videos. The cupboards were stacked with cans of diet mixes, the refrigerator full of diet drinks. Hidden in my underwear drawer were stacks of diet pills that I popped along with my vitamins. At my worst, I would quietly excuse myself from family activities to turn on the bathroom faucet full blast and vomit into the toilet. Every day I stood in front of the mirror, a ritual not unlike brushing my teeth, and scrutinized my body. My face, arms, stomach, buttocks, hips, and thighs could never be small enough.

—Paula Treick

Illustration/Elaboration

additionally	besides	next
again	finally	other
along with	for example	that is
also	for instance	
and	in addition	
another	in other words	
as well	moreover	

Analogy

An analogy is a comparison that a writer uses to explain a complex or unfamiliar phenomenon (how the immune system works) in terms of a familiar one (how mall security works).

The human body is like a mall, and the immune system is like mall security. Because the mall has hundreds of employees and thousands of customers, security guards must rely on photo IDs, name tags, and uniforms to decide who should be allowed to open cash registers and who should have access to the vault. In the same way, white blood cells and antibodies need to use DNA cues to recognize which cells belong in a body and which do not. Occasionally security guards make mistakes, wrestling Kookie the Klown to the ground while DVD players "walk" out of the service entrance, but these problems amount only to allergic reactions or little infections. If security guards become hypervigilant, detaining every customer and employee, the situation is akin to leukemia, in which white blood cells attack healthy cells. If security guards become corrupt, letting thieves take a "five-finger discount," the situation is akin to AIDS. Both systems—mall security and human immunity—work by correctly differentiating friend from foe.

—Rob King

Cause and Effect

Cause-and-effect organization shows how events are linked to their results. If you start with effects, follow with specific causes; if you begin with causes, follow with specific effects. The example below discusses the effects of hypothermia on the human body.

> Even a slight drop in the normal human body temperature of 98.6 degrees Fahrenheit causes hypothermia. Often produced by accidental or prolonged exposure to cold, the condition forces all bodily functions to slow down. The heart rate and blood pressure decrease. Breathing becomes slower and shallower. As the body temperature drops, these effects become even more dramatic until it reaches somewhere between 86 and 82 degrees Fahrenheit and the person lapses into unconsciousness. When the temperature reaches between 65 and 59 degrees Fahrenheit, heart action, blood flow, and electrical brain activity stop. Normally such a condition would be fatal. However, as the body cools down, the need for oxygen also slows down. A person can survive in a deep hypothermic state for an hour or longer and be revived without serious complications.

—Laura Black

Cause and Effect

as a result	inevitably
because	resulting in
consequently	since
due to the fact that	therefore
every time that	

Narration

In the paragraph below, the writer uses narration and chronological order to relate an anecdote—a short, illustrative story.

> When I was six or seven years old, growing up in Pittsburgh, I used to take a precious penny of my own and hide it for someone else to find. It was a curious compulsion; sadly, I've never been seized by it since. For some reason I always "hid" the penny along the same stretch of sidewalk up the street. I would cradle it at the roots of a sycamore, say, or in a hole left by a chipped-off piece of sidewalk. Then I would take a piece of chalk, and, starting at either end of the block, draw huge arrows leading up to the penny from both directions. After I learned to write I labeled the arrows: surprise ahead or money this way. I was greatly excited, during all this arrow-drawing, at the thought of the first lucky passer-by who would receive in this way, regardless of merit, a free gift from the universe. But I never lurked about. I would go straight home and not give the matter another thought, until, some months later, I would be gripped again by the impulse to hide another penny.

—W. Somerset Maugham, *Of Human Bondage*

Process

In the paragraph that follows, a student writer describes the process of entering the "tube," or "green room," while surfing.

> At this point you are slightly ahead of the barreling part of the wave, and you need to "stall," or slow yourself, to get into the tube. There are three methods of stalling used in different situations. If you are slightly ahead of the tube, you can drag your inside hand along the water to stall. If you are a couple of feet in front of the barrel, apply all your weight onto your back foot and sink the tail of the board into the water. This is known as a "tail stall" for obvious reasons, and

its purpose is to decrease your board speed. If you are moving faster than the wave is breaking, you need to do what is called a "wrap-around." To accomplish this maneuver, lean back away from the wave while applying pressure on the tail. This shifts your forward momentum away from the wave and slows you down. When the wave comes, turn toward the wave and place yourself in the barrel.

—Luke Sunukjian, "Entering the Green Room"

Chronological Order

Chronological (time) order helps you tell a story or present steps in a process. For example, the following paragraph describes how cement is made. Notice how the writer explains every step and uses transitional words to lead readers through the process.

The production of cement is a complicated process. The raw materials that go into cement consist of about 60 percent lime, 25 percent silica, and 5 percent alumina. The remaining 10 percent is a varying combination of gypsum and iron oxide (because the amount of gypsum determines the drying time of the cement). First, this mixture is ground up into very fine particles and fed into a kiln. Cement kilns, the largest pieces of moving machinery used by any industry, are colossal steel cylinders lined with firebricks. They can be 25 feet in diameter and up to 750 feet long. The kiln is built at a slant and turns slowly as the cement mix makes its way down from the top end. A flame at the bottom heats the kiln to temperatures of up to 3,000 degrees Fahrenheit. When the melted cement compound emerges from the kiln, it cools into little marble-like balls called clinker. Finally, the clinker is ground to a consistency finer than flour and packaged as cement.

—Kevin Maas

Deyan Georgiev, 2011 / Used under license from Shutterstock.com

Narration/Process/Chronological

a day before	during	second
about	finally	soon
after	first	then
afterward	in the end	today
as soon as	later	tomorrow
at	meanwhile	until
before	next	yesterday

Classification

When classifying a subject, place the subject in its appropriate category and then show how this subject is different from other subjects in the same category. In the following paragraph, a student writer uses classification to describe the theory of temperament.

Medieval doctors believed that "four temperaments rule mankind wholly." According to this theory, each person has a distinctive temperament or personality (sanguine, phlegmatic, melancholy, or choleric) based on the balance of four elements in the body, a balance peculiar to the individual. The theory was built on Galen's and Hippocrates' notion of "humors," which stated that the body contains blood, phlegm, black bile, and yellow bile—four fluids that maintain the balance within the body. The sanguine person was dominated by blood, associated with fire: Blood was hot and moist, and the person was fat and prone to laughter. The phlegmatic person was dominated by phlegm (associated with earth) and was squarish and slothful—a sleepy type. The melancholy person was dominated by cold, black bile (connected with the element of water) and as a result was pensive, peevish, and solitary. The choleric person was dominated by hot, yellow bile (air) and thus was inclined to anger.

—Jessica Radsma

Classification

a typical type	rarest of all
another kind	the third variety
a second variety	the most common
in one category	the most popular
one type	

Climax

Climax is a method in which you first present details and then provide a general climactic statement or conclusion drawn from the details.

> As I walked home, I glanced across the road to see a troubling scene unfold. A burly man strode along the curb, shoulders rounded and face clenched in anger or grief. Behind him, a slim little girl sat on her heels on the sidewalk, hands in her lap and tears streaming down white cheeks. I glanced back at that brute, who climbed into his big black truck and started up the engine. I almost ran across the road to stop him, to set right whatever he'd done. But then I spotted the little dog lying very still in the gutter. The man in the truck must have hit the poor creature, stopped to see if he could help, realized he couldn't, apologized, and left the little girl to grieve. There was nothing I could do, either. Face clenched, I looked back to my side of the street and walked on.

—Jamal Kendal

Compare-Contrast

To compare and contrast, show how two or more subjects are similar and different.

> The old man behind the counter is no doubt Pappy, after which Pappy's Grocery is named. He leans on the glass display case, world weary and watchful, tracking the youth by the snack display. The folds deepen around Pappy's intense eyes as the young customer picks lightly at a bag of potato chips, lifts a can of cashews, runs lithe fingers over the packs of gum. He crouches for a better look at the snack cakes, his pants sliding below colorful boxers. Pappy hitches his own belt higher over his tucked-in shirt. "You gonna buy anything?" The young customer startles, looks up with a smooth face and wide eyes, stands, and walks from Pappy's Grocery.

—Tina Jacobs

Jiri Hera, 2011 / Used under license from Shutterstock.com

Comparison/Contrast

as	like
also	likewise
although	one way
both	on the one hand
but	on the other hand
by contrast	otherwise
even though	similarly
however	still
in the same way	yet

Writing with Sources: Advance and deepen your thesis with reliable reasons and evidence. A typical supporting paragraph starts with a topic sentence and elaborates it with detailed evidence and careful reasoning. Make sure to smoothly integrate quotations into the flow of the writing. Also, avoid dropping in quotations without setting them up and explaining them.

Closing: Complete, clarify, and unify your message.

LO4

Closing paragraphs can be important for tying up loose ends, clarifying key points, or signing off with the reader. In a sense, the entire essay is a preparation for an effective ending; the ending helps the reader look back over the essay with new understanding and appreciation.

Advice:	Because the ending can be so important, draft a variety of possible endings. Choose the one that flows best from a sense of the whole.
Cautions:	If your thesis is weak or unclear, you will have a difficult time writing a satisfactory ending. To strengthen the ending, strengthen the thesis.
	You may have heard this formula for writing an essay: "Say what you're going to say, say it, then say what you've just said." Remember, though, if you need to "say what you've just said," say it in new words.

The information on this page will help you develop your ending. For additional strategies, refer to the sample essays elsewhere in this book.

Reassert the main point.

If an essay is complicated, the reader may need reclarification at the end. Show that you are fulfilling the promises you made in the beginning.

Remind the reader. Recall what you first set out to do; check off the key points you've covered; or answer any questions left unanswered.

Rephrase the thesis. Restate your thesis in light of the most important support you've given. Deepen and expand your original thesis.

Urge the reader.

Your reader may still be reluctant to accept your ideas or argument. The ending is your last chance to gain the reader's acceptance. Here are some possible strategies:

Show the implications. Follow further possibilities raised by your train of thought; be reasonable and convincing.

Look ahead. Suggest other possible connections.

List the benefits. Show the reader the benefits of accepting or applying the things you've said.

> Insight: When your writing comes to an effective stopping point, conclude the essay. Don't tack on another idea.

Complete and unify your message.

Your final paragraphs are your last opportunity to refocus, unify, and otherwise reinforce your message. Draft the closing carefully, not merely to finish the essay but to further advance your purpose and thesis.

Weak Ending

The ending below does not focus on and show commitment to the essay's main idea. Rather than reinforcing this idea, the writing leads off in a new direction.

I realize I've got to catch my bus. I've spent too much time talking to this woman whose life is a wreck. I give her some spare change and then head off. She doesn't follow me. It's kind of a relief. Toronto is a great city, but sometimes you have weird experiences there. Once a street vendor gave me a free falafel. I didn't want to eat it because maybe something was wrong with it. What a weird city!

Strong Endings

Below are final paragraphs from two essays in this book. Listen to their tone, watch how they reconsider the essay's ideas, and note how they offer further food for thought. (The first example is a revision of the weak paragraph above.)

I tell her I need to get going. She should go, too, or she'll be late for the hearing. Before getting up, I reach into my wallet and give her two TTC passes and some spare change. I walk her to the street and point her toward Old City Hall. She never thanks me, only looks at me one last time with immense vulnerability and helplessness. Then she walks away.

I wonder as I hurry towards the station if she'll be okay, if her boyfriend really will get out of jail, and if her grandmother will ever take her back. Either way, I think as I cross Bay Street, what more can I do? I have a bus to catch.

(See the full essay on pages 103–105.)

Passion and power permeate all of Latin America's music. The four major types of music— indigenous, Iberian and Mestizo folk, Afro-American, and popular urban—are as diverse as the people of Latin America, and each style serves a valued need or function in Latinos' everyday lives. As a result, those listening to Latin American music—whether it is a Peruvian Indian's chant, a Venezuelan farmer's whistled tune, a Cuban mambo drummer's vivacious beat, or the Bogotá rock concert's compelling rhythms—are hearing much more than music. They are hearing the passion and power of the Latin American people.

> **Writing with Sources:** Save the best for last. Consider using an especially thought-provoking statement, quotation, or detail in your conclusion. Doing so can help you clinch your point.

Use sources effectively.

LO5

Working with Sources: If you are using sources, take care not to overwhelm your draft with source material. Keep the focus on your own ideas:

- Avoid strings of references and chunks of source material with no discussion, explanation, or interpretation on your part in between.
- Don't offer entire paragraphs of material from a source (whether paraphrased or quoted) with a single in-text citation at the end. When you do so, your thinking disappears.
- Be careful not to overload your draft with complex information and dense data lacking explanation.
- Resist the urge to simply copy and paste big chunks from sources. Even if you document the sources, your paper will quickly become a patchwork of source material with a few weak stitches (your contribution) holding it together.
- Note the careful use of source material in the following paragraph.

Sample Paragraph Showing Integration of Source Material

(A)   Antibiotics are effective only against infections caused by bacteria and should never be used against infections caused by viruses. Using an antibiotic against a viral infection is like throwing water on a grease fire—water may normally put out fires but will only worsen the situation for a grease fire. In the same way, antibiotics fight infec-

(B) tions, but they cause the body harm only when they are used to fight infections caused by viruses. Viruses cause the common cold, the flu, and most sore throats, sinus infections, coughs, and bronchitis. Yet antibiotics are commonly prescribed for these viral infections.

(C) The *New England Journal of Medicine* reports that 22.7 million kilograms (25,000 tons) of antibiotics is prescribed each year in the United States alone (Wenzel and Edmond, 1962). Meanwhile, the CDC reports that approximately 50 percent of those prescriptions are completely unnecessary ("Antibiotic Overuse" 25). "Every year, tens of millions of prescriptions for antibiotics are written to treat

(D) viral illnesses for which these antibiotics offer no benefits," says the CDC's antimicrobial resistance director David Bell, M.D. (qtd. in Bren 30). Such mis-prescribing is simply bad medical practice that contributes to the problem of growing bacterial infection.

(A) Topic sentence: idea elaborating and supporting thesis
(B) Development of idea through reasoning
(C) Support of idea through reference to source material
(D) Concluding statement of idea

Critical-Thinking and Writing Activities

As directed by your instructor, complete the following critical-thinking and writing activities by yourself or with classmates.

1. Patricia T. O'Connor says, "All writing begins life as a first draft, and first drafts are never any good. They're not supposed to be." Is this claim true? Why or why not? What do you hope to accomplish with a first draft?

2. Read the final paragraphs of any three essays included in this book. Write a brief analysis of each ending based on the information on pages 61–62.

3. Imagine that you are a journalist who has been asked to write an article about a wedding, a funeral, or another significant event you have experienced. Choose an event and sketch out a plan for your article. Include the main writing moves and the type of information at each stage of your writing.

Checklist: Learning Outcomes

Use the checklist below to assess what you have learned about taking a position in writing.

____ I have reconsidered the rhetorical situation, thinking about my role, the subject, my purpose, my audience, the medium, and the context.

____ I understand the essay structure—opening, middle, and closing.

____ I have created a strong opening.
  - The opening engages the reader.
  - The opening establishes a focus and states a main point.

____ I have developed the ideas in the middle of my essay.
  - The middle advances my thesis by developing and testing ideas.
  - The middle orders supporting details in a clear, logical way.

____ I have created an effective closing.
  - The closing reasserts the main point and completes the message.

____ I understand how to use sources to best effect in a draft.

"To achieve style, begin by affecting none—that is, begin by placing yourself in the background."
—E. B. White

6

Revising

The word *revising* means "taking another look," so revising is best done after a brief break. Set aside your writing and return to it later with fresh eyes. Also, enlist the fresh eyes of another reader, whether a roommate, a classmate, or someone at the writing center. Revising is all about getting perspective.

Of course, once you have perspective, you need to figure out how to make improvements. This chapter provides numerous strategies for focusing on the global traits of your writing—ideas, organization, and voice. The changes you make should improve the work significantly, perhaps even reshaping it.

Learning Outcomes

LO1 Address whole-paper issues.

LO2 Assess your ideas, organization, and voice.

LO3 Revise for ideas and organization.

LO4 Revise for voice and style.

LO5 Address paragraph issues.

LO6 Revise collaboratively.

LO7 Use the writing center.

Address whole paper issues. LO1

When revising, first look at the big picture. Take it all in. Determine whether the content is interesting, informative, and worth sharing. Note any gaps or soft spots in your line of thinking. Ask yourself how you can improve what you have done so far. The information that follows will help you address whole-paper issues such as these.

Revisit the rhetorical situation.

Just as the rhetorical situation helped you to set your direction in writing, it can help you make course corrections. Think about each part of the rhetorical situation.

Consider your role. How are you coming across in this draft? Do you sound authoritative, engaged, knowledgeable, confident? How do you want to come across?

Think about your subject. Have you stated a clear focus? Have you supported it with a variety of details? Have you explored the subject fully?

Remember your purpose. Are you trying to analyze, describe, explain, propose? Does the writing succeed? Do the ideas promote your purpose? Does your organization support the purpose? Is your writing voice helpful in achieving your purpose?

Check the form. Have you created writing that matches the form that your instructor requested? Have you taken best advantage of the form, including graphics or other media, if appropriate?

Consider your audience. Have you captured their attention and interest? Have you provided them the information they need to understand your writing? Have you considered their values, needs, and opinions, and used them to connect?

Think about the context. Is this piece of writing the correct length and level of seriousness for the assignment? Is it on schedule? How does it match up to what others are doing?

Writing with Sources: Make sure that your sources work well for each part of the rhetorical situation. Choose sources that

- reflect well on you, showing that you understand and care about the topic.
- illuminate the subject with accurate, precise, substantial information.
- help you achieve your purpose, whether to inform, persuade, or reflect.
- work well within the form and can be appropriately credited.
- are seen as authoritative by the audience.
- are timely and credible in the context.

Consider your overall approach.

Sometimes it's better to start fresh if your writing contains stretches of uninspired ideas. Consider a fresh start if your first draft shows one of these problems:

The topic is worn-out. An essay titled "Lead Poisoning" may not sound very interesting. Unless you can approach it with a new twist ("Get the Lead Out!"), consider cutting your losses and finding a fresh topic.

The approach is stale. If you've been writing primarily to get a good grade, finish the assignment, or sound cool, start again. Try writing to learn something, prompt real thinking in readers, or touch a chord.

Your voice is predictable or fake. Avoid the bland "A good time was had by all" or the phony academic "When one studies this significant problem in considerable depth . . . " Be real. Be honest.

The draft sounds boring. Maybe it's boring because you pay an equal amount of attention to everything and hence stress nothing. Try condensing less important material and expanding what's important.

The essay is formulaic. In other words, it follows the "five-paragraph" format. This handy organizing frame may prevent you from doing justice to your topic and thinking. If your draft is dragged down by rigid adherence to a formula, try a more original approach.

Writing with Sources: Test the balance of reasoning and sources. Make sure your draft is not thin on source material, but also make sure that the source material does not dominate the conversation. Use these tips for balancing reasoning and sources:

1. Before diving into source material within a paragraph or section of your paper, flesh out your thinking more fully. Offer reasoning that elaborates the claim and effectively leads into the evidence.

2. As you present evidence from source material, build on it by explaining what it means. Evidence doesn't typically speak for itself: through analysis, synthesis, illustration, contrast, and other means, you need to show how or why your sources advance your thesis.

3. After you have presented evidence that elaborates on and supports your idea, extend your thoughts by addressing the reader's "So what?" or "Why does this matter?" skepticism.

Assess your ideas, organization, and voice. LO2

Revising helps you turn your first draft into a more complete, thoughtful piece of writing. The following information will help you do that.

Prepare to revise.

Once you've finished a first draft, set it aside (ideally for a few days) until you can look at the draft objectively and make needed changes. If you drafted on paper, photocopy the draft. If you drafted on a computer, print your paper (double-spaced). Then make changes with a good pencil or colored pen. If you prefer revising on the computer, consider using your software editing program. In all cases, save your first draft for reference.

Think globally.

When revising, focus on the big picture—the overall strength of the ideas, organization, and voice.

Ideas: Check your thesis, focus, or theme. Has your thinking on your topic changed? Also think about your readers' most pressing questions concerning this topic. Have you answered these questions? Finally, consider your reasoning and support. Are both complete and sound?

Organization: Check the overall design of your writing, making sure that ideas move smoothly and logically from one point to the next. Does your essay build effectively? Do you shift directions cleanly? Fix structural problems in one of these ways:

- Reorder material to improve the sequence.
- Cut information that doesn't support the thesis.
- Add details where the draft is thin.
- Rewrite parts that seem unclear.
- Improve links between points by using transitions.

Voice: Voice is your personal presence on the page, the tone and attitude that others hear when reading your work. In other words, voice is the between-the-lines message your readers get (whether you want them to or not). When revising, make sure that the tone of your message matches your purpose, whether it is serious, playful, or satiric.

Insight: Don't pay undue attention to spelling, grammar, and punctuation at this early stage in the process. Otherwise, you may become distracted from the task at hand: improving the content of your writing. Editing and proofreading come later.

Sportstock, 2011 / Used under license from Shutterstock.com

Revise for ideas and organization.   LO3

As you review your draft for content, make sure the ideas are fully developed and the organization is clear. From your main claim or thesis to your reasoning and your evidence, strengthen your thinking and sequencing.

Examine your ideas.

Review the ideas in your writing, making sure that each point is logical, complete, and clear. To test the logic in your writing, see pages 182–185.

Complete Thinking

Have you answered readers' basic questions? Have you supported the thesis? The original passage below is too general; the revision is clearly more complete.

Original Passage *(Too general)*

As soon as you receive a minor cut, the body's healing process begins to work. Blood from tiny vessels fills the wound and begins to clot. In less than 24 hours, a scab forms.

Revised Version *(More specific)*

As soon as you receive a minor cut, the body's healing process begins to work. In a simple wound, the first and second layers of skin are severed along with tiny blood vessels called capillaries. As these vessels bleed into the wound, minute structures called platelets help stop the bleeding by sticking to the edges of the cut and to one another, forming a plug. The platelets then release chemicals that react with certain proteins in the blood to form a clot. The blood clot, with its fiber network, begins to join the edges of the wound together. As the clot dries out, a scab forms, usually in less than 24 hours.

Clear Thesis

Make sure that your writing centers on one main issue or thesis. Although this next original passage lacks a thesis, the revision has a clear one.

Original Passage *(Lacks a thesis)*

Teen magazines are popular with young girls. These magazines contain a lot of how-to articles about self-image, fashion, and boy-girl relationships. Girls read them to get advice on how to act and how to look. Girls who don't really know what they want are the most eager readers.

Revised Version *(Identifies a specific thesis statement)*

Adolescent girls often see teen magazines as handbooks on how to be teenagers. These magazines influence the ways they act and the ways they look. For girls who are unsure of themselves, these magazines can exert an enormous amount of influence. Unfortunately, the advice these magazines give about self-image, fashion, and boys may do more harm than good.

Examine your organization.

Good writing has structure. It leads readers logically and clearly from one point to the next. When revising for organization, consider four areas: the overall plan, the opening, the flow of ideas, and the closing.

Overall Plan

Look closely at the sequence of ideas or events that you share. Does that sequence advance your thesis? Do the points build effectively? Are there gaps in the support or points that stray from your original purpose? If you find such problems, consider the following actions:

- Refine the focus or emphasis by rearranging material within the text.
- Fill in the gaps with new material. Go back to your planning notes.
- Delete material that wanders away from your purpose.
- Use an additional (or different) method of organization. For example, if you are comparing two subjects, add depth to your analysis by contrasting them as well. If you are describing a complex subject, show the subject more clearly and fully by distinguishing and classifying its parts. (See pages 56–61 for more on organizational methods.)

> **Insight:** What is the best method of organization for your essay? The writing you are doing will usually determine the choice. As you know, a personal narrative is often organized by time. Typically, however, you combine and customize methods to develop a writing idea. For example, within a comparison essay you may do some describing or classifying. See pages 57 and 58–61 for more on the common methods of development.

Opening Ideas

Reread your opening paragraph(s). Is the opening organized effectively? Does it engage readers, establish a direction for your writing, and express your thesis or focus? The original opening below doesn't build to a compelling thesis statement, but the revised version engages the reader and leads to the thesis.

> **Original Opening** *(Lacks interest and direction)*
>
> The lack of student motivation is a common subject in the news. Educators want to know how to get students to learn. Today's higher standards mean that students will be expected to learn even more. Another problem in urban areas is that large numbers of students are dropping out. How to interest students is a challenge.
>
> **Revised Version**
> *(Effectively leads readers into the essay)*
>
> How can we motivate students to learn? How can we get them to meet today's rising standards of excellence? How can we, in fact, keep students in school long enough to learn? The answer to these problems is quite simple. Give them money. Pay students to study and learn and stay in school.

Shevel Artur, 2011 / Used under license from Shutterstock.com

Flow of Ideas

Look closely at the beginnings and endings of each paragraph. Have you connected your thoughts clearly? (See pages 75–76 for a list of transition words.) The original opening words of the paragraph sequence below, from an essay of description, offer no links for readers. The revised versions use strong transitions indicating spatial organization (order by location).

> **Original First Words in the Four Middle Paragraphs**
>
> There was a huge, steep hill . . .
>
> Buffalo Creek ran . . .
>
> A dense "jungle" covering . . .
>
> Within walking distance from my house . . .
>
> **Revised Versions**
> *(Words and phrases connect ideas)*
>
> Behind the house, there was a huge, steep hill . . .
>
> Across the road from the house, Buffalo Creek ran . . .
>
> On the far side of the creek bank was a dense "jungle" covering . . .
>
> Up the road, within walking distance from my house . . .

> **Insight:** Review "Supporting Your Claims" (pages 180–182) and use those strategies to strengthen weak or unconvincing passages.

Closing Ideas

Reread your closing paragraph(s). Do you offer an effective summary, reassert your main point in a fresh way, and provide readers with food for thought as they leave your writing? Or is your ending abrupt, repetitive, or directionless? The original ending that follows is uninspiring; it adds little to the main part of the writing. The revision summarizes the main points in the essay and then urges the reader to think again about the overall point of writing.

Original Ending *(Sketchy and flat)*

Native Son deals with a young man's struggle against racism. It shows the effects of prejudice. Everyone should read this book.

Revised Version *(Effectively ends the writing)*

Native Son deals with a young man's struggle in a racist society, but also with so much more. It shows how prejudice affects people, how it closes in on them, and what some people will do to find a way out. Anyone who wants to better understand racism in the United States should read this book.

 Tip To generate fresh ideas for your closing, freewrite answers to questions like these: Why is the topic important to me? What should my readers have learned? Why should this issue matter to readers? What evidence or appeal (pages 180–182) will help readers remember my message and act on it? How does the topic relate to broader issues in society, history, or life?

Revise for voice and style.

LO4

Generally, readers more fully trust writing that speaks in an informed voice and a clear, natural style. To develop an informed voice, make sure that your details are correct and complete; to develop a clear style, make sure that your writing is well organized and unpretentious. Check the issues below.

Check the level of commitment.

Consider how and to what degree your writing shows that you care about the topic and reader. For example, note how the following original passage lacks a personal voice, revealing nothing about the writer's connection to—or interest in—the topic. In contrast, the revision shows that the writer cares about the topic.

Original Passage *(Lacks voice)*

Cemeteries can teach us a lot about history. They make history seem more real. There is an old grave of a Revolutionary War veteran in the Union Grove Cemetery. . . .

Revised Version *(Personal, sincere voice)*

I've always had a special feeling for cemeteries. It's hard to explain any further than that, except to say history never seems quite as real as it does when I walk among many old gravestones. One day I discovered the grave of a Revolutionary War veteran. . . .

Check the intensity of your writing.

All writing—including academic writing—is enriched by an appropriate level of intensity, or even passion. In the original passage below, the writer's concern for the topic is unclear because the piece sounds neutral. In contrast, the revised version exudes energy.

Original Passage *(Lacks feeling and energy)*

The Dream Act could make a difference for people. It just takes a long time to get any bill through Congress. This bill probably will never get approved. Instead of passing the Dream Act, the country will probably just deport high school students from other countries.

Revised Passage *(Expresses real feelings)*

Given such debates, it might be a long time before the bill becomes law, thereby dashing the dreams of nearly 65,000 high school students like Maria who can't wait another year because they may already be in deportation proceedings. We need to step up and educate our representatives and senators about the importance of passing the Dream Act on its own instead of including the bill along with CIR. We need to urge them to debate and approve the Dream Act now, thereby making Maria's dreams—and the dreams of thousands of students like her—a reality!

Develop an academic style.

Most college writing requires an academic style. Such a style isn't stuffy; you're not trying to impress readers with ten-dollar words. Rather, you are using language that facilitates a thoughtful, engaged discussion of the topic. To choose the best words for such a conversation, consider the issues that follow.

Personal Pronouns

In some academic writing, personal pronouns are acceptable. This is the case in informal writing, such as reading responses; personal essays involving narration, description, and reflection; and opinion-editorial essays written for a broad audience. In addition, *I* is correctly used in academic writing rooted in personal research, sometimes called an *I-search paper*.

Generally, however, avoid using *I, we,* and *you* in traditional academic writing. The concept, instead, is to focus on the topic itself and let your attitude be revealed indirectly. As E. B. White puts it, "To achieve style, begin by affecting none—that is, begin by placing yourself in the background."

> **No:** I really think that the problem of the homeless in Chicago is serious, given the number of people who are dying, as I know from my experience where I grew up.
>
> **Yes:** Homelessness in Chicago often leads to death. This fact demands the attention of more than lawmakers and social workers; all citizens must address the problems of their suffering neighbors.

> **Tip** Use the pronoun *one* carefully in academic prose. When it means "a person," *one* can lead to a stilted style if overused. In addition, the pronoun *their* (a plural pronoun) should not be used with *one* (a singular pronoun).

Technical Terms and Jargon

Technical terms and jargon—"insider" words—can be the specialized vocabulary of a subject, a discipline, a profession, or a social group. As such, jargon can be difficult to read for "outsiders." Follow these guidelines:

- Use technical terms to communicate with people within the profession or discipline as a kind of shorthand. However, be careful that such jargon doesn't devolve into meaningless buzzwords and catchphrases.
- Avoid jargon when writing for readers outside the profession or discipline. Use simpler terms and define technical terms that must be used.

> **Technical:** Bin's Douser power washer delivers 2200 psi p.r., runs off standard a.c. lines, comes with 100 ft. h.d. synthetic-rubber tubing, and features variable pulsation options through three adjustable s.s. tips.
>
> **Simple:** Bin's Douser power washer has a pressure rating of 2200 psi (pounds per square inch), runs off a common 200-volt electrical circuit, comes with 100 feet of hose, and includes three nozzles.

Level of Formality

Most academic writing (especially research papers, literary analyses, lab reports, and argumentative essays) should meet the standards of formal English. Formal English is characterized by a serious tone; careful attention to word choice; longer and more complex sentences reflecting complex thinking; strict adherence to traditional conventions of grammar, mechanics, and punctuation; and avoidance of contractions.

> Formal English, modeled in this sentence, is worded correctly and carefully so that it can withstand repeated readings without seeming tiresome, sloppy, or cute.

You may write other papers (personal essays, commentaries, journals, and reviews) in which informal English is appropriate. Informal English is characterized by a personal tone, the occasional use of popular expressions, shorter sentences with slightly looser syntax, contractions, and personal references (*I, we, you*), but it still adheres to basic conventions.

> Informal English sounds like one person talking to another person (in a somewhat relaxed setting). It's the type of language that you're reading now. It sounds comfortable and real, not affected or breezy.

Unnecessary Qualifiers

Using qualifiers (such as *mostly, often, likely,* or *tends to*) is an appropriate strategy for developing defendable claims in argumentative writing. (See pages 179–180.) However, when you "overqualify" your ideas or add intensifiers (*really, truly*), the result is insecurity—the impression that you lack confidence in your ideas. The cure? Say what you mean, and mean what you say.

Insecure: I totally and completely agree with the new security measures at sporting events, but that's only my opinion.

Secure: I agree with the new security measures at sporting events.

fyi Each academic discipline has its own vocabulary and its own vocabulary resources. Such resources include dictionaries, glossaries, or handbooks. Check your library for the vocabulary resources in your discipline. Use them regularly to deepen your grasp of that vocabulary.

Know when to use the passive voice.

Most verbs can be in either the active or the passive voice. When a verb is active, the sentence's subject performs the action. When the verb is passive, the subject is acted upon.

Active: If you *can't attend* the meeting, *notify* Richard by Thursday.

Passive: If a meeting *can't be attended* by you, Richard *must be notified* by Thursday.

Weaknesses of Passive Voice: The passive voice tends to be wordy and sluggish because the verb's action is directed backward, not ahead. In addition, passive constructions tend to be impersonal, making people disappear.

Passive: The sound system *can* now *be used* to listen in on sessions in the therapy room. Parents *can be helped* by having constructive one-on-one communication methods with children modeled by therapists.

Active: Parents *can* now *use* the sound system to listen in on sessions in the therapy room. Therapists *can help* parents by modeling constructive one-on-one communication methods with children.

Strengths of Passive Voice: Using the passive voice isn't wrong. In fact, the passive voice has some important uses: (1) when you need to be tactful (say, in a bad-news letter), (2) if you wish to stress the object or person acted upon, and (3) if the actual actor is understood, unknown, or unimportant.

Active: Our engineers determined that you bent the bar at the midpoint.

Passive: Our engineers determined that the bar had been bent at the midpoint. (tactful)

Active: Congratulations! We *have approved* your scholarship for $2,500.

Passive: Congratulations! Your scholarship for $2,500 *has been approved.* (emphasis on receiver; actor understood)

Writing with Sources: Academic writing must be free of plagiarism. Check that you have clearly indicated which material in your draft is summarized, paraphrased, or quoted from another source. (For more help, see pages 354–356.)

Address paragraph issues. LO5

While drafting, you may have constructed paragraphs that are loosely held together, poorly developed, or unclear. When you revise, take a close look at your paragraphs for focus, unity, and coherence (pages 73–77).

Remember the basics.

A paragraph should be a concise unit of thought. Revise a paragraph until it . . .

- is organized around a controlling idea—often stated in a topic sentence.
- consists of supporting sentences that develop the controlling idea.
- concludes with a sentence that summarizes the main point and prepares readers for the next paragraph or main point.
- serves a specific function in a piece of writing—opening, supporting, developing, illustrating, countering, describing, or closing.

Sample Paragraph

A   Tumor cells can hurt the body in a number of ways. First, a tumor can grow so big that it takes up space needed by other organs. Second, some cells may detach from the original tumor and spread throughout the body, creating new tumors elsewhere. This happens with lymphatic cancer—a cancer that's hard to control because it spreads so quickly. A third way

B that tumor cells can hurt the body is by doing work not called for in their DNA. For example, a gland cell's DNA code may tell the cell to produce a necessary hormone in the endocrine system. However, if cancer damages or distorts that code, sick cells may produce more of the hormone than the body can use—or even tolerate (Braun 4).

C Cancer cells seem to have minds of their own, and this is why cancer is such a serious disease.

(A) Topic sentence
(B) Supporting sentences
(C) Closing sentence

Keep the purpose in mind.

Use these questions to evaluate the purpose and function of each paragraph:

- What function does the paragraph fulfill? How does it add to your line of reasoning or the development of your thesis?
- Would the paragraph work better if it were divided in two—or combined with another paragraph?
- Does the paragraph flow smoothly from the previous paragraph, and does it lead effectively into the next one?

Check for unity.

A unified paragraph is one in which all the details help to develop a single main topic or achieve a single main effect. Test for unity by following these guidelines.

Topic Sentence

Very often the topic of a paragraph is stated in a single sentence called a "topic sentence." Check whether your paragraph needs a topic sentence. If the paragraph has a topic sentence, determine whether it is clear, specific, and well focused. Here is a formula for writing good topic sentences:

Formula:	A topic sentence = a limited topic + a specific feeling or thought about it.
Example:	The fear that Americans feel (limited topic) comes partly from the uncertainty related to this attack (a specific thought).

Placement of the Topic Sentence

Normally the topic sentence is the first sentence in the paragraph. However, it can appear elsewhere in a paragraph.

Middle Placement: Place a topic sentence in the middle when you want to build up to and then lead away from the key idea.

During the making of *Apocalypse Now,* Eleanor Coppola created a documentary about the filming called *Hearts of Darkness: A Filmmaker's Apocalypse.* In the first film, the insane Colonel Kurtz has disappeared into the Cambodian jungle. As Captain Willard searches for Kurtz, the screen fills with horror. **However, as *Hearts of Darkness* relates, the horror portrayed in the fictional movie was being lived out by the production company.** For example, in the documentary, actor Larry Fishburne shockingly says, "War is fun. . . . Vietnam must have been so much fun." Then toward the end of the filming, actor Martin Sheen suffered a heart attack. When an assistant informed investors, the director exploded, "He's not dead unless I say he's dead."

End Placement: Place a topic sentence at the end when you want to build to a climax, as in a passage of narration or persuasion.

When sportsmen stop to reflect on why they find fishing so enjoyable, most realize that what they love is the feel of a fish on the end of the line, not necessarily the weight of the fillets in their coolers. Fishing has undergone a slow evolution over the last century. While fishing used to be a way of putting food on the table, most of today's fishermen do so only for the relaxation that it provides. The barbed hook was invented to increase the quantity of fish a man could land so that he could better feed his family. **This need no longer exists, so barbed hooks are no longer necessary.**

Use supporting sentences.

All the sentences in the body of a paragraph should support the topic sentence. The closing sentence, for instance, will often summarize the paragraph's main point or emphasize a key detail. If any sentences shift the focus away from the topic, revise the paragraph in one of the following ways:

- Delete the material from the paragraph.
- Rewrite the material so that it clearly supports the topic sentence.
- Create a separate paragraph based on the odd-man-out material.
- Revise the topic sentence so that it relates more closely to the support.

Consistent Focus

Examine the following paragraph about fishing hooks. The original topic sentence focuses on the point that some anglers prefer smooth hooks. However, the writer leaves this initial idea unfinished and turns to the issue of the cost of new hooks. In the revised version, unity is restored: The first paragraph completes the point about anglers who prefer smooth hooks; the second paragraph addresses the issue of replacement costs.

Original Paragraph *(Lacks unity)*

According to some anglers who do use smooth hooks, their lures perform better than barbed lures as long as they maintain a constant tension on the line. Smooth hooks can bite deeper than barbed hooks, actually providing a stronger hold on the fish. Some people have argued that replacing all of the barbed hooks in their tackle would be a costly operation.

Revised Version *(Unified)*

According to some anglers who do use smooth hooks, their lures perform better than barbed lures as long as the anglers maintain a constant tension on the line. Smooth hooks can bite deeper than barbed hooks, actually providing a stronger hold on the fish. These anglers testify that switching from barbed hooks has not noticeably reduced the number of fish that they are able to land. In their experience, and in my own, enjoyment of the sport is actually heightened by adding another challenge to playing the fish (maintaining line tension).

Some people have argued that replacing all of the barbed hooks in their tackle would be a costly operation. While this is certainly a concern, barbed hooks do not necessarily require replacement. With a simple set of pliers, the barbs on most conventional hooks can be bent down, providing a cost-free method of modifying one's existing tackle. . . .

fyi Paragraphs that contain unrelated ideas lack unity and are hard to follow. As you review each paragraph for unity, ask yourself these questions: Is the topic of the paragraph clear? Does each sentence relate to the topic? Are the sentences organized in the best possible order?

Check for coherence.

When a paragraph is coherent, the parts stay together. A coherent paragraph flows smoothly because each sentence is connected to others by patterns in the language such as repetition and transitions. To strengthen the coherence in your paragraphs, check for the issues discussed below.

Effective Repetition

To achieve coherence in your paragraphs, consider using repetition—repeating words or synonyms where necessary to remind readers of what you have already said. You can also use parallelism—repeating phrase or sentence structures to show the relationships among ideas. At the same time, you will add a unifying rhythm to your writing.

> **Ineffective:** The floor was littered with discarded soda cans, newspapers that were crumpled, and wrinkled clothes.
>
> **Effective:** **The floor was littered with discarded soda cans, crumpled newspapers, and wrinkled clothes.** (Three parallel phrases are used.)
>
> **Ineffective:** Reading the book was enjoyable; to write the critique was difficult.
>
> **Effective:** **Reading the book was enjoyable; writing the critique was difficult.** (Two similar structures are repeated.)

Clear Transitions

Linking words and phrases like "next," "on the other hand," and "in addition" connect ideas by showing the relationship among them. There are transitions that show location and time, compare and contrast things, emphasize a point, conclude or summarize, and add or clarify information. (See the table to the right for a list of linking words and phrases.) Note the use of transitions in the following examples:

> The paradox of Scotland is that violence had long been the norm in this now-peaceful land. *In fact,* the country was born, bred, and came of age in war.
> (The transition is used to emphasize a point.)
>
> The production of cement is a complicated process. *First,* the mixture of lime, silica, alumina, and gypsum is ground into very fine particles.
> (The transition is used to show time or order.)

> **Insight:** Another way to achieve coherence in your paragraphs is to use pronouns effectively. A pronoun forms a link to the noun it replaces and ties that noun (idea) to the ideas that follow. As always, don't overuse pronouns or rely too heavily on them in establishing coherence in your paragraphs.

Transitions and Linking Words

The words and phrases below can help you tie together words, phrases, sentences, and paragraphs.

Show location: above, behind, down, on top of, across, below, in back of, onto, against, beneath, in front of, outside, along, beside, inside, over, among, between, into, throughout, around, beyond, near, to the right, away from, by, off, under

Show time: about, during, next, today, after, finally, next week, tomorrow, afterward, first, second, until, as soon as, immediately, soon, when, at, later, then, yesterday, before, meanwhile, third

Show similarities: also, in the same way, likewise, as, like, similarly

Show differences: although, even though, on the other hand, still, but, however, otherwise, yet

Emphasize a point: again, for this reason, particularly, to repeat, even, in fact, to emphasize, truly

Conclude or summarize: all in all, finally, in summary, therefore, as a result, in conclusion, last, to sum up

Add information: additionally, and, equally important, in addition, again, another, finally, likewise, along with, as well, for example, next, also, besides, for instance, second

Clarify: for instance, in other words, put another way, that is

Note: Use transitions to link, expand, or intensify an idea, but don't add elements carelessly, creating run-on or rambling sentences (pages 422–423).

Check for completeness.

The sentences in a paragraph should support and expand on the main point. If your paragraph does not seem complete, you will need to add information.

Supporting Details

If some of your paragraphs are incomplete, they may lack details. There are numerous kinds of details, including the following:

facts	anecdotes	analyses	paraphrases
statistics	quotations	explanations	comparisons
examples	definitions	summaries	analogies

Add details based on the type of writing you are engaged in.

Describing: Add details that help readers see, smell, taste, touch, or hear it.

Narrating: Add details that help readers understand the events and actions.

Explaining: Add details that help readers understand what it means, how it works, or what it does.

Persuading: Add details that strengthen the logic of your argument.

Specific Details

The original paragraph below fails to answer fully the question posed by the topic sentence. In the revised paragraph, the writer uses an anecdote to answer the question.

Original Paragraph *(Lacks completeness)*
So what is stress? Actually, the physiological characteristics of stress are some of the body's potentially good self-defense mechanisms. People experience stress when they are in danger. In fact, stress can be healthy.

Revised Version *(Full development)*
So what is stress? Actually, the physiological characteristics of stress are some of the body's potentially good self-defense mechanisms. Take, for example, a man who is crossing a busy intersection when he spots an oncoming car. Immediately his brain releases a flood of adrenaline into his bloodstream. As a result, his muscles contract, his eyes dilate, his heart pounds faster, his breathing quickens, and his blood clots more readily. Each one of these responses helps the man leap out of the car's path. His muscles contract to give him exceptional strength. His eyes dilate so that he can see more clearly. His heart pumps more blood and his lungs exchange more air—both to increase his metabolism. If the man were injured, his blood would clot faster, ensuring a smaller amount of blood loss. In this situation and many more like it, stress symptoms are good (Curtis 25–26).

Insight: If a paragraph is getting long, divide it at a natural stopping point. The topic sentence can then function as the thesis for that part of your essay or paper.

Minerva Studio, 2011 / Used under license from Shutterstock.com

Working with Sources: Test your evidence to make certain that it provides the support you need.

- **accurate:** The information is all correct.
- **precise:** The data are concrete and specific, not vague and general.
- **substantial:** The amount of evidence reaches a critical mass—enough to convey the idea and convince readers of its validity.
- **authoritative:** The evidence comes from a reliable source. Moreover, the information is as close to the origin as possible; it is not a report conveying thirdhand or fourthhand information.
- **representative:** The information fairly represents the range of data on the issue. Your presentation of evidence is balanced.
- **fitting:** Given your purpose, the topic, and your reader, the evidence is appropriate and relevant for the question or issue you are discussing.

The reference page below comes from the APA paper, "Running on Empty" (see pages 390–396)." Note how student writers Thomas I. DeJong and Adam B. Smit used a variety of sources that meet the criteria listed above.

Running on Empty   11

References

Costa, A. L. (1984). Thinking: How do we know students are getting better at it? *Roeper Review, 6,* 197–199.   **(A)**

Crumpton, E., Wine, D. B., & Drenick, E. J. (1966). Starvation: Stress or satisfaction? *Journal of the American Medical Association, 196,* 394–396.

D'Agostino, C. A. F. (1996). Testing a social-cognitive model of achievement motivation. *Dissertation Abstracts International Section A: Humanities & Social Sciences, 57,* 1985.

Eisenberger, R., & Leonard, J. M. (1980). Effects of conceptual task difficulty on generalized persistence. *American Journal of Psychology, 93,* 285–298.   **(B)**

Green, M. W., Elliman, N. A., & Rogers, P. J. (1995). Lack of effect of short-term fasting on cognitive function. *Journal of Psychiatric Research, 29,* 245–253.

Green, M. W., Elliman, N. A., & Rogers, P. J. (1996). Hunger, caloric preloading, and the selective processing

(A) All works referred to in the paper appear on the reference page, listed alphabetically by author (or title).
(B) Each entry follows APA guidelines for listing authors, dates, titles, and publishing information.

of food and body shape words. *British Journal of Clinical Psychology, 35,* 143–151.

Green, M. W., Elliman, N. A., & Rogers, P. J. (1997). The study effects of food deprivation and incentive motivation on blood glucose levels and cognitive function. *Psychopharmacology, 134,* 88–94.

Hickman, K. L., Stromme, C., & Lippman, L. G. (1998). Learned industriousness: Replication in principle. *Journal of General Psychology, 125,* 213–217.   **(C)**

Keys, A., Brozek, J., Henschel, A., Mickelsen, O., & Taylor, H. L. (1950). *The biology of human starvation* (Vol. 2). Minneapolis: University of Minnesota Press.

Kollar, E. J., Slater, G. R., Palmer, J. O., Docter, R. F., & Mandell, A. J. (1964). Measurement of stress in fasting man. *Archives of General Psychology, 11,* 113–125.

Pinel, J. P. (2000). *Biopsychology* (4th ed.). Boston: Allyn and Bacon.

(C) Capitalization, punctuation, and hanging indentation are consistent with APA format.

Revise collaboratively. LO6

Every writer can benefit from feedback from an interested audience, especially one that offers constructive and honest advice during a writing project. Members of an existing writing group already know how valuable it is for writers to share their work. Others might want to start a writing group to experience the benefits. Your group might collaborate online or in person. In either case, the information on the next two pages will help you get started.

Know your role.

Writers and reviewers should know their roles and fulfill their responsibilities during revising sessions. Essentially, the writer should briefly introduce the draft and solicit honest responses. Reviewers should make constructive comments in response to the writing.

Provide appropriate feedback.

Feedback can take many forms, including the three approaches described here.

Basic Description: In this simple response, the reviewer listens or reads attentively and then simply describes what she or he hears or sees happening in the piece. The reviewer offers no criticism of the writing.

> **Ineffective:** "That was interesting. The piece was informative."
>
> **Effective:** "First, the essay introduced the challenge of your birth defect and how you have had to cope with it. Then in the next part you . . ."

Summary Evaluation: Here the reviewer reads or listens to the piece and then provides a specific evaluation of the draft.

> **Ineffective:** "Gee, I really liked it!" or "It was boring."
>
> **Effective:** "Your story at the beginning really pulled me in, and the middle explained the issue strongly, but the ending felt a bit flat."

Thorough Critique: The reviewer assesses the ideas, organization, and voice in the writing. Feedback should be detailed and constructive. Such a critique may also be completed with the aid of a review sheet or checklist. As a reviewer, be prepared to share specific responses, suggestions, and questions. But also be sure to focus your comments on the writing, rather than the writer.

> **Ineffective:** "You really need to fix that opening! What were you thinking?"
>
> **Effective:** "Let's look closely at the opening. Could you rewrite the first sentence so it grabs the reader's attention? Also, I'm somewhat confused about the thesis statement. Could you rephrase it so it states your position more clearly?"

Respond according to a plan.

Using a specific plan or scheme like the following will help you give clear, helpful, and complete feedback.

OAQS Method: Use this simple four-step scheme—Observe, Appreciate, Question, and Suggest—to respond to your peers' writing.

1. Observe means to notice what another person's essay is designed to do and say something about its design or purpose. For example, you might say, "Even though you are writing about your boyfriend, it appears that you are trying to get a message across to your parents."

2. Appreciate means to praise something in the writing that impresses or pleases you. You can find something to appreciate in any piece of writing. For example, you might say, "You make a very convincing point" or "With your description, I can actually see his broken tooth."

3. Question means to ask whatever you want to know after you've read the essay. You might ask for background information, a definition, an interpretation, or an explanation. For example, you might say, "Can you tell us what happened when you got to the emergency room?"

4. Suggest means to give helpful advice about possible changes. For example, you might say, "With a little more physical detail—especially more sounds and smells—your third paragraph could be the highlight of the whole essay. What do you think?"

Asking the Writer Questions

Reviewers should ask the following types of questions while reviewing a piece of writing:

- **To help writers reflect on their purpose and audience . . .**

  Why are you writing this?

  Who will read this, and what do they need to know?

- **To help writers focus their thoughts . . .**

  What message are you trying to get across?

  Do you have more than one main point?

  What are the most important examples?

- **To help writers think about their information . . .**

  What do you know about the subject?

  Does this part say enough?

  Does your writing cover all of the basics (Who? What? Where? When? Why? and How?)?

- **To help writers with their openings and closings . . .**

  What are you trying to say in the opening?

  How else could you start your writing?

  How do you want your readers to feel at the end?

Use the writing center. LO7

A college writing center or lab is a place where a trained adviser will help you develop and strengthen a piece of writing. You can expect the writing center adviser to do certain things; other things only you can do. For quick reference, refer to the chart below.

Adviser's Job	Your Job
Make you feel at home	Be respectful
Discuss your needs	Be ready to work
Help you choose a topic	Decide on a topic
Discuss your purpose and audience	Know your purpose and audience
Help you generate ideas	Embrace the best ideas
Help you develop your logic	Consider other points of view; stretch your own perspective
Help you understand how to research your material	Do the research
Read your draft	Share your writing
Identify problems in organization, logic, expression, and format	Recognize and fix problems
Teach ways to correct weaknesses	Learn important principles
Help you with grammar, usage, diction, vocabulary, and mechanics	Correct all errors

Tip TIPS for getting the most out of the writing center

- Visit the center at least several days before your paper is due.
- Take your assignment sheet with you to each advising session.
- Read your work aloud, slowly.
- Expect to rethink your writing from scratch.
- Do not defend your wording—if it needs defense, it needs revision.
- Ask questions. (No question is "too dumb.")
- Request clarification of anything you don't understand.
- Ask for examples or illustrations of important points.
- Write down all practical suggestions.
- Ask the adviser to summarize his or her remarks.
- Rewrite as soon as possible after—or even during—the advising session.
- Return to the writing center for a response to your revisions.

Critical-Thinking and Writing Activities

As directed by your instructor, complete the following critical-thinking and writing activities by yourself or with classmates.

1. Doris Lessing has stated that when it comes to writing, "The more a thing cooks, the better." In what sense is revision a crucial stage in that cooking process? Using Lessing's cooking metaphor as a starting point, explore how revision should function in your own writing.

2. Review the opening and closing paragraphs of one of your essays. Then come up with fresh and different approaches for those paragraphs using the information on pages 70–77 as a guide.

3. For your current writing assignment, ask a peer to provide detailed feedback using the information in this chapter as a guide. Then take a fresh copy of your paper to the writing center and work through your draft with an adviser. Revise the draft as needed.

Checklist: Learning Outcomes

____ I have thought about my overall approach, reconsidering the rhetorical situation—my role, subject, purpose, form, audience, and context.

____ I have thought about the three global traits: ideas, organization, and voice.

____ I have revised for ideas and organization.

Ideas: I have a clear thesis and have provided excellent support.

Organization: I have an opening, a middle, and a closing, and I use a consistent pattern of organization.

____ I have revised for voice and style.

Voice: My voice reflects the rhetorical situation.

____ I have made sure paragraphs are unified, coherent, and complete.

____ I have gotten and used a peer review.

____ I have made use of the writing center.

"Mistakes are a fact of life. It is the response to the error that counts."

—Nikki Giovanni

7

Editing

Editing and proofreading allow you to fine-tune your writing, making it ready to hand in. When you edit, look first for words, phrases, and sentences that sound awkward, uninteresting, or unclear. When you proofread, check your writing for spelling, mechanics, usage, and grammar errors. Ask one of your writing peers to help you.

The guidelines and strategies given in this chapter will help you edit your writing for style and clarity and proofread it for errors.

Learning Outcomes

LO1 Review your overall writing style.

LO2 Combine short, simplistic sentences.

LO3 Expand sentences to add details.

LO4 Edit sentences for variety and style.

LO5 Replace imprecise, misleading, and biased words.

LO6 Edit and proofread for correctness.

Review your overall writing style. — LO1

When you have thoroughly revised your writing, you need to edit it so as to make it clear and concise enough to present to readers. Use the editing guidelines below to check your revised draft.

Review the sentence structure and word choice.

1. **Read your revised writing aloud.** Better yet, have a writing peer read it aloud to you. Highlight any writing that doesn't read smoothly and naturally.
2. **Check that your style fits the rhetorical situation.**

> **Goal:** Does your writing sound as if you wrote it with a clear aim in mind? Do the sentence style and word choice match the goal?
>
> **Reader:** Is the tone sincere? Does the writing sound authentic and honest?
>
> **Subject:** Does the writing suit the subject and your treatment of it in terms of seriousness or playfulness, complexity or simplicity?

3. **Examine your sentences.** Check them for clarity, conciseness, and variety. Replace sentences that are wordy or rambling; combine or expand sentences that are short and choppy. Also, vary the beginnings of your sentences and avoid sentence patterns that are too predictable.

Consider word choice.

1. **Avoid redundancy.** Be alert for words or phrases that are used together but mean nearly the same thing.

> repeat again   red in color   refer back

2. **Watch for repetition.** When used appropriately, repetition can add rhythm and coherence to your writing. When used ineffectively, however, it can be a real distraction.

> **The man** looked as if he were in his late seventies. **The man** was dressed in an old suit. I soon realized that **the man** was homeless. . . .

3. **Look for general nouns, verbs, and modifiers.** Specific words are much more effective than general ones. (See pages 87–88.)

> The girl moved on the bench. (general)
> Rosie slid quietly to the end of the park bench. (specific)

4. **Avoid highly technical terms.** Check for jargon or technical terms that your readers will not know or that you haven't adequately explained. (See page 88.)

> As the **capillaries** bleed, **platelets** work with **fibrinogens** to form a clot.

5. **Use fair language.** Replace words or phrases that are biased or demeaning. (See pages 87–90.)

Combine short, simplistic sentences. — LO2

Effective sentences often contain several basic ideas that work together to show relationships and make connections. Here are five basic ideas followed by seven examples of how the ideas can be combined into effective sentences.

1. The longest and largest construction project in history was the Great Wall of China.
2. The project took 1,700 years to complete.
3. The Great Wall of China is 1,400 miles long.
4. It is between 18 and 30 feet high.
5. It is up to 32 feet wide.

Edit sentences for clarity and style.

Combine your short, simplistic sentences into longer, more detailed sentences. Sentence combining is generally carried out in the following ways:

- Use a **series** to combine three or more similar ideas.

  The Great Wall of China is **1,400 miles long,** between **18 and 30 feet high,** and up to **32 feet wide.**

- Use a **relative pronoun** (*who, whose, that, which*) to introduce subordinate (less important) ideas.

  The Great Wall of China, **which is 1,400 miles long and between 18 and 30 feet high,** took 1,700 years to complete.

- Use an **introductory phrase** or **clause**.

  Having taken 1,700 years to complete, the Great Wall of China was the longest construction project in history.

- Use a **semicolon** (and a conjunctive adverb if appropriate).

  The Great Wall took 1,700 years to complete; it is 1,400 miles long and up to 30 feet high and 32 feet wide.

- Repeat a **key word** or phrase to emphasize an idea.

  The Great Wall of China was the longest construction **project** in history, a **project** that took 1,700 years to complete.

- Use **correlative conjunctions** (*either, or; not only, but also*) to compare or contrast two ideas in a sentence.

  The Great Wall of China is **not only** up to 30 feet high and 32 feet wide, **but also** 1,400 miles long.

- Use an **appositive** (a word or phrase that renames) to emphasize an idea.

  The Great Wall of China—**the largest construction project in history**—is 1,400 miles long, 32 feet wide, and up to 30 feet high.

Expand sentences to add details.

LO3

Expand sentences when you edit so as to connect related ideas and make room for new information. Length has no value in and of itself: The best sentence is still the shortest one that says all it has to say. An expanded sentence, however, is capable of saying more—and saying it more expressively.

Use cumulative sentences.

Modern writers often use an expressive sentence form called the cumulative sentence. A cumulative sentence is made of a general "base clause" that is expanded by adding modifying words, phrases, or clauses. In such a sentence, details are added before and after the main clause, creating an image-rich thought. Here's an example of a cumulative sentence, with the base clause or main idea in boldface:

> In preparation for her Spanish exam, **Julie was studying** at the kitchen table, completely focused, memorizing a list of vocabulary words.

Discussion: Notice how each new modifier adds to the richness of the final sentence. Also notice that each of these modifying phrases is set off by a comma. Here's another sample sentence:

> With his hands on his face, **Tony was laughing** halfheartedly, looking puzzled and embarrassed.

Discussion: Such a cumulative sentence provides a way to write description that is rich in detail, without rambling. Notice how each modifier changes the flow or rhythm of the sentence.

Expand with details.

Here are seven basic ways to expand a main idea:

- **Adjectives and Adverbs:**
  halfheartedly, once again
- **Prepositional Phrases:**
  with his hands on his face
- **Absolute Phrases:**
  his head tilted to one side
- **Participial** (*ing* or *ed*) **Phrases:**
  looking puzzled
- **Infinitive Phrases:**
  to hide his embarrassment
- **Subordinate Clauses:**
  while his friend talks
- **Relative Clauses:**
  who isn't laughing at all

Edit sentences for variety and style. ___ LO4

Writer E. B. White advised young writers to "approach sentence style by way of simplicity, plainness, orderliness, and sincerity." That's good advice from a writer steeped in style. It's also important to know what to look for when editing your sentences. The information on this page and the following three pages will help you edit your sentences for style and correctness.

Avoid these sentence problems.

Always check for and correct the following types of sentence problems. Turn to the pages listed below for guidelines and examples when attempting to fix problems in your sentences.

Short, Choppy Sentences: Combine or expand any short, choppy sentences; use the examples and guidelines on pages 82–83.

Flat, Predictable Sentences: Rewrite any sentences that sound predictable and uninteresting by varying their structures and expanding them with modifying words, phrases, and clauses. (See pages 84–87.)

Incorrect Sentences: Look for and correct fragments, run-ons, and comma splices.

Unclear Sentences: Edit any sentences that contain unclear wording, misplaced modifiers, dangling modifiers, or incomplete comparisons.

Unacceptable Sentences: Change sentences that include nonstandard language, double negatives, or unparallel constructions.

Unnatural Sentences: Rewrite sentences that contain jargon, cliches, or flowery language.

Review your writing for sentence variety.

Use the following strategy to review your writing for variety in terms of sentence beginnings, lengths, and types.

- In one column on a piece of paper, list the opening words in each of your sentences. Then decide if you need to vary some of your sentence beginnings.
- In another column, identify the number of words in each sentence. Then decide if you need to change the lengths of some of your sentences.
- In a third column, list the kinds of sentences used (exclamatory, declarative, interrogative, and so on). Then, based on your analysis, use the instructions on the next two pages to edit your sentences as needed.

Writing with Sources: When you integrate a quotation into the flow of text, make sure that the quotation works with the material around it. Either make the quotation a grammatical part of the sentence, or introduce the quotation with a complete sentence followed by a colon.

Vary sentence structures.

To energize your sentences, vary their structures using one or more of the methods shown on this page and the next two.

1. **Vary sentence openings.** Move a modifying word, phrase, or clause to the front of the sentence to stress that modifier. However, avoid creating dangling or misplaced modifiers.

The norm:	We apologize for the inconvenience this may have caused you.
Variation:	For the inconvenience this may have caused you, we apologize.

2. **Vary sentence lengths.** Short sentences (ten words or fewer) are ideal for making points crisply. Medium sentences (ten to twenty words) should carry the bulk of your information. When well crafted, occasional long sentences (more than twenty words) can develop and expand your ideas.

Short:	Welcome back to Magnolia Suites!
Medium:	Unfortunately, your confirmed room was unavailable last night when you arrived. For the inconvenience this may have caused you, we apologize.
Long:	Because several guests did not depart as scheduled, we were forced to provide you with accommodations elsewhere; however, for your trouble, we were happy to cover the cost of last night's lodging.

3. **Vary sentence kinds.** The most common sentence is declarative—it states a point. For variety, try exclamatory, imperative, interrogative, and conditional statements.

Exclamatory:	Our goal is providing you with outstanding service!
Declarative:	To that end, we have upgraded your room at no expense.
Imperative:	Please accept, as well, this box of chocolates as a gift to sweeten your stay.
Interrogative:	Do you need further assistance?
Conditional:	If you do, we are ready to fulfill your requests.

INSIGHT: In creative writing (stories, novels, plays), writers occasionally use fragments to vary the rhythm of their prose, emphasize a point, or create dialogue. Avoid fragments in academic or business writing.

Writing with Sources: When you refer to ideas from a source, use the "historical present tense." That is, refer to the person and her or his work in the present tense—"Einstein **writes** that relativity . . ." Use past tense only if you want to emphasize the pastness of the source.

4. **Vary sentence arrangements.** Where do you want to place the main point of your sentence? You make that choice by arranging sentence parts into loose, periodic, balanced, or cumulative patterns. Each pattern creates a specific effect.

Loose Sentence
The Travel Center offers an attractive flight-reservation plan for students, one that allows you to collect bonus miles and receive $150,000 in life insurance per flight.

Analysis: This pattern is direct. It states the main point immediately (bold), and then tacks on extra information.

Periodic Sentence
Although this plan requires that you join the Travel Center's Student-Flight Club and pay the $10 admission fee, **in the long run you will save money!**

Analysis: This pattern postpones the main point (bold) until the end. The sentence builds to the point, creating an indirect, dramatic effect.

Balanced Sentence
Joining the club in your freshman year will save you money over your entire college career; in addition, accruing bonus miles over four years will earn you a free trip to Europe!

Analysis: This pattern gives equal weight to complementary or contrasting points (bold); the balance is often signaled by a comma and a conjunction (*and, but*) or by a semicolon. Often a conjunctive adverb (*however, nevertheless*) or a transitional phrase (*in addition, even so*) will follow the semicolon to further clarify the relationship.

Cumulative Sentence
Because the club membership is in your name, **you can retain its benefits** as long as you are a student, even if you transfer to a different college or go on to graduate school.

Analysis: This pattern puts the main idea (bold) in the middle of the sentence, surrounding it with modifying words, phrases, and clauses.

5. Use positive repetition. Although you should avoid needless repetition, you might use emphatic repetition to repeat a key word to stress a point.

Repetitive Sentence
Each year, more than a million young people who read poorly leave high school unable to read well, functionally illiterate.

Emphatic Sentence
Each year, more than a million young people leave high school functionally illiterate, so **illiterate** that they can't read daily newspapers, job ads, or safety instructions.

Use parallel structure.

Coordinated sentence elements should be parallel—that is, they should be written in the same grammatical forms. Parallel structures save words, clarify relationships, and present the information in the correct sequence. Follow these guidelines.

1. For words, phrases, or clauses in a series, keep elements consistent.

Not parallel:	I have tutored students in Biology 101, also Chemistry 102, not to mention my familiarity with Physics 200.
Parallel:	I have tutored students in *Biology 101, Chemistry 102,* and *Physics 200.*

Not parallel:	I have volunteered as a hospital receptionist, have been a hospice volunteer, and as an emergency medical technician.
Parallel:	I have done volunteer work as *a hospital receptionist, a hospice counselor,* and *an emergency medical technician.*

2. Use both parts of correlative conjunctions (*either, or; neither, nor; not only, but also; as, so; whether, so; both, and*) so that both segments of the sentence are balanced.

Not parallel:	*Not only* did Blake College turn 20 this year. Its enrollment grew by 16 percent.
Parallel:	*Not only* did Blake College turn 20 this year, *but* its enrollment *also* grew by 16 percent.

3. Place a modifier correctly so that it clearly indicates the word or words to which it refers.

Confusing:	MADD promotes severely punishing and eliminating drunk driving because this offense leads to a *great number* of deaths and sorrow.
Parallel:	MADD promotes eliminating and severely punishing drunk driving because this offense leads to *many* deaths and *untold* sorrow.

4. Place contrasting details in parallel structures (words, phrases, or clauses) to stress a contrast.

Weak contrast:	The average child watches 24 hours of television a week and reads for 36 minutes.
Strong contrast:	Each week, the average child watches television for 24 hours but reads for only about half an hour.

Writing with Sources: When using sources, smoothly integrate text references to those sources. (For MLA and APA guidelines, see pages 370–397.)

Avoid weak constructions.

Avoid constructions (like those below) that weaken your writing.

Nominal Constructions — The nominal construction is both sluggish and wordy. Avoid it by changing the noun form of a verb *(description* or *instructions)* to a verb *(describe* or *instruct).* At the same time, delete the weak verb that preceded the noun.

Nominal Constructions (noun form underlined)

Tim gave a <u>description</u> . . .

Lydia provided <u>instructions</u> . . .

Strong Verbs

Tim *described* . . .

Lydia *instructed* . . .

Sluggish: John *had a discussion* with the tutors regarding the incident. They gave him their *confirmation* that similar developments had occurred before, but they had not provided *submissions* of their reports.

Energetic: John *discussed* the incident with the tutors. They *confirmed* that similar problems had developed before, but they hadn't *submitted* their reports.

Expletives — Expletives such as "it is" and "there is" are fillers that serve no purpose in most sentences—except to make them wordy and unnatural.

Sluggish: *It is* likely that Nathan will attend the Communication Department's Honors Banquet. *There is* a journalism scholarship that he might win.

Energetic: Nathan will likely attend the Communication Department's Honors Banquet and might win a journalism scholarship.

Negative Constructions — Sentences constructed upon the negatives *no, not, neither/nor* can be wordy and difficult to understand. It's simpler to state what is the case.

Negative: During my four years on the newspaper staff, *I have not been* behind in making significant contributions. My editorial skills *have* certainly *not deteriorated,* as I have *never failed* to tackle challenging assignments.

Positive: During my four years on the newspaper staff, *I have made* significant contributions. My editorial skills *have* steadily *developed* as I *have tackled* difficult assignments.

Replace imprecise, misleading, and biased words. — LO5

As you edit your writing, check your choice of words carefully. The information on the next four pages will help you edit for word choice.

Substitute specific words.

Replace vague nouns and verbs with words that generate clarity and energy.

Specific Nouns — Make it a habit to use specific nouns for subjects. General nouns *(woman, school)* give the reader a vague, uninteresting picture. More specific nouns *(actress, university)* give the reader a better picture. Finally, very specific nouns *(Meryl Streep, Notre Dame)* are the type that can make your writing clear and colorful.

General to Specific Nouns

Person	Place
woman	school
actor	university
Meryl Streep	Notre Dame

Thing	Idea
book	theory
novel	scientific theory
Pride and Prejudice	relativity

Vivid Verbs

Vivid Verbs — Like nouns, verbs can be too general to create a vivid word picture. For example, the verb *looked* does not say the same thing as *stared, glared, glanced,* or *peeked.*

- Whenever possible, use a verb that is strong enough to stand alone without the help of an adverb.
  Verb and adverb: John *fell down* in the student lounge.
  Vivid verb: John **collapsed** in the student lounge.

- Avoid overusing the "be" verbs (*is, are, was, were*) and helping verbs. Often a main verb can be made from another word in the same sentence.
  A "be" verb: Cole *is* someone who follows international news.
  A stronger verb: Cole **follows** international news.

- Use active rather than passive verbs. (Use passive verbs only if you want to downplay who is performing the action in a sentence. See page 72.)
  Passive verb: Another provocative essay *was submitted* by Kim.
  Active verb: Kim **submitted** another provocative essay.

- Use verbs that show rather than tell.
  A verb that tells: Dr. Lewis *is* very thorough.
  A verb that shows: Dr. Lewis **prepares** detailed, interactive lectures.

Replace jargon and cliches.

Replace language that is overly technical or difficult to understand. Also replace overused, worn-out words.

Understandable Language

Understandable Language — Jargon is language used in a certain profession or by a particular group of people. It may be acceptable to use if your audience is that group of people, but to most ears jargon will sound technical and unnatural.

Jargon:	The bottom line is that our output is not within our game plan.
Clear:	Production is not on schedule.

Jargon:	I'm having conceptual difficulty with these academic queries.
Clear:	I don't understand these review questions.

Jargon:	Pursuant to our conversation, I have forwarded you a remittance attached herewith.
Clear:	As we discussed, I am mailing you the check.

Fresh and Original Writing

Fresh and Original Writing — Cliches are overused words or phrases. They give the reader no fresh view and no concrete picture. Because cliches spring quickly to mind (for both the writer and the reader), they are easy to write and often remain unedited.

an axe to grind	piece of cake
as good as dead	planting the seed
beat around the bush	rearing its ugly head
between a rock and a hard place	stick your neck out
burning bridges	throwing your weight around
easy as pie	up a creek

Purpose and Voice

Purpose and Voice — Other aspects of your writing may also be tired and overworked. Be alert to the two types of cliches described below.

Cliches of Purpose:

- Sentimental papers gushing about an ideal friend or family member, or droning on about a moving experience
- Overused topics with recycled information and predictable examples

Cliches of Voice:

- Writing that assumes a false sense of authority: "I have determined that there are three basic types of newspapers. My preference is for the third."
- Writing that speaks with little or no sense of authority: "I flipped when I saw *Viewpoints.*"
- Writing that is pretentious: "Because I have researched the topic thoroughly, readers should not question my conclusion."

Change biased words.

When depicting individuals or groups according to their differences, use language that implies equal value and respect for all people.

Quick Guide: Biased Words

Words Referring to Ethnicity

General Terms	Specific Terms
American Indians, Native Americans	Cherokee people, Inuit people, and so forth
Asian Americans (not Orientals)	Chinese Americans, Japanese Americans, and so forth
Latinos, Latinas, Hispanics	Mexican Americans, Cubans Americans, and so forth

African Americans, blacks: "African American" has come into wide acceptance, though the term "black" is preferred by some individuals.

Anglo Americans (English ancestry), **European Americans:** Use these terms to avoid the notion that "American," used alone, means "white."

Not Recommended	Preferred
Eurasian, mulatto	**person of mixed ancestry**
nonwhite	**person of color**
Caucasian	**white**
American (to mean U.S. citizen)	**U.S. citizen**

Words Referring to Age

Age Group	Acceptable Terms
up to age 13 or 14	**boys, girls**
between 13 and 19	**youth, young people, young men, young women**
late teens and 20s	**young adults, young women, young men**
30s to age 60	**adults, men, women**
60 and older	**older adults, older people** (not elderly)
66 and older	**seniors** (**senior citizens** also acceptable)

Insight: Whenever you write about a person with a disability, an impairment, or other special condition, give the person and your readers the utmost respect. Nothing is more distracting to a reader than an insensitive or outdated reference.

Words Referring to Disabilities or Impairments

— In the recent past, some writers were choosing alternatives to the term *disabled*, including *physically challenged, exceptional,* or *special.* However, it is not generally held that these new terms are precise enough to serve those who live with disabilities. Of course, degrading labels such as *crippled, invalid,* and *maimed,* as well as overly negative terminology, must be avoided.

Not Recommended	Preferred
handicapped	**disabled**
birth defect	**congenital disability**
stutter, stammer, lisp	**speech impairment**
an AIDS victim	**person with AIDS**
suffering from cancer	**person who has cancer**
mechanical foot	**prosthetic foot**
false teeth	**dentures**

Words Referring to Conditions

— People with various disabilities and conditions have sometimes been referred to as though they were their condition (*quadriplegics, depressives, epileptics*) instead of people who happen to have a particular disability. As much as possible, remember to refer to the person first, the disability second.

Not Recommended	Preferred
the disabled	**people with disabilities**
cripples	**people who have difficulty walking**
the retarded	**people with a developmental disability**
dyslexics	**students with dyslexia**
neurotics	**patients with neuroses**
subjects, cases	**participants, patients**
quadriplegics	**people who are quadriplegic**
wheelchair users	**people who use wheelchairs**

Make sure you understand the following terms that address specific impairments:

hearing impairment	=	partial hearing loss, hard of hearing (not deaf, which is total loss of hearing)
visual impairment	=	partially sighted (not blind, which is total loss of vision)
communicative disorder	=	speech, hearing, and learning disabilities affecting communication

Words Referring to Gender

- **Use parallel language for both sexes:**
    The **men** and the **women** rebuilt the school together.
    Hank and **Marie**
    Mr. Robert Gumble, **Mrs. Joy Gumble**

Note: The courtesy titles *Mr., Ms., Mrs.,* and *Miss* ought to be used according to the person's preference.

- **Use nonsexist alternatives** to words with masculine connotations:
    humanity (not *mankind*)
    synthetic (not *man-made*)
    artisan (not *craftsman*)

- **Do not use masculine-only or feminine-only pronouns** *(he, she, his, her)* when you want to refer to a human being in general:
    A politician can kiss privacy good-bye when **he** runs for office. (not recommended)

Instead, use *he or she,* change the sentence to plural, or eliminate the pronoun:
    A politician can kiss privacy good-bye when **he or she** runs for office.
    Politicians can kiss privacy good-bye when **they** run for office.
    A politician can kiss privacy good-bye when running for office.

- **Do not use gender-specific references** in the salutation of a business letter when you don't know the person's name:
    Dear Sir:
    Dear Gentlemen: (neither is recommended)
    Instead, address a position:
    Dear Personnel Officer:
    Dear Members of the Economic Committee

Occupational Issues

Not Recommended	Preferred
chairman	chair, presiding officer, moderator
salesman	sales representative, salesperson
clergyman	minister, priest, rabbi
male/female nurse	nurse
male/female doctor	doctor, physician
mailman	mail carrier, postal worker, letter carrier
insurance man	insurance agent
fireman	firefighter
businessman	executive, manager, businessperson
congressman	member of Congress, representative, senator
steward, stewardess	flight attendant
policeman, policewoman	police officer

Edit and proofread for correctness. LO6

Correct errors in spelling, mechanics, usage, grammar, and form.

Review punctuation and mechanics.

1. **Check for proper use of commas** before coordinating conjunctions in compound sentences, after introductory clauses and long introductory phrases, between items in a series, and so on.
2. **Look for apostrophes** in contractions, plurals, and possessive nouns.
3. **Examine quotation marks** in quoted information, titles, or dialogue.
4. **Watch for proper use of capital letters** for first words in written conversation and for proper names of people, places, and things.

Look for usage and grammar errors.

1. **Look for words that writers commonly misuse:** *there/their/they're; accept/except.*
2. **Check for verb use.** Subjects and verbs should agree in number: Singular subjects go with singular verbs; plural subjects go with plural verbs. Verb tenses should be consistent throughout.
3. **Review for pronoun/antecedent agreement problems.** A pronoun and its antecedent must agree in number.

Check for spelling errors.

1. **Use a spell checker and dictionary.** Your spell checker will catch most errors.
2. **Check each spelling you are unsure of.** Especially check those proper names and other special words your spell checker won't know.

Check the writing for form and presentation.

1. **Note the title.** A title should be appropriate and lead into the writing.
2. **Examine any quoted or cited material.** Are sources properly presented and documented? (See pages 354–359 and 370–396.)
3. **Check for correct page design.** (See page 94.)

Critical-Thinking and Writing Activities

As directed by your instructor, complete the following activities.

1. The nineteenth-century British writer Matthew Arnold offers this advice to writers about refining their writing: "Have something to say and say it as clearly as you can. That is the only secret of style." Does your own writing clearly communicate a meaningful message? Explain why or why not.
2. Choose a writing assignment that you have recently completed. Edit the sentences in this writing for style and correctness using pages 82–91 as a guide. Then use pages 87–90 in this chapter to edit the piece of writing for vague words, jargon, cliches, and biased language.

Cross-Curricular Connections

Different disciplines have different documentation systems, each with its own conventions, formats, and punctuation practices. For MLA and APA styles, see pages 370–397.

Checklist: Learning Outcomes

____ I understand that editing involves checking overall sentence style and word choice.

____ I have combined short, simplistic sentences.

____ I have expanded sentences, where appropriate, to create a more expressive style.

____ I have avoided sentence problems and improved sentence style.
 - Varying sentence structures
 - Varying sentence arrangements
 - Using parallel structure
 - Avoiding weak constructions

____ I have made sure that I use strong, effective words.
 - Using specific nouns and vivid verbs
 - Replacing jargon and cliches
 - Changing biased words

____ I have proofread my writing, checking punctuation, mechanics, usage, grammar, and spelling—as well as form and presentation.

"Start with something interesting and promising; wind up with something the reader will remember."
—Rudolf Flesch

8

Publishing

Submitting your writing might be as simple as handing it in to your instructor or posting it to a class wiki, or it might be as involved as submitting it to a journal in your area of study or assembling it with your other works to publish in a portfolio. Whatever the case, sharing your writing makes all the work you have done worthwhile. As writer Tom Liner states, "You learn ways to improve your writing by seeing its effect on others."

This chapter will help you prepare your writing for submission and sharing. When you make your writing public—in whatever form—you are *publishing* it.

Learning Outcomes

LO1 Format your writing.

LO2 Create a writing portfolio.

Format your writing.

A good page design makes your writing clear and easy to follow. Keep that in mind when you produce a final copy of your writing.

Strive for clarity in page design.

Examine the following design elements, making sure that each is appropriate and clear in your project and in your writing.

Format and Documentation

- **Keep the design clear and uncluttered.** Aim for a sharp, polished look in all your assigned writing.
- **Use the designated documentation form.** Follow all the requirements outlined in the MLA or APA style guides (see pages 370–397).

Typography

- **Use an easy-to-read serif font for the main text.** Serif type, **like this**, has "tails" at the tops and bottoms of the letters. For most types of writing, use a 10- or 12-point type size.
- **Consider using a sans serif font for the title and headings.** Sans serif type, **like this**, does not have "tails." Use larger, perhaps 18-point, type for your title and 14-point type for any headings. You can also use boldface for headings if they seem to get lost on the page. (Follow your instructor's formatting guidelines.)

Because most people find a sans serif font easier to read on screen, consider a sans serif font for the body and a serif font for the titles and headings in any writing you publish online.

Spacing

- **Follow all requirements for indents and margins.** This usually means indenting the first line of each paragraph five spaces, maintaining a one-inch margin around each page, and double-spacing throughout the paper.
- **Avoid widows and orphans.** Avoid leaving headings, hyphenated words, or single lines (widows) of new paragraphs alone at the bottom of a page.

Also avoid single words (orphans) at the bottom of a page or carried over to the top of a new page.

Graphic Devices

- **Create bulleted or numbered lists to highlight individual items in a list.** However, be selective, using traditional paragraphs when they help you more effectively communicate your message. Writing should not include too many lists.
- **Include charts or other graphics.** Graphics should be neither so small that they get lost on the page, nor so large that they overpower the page.

Create a writing portfolio.

Once you have formatted and proofread your final draft, you should be ready to share your writing. For college assignments, you will often simply turn in your paper to your instructor. However, you should also think about sharing your writing with other audiences, including those who will want to see your writing portfolio.

Consider potential audiences.

You could receive helpful feedback by taking any of the following steps:

- Share your writing with peers or family members.
- Submit your work to a local publication or an online journal.
- Post your writing on an appropriate Web site, including your own.
- Turn in your writing to your instructor.

Select appropriate submission methods.

There are two basic methods for submitting your work.

- **Paper submission:** Print an error-free copy on quality paper.
- **Electronic submission:** If allowed, send your writing as an e-mail attachment.

Use a writing portfolio.

There are two basic types of writing portfolios: (1) *a working portfolio* in which you store documents at various stages of development, and (2) *a showcase portfolio* with which you share appropriate finished work. For example, you could submit a portfolio to complete course requirements or to apply for a scholarship, graduate program, or job. The documents below are commonly included in a showcase portfolio:

A table of contents listing the pieces included in your portfolio

An opening essay or letter detailing the story behind your portfolio (how you compiled it and why it features the qualities expected by the intended reader)

A specified number of—and types of—finished pieces

A cover sheet attached to each piece of writing, discussing the reason for its selection, the amount of work that went into it, and so on

Evaluation sheets or checklists charting the progress or experience you want to show related to issues of interest to the reader

Modella, 2011 / Used under license from Shutterstock.com

Critical-Thinking and Writing Activities

As directed by your instructor, complete the following critical-thinking and writing activities by yourself or with classmates.

1. Catherine Drinker Bowen has argued the following: "Writing is not apart from living. Writing is a kind of double living." As you think about sharing your own writing and adding it to your writing portfolio, does this claim ring true? Why or why not?

2. Choose one of your recent writing assignments and use the instructions on page 94 to assess the quality of your formatting and page design. Edit and redesign the paper as needed.

3. For the class in which you are using this book, begin two working portfolios: (1) an electronic portfolio on your computer and (2) a paper portfolio in a sturdy folder or binder. In the electronic portfolio, store all drafts of your assignments, as well as all related electronic correspondence with your instructor. In your paper portfolio, store all printed drafts of your work, including copies that show your instructor's notations and grades.

Checklist: Learning Outcomes

_____ I have formatted my writing according to assignment and submission guidelines.
- Using appropriate headings, layout, margins, typography, and documentation

_____ I have added my writing to my portfolio.
- Demonstrating an appropriate level of scholarship and research
- Using appropriate voice and style
- Including an attractive design

"If you don't understand yourself
you don't understand anybody else."
Nikki Giovanni

9

Narration, Description, and Reflection

Personal narratives tell stories—not ones that the writers made up, but ones that they lived. Whatever the topics, the stories should help readers see, hear, touch, and taste those details that make the experiences come alive. To do that, writers must carefully describe key aspects of the experience. But they might also reflect on why the experiences are important—exploring their personal and shared meanings.

When reading such personal essays, do so with an open mind—seeking to go where writers guide you, to experience what they carefully describe, and to analyze how they craft their work.

As you prepare to write your own story, get ready to relive it yourself—to reexperience all that you felt, thought, or sensed during the event. In addition, be ready to learn something new about the experience, about others, and even about yourself.

Learning Outcomes

LO1 Understand how to read personal essays.

LO2 Understand how to use anecdotes.

LO3 Establish setting, describe people, and narrate action.

LO4 Reflect on an experience.

LO5 Use narration, description, and reflection to write a personal essay.

Understand how to read personal essays.

The strategies below will help you read personal essays—writing that blends narration, description, and reflection.

Consider the rhetorical situation.

Think about the writer's purpose, audience, and topic, and how these might be linked.

Purpose: Writers develop personal essays to explore meaningful aspects of life—people, experiences, and things that they care for and are shaped by.

Audience: Most personal essays are written for a general audience, with the writer hoping that readers will empathize with and connect to the writer's experience.

Topic: In personal essays, writers address any topics that they find meaningful and worth exploring through the lens of personal reflection.

Consider the writer's strategies.

For personal essays, writers primarily use **narration, description,** and **reflection,** but they often combine these strategies with others such as compare/contrast and definition.

Narration: Well-written narratives are stories that include the following:

- **Characters** who are well-developed, often complex, and engaging
- **Dialogue** that indicates who characters are and what they think and say about themselves, others, and life itself
- **Action** that includes conflicts and shows what characters do; usually it is organized chronologically, though it may start in the middle or flash back; often the action reveals that characters are not who they think or say they are
- **Settings** that often influence—and sometimes reflect—the characters and action; time and place anchor the experience naturally and culturally

Description: Effective descriptive passages offer precise details that help readers sensually and thoughtfully experience the topic. In addition, figurative language such as metaphors, similes, and symbols commonly enrich the text.

Reflection: Strong reflective passages relay the writers' observations and insights regarding the nature, impact, and value of their experiences.

Checklist: Personal Essays

- ✔ Why does the writer care about the topic, and how is he or she affected by it?
- ✔ What ideas or themes evolve from the story? Explain.
- ✔ Are the characters' actions and dialogue believable and consistent?
- ✔ Is the description concise, precise, informing, and engaging?

Understand how to use anecdotes.

A common narrative is the anecdote—a brief story that enlivens your writing while introducing a topic or illustrating an idea. Read the anecdotes below, along with the essays from which they are taken. Then assess the anecdotes' effectiveness.

Anecdote Introducing a Topic

The other day, my wife, watching our son-in-law with his large hands gracefully tie the shoelaces of his little daughter, remarked, "You really are deft." Ever the cynic, I remarked, "He's not only deft, he's daft." I talk that sort of nonsense frequently, but as I said this, I began to wonder. What if *deft* and *daft* come from the same root and once meant the same thing? A quick trip to the dictionary showed that, indeed, they did once mean the same thing (though my wife thought me daft when I first suggested it).

From "Deft or Daft," page 118

Anecdote Illustrating a Point

LAST week, the Senate majority leader, Harry Reid, found himself in trouble for once suggesting that Barack Obama had a political edge over other African-American candidates because he was "light-skinned" and had "no Negro dialect, unless he wanted to have one." Mr. Reid was not expressing sadness but a gleeful opportunism that Americans were still judging one another by the color of their skin, rather than—as the Rev. Dr. Martin Luther King Jr., whose legacy we commemorated on Monday, dreamed—by the content of their character.

From "Shades of Prejudice," pages 157–159

Anecdote Illustrating a Trait

Jackie Thomas, Nike's associate director of sports marketing, usually spends her lunch hour on the sports-shoe company's basketball courts charging for the basket, always outnumbered by male colleagues. "I hold my own," boasts the 33-year-old executive.

She also does well playing the corporate game back inside the headquarter's offices. Thomas, a former University of California-Berkeley college basketball point guard, says her success is due in large part to the lessons she learned growing up playing competitive team sports. "It's taught me that if you lose a game, you go back afterward and figure out what went wrong and how to overcome it the next time," says the former tomboy from Kingston, Jamaica.

While most of America's corporations are still commanded by male chief executives, women are gaining ground, winning vice-presidential and top management slots and, in a few cases, the highest leadership roles. Many of these young female executives say playing team sports helped them get ahead.

From "If You Let Me Play . . . ," pages 169–171

Establish setting, describe people, and narrate action. LO3

In this essay, student writer Robert Minto recalls a series of events through which he learned something about his community, himself, and the nature of life. Note how the details he cites help you visualize places, people, and events. Note also how direct dialogue reveals personalities and feelings.

Essay Outline

Introduction: Setting, key characters, and conflict: moths (such as Ryan) vs. spiders (such as Old Jack)

1. Narrator goes to Ryan's house.
2. They stop at narrator's house, pass church, arrive at cemetery.
3. They explore cemetery and discuss spirits.
4. They hear moaning and move toward it.
5. They see Old Jack's grandson and a girl.
6. They return to bikes and ride past church to Ryan's house.

Closing: Narrator tells Old Jack about grandson and girl and then reflects on the moth/spider conflict.

Symbiot, 2011 / Used under license from Shutterstock.com

The Entomology (A) of Village Life

1 (B) Buddy didn't know that we were **cliches**. I knew. I liked it that way. We spent our days together—me too inquisitive and his tail always wagging. My neighbor, Old Jack, who was forever pulling weeds in his garden, self-exiled from a sharp-tongued wife, was a cliché too. So was the **grange** on the other side of my house. Most of the men in Naymari, Pennsylvania, never missed a grange meeting, mainly to supervise the village's one employee, Pedro, who mowed the grass in the park. Within this small web of places and personalities, life abounded. Some people were the moths, tied down and struggling; some were the spiders, growing fat on gossip.

2 (C) One of the moths lived across the street. He was my friend Ryan. Ryan lived in the dirtiest house I've ever seen. His mother cared for him and for two younger, mentally disabled boys as well. She had a big heart but too few hands and no husband. In the winter, they all huddled around a kerosene heater, wearing most of the clothing they owned, the two youngest boys often licking the snot that dripped from their cold noses. They couldn't afford oil. Through a government program, Ryan had received an old IBM computer. He spent most of his time playing Tetris on it in his room. Sometimes when Buddy and I got up early in the morning to roam the village, we'd stop outside Ryan's window, and I'd toss pebbles at it. (His mother and I had this understanding that I could get him up to play, but because she slept in later than we did, I couldn't yell.) Soon his bleary eyes would peer over the sill. Eventually he'd come out, and I'd lead him off on some adventure.

3 (D) Old Jack, on the other hand, was one of Naymeri's spiders. His garden wasn't merely a refuge from his wife, but it was also the **epicenter** of his web. At the slightest hint of gossip, he'd scurry down the street with a twine-wrapped bundle of asparagus, his specialty, to gain entry into whatever home promised the best information. With most people, me included, Jack gossiped on a strictly business model. He'd tell me his latest and juiciest stories and in return, I'd offer him— as keeper of the town's skeleton closet—whatever my wandering uncovered. It was Jack who told me, with relish, the **acrimonious** story of how Ryan's family had broken apart. He enjoyed the telling.

4 Old Jack also hated abortion, but not because of religion—he hated that too. One time, standing in his asparagus and gesturing with a weed, he told me why.

5 "You seen those hooded graves?" he asked.

6 "What graves?" I said, holding Buddy so he wouldn't pee on Jack's onions.

7 "You haven't seen 'em? The graves with cages across the way at the Methodist church?"

8 "Oh, *those*. Sure, I've seen 'em."

9 "Do you know why they got cages?"

10 "Why?"

11 Jack shook his weed again, and a little shower of dirt crumbled off it. "Because," he said, "if you go over there at night and listen, you can hear the spirits of aborted children screaming to get out and hurt the people who killed 'em!"

12 I shivered. Buddy licked my face.

13 (E) A few minutes later I was tossing pebbles at Ryan's window. Eventually he staggered out of the house.

14 "Hey Ryan," I said quietly, "want an adventure?"

15 Ryan thought that was a good idea, but he wanted to know if he should bring anything. Last adventure we got all wet in a stream, and he wished he'd brought some boots.

(A) The title forecasts a study of insects.
(B) Introduction: setting, key characters, and conflict: moths (such as Ryan) vs. spiders (such as Old Jack)
(C) Ryan, a moth

cliches
a term that has lost its effectiveness from overuse

grange
a local lodge in the Grange, an organization that promotes agriculture

epicenter
a center of influence, as in an earthquake

acrimonious
full of anger or resentment

(D) Old Jack, a spider
(E) Narrator goes to Ryan's house.

16 "Nah," I told him, "we're just gonna listen to some
(F) spirits."

17 We stopped by my house to get a paper bag filled with Swiss-and-ham-on-rye and a smoked pig's ear for Buddy. Then we grabbed our bikes and headed east toward the park, the cemetery, and the Methodist church. We left our bikes in the gravel parking lot by the church. We could see the pastor in the big glass window of his study. He had his head on his arms, sleeping.

18 The hooded graves were at the far edge of the cem-
(G) etery, right beside the woods that harbored our park. The unmowed grass beside these graves suggested that they might not be part of the cemetery. Ryan and I waded through the grass and peered past the wire mesh that caged the white stones. Because they were worn smooth by rain, any carved writing on the stones was long gone. I tugged on one of the cages until Ryan nervously told me to stop. He needn't have—I couldn't budge it. It was firmly planted in the hard earth.

19 "When do we hear the spirits?" asked Ryan.

20 "When the sun goes down," I told him, "I think." We walked over to a big oak tree on the edge of the woods where we could see the graves better. The tree had several nice boles to sit in. I told Ryan the rest of what Jack had told me. We agreed that the children's spirits might want to get even, but Ryan doubted that the spirits could really do that.

21 "Don't you believe in spirits?" I asked. Of course he did—he went to the Presbyterian church.

22 "I've *seen* one, too!" said Ryan. "I was in my room when we lived in Florida. That was before we left my dad. I slept upstairs in the attic there, just like here. I was laying in bed when I heard something coming up the stairs and scratching at the door. Then the door opened and a big white thing came in and stood by the bed. I closed my eyes and prayed, and when I opened 'em the thing was gone."

23 I told him it was probably just his dad. Or maybe his mom.

24 "No," he said, "because I got really cold when it came in, and I felt like I couldn't move." We were silent, me imagining, him remembering.

25 "Then why don't you believe that we'll hear the spirits?" I asked.

26 "Why don't you believe in the ghost I saw?" he replied.

27 I saw his point. But somehow his story just didn't seem as vivid as Old Jack's story about children's spirits out for revenge. Now *that* one would give me nightmares!

28 Suddenly I noticed that I couldn't hear Buddy. He'd been nosing around the trees, scratching at the dirt, sniffing at mole-holes, snapping at dandelions. I looked around and saw him standing, stiff. He was staring into the woods. As I turned to follow his gaze (H) I heard a moan.

29 Ryan jumped. We looked at each other. The moan again. We looked at the hooded graves, but there was nothing to see.

30 "Did you let it out when you pulled on the cage?" asked Ryan. Then he added, "But didn't you say we wouldn't hear 'em til the sun went *down?*"

31 The moan again. It seemed to be coming from the grove of trees at our back. We turned toward the sound, and I started to worm forward on my belly into the trees. "Stay," I told Buddy. Ryan obeyed the command as well for about ten seconds, and then he started worming forward too, grumbling quietly. The damp earth was covered with crunchy leaves, but we were small and had practice sneaking.

32 As we neared the sound, it became more frequent, and then we heard a sort of ragged breathing joining in, like a duet. But it didn't sound like spirits.

33 Then we came to a place where we could see some-
(I) thing through the trees. It was a zebra-striped car with spinners on the wheels. On top of the car, awkwardly straddling a dark-haired girl, Old Jack's grandson, Jim, was doing his best to make her moan louder. The ragged breathing was his. He jerked up and down, and I could see the silver flash of the car's antenna between

---

(F) They stop at narrator's house, pass the church, and arrive at cemetery.
(G) They explore cemetery and discuss spirits.

(H) They hear moaning and move toward it.
(I) They see Old Jack's grandson and a girl.

them each time they separated. Me and Ryan froze for a few seconds before comprehension struck. Glancing wildly at each other, we squirmed away.

34 When we reached the edge of the wood, we stood
(J) up and made our way back to our bikes. Somehow, waiting for the spirits had lost its appeal. I glanced at the Methodist church and saw the pastor was awake, waving at us through the window. We pedaled quietly back to town. I imagined that even Buddy seemed subdued. When we reached Ryan's house, he stopped and laid his bike on the grass. We could hear his mom inside, talking to his brothers.

35 Ryan began to walk up the lawn, back to his Tetris. Then he stopped, turned around and asked, "What are you gonna do?"

36 I thought for a moment. Then I told him.

37 About an hour later, I finished telling Old Jack what we'd seen. He was watering his tomatoes, and as I talked, I noticed that one of the plants was nearly floating even though he was staring right at it. I finished up, and he went right on watering that same plant.

38 Then he glanced over at me and said, "That's very
(K) interesting." He contemplated the drowning plant again and added, "But this isn't something to get around town, you know. You wouldn't tell anybody else, would ya?"

39 I thought for a moment. Then I smiled.

40 Somewhere, a spider was about to become a moth.

(J) They return to bikes and ride past church to Ryan's house.
(K) Closing: Narrator tells Old Jack about grandson and girl and then reflects on the moth/spider conflict.

Peter Waters, 2011 / Used under license from Shutterstock.com

Reading for Better Writing

Working by yourself or with a group, answer these questions:

1. Review the title, "The Entomology of Village Life." Then explain what *entomology* is and why it is (or is not) a good choice for this essay.

2. In the opening paragraph, the writer refers to himself and other village residents as *cliches*. Explain why the writer might use this term. Does the essay show the characters to be cliches? Explain.

3. In the second paragraph, the writer refers to village residents as moths and spiders. Explain what he might mean by these metaphors and the effect of his using them to open and close the essay.

4. Identify a narrative passage, a descriptive passage, and a reflective passage that you consider well written. Explain why.

5. What is the essay's main idea or theme? How does the writer introduce the idea and develop it?

6. Re-read the essay's last sentence and explain why it is (or is not) an effective closing.

Reflect on an experience. ___LO4

Often, the meaning of an experience can simply be implied through the action and descriptions. Sometimes, however, such meaning can be accented through reflection. Study how descriptive and reflective passages are used in the following essays.

Reflecting on an Encounter

"Spare Change" is the first part of student writer Teresa Zsuffa's "A Diary of Chance Encounters," an essay that explores her experiences of living in Toronto. The piece below recounts a challenging encounter with the face of poverty.

"Spare Change"

Survey · Question · Read · Recite · Review **SQ3R**

1 This grime is infectious. The smell of old cigarettes and expired perfume is constricting my throat
(A) and turning my stomach. But here I am again on the underground subway platform, changing trains at Bloor-Yonge in Toronto, the weight of my backpack thrusting me forward with the Friday morning rush hour crowd. When the subway doors open, I hurry inside and look around frantically, as usual. There is an empty seat to my left, but everyone is keeping a safe four-foot distance, as if the seat will suck them in and destroy them if they sit down. Or at least destroy the **facade** put on with a Ralph Lauren suit, a Coach handbag, or a pair of authentic Gucci sunglasses. Not like the fake five-dollar ones I picked up from a Chinatown vendor just yesterday. The others keep their starry distance; when I sit down, I see why.

2 She must be about twenty-nine. Her orange track-
(B) pants are worn and faded, her T-shirt is far too big, and her powder blue sweatshirt is tied around her waist. Her face and teeth are stained, hair greasy and unkempt. A part of me feels sorry for her. Another part follows the crowd and is careful not to make eye contact.

3 "Excuse me," she says, perching on the edge of her seat, leaning forward and clasping the metal pole with two hands. No one turns. "Excuse me, which stop do I take to the Old City Hall?" One man shrugs and

shakes his head while pretending to check his phone. I feel guilt, but it's easily subdued. After all, she wasn't asking me.

4 I am deeply engrossed in my Nicholas Sparks novel by the time the driver announces "Dundas Station." As I stuff the book back into my purse and make my way towards the doorway, I'm irritated to see that she also stands up—one stop early for Old City Hall. Doesn't she know she should stay on until Queen? Oh well, she'll figure it out, I reason. The Toronto Transit Commission officers can help her.

5 I let her off the subway before me. Finally I'm free.

6 But then she stops on the platform and turns her head, like a puppy making sure her owner is following
(C) close behind. No eye contact, I remind myself, and try to walk past but she falls into step with me.

7 "Can I help you carry your bag?"

8 I may look like a tourist, but I'm smarter. "No, thanks," I reply.

9 "Well it just looks pretty heavy." We reach the escalator and the staircase and I take the left side, where I can climb the steps and go up twice as fast as those just standing there on the right and enjoying the ride. But it doesn't work; the woman is still at my heels.

10 "Are you going somewhere?" she asks.

11 "Yeah, I have to get to the Greyhound station, I'm going out of town."

12 "Oh." Now we are standing in front of the underground entrance to the Eaton Center. The Atrium on
(D) Bay is to my right, on the other side of which is the bus station and my ticket out of this alien city that is now my home. The woman stands frozen and looks around trying to get her bearings. I start to walk away but hesitate. Looking back, I see her blinking and flinching as people shove past her. She reminds me of a small child lost at a summer carnival.

(A) The writer describes an urban setting and a common situation.
(B) She introduces the central person through concrete details, her words, and the reactions of others (including the writer's own mixed feelings).

(C) The writer narrates the events and dialogue that lead her to offer help.
(D) Details describe the urban setting, and the writer's acclimation to it.

facade
a false image

13   I check my watch—quarter past eight. I just missed an express shuttle, and the next bus to Niagara Falls, where my father lives, won't be leaving for another forty-five minutes. Something pulls me back to the woman, and against all sworn Torontonian rules, I ask if she needs help.

(E)

14   Her dull brown eyes light up. "I need to find the Old City Hall."

15   "Okay," I nod. "I'll take you." I lead her through the glass doors into the city's busiest mall. It's the fastest way from Dundas to Queen Street, and from there she will need to walk only a few blocks west. As we're walking, I'm aware of the stares I'm getting from people I'll never see again.

16   "So where are you from?" I ask.

17   "Sudbury." And I'm instantly speechless. What is this woman doing so far from home? How did she get here? I ask why she's in the city.

(F)

18   "My boyfriend. He's in jail, and they're letting him go today. I came to take him back home with me after his hearing."

19   While we walk past Mexx, Aritzia, and Abercrombie, I learn that she had taken a bus from Sudbury the day before and spent the night on a park bench. Her boyfriend is forty-two years old and has been in jail for the past ten months. I don't ask why. She proudly tells me she was a crack addict and that she's been clean for three months.

20   "I just got out of rehab," she says. "Now maybe my grandma will take me back in."

(G)

21   "Back in?"

22   "Yeah, she kicked me out. She told me I wasn't allowed to be a hooker anymore, but I got caught bringing someone home once."

23   I have no idea how to talk to a prostitute, never mind one who is so open about everything she's done,

(H)

(E) She refers to the city's cultural "rules."
(F) The writer uses dialogue to describe the woman's life and her journey.
(G) Short quotes create a tensive rhythm.
(H) The writer describes her confusion, sympathy, and guilt.

providence
care and guidance provided by God

but this woman seems to like me and trust me. The next thing I know, I'm offering to buy her breakfast before she meets up with her boyfriend.

24   There's a McDonald's at the southernmost side of the Eaton Centre, overlooking the Queen Street entrance. I tell her she can have anything she wants. An Egg McMuffin? Fruit and yogurt? But all she wants is Coke and a hash-brown. I order her two.

25   We sit down at a freshly wiped table by the window. Beside us, two men in grey suits sip coffee over an array of files and spreadsheets. They pause in their conversation to stare at us—the student traveler and the bedraggled prostitute. I tell the woman a little about my life, and ask more about hers and her grandmother. She says that they used to go to church together, when she was little, but she hasn't been since. She takes another bite of her hash-brown and tells me she's now twenty-one. Only twenty-one, and her boyfriend is forty-two. She talks about the drugs and the **providence** of God.

(I)

26   "I know that he helped me stop," she says. "I've been clean for three months, can you believe that? That's a miracle! It has to be a miracle."

27   At this point all I can do is smile.

28   "I wish I could get my boyfriend to quit," she says, staring off. Then she suddenly leans forward and asks, "Do you know how hard it is? Have you ever done crack?"

29   "No."

30   "Pot, at least?"

31   "No. Sorry." I'm not sure why I'm apologizing for never having tried drugs, but the way her face drops and she shifts her eyes makes me feel guilty. As though I can never fully understand her because I've never experienced the things she has.

(J)

32   "Well you should try it," she urges. "It's really good."

33   "Maybe one day." I glance at my watch. It's now quarter-to, and I still need to stand in line to buy my

---

(I) A dash accents the irony of this unlikely pair sharing personal time and stories.
(J) The writer acknowledges her own inexperience and confusion.

ticket and get to the right platform. I wonder why I'm not panicking yet.

34   I tell her I need to get going. She should go, too,
(K) or she'll be late for the hearing. Before getting up, I reach into my wallet and give her two TTC passes and some spare change. I walk her to the street and point her toward Old City Hall. She never thanks me, only looks at me one last time with immense vulnerability and helplessness. Then she walks away.

35   I wonder as I hurry towards the station if she'll be okay, if her boyfriend really will get out of jail, and if her grandmother will ever take her back. Either way, I think as I cross Bay Street, what more can I do? I have a bus to catch.

(K) The writer offers spare change, a gift that is cited in the title and that symbolizes the women's distanced relationship.

Reading for Better Writing

Working by yourself or with a group, answer these questions:

1. Teresa's essay focuses on an urban setting. What does she evoke about the city, and what descriptions create that feeling?

2. The central character in the essay is presented primarily through description, comparisons, and dialogue. Identify such passages, exploring what they communicate about the woman and how effectively they work.

3. One focus of the essay is the writer's experience of the city and of her encounter with the prostitute. Describe Teresa's reflections and feelings about both. How does she communicate these? Identify and analyze specific passages, sentences, and phrases.

Narrating a Comic Event

Elizabeth Fuller writes this essay to describe her one-time experience as a stowaway flight attendant—an experience that she enjoys describing but likely does not want to relive. Consider how she opens her essay by reflecting on how she felt about her job.

When Dreams Take Flight   (A)

Survey · Question · Read · Recite · Review   **SQ3R**

In my 20s I was a flight attendant for Northwest   1
Airlines, and I remember the holiday season as the (B)
most exhausting of the year. But I loved my job. From the first day Northwest hired me in Minneapolis in 1969, I tried to be a model flight attendant, to develop the qualities my operations manual demanded: poise, good judgment, initiative, adaptability and a spotless appearance.

But one time I slipped up: I fell asleep. It happened   2
one dreary morning around Thanksgiving. We'd just (C)
landed in Washington and I was dog-tired. The crew had disembarked for breakfast; the new passengers wouldn't board for two hours. For some reason, my eye drifted toward the overhead racks. Back then, the racks in Boeing 727's had no doors and were used only for storing pillows, blankets and passengers' coats and hats. I looked at all the little pillows up there, snuggled next to the blankets. And then I climbed up.

This was not easy in a pencil skirt and regulation   3
red half-slip. But I did it. And it was heaven. I lay back on the mountain of pillows and pulled a blanket up over my head. Just before I drifted off, the thought crossed my mind that I ought to set my portable alarm (D)
clock—but it was too late.

I certainly wasn't worrying about our operations   4
manual, though I knew, of course, that flight atten- (E)
dants caught sleeping on duty could lose their wings. But I wasn't on duty, not in the strict sense. What's more, I was exhibiting initiative and adaptability, some of those attributes most cherished by Northwest Airlines.

It was a sound sleep. Suddenly I woke to a voice   5
on the public address system: "Morning, folks. This (F)
is your captain speaking. We're No. 4 for takeoff, up

(A) A playful title forecasts what will happen.
(B) The writer describes herself.
(C) A transition and short clause introduce the action.
(D) A dash and short clause forecast trouble.
(E) She reflects on and rationalizes her choice.
(F) The quotation builds tension and tells what is happening.

near the end of the runway. So if you'll just sit back and relax, we'll be taking off in a few minutes. The flight attendants will do the best they can for you this morning, even though they are one short in the second cabin."

6   I opened my eyes and gasped. The passengers and
(G) crew had boarded, and no one had checked my overhead bunk. If only someone had tried to store a coat up there or grab a blanket! I should have been down on the cabin floor, on duty and with my one-inch **grosgrain** ribbon tying my hair in place, my gold logo centered on the front of my hat. Instead, I was up on that rack, breaking into a cold sweat.

7   If I ever needed that Northwest Airlines initiative, it was then. I poked my head out and down. The cabin
(H) was packed with businessmen reading the financial papers. I hitched up my skirt—hemmed precisely one and three-quarter inches above the knee—and lowered a leg. This snagged the attention of the last 10 rows, as well as my pantyhose. Then I lowered my other leg. By this time, the rows in front had turned around and were watching too. Luckily, no one laughed.

8   I swung down and planted my navy blue pump
(I) half on a passenger's armrest and half on his pin-striped leg. My hat was in the overhead rack, I told him, and I had been digging around for a long time trying to find it. I pointed out that I had to wear my hat, or I would be fired.

9   He cleared his throat but didn't say anything. I thanked him for his understanding and walked up the aisle toward my two fellow flight attendants, who were
(J) howling with laughter. We were sobered only by the realization that somebody had to notify the captain.

(G) A series of short sentences suggest her thoughts and fears.
(H) She describes her cautious and embarrassing descent.
(I) She summarizes her excuse and notes his suspicion.
(J) Mention of the captain sets up the conclusion.

grosgrain
a corded silk or rayon fabric used for trimmings

As the plane rose to cruising altitude, the senior   *10*
flight attendant went to the cockpit and explained that I was back in the cabin. Meanwhile, I put on my smock and began pouring coffee, trying to avoid the rows near my overhead bunk. As I headed back to the galley to refill my coffeepot, I found the captain waiting for me with a stern and unforgiving look. I was getting ready to try to explain when he snapped the galley curtain closed and doubled over with laughter. "All's well that ends well," he said with a wink.   **(K)**

(K) The captain responds by quoting Shakespeare.

Reading for Better Writing

Working by yourself or with a group, answer these questions:

1. Review the title and explain why it is (or is not) a good choice.

2. Re-read the opening paragraph and note what the writer says about her age, employer, the season, her employer's expectations, and her desire to excel. Then explain how this reflection helps set up the story, build interest in the action, and create humor.

3. Cite a descriptive passage that you find particularly engaging and explain why.

4. Compare what the captain says in paragraph 5 with what he says in paragraph 10. What does each statement tell you about his personality, role on the plane, and relationship with the crew? Would paraphrasing the captain have been more effective than quoting him?

5. Review paragraphs 7-9 in which the writer describes her descent from the luggage bin, the passenger whom she steps on, her excuse, and his response. Do the details she offers adequately describe her action and his response? Explain.

6. Do you find the story funny? Why or why not?

Reflecting on a Cultural Practice

The following essay by Barbara Kingsolver is taken from her book *High Tide in Tucson.* In the essay, she describes her brief experience as a bodybuilding wannabe, and she reflects on how she "outgrew" her need to buff up. Study not only her use of narration and description to present her experiences but also her comic reflections on bodybuilding practices.

The Muscle Mystique

Survey • Question • Read • Recite • Review   **SQ3R**

1   The baby-sitter surely thought I was having an affair. Years ago, for a period of three whole months, I would dash in to pick up my daughter after "work" with my cheeks flushed, my heart pounding, my hair damp from a quick shower. I'm loath to admit where I'd really been for that last hour of the afternoon. But it's time to come clean.

2   I joined a health club.

3   I went downtown and sweated with the masses. I rode a bike that goes nowhere at the rate of five hundred calories per hour. I even pumped a little iron. I can't deny the place was a **lekking** ground: guys stalking around the weight room like prairie chickens, nervously eying each other's pectorals. Over by the abdominal machines I heard some of the frankest pickup lines since eighth grade ("You've got real defined deltoids for a girl"). A truck perpetually parked out front had vanity plates the read: LFT WTS. Another one, PRSS 250, I didn't recognize as a vanity plate until I understood the prestige of bench pressing 250 pounds.

4   I personally couldn't bench press a fully loaded steam iron. I didn't join the health club to lose weight, or to meet the young **Adonis** who admired my (dubiously defined) deltoids. I am content with my lot in life, save for one irksome affliction: I am what's known in comic-book jargon as the ninety-eight-pound weakling. I finally tipped the scales into three digits my last year of high school, but "weakling" I've remained, pretty much since birth. In polite terminology I'm cerebral; the muscles between my ears are what I get by on. The last great body in my family was my Grandfather Henry. He wore muscle shirts in the days when they were known as BVDs, under his cotton work shirt, and his bronze tan stopped mid-biceps. He got those biceps by hauling floor joists and hammering up roof beams every day of his life, including his last. How he would have guffawed to see a roomful of nearly naked bankers and attorneys, pale as plucked geese, heads down, eyes fixed on a horizon beyond the water cooler, pedaling like bats out of hell on bolted-down bicycles. I expect he'd offer us all a job. If we'd pay our thirty dollars a month to *him,* we could come out to the construction site and run up and down ladders bringing him nails. That's why I'm embarrassed about all this. I'm afraid I share his opinion of unproductive sweat.

lekking
an area of ground used by male fowl for mating displays
Adonis
an extremely handsome young man from Greek mythology

5 Actually, he'd be more amazed than scornful. His idea of fun was watching Ed Sullivan or snoozing in a recliner, or ideally, both at once. Why work like a maniac on your day off? To keep your heart and lungs in shape. Of course. But I haven't noticed any vanity plates that say GD LNGS. The operative word here is vanity.

6 Standards of beauty in every era are things that advertise, usually falsely: "I'm rich and I don't have to work." How could you be a useful farmhand, or even an efficient clerk-typist, if you have long, painted fingernails? Four-inch high heels, like the bound feet of Chinese aristocrats, suggest you don't have to do *anything* efficiently, except maybe put up your tootsies on an ottoman and eat **bonbons**. (And I'll point out here that aristocratic *men* wore the first high heels.) In my grandmother's day, women of all classes lived in dread of getting a tan, since that betrayed a field worker's station in life. But now that the field hand's station is occupied by the office worker, a tan, I suppose, advertises that Florida and Maui are within your reach. Fat is another peculiar cultural flip-flop: in places where food is scarce, beauty is three inches of **subcutaneous** fat deep. But here and now, jobs are sedentary and calories are relatively cheap, while the luxury of time to work them off is very dear. It still gives me pause to see an ad for a weight-loss program that boldly enlists: "First ten pounds come off free!" But that is about the size of it, in the strange food-drenched land of ours. After those first ten, it gets expensive.

7 As a writer I could probably do my job fine with no deltoids at all, or biceps or triceps, so long as you left me those **vermicelli**-sized muscles that lift the fingers to the keyboard. (My vermicellis are *very* well defined.)

bonbons
a candy

subcutaneous
below the skin

vermicelli
a long, thin pasta noodle

mortification
shame and humiliation

bougainvilleas
a type of climbing plant with colorful leaves

So when I've writ my piece, off I should merrily go to build a body that says I don't really have a financial obligation to sit here in video-terminal bondage.

8 Well, yes. But to tell the truth, the leisure body and even the GD LNGS are not really what I was after when I signed up at Pecs-R-Us. What I craved, and long for still, is to be *strong.* I've never been strong. In childhood, team sports were my most reliable source of humiliation. I've been knocked breathless to the ground by softballs, basketballs, volleyballs, and once, during a wildly out-of-hand game of Red Rover, a sneaker. In every case I knew my teammates were counting on me for a volley or a double play or anyhow something more than clutching my stomach and rolling upon the grass. By the time I reached junior high I wasn't even the last one picked anymore. I'd slunk away long before they got to the bottom of the barrel.

9 Even now, the great **mortification** of my life is that visitors to my home sometimes screw the mustard and pickle jar lids back on so tightly *I can't get them open!* (The visitors probably think they are just closing them enough to keep the bugs out.) Sure, I can use a pipe wrench, but it's embarrassing. Once, my front gate stuck, and for several days I could only leave home by clambering furtively through the **bougainvilleas** and over the garden wall. When a young man knocked on my door to deliver flowers one sunny morning, I threw my arms around him. He thought that was pretty emotional, for florists' mums. He had no idea he'd just casually pushed open the Berlin Wall.

10 My inspiration down at the health club was a woman fire-fighter who could have knocked down my garden gate with a karate chop. I still dream about her tri-

ceps. But I've mostly gotten over my brief fit of muscle envy. Oh, I still make my ongoing, creative stabs at bodybuilding: I do "girl pushups," and some of the low-impact things from Jane Fonda's pregnant-lady workout book, even if I'm not. I love to run, because it always seems like there's a chance you might actually get somewhere, so I'll sometimes cover a familiar mile or so of our county road after I see my daughter onto the school bus. (The driver confessed that for weeks he thought I was chasing him; he never stopped.) And finally, my friends have given me an official item of exercise equipment that looks like a glob of blue putty, which you're supposed to squeeze a million times daily to improve your grip. That's my current program. The so-called noncompetitive atmosphere of the health club whipped me, hands down. Realistically, I've always known I was born to be a "before" picture. So I won't be seen driving around with plates that boast: PRSS 250.

11   Maybe: OPN JRS.

Reading for Better Writing

Working by yourself or with a group, answer these questions:

1. Kingsolver entitles her essay, "The Muscle Mystique." What does "mystique" mean and in what sense are muscles or bodybuilding a "mystique"?

2. Review the opening few paragraphs and explain how the writer introduces her subject and sets the tone for the essay. Cite words and phrases that you find interesting, engaging, or funny.

3. In the third paragraph, Kingsolver describes the health club as a "lekking ground." What does this phrase suggest about the "muscle mystique"?

4. Re-read paragraph 4 in which the writer compares her own physique with that of her grandfather's. Cite details that help you envision each.

5. Kingsolver contrasts (1) current bodybuilders' focus on playful lekking with (2) her fit grandfather's focus on hard work. What's her point? And how does this point relate to what she says in paragraph 6 about the "standards of beauty" in her time versus. "standards of beauty" in her grandmother's time?

6. Define "self-deprecating humor" and cite examples in paragraphs 7-11. Would these passages be as funny if the writer were describing others' foibles rather than her own?

7. Find two or three passages that you consider reflective writing and explain how they enrich the text.

8. Re-read Kingsolver's last sentence in which she suggests a license-plate inscription that relays her bodybuilding goal. Then work with a classmate to create comic inscriptions that relay your goals.

Use narration, description, and reflection to write a personal essay. LO5

Writing Guidelines

Planning

1. **Select a topic.** The most promising topics are experiences that gave you insights into yourself, and possibly into others as well. To identify such topics, consider the categories below and then list whatever experiences come to mind:

   - Times when you felt *secure, hopeful, distraught, appreciated, confident, frightened, exploited,* or *misunderstood.*
   - Times when you made a decision about *lifestyles, careers, education,* or *religion.*
   - Events that tested your *will, patience, self-concept,* or *goals.*
   - Events that changed or confirmed your assessment of *a person, a group,* or *an institution.*

   Tip List topics in response to the following statement: *Reflect on times when you first discovered that the world was strange, wonderful, complex, frightening, small, full, or empty.* How did these experiences affect you?

2. **Get the big picture.** Once you have chosen a topic, gather your thoughts by brainstorming or freewriting in response to questions like these:

   - Where did the experience take place and what specific sights, sounds, and smells distinguish the place?
   - Who else was involved, and what did they look like, act like, do, and say?
   - What were the key or pivotal points in your experiences and why?
   - What led to these key moments and what resulted from them?
   - How did your or others' comments or actions affect what happened?

   - What did others learn from this experience—and what did you learn?
   - Did the experience end as you had hoped? Why or why not?
   - What themes, conflicts, and insights arose from the experience?
   - How do your feelings now differ from your feelings then? Why?

   To find out more details about the event or people involved, sort through photo albums and home videos to trigger memories; talk to someone who shared your experiences; consult your journal, old letters, and saved e-mail.

3. **Probe the topic and reveal what you find.** The mind-searching aspect of writing this essay happens while asking so-why questions: *So why does this picture still make me smile?* or *Why does his comment still hurt?* or *Why did I do that when I knew better—or Did I know better?* Your readers need to experience what you experienced, so don't hide what's embarrassing, or painful, or still unclear.

4. **Get organized.** Review your brainstorming or freewriting, and highlight key details, quotations, or episodes. Then list the main events in chronological order, or use a cluster to help you gather details related to your experiences.

Drafting

5. **Write the first draft.** Rough out the first draft. Then test your narration and description by asking whether the quotations, details, and events are accurate and clear. Test your reflection by asking whether it explains how the experience affected you. If appropriate, integrate photos or other images into the draft.

Revising

6. **Review the draft.** After taking a break, read your essay for truthfulness and completeness. Does it include needed details and questions?

7. **Get feedback.** Ask a classmate to read your paper and respond to it.

8. **Improve the ideas, organization, and voice.** Use your own review and peer review to address these issues:

- **Ideas:** Does the essay offer readers an engaging, informative look into your life, personality, and perspective?
- **Organization:** Does the essay include (1) an inviting opening that pictures the setting, introduces the characters, and forecasts the themes; (2) a rich middle that develops a clear series of events, nuanced characters, and descriptions; and (3) a satisfying closing that completes the experience and unifies the essay's ideas?
- **Voice:** Is the tone fair, and does it fit the experience? Is your voice genuine, thoughtful, and inviting?

Editing

9. **Edit and proofread your essay.** Polish your writing by addressing these items:
   - **Words:** The words in descriptive and narrative passages *show* instead of *tell about*; they are precise and rich, helping readers imagine the setting, envision the characters, and vicariously experience the action. The words in reflective passages are insightful and measured.
   - **Sentences:** The sentences in descriptive and reflective passages are clear, varied in structure, and smooth. The sentences in dialogue accurately reflect the characters' personalities, regional diction, and current idioms.
   - **Correctness:** The copy includes no errors in spelling, mechanics, punctuation, or grammar.
   - **Page Design:** The design is attractive and follows assigned guidelines. If photos are used, they are effectively reproduced and positioned in the text.

Publishing

10. **Publish your writing** by sharing your essay with friends and family, posting it on a Web site, or submitting it to a journal or newspaper.

Critical-Thinking and Writing Activities

As directed by your instructor, complete the following activities by yourself or with classmates.

1. Review "The Entomology of Village Life," noting how the essay centers on what the writer and his friend witness. Think about what it means to be a witness—to a crime, a tragedy, a triumph, a performance, an encounter, and so on. Then write an essay in which you explore a time that you were a witness.

2. In "Spare Change," Teresa Zsuffa describes her encounter with someone whose qualities, experiences, and values are different from her own. Write a personal essay in which you explore such an encounter in your life.

3. Elizabeth Fuller in "When Dreams Take Flight" and Barbara Kingsolver in "The Muscle Mystique" write about themselves with self-deprecating humor. As readers, we laugh with them because we also have had experiences in which we made mistakes, did something silly, or found that we didn't measure up to our own or others' goals or standards. Choose such an experience that you feel comfortable sharing with others. Then write an essay in which you describe what happened, reflect on its impact, and share the mirth.

Checklist: Learning Outcomes

Use this checklist to assess how effectively you achieved the learning outcomes for this chapter:

_____ I understand how to read personal essays.

_____ I understand when and how to use anecdotes in different writing forms and for different writing occasions.

_____ I understand how to establish setting, describe people, and narrate action.

_____ I can effectively reflect on an experience's impact or value.

_____ I have effectively blended techniques of narration, description, and reflection to craft a personal essay that shares with readers something of my particular experiences in such a way that readers can understand and relate to the broader significance of that experience.

"Culture is a way of coping with the world by defining it in detail."

—Malcolm Bradbury

10

Definition

Most forms of academic and workplace writing—from essays and reports to proposals and literature reviews—include brief (one- or two-sentence) definitions of terms. Although this chapter will help you read and write those (see pages 114–123), its main purpose is to help you understand and write longer, essay-length pieces sometimes called extended definitions.

Such definitions clarify and deepen readers' understanding of a term—whether the term refers to something concrete or abstract. When reading such essays, consider how the writers "extend" your understanding of their topics, often using examples and stories to do so.

Learning Outcomes

LO1 Understand how to read definition essays.

LO2 Define a term through distinction from related terms.

LO3 Define a term by examining denotation and connotation.

LO4 Define a term through etymology.

LO5 Define a term through cultural and philosophical analysis.

LO6 Write, revise, and edit an extended definition.

Understand how to read definition essays. LO1

To effectively read extended definitions, consider the essays' rhetorical situation and the specific definition strategies the writers use—and why.

Consider the rhetorical situation.

To understand a definition, consider the writer's purpose, audience, and topic.

Purpose: Writers compose definitions for many reasons—to correctly define a misunderstood term, to deepen or re-direct its meaning, to plumb a term's history, or to entertain readers. Look for the point of the definition.

Audience: For some readers, the term may be new; while for others, the term may be familiar but misunderstood. Determine the target audience and think through its relationship to the term being defined.

Topic: For any definition, the topic is a term. But what terms do writers typically focus on? Terms may be technical, unusual, complex, comical, or new. They may have changed through time. They may be crucial to a larger analysis or argument. As you read a definition, ask "Why this term?"

Consider definition-writing strategies.

To understand a definition, identify the writer's strategies. Consider, for example, what the writer conveys about the term's **denotative** (or literal) meaning, its **connotative** (or suggested) meaning, and its **etymological** (or historical) meaning. Examine, as well, the use of anecdotes, comparisons, contrasts, and visuals.

denotative
literal meaning

connotative
suggested meaning

etymological
historical meaning

Consider the Following — The writers whose essays are included in this chapter make the following choices:

Shon Bogar defines his topic (human trafficking) in part by distinguishing it from related practices. In other words, he explains what the practice is by showing what it is not.

Mary Beth Bruins uses an etymological approach to define *gullible*. She also integrates anecdotes about the word in her opening and closing paragraphs.

David Schelhaas explains the meanings of *deft* and *daft* by sharing a funny anecdote and analyzing the words' etymologies—or historical development.

Simon L Garfinkle, in his extended definition entitled "Wikipedia and the Meaning of *Truth*," shares anecdotes and cites historical phenomena to explain how we determine what *is*—or is *not*—truth.

Checklist: Reading Definitions

Use the following questions to evaluate your main questions.

- ✔ Precisely what does the writer claim about the term's meaning?
- ✔ Is the definition current, relevant, complete, and clear?
- ✔ Is the definition accurate in terms of its past and current usage?

Define a term through distinction from related terms. LO2

The excerpt on the next two pages comes from a research paper by student writer Shon Bogar. The paper focuses on the problems of human trafficking and slavery as phenomena associated with current trends in globalization. To help readers understand human trafficking, he compares and contrasts its meaning with the meaning of related terms.

Economic Disparities Fuel Human Trafficking

Survey • Question • Read • Recite • Review SQ3R

1

(A) . . . . These great economic disparities, from extreme poverty to fabulous wealth, have helped fuel the international trade in human cargo, as those people with nothing seek a better life serving those with excess.

2

(B) The buying, selling, and forced exploitation of people—slavery—is not a new phenomenon. Most nations and most cultures have, at one time or another, enslaved others and been themselves enslaved in turn. The pattern continues today; in fact, slavery exists far beyond the developing world and reaches into the comfortable First World of the United States, Europe, Japan, and Australia. However, examining current trends in the trade of human cargo shows that trafficking and slavery are extremely difficult to define and understand, and that they coexist with and are codependent upon each other. These problems, moreover, have a variety of complex causes and too few solutions that offer a realistic possibility of ending this global **abomination**.

3

(C) Human trafficking, in particular, is a term that is difficult to define properly, but it must first be clarified if the problem itself is to be addressed. To begin, migration, human smuggling, and human trafficking are distinct but related phenomena, and incorrect definitions would put different groups of people in the wrong category, with potentially dire consequences. For example, the Trafficking Victims Prevention Act (TVPA), which came into law in 2000, requires the U.S. government to ensure that victims of trafficking are not jailed or "otherwise penalized solely for unlawful acts as a direct result of being trafficked" (U.S. Department of State, 2004), whereas illegal immigrants are still subject to deportation and criminal proceedings. The U.S. State Department recognizes the potentially "confusing" difference between smuggling and human trafficking, so it defines human smuggling as "the procurement or transport for profit of a person for illegal entry in a country" (2004). However, even if the smuggling involves "dangerous or degrading conditions," the act is still considered smuggling, not human trafficking, and so smuggling is considered an immigration matter, not necessarily a human rights issue (2004).

4

(D) What distinguishes trafficking from smuggling is the element of exploitation, including but not limited to "fraud, force, or coercion" (U.S. Department of

(D) The writer offers a formal definition of the key term "human trafficking" by going to official sources.

Elnur, 2011 / Used under license from Shutterstock.com

(A) At the end of the introduction, the writer transitions to the extended definition.

(B) An informal definition of the broader concept of slavery prefaces the extended definition.

(C) The main term is distinguished from related terms using reliable source material.

abomination
something shameful or greatly disliked

State, 2004). With this distinction in mind, the United Nations Convention Against Transnational Organized Crime has developed this standard definition of human trafficking: "the recruitment, transportation, transfer, harbouring or receipt of persons, by means of the threat or use of force or other forms of coercion, of abduction, of fraud, of deception, of the abuse of power, or of a position of vulnerability or of the giving or receiving of payments or benefits to achieve the consent of a person having control over another person, for the purpose of exploitation" (U.N. Resolution 25, 2001). To unravel the U.N. legalese, human trafficking involves any use of force, **coercion**, fraud, or deception by those with power so as to exploit people, primarily by moving them into some form of slavery. Under this definition, smuggling can become trafficking if the smugglers have used any means of deception. Unfortunately, the requirement that the smuggler/trafficker be aware of the "victim's final circumstances" makes distinguishing between smuggling and trafficking an inexact science (U.S. Department of State, 2004), and it creates a new set of problems in combating trafficking apart from smuggling. Nevertheless, this definition of human trafficking is a helpful starting point from which the United Nations and governments around the globe can start to fight the trafficking and eventual enslavement of people.

5   All difficulties of definition aside, human trafficking and slavery are real problems—historical problems that have taken new shapes due to globalization. In fact, today human trafficking is linked to millions of people experiencing multiple forms of slavery, from traditional "**chattel** slavery" to sexual slavery to debt bondage. . . .

(E) The writer restates a complex legal definition in terms readers will understand.

(F) While admitting a difficulty in the definition, the writer stresses the definition's usefulness.

coercion
the use of force or intimidation to gain control

chattel
a slave

Reading for Better Writing

Working by yourself or with a group, answer these questions:

1. Without looking back at the model, define "human trafficking" in a sentence or two.

2. Examine each of the three main paragraphs of Bogar's extended definition. What does each paragraph accomplish? How do the paragraphs build on each other?

3. Identify the strategies that the author uses to argue that the definition is necessary. Is the reasoning compelling? Why or why not?

4. Look again at the sources that the writer uses to develop the necessary definitions. Why are these sources appropriate for the terms in question? Which other types of sources might be useful?

5. Examine how the writer transitions into and out of the extended definition. Are these transitions effective? Why or why not?

6. The writer makes fine distinctions between complex, closely related terms. How might he have represented these distinctions graphically or visually?

Define a term by examining denotation and connotation.

LO3

In this essay, student writer Mary Beth Bruins describes how she earned the name "Gullible" and what the name means to most people—and specifically what it means to her. Notice how she defines the term by examining both its denotative and connotative meaning.

The Gullible Family

1
(A) The other day, my friend Loris fell for the oldest trick in the book: "Hey, somebody wrote 'gullible' on the ceiling!" Shortly after mocking "Gullible Loris" for looking up, I swallowed the news that Wal-Mart sells popcorn that pops into the shapes of cartoon characters. And so, as "Gullible Mary," I decided to explore what our name means, and who else belongs to the Gullible family. What I learned is that our family includes both people and birds, related to each other by our willingness to "swallow."

2
A gullible person will swallow an idea or argument without questioning its truth. Similarly, the *gull* (a long-winged, web-footed bird) will swallow just about anything thrown to it. In fact, the word *gullible* comes from *gull*, and this word can be traced back to the
(B) Germanic word *gwel* (to swallow). Both *gull* and *gwel* are linked to the modern word *gulp*, which means, "to swallow greedily or rapidly in large amounts." It's not surprising then that Loris and I, sisters in the Gullible family, both eagerly gulped (like gulls) the false statements thrown to us.

3
Swallowing things so quickly isn't too bright, and *gull* (when referring to a bird or person) implies that the swallower is immature and foolish. For example, *gull* refers to an "unfledged" fowl, which the
(C) *Grolier Encyclopedia* describes as either "an immature bird still lacking flight feathers" or something that is "inexperienced, immature, or untried." These words describe someone who is fooled easily, and that's why *gull*, when referring to a human, means "dupe" or "simpleton." In fact, since 1550, *gullet*, which means "throat," has also meant "fooled."

4
To illustrate this usage, the *Oxford English Dic-*
(D) *tionary* quotes two authors who use *gull* as a verb meaning to *fool*. "Nothing is so easy as to *gull* the public, if you only set up a **prodigy**," writes Washington Irving. William Deal Howells uses the word similarly when he writes, "You are perfectly safe to go on and *gull* imbeciles to the end of the time, for all I care."

5
(E) Both of these authors are pretty critical of *gullible* people, but does gullible have only negative connotations? Is there no hope for Gullibiles like Loris and me? C. O. Sylvester Marson's comments about *gullible* may give us some comfort. He links *gullible* to "credulous, confiding, and easily deceived." At first, these adjectives also sound negative, but *credulous* does mean "to follow implicitly." And the word *credit* comes from the Latin word *credo* (meaning "I believe"). So what's bad about that? In other words, isn't *wanting to believe* other people a good thing? Why shouldn't Loris and I be proud of at least that aspect of our gull blood? We want to be positive—and we don't want to be cynics!

(A) The writer uses the title and an anecdote to introduce the topic.
(B) She gives an example and the word's Germanic root.
(C) She cites details from an encyclopedia.
(D) She quotes two writers.
(E) She closes with a playful, positive spin.

Reading for Better Writing

Working by yourself or with a group, answer these questions:

1. The writer tells anecdotes about herself and Loris. Find each anecdotal reference and explain how it does or doesn't help define *gullible*.

2. Identify passages that focus on the term's denotations and passages that focus on connotations. How effectively does the essay address and related both?

3. Describe the writer's voice and explain why it does or doesn't fit the topic.

4. The writer uses "family" as a metaphor for a group that includes both birds and people. Explain why this metaphor is or isn't effective.

prodigy
someone particularly skilled at a certain craft

Define a term through etymology.

LO4

Professor David Schelhaas delivered the following definition on his weekly radio program, *What's the Good Word?* Watch how he defines *deft* and *daft* by examining their roots.

Deft or Daft

Survey · Question · Read · Recite · Review **SQ3R**

1
(A) The other day, my wife, watching our son-in-law with his large hands gracefully tie the shoelaces of his little daughter, remarked, "You really are deft." Ever the cynic, I remarked, "He's not only deft, he's daft." I talk that sort of nonsense frequently, but as I said this, I began to wonder. What if *deft* and *daft* come from the same root and once meant the same thing? A quick trip to the dictionary showed that, indeed, they did once mean the same thing (though my wife thought me daft when I first suggested it).

2
(B) Let me see if I can explain the original meaning and also how *daft* and *deft* came to part company. *Daft* originally meant mild or gentle. The Middle English *dafte* comes from the Old English *gadaefte,* which has as its underlying sense fit or suitable. Quite likely, mild or gentle people were seen as behaving in a way that was fit and suitable.

3 Gradually, however, the mild, gentle meaning descended in connotation to mean crazy or foolish. First, animals were described as daft—that is, without reason—and eventually people also. The word *silly,* which once meant happy or blessed, slid down the same slope. So that explains where *daft* got its present meaning.

4
(C) But how does *deft,* meaning skillful or **dexterous,** fit into the picture? Again, if we start with the Old English meaning of *fit* or *suitable,* we can see a connection to skillful. In fact, the root of *gadaefte,* which is *dhabh,* to fit, carries with it the sense of a joiner or an artisan, someone who skillfully made the ends or corners of a cupboard or piece of furniture fit neatly together. From *fit* to *skillful* to *dexterous.* Thus we see how one root word meaning *fit* or *suitable* went in two different directions—one meaning crazy, the other meaning skillful.

5 These days it is usually considered much better to be deft than to be daft. But don't be too sure. It is good to remind ourselves that one person's deftness might very well appear as daftness to another.

6
(D) This is David Schelhaas asking, "What's the Good Word?"

(A) The writer introduces the topic with an anecdote.
(B) He describes the history of *daft.*
(C) He compares and contrasts the two words.

dexterous
skillful use of the hands

(D) He closes with a reflection and his usual sign-off.

Ilya Andriyanov, 2011 / Used under license from Shutterstock.com

Reading for Better Writing

Working by yourself or with a group, answer these questions:

1. Explain how the opening attempts to engage the reader. In what ways does it succeed?

2. Describe how the writer goes to root meanings and shows that the meanings have changed. Is his explanation clear? Why or why not?

4. Describe the writer's tone. Is it effective for a radio program? Explain.

5. Imagine turning this radio broadcast into a short video. What film would you create to deepen the definition? Explain.

Define a term through cultural and philosophical analysis. LO5

Simson L. Garfinkle is a contributing editor to *Technology Review;* an associate professor at the Naval Postgraduate School in Monterey, California; and an associate of the School of Engineering and Applied Sciences at Harvard. In the following essay, published in 2008, he analyzes how the nature and use of Wikipedia affect how we discern what is true. Notice how he makes philosophical distinctions as he analyzes the cultural significance of Wikipedia.

Wikipedia and the Meaning of *Truth*

Why the online encyclopedia's **epistemology** *should worry those who care about traditional notions of accuracy.*

Survey · Question · Read · Recite · Review **SQ3R**

1 (A) With little notice from the outside world, the community-written encyclopedia Wikipedia has redefined the commonly accepted use of the word "truth."

2 Why should we care? Because Wikipedia's articles are the first- or second-ranked results for most Internet searches. Type "iron" into Google, and Wikipedia's article on the element is the top-ranked result; likewise, its article on the Iron Cross is first when the search words are "iron cross." Google's search algorithms rank a story in part by how many times it has been linked to; people are linking to Wikipedia articles a lot.

3 This means that the content of these articles really matters. Wikipedia's standards of inclusion—what's in and what's not—affect the work of journalists, who routinely read Wikipedia articles and then repeat the wikiclaims as "background" without bothering to cite them. These standards affect students, whose research

on many topics starts (and often ends) with Wikipedia. And since I used Wikipedia to research large parts of this article, these standards are affecting you, dear reader, at this very moment.

4 Many people, especially academic experts, have argued that Wikipedia's articles can't be trusted, because they are written and edited by volunteers who have never been **vetted**. Nevertheless, studies have found that the articles are remarkably accurate. The reason is that Wikipedia's community of more than seven million registered users has organically evolved a set of policies and procedures for removing untruths. This also explains Wikipedia's explosive growth: if the stuff in Wikipedia didn't seem "true enough" to most readers, they wouldn't keep coming back to the Web site.

5 These policies have become the social contract for Wikipedia's army of apparently **insomniac** volunteers. Thanks to them, incorrect information generally disappears quite quickly.

6 So how do the Wikipedians decide what's true and what's not? On what is their epistemology based?

7 Unlike the laws of mathematics or science, wikitruth isn't based on principles such as consistency or observability. It's not even based on common sense or firsthand experience. Wikipedia has evolved a radically different set of epistemological standards— standards that aren't especially surprising given that the site is rooted in a Web-based community, but that should concern those of us who are interested in traditional notions of truth and accuracy. On Wikipedia, objective truth isn't all that important, actually. What makes a fact or statement fit for inclusion is that it appeared in some other publication—ideally, one that is in English and is available free online. "The threshold for inclusion in Wikipedia is **verifiability**, not truth," states Wikipedia's official policy on the subject.

(A) As you read this essay, annotate it and take notes— identifying strategies the writer uses to develop an extended definition.

> **epistemology**
> the study of the origin and limits of human knowledge
>
> **vetted**
> to verify or check the accuracy of something
>
> **insomniac**
> a person who has extreme difficulty falling sleep
>
> **verifiability**
> the ability to prove the truth

8   Verifiability is one of Wikipedia's three core content policies; it was codified back in August 2003. The two others are "no original research" (December 2003) and "neutral point of view," which the Wikipedia project inherited from Nupedia, an earlier volunteer-written Web-based free encyclopedia that existed from March 2000 to September 2003 (Wikipedia's own NPOV policy was codified in December 2001). These policies have made Wikipedia a kind of academic **agora** where people on both sides of politically charged subjects can rationally discuss their positions, find common ground, and unemotionally document their differences. Wikipedia is successful because these policies have worked.

9   Unlike Wikipedia's articles, Nupedia's were written and vetted by experts. But few experts were motivated to contribute. Well, some wanted to write about their own research, but Larry Sanger, Nupedia's editor in chief, immediately put an end to that practice.

10   "I said, 'If it hasn't been vetted by the relevant experts, then basically we are setting ourselves up as a frontline source of new, original information, and we aren't set up to do that,'" Sanger (who is himself, ironically or not, a former philosophy instructor and by training an epistemologist) recalls telling his fellow Nupedians.

11   With experts barred from writing about their own work and having no incentive to write

agora
a meeting place

© Wikimedia Foundation Inc.

about anything else, Nupedia struggled. Then Sanger and Jimmy Wales, Nupedia's founder, decided to try a different policy on a new site, which they launched on January 15, 2001. They adopted the newly invented "wiki" technology, allowing anybody to contribute to any article—or create a new one—on any topic, simply by clicking "Edit this page."

12 Soon the promoters of oddball hypotheses and outlandish ideas were all over Wikipedia, causing the new site's volunteers to spend a good deal of time repairing damage—not all of it the innocent work of the misguided or deluded. (A study recently published in Communications of the Association for Computing Machinery found that 11 percent of Wikipedia articles have been vandalized at least once.) But how could Wikipedia's volunteer editors tell if something was true? The solution was to add references and footnotes to the articles, "not in order to help the reader, but in order to establish a point to the satisfaction of the [other] contributors," says Sanger, who left Wikipedia before the verifiability policy was formally adopted. (Sanger and Wales, now the chairman emeritus of the Wikimedia Foundation, fell out about the scale of Sanger's role in the creation of Wikipedia. Today, Sanger is the creator and editor in chief of Citizendium, an alternative to Wikipedia that is intended to address the inadequacy of its "reliability and quality.")

13 Verifiability is really an appeal to authority—not the authority of truth, but the authority of other publications. Any other publication, really. These days, information that's added to Wikipedia without an appropriate reference is likely to be slapped with a "citation needed" badge by one of Wikipedia's self-appointed editors. Remove the badge and somebody else will put it back. Keep it up and you might find yourself face to face with another kind of authority—one of the English-

language Wikipedia's 1,500 administrators, who have the ability to place increasingly restrictive protections on contentious pages when the policies are ignored.

14 To be fair, Wikipedia's verifiability policy states that "articles should rely on reliable, third-party published sources" that themselves adhere to Wikipedia's NPOV policy. Self-published articles should generally be avoided, and non-English sources are discouraged if English articles are available, because many people who read, write, and edit En.Wikipedia (the English-language version) can read only English.

Mob Rules

15 In a May 2006 essay on the technology and culture Web site Edge.org, **futurist** Jaron Lanier called Wikipedia an example of "digital **Maoism**"—the closest humanity has come to a functioning mob rule.

16 Lanier was moved to write about Wikipedia because someone kept editing his Wikipedia entry to say that he was a film director. Lanier describes himself as a "computer scientist, composer, visual artist, and author." He is good at all those things, but he is no director. According to his essay, he made one short experimental film in the 1990s, and it was "awful."

17 "I have attempted to retire from directing films in the alternative universe that is the Wikipedia a number of times, but somebody always overrules me," Lanier wrote. "Every time my Wikipedia entry is corrected, within a day I'm turned into a film director again."

18 Since Lanier's attempted edits to his own Wikipedia entry were based on firsthand knowledge of his own career, he was in direct violation of Wikipedia's three core policies. He has a point of view; he was writing on the basis of his own original research; and what he wrote couldn't be verified by following a link to some kind of legitimate, authoritative, and verifiable publication.

19 Wikipedia's standard for "truth" makes good technical and legal sense, given that anyone can edit

futurist
one who studies and predicts the future

Maoism
communist philosophy of Chinese political leader Mao Zedong

its articles. There was no way for Wikipedia, as a community, to know whether the person revising the article about Jaron Lanier was really Jaron Lanier or a vandal. So it's safer not to take people at their word, and instead to require an appeal to the authority of another publication from everybody who contributes, expert or not.

20   An interesting thing happens when you try to understand Wikipedia: the deeper you go, the more convoluted it becomes. Consider the verifiability policy. Wikipedia considers the "most reliable sources" to be "peer-reviewed journals and books published in university presses," followed by "university-level textbooks," then magazines, journals, "books published by respected publishing houses," and finally "mainstream newspapers" (but not the opinion pages of newspapers).

21   Once again, this makes sense, given Wikipedia's inability to vet the real-world identities of authors. Lanier's complaints when his Wikipedia page claimed that he was a film director couldn't be taken seriously by Wikipedia's "contributors" until Lanier persuaded the editors at Edge to print his article bemoaning the claim. This Edge article by Lanier was enough to convince the Wikipedians that the Wikipedia article about Lanier was incorrect—after all, there was a clickable link! Presumably the editors at Edge did their fact checking, so the wikiworld could now be corrected.

22   As fate would have it, Lanier was subsequently criticized for engaging in the wikisin of editing his own wikientry. The same criticism was leveled against me when I corrected a number of obvious errors in my own Wikipedia entry.

23   "Criticism" is actually a mild word for the kind of wikijustice meted out to people who are foolish enough to get caught editing their own Wikipedia entries: the entries get slapped with a banner headline that says "A major contributor to this article, or its creator, may have a conflict of interest regarding its subject matter." The banner is accompanied by a little picture showing the scales of justice tilted to the left. Wikipedia's "Autobiography" policy explains in great detail how drawing on your own knowledge to edit

the Wikipedia entry about yourself violates all three of the site's cornerstone policies—and illustrates the point with yet another appeal to authority, a quotation from *The Hitchhiker's Guide to the Galaxy.*

24   But there is a problem with appealing to the authority of other people's written words: many publications don't do any fact checking at all, and many of those that do simply call up the subject of the article and ask if the writer got the facts wrong or right. For instance, Dun and Bradstreet gets the information for its small-business information reports in part by asking those very same small businesses to fill out questionnaires about themselves.

"No Original Research"

25   What all this means is hard to say. I am infrequently troubled by Wiki's unreliability. (The quality of the writing is a different subject.) As a computer scientist, I find myself using Wikipedia on a daily basis. Its discussions of algorithms, architectures, microprocessors, and other technical subjects are generally excellent. When they aren't excellent and I know better, I just fix them. And when they're wrong and I don't know better—well, I don't know any better, do I?

26   I've also spent quite a bit of time reviewing Wikipedia's articles about such things as the "Singularity Scalpel," the "Treaty of Algeron," and "Number Six." Search for these terms and you'll be directed to Wikipedia articles with the titles "List of Torchwood items" and "List of treaties in Star Trek," and to one about a Cylon robot played by Canadian actress Tricia Helfer. These articles all hang their wikiexistence upon scholarly references to original episodes of *Dr. Who, Torchwood, Star Trek,* and *Battlestar Galactica*—popular television shows that the Wikipedia contributors dignify with the word "canon."

27   I enjoy using these articles as sticks to poke at Wikipedia, but they represent a tiny percentage of Wikipedia's overall content. On the other hand, they've been an important part of Wikipedia culture from the beginning. Sanger says that early on, Wikipedia made a commitment to having a wide variety of articles: "There's plenty of disk space, and as long

as there are people out there who are able to write a decent article about a subject, why not let them? . . . I thought it was kind of funny and cool that people were writing articles about every character in *The Lord of the Rings*. I didn't regard it as a problem the way some people do now."

28   What's wrong with the articles about fantastical worlds is that they are at odds with Wikipedia's "no original research" rule, since almost all of them draw their "references" from the fictions themselves and not from the allegedly more reliable secondary sources. I haven't nominated these articles for speedy deletion because Wikipedia makes an exception for fiction— and because, truth be told, I enjoy reading them. And these days, most such entries are labeled as referring to fictional universes.

29   So what is Truth? According to Wikipedia's entry on the subject, "the term has no single definition about which the majority of professional philosophers and scholars agree." But in practice, Wikipedia's standard for inclusion has become its **de facto** standard for truth, and since Wikipedia is the most widely read online reference on the planet, it's the standard of truth that most people are **implicitly** using when they type a search term into Google or Yahoo. On Wikipedia, truth is received truth: the consensus view of a subject.

30   That standard is simple: something is true if it was published in a newspaper article, a magazine or journal, or a book published by a university press—or if it appeared on Dr. Who.

Reading for Better Writing

Working by yourself or with a group, answer these questions:

1. What does Garfinkle's subtitle convey about his essay and his purpose?

2. Garfinkle says that wiki readers "repeat the wikiclaims as 'background' without bothering to cite them." Is he correct, and is the practice a problem? Explain.

3. Review Garfinkle's subheadings "Mob Rules" and "No Original Research." Then explain what they mean and why they do or do not help readers understand his argument.

4. Review paragraph 29 in which the writer quotes Wikipedia's definition of truth and then says, "On Wikipedia, truth is received truth: the consensus view of a subject." Explain what he means, and whether this issue is a serious one.

5. Review a Wikipedia entry on a topic that interests you, studying especially the entry's design, appearance on the screen, and use of graphics. What do these elements contribute to the entry's sense of authority and truthfulness?

Diego Cervo, 2011 / Used under license from Shutterstock.com

de facto
in reality

implicitly
implying, rather than stating outright

Write, revise, and edit an extended definition. LO6

Writing Guidelines

Planning

1. **Select a topic.** Beneath headings like these, list words that you'd like to explore:

> **Words that ...**
> - ► are related to an art or a sport.
> - ► are in the news (or should be).
> - ► are overused, underused, or abused.
> - ► make you chuckle, frown, or fret.
> - ► do or do not describe you.

 Tip The best topics are abstract nouns (*truth, individualism*), complex terms (*code blue, dementia*), or words connected to a personal experience (*excellence, deft, daft*).

2. **Identify what you know.** To discern what you already know about the topic, write freely about the word, letting your writing go where it chooses. Explore both your personal and your academic connections with the word.

3. **Gather information.** To find information about the word's history, usage, and grammatical form, use strategies such as these:
   - Consult a general dictionary, preferably an unabridged dictionary; list both denotative (literal) and connotative (associated) meanings for the word.
   - Consult specialized dictionaries that define words from specific disciplines or occupations: music, literature, law, medicine, and so on.
   - If helpful, interview experts on your topic.
   - Check reference books such as *Bartlett's Familiar Quotations* to see how famous speakers and writers have used the word.
   - Research the word's etymology and usage by consulting appropriate Web sources such as dictionary.com, m-w.com, or xrefer.com.

- Do a general search on the Web to see where the word pops up in titles of songs, books, or films; company names, products, and ads; nonprofit organizations' names, campaigns, and programs; and topics in the news.
- List synonyms (words meaning the same—or nearly the same) and antonyms (words meaning the opposite).
- Identify graphics that could clarify the term visually.

4. **Compress what you know.** Based on your freewriting and research, try writing a formal, one-sentence definition that satisfies the following equation:

Equation:

Term = larger class + distinguishing characteristics

Examples:

> **Swedish pimple** = fishing lure + silver surface, tubular body, three hooks
>
> **melodrama** = stage play + flat characters, contrived plot, moralistic theme
>
> **Alzheimer's** = dementia + increasing loss of memory, hygiene, social skills

5. **Get organized.** To organize the information that you have, and to identify details that you may want to add, fill out a graphic organizer like the one on page 51.

Drafting

6. **Draft the essay.** Review your outline as needed to write the first draft.

Opening: Get the reader's attention and introduce the term. If you are organizing the essay from general to specific, consider using an anecdote, an illustration, or a quotation to set the context. If you are organizing the essay from specific to general, consider including an interesting detail from the word's history or usage. When using a dictionary definition, avoid the dusty phrase "According to Webster . . ."

Middle: Show your readers precisely what the word means. Build the definition in paragraphs that address distinct aspects of the word: common definitions, etymology, usage by professional writers, and so on. Link paragraphs so that the essay unfolds the word's meaning layer by layer.

Closing: Review your main point and close your essay. (You might, for example, conclude by encouraging readers to use—or not use—the word.)

Revising

7. Improve the ideas, organization, and voice. Ask a classmate or someone from the college's writing center to read your essay for the following:

Ideas: Is each facet of the definition clear, showing precisely what the word does and does not mean? Is the definition complete, telling the reader all that she or he needs to know in order to understand and use the word?

Organization: Does the opening identify the word and set the context for what follows? Are the middle paragraphs cohesive, each offering a unit of meaningful information? Does the closing wrap up the message and refocus on the word's core meaning?

Voice: Is the voice informed, engaging, instructive, and courteous?

Editing

8. Edit the essay by addressing these issues:

Words: The words are precise and clear to the essay's audience.

Sentences: The sentences are complete, varied in structure, and readable.

Correctness: The copy includes no errors in spelling, usage, punctuation, grammar, or mechanics.

Design: The page design is correctly formatted and attractive. Visuals and diagrams are clearly presented and effectively integrated.

Publishing

9. Publish the essay. Share your writing with interested readers, including friends, family, and classmates. Submit the essay to your instructor. If appropriate, use what you learned to edit a wiki article on your topic.

Critical-Thinking and Writing Activities

As directed by your instructor, complete the following critical-thinking and writing activities.

1. In the passage excerpted from "Economic Disparities Fuel Human Trafficking," the writer defines terms that readers must grasp in order to understand the rest of his essay. Choose an essay that includes a word or concept needing clarification. Define the topic and insert the definitions into the text.

2. Review "The Gullible Family" and think of a word that similarly defines you. Research the word and write an essay that defines the term.

3. Review "Deft or Daft" and choose a pair of words that similarly mirror each other's meaning. Research the words, and write an essay comparing and contrasting their etymologies and meanings.

4. "Wikipedia and the Meaning of *Truth*" explores how a relatively new phenomenon challenges a traditional concept. Write an extended definition exploring how a similar phenomenon has challenged a traditional term.

5. Write an essay defining a word or phrase that is understood by people in a particular field of study but not by "outsiders." Write for the audience of outsiders.

Checklist: Learning Outcomes

Use this checklist to assess how effectively you achieved the learning outcomes for this chapter.

____ I understand how to read definition writing.

____ I can define a term by distinguishing it from related terms.

____ I can define a term by exploring both denotation and connotation.

____ I can define a term through etymology.

____ I can explore a term's cultural and philosophical meaning.

____ I have written an effective extended definition.

"Nothing in life is to be feared.
It is only to be understood."
Madame Curie

11

Classification

Classification is an organizational strategy that helps writers make sense of large or complex sets of things. A writer using this strategy breaks the topic into individual items or members that can be sorted into clearly distinguishable groups or categories. For example, if writing about the types of residents who live in assisted-care facilities, a nursing student might classify them according to various physical and/or mental limitations.

By sorting residents in this way, the writer can discuss them as individuals, as representatives of a group, or as members of the body as a whole. By using an additional strategy such as compare-contrast, she or he can show both similarities and differences between individuals within a group, or between one group and another.

Learning Outcomes

LO1 Understand how to read classification essays.

LO2 Create categories that are consistent, exclusive, and complete.

LO3 Use precise terms for categories.

LO4 Illustrate distinctive and shared traits of categories.

LO5 Write, revise, and edit a classification essay.

Understand how to read classification essays. LO1

Use the information that follows as a basic guide when reading and analyzing classification essays.

Consider the rhetorical situation.

When reading classification essays, examine the writers' classification schemes—how they break their subjects into groups and why they sort them as they do. Explore whether the classification schemes fit the writer's purpose, audience, and topic.

Purpose: Writers classify a body of information to explain its order, to clarify relationships, and to "locate" specific items within a larger structure. For example, in her essay, "Latin American Music . . ." (pages 129–131), Kathleen Kropp wants to explain how the music reflects Latinos' cultural identity and impacts social change.

Audience: While readership can vary greatly, writers using classification are seeking to illuminate the deeper order of a topic, either to enhance readers' understanding or to support an argument. For example, Kropp's criteria instruct her college-student audience about the history and diversity of Latin American music.

Topic: Writers typically use classification with topics that include a complex body of individual items or members. For example, Kropp's classification takes the large body of Latin American music (made up of many individual songs) and makes sense of it all through four categories that clarify music's role in Latino culture.

Consider classification principles.

The principles that follow help writers sort items into unified and distinct categories.

Consistency: The same criteria should be used in the same way when one sorts items into groups. For example, John Van Rys sorts approaches to literary criticism based on one criterion: the critic's focus when reading (see "Four Ways . . . ," pages 134–135).

Exclusivity: Groups should be distinct. For example, Van Rys identifies four main approaches to literary criticism, and whereas they do share some traits, yet each approach is substantially different from the others.

Completeness: All individual items or members of the larger body should fit into a category with no items left over. For example, any common approach to literary criticism will fit into one of Van Rys's four categories.

Checklist: Classification Writing

- ✔ Does the writer's classification scheme effectively explain the order of this topic for the target audience?
- ✔ Are the categories consistent, exclusive, and complete?
- ✔ Do the writer's classification strategies help you understand the subject?

criteria
the traits or features of a topic used to create subgroups

literary criticism
evaluation of literature

Create categories that are consistent, exclusive, and complete.

LO2

In the essay below, student writer Kathleen Kropp uses classification strategies to describe the nature of Latin American music and to explain how the music both reflects and affects Latin American culture. As you read, assess whether she creates consistent, exclusive, and complete categories.

Essay Outline

> *Introduction:* Latin American music's unifying power
> 1. Category 1: indigenous music
> 2. Category 2: Iberian and Mestizo folk music
> 3. Category 3: Afro-American music
> 4. Category 4: urban popular music
>
> *Closing:* These diverse types together express the passion and power of Latin-American people.

(A) Latin American Music: A Diverse and Unifying Force

> Survey · Question · Read · Recite · Review **SQ3R**

1   On September 20, 2009, Latin pop, rock, and salsa
(B) rhythms danced through the air in Havana's Plaza de la Revolución as more than one million people gathered to witness Paz Sin Fronteras II (Peace Without Borders II). These benefit concerts brought together performers from Cuba, Puerto Rico, Ecuador, and Venezuela. Juanes, a popular Colombian singer who headlined the concerts, explained the event's passion and power like this: "Music becomes an excuse to send a message that we're all here together building peace, that we are here as citizens and this is what we want, and we have to be heard" (Hispanic 17). His statement demonstrates Latinos' belief that their music has the power to unify Latin American people, **synthesize** their

cultural activities, and address their diverse needs. To understand how the music (which is as diverse as Latin America's people) can do this, it is helpful to sort the many forms of music into four major types and consider what each type contributes to Latin American society.

     One type is **indigenous** music, a group of musical *2* forms that connect the human and the spiritual. Ar- **(C)** cheological evidence indicates that indigenous musical cultures of the Americas began over 30,000 years ago. Over time the first instruments, which were stone and clay sound-producing objects, evolved into wind instruments such as flutes and windpipes. An example of indigenous music connecting the human and spiritual is found among Aymara-speaking musicians in the Lake Titicaca Region of Peru. The people of this region use music to mesh pre-Columbian agricultural rites with current Catholic practices. For instance, during feasts such as the annual Fiesta de la Candelaria (Candlemas Feast), celebrants use Sicus (panpipes), pincullos (vertical duct flutes), cajas (drums), chants, dances, and costumes—in combination with Catholic

---

(A) Title: the larger topic and the classification theme
(B) Introduction: Latin American music's unifying power
(C) 1 Indigenous music

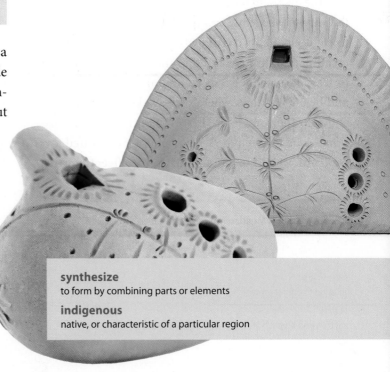

> **synthesize**
> to form by combining parts or elements
> **indigenous**
> native, or characteristic of a particular region

symbolism—to celebrate the gift of staple crops such as corn and potatoes (Indigenous 328, 330).

3   A second type, Iberian and Mestizo (mixed) folk
(D) music, enriches Latinos' everyday lives in a variety of forms, including liturgical music, working songs, and mariachi tunes. For example, whereas the traditional Catholic mass featured organ music, more recent Catholic services such as the Nicaraguan Peasant Mass use the acoustic guitar along with the colorful sounds of the marimba, maracas, and melodies from popular festivals. As a result, worshipers find the music inviting and the passionate lyrics (like those that follow, translated by Mike Yoder, October 2, 1989) socially relevant:

4   You are the God of the poor, the simple and human God, the God who sweats in the street;
You eat food scrapings there in the park. I've seen you in a corner grocery working behind the counter.

5   Another form of folk music known as tonadas (or tunes) are used as serenades and working songs. For example, in Venezuela, workers might whistle or sing tonadas while milking, plowing, or fishing (Tonadas). These vocal duets, which also can be accompanied by guitar, have pleasant harmonies, two main melodies, and faster tempos ("Iberian and mestizo folk music" 338, 341).

6   The mariachi band, a final form of folk music, adds festivity to Mexicans' many celebrations. With its six to eight violins, two trumpets, and a guitar, the band creates a vibrant, engaging sound. During birthdays or feast days, these bands commonly set up on streets and below windows where they awaken the residents above to the sounds of "Las Mañ Anitas," the traditional song for such days. Mariachis are also hired for baptisms, weddings, quinceañeras (the fifteenth birthday for a Mexican girl), patriotic holidays, and funerals (History of the Mariachi).

7   Afro-American music, the third type of Latin
(E) American music, infuses passion and power in its percussion-driven dances and complex rhythm structures. These songs and dances, performed throughout the Caribbean, function as an entertaining, unifying force among Latin people ("Afro-American" 345-6). The energy of Afro-American music is clear in genres such as the mambo and the rumba dances. The rumba, an Afro-Caribbean dance, is highly improvisational and exciting. The quinto (a high-pitched drum) establishes a dialogue with a solo voice and challenges the male dancer, while the tumbadora and palitos (sticks on woodblock) provide a contrast with regular, unchanging rhythm patterns.

8   The mambo, an Afro-Cuban dance, became popular in Havana, Cuba. In the 1940s, nightclubs throughout Latin America caught the energy of this fast tempo song and dance. Arsenio Rodríguez' "Bruca Managuá" exemplifies this form. Because of the song's sound and lyrics, many black Cubans consider the piece to be an anthem of Afro-Cuban pride and resistance:

9   I am Calabrí, black by birth/nation,
Without freedom, I can't live,
Too much abuse, the body is going to die.

(*Oxford Encyclopedia for Latinos and Latinas in the United States* 218)

10   Urban popular music, the fourth type of Latin
(F) American music, combines a dynamic sound with poignant appeals for social change, appeals that resonate with many listeners. The styles of this type of music include rock, heavy metal, punk, hip-hop, jazz, reggae, and **R & B**. During the September 20, 2009 Paz Sin Fronteras II concerts described earlier, urban popular music was common fare. As U.S. representative Jim McGovern observed, the message of the concerts was to "circumvent politics . . . using the medium of music

---

(**D**) 2 Iberian and Mestizo (mixed) folk music

liturgical
relating to church or worship
R & B
rhythm and blues

(**E**) 3 Afro-American music
(**F**) 4 Urban popular music

to speak directly to young people, to change their way of thinking, and leave behind the old politics, hatred, prejudices, and national enmities that have locked too many people in patterns of conflict, violence, poverty, and despair. It is an attempt to break down barriers and ask people to join in common purpose" (Paz Sin Fronteras II). Popular urban musicians such as Juanes utilize music not only to entertain but also to unite Latinos in a universal cause.

11   Passion and power permeate all of Latin America's
(G) music. The four major types of music—indigenous, Iberian and Mestizo folk, Afro-American, and popular urban—are as diverse as the people of Latin America, and each style serves a valued need or function in Latinos' everyday lives. As a result, those listening to Latin American music—whether it is a Peruvian Indian's chant, a Venezuelan farmer's whistled tune, a Cuban mambo drummer's vivacious beat, or the Bogotá rock concert's compelling rhythms—are hearing much more than music. They are hearing the passion and power of the Latin American people.

Note: The Works Cited page is not shown. For sample pages, see MLA (pages 368–369) and APA (page 396).

(G) Conclusion: passion and power of Latin American music and culture

Reading for Better Writing

Working by yourself or with a group, do the following:

1. Review the opening in which Kropp introduces her topic, thesis, and choice to sort the music into four categories. Then explain (a) why the passage is clear or unclear and (b) whether sorting forms into categories seems necessary or helpful.

2. Cite three strategies that Kropp uses to distinguish the four types of music and the various forms within those groups. Are the strategies effective? Why?

3. Identify language that Kropp uses to help you imagine the tone and tenor of the music. Is the word choice helpful? Why?

4 In the last sentence, Kropp re-states—and re-phrases—her thesis. Review the sentence: Is it an effective closing? Why or why not?

5 Using Kropp's essay as a guide, research your own music library and other sources to find representative pieces of music for each category. Then create an audio mix that captures the diversity of Latin American music.

Use precise terms for categories.

LO3

Stewart Brand, author of *Whole Earth Discipline: An Ecopragmatist Manifesto*, published this essay in December 2009. In the piece, he argues that the climate-change debate is better understood as advocating four main perspectives—not two. As you read, note his category titles and assess if they are sufficiently clear and informative.

Four Sides to Every Story

Survey • Question • Read • Recite • Review   **SQ3R**

1

(A) Climate talks have been going on in Copenhagen for a week now, and it appears to be a two-sided debate between alarmists and skeptics. But there are actually *four* different views of global warming. A **taxonomy** of the four:

2

(B) **DENIALISTS** They are loud, sure and political. Their view is that climatologists and their fellow travelers are engaged in a vast conspiracy to panic the public into following an agenda that is political and **pernicious**. Senator James Inhofe of Oklahoma and the columnist George Will wave the banner for the hoax-callers.

3

(C) "The claim that global warming is caused by man-made emissions is simply untrue and not based on sound science," Mr. Inhofe declared in a 2003 speech to the Senate about the Kyoto accord that remains emblematic of his position. "CO2 does not cause catastrophic disasters—actually it would be beneficial to our environment and our economy. . . . The motives for Kyoto are economic, not environmental—that is, proponents favor handicapping the American economy through carbon taxes and more regulations."

4

(D) **SKEPTICS** This group is most interested in the limitations of climate science so far: they like to examine in detail the contradictions and shortcomings in climate data and models, and they are wary about any "consensus" in science. To the skeptics' discomfort, their arguments are frequently quoted by the denialists.

5

(E) In this mode, Roger Pielke, a climate scientist at the University of Colorado, argues that the scenarios presented by the United Nations Intergovernmental Panel on Climate Change are overstated and underpredictive. Another prominent skeptic is the physicist Freeman Dyson, who wrote in 2007: "I am opposing

(F) the holy brotherhood of climate model experts and the crowd of deluded citizens who believe the numbers predicted by the computer models. . . . I have studied the climate models and I know what they can do. The models solve the equations of fluid dynamics, and they do a very good job of describing the fluid motions of the atmosphere and the oceans. They do a very poor job of describing the clouds, the dust, the chemistry and the biology of fields and farms and forests."

6

(G) **WARNERS** These are the climatologists who see the trends in climate headed toward planetary disaster, and they blame human production of greenhouse gases as the primary culprit. Leaders in this category are the scientists James Hansen, Stephen Schneider and James Lovelock. (This is the group that most persuades me and whose views I promote.)

7

(H) "If humanity wishes to preserve a planet similar to that on which civilization developed and to which life on earth is adapted," Mr. Hansen wrote as the lead author of an influential 2008 paper, then the concentration of carbon dioxide in the atmosphere would have to be reduced from 395 parts per million to "at most 350 p.p.m."

(A) The writer introduces his topic and thesis.
(B) He distinguishes the four viewpoints with descriptive names.
(C) A hyperlink helps readers access the speech.

taxonomy
the classification technique

pernicious
causing harm

(D) The writer names and describes the second group.
(E) He offers examples illustrating the group's viewpoint.
(F) The quotation relays the speaker's argument and tone.
(G) The writer names and describes the group.
(H) A hyperlink helps readers access the paper.

8

(I) **CALAMATISTS** There are many environmentalists who believe that industrial civilization has committed crimes against nature, and retribution is coming. They quote the warners in **apocalyptic** terms, and they view denialists as deeply evil. The technology critic Jeremy Rifkin speaks in this manner, and the writer-turned-activist Bill McKibben is a (fairly gentle) leader in this category.

9

(J) In his 2006 introduction for *The End of Nature*, his famed 1989 book, Mr. McKibben wrote of climate change in religious terms: "We are no longer able to think of ourselves as a species tossed about by larger forces—now we are those larger forces. Hurricanes and thunderstorms and tornadoes become not acts of God but acts of man. That was what I meant by the 'end of nature.'"

10

(K) The calamatists and denialists are primarily political figures, with firm ideological loyalties, whereas the warners and skeptics are primarily scientists, guided by ever-changing evidence. That distinction between ideology and science not only helps clarify the strengths and weaknesses of the four stances, it can also be used to predict how they might respond to future climate developments.

(I) The writer identifies the fourth group.
(J) He quotes McKibben and cites the source.
(K) He compares two groups and contrasts them with two others.

If climate change were to suddenly reverse itself **11** (because of some yet undiscovered mechanism of **(L)** balance in our climate system), my guess is that the denialists would be triumphant, the skeptics would be skeptical this time of the apparent good news, the warners would be relieved, and the calamatists would seek out some other doom to proclaim.

If climate change keeps getting worse, then I **12** would expect denialists to grasp at stranger straws, many skeptics to become warners, the warners to start pushing geoengineering schemes like sulfur dust in the stratosphere, and the calamatists to push liberal political agendas—just as the denialists said they would.

(L) The writer distinguishes the groups by projecting how they might respond to good news or bad news.

Reading for Better Writing

Working by yourself or with a group, do the following:

1. Identify Brand's thesis. How does his classification thinking make sense of the topic?

2. Cite three strategies that he uses to distinguish the four viewpoints. To visualize these strategies, create a classification grid like the one on page 136. Do you find these strategies effective? Why or why not?

3. Identify two of Brand's claims, describe how he supports each claim, and then explain why that support is or is not convincing (for information about claims, see pages 179–187).

apocalyptic
impending doom; total destruction

mevert, 2011 / Used under license from Shutterstock.com

Illustrate distinctive and shared traits of categories.

_LO4_

In this essay, John Van Rys, a college professor, classifies four approaches to literary criticism. To illustrate similarities and differences, he shows how a critic using each approach might analyze Robert Browning's "My Last Duchess."

Four Ways to Talk About Literature

Survey · Question · Read · Recite · Review   **SQ3R**

_1_

_(A)_ Have you ever been in a conversation in which you suddenly felt lost—out of the loop? Perhaps you feel that way in your literature class. You may think a poem or short story means one thing, and then your instructor suddenly pulls out the "hidden meaning." Joining the conversation about literature—in class or in an essay—may indeed seem daunting, but you can do it if you know what to look for and what to talk about. There are four main perspectives, or approaches, that you can use to converse about literature.

_2_

_(B)_ Text-centered approaches focus on the literary piece itself. Often called _formalist criticism,_ such approaches claim that the structure of a work and the rules of its **genre** are crucial to its meaning. The formalist critic determines how various elements (plot, character, language, and so on) reinforce the mean-

ing and unify the work. For example, the formalist may ask the following questions concerning Robert Browning's poem "My Last Duchess": How do the main elements in the poem—irony, symbolism, and verse form—help develop the main theme (deception)? How does Browning use the dramatic monologue genre in this poem?

_3_

_(C)_ Audience-centered approaches focus on the "transaction" between text and reader—the dynamic way the reader interacts with the text. Often called _rhetorical_ or _reader-response criticism,_ these approaches see the text not as an object to be analyzed, but as an activity that is different for each reader. A reader-response critic might ask these questions of "My Last Duchess": How does the reader become aware of the duke's true nature if it's never actually stated? Do men and women read the poem differently? Who were Browning's original readers?

_4_

_(D)_ Author-centered approaches focus on the origins of a text (the writer and the historical background). For example, an author-centered study examines the writer's life—showing connections, contrasts, and conflicts between his or her life and the writing. Broader historical studies explore social and intellectual currents, showing links between an author's work and the ideas, events, and institutions of that period. Finally, the literary historian may make connections between the text in question and earlier and later liter-

---

(C) He describes the second subgroup and gives an example.
(D) He describes the third subgroup and gives examples.

(A) The writer introduces the topic and criterion for creating four subgroups.
(B) He describes the first subgroup and gives an example.

genre
class or category of something

ary works. The author-centered critic might ask these questions of "My Last Duchess": What were Browning's views of marriage, men and women, art, class, and wealth? As an institution, what was marriage like in Victorian England (Browning's era) or Renaissance Italy (the duke's era)? Who was the historical Duke of Ferrara?

5
(E) The fourth approach to criticism applies ideas outside of literature to literary works. Because literature mirrors life, argue these critics, disciplines that explore human life can help us understand literature. Some critics, for example, apply psychological theories to literary works by exploring dreams, symbolic meanings, and motivation. Myth or archetype criticism uses insights from psychology, cultural anthropology, and classical studies to explore a text's universal appeal. Moral criticism, rooted in religious studies and ethics, explores the moral dilemmas literary works raise. Marxist, feminist, and minority criticism are, broadly speaking, sociological approaches to interpretation. While the Marxist examines the themes of class struggle, economic power, and social justice in texts, the feminist critic explores the just and unjust treatment of women as well as the effect of gender on language, reading, and the literary canon. The critic interested in race and ethnic identity explores similar issues, with the focus shifted to a specific cultural group.

6
(F) Such ideological criticism might ask a wide variety of questions about "My Last Duchess": What does the poem reveal about the duke's psychological state and his personality? How does the reference to **Neptune** deepen the poem? What does the poem suggest about the nature of evil and injustice? In what ways are the duke's motives class-based and economic? How does the poem present the duke's power and the duchess's weakness? What is the status of women in this society?

7
(G) If you look at the variety of questions critics might ask about "My Last Duchess," you see both the diver-

sity of critical approaches and the common ground between them. In fact, interpretive methods actually share important characteristics: (1) a close attention to literary elements such as character, plot, symbolism, and metaphor; (2) a desire not to distort the work; and (3) a sincere concern for increasing interest and understanding in a text. In actual practice, critics may develop a **hybrid** approach to criticism, one that matches their individual questions and concerns about a text. Now that you're familiar with some of the questions defining literary criticism, exercise your own curiosity (and join the ongoing literary dialogue) by discussing a text that genuinely interests you.

Reading for Better Writing

Working by yourself or with a group, do the following:

1. Explain how the writer introduces the subject and attempts to engage the reader. Is this strategy effective? Why or why not?

2. The writer uses one poem to illustrate how each of the four critical approaches works. Explain why this strategy is or is not effective.

3. Review the last paragraph and explain why it does or does not unify the essay.

4. How might this classification of critical approaches apply to other forms of art or narrative? Modify this scheme for viewing films or listening to music.

5. Study the graphic organizers on pages 49–51. Does it help you visualize and understand the scheme used by Van Rys? Would you use a different kind of visual?

(E) He describes the fourth approach and gives examples of each subgroup in it.
(F) He cites sample questions.
(G) The closing presents qualities shared by all four approaches.

Neptune
ancient Roman god of the sea
hybrid
a fusion of two or more sources

Write, revise, and edit a classification essay. LO5

Writing Guidelines

Planning

1. **Select a topic.** Start by writing a few general headings like the academic headings below; then list two or three related topics under each heading. Finally, pick a topic that is characterized by a larger set of items or members that can best be explained by ordering them into categories.

Engineering	Biology	Social Work
Machines	Whales	Child welfare
Bridges	Fruits	Organizations

2. **Look at the big picture.** Do preliminary research to get an overview of your topic. Review your purpose (to explain, persuade, inform, and so on), and consider which classification criteria will help you divide the subject's content into distinct, understandable categories.

3. **Choose and test your criterion.** Choose a criterion for creating categories. Make sure it produces groups that are *consistent* (the same criterion are used throughout the sorting process), *exclusive* (groups are distinct—no member fits into more than one group), and *complete* (each member fits into a category with no member left over).

4. **Gather and organize information.** Gather information from reliable sources. To organize your information, take notes, possibly using a classification grid like the one shown below or the one on page 51. Set up the grid by listing the classification criteria down the left column and listing the groups in the top row of the columns. Then fill in the grid with appropriate details. (The grid at the bottom of this page lists the classification criterion and groups discussed in "Four Ways to Talk About Literature," pages 134–135.)

Note: If you do not use a grid, consider using an outline to organize your thoughts.

5. **Draft a thesis.** Draft a working thesis (you can revise it later as needed) that states your topic and identifies your classification scheme. Include language introducing your criteria for classifying groups.

Drafting

6. **Draft the essay.** Write your first draft, using organization planned earlier.

   Opening: Get the readers' attention, introduce the subject and thesis, and give your criteria for dividing the subject into categories.

   Middle: Develop the thesis by discussing each category, explaining its traits, and showing how it is distinct from the other groups. For example, in the middle section of "Four Ways to Talk About Literature," the writer first shows the unique focus of each of the four approaches to literary criticism, and then illustrates each approach by applying it to the same poem, "My Last Duchess" (see pages 134–135).

   Closing: Reflect on and tie together the classification scheme. While the opening and middle of the essay separate the subject into distinct categories, the closing may bring the groups back together. For example, Van Rys closes by identifying characteristics that the four subgroups have in common (see page 128).

Classification Criteria	Group #1	Group #2	Group #3	Group #4
	Text-centered approach	Audience-centered approach	Author-centered approach	Ideas outside literature
focus of the critical approach	• Trait #1 • Trait #2 • Trait #3	• Trait #1 • Trait #2 • Trait #3	• Trait #1 • Trait #2 • Trait #3	• Trait #1 • Trait #2 • Trait #3

Revising

7. Improve the ideas, organization, and voice. Ask a classmate or someone from the writing center to read your essay, looking for the following:

Ideas: Are the classification criteria logical and clear, resulting in categories that are consistent, exclusive, and complete? Does the discussion include appropriate examples that clarify the nature and function of each group?

Organization: Does the essay include (1) an engaging opening that introduces the subject, thesis, and criteria for classification, (2) a well-organized middle that distinguishes groups, shows why each group is unique, and supports these claims with evidence, and (3) a unifying conclusion that restates the main idea and its relevance?

Voice: Is the tone informed, courteous, and rational?

Editing

8. Edit the essay. Polish your writing by addressing these issues:

Words: The words distinguishing classifications are used uniformly.

Sentences: The sentences and paragraphs are complete, varied, and clear.

Correctness: The usage, grammar, and mechanics are correct.

Page Design: The design follows MLA, APA, CMS, or CSE formatting rules.

Publishing

9. Publish the essay by sharing it with your instructor and classmates, publishing it on your Web site, or submitting it to a print or online journal.

Critical-Thinking and Writing Activities

As directed by your instructor, complete the following activities.

1. In "Latin American Music: A Diverse and Unifying Force," Kathleen Kropp uses classification to analyze the nature and impact of an art form. Choose an art form that interests you, research the topic, and write an essay that uses classification to explain the art form's historical development and social impact.

2. "Four Ways to Talk About Literature" examines four approaches to reading and understanding a piece of literature. Identify a similar group of approaches to analysis or problem solving in your program or major. Write an essay in which you break your topic into categories, sort the groups, and explain the topic to the reader.

3. In "Four Sides to Every Story," Steward Brand uses classification to show that the climate-change debate is more complex than a two-position argument. Select an argument in the news or in your major that is erroneously presented as a two-option issue. Then research the topic and write a classification essay that accurately addresses the topic.

4. Find an article in a newspaper or an academic journal that uses classification to develop a thesis. Note the writer's criteria for sorting elements of the topic into categories. Then write a brief essay explaining why the criteria do or do not lead to groups that are consistent, exclusive, and complete. Share your writing with the class.

Checklist: Learning Outcomes

Use this checklist to assess how effectively you achieved the learning outcomes for this chapter.

_____ I know how to read a classification essay.

_____ I can create categories that are consistent, exclusive, and complete.

_____ I use precise terms for categories.

_____ I can effectively illustrate distinctive and shared traits of categories.

"I was brought up to believe that the only
thing worth doing was to add to the sum of
accurate information in the world."

Margaret Mead

12

Process

Process writing helps us understand ourselves and the world around us by answering interesting questions such as these: How does cancer spread? How do you download photographs from a camera? or What does Barack Obama's presidency indicate about America's progress toward racial reconciliation?

Writing that answers questions like these analyzes a process by breaking it down into steps, often grouped into stages or phases. Sometimes, the analysis also explains the process's causes and effects.

The two basic forms of process writing are a process essay and instructions. This chapter includes guidelines and models that will help you read and write both forms.

Learning Outcomes

LO1 Understand how to read process essays and instructions.

LO2 Study chronological structure.

LO3 Describe and analyze steps in a process.

LO4 Understand and use signal terms.

LO5 Write, revise, and edit a process essay.

Understand how to read process essays and instructions.

LO1

Process writing is analytical prose in which authors break a process into a clear series of steps (often organized into phases or stages) and then explain how and why those steps lead to a specific outcome. As you read process analyses, note how writers both describe and analyze the process, often using cause-effect reasoning.

Consider the rhetorical situation.

Depending on the writer's purpose, audience, and topic, process writing usually takes one of two forms: an essay that describes and analyzes the nature and function of a process, or a set of instructions that tells readers precisely how to do the process.

Purpose: If the writer intends to explain the topic, he or she writes an essay. The essay first offers an overview of the process and then explains how each step leads logically to the next, and how all the steps together complete the process. If the writer wants to help readers work through a process themselves, he or she writes instructions. These documents begin with a list of materials, and then follow with a detailed list of directives, often including precise signal terms such as "Note:" **"Warning!" "CAUTION!"** or **"DANGER!"**

Audience: Whether the form is an essay or a set of instructions, the text should meet the needs of all its readers, including those who know the least about the topic. To do this, writers should (1) include all the information that readers need, (2) use language that they understand, and (3) define unfamiliar or technical terms.

Topic: Topics addressed in academic process writing are usually course-related phenomena that interest the writer and offer readers insight into their discipline. For an example, see Kerry Mertz's essay, "Wayward Cells" (pages 141–142). Topics addressed in professional publications should interest and educate their readers.

Note signal terms.

In instructions, writers use signal terms (like those cited previously) to help users complete a process safely and successfully. Three organizations—the American National Standards Institute (ANSI), the International Organization for Standardization (ISO), and the U.S. military (MILSPEC)—set the standards for how signal terms must be used in instructions for these and other businesses. To learn more about how these organizations define, design, and use signal terms and related icons, check their Web sites.

Stephen Lynch, 2011 / Used under license from Shutterstock.com

Checklist: Process Writing

✔ Does the essay clearly identify the process, outline its stages, explain individual steps, and (if appropriate) discuss causes and effects?

✔ Do the instructions clearly and accurately explain the process, the tools and parts needed, the steps required, and the necessary precautions?

✔ Does the document use clear, precise language and define unfamiliar terms?

Study chronological structure.

Student writer Kerri Mertz wrote the following essay to explain how cancer cells affect the body. Note how she uses chronological order and transitions to distinguish steps in the process.

Essay Outline

Introduction: analogy of workers in room as cells in body

1. First step of cancer development: cell undifferentiating
2. Second step: reproduction of cancer cells, "autonomy"
3. Third step: varieties of damage to the body
4. The development of promising treatments

Closing: restate analogy—wayward cells as wayward workers

(A) # Wayward Cells

Survey · Question · Read · Recite · Review **SQ3R**

1
(B) Imagine a room containing a large group of people all working hard toward the same goal. Each person knows his or her job, does it carefully, and cooperates with other group members. Together, they function smoothly—like a well-oiled machine.

2
Then something goes wrong. One guy suddenly drops his task, steps into another person's workstation, grabs the material that she's working with, and begins something very different—he uses the material to make little reproductions of himself, thousands of

---

(A) Title: metaphor for process
(B) Introduction: cells-workers analogy

---

them. These look-alikes imitate him—grabbing material and making reproductions of themselves. Soon the bunch gets so big that they spill into other people's workstations, getting in their way, and interrupting their work. As the number of look-alikes grows, the work group's activity slows, stutters, and finally stops.

A human body is like this room, and the body's *3* cells are like these workers. If the body is healthy, each cell has a necessary job and does it correctly. For example, right now red blood cells are running throughout your body carrying oxygen to each body part. Other cells are digesting that steak sandwich that you had for lunch, and others are patching up that cut on your left hand. Each cell knows what to do because its genetic code—or DNA—tells it what to do. When a cell begins to function abnormally, it can initiate a process that results in cancer.

The problem starts when one cell "forgets" what *4* it should do. Scientists call this "undifferentiating"— (C) meaning that the cell loses its identity within the body (Pierce 75). Just like the guy in the group who decided to do his own thing, the cell forgets its job. Why this happens is somewhat unclear.

The problem could be caused by a defect in the *5* cell's DNA code or by something in the environment, such as cigarette smoke or asbestos (German 21). Causes from inside the body are called genetic, whereas causes from outside the body are

---

(C) 1 Cancer starts with cell undifferentiating.

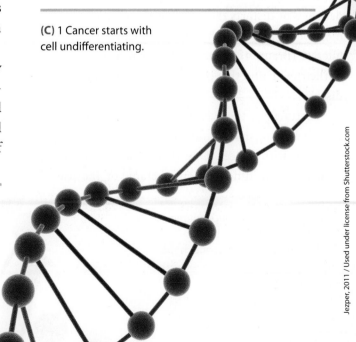

Jezper, 2011 / Used under license from Shutterstock.com

called carcinogens, meaning "any substance that causes cancer" (Neufeldt and Sparks 90). In either case, an undifferentiated cell can disrupt the function of healthy cells in two ways: by not doing its job as specified in its DNA and by not reproducing at the rate noted in its DNA.

6

(D) Most healthy cells reproduce rather quickly, but their reproduction rate is controlled. For example, your blood cells completely die off and replace themselves within a matter of weeks, but existing cells make only as many new cells as the body needs. The DNA codes in healthy cells tell them how many new cells to produce. However, cancer cells don't have this control, so they reproduce quickly with no stopping point, a characteristic called "autonomy" (Braun 3). What's more, all their "offspring" have the same qualities as their messed-up parent, and the resulting overpopulation produces growths called tumors.

7

(E) Tumor cells can hurt the body in a number of ways. First, a tumor can grow so big that it takes up space needed by other organs. Second, some cells may detach from the original tumor and spread throughout the body, creating new tumors elsewhere. This happens with lymphatic cancer—a cancer that's hard to control because it spreads so quickly. A third way that tumor cells can hurt the body is by doing work not called for in their DNA. For example, a gland cell's DNA code may tell the cell to produce a necessary hormone in the **endocrine system**. However, if cancer damages or distorts that code, sick cells may produce more of the hormone than the body can use—or even tolerate (Braun 4). Cancer cells seem to have minds of their own, and this is why cancer is such a serious disease.

8

(F) Fortunately, there is hope. Scientific research is already helping doctors do amazing things for people suffering with cancer. One treatment that has been used for some time is chemotherapy, or the use of chemicals to kill off all fast-growing cells, including cancer cells. (Unfortunately, chemotherapy can't distinguish between healthy and unhealthy cells, so it may cause negative side effects such as damaging fast-growing hair follicles, resulting in hair loss.) Another common treatment is radiation, or the use of light rays to kill cancer cells. One of the newest and most promising treatments is gene therapy—an effort to identify and treat chromosomes that carry a "wrong code" in their DNA. A treatment like gene therapy is promising because it treats the cause of cancer, not just the effect. Year by year, research is helping doctors better understand what cancer is and how to treat it.

9

(G) Much of life involves dealing with problems like wayward workers, broken machines, or dysfunctional organizations. Dealing with wayward cells is just another problem. While the problem is painful and deadly, there is hope. Medical specialists and other scientists are making progress, and some day they will help us win our battle against wayward cells.

(H)

(G) Conclusion: wayward cells as wayward workers
(H) Note: The Works Cited page is not shown.

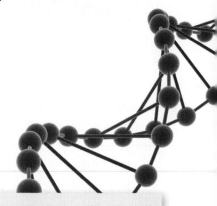

(D) 2 Cancer cells reproduce autonomously.
(E) 3 Tumors damage the body.
(F) 4 Promising treatments offer hope.

endocrine system
the body's glands

Reading for Better Writing

Working by yourself or with a group, do the following:

1. Explain why the analogy in the opening and closing is or is not effective.

2. Explain how transitions are used to lead into and out of each step.

3. Explain how the essay both describes and analyzes the process.

Describe and analyze steps in a process. LO3

In the following essay, published one month before Barack Obama was elected president, award-winning writer Gerald L. Early analyzes the process that led him and others to ask whether Obama's presidency marks the end of racism as we know it.

The End of Race as We Know It

1 **"And could politics ever be an expression of love?"**
   Ralph Ellison, *Invisible Man* **(1952)**

Survey • Question • Read • Recite • Review SQ3R

2 The controversial *New Yorker* cover of July 21, 2008—showing the Democratic presidential nominee, Barack Obama, as a Muslim jihadist and his wife, Michelle, as a gun-toting, Afro-wearing black militant—actually missed its target. It was funny as a kind of political and cultural satire, but only if you view the Obamas as **channeling** the first generation of black students to attend elite, white universities.

3 That was my generation—we're about 10 to 15 years older. We started attending college in 1970, almost as soon as black-studies programs, special black dorms, and special black admissions were instituted. Many of us were secretly, in our imagination, Muslim back in those days, or we adopted certain superficial Muslim pieties. We didn't eat pork, castigating it as slave food, and we sometimes called God "Allah." Among our heroes were the late, martyred Malcolm X and the living but also martyred Muhammad Ali, both Muslims. Ali himself kept the image of holy war alive in popular culture in the way he promoted many of his fights: as a cosmic battle between the good Muslim and the **reprobate**, pork-eating, **Uncle Tom** Christian. He did this especially against black opponents like Floyd Patterson, Joe Frazier, and George Foreman. *The Autobiography of Malcolm X* was the central book of our generation, the story of how true Islam spiritually and politically reawakened an African-American. The basketball great Lew Alcindor became Kareem Abdul-Jabbar in

1971. The Nation of Islam was highly respected, even highly feared by some. Amiri Baraka, our poet laureate and leading **agitprop** dramatist, was publishing work with the alternative Jihad Press, based in Newark, N.J., his hometown, and his form of cultural nationalism gave a respectful nod to Islam. The jazz pianist Doug Carn wrote a tune, "Jihad," that appeared on his popular (with black college students) 1973 album, *Revelation*. Other hip black-college-student music of the period: The tenor saxophonist Pharoah Sanders and the singer Leon Thomas recorded a tune called "Hum-Allah-Hum-Allah-Hum-Allah" on their 1969 album, *Jewels of Thought*. A 1966 album of Sanders was called *Tauhid*, an Islamic theological term.

4 In our bull sessions, some of us would talk about jihad, or righteous war, against the whites. (It was all talk.) Some of us actually became Muslims (very few—we were Christians to the bone, despite our chatter about "the white man's religion") or joined some Eastern religious sect and adopted certain garb and mannerisms. Many of us wore wild **Afros**, making them wilder with blowout kits, and thought we were revolutionaries of a sort. After all, some of the black upperclassmen among us had seized buildings in protest, and a few even brandished weapons during the sieges.

5 Looking at *The New Yorker* cover as a middle-aged, black baby boomer, far removed from any of the Orientalism and racial and political romanticism of my youth, reminded me of a certain kind of silliness, but it also, strangely, moved me deeply. The cover told the story of a rite of African-American passage that occurred at a particular time for the generation of blacks who would become the most successful in the history of the group, and the most integrated. The relatively

channeling
to allow another person's spirit to speak or act through one's body

reprobate
immoral or disreputable

Uncle Tom
a subservient black person, from the title character of *Uncle Tom's Cabin*

agitprop
political propaganda

Afros
a large, bushy hairstyle, trimmed to be round

difficult years that my generation endured integrating white institutions—difficult not in any material sense, but in the sense that we were not very well prepared academically or emotionally to cope with our surroundings (we were given more than we knew what to do with, so much that one felt simultaneously intoxicated by the riches and stressed to the breaking point by how alien it all felt)—made us clutch at any sort of feeble identity protection we could muster. We had to "act black" because, after all, that is why we were at the university in the first place: to provide diversity in the only way we knew how.

6   Basically, entrapped in our excessive and youthful self-consciousness, our special sort of juvenile insecurity, we were trying, ironically, to show that we belonged, to protect ourselves from being considered "dumb niggers," or, even worse, "charity cases," the ragtag tail end of the American bourgeois elite. Some succeeded (by graduating). Many didn't. It is a modern story about integration in America—not the bloody civil-rights struggle of gaining access, but rather how people can sometimes be killed by kindness, paddled by paternalism, undone by **philanthropy**. I think back on it all as a remarkable form of self-hazing.

7   In looking at that *New Yorker* cover, it occurred to me that an important dimension of black identity politics was the memory of being something you never were but that you needed to think you might have been. Middle-aged black yuppies, like me—we, the generation of the Talented Tenth, the recipients of the gifts of the civil-rights struggle, those to whom much was given—see a great deal of ourselves in the Obamas. Whether we are elitists is unclear (many of us probably are—there is no shortage of black snobs), but we were surely educated to be an elite, a professional cadre for the race, gate-crashers turned gatekeepers—guardians who ensure diversity at predominantly white institutions rather than exult in and maintain the precarious, tarnished glory of black, "shadow" institutions.

The New Yorker cover reminds me how much we   8 have, as integrationists, tried to fit in and how much we may secretly feel (or hope) we haven't. But the cover not only reminds me how much this group has done to make whites feel comfortable around us by adopting "secret identities" (the exotic nature of which were meant to nonplus and annoy whites, while **titillating** their sense of romantic racialism). It also posed an important question: How comfortable are we with ourselves? Did we, in our desperation, ask race to do more work, support more of a psychological burden, than such a limited concept could ever hope to do because, alas, it was all we had: white people's crazy, self-serving idea of what human difference means? As Kwame Anthony Appiah wrote: "There is nothing in the world that can do all we ask race to do for us." We even hoped it would make us Americans while it would protect us from America.

As black people know better than many, it is, as   9 Henry James acknowledged, a complex fate to be an American, especially to pose as being an American against one's will, the forever skeptical **quasi**-American, as most of us did. Anti-Americanism—not saluting the flag, ignoring the playing of the national anthem, decrying the United States and its policies at any and every opportunity—was common among black college students at the time, particularly those with any intellectual pretension. As influenced as we were by black cultural nationalism and trickle-down Marxism, this is hardly surprising.

But the irony of our anti-Americanism was that it   10 masked our yearning for inclusion, which is why we were attending white colleges and universities in the first place. We grasped an identity of "blackness," of the superficially non-Western, in our confused hunt to fit into somebody's scheme and our reflexive fear that we would certainly not fit into a Western or white scheme. We did not want to be, in James Baldwin's words, "bastards of the West," but the very nature of our identity quest was propelled by the fact that we knew, inescapably, we were just that. It was the West, America, that we knew and by which we measured and understood reality. We had a complicated, un-

philanthropy
beneficial action toward humankind

titillating
to cause a pleasurably tingling sensation, often sexually

quasi
bearing a resemblance to something but not the same

certain place in the American scheme, a scheme we desired but that did not desire us. Suppose one day our place would become more assured in the scheme, suppose one day we could be unconditionally loyal to the scheme. Would we recognize that day, or would we be so historically conditioned that we would not know when history had finally turned a page, ended a chapter, entered a new phase of its unfolding?

11   Dinesh D'Souza's controversial 1995 book, *The End of Racism,* proposed that if racism has a historical beginning (which it does), then it must be reasonable to think it would have a historical end. The book then proposes: Suppose there is sufficient evidence to show that we have now reached that endpoint? The end of racism would mean that blacks can live their lives as fully as whites can, that any existing racism is **residual** and has no impact on the quality of black life. Thus the end of racism means the end of the claim of black victimization. But how would we know when we have reached it? What sign would show that we have arrived at, in effect, the end of America's racial history?

12   Considering the vociferous responses by black intellectuals and leftists to D'Souza, we had not unambiguously arrived at that point in 1995. Apparently, for many black leaders, pundits, and scholars, the signs were not the success of Bill Cosby or Oprah Winfrey, not the Nobel Prize of Toni Morrison or the career of Spike Lee, not the crossover achievement of Serena and Venus Williams and Tiger Woods, not the political careers of Condoleezza Rice or Colin Powell, not the stardom of Will Smith and Morgan Freeman, not the Ivy League college presidency of Ruth Simmons or the arrival of such black public intellectuals as Henry Louis Gates Jr., Michael Eric Dyson, Orlando Patterson, and Cornel West.

13   None of those have been the tipping point. The accomplishments of those people and thousands more did not indicate to many African-Americans that America had advanced beyond racism and that blacks had transcended their victimization. We had the anxiety of the paranoid: Whites are always out to get us, no matter how much we might succeed. In fact, they are out to get you all the more if you do succeed. We had the self-deprecating, cynical view of our elite status that spoke of guilt because of our lack of solidarity (we kill each other at an alarming clip) and our continuing need for white philanthropy (our dependency undermines our sense of power as a group): Successful blacks are nothing more than social and political tranquilizers that mask the continued existence of racism and the brutal victimization of black people. The thought crosses my mind from time to time: Am I doing good by doing well?

14   Might the presidency of Barack Obama be the tipping point? Blacks may become famous authors, film directors, diplomats, CEO's, fashion models, entertainers, and physicists. But the presidency of the country, the most powerful person in the world, is the ultimate—to have authority that all whites, everyone in the world, would be bound to respect. What could mean more to a people who have endured a history of powerlessness? Black people were convinced that no black would become president of the United States during the lifetime of the baby-boom generation, not in the lifetime of any African-American adult currently living. That may change in a matter of weeks. My mother, who is 79 years old, summed it up: "I never thought I would live to see the day when I could vote for a black man for president and he actually has a chance to win." My mother says this as if that fact signifies the end of America's racial history, or at least the end of race as we once knew it.

15   The presidential campaign of Barack Obama has raised the question of what happens to the black American **meta**-narrative of heroic or noble victimization if he wins. (Presumably nothing happens to it if he loses; the loss can be blamed on racism, as it will, in fact, be another example of victimization. White folks will always find a way to cut down a successful black man, to not let him get too far, is the common belief. That sort of black cynicism, expressed in different political and aesthetic modalities, underscores both the blues and rap. If Obama loses, he becomes, in black folklore, John Henry, the "natural" man with the courage to go up against the political machine. The moral of the tale,

residual
something that remains when the original is gone

meta
transcending

in politics as in life, is that the machine always wins.)

16   The author Charles Johnson, in an essay that appeared in the summer 2008 issue of *The American Scholar*, argued that the black American narrative of victimization has already reached its end: "It simply is no longer the case that the essence of black American life is racial victimization and **disenfranchisement**, a curse and a condemnation, a destiny based on color in which the meaning of one's life is thinghood, created even before one is born." Perhaps black conservatism, the first sustained attempt by blacks to de-emphasize racism as a factor in black life, arose in the 1970s and 1980s as a way around the victimization narrative, as a way to move beyond civil rights. Perhaps it was the beginning of victimization fatigue. Afrocentrism re-energized the victim narrative in the 1990s by designating the achievements and destruction of Africanity as the core reality of Western civilization.

17   Many of us black professionals, members of the black elite, keep the embers of our victimization burning for opportunistic reasons: to leverage white patronage, to maintain our own sense of identity and tradition. In some respects, this narrative has something of the power in its endurance that original sin does for Christians. In fact, our narrative of victimization is America's original sin, or what we want to serve as the country's original sin, which may be why we refuse to give it up.

18   We have used it shamelessly—especially those who are least entitled to do so, as we have suffered the least—hustled it to get over on whites, to milk their guilt, to excuse our excesses and failures. Being the victim justifies all ethical lapses, as the victim becomes morally reprehensible in the guise of being morally outraged. Being the victim has turned into a sucker's game, the only possible game that the weak can play against the strong with any chance of winning. Nonetheless, the narrative does a kind of cultural work that serves our purposes in some profound ways, and it may be good for the country as a whole in reminding everyone about the costs of American democracy, its fragile foundation, its historically based hypocrisy.

disenfranchisement
to deprive of rights

The conservatives are right: Freedom isn't free, and the black victim narrative reminds us all of that.

In the end, black people chose to see themselves   19
as America's exceptionalist people, the only ones who came to the land of freedom as perpetually unfree, who came to the land that welcomed the exile and the outcast against their will and who remained in that land as exiles and outcasts. In the grand scheme of American exceptionalism, the God-designed empire meant to do good, were African-Americans who troubled the waters with their own exceptionalist claims that went counter to the story of American triumphalist history. How could the country claim to be good and do good when it so mistreated blacks? The African-American story, perforce, had to be the tale of America's tragedy.

But of course that is not quite the case: The black   20
American story of victimization, our exceptionalism, was meant to be a triumphalist story of its own sort. Black Americans have survived, persevered, and even thrived despite the enormous obstacles thrown in our way. In a way, the black American narrative revealed American hypocrisy but simultaneously reinscribed American greatness, for blacks were heroic victims, and only in America could the heroism of the weak win a victory able to humble a nation into recognition of its wrongs.

The black narrative of victimization may have out-   21
lived its historical need and its psychological urgency, but it still may have a kind of cultural work to do as a tale of redemption and an example of salvation history. If we are the shining city on a hill, part of that city must be the quarters of bondage, the world the slaves made, and America's true greatness might be that it is the only nation that symbolizes itself in this way, the grand city as the uplift of all people, even those it has enslaved. In the tale of heroism in adversity, perhaps best exemplified in spirituals, black-American Christianity, and the secular humanism of the blues, the narrative of victimization reminds all Americans of the need, from time to time, to lift every voice and sing in tribute to who we are, however inadequate, and to what we hope we can be when we arrive at that day when, as Martin Luther King Jr. prophesied in his vision of America as a beloved community, politics becomes an expression of love.

Reading for Better Writing

Working by yourself or with a group, do the following:

1. In this essay, Gerald L. Early describes and analyzes a process. What is the process, and how does he introduce it?

2. In paragraphs 2, 5, 7, and 8, Early refers to the July 21, 2008 front cover of *The New Yorker*. Explain how Early uses it to introduce and develop his thesis.

3. In paragraph 10, Early says, "But the irony of our anti-Americanism was that it masked our yearning for inclusion." What is irony and how is "our anti-Americanism" ironic?

4. In paragraphs 13 and 14, Early uses the phrase, "tipping point." Explain what the phrase means and how he uses it to develop his thesis.

5. In paragraph 20, Early says, "In a way, the black American narrative revealed American hypocrisy but simultaneously reinscribed American greatness." Explain what the sentence means and why you do or do not agree.

6. Review Early's final paragraph. In what ways does it bring his process analysis to a conclusion?

Understand and use signal terms.

LO4

Instructions like the ones that follow are written to help readers understand and complete a process successfully and safely. To help readers succeed, state the steps in the process clearly, organize the steps in chronological order, and insert mild signal terms (e.g., "Note.") that alert readers to special details. To help readers complete a process safely, use strong signal terms such as **"Warning!" "CAUTION!"** or **"DANGER!"** (For more information on signal terms, see pages 140 and 148.)

Downloading Photographs from a Digital Camera (A)

Survey • Question • Read • Recite • Review **SQ3R**

Note: MC-150 software must be loaded on your computer to download photographs from the camera.

1. Turn your computer on. (B)
2. Plug the camera's USB cable into your computer.
3. Turn the camera's mode dial to the **data transfer setting** (Figure 1). (C)
4. Open the camera's flash-card door and plug the other end of the USB cable into the **camera port** (Figure 2). (D)

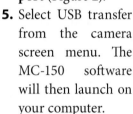

Figure 1: Data Transfer Setting

5. Select USB transfer from the camera screen menu. The MC-150 software will then launch on your computer. (E) (F)

Figure 2: Camera Port

© Sebranek Inc.

6. Follow the instructions on the computer screen to download all of your photos or specific photos.
7. When your download is complete, turn the camera off and unplug the USB cable from the camera and the computer.

Note: If the MC-150 software doesn't launch, disconnect the camera (step 7), and then restart the computer and continue on from step 2. (G)

(A) Opening: Use a descriptive title. Note or list materials needed.
(B) Middle: State steps in chronological order and parallel from.
(C) Add graphics (such as the arrow) to create a quick visual cue.
(D) Boldface words that need special attention.
(E) To show an object's size, use a reference (such as the fingers).
(F) Use only well-focused photographs.
(G) Closing: Note common problems.

Write, revise, and edit a process essay. LO5

Writing Guidelines

Planning

1. **Select a topic.** Use prompts like those below to generate a list of topics.
   - A course-related process
   - A process in nature
   - A process in the news
   - A process that helps you get a job

2. **Review the process.** Use your knowledge of the topic to fill out an organizer like the one on the right. List the subject at the top, each of the steps in chronological order, and the outcome

   > Process Analysis
   > Subject:
   > - Step #1
   > - Step #2
   > - Step #3
   > Outcome:

   at the bottom. For a complex process, break it down into stages or phases first; then outline the steps within each phase.

3. **Research as needed.** Find information that helps you explain the process: what it is, what steps are required, what order the steps follow, how the steps are done, what outcome the process produces, and what safety precautions are needed. If possible, observe the process or perform it yourself. Carefully record correct names, materials, tools, and safety or legal issues.

4. **Organize information.** Revise the organizer as needed. Then develop an outline, including steps listed in the organizer, as well as supporting details from your research.

Drafting

5. **Draft the document.** Write the document using the guidelines below.

Describing and Explaining a Process

Opening: Introduce the topic; give an overview of the process, possibly forecasting its main stages; and explain why the process is important.

Middle: Order the process into phases if necessary, clearly describe each step in the process, and link steps with transitions such as *first, second, next, finally,* and *while.* Explain the importance of each step, and how it is linked to other steps in the process. Describe the overall outcome of the process and explain its relevance.

Closing: Summarize the process and restate key points as needed; if appropriate, explain follow-up activity.

Writing Instructions

Opening: Name the process in the title, summarize the process's goal, and list any materials and tools needed.

Middle: Present each step in a separate—usually one- or two-sentence—paragraph. Number the steps and state each clearly, using firm commands directed to the reader. Where appropriate, include signal terms indicating **Caution! WARNING!** or **DANGER!**

Closing: In a short paragraph, explain how and when follow-up action should be completed.

Note: To state instructions as direct commands, use action verbs in the imperative mood. The mood of a verb indicates the tone or attitude it conveys.

Revising

6. **Improve the ideas, organization, and voice.** Ask a classmate or someone from the writing center to evaluate the following:

   Ideas: Is the process presented as a unified phenomenon that includes a logical series of stages and steps? If causes and effects are addressed, are the claims clear and supported with well-researched details?

Organization: Does the *process essay* include an opening that introduces the process and thesis; a middle that describes stages and steps clearly and correctly; and a closing that unifies the essay by accenting key points?

Do the *instructions* include an opening that correctly names the process and lists materials needed; a middle that states each step (or directive) correctly and in the required order; and a closing that specifies follow-up action?

Voice: Is the tone informed, concerned, and objective? Are instructions stated as firm, direct commands using action verbs in the imperative mood?

Tip   Test instructions by using them to perform the process.

Editing

7. **Edit the essay.** Polish your writing by addressing the following:

   Words: The words are precise, clear, and correct.
   - Technical terms are correct, used uniformly, and defined.
   - Transitions link steps, and a consistent verb tense is used.

   Sentences: The sentences are smooth, varied in structure, and engaging. In instructions, sentences are shaped as clear, brief commands formatted in accordance with standards set by regulatory agencies such as the American National Standards Institute (ANSI).

   Correctness: The finished copy includes correct usage, grammar, punctuation, and spelling.

   Page Design: The design features steps in the process. In instructions, signal terms and symbols conform to regulatory standards.

Publishing

8. **Publish the essay** by offering it to instructors, students, and nonprofit agencies working with the process. Also consider posting the writing on a suitable Web site.

Critical-Thinking and Writing Activities

As directed by your instructor, complete the following activities by yourself or in a group.

1. Reread the topics that you listed under "Select a Topic" on page 148. Choose a topic and write about it as an essay or as a set of instructions.

2. Review "Wayward Cells," the essay that analyzes what cancer is and how it progresses. Then choose another natural- or social-science process that interests you and write an essay describing and analyzing that process. Conversely, think of a process within the arts and humanities (e.g., a historical movement, a cultural change, a plot pattern in fiction or film, an artistic method).

3. Review the instructions "Downloading Photographs from the MC-150 Digital Camera," considering how the written and visual elements on the page work together. Draft or revise a process document in which visual elements are essential to effectively communicate your ideas. Integrate relevant, high-quality visuals (photos, illustrations, diagrams) that will help readers to better understand the process.

4. In his essay, "The End of Race as We Know It," Gerald L. Early analyzes a process through which he came to a new and deeper understanding of himself and others. Think about a time or phase in your own life during which you came to know yourself more fully. Then write an essay in which you analyze the transition, identify related stages, and explain their causes and effects.

Checklist: Learning Outcomes

Use this checklist to assess what you have learned about process writing:

_____ I understand how to read process essays and instructions.

_____ I understand chronological structure.

_____ I describe and analyze steps in the process.

_____ I understand and use signal terms.

_____ I can draft, revise, edit, design, and publish both a process essay and a set of instructions.

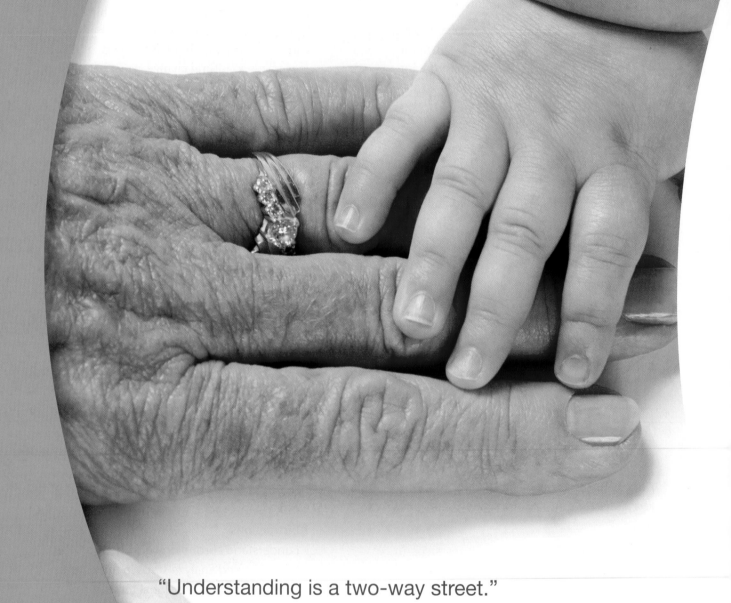

"Understanding is a two-way street."
Eleanor Roosevelt

13

Comparison-Contrast

In his plays, William Shakespeare creates characters, families, and even plot lines that mirror each other. As a result, we see Hamlet in relation to Laertes and the Montagues in relation to the Capulets. In the process, we do precisely what the writer wants us to do—we compare and contrast the subjects. The result is clarity and insight: by thinking about both subjects in relation to each other, we understand each one more clearly.

But writers in college and in the workplace also use comparison-contrast as an analytical strategy. To help you read and write such documents, the following pages include writing guidelines and three model essays.

Learning Outcomes

LO1 Understand how to read comparison-contrast writing.

LO2 Use subject-by-subject or trait-by-trait organization.

LO3 Cite details to support and clarify compare-contrast claims.

LO4 Use comparison-contrast strategies to analyze, illustrate, or define concepts.

LO5 Write, revise, and edit a compare-contrast essay.

Understand how to read comparison-contrast writing. LO1

When writers use compare-contrast, what should you as a reader look for? The instruction below will help you read essays like those that follow.

Consider the rhetorical situation.

Think about how a writer might use comparison-contrast to achieve her or his purpose, address an audience, and analyze a topic.

Purpose: Writers compare and contrast subjects in order to understand their similarities and differences. Their purpose may be to stress the similarities between seemingly dissimilar things or the differences between things that seem quite similar.

Audience: A writer using this strategy may have virtually any reader in mind—the instructor for a student essay or potential clients for a marketing document. Whatever the situation, the writer sees readers as people whose understanding of a topic, an issue, or a phenomenon can be deepened with comparative analysis.

Topics: Writers address a wide range of topics through compare-contrast: people, events, phenomena, technologies, problems, products, stories, and so on. The writer simply thinks through what aspects of the topic may be illuminated through comparison and/or contrast.

Consider the compare-contrast practices used.

As you read an essay using compare-contrast, look for the following:

Criteria Used for Comparison: Writers anchor their analyses in specific points of comparison. For example, a comparison of two characters in a play might focus on their backgrounds, their actions in the play, their psychology, their fate, and so on. As you read, trace the features compared, thinking through the writer's choices.

Organization of the Comparison: Such writing is generally structured either subject by subject (first dealing with one topic fully and then the other) or trait by trait (holding up the topics side by side, feature by feature).

The Point of the Comparison: Writers use comparison to illuminate topics through a key idea about connections and distinctions. Identify the essential insight of the comparison, whether the writer states it at the beginning or leaves it to the end.

> ## Checklist: Comparison-Contrast
>
> ✔ Why is the writer comparing these topics? Is the goal to stress similarities, differences, or both? How does the comparison speak to specific readers?
>
> ✔ What features or traits of the topics are compared? Why?
>
> ✔ How does the writer present the topics and the criteria for comparison?
>
> ✔ What conclusion does the writer develop through analysis?

Use subject-by-subject or trait-by-trait organization. LO2

In the essay that follows, student writer Rachel De Smith uses trait-by-trait organization to analyze characters from two novels. Note how she introduces her characters, and then compares and contrasts their isolation, haunting experiences, and escape.

Essay Outline

Introduction: Sethe and Orleanna as surprisingly similar characters
1. Living and isolation and loneliness
2. Haunted by the past
3. Grueling journeys of escape

Conclusion: Sethe and Orleanna as suffering but strong women

Sethe in *Beloved* and Orleanna in *Poisonwood Bible:* Isolation, Children, and Getting Out

Survey · Question · Read · Recite · Review **SQ3R**

1 Toni Morrison's Sethe and Barbara Kingsolver's
(B) Orleanna Price seem to be vastly different women, living in different times and cultures, descended from different races. One has had a faithful spouse forced away from her by circumstances; the other lives in a devastating marriage. One is a former slave, while the other is a comparatively well-off minister's wife. However, these two women are more alike than they first appear. Both live in isolation and loneliness, both are haunted by the past, both risk everything to get their children out of devastating circumstances—and both reap the consequences of such risks.

2 Sethe lives in house number 124, a house generally
(C) believed to be haunted, "full of a baby's venom" (Mor-
(D) rison 3). The child's ghost inhabiting the house throws things around, makes spots of colored light appear, shakes floors, and stomps up the stairs. The people of the surrounding community—remembering Sethe's past, fearing ghostly retribution, and resenting the long-ago extravagance of Sethe's mother-in-law, Baby Suggs—diligently avoid the house and its residents. Sethe's one remaining daughter, Denver, will not leave the yard (Morrison 205). The two of them live with the ghost, ostracized.

3 Orleanna lives in a less malignant but equally iso-
(E) lated situation. When she and her daughters follow her husband on his zealous missionary trip to the **Congo**, she is the only white woman in a village of people with whom she shares nothing, not even a word of their language. Preoccupied with the troubles in her own house, she remains separated from the villagers by a gulf of cultural misunderstanding—from how to behave in the marketplace to where to get her drinking water (Kingsolver 89, 172). Even when she returns to the United States, Orleanna lives in isolation, hidden among her flower gardens, set apart by the stigma of her past (Kingsolver 407).

4 The cause of all this isolation, for both women, is
(F) the past. When Sethe saw a slave catcher coming for
(G) her, she attempted to kill all four of her young children in order to prevent them from becoming slaves (Morrison 149, 163). She succeeded in killing only her second-youngest, known as Beloved. No one went back to the plantation; Sethe went to jail instead. Years later, her two oldest children (sons) run off, unable to face the specter of their dead sister knocking over jars and leaving handprints in cakes. Beloved's death is thus the defining moment not only for Sethe's haunted life but also for Denver's, Baby Suggs', and, in many ways, the entire community's.

5 Orleanna, like Sethe, has lost a child, though not
(H) by her own hand. Her youngest daughter, Ruth May, died of snakebite after an ugly disagreement (involving much shouting and plenty of **voodoo**) between the Price family and the rest of the village. Orleanna is not immediately responsible for Ruth May's death—in fact, she has recently brought the girl miraculously through a bout with malaria (Kingsolver 276). However, Orleanna still feels tremendous guilt about Ruth May's death, and even about being in Africa at all. In much of Orleanna's narration, she attempts to move past this guilt, periodically asking her absent daughter's forgiveness. Sethe, also hoping for reconciliation, explains herself in a similar way to Beloved. But Beloved seems to feed off of Sethe's remorse, whereas

---

(F) 2 Isolation for both women is rooted in a haunting past.
(G) (a) Sethe
(H) (b) Orleanna

Congo
republic in central Africa
voodoo
magical worship

(A) The title identifies the topics compared and the traits examined.
(B) Introduction: two seemingly different characters share similar lives.
(C) 1 Both women live in isolation and loneliness.
(D) (a) Sethe
(E) (b) Orleanna

Lucian Coman, 2011 / Used under license from Shutterstock.com

Ruth May, as portrayed in the final chapter of the novel, bears no such ill-will. Ruth May says, "Mother, you can still hold on but forgive, forgive . . . I forgive you, Mother" (Kingsolver 537, 543). Beloved continually punishes Sethe for leaving her behind, but Ruth May is willing to forgive.

6   Both Sethe and Orleanna endure grueling jour-
(I) neys of escape, though the journeys begin very differ-
(J) ently. Sethe has spent a long time planning an escape with her fellow slaves. When the opportunity finally comes, Sethe sends her children on ahead and then follows, pausing on the way to give birth to Denver. Oddly enough, the final stage of her journey to "free-

---

(I) (3) Both women take journeys to escape.
(J) (a) Sethe

estrangement
removal or distance

dom" seems to be her time in jail, an episode that kept her from going back to the Sweet Home plantation. However, even after Sethe leaves jail and begins a life free from the degradations of the plantation, she cannot escape the stigma of her past, particularly Beloved's violent death.

     Orleanna's journey, though also long-anticipated   7
or at least long-desired, is a spontaneous event. Follow- (K)
ing Ruth May's tragic death (the impetus for her jour-
ney), Orleanna simply walks away: her daughter Leah recalls that "Mother never once turned around to look over her shoulder" (Kinsolver 389). Their unplanned journey ends up as a fiasco, culminating in malaria during the rainy season somewhere in the depths of the Congo, but all of Orleanna's remaining daughters survive. Though obvious differences exist between the deaths of Ruth May and Beloved, both deaths allow their families some form of escape. In addition, Orleanna, like Sethe, is willing to give up her children in order for them to escape; she sends Rachel with Eeben Axelroot and leaves Leah with Anatole when she and Adah leave the country for good. Orleanna's actions parallel Sethe's, as Sethe sends her children ahead of her (in escape or death) in order for them to leave the plantation. Orleanna sees very little of Rachel and Leah for the rest of her life, but they have escaped the devastation of their lives in the Congo, or at least their lives under Nathan Price, and that is—or must be— enough for her.

     Sethe and Orleanna are both haunted women. The   8
deaths of their daughters and **estrangement** from their (L)
remaining children prevent these women from finding peace. Both are haunted by guilt—Sethe for her own actions in the murder of Beloved, and Orleanna for her complicity both in Ruth May's death and in the chaos that enveloped the Congo at the same time. Both women are also isolated and lonely, distanced by distrust and misunderstanding from the people around them. And both women, in the long run, risk everything to gain freedom for their children. Distrust, rage, fear, and bad dreams accompany that

---

(K) (b) Orleanna
(L) Conclusion: These two haunted characters are strong women who eventually move beyond guilt.

risk, but both women keep their children from the evil awaiting them—a plantation, a father's oppression. Paul D. questions Sethe on this point, wondering if other circumstances might be even worse than the plantation. Sethe responds, "It ain't my job to know what's worse. It's my job to know what is and to keep them away from what I know is terrible" (Morrison 165). Sethe is never able to achieve true reconciliation with Beloved, but her relationships with Denver and Paul D. help to make up for this loss, while Orleanna is forgiven by Ruth May and eventually reunited (albeit briefly) with her other children. Despite the attendant circumstances, both Sethe and Orleanna are revealed to be strong women, and both eventually move past their paralyzing guilt in their efforts to "walk forward into the light" (Kingsolver 543).

Note: The Works Cited page is not shown. For sample pages, see MLA (pages 368–369 and APA (page 396).

Reading for Better Writing

Working by yourself or with a group, do the following:

1. Review the title and opening paragraph, describe how the writer focuses her essay, and explain why you do or do not find that introduction well written.
2. A thesis is a type of contract in which the writers states what he or she will do in the essay. Review the writer's thesis and explain whether she does what she promises.
3. Cite passages in the essay that illustrate trait-by-trait organization. Then explain why you think this approach is or is not an effective strategy for analyzing literature.
4. Explain why you think that compare-contrast reasoning is or is not an effective strategy for analyzing literature.
5. Explain why the writer's voice is or is not appropriate for this essay. For example is the voice informed or uninformed, objective or manipulative, respectful or disrespectful?
6. Review the visual on page 154 and assess why it does or does not support your reading experience.

Cite details to support and clarify compare-contrast claims.

LO3

In the following essay, writer Gelareh Asayesh analyzes how the traditional Islamic clothing that she must wear in Iran affects her sense of self. To that end, she compares and contrasts its advantages and disadvantages, and supports her claims with details, anecdotes, and keen observations.

Shrouded in Contradiction

Survey • Question • Read • Recite • Review **SQ3R**

I grew up wearing the miniskirt to school, the veil to the mosque. In the Tehran of my childhood, women in bright sundresses shared the sidewalk with women swathed in black. The tension between the two ways of life was palpable. As a schoolgirl, I often cringed when my bare legs got leering or contemptuous glances. Yet, at times, I long for the days when I could walk the streets of my country with the wind in my hair. When clothes were clothes. In today's Iran, whatever I wear sends a message. If it's a **chador**, it embarrasses my Westernized relatives. If it's a skimpy scarf, I risk being accused of stepping on the blood of the martyrs who died in the war with Iraq. Each time I return to Tehran, I wait until the last possible moment, when my plane lands on the tarmac, to don the scarf and long jacket that many Iranian women wear in lieu of a veil. To wear *hijab*—Islamic covering—is to invite contradiction. Sometimes I hate it. Sometimes I value it.

Most of the time, I don't even notice it. It's annoying, but so is wearing panty hose to work. It ruins my hair, but so does the humidity in Florida, where I live.

1
(A)
(B)
2

(A) Two contrasting scenes appear in the first sentence.
(B) Italics distinguish *hijab* as a non-English word.

chador
long, black cloth or veil covering the entire body; traditionally worn by Muslim and Hindu women

For many women, the veil is neither a symbol nor a statement. It's simply what they wear, as their mothers did before them. Something to dry your face with after your **ablutions** before prayer. A place for a toddler to hide when he's feeling shy. Even for a woman like me, who wears it with a hint of rebellion, *hijab* is just not that big a deal.

3   Except when it is.

4   "Sister, what kind of get-up is this?" a woman in black, one of a pair, asks me one summer day on the Caspian shore. I am standing in line to ride a gondola up a mountain, where I'll savor some ice cream along with vistas of sea and forest. Women in chadors stand wilting in the heat, faces gleaming with sweat. Women in makeup and clunky heels wear knee-length jackets with pants, their hair daringly exposed beneath sheer scarves.

5   None have been more daring than I. I've wound my scarf into a turban, leaving my neck bare to the breeze. The woman in black is a government employee paid to police public morals. "Fix your scarf at once!" she snaps.

6   "But I'm hot," I say.

7   "You're hot?" she exclaims. "Don't you think we all are?"

8   I start unwinding my makeshift turban. "The men aren't hot," I mutter.

9   Her companion looks at me in shocked reproach. "Sister, this isn't about men and women," she says, shaking her head. "This is about Islam."

10   I want to argue. I feel like a child. Defiant, but
(D) powerless. Burning with injustice, but also with a hint of shame. I do as I am told, feeling acutely conscious of the bare skin I am covering. In policing my sexuality, these women have made me more aware of it.

11   The veil masks erotic freedom, but its advocates
(E) believe *hijab* transcends the erotic—or expands it. In the West, we think of passion as a fever of the body, not the soul. In the East, Sufi poets used earthly passion as a metaphor; the beloved they celebrated was God. Where I come from, people are more likely to find delirious passion in the mosque than in the bedroom.

12   There are times when I feel a hint of this passion. A few years after my encounter on the Caspian, I go to the wake of a family friend. Sitting in a mosque in Mashhad, I grip a slippery black veil with one hand and a prayer book with the other. In the center of the hall, there's a stack of Koranic texts decorated with green-and-black calligraphy, a vase of white gladioluses and a large photograph of the dearly departed. Along the walls, women wait quietly.

13   From the men's side of the mosque, the **mullah's** voice rises in lament. His voice is deep and plaintive, oddly compelling. I bow my head, sequestered in my veil while at my side a community of women pray and weep with increasing abandon. I remember from girlhood this sense of being exquisitely alone in the company of others. Sometimes I have cried as well, free to weep without having to offer an explanation. Perhaps **(F)** they are right, those mystics who believe that physical love is an obstacle to spiritual love; those architects of mosques who abstained from images of earthly life, decorating their work with geometric shapes that they believed freed the soul to slip from its worldly moorings. I do not aspire to such lofty sentiments. All I know is that such moments of passionate abandon, within the circle of invisibility created by the veil, offer an emotional catharsis every bit as potent as any sexual release.

14   Outside, the rain pours from a sullen sky. I make my farewells and walk toward the car, where my driver waits. My veil is wicking muddy water from the sidewalk. I gather up the wet and grimy folds with distaste, longing to be home, where I can cast off this **(G)** curtain of cloth that gives with one hand, takes away with the other.

(D) Contradictory feelings are pushed together in a compact list.
(E) The writer offers definitions of passion reflecting three different perspectives.

ablutions
washing of the body with water

mullah's
a Muslim man educated in Islamic theology

(F) The writer uses terms of limited certainty, such as *perhaps* and *all I know.*
(G) The final line summarizes the contradictions described in the essay.

Reading for Better Writing

Working by yourself or with a group, do the following:

1. Sometimes writers use comparison-contrast organization to take a position on an issue—in some cases to show that one side is better than the other, but in others, to show the difficulty of choosing one side over the other. What do you think is Asayesh's position on hijab, and why?

2. Find Asayesh's one-sentence paragraph (paragraph 3). Why might the writer have constructed the paragraph in this way? How would this excerpt differ if that sentence had been part of either the preceding or the following paragraph?

3. What contrasts are listed in paragraph 4? How does the writer use sentence structure and punctuation to mark the contrasts?

4. In paragraph 13, Asayesh uses words that indicate limited certainty, such as *perhaps* and *all I know.* How do these phrases temper her claims?

5. In what ways are the opening and closing sentences alike? How are these similarities significant for readers?

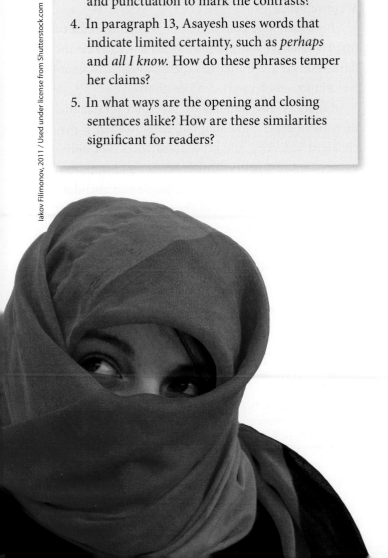

Iakov Filimonov, 2011 / Used under license from Shutterstock.com

Use comparison-contrast strategies to analyze, illustrate, or define concepts.

LO 4

Shanker Vedantam, a Nieman Fellow at Harvard University and science reporter for the *Washington Post,* wrote the following essay to define and analyze colorism. Note how he introduces his topic with an anecdote, supports his claims by citing academic studies, and uses comparison-contrast to analyze illustrate, or define concepts.

Shades of Prejudice

Survey • Question • Read • Recite • Review **SQ3R**

LAST week, the Senate majority leader, Harry Reid, found himself in trouble for once suggesting that Barack Obama had a political edge over other African-American candidates because he was "light-skinned" and had "no Negro dialect, unless he wanted to have one." Mr. Reid was not expressing sadness but a gleeful opportunism that Americans were still judging one another by the color of their skin, rather than—as the Rev. Dr. Martin Luther King Jr., whose legacy we commemorated on Monday, dreamed—by the content of their character. **1** **(A)**

The Senate leader's choice of words was flawed, but positing that black candidates who look "less black" have a leg up is hardly more controversial than saying wealthy people have an advantage in elections. Dozens of research studies have shown that skin tone and other racial features play powerful roles in who gets ahead and who does not. These factors regularly determine who gets hired, who gets convicted and who gets elected. **2** **(B)**

(A) The writer uses an anecdote to introduce and illustrate his thesis.

(B) He asserts that research supports his thesis, but he cites no sources.

3
(C)   Consider: Lighter-skinned Latinos in the United States make $5,000 more on average than darker-skinned Latinos. The education test-score gap between light-skinned and dark-skinned African-Americans is nearly as large as the gap between whites and blacks.

4
(D)   The Harvard neuroscientist Allen Counter has found that in Arizona, California and Texas, hundreds of Mexican-American women have suffered mercury poisoning as a result of the use of skin-whitening creams. In India, where I was born, a best-selling line of women's cosmetics called Fair and Lovely has recently been supplemented by a product aimed at men called Fair and Handsome.

5
(E)   This isn't racism, per se: it's colorism, an unconscious prejudice that isn't focused on a single group like blacks so much as on blackness itself. Our brains, shaped by culture and history, create intricate caste hierarchies that privilege those who are physically and culturally whiter and punish those who are darker.

6   Colorism is an **intraracial** problem as well as an **interracial** problem. Racial minorities who are alert to white-black or white-brown issues often remain silent about a colorism that asks "how black" or "how brown" someone is within their own communities.

7
(F)   If colorism lives underground, its effects are very real. Darker-skinned African-American defendants are more than twice as likely to receive the death penalty as lighter-skinned African-American defendants for crimes of equivalent seriousness involving white victims. This was proven in rigorous, peer-reviewed research into hundreds of capital punishment-worthy cases by the Stanford psychologist Jennifer Eberhardt.

(C) He offers examples.
(D) He supports his point by referring to his colleague's research.
(E) The writer distinguishes racism and colorism by comparing and contrasting the nature and effects of each.
(F) To support his claim, he gives an example and cites a study.

intraracial
within the same race
interracial
involving different races

8   Take, for instance, two of Dr. Eberhardt's murder cases, in Philadelphia, involving black defendants—one light-skinned, the other dark. The lighter-skinned defendant, Arthur Hawthorne, ransacked a drug store for money and narcotics. The pharmacist had complied with every demand, yet Mr. Hawthorne shot him when he was lying face down. Mr. Hawthorne was independently identified as the killer by multiple (G) witnesses, a family member and an accomplice.

9   The darker-skinned defendant, Ernest Porter, pleaded not guilty to the murder of a beautician, a crime that he was linked to only through a circuitous chain of evidence. A central witness later said that prosecutors forced him to finger Mr. Porter even though he was sure that he was the wrong man. Two people who provided an alibi for Mr. Porter were mysteriously never called to testify. During his trial, Mr. Porter revealed that the police had even gotten his name wrong—his real name was Theodore Wilson—but the court stuck to the wrong name in the interest of convenience.

10   Both men were convicted. But the lighter-skinned (H) Mr. Hawthorne was given a life sentence, while the dark-skinned Mr. Porter has spent more than a quarter-century on Pennsylvania's death row.

11   Colorism also influenced the 2008 presidential (I) race. In an experiment that fall, Drew Westen, a psychologist at Emory, and other researchers shot different versions of a political advertisement in support of Mr. Obama. One version showed a light-skinned black family. Another version had the same script, but used a darker-skinned black family. Voters, at an unconscious level, were less inclined to support Mr. Obama after watching the ad featuring the darker-skinned family than were those who watched the ad with the lighter-skinned family.

(G) The writer compares and contrasts how people are treated by the legal system.
(H) He cites a similarity and a difference.
(I) He compares colorism in the legal system with colorism in politics.

12   Political operatives are certainly aware of this dynamic. During the campaign, a conservative group created attack ads linking Mr. Obama with Kwame

(J) Kilpatrick, the disgraced former mayor of Detroit, which darkened Mr. Kilpatrick's skin to have a more persuasive effect. Though there can be little doubt that as a candidate Mr. Obama faced voters' conscious and unconscious prejudices, it is simultaneously true that unconscious colorism subtly advantaged him over darker-skinned politicians.

13   In highlighting how Mr. Obama benefited from

(K) his links to whiteness, Harry Reid punctured the myth that Mr. Obama's election signaled the completion of the Rev. King's dream. Americans may like to believe that we are now color-blind, that we can consciously choose not to use race when making judgments about other people. It remains a worthy aspiration. But this belief rests on a profound misunderstanding about how our minds work and perversely limits our ability to discuss prejudice honestly.

(J) To support his claim, he offers an example.
(K) To restate his thesis and unify his essay, the writer refers to the anecdote used in the opening.

Reading for Better Writing

Working by yourself or with a group, do the following:

1. Describe how Shankar Vedantam uses an anecdote to open and close his essay. Then explain why you do or do not find that strategy effective.

2. The writer asserts that (a) colorism and racism are different and that (b) colorism is both an intraracial problem and an interracial problem. Explain what he means by each assertion and why you do or do not agree.

3. Review paragraphs 7–10 in which the writer compares and contrasts penalties meted out by the legal system. Then explain why this strategy does or does not help develop his thesis.

4. Note how the writer uses dashes in paragraphs 8 and 9, and then explain why that use is or is not correct.

5. In January 18, 2010, the writer published this essay in *The New York Times*. Cite words or sentences showing that his voice is or is not appropriate for his subject and audience.

6. In paragraphs 11 and 12, Vedantam describes two advertisements that displayed colorism. What is your reaction to the tactics displayed by the advertisers?

Write, revise, and edit a compare-contrast essay.

LO5

Writing Guidelines

Planning

1. **Select a topic.** List subjects that are similar and/ or different in ways that you find interesting, perplexing, disgusting, infuriating, charming, or informing. Then choose two subjects whose comparison and/or contrast gives the reader some insight into who or what they are. *Note:* Make sure that the items have a solid *basis* for comparison. Comparable items are types of the same thing (e.g., two rivers, two characters, two films, two mental illnesses, two banking regulations, two search engines, two theories).

2. **Get the big picture.** Using a computer or a paper and pen, create three columns as shown below. Brainstorm a list of traits under each heading. (Also see the Venn diagram on page 50.)

Features Peculiar to Subject #1	Shared Features	Features Peculiar to Subject #2

3. **Gather information.** Review your list of features, highlighting those that could provide insight into one or both subjects. Research the subjects, using hands-on analysis when possible. Consider writing your research notes in the three-column format shown above.

4. **Draft a working thesis.** Review your expanded list of features and eliminate those that now seem unimportant. Write a sentence stating the core of what you learned about the subjects: what essential insight have you reached about the similarities and/or differences between the topics? If you're stuck, try completing the sentence below. (Switch around the terms "similar" and "different" if you wish to stress similarities.)

Whereas _____ and _____ seem similar, they are different in several ways, and the differences are important because _____ .

5. **Get organized.** Decide how to organize your essay. Generally, *subject by subject* works better for short, simple comparisons. *Trait by trait* works better for longer, more complex comparisons, in that you hold up the topics side by side, trait by trait. Consider, as well, the order in which you will discuss the topics and arrange the traits, choices that depend on what you want to feature and how you want to build and deepen the comparison.

Subject by Subject:	**Trait by Trait:**
Introduction	Introduction
Subject #1	Trait A
▪ Trait A	▪ Subject #1
▪ Trait B	▪ Subject #2
Subject #2	Trait B
▪ Trait A	▪ Subject #1
▪ Trait B	▪ Subject #2

Drafting

6. **Write your first draft.** Review your outline and draft the paper.

Subject-by-subject pattern:

Opening: get readers' attention, introduce the subjects, and offer a thesis.

Middle: discuss the first subject, then analyze the second subject, discussing traits parallel to those you addressed with the first subject.

Conclusion: summarize similarities, differences, and implications.

Trait-by-trait pattern:

Opening: get readers' attention, introduce the subjects, and offer a thesis.

Middle: compare and/or contrast the two subjects trait by trait; include transitions that help readers look back and forth between the two subjects.

Conclusion: summarize the key relationships and note their significance.

Revising

7. Get feedback. Ask someone to read your paper, looking for a clear thesis, an engaging introduction, a middle that compares and/or contrasts parallel traits in a logical order, and a unifying closing.

8. Rework your draft. Based on feedback, revise for the following issues:

Ideas: The points made and conclusions drawn from comparing and contrasting provide insight into both subjects.

Organization: The structure, whether subject by subject or trait by trait, helps readers grasp the similarities and differences between the subjects.

Voice: The tone is informed, involved, and genuine.

Editing and Proofreading

9. Carefully edit your essay. Look for the following issues:

Words are precise, clear, and defined as needed.

Sentences are clear, well reasoned, varied in structure, and smooth.

The **copy** is **correct**, clean, and properly formatted. Graphics are well-placed.

Page design is attractive and follows MLA or APA guidelines.

Publishing

10. Publish the essay. Share your writing by submitting it to your instructor, posting it on a Web site, sharing it with friends and family who might be interested in the topic, crafting a presentation or demonstration, or reshaping your writing as a blog.

Critical-Thinking and Writing Activities

As directed by your instructor, complete the following activities.

1. Review Rachel De Smith's analysis of Toni Morrison's Sethe and Barbara Kingsolver's Orleanna Price. Then choose two characters from other literary works and write an analysis of them using compare and/or contrast organization.

2. Review Gelareh Asayesh's article "Shrouded in Contradiction," noting how she uses comparison-contrast strategies in order to take a position. Draft or revise an essay in which you use comparison-contrast to develop or support your thesis.

3. Re-examine how Shankar Vedantam opens and closes "Shades of Prejudice" with an anecdote (or a news story) that was current when he wrote the essay. Revise one of your recent essays by selecting a recent news story that you can use to develop your thesis. For example, you might use the story to get readers' attention or to compare the story with a parallel situation addressed in your paper.

4. Write an essay in which you compare and contrast two people, using subject-by-subject organization. Then revise the essay using trait-by-trait organization. Finally, discuss the essays with a classmate to determine which strategy works better.

Checklist: Learning Outcomes

After reading the essays in this chapter, developing your own comparison-contrast essay, and getting feedback from classmates and your instructor, use this checklist to assess how effectively you achieved the learning outcomes for this chapter:

_____ I understand comparison-contrast reasoning, both as a reader and a writer.

_____ I am able to structure compare-contrast writing either subject by subject or trait by trait, and I understand when to use which pattern.

_____ I know how to support compare-contrast reasoning with concrete and precise details, as well as with transitional words that clarify similarities and differences.

_____ I can use comparison-contrast to analyze, illustrate, and define a concept.

_____ I have effectively planned, drafted, revised, and polished a compare-contrast essay.

"Shallow men believe in luck.
Strong men believe in cause and effect."
Ralph Waldo Emerson

14

Cause-Effect

Now, why did that happen? We ask this question every day at home, in college, and on the job in order to understand and cope with things that happen in our lives. For example, knowing why a computer crashed will help us avoid that problem, and knowing the causes and effects of a disease such as diabetes can help us control the condition. In other words, cause and effect reasoning helps us deal with everyday issues, whether large or small.

In a cause and effect essay, the writer develops the thesis through cause and effect reasoning. That is, she or he analyzes and explains the causes, the effects, or both the causes and the effects of a **phenomenon**. This chapter includes instructions and models that will help you read and write cause-effect analyses.

Learning Outcomes

LO1 Understand how to read cause-effect writing.

LO2 Make limited and logical cause-effect claims.

LO3 Support cause-effect reasoning with relevant, reliable evidence.

LO4 Avoid logical fallacies.

LO5 Write, revise, and edit a cause-effect essay.

phenomenon
a fact, occurrence, or circumstance

Understand how to read cause-effect writing. LO1

When reading cause-effect writing, note the writer's rhetorical situation and study his or her logic.

Consider the rhetorical situation.

Assess how the writer's purpose, audience, and topic affect his or her writing strategies.

Purpose. Writers use cause-effect analysis to deepen understanding about how specific forces work to bring about particular results. In academia and the workplace, cause-effect logic operates in many forms of writing—from persuasive essays and lab reports to project proposals and market analyses. In each situation, writers use cause-effect thinking to explain a phenomenon or to prove a point.

Audience. The audience for cause-effect writing typically have a basic understanding of the topic but want or need a deeper understanding of the forces operating within it—understanding that may help them make decisions about or take positions on the issue.

Topic. Cause-effect topics are phenomena—events, occurrences, developments, processes, problems, conditions, and so on—that need to be more fully explained in terms of their operating forces.

Consider the analytical logic.

As you read essays using cause-effect reasoning, identify the problem or phenomenon addressed and look for the following elements of strong cause-effect logic.

Clear Reasoning: The thesis clearly identifies a cause-effect idea, and the essay's body carefully and systematically explores and supports this idea. The writer also distinguishes between primary and secondary causes and effects.

Supporting Details: Claims identifying causes, effects, and the links between causes and effects are fully supported with reliable, detailed evidence. When appropriate, the writer uses visuals, tables, or multime-

dia elements effectively. Conversely, the writer avoids relying extensively on circumstantial evidence.

Logical Analyses: The reasoning is transparent, unified, and free of logical fallacies such as Bare Assertion (see 183), False Cause (see 184), Slippery Slope (see 184), and False Analogy (see 185).

Checklist: Cause-Effect Writing

- ✔ Is the writer's rationale for writing informed, reasonable, and convincing?
- ✔ Who is the intended audience, and does the essay present all the information that they need to understand and respond to the analysis?
- ✔ Is the topic clearly identified and explored as a phenomenon?
- ✔ Is the thesis clear, and is the argument free of logical fallacies?
- ✔ What claims does the writer make regarding causes and effects, and are the statements sufficiently limited, focused, and logical?
- ✔ Are supporting details well researched, relevant, and strong?

Make limited and logical cause-effect claims. LO2

To build a convincing cause-effect analysis, writers need to start with reasonable, measured claims about cause-effect links. When she wrote the essay below, Sarah Hanley was a college student who was also in the military. In the essay, Sarah uses both research and her military experience to explore the causes and effects of adrenaline highs. As you read her essay, note how she makes measured claims about the workings of adrenaline.

Adrenaline Junkies

Survey • Question • Read • Recite • Review   **SQ3R**

1 **(A)** Who are "adrenaline junkies"? Bungee jumpers hurling themselves from bridges? Mythbusters blowing up anything they can get hold of? Retirees excitedly stuffing quarters in slot machines? Actually, all three qualify as adrenaline junkies if they do the activities to get their adrenaline highs. But what, exactly, is an adrenaline high, what causes it, what are its effects, and are the effects positive?

2 **(B)** Adrenaline (also called epinephrine) is a hormone linked to the two adrenal glands located on top of the kidneys. Each gland has two parts: the outer portion called the cortex, and the inner portion called the medulla. When a person experiences an unusual exertion or a crisis situation, his or her brain triggers the medullas, which release little packets of adrenaline into the bloodstream (Nathan). The rush of adrenaline in the blood leads to increased blood pressure, heart rate, sugar **metabolism**, oxygen intake, and muscle strength. All these phenomena cause an adrenaline high: feeling highly alert and very energetic (Scheuller 2).

3 However, while all healthy people experience adrenaline highs, different people need different levels of **stimuli** to trigger the highs. The level of stimulus that a person

needs depends on the amount of protein in his or her medullas. In other words, the medullas release adrenaline through channels containing a certain protein. If the channels contain a large amount of the protein, they release adrenaline more easily than channels containing less protein. Therefore, a person with a higher level of protein in the channels of his or her medullas experiences an adrenaline release more easily than someone with a lower level of the protein (Scheuller 4).

4 To illustrate this difference, we'll call the people with a higher level of protein (and a more easily stimulated output of adrenaline) Type N, for nervous; the others we'll call Type C, for calm. Because Type N people release adrenaline more easily than Type C people do, Type Ns require a lesser stimulus to trigger an adrenaline release. For example, a Type N person may get an adrenaline high from finishing his research paper on time, whereas a Type C person will get a similar buzz only when she parachutes from a plane at 10,000 feet!

5 **(C)** While different people get their adrenaline highs differently, any person's highs can be channeled for healthy or harmful effects. For example, the Type N person who gets a rush from finishing the research project could do good work as a research technician in a science lab. As long as he avoids becoming a workaholic, seeking the highs won't threaten his health, and the work may contribute to the overall welfare of society. Similarly, the Type C person who gets her highs by jumping out of airplanes could do good work as a fire-fighter or a brain surgeon. As long as she gets periodic relief from the tension, the highs won't hurt her health, and the work could help her community.

6 **(D)** On the other hand, pursuing the wrong type of adrenaline high, or seeking too many highs, can be destructive. Examples of this kind of behavior include compulsive gambling, drug use, careless risk taking in sports, and win-at-all-cost business practices. De-

(C) She uses an illustration to clarify a point.
(D) An introductory phrase signals a shift in focus.

(A) The writer introduces the topic by asking a series of questions.
(B) She describes the causes and effects of an adrenaline high.

metabolism
chemical change of a substance in a living organism
stimuli
plural of "stimulus," something that provokes a change

structive pursuits have many high-cost results including bankruptcy, broken relationships, physical injury, drug addiction, and death (Lyons 3).

7
(E) Because adrenaline highs can lead to positive results, maybe people shouldn't worry about becoming adrenaline junkies. Instead, they should ask how to pursue those highs positively. In other words, the proteins, hormones, and chemical processes that produce adrenaline highs are, themselves, very good—and they can be used for good. In fact, someone may figure out how to bottle the stuff and put it on the market! *Note:* The works-cited page is not shown.

(E) The writer concludes by reviewing her main points.

Reading for Better Writing

1. Name two or more ways that the opening paragraph engages you and effectively introduces the topic and thesis.

2. Paragraphs 3 and 4 explain how different people need different levels of stimulus to trigger adrenaline highs. Is this explanation clear and believable? Why or why not?

3. In one sentence, summarize the writer's explanation of the causes and effects of an adrenaline high. Explain why you do or do not find these claims convincing.

4. The writer concludes the essay with a playful sentence suggesting that someday adrenaline may be bottled and sold. Explain why you think the sentence is or is not an effective closing.

5. The photograph to your right represents an adrenaline rush in the image of skydivers. If you were to choose an image to represent an adrenaline high, what would it be?

Support cause-effect reasoning with relevant, reliable evidence.

LO3

Writers need to back up cause-effect links with sound evidence. The following two essays model this process.

Use evidence from traditional research.

Student writer Brittany Korver wrote the following essay in 2008. In the paper, she analyzes how the increasing number of Muslim residents in the Netherlands is impacting Dutch culture and raising tension within a society known for its diversity and tolerance.

Dutch Discord

(A)

Survey • Question • Read • Recite • Review **SQ3R**

1 When people outside the Netherlands think of the Dutch, what do they envision? Some may picture **stoic** (B) windmills, grass-covered **dikes**, and tidy row houses. Others may see barge-filled canals, gay parades, and red-light districts. Still others may envision the Free University in Amsterdam, the harbor in Rotterdam, and the International Court of Justice in The Hague. But when people inside the Netherlands think of common sites in their country, they likely also picture the growing number of domed mosques in Dutch city skylines, veiled faces in the streets, or scarf-covered heads in the classrooms. The fact is, these images are

(A) The title identifies the phenomenon.
(B) Introduction: Dutch symbols and ethnic tensions

increasingly common in the Netherlands as its Muslim population continues to grow and spread ("One Million Muslims"). More importantly, however, this **diffusion** appears to have increased tension between the progressive ethnic Dutch—long known for tolerating cultural differences—and their new neighbors.

2   The first, most notable influx of Muslims was drawn to the Netherlands after World War II by job offers (Shadid 10). The Dutch, looking for cheap labor, recruited large numbers of unskilled laborers from poorer countries (10). These immigrants were typically guest workers who expected to stay temporarily and then return to their homelands, as many of them did (Sunier 318).

3   By 1973, an economic crisis hit Europe, and the Netherlands no longer needed extra workers (Van Amersfoort 179). Many Muslims, however, decided to stay because the economic conditions in their home countries were even less desirable than conditions in the Netherlands (Ketner 146). Numerous immigrants became permanent residents and were joined by their families. When the Dutch finally tightened restrictions by lowering quotas and raising standards for refugees, marriages continued between Dutch-Muslim citizens and Muslim foreigners. Since family reunification is a Dutch migration priority, these spouses continued to flow into the Netherlands (Van Amersfoort 179). In addition, the Netherlands experienced increased illegal immigration (179).

4   However, while legal and illegal immigrants increased the Netherlands' Muslim population significantly, the population swelled even more because of Muslims' relatively high fertility rates (Kent). For example, as of 2004, CBS (the Netherlands' statistics bureau) reported 945 thousand Muslims living in the country, a jump of over 339 thousand from ten years earlier ("One Million Muslims"). They currently account for at least 5.8 percent of the population, which makes Muslims the fourth largest religious group in the Netherlands, trailing just behind Dutch Calvinists ("As many Muslims as Calvinists"). While Muslims are distributed quite sparsely in some provinces

(e.g., less than 3 percent in Friesland), they make up as much as one third of the population in cities such as Amsterdam (Rawstome 30).

5   Not surprisingly, this growing minority is both affecting and being affected by Dutch culture. Ethnic foods are increasingly available in stores and restaurants (Wagensveld). New shops and market stands accommodate the demand for folk clothing (Wagensveld). Private Islamic schools are available, and mosques dot the landscape (Landman 1125). Coverage of Turk and Moroccan culture, including their religious festivals, fill many pages in the Netherlands' souvenir books (DeRooi 107). In addition, businesses cater to their new consumers by including dark-haired people in their ads and abandoning potentially offensive practices, such as distributing piggy-banks (Charter 40).

6   Dutch culture also leaves its mark on this new community. For example, many Muslims find themselves forgetting Islamic holidays because they are too busy or do not know the Arabic calendar ("Time and Migration" 387). Many have adjusted to the Dutch view of time, making their lives faster paced. Some save religious prayers for after work, disrupting the normal prayer schedule (390). In fact, even some mosques encourage change by offering immigrants Dutch language classes, computer courses, and bicycle lessons (Van Amersfoort 185–186).

7   Though assimilation between most cultural groups in the Netherlands is common, the ethnic Dutch and those who trace their roots to Muslim countries retain **conspicuous** differences, sometimes leading to tensions between them. For example, fertility runs

---

(D) 2 Impact of Dutch and Muslim cultures on each other
(E) 3 Secondary differences between Dutch and Muslim cultures

stoic
steadfast, displaying no emotion

dike
an embankment of earth to prevent flooding

diffusion
the slow spread of one thing into another

conspicuous
noticeable

(C) 1 Social changes brought about by immigration: history

higher among these immigrants, prompting some ethnic Dutch to fear that they will eventually become a minority (Kent). Muslims still have lower education levels, high levels of unemployment, and poorer housing than most other residents. And among second generation Muslims, dropout rates and delinquencies run high (Mamadouh 198).

8
(F) However, the chief challenges that ethnic Dutch have in relating to their Muslim neighbors have little to do with **demographic** characteristics or economic standing, and more to do with cultural practices and worldviews. For example, ethnic Dutch have difficulty accepting or respecting traditional Muslim views regarding women's roles in society and homosexual lifestyles, as well as resident Muslims' high crime rate and violent Islamic extremism ("Veils and Wooden Clogs" 230). The ethnic Dutch are repulsed by stories of wife beating, arranged marriages, women forbidden to hold jobs, homosexuals put to death in the immigrants' home countries, terrorist attacks in Western countries, and violent crimes committed by immigrants in the Netherlands (230). This cultural clash has led the Netherlands to re-evaluate and in some ways re-direct its pursuit of a multi-cultural state and return to the nation-state model as the ideal (198 Mamadouh).

9
(G) In some cases, tensions have evolved into an "us" vs. "them" mentality that includes covert and overt racism and hostility (Shadid16). In the journal *European Education,* Wasif A. Shadid makes this point by comparing some attitudes in Holland with what appear to be parallel attitudes in South Africa's **apartheid** system. Examples of these tensions or attitudes include increasing differentiation between the native Dutch and immigrant groups, politicians speaking negatively of Muslim residents (11-16), and sometimes violent acts between Muslims and non-Muslims (Esman 12).

(F) 4 Major differences: cultural practices and world view
(G) (a) us vs. them mentality

demographic
characteristics of a population

apartheid
a system of racial separation

Since the turn of the millennium, the ethnic 10
Dutch fear of Islamic extremism has also increased, (H) brought on in part by international events such as the September 11, 2001 attacks in the United States, and the subsequent strikes in Madrid and London. This fear was further intensified when two well-known anti-Islam Dutch politicians were assassinated inside the Netherlands. The first was Pim Fortuyn, who was shot in 2002 (Shadid 17). Fortuyn had his own political party, which called for "stopping all immigration" and a "cold war against Islam" (Esman 12). His assassination created a stir because the Dutch suddenly found their freedom of speech jeopardized, thereby widening the rift between the Dutch and Muslim cultures (Wagensveld).

The second Dutch politician assassinated was Theo 11
Van Gogh in 2004, and this event is often referred to as the September 11 of the Netherlands (Esman 12). Like Fortuyn, Van Gogh was very outspoken. He also used offensive language, gained many young followers (Margaronis 6), and went on to make the movie *Submission* with ex-Muslim and screen writer, Ayaan Hirsi Ali, a film that exposed Dutch-Muslim domestic abuse (6). Van Gogh was shot and stabbed to death, resulting in a martyr-like legacy for his cause (Rawstome 30).

The most recent tension-building event was the 12
March 2008 release of the controversial movie *Fitna* (Arabic for strife), directed by Dutch MP Geert Wilders (Rawstome 30). The short movie displays graphic and disturbing images of terrorism and abuse, and it uses quotes from the Koran and Islamic leaders, suggesting that both sources support these violent actions (*Fitna*). The movie is so controversial that fear of violent repercussions is widespread, and many Netherlanders think that Wilders was irresponsible for releasing it (Rawstome 30). Wilders received six hundred death threats by late March, has six body guards, and at times he and his wife live in prison cells for safety (30).

As events like these suggest, the growth of the 13
Muslim community in the Netherlands appears to (I) have increased the tension between the ethnic Dutch

---

(H) (b) fear of extremism, terrorism, and assassinations
(I) Conclusion: Tensions lead to fear and alienation.

and Muslims. As a result, many ethnic Dutch feel disconcerted, and many Dutch Muslims feel alienated (Shadid 20). Whether those who built windmills and those who build mosques will ever live together in unity remains unclear. But what is clear is that such unity never will happen until the two groups learn to live with the differences that now separate them.

Reading for Better Writing

Working by yourself or with a group, do the following:

1. Do the title and opening paragraph effectively get your attention and introduce the topic? Explain. How do the opening and closing paragraphs unite the essay?

2. Brittany Korver wrote this essay expecting that it would be read by other college students and her professor. Review her topic, thesis, and core argument; then explain why they are or are not fitting choices for her audience.

3. In paragraphs 2–4, Brittany uses chronological order to explain how the Muslim population in the Netherlands increased. Review those paragraphs and explain whether her organization and details adequately describe the increase.

4. Note how the writer builds paragraphs 7–9 by opening each with a topic sentence and following with documented supporting details. Then explain why these choices do or do not strengthen her argument.

5. In paragraphs 10–12, the writer describes three violent events that transpired since 2002. Explain why she might cite these events and whether she uses them effectively to develop her thesis.

6. If Brittany's essay were a magazine article, what visuals might deepen readers' understanding of the causes and effects she analyzes? What visuals would be counterproductive?

Use statistics and interviews as evidence.

In the essay below (originally published as an article in *US News & World Report*), Mary Brophy Marcus describes successful businesswomen and argues that the skills they learned from organized sports helped them achieve that success. Notice how she uses legal changes, statistics, and individual cases and testimonies as evidence to support her cause-effect reasoning.

If You Let Me Play . . .

Survey • Question • Read • Recite • Review   **SQ3R**

Jackie Thomas, Nike's associate director of sports marketing, usually spends her lunch hour on the sports-shoe company's basketball courts charging for the basket, always outnumbered by male colleagues. "I hold my own," boasts the 33-year-old executive. **(1)** **(A)**

She also does well playing the corporate game back inside the headquarters' offices. Thomas, a former University of California–Berkeley college basketball point guard, says her success is due in large part to the lessons she learned growing up playing competitive team sports. "It's taught me that if you lose a game, you go back afterward and figure out what went wrong and how to overcome it the next time," says the former tomboy from Kingston, Jamaica. **(2)**

While most of America's corporations are still commanded by male chief executives, women are gaining ground, winning vice-presidential and top management slots and, in a few cases, the highest leadership roles. Many of these young female executives say playing team sports helped them get ahead. A University of Virginia study conducted in the late 1980s showed that 80 percent of key female leaders from *Fortune* 500 companies said they participated in sports and considered themselves tomboys. **(3)** **(B)**

(A) The writer uses an anecdote to introduce the topic and focus the essay.
(B) A dependent clause links the second and third paragraphs.

4

(C) A lot of credit, female executives say, has to go to Title IX, part of the Federal Education Amendments Act of 1972. It mandated that federally funded schools give women's sports the same treatment as men's games receive. That meant that in schools and colleges across the United States, for every boy's **varsity** soccer team, there must be a girl's varsity soccer team; for every male basketball scholarship, there must be a female basketball scholarship of equal dollars. Since the early 1970s, the law has increased money for new equipment, coaches, and travel for women's teams. More college scholarships have translated into more diplomas and better jobs for women. Thomas earned a partial academic scholarship when she applied to Berkeley, one of the country's top universities, but without an additional basketball scholarship awarded in her junior and senior years, she would have had a hard time paying for the education.

5

(D) Girls' participation in high school sports has spiked from about 300,000 in 1971 to 2.4 million in 1996. At the college level, where competition is tougher, the number of female athletes has increased to 123,832 from 80,040 in 1982, says the National Collegiate Athletic Association.

6

(E) "No other experience I know of can prepare you for the high-level competition of business," says Anh Ngyuen, 25, a former Carnegie Mellon University varsity soccer star. She should know. Now she battles Microsoft as a product manager for Netscape Communications. "My colleagues can't believe how aggressive I am," she says.

7

Sports helped these women master the interpersonal skills, like teamwork, that many men take for

starfotograf © iStockphoto

granted. "I've seen firsthand hundreds and hundreds of times that one person can't win a soccer or softball game," says Maria Murnane, a 28-year-old senior account executive for a San Francisco public-relations firm. "Same goes for work. You have to learn to trust the people on your team, let them run with projects," the former Northwestern soccer center midfielder says. Her boss, William Harris, the president of Strategy Associates, agrees: "We don't want Lone Rangers. She's a team player—a captain and cheerleader."

8

Playing team sports helps with the little things, too. Women learn to speak in sports **metaphors** as many men do. Lisa Delpy, professor of sports management at George Washington University in Washington, D.C., also notes that in many companies a lot of business is conducted on the golf course, at ball games, or at other sports events. Women who know the difference between a slide tackle and a sweeper at a World Cup soccer match can fit right in.

9

(F) Stephanie Delaney, now 31, captained the varsity soccer team at Franklin and Marshall College in Lancaster, Pennsylvania, when it won the Mid-Atlantic Conference championship her senior year. Now the sales manager for the Caribbean and Latin Ameri-

---

(C) The writer describes events (or causes) that helped women gain valuable skills in sports.
(D) Using statistical evidence, she cites effects of the causes described in the previous paragraph.
(E) A quotation supports the writer's thesis: Skills learned in sports help one succeed in business.

varsity
the primary sports team of a high school, college, or university

metaphors
figures of speech using one thing to represent another

(F) The writer supports her thesis with an anecdote.

can division of ConAgra's Lamb-Weston, one of the world's largest frozen-french-fry producers, she was the only woman to play a game of basketball with potential clients at a big food conference last year in Jamaica. "I was the high scorer," she notes.

10 And yes, it helped sell french fries. "I didn't close (G) the deal on the court, but afterward when we were hanging out drinking water and shooting the breeze, they agreed to test my product. Now we have Kentucky Fried Chicken's business in Jamaica," says Delaney.

11 Female executives say that Title IX had another subtle, but important, effect. For the first time, many boys, coaches, and parents opened their eyes to the fact that their sisters and daughters could be just as strong, fast, and nimble on the field as their brothers and sons. Likewise, girls whose talents had formerly gone unnoticed under driveway basketball nets and (H) on back lots began realizing their own power—that they could compete with boys and win. "When my girlfriends and I formed a softball team back in college, we were dreadful—like the **Keystone Kops**," recalls Penny Cate, 45, now a vice president at Quaker Oats. "There'd be four of us in the outfield and the ball would go through our legs. But after a few years, we became very good. It built my confidence, made me realize I could accomplish anything in sports or out," she says.

12 That point is repeatedly brought home when Nike executives ask schoolgirls what they think of one of (I) the company's TV ads. The ad begins with the voice of a young girl saying, "If you let me play . . . ." The phrase is finished by other little girls saying things like, "I will have greater self-confidence" or "I will be more likely to stay in school."

13 The girls often reply, in a tone of genuine befuddlement, "If who lets me play?" They don't see any barriers between themselves and America's playing fields. Twenty years from now, might they say, "*What* glass ceiling?"

(G) A lively quotation offers interesting details.

(H) The dash links the word *power* to the defining clause that follows.

(I) The writer cites an advertisement from which she created the essay's title and with which she advances her thesis.

Reading for Better Writing

Working by yourself or with a group, do the following:

1. Review the writer's title and her reference to it late in the essay. How does the writer use the title to introduce and advance her thesis?

2. Mary Brophy Marcus is a journalist who wrote this essay and many others for publications such as *US News & World Report* and *USA Today*. Review three or four paragraphs from the essay and explain how her word choice, sentence structure, and use of quotations are or are not appropriate for readers of periodicals like these.

3. Review the qualities of an academic style as discussed on pages 71–72. Then explain why Marcus's essay does or does not reflect this style. Cite specific passages to support your answer.

4. Marcus uses cause-effect reasoning to argue that (1) women's participation in sports produces valuable skills and (2) these skills help women succeed in business. Examine three points, along with the evidence (statistics, interviews, quotations, and other elements), that Marcus uses to support either of these claims. Finally, explain why each supporting point and its related evidence are or are not convincing.

5. Marcus concludes her essay with the question, "*What* glass ceiling?" Explain why the quotation does or does not (1) advance her thesis and (2) close the essay effectively.

6. Working with a classmate, review the checklist under Step 8, "Revise the essay," found on page 175. Then analyze to what degree this article reflects these traits.

Keystone Kops
an inept group of police in silent movies

Avoid logical fallacies. LO4

Steven Pinker teaches in the Department of Psychology at Harvard University where he also conducts research on language and cognition. He writes regularly for publications such as *Time* and *The New Republic,* and he is the author of seven books, including *How the Mind Works.* In the essay below, published as an op-ed piece in the *New York Times* on January 10, 2010, Pinker analyzes how our current use of electronic technologies affects our ability to think deeply and process information. Before you read his essay, review common logical fallacies such as bare assertion (page 183), false cause (page 184), slippery slope (page 184), and false analogy (page 185). As you read, mark up the article with your thoughts and questions tracking the cause-effect thinking Pinker uses.

Mind Over Mass Media

Survey · Question · Read · Recite · Review **SQ3R**

1   NEW forms of media have always caused moral panics: the printing press, newspapers, paperbacks and television were all once denounced as threats to their consumers' brainpower and moral fiber.

2   So too with electronic technologies. PowerPoint, we're told, is reducing **discourse** to bullet points. Search engines lower our intelligence, encouraging us to skim on the surface of knowledge rather than dive to its depths. Twitter is shrinking our attention spans.

3   But such panics often fail basic reality checks. When comic books were accused of turning juveniles into delinquents in the 1950s, crime was falling to record lows, just as the **denunciations** of video games in the 1990s coincided with the great American crime decline. The decades of television, transistor radios and rock videos were also decades in which I.Q. scores rose continuously.

4   For a reality check today, take the state of science, which demands high levels of brainwork and is measured by clear benchmarks of discovery. These days scientists are never far from their e-mail, rarely touch paper and cannot lecture without PowerPoint. If electronic media were hazardous to intelligence, the quality of science would be plummeting. Yet discoveries are multiplying like fruit flies, and progress is dizzying. Other activities in the life of the mind, like philosophy, history and cultural criticism, are likewise flourishing, as anyone who has lost a morning of work to the Web site *Arts & Letters Daily* can attest.

5   Critics of new media sometimes use science itself to press their case, citing research that shows how "experience can change the brain." But **cognitive** neuroscientists roll their eyes at such talk. Yes, every time we learn a fact or skill the wiring of the brain changes; it's not as if the information is stored in the pancreas. But the existence of **neural plasticity** does not mean the brain is a blob of clay pounded into shape by experience.

6   Experience does not revamp the basic information-processing capacities of the brain. Speed-reading programs have long claimed to do just that, but the verdict was rendered by Woody Allen after he read *War and Peace* in one sitting: "It was about Russia." Genuine multitasking, too, has been exposed as a myth, not just by laboratory studies but by the familiar sight of an S.U.V. undulating between lanes as the driver cuts deals on his cellphone.

7   Moreover, as the psychologists Christopher Chabris and Daniel Simons show in their new book *The Invisible Gorilla: And Other Ways Our Intuitions Deceive Us,* the effects of experience are highly specific to the experiences themselves. If you train people to

discourse
communication, discussion

denunciation
condemnation

cognitive
having to do with thinking

neural plasticity
adaptability of nerve cells

Angela Waye , 2011 / Used under license from Shutterstock.com

do one thing (recognize shapes, solve math puzzles, find hidden words), they get better at doing that thing, but almost nothing else. Music doesn't make you better at math, conjugating Latin doesn't make you more logical, brain-training games don't make you smarter. Accomplished people don't bulk up their brains with intellectual **calisthenics**; they immerse themselves in their fields. Novelists read lots of novels, scientists read lots of science.

8   The effects of consuming electronic media are also likely to be far more limited than the panic implies. Media critics write as if the brain takes on the qualities of whatever it consumes, the informational equivalent of "you are what you eat." As with primitive peoples who believe that eating fierce animals will make them fierce, they assume that watching quick cuts in rock videos turns your mental life into quick cuts or that reading bullet points and Twitter postings turns your thoughts into bullet points and Twitter postings.

9   Yes, the constant arrival of information packets can be distracting or addictive, especially to people with **attention deficit disorder**. But distraction is not a new phenomenon. The solution is not to bemoan technology but to develop strategies of self-control, as we do with every other temptation in life. Turn off e-mail or Twitter when you work, put away your Blackberry at dinner time, ask your spouse to call you to bed at a designated hour.

10   And to encourage intellectual depth, don't rail at PowerPoint or Google. It's not as if habits of deep reflection, thorough research and rigorous reasoning ever came naturally to people. They must be acquired in special institutions, which we call universities, and maintained with constant upkeep, which we call analysis, criticism and debate. They are not granted by propping a heavy encyclopedia on your lap, nor are they taken away by efficient access to information on the Internet.

11   The new media have caught on for a reason. Knowledge is increasing **exponentially**; human brainpower and waking hours are not. Fortunately, the Internet and information technologies are helping us manage, search and retrieve our collective intellectual output at different scales, from Twitter and previews to e-books and online encyclopedias. Far from making us stupid, these technologies are the only things that will keep us smart.

Reading for Better Writing

Working by yourself or with a group, do the following:

1. Review Pinker's opening paragraph in which he introduces his topic by suggesting that current allegations regarding the negative impact of electronic technologies are similar to past allegations regarding the impact of the printing press, newspapers, paperbacks, and television. Paraphrase his claim, explain why you do or do not agree, and explain whether the opening is or is not effective.

2. The essay is organized as a series of critics' arguments asserting the negative impact of new media, followed by Pinker's counterarguments. Identify three of these exchanges and explain how the point-counterpoint format clarifies both sides of the argument while also making Pinker's position more convincing.

3. Note that Pinker uses cause-effect logic to identify weaknesses in others' claims and to assert the value of his own claims. Identify an example of each that you find persuasive and explain why.

4. Pinker is a scholar aiming to analyze an academic topic with thoughtful, well-researched arguments in an informed, academic tone. Cite passages that illustrate this voice.

5. Study the image on the previous page. How does the image relate to Pinker's analysis? Does the visual content effectively reinforce his claims?

calisthenics
physical exercises

attention deficit disorder
a condition making concentration difficult and often causing hyperactivity

exponential
a number increasing by a curve rather than linearly

Write, revise, and edit a cause-effect essay. LO5

Writing Guidelines

Planning

1. **Select a topic.** Begin by thinking about categories such as those listed below and listing phenomena related to each category. From this list, choose a topic and analyze its causes, its effects, or both.

   - **Family Life:** adult children living with parents, more stay-at-home dads, families simplifying their lifestyles, adults squeezed by needs of children and parents
   - **Politics:** fewer student voters, increasing support for green-energy production, increased interest in third-party politics, tension between political-action groups
   - **Society:** nursing shortage, doctor shortage, terrorist threats, increasing immigrant-advocacy efforts, shifting ethnic ratios, decreasing number of newspapers
   - **Environment:** common water pollutants, new water-purification technology, decreasing U.S. space exploration, increasing number of wind turbines

2. **Narrow and research the topic.** State your topic and below it, list related causes and effects in two columns. Next, do preliminary research to expand the list and distinguish primary causes and effects from secondary ones. Revise your topic as needed to address only primary causes and/or effects that research links to a specific phenomenon.

Cause/Effect Topic: _____

Causes (Because of)	Effects (this results)
1. _____	1. _____
2. _____	2. _____
3. _____	3. _____

3. **Draft and test your thesis.** Based on your preliminary research, draft a working thesis (you may revise it later) that introduces the topic, along with the causes and/or effects you intend to discuss. Limit your argument to only those points you can prove.

4. **Gather and analyze information.** Research your topic, looking for clear evidence that links specific causes to specific effects. As you study the phenomenon, distinguish between primary and secondary causes (main and contributing), direct and indirect results, short-term and long-term effects, and so on. At the same time, test your analysis to avoid mistaking a coincidence for a cause-effect relationship. Use the list of logical fallacies (see pages 182–185) to weed out common errors in logic. For example, finding chemical pollutants in a stream running beside a chemical plant does not "prove" that the plant caused the pollutants. In addition, carefully study any tables, diagrams, graphs, images, or videos that clarify the topic's causes and/or effects.

5. **Get organized.** Develop an outline that lays out your thesis and argument in a clear pattern. Under each main point asserting a cause-effect connection, list details from your research that support the connection.

Point #1	Point #2	Point #3
▪ Supporting details	▪ Supporting details	▪ Supporting details
▪ Supporting details	▪ Supporting details	▪ Supporting details

Drafting

6. **Use your outline to draft the essay.** Try to rough out the essay's overall argument before you attempt to revise it. As you write, show how specific causes led to specific effects, citing examples as needed. To show those cause-effect relationships, use transitional words like the following:

accordingly	since
as a result	so
because	such as
consequently	thereby
for this purpose	therefore
for this reason	thus
hence	to illustrate
just as	whereas

Revising

7. Get feedback. Ask a peer reviewer or someone from the college's writing center to read your essay for an engaging opening, a thoughtful cause-effect thesis, clear and convincing reasoning that links specific causes to specific effects, and a closing that deepens and extends the cause-effect analysis of the phenomenon.

8. Revise the essay. Whether your essay presents causes, effects, or both, use the checklist below to trace and refine your argument.

Ideas: The essay explains the causes and/or effects of the topic in a clear, well-reasoned analysis. The analysis is supported by credible information and is free of logical fallacies.

Organization: The structure helps clarify the cause-effect relationships through a well-traced line of thinking; and the links between the main points, supporting points, and evidence are clear.

Voice: The tone is informed, polite, logical and measured.

Editing and Proofreading

9. Edit the essay for clarity and correctness. Check for the following:

Words: The diction is precise and clear, and technical or scientific terms are defined. Causes are linked to effects with transitional words and phrases.

Sentences: Structures are clear, varied, and smooth.

Correctness: The writing is correct in terms of grammar, punctuation, mechanics, usage, and spelling.

Design: The format, layout, and typography adhere to expectation; any visuals used enhance the written analysis and clarify the paper's cause-effect reasoning.

Publishing

10. Publish your essay. Share your writing by submitting it to your instructor, posting it on the class's or department's Web site, or turning it into a presentation.

Critical-Thinking and Writing Activities

As directed by your instructor, complete the following activities.

1. In "Dutch Discord," Brittany Korver analyzes the causes and effects of a shift in the Netherlands' immigration practices. Identify a similar shift in the policies or practices of a city, state, or country that interests you. Then write an essay in which you analyze the causes and effects of this shift.

2. In "If You Let Me Play . . . ," Mary Brophy Marcus uses cause-effect reasoning to analyze how Jackie Thomas's experience in college athletics helped her prepare for a successful business career. Identify experiences that will help you prepare for your career. Then write an essay in which you use cause-effect reasoning to prove your claim.

3. "Mind Over Mass Media" analyzes changes brought by technology. Identify a technological change that has impacted your life; then analyze the causes or effects of that change.

4. Scan editorials in two or three newspapers, looking for arguments based on cause-effect reasoning. Then examine the arguments for logical fallacies such as false-cause or slippery-slope claims (for help, see page 184). Present your findings to the class.

5. List the kinds of documents written by workers in your planned career and identify which ones are likely based on cause-effect reasoning. Then find examples of two or three of these documents, analyze the quality of the writing, and share your findings with the class.

Checklist: Learning Outcomes

Use this checklist to assess how effectively you achieved the learning outcomes for this chapter:

_____ I understand how to read cause-effect writing.

_____ I can make limited and logical cause-effect claims.

_____ I can support cause-effect reasoning with relevant, reliable evidence.

_____ I can avoid logical fallacies that derail cause-effect reasoning.

_____ I have effectively written, revised, and edited a cause-effect essay.

WRITE

"Put the argument in concrete shape . . .
and the cause is half won."

—Ralph Waldo Emerson

15

Strategies for Argumentation and Persuasion

"I wasn't convinced." "I just didn't buy it." Maybe you've said something similar while watching a political debate, viewing a TV ad, or discussing an issue in class or at work. You simply didn't find the argument logical or convincing.

College is a place where big issues get argued out—in class and out. To participate in that dialogue, you must be able to read and listen to others' arguments, analyze them, and build your own.

This chapter will help you do that. It explains what argumentation is, how to identify weak arguments, and how to construct strong ones. The three ensuing chapters then explain and model three forms of written argumentation: taking a position, persuading readers to act, and proposing a solution.

Learning Outcomes

LO1 Understand how to build an argument.

LO2 Prepare your argument.

LO3 Make and qualify your claims.

LO4 Support your claims.

LO5 Identify and avoid logical fallacies.

LO6 Engage the opposition.

LO7 Use appropriate appeals.

Understand how to build an argument. _____ LO1

What is an argument? Formally, an *argument* is a series of statements arranged in a logical sequence, supported with sound evidence, and expressed powerfully so as to sway your reader or listener. Arguments appear in a variety of places:

- A research paper about e-mail surveillance by the FBI.
- An analysis of "Good Country People" (short story) or *Poisonwood Bible* (novel).
- A debate about the ethics of transferring copyrighted music over the Internet.

Follow a process.

Step 1: Consider your audience, purpose, and topic.

- Identify your audience and purpose. Who is your audience and what is your goal? Do you want to take a position, persuade readers to act, or offer a solution?
- Generate ideas and gather solid evidence. You can't base an argument on opinions. Find accurate, pertinent information about the issue and uncover all viewpoints on it.
- Develop a line of reasoning. To be effective, you need to link your ideas in a clear, logical sequence.

Step 2: Make and qualify your claim.

- Draw reasonable conclusions from the evidence. State your claim (a debatable idea) as the central point for which you will argue. For example, you might assert that something is true, has value, or should be done.
- Add qualifiers. Words such as "typically" and "sometimes" soften your claim, making it more reasonable and acceptable.

Step 3: Support your claim.

- Support each point in your claim with solid evidence.
- Identify logical fallacies. Test your thinking for errors in logic (See pages 182–185.)

Step 4: Engage the opposition.

- Make concessions, if needed, by granting points to the opposition.
- Develop rebuttals that expose the weaknesses of the opposition's position, whenever possible.
- Use appropriate appeals—emotional "tugs" that ethically and logically help readers see your argument as convincing.

Prepare your argument. _____ LO2

An argument is a reason or chain of reasons used to support a claim. To use argumentation well, you need to know how to draw logical conclusions from sound evidence. Preparing an effective argument involves a number of specific steps, starting with those discussed below.

Consider the situation.

- Clearly identify your purpose and audience. This step is essential for all writing, but especially true when building an argument. (See pages 33–34.)
- Consider a range of ideas to broaden your understanding of the issue and to help focus your thinking on a particular viewpoint. (See pages 179–180.)
- Gather sound evidence to support your viewpoint. (See pages 180–182.)

Develop a line of reasoning.

Argumentative writing requires a clear line of reasoning with each point logically supporting your argument. Develop the line of reasoning as you study the issue, or use either of the following outlines as a guide.

Sample Argumentative Outlines

Outline 1: **Present your supporting arguments, then address counterarguments, and conclude with the strongest argument.**

Introduction: question, concern, or claim

1. Strong argument-supporting claim
   - Discussion and support
2. Other argument-supporting claims
   - Discussion of and support for each argument
3. Objections, concerns, and counterarguments
   - Discussion, concessions, answers, and rebuttals
4. Strongest argument-supporting claim
   - Discussion and support

Conclusion: argument consolidated—claim reinforced

Outline 2: **Address the arguments and counterarguments point by point.**

Introduction: question, concern, or claim

1. Strong argument-supporting claim
   - Discussion and support
   - Counterarguments, concessions, and rebuttals
2. Other argument-supporting claims
   - For each argument, discussion and support
   - For each argument, counterarguments, concessions, and rebuttals
3. Strongest argument-supporting claim
   - Discussion and support
   - Counterarguments, concessions, and rebuttals

Conclusion: argument consolidated—claim reinforced

Sergey Dubrov, 2011 / Used under license from Shutterstock.com

Make and qualify your claims.
LO3

An argument centers on a claim—a debatable statement. That claim is the thesis, or key point you wish to explain and defend so well that readers agree with it. A strong claim has the following traits:

- It's clearly arguable—it can be vigorously debated.
- It's defendable—it can be supported with sufficient arguments and evidence.
- It's responsible—it takes an ethically sound position.
- It's understandable—it uses clear terms and defines key words.
- It's interesting—it is challenging and worth discussing, not bland and easily accepted.

Distinguish claims from facts and opinions.

A claim is a conclusion drawn from logical thought and reliable evidence. A fact, in contrast, is a statement that can be checked for accuracy. An opinion is a personally held taste or attitude. A claim can be debated, but a fact or an opinion cannot.

Fact: *The Fellowship of the Ring* is the first book in J. R. R. Tolkien's trilogy *The Lord of the Rings*.

Opinion: I liked the movie almost as much as the book.

Claim: While the film version of *The Fellowship of the Ring* does not completely follow the novel's plot, the film does faithfully capture the spirit of Tolkien's novel.

Note: While the fact's accuracy can easily be checked, the opinion statement simply offers a personal feeling. Conversely, the claim states an idea that can be supported with reasoning and evidence.

Distinguish three types of claims.

Truth, value, and policy—these types of claims are made in an argument. The differences among them are important because each type has a distinct goal.

Claims of truth state that something is or is not the case. As a writer, you want readers to accept your claim as trustworthy.

> The Arctic ice cap will begin to disappear as early as 2050.
>
> The cholesterol in eggs is not as dangerous as previously feared.

Comment: Avoid statements that are (1) obviously true or (2) impossible to prove. Also, truth claims must be argued carefully because accepting them (or not) can have serious consequences.
Sample Essay: "Ah, the Power of Women," pages 191–193.

Claims of value state that something does or does not have worth. As a writer, you want readers to accept your judgment.

> Volunteer reading tutors provide a valuable service.
>
> Many music videos fail to present positive images of women.

Comment: Claims of value must be supported by referring to a known standard or by establishing an agreed-upon standard. To avoid a bias, base your judgments on the known standard, not on your feelings.
Sample Essay: "Our Wealth: Where Is It Taking Us?" pages 212–214

Claims of policy state that something ought or ought not to be done. As a writer, you want readers to approve your course of action.

> Special taxes should be placed on gas-guzzling SUVs.
>
> The developer should not be allowed to fill in the pond where the endangered tiger salamander lives.

Comment: Policy claims focus on action. To arrive at them, you must often first establish certain truths and values; thus an argument over policy may include both truth and value claims.
Sample Essay: "In Africa, AIDS Has a Woman's Face," pages 218–219

Develop supportable claims.

An effective claim balances confidence with common sense. Follow these tips:

Avoid all-or-nothing, extreme claims. Propositions using words that are overly positive or negative—such as *all*, *best*, *never*, and *worst*—may be difficult to support. Statements that leave no room for exceptions are easy to attack.

> **Extreme:** All people charged even once for DUI should never be allowed to drive again.

Make a truly meaningful claim. Avoid claims that are obvious, trivial, or unsupportable. None is worth the energy needed to argue the point.

> **Obvious:** College athletes sometimes receive special treatment.
>
> **Trivial:** The College Rec Center is a good place to get fit.
>
> **Unsupportable:** Athletics are irrelevant to college life.

Use qualifiers to temper your claims. Qualifiers are words or phrases that make claims more reasonable. Notice the difference between these two claims:

> **Unqualified:** Star athletes take far too many academic shortcuts.
>
> **Qualified:** Some star athletes take improper academic shortcuts.

Note: The "qualified" claim is easier to defend because it narrows the focus and leaves room for exceptions. Use qualifier words like these:

almost	many	often	tends to
frequently	maybe	probably	typically
likely	might	some	usually

Support your claims.

A claim stands or falls on its support. It's not the popular strength of your claim that matters, but rather the strength of your reasoning and evidence. To develop strong support, consider how to select and use evidence.

Gather evidence.

Several types of evidence can support claims. To make good choices, review each type, as well as its strengths and weaknesses.

Observations and anecdotes share what people (including you) have seen, heard, smelled, touched, tasted, and experienced. Such evidence offers an "eye-witness" perspective shaped by the observer's viewpoint, which can be powerful but may also prove narrow and subjective.

> Most of us have closets full of clothes: jeans, sweaters, khakis, T-shirts, and shoes for every occasion.

Statistics offer concrete numbers about a topic. Numbers don't "speak for themselves," however. They need to be interpreted and compared properly—not slanted or taken out of context. They also need to be up-to-date, relevant, and accurate.

> Pennsylvania spends $30 million annually in deer-related costs.
>
> Wisconsin has an estimated annual loss of $37 million for crop damage alone.

Tests and experiments provide hard data developed through the scientific method, data that must nevertheless be carefully studied and properly interpreted.

> According to the two scientists, the rats with unlimited access to the functional running wheel ran each day and gradually increased the amount of running; in addition, they started to eat less.

Graphics provide information in visual form—from simple tables to more complex charts, maps, drawings, and photographs. When poorly done, however, graphics can distort the truth.

Analogies compare two things, creating clarity by drawing parallels. However, every analogy breaks down if pushed too far.

> It is obvious today that America has defaulted on this promissory note insofar as her citizens of color are concerned. Instead of honoring this sacred obligation, America has given the Negro people a bad check; a check which has come back marked "insufficient funds." But we refuse to believe that the bank of justice is bankrupt.
> —Martin Luther King, Jr.

Expert testimony offers insights from an authority on the topic. Such testimony always has limits: Experts don't know it all, and they work from distinct perspectives, which means that they can disagree.

> One specialist opposed to drilling is David Klein, a professor at the Institute of Arctic Biology at the University of Alaska–Fairbanks. Klein argues that if the oil industry opens up the ANWR for drilling, the number of caribou will likely decrease because the calving locations will change.

Illustrations, examples, and demonstrations support general claims with specific instances, making such statements seem concrete and observable. Of course, an example may not be your best support if it isn't familiar.

> Think about how differently one can frame Rosa Parks' historic action. In prevailing myth, Parks—a holy innocent—acts almost on whim.... The real story is more empowering: It suggests that change is the product of deliberate, incremental action.

Analyses examine parts of a topic through thought patterns—cause/effect, compare/contrast, classification, process, or definition. Such analysis helps make sense of a topic's complexity, but muddles the topic when poorly done.

> If colorism lives underground, its effects are very real. Darker-skinned African-American defendants are more than twice as likely to receive the death penalty as lighter-skinned African-American defendants for crimes of equivalent seriousness....

Predictions offer insights into possible outcomes or consequences by forecasting what might happen under certain conditions. Like weather forecasting, predicting can be tricky. To be plausible, a prediction must be rooted in a logical analysis of present facts.

> While agroterrorist diseases would have little direct effect on people's health, they would be devastating to the agricultural economy, in part because of the many different diseases that could be used in an attack.

Use evidence.

Finding evidence is one thing; using it well is another. To marshal evidence in support of your claim, follow three guidelines:

1. **Go for quality and variety, not just quantity.** More evidence is not necessarily better. Instead, support your points with sound evidence in different forms. Quality evidence is . . .

   - *accurate:* correct and verifiable in each detail.
   - *complete:* filled with pertinent facts.
   - *concrete:* filled with specifics.
   - *relevant:* clearly related to the claim.
   - *current:* reliably up-to-date.
   - *authoritative:* backed by expertise, training, and knowledge.
   - *appealing:* able to influence readers.

2. **Use inductive and deductive patterns of logic.** Depending on your purpose, use inductive or deductive reasoning. (See page 12.)

   Induction: Inductive reasoning works from the particular toward general conclusions. In a persuasive essay using induction, look at facts first, find a pattern in them, and then lead the reader to your conclusion.

   > For example, in "Nuclear Is Not the Answer," Alyssa Woudstra first examines the benefits and liabilities of nuclear energy versus fossil fuels before asserting her claim that using the latter is a better choice. (See pages 194–196.)

   Deduction: Deductive reasoning—the opposite of inductive reasoning—starts from accepted truths and applies them to a new situation so as to reach a conclusion about it. For deduction to be sound, be sure the starting principles or facts are true, the new situation is accurately described, and the application is logical.

   > For example, Martin Luther King opened his 1963 "I Have a Dream" speech by noting that more than one hundred years earlier, the Emancipation Proclamation promised African Americans justice and freedom. He then described the continuing unjust treatment of African Americans, deducing that the promises in the Proclamation remained unfulfilled. (See pages 215–217.)

3. **Reason using valid warrants.** To make sense, claims and their supporting reasons must have a logical connection. That connection is called the warrant—the often unspoken thinking used to relate the reasoning to the claim. If warrants are good, arguments hold water; if warrants are faulty, then arguments break down. In other words, beware of faulty assumptions.

Check the short argument outlined below. Which of the warrants seem reasonable and strong, and which seem weak? Where does the argument fail?

> **Reasoning:** If current trends in water usage continue, the reservoir will be empty in two years.
>
> **Claim:** Therefore, Emeryville should immediately shut down its public swimming pools.

Unstated Warrants or Assumptions:

> It is not good for the reservoir to be empty.
>
> The swimming pools draw significant amounts of water from the reservoir.
>
> Emptying the pools would help raise the level of the reservoir.
>
> No other action would better prevent the reservoir from emptying.
>
> It is worse to have an empty reservoir than an empty swimming pool.

> **Insight:** Because an argument is no stronger than its warrants, you must make sure that your reasoning clearly and logically supports your claims.

Identify and avoid logical fallacies. LO5

Fallacies are false arguments—that is, bits of fuzzy, dishonest, or incomplete thinking. They may crop up in your own thinking, in your opposition's thinking, or in such public "arguments" as ads, political appeals, and talk shows. Because fallacies may sway an unsuspecting audience, they are dangerously persuasive. By learning to recognize fallacies, however, you may identify them in opposing arguments and eliminate them from your own writing. In this section, logical fallacies are grouped according to how they falsify an argument.

Distorting the Issue

The following fallacies falsify an argument by twisting the logical framework.

Bare Assertion The most basic way to distort an issue is to deny that it exists. This fallacy claims, "That's just how it is."

> The private ownership of handguns is a constitutional right. (*Objection:* The claim shuts off discussion of the U.S. Constitution or the reasons for regulation.)

Begging the Question Also known as circular reasoning, this fallacy arises from assuming in the basis of your argument the very point you need to prove.

> We don't need a useless film series when every third student owns a DVD player or VCR. (*Objection:* There may be uses for a public film series that private video viewing can't provide. The word "useless" begs the question.)

Oversimplification This fallacy reduces complexity to simplicity. Beware of phrases like "It's a simple question of." Serious issues are rarely simple.

> Capital punishment is a simple question of protecting society.

Either/Or Thinking Also known as black-and-white thinking, this fallacy reduces all options to two extremes. Frequently, it derives from a clear bias.

> Either this community develops light-rail transportation or the community will not grow in the future. (*Objection:* The claim ignores the possibility that growth may occur through other means.)

Complex Question Sometimes by phrasing a question a certain way, a person ignores or covers up a more basic question.

> Why can't we bring down the prices that corrupt gas stations are charging? (*Objection:* This question ignores a more basic question—"Are gas stations really corrupt?")

Straw Man In this fallacy, the writer argues against a claim that is easily refuted. Typically, such a claim exaggerates or misrepresents the opponents' position.

> Those who oppose euthanasia must believe that the terminally ill deserve to suffer.

Sabotaging the Argument

These fallacies falsify the argument by twisting it. They destroy reason and replace it with something hollow or misleading.

Red Herring This strange term comes from the practice of dragging a stinky fish across a trail to throw tracking dogs off the scent. When a person puts forth a volatile idea that pulls readers away from the real issue, readers become distracted. Suppose the argument addresses drilling for oil in the Arctic National Wildlife Refuge (ANWR) of Alaska, and the writer begins with this statement:

> In 1989, the infamous oil spill of the *Exxon Valdez* led to massive animal deaths and enormous environmental degradation of the coastline. (*Objection:* Introducing this notorious oil spill distracts from the real issue—how oil drilling will affect the ANWR.)

Misuse of Humor Jokes, satire, and irony can lighten the mood and highlight a truth; when humor distracts or mocks, however, it undercuts the argument. What effect would the mocking tone of this statement have in an argument about tanning beds in health clubs?

> People who use tanning beds will just turn into wrinkled old prunes or leathery sun-dried tomatoes!

Appeal to Pity This fallacy engages in a misleading tug on the heartstrings. Instead of using a measured emotional appeal, an appeal to pity seeks to manipulate the audience into agreement.

> Affirmative action policies ruined this young man's life. Because of them, he was denied admission to Centerville College.

Use of Threats A simple but unethical way of sabotaging an argument is to threaten opponents. More often than not, a threat is merely implied: "If you don't accept my argument, you'll regret it."

> If we don't immediately start drilling for oil in the ANWR, you will soon face hour-long lines at gas stations from New York to California.

Bandwagon Mentality Someone implies that a claim cannot be true because a majority of people are opposed to it, or it must be true because a majority support it. (History shows that people in the minority have often had the better argument.) At its worst, such an appeal manipulates people's desire to belong or be accepted.

> It's obvious to intelligent people that cockroaches live only in the apartments of dirty people. (*Objection:* Based on popular opinion, the claim appeals to a kind of prejudice and ignores scientific evidence about cockroaches.)

Appeal to Popular Sentiment This fallacy consists of associating your position with something popularly loved: the American flag, baseball, apple pie. Appeals to popular sentiment sidestep thought to play on feelings.

> Anyone who has seen *Bambi* could never condone hunting deer.

Drawing Faulty Conclusions from the Evidence

This group of fallacies falsifies the argument by short-circuiting proper logic in favor of assumptions or faulty thinking.

Appeal to Ignorance This fallacy suggests that because no one has proven a particular claim, it must be false; or, because no one has disproven a claim, it must be true. Appeals to ignorance unfairly shift the burden of proof onto someone else.

> Flying saucers are real. No scientific explanation has ruled them out.

Hasty or Broad Generalization Such a claim is based on too little evidence or allows no exceptions. In jumping to a conclusion, the writer may use intensifiers such as *all*, *every*, or *never*.

> Today's voters spend too little time reading and too much time being taken in by 30-second sound bites. (*Objection:* Quite a few voters may, in fact, spend too little time reading about the issues, but it is unfair to suggest that this is true of everyone.)

False Cause This well-known fallacy confuses sequence with causation: If *A* comes before *B*, *A* must have caused *B*. However, *A* may be one of several causes, or *A* and *B* may be only loosely related, or the connection between *A* and *B* may be entirely coincidental.

> Since that new school opened, drug use among young people has skyrocketed. Better that the school had never been built.

Slippery Slope This fallacy argues that a single step will start an unstoppable chain of events. While such a slide may occur, the prediction lacks evidence.

> If we legalize marijuana, it's only a matter of time before hard drugs follow and America becomes a nation of junkies and addicts.

Misusing Evidence

These fallacies falsify the argument by abusing or distorting the evidence.

Impressing with Numbers In this case, the writer drowns readers in statistics and numbers that overwhelm the readers into agreement. In addition, the numbers haven't been properly interpreted.

> At 35 ppm, CO levels factory-wide are only 10 ppm above the OSHA recommendation, which is 25 ppm. Clearly, that 10 ppm is insignificant in the big picture, and the occasional readings in some areas of between 40 and 80 ppm are aberrations that can safely be ignored. (*Objection:* The 10 ppm may be significant, and higher readings may indicate real danger.)

Half-Truths A half-truth contains part of but not the whole truth. Because a half-truth leaves out "the rest of the story," the assertion is both true and false simultaneously.

> The new welfare bill is good because it will get people off the public dole. (*Objection:* This may be true, but the bill may also cause undue suffering for some truly needy individuals.)

Unreliable Testimonial An appeal to authority has force only if the authority is qualified in the proper field. If he or she is not, the testimony is irrelevant. Note that fame is not the same thing as authority.

On her talk show, Alberta Magnus recently claimed that most pork sold in the United States is tainted. (*Objection:* Although Magnus may be an articulate talk show host, she is not an expert on food safety.)

Attack Against the Person This fallacy directs attention to a person's character, lifestyle, or beliefs rather than to the issue.

Would you accept the opinion of a candidate who experimented with drugs in college?

Hypothesis Contrary to Fact This fallacy relies on "if only" thinking. It bases the claim on an assumption of what would have happened if something else had, or had not, happened. Being pure speculation, such a claim cannot be tested.

If only multiculturalists hadn't pushed through affirmative action, the United States would be a united nation.

False Analogy Sometimes a person will argue that X is good (or bad) because it is like Y. Such an analogy may be valid, but it weakens the argument if the grounds for the comparison are vague or unrelated.

Don't bother voting in this election; it's a stinking quagmire. (*Objection:* Comparing the election to a "stinking quagmire" is unclear and exaggerated.)

Misusing Language

Essentially, all logical fallacies misuse language. However, three fallacies falsify the argument, especially by the misleading use of words.

Obfuscation This fallacy involves using fuzzy terms like *throughput* and *downlink* to muddy the issue. These words may make simple ideas sound more profound than they really are, or they may make false ideas sound true.

Through the fully functional developmental process of a streamlined target-refractory system, the U.S. military will successfully reprioritize its data throughputs. (*Objection:* What does this sentence mean?)

Ambiguity Ambiguous statements can be interpreted in two or more opposite ways. Although ambiguity can result from unintentional careless thinking, writers sometimes use ambiguity to obscure a position.

Many women need to work to support their children through school, but they would be better off at home. (*Objection:* Does *they* refer to *children* or *women*? What does *better off* mean? These words and phrases can be interpreted in opposite ways.)

Slanted Language By choosing words with strong positive or negative connotations, a writer can draw readers away from the true logic of the argument. Here is an example of three synonyms for the word *stubborn* that the philosopher Bertrand Russell once used to illustrate the bias in slanted language:

I am firm. You are obstinate. He is pigheaded.

Engage the opposition. LO6

Think of an argument as an intelligent, lively dialogue with readers. Anticipate their questions, concerns, objections, and counterarguments. Then follow these guidelines.

Make concessions.

By offering concessions—recognizing points scored by the other side—you acknowledge your argument's limits and the truth of other positions. Paradoxically, such concessions strengthen your overall argument by making it seem more credible. Concede your points graciously, using words such as the following:

Admittedly	Granted	I agree that
I cannot argue with	It is true that	You're right
I accept	No doubt	Of course
Certainly it's the case	I concede that	Perhaps

While foot-and-mouth disease is not dangerous to humans, other animal diseases are.

Develop rebuttals.

Even when you concede a point, you can often answer that objection by rebutting it. A good rebuttal is a small, tactful argument aimed at a weak spot in the opposing argument. Try these strategies:

1. **Point out the counterargument's limits** by putting the opposing point in a larger context. Show that the counterargument leaves something important out of the picture.
2. **Tell the other side of the story.** Offer an opposing interpretation of the evidence, or counter with stronger, more reliable, more convincing evidence.
3. **Address logical fallacies in the counterargument.** Check for faulty reasoning or emotional manipulation. For example, if the counterargument presents a half-truth, offer information that presents "the rest of the story."

> It is true that Chernobyl occurred more than twenty years ago, so safety measures for nuclear reactors have been greatly improved. However, that single accident is still affecting millions of people who were exposed to the radiation.

Consolidate your claim.

After making concessions and rebutting objections, you may need to regroup. Restate your claim so carefully that the weight of your whole argument can rest on it.

> One of these is bovine spongiform encephalopathy, better known as mad-cow disease.

Use appropriate appeals. _____ LO7

For your argument to be persuasive, it must not only be logical, but also "feel right." It must treat readers as real people by appealing to their common sense, hopes, pride, and notion of right and wrong. How do you appeal to all these concerns? Do the following: (1) build credibility, (2) make logical appeals, and (3) focus on readers' needs.

Build credibility.

A persuasive argument is credible—so trustworthy that readers can change their minds painlessly. To build credibility, observe these rules:

Be thoroughly honest. Demonstrate integrity toward the topic—don't falsify data, spin evidence, or ignore facts. Document your sources and cite them wherever appropriate.

Make realistic claims, projections, and promises. Avoid emotionally charged statements, pie-in-the-sky forecasts, and undeliverable deals.

Develop and maintain trust. From your first word to your last, develop trust—in your attitude toward the topic, your treatment of readers, and your respect for opposing viewpoints.

Make logical appeals.

Arguments stand or fall on their logical strength, but your readers' acceptance of those arguments is often affected more by the emotional appeal of your ideas and evidence. To avoid overly emotional appeals, follow these guidelines:

Engage readers positively. Appeal to their better natures—to their sense of honor, justice, social commitment, altruism, and enlightened self-interest. Avoid appeals geared toward ignorance, prejudice, selfishness, or fear.

Use a fitting tone. Use a tone that is appropriate for the topic, purpose, situation, and audience.

Aim to motivate, not manipulate, readers. While you do want them to accept your viewpoint, it's not a win-at-all-costs situation. Avoid bullying, guilt-tripping, and exaggerated tugs on heartstrings.

Don't trash-talk the opposition. Show tact, respect, and understanding. Focus on issues, not personalities.

Use arguments and evidence that readers can understand and appreciate. If readers find your thinking too complex, too simple, or too strange, you've lost them.

Focus on readers' needs.

Instead of playing on readers' emotions, connect your argument with readers' needs and values. Follow these guidelines:

Know your real readers. Who are they—peers, professors, or fellow citizens? What are their allegiances, their worries, their dreams?

Picture readers as resistant. Accept that your readers, including those inclined to agree with you, need convincing.

Use appeals that match needs and values. Your argument may support or challenge readers' needs and values. To understand those needs, study the table below, which is based loosely on the thinking of psychologist Abraham Maslow. Maslow's hierarchy ranks people's needs on a scale from the most basic to the most complex. The table begins at the bottom with *having necessities* (a basic need) and ends at the top with helping others (a more complex need). For example, if you're writing to argue for more affordable housing for the elderly, you'd argue differently to legislators (whose focus is on *helping others*) than to the elderly who need the housing (whose focus is on *having necessities*). Follow these guidelines:

- Use appeals that match the foremost needs and values of your readers.
- If appropriate, constructively challenge those needs and values.
- Phrase your appeals in positive terms.
- After analyzing your readers' needs, choose a persuasive theme for your argument—a positive benefit, advantage, or outcome that readers can expect if they accept your claim.

Reader needs . . .	Use persuasive appeals to . . .
To make the world better by helping others	values and social obligations
To achieve by being good at something getting recognition	self-fulfillment, status appreciation
To belong by being part of a group	group identity, acceptance
To survive by avoiding threats, having necessities	safety, security physical needs

Critical-Thinking and Writing Activities

As directed by your instructor, complete the following critical-thinking and writing activities by yourself or with classmates.

1. Select an essay from chapters 16–18, "Taking a Position," "Persuading Readers to Act," or "Proposing a Solution." Read the essay carefully. Then describe and evaluate the essay's argumentative strategies by answering the questions below:
   - What is the main claim the writer makes? Is it a claim of truth, value, or policy?
   - Is the claim arguable—that is, is it supportable, qualified, and effectively phrased?
   - What arguments does the writer develop in support of the claim? Are these arguments logical?
   - What types of evidence does the writer provide to support her or his discussion?
   - Is the evidence valid, sufficient, and accurate?
   - Does the writer effectively address questions, alternatives, objections, and counterarguments?

2. Review the essay that you read for the first activity, and then answer the following questions:
   - Describe the writer's tone. Is it engaging?
   - Does the argument seem credible and authoritative? Explain.

3. Find a quality article in a respected journal in your major. Read the article and then answer these questions: What forms of reasoning, appeals, and evidence does the author use? What forms does she or he avoid? Is the reasoning convincing? Why?

Checklist: Learning Outcomes

Use this checklist to assess your grasp of argumentative and persuasive strategies.

_____ I understand how to build an argument.

_____ I understand how to prepare an argument by analyzing my writing situation and developing my line of reasoning.

_____ I can make factual claims of truth, value, and policy.

_____ I can support my claims with quality evidence and valid warrants.

_____ I can identify and avoid logical fallacies.

_____ I can engage the opposition by making concessions, developing rebuttals, and consolidating my claims.

_____ I can use credible and logical appeals, focused on readers' needs.

"The ultimate measure of man is not where he stands in moments of comfort and convenience, but where he stands at times of challenge and controversy."
—Martin Luther King Jr.

16

Taking a Position

Sometimes you just have to take a stand. An issue comes up that upsets you or challenges your thinking, and in response, you say, "Okay, this is what I believe, and this is why I believe it."

Learning to read and write position papers enables you to do this. The reading skills help you analyze others' positions, recognize their strengths, and identify their weaknesses. The writing skills help you probe a topic, refine your own perspective on the issues, educate others about the topic, and convince them that your position has value.

This chapter will help you refine both skills. In addition, because both skills are used across the college curriculum and at work, learning this chapter's writing skills and strategies will help you succeed in the classroom today and in the workplace throughout your career.

Learning Outcomes

LO1 Understand how to read position papers.

LO2 Develop sound claims with reliable evidence.

LO3 Make concessions and rebut opposing arguments.

LO4 Make effective appeals.

LO5 Write, revise, and edit a logical position paper.

Understand how to read position papers. LO1

How should you read a position paper? The instructions below will guide you.

Consider the rhetorical situation.

Think first about how the writer uses persuasion to achieve a specific purpose, affect a particular audience, and address a given topic.

Purpose: In most cases, writers produce position papers in order to educate and to persuade: they want (1) to inform you about the nature and relevance of a topic and (2) to persuade you that their position on the topic is the best, most reasonable option.

Audience: A writer may address a variety of readers: people opposed to the writer's position, people uncertain of what position to take, people unaware that an issue exists, or even people who agree with the writer's position but are looking for sensible reasons. Good writers shape the content, organization, and tone of position essays to effectively address such intended readers.

Topic: The topics addressed in meaningful position papers are debatable issues about which informed people can reasonably disagree. Therefore, as a reader, you will learn more about a paper's topic by focusing not only on the writer's position, but also on the reasoning that she or he uses to develop that position, including her or his attention to alternative positions.

pontificating
speaking in an arrogant manner

Consider qualities of strong arguments.

When reading a position paper, look for the following:

Informed Writing: The writer has researched the topic thoroughly and understands it fully, including positions other than his or her own.

Logical Writing: The writer presents the topic objectively, describes alternative positions fairly, and takes the position supported by the best evidence and strongest logic. The writing avoids logical fallacies such as oversimplification, either/or thinking, straw-man claims, red-herring assertions, appeals to pity, or attacks against opponents. (For information on these and other fallacies, see pages 182–185.) If the writer uses visuals, they should fairly represent the issue.

Engaging Writing: Rather than quarreling or **pontificating**, the writer converses with readers by making reasonable concessions, rebutting opposing arguments, and consolidating or refocusing claims. (For details on these strategies, see pages 185–187.)

Checklist: Reading Positions

Use the following questions to guide your reading of a position paper.

✔ What is the topic, and is it debatable, stated fairly, and addressed fully?

✔ What are the writer's claims, and are they supported by reliable evidence?

✔ Is the overall argument clear, unified, and free of logical fallacies and manipulative visuals?

✔ Is the tone measured, reasonable, and free of manipulative language?

Diego Cervo, 2011 / Used under license from Shutterstock.com

Develop sound claims with reliable evidence. ___ LO2

Student writer Aleah Stenberg wrote the following essay to explain and promote her interpretation of (or position on) the characters and themes in Louise Erdrich's *Love Medicine*. A convincing interpretive position is built on sound, measured claims backed up by clear, reliable evidence. As you read Aleah's essay, study especially her claims and evidence.

(A) # Ah, the Power of Women

| Survey · Question · Read · Recite · Review | **SQ3R** |

1   While most American literature commonly portrays a negative view of women, Louise Erdrich's Na-
(B) tive American novel, *Love Medicine,* does just the opposite. Her female characters are the **catalyst** around which the action of the book revolves. The two strongest women, Lulu Lamartine and Marie Kashpaw, create the **dissonant nucleoli** that give rise to the conflict in the novel and also trump the men in most forms of power. The **matriarchal** Native American culture depicted by Erdrich provides a setting in which these women can roar.

2   The culture of the Chippewa highly regards mothers in particular and women in general. As a child,
(C) Lulu learns this lesson by noting the respect allotted her mother. Lulu acknowledges, "I never grew from the curve of my mother's arms" (Erdrich 68), and finds in nature **manifestations** of her connection to her mother's person and power. This mother/daughter bond is **impenetrable** for men. While Lulu mourns her mother's passing, she never mentions a father. The closest father figure she has is Uncle Nanapush, but even when conversing about his death ceremony, she does so by referencing her feelings for her mother: "I couldn't bear to think of losing him the way I had lost

my mother" (71). The oldest clan matron, Rushes Bear, also alludes to the matriarchal culture of the tribe as she laments about Nector Kashpaw: "My son is marrying one of that lowlife family that insulted me. Those Lazarres breed fast and die young. I hope I'll outlive her tough bread and Nector Kashpaw will once again respect his mother" (72). Nector's actions don't insult his father or his family in a European sense; instead, he disgraces his mother. By recognizing mothers as the beating heart of the family, the Chippewa respect them accordingly.

3   In light of the reverence for women in Chippewa society, Erdrich's strongest, most prominent characters are Marie Kashpaw and Lulu Lamartine. These two are in charge of the house and rule over their husbands. Other female characters are also strong, although they play lesser roles. Rushes Bear and Sister Leopolda are strongly influential but in different times or spheres; for example, Sister Leopolda rules with a cruel hand at the Sacred **(D)** Heart Convent. Erdrich's male characters have less prominent roles, and their main purpose—many times—is to be **subordinated** by **domineering** females.

(D) Marie and Lulu, like less prominent female characters, control males.

catalyst
a force that puts an event or a change into motion

dissonant nucleoli
force of disagreement

matriarchal
a culture in which a female is the head of the family

manifestations
indicators

impenetrable
not accessible; cannot be penetrated

subordinated
less important; under the authority of a superior

domineering
inclined to rule strictly or harshly

(A) Title introduces theme.
(B) Introduction: Erdrich's setting warrants her depicting women as the dominant gender.
(C) Characters refer to and support women's dominant role.

4　The women in *Love Medicine* have supremacy over the men in many aspects. Sexual power over males guides much of the story in both Lulu and Marie's lives. Lulu, particularly, has many affairs; she knows what she wants, gets it, and then does away with what she doesn't like. Each of her boys and daughter is symbolic of her conquering another man. At a young age, Lulu learned about sexual power while listening to **(E)** older women. Lulu remembers, "Rushes Bear always said that a man has to enter and enter, repeatedly, as if in punishment for having ever left the woman's body. She said that the woman is complete. Men must come through us to live" (82). The idea that men are incomplete because they left the woman's body gives females the edge in sexual relations. The man needs her; the woman is not dependant on the man; on the contrary, she has command of the relationship. This same idea also points to the reverence of women in Chippewa culture. The mother is the creator of new life and the sustainer of the men she beds (whether her husband or not), and as such, she is given great honor.

5　The sexual power of women in *Love Medicine* also gives them political and social clout. Lulu wields her **(F)** political power when she denounces the proposed tomahawk factory which would require moving her house: "Before I'd move the Lamartine household I'd hit the tribe with a fistful of paternity suits that would make their heads spin. Some of them had forgotten until then that I'd even had their son. Still others must have wondered. I could see the back neck hair on the wives all over that room prickle" (285). Lulu's sexual power gives her a platform to preside over political decisions. Because of women's power sexually, they also are given social influence. One of the examples in Lulu's life is deciding which Lamartine to marry. She

Petr Nad, 2011 / Used under license from Shutterstock.com

tells Beverly, "I am a woman of detachable parts. You should know by now. You simply weren't playing in your league with strip poker" (115). And she adds, "It was after I won your shorts with my pair of deuces and Henry's with my eights, and you were naked except for your hat, that I decided which one to marry" (115). So many men are sexually attracted to Lulu that she can pick and choose whom she wants. In the culture the novel describes, women are **venerated** for their sexuality. They can then use that given power to gain influence in tribal society and politics.

(E) The women learn about their power by listening to elders and observing Chippewa culture.
(F) Through their sexual power, they garner social and political influence.

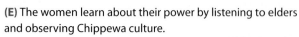

venerated
respected

6   Matriarchal Chippewa culture; the sexual, political, and social power given to women; and Erdrich's use of strong female characters **culminate** in Lulu and Marie forming the central conflict of the piece. Both these women are strong and at odds, the nuclei of opposing forces, two different pressure systems raging over North Dakota. Nector Kashpaw is a main object of competition for these two. Like the arms race of the Cold War, Marie and Lulu also engage in a race to have the most children. Lulu has many children, all by different fathers. Marie, after two of her and Nector's offspring die in childhood, rapidly adopts children and takes in young family members. These women are constantly vying for supremacy over each other. Even when they become friends, Lyman Lamartine notes, "Their statures had to be completely equal. . . . They each needed territory to control. . . . Their friendship, if that's what you'd call it, was hard to figure. Set free by Nector's death, they couldn't get enough of their own differences. They argued unceasingly about the past, and didn't agree on the present either" (311). In addition to these battles within their friendship, all other conflicts in *Love Medicine* stem from Lulu and Marie's on-going war or are in some way linked to it.

7   Erdrich gives women center stage in *Love Medicine*. By choosing the matriarchal Chippewa tribe as her setting, she is able to create powerful female characters with dissonant relationships. Writing against the typical, American, male-dominated social order, Erdrich constructs a world in which women are in charge. Even though the female characters in the book are mothers who do laundry, cook meals, and finish long "to-do" lists, they are not held to this position. They have the power to rise above and take **jurisdiction**. Full of strong females, *Love Medicine* asserts a positive feminist message: women—hear them roar.

Note: The Works Cited pages is not shown. For sample, pages, see MLA (pages 368–369) and APA (page 396).

(G) Culture, power, and prominence generate conflict.
(H) Edrich's setting warrants her depicting women as the stronger, controlling gender.

Reading for Better Writing

Working by yourself or with a group, do the following:

1. Stenberg's essay introduces a novel (her topic) and analyzes its setting, characters, and themes. Describe how she uses the title and opening paragraphs to introduce this topic. Then trace how the body of the essay develops a sound analysis of the novel.

2. Stenberg's paper is also a persuasive essay in which she explains and advocates her interpretation of—or position on—one issue in the novel. Explain how the writer uses the title and opening sentences to introduce and focus her argument.

3. In your own words, state her core argument or claim—her position on the novel.

4. Review paragraphs 2-6, identify the supporting claim developed in each paragraph, and explain how Stenberg uses these points to support and clarify her main claim.

5. Describe how the writer uses her closing paragraph to refine and clarify her position. Does the paragraph accomplish these goals? Explain.

6. Study the image on page 192. Does the image relate in any way to Aleah's position about the power of women in the novel? If yes, how so? If not, what kind of image would you choose to emphasize this theme?

culminate
to reach the highest level

jurisdiction
power or authority

Make concessions and rebut opposing arguments. ─── LO3

Student writer Alyssa Woudstra wrote the following essay to take a position on an environmental issue—energy production. Part of taking a position is acknowledging other positions and conceding their strengths, but then rebutting their claims in order to strengthen your own position. As you read Alyssa's essay, observe how she makes concessions concerning nuclear power but then rebuts those arguments.

(A) # Nuclear Is Not the Answer

Survey • Question • Read • Recite • Review SQ3R

1   In recent years, it has become popular to be "green" in all areas of life. Celebrities and corpora-
(B) tions constantly advertise natural cleaning products, fuel-efficient cars, and energy-efficient light bulbs. Governments offer home-improvement grants to people who renovate their homes to include low-flush toilets, weather-proof windows, and additional insulation. Due to climate change and pollution, concern for the environment is rising. One major issue centers on which type of energy production is best for the environment. Nuclear power and **fossil fuels** are two major methods for energy production, and nuclear power could be seen as the "greener" option. However, the risks of nuclear power far outweigh its benefits, making fossil fuels the safer and more environmentally responsible option.

2   As a significant method of energy production, nuclear power does offer distinct advantages. The Nuclear Energy Institute's statistics show that nuclear **(C)** energy accounted for fourteen percent of the world's electricity production in 2008, and that as of September 2009, thirty countries were using nuclear power ("Around the World"). This popularity speaks to nuclear power's advantages over fossil fuels. First, nuclear power plants do not release the harmful emissions that coal-burning plants do, so nuclear power does not contribute greatly to global warming (Evans 115). Second, a single nuclear power plant can produce a large amount of energy, making nuclear an efficient source ("Pros and Cons"). In fact, according to Robert Evans, "The amount of **thermal** energy released from just one kilogram of U235 undergoing **fission** is equivalent to that obtained by burning some 2.5 million kilograms, or 2500 tonnes, of coal" (116).

3   Nevertheless, these advantages of nuclear power are outweighed by its disadvantages. Nuclear power plants produce radioactive waste, which is an enor- **(D)** mous health and safety concern. The waste cannot simply be disposed of but must be carefully stored for hundreds of generations. The **isotopes** used in nuclear reactions have **half-lives** of thousands of years. For example, plutonium-239 has a half-life of around 24,000 years (American Assembly 24). This radioactive waste must be stored safely to prevent radiation poisoning, but it would be nearly impossible to do so for that long.

(A) The title partly declares the position.
(B) Alyssa starts with common ground and narrows to her position on energy production.

(C) She examines the positives of what she actually opposes.
(D) She turns to the disadvantages of nuclear energy: its risks and dangers.

---

fossil fuels
natural fuels that come from the earth

thermal
heat

fission
a splitting of parts that produces energy

isotopes
chemical elements that have almost identical properties

half-lives
the time it takes an isotope to undergo radioactive decay

4 A further danger of nuclear power is that while every safety precaution might be in place, it is possible for terrible accidents to happen. The most famous nuclear accident took place on April 26, 1986, when reactor number four at the Chernobyl Nuclear Power Plant in the Ukraine, which was then part of the Soviet Union, exploded after a **power excursion**. That explosion then caused the rest of the plant to explode (Hawks et. al. 98-102). This accident released one hundred times more radiation than the bombing of Hiroshima and Nagasaki combined ("No More Chernobyls"). Chernobyl's radiation spread all over Europe, affecting people as far away as Romania and Bulgaria, exposing more than 600,000 to the effects of radiation poisoning (Medvedev 194-216). More than twenty years after Chernobyl, people are still dying from cancer that was likely caused by the disaster.

5 It is true that Chernobyl occurred more than twenty years ago, so safety measures for nuclear reactors have since been greatly improved. However, that single accident is still affecting millions of people who were exposed to the radiation. Moreover, the accident had a devastating impact on the environment: even now, vegetation in the area around Chernobyl is practically non-existent. If more nuclear power plants are built, the risk of similar accidents will rise.

6 Beyond accidents, however, is the possibility of deliberate sabotage in the form of terrorism ("Pros and Cons"). If terrorists wanted to cause mass devastation, they could attack a nuclear power plant or become employees that purposely cause errors to create an explosion. On September 11, 2001, millions of people were affected at once. If a power plant were attacked, it would also affect millions, since it would cause the loss of not only many jobs but also many lives. Moreover, the risk of terrorism also surrounds the nuclear waste left behind after the reactions. Easier to obtain than pure uranium, such waste could be used to build "dirty bombs" (Evans 133).

7 Beyond the risks and dangers of nuclear power, still another argument against it is that it is nonrenewable. Fossil fuels are also nonrenewable, but nuclear power is not an alternative in this way. In their reactors, nuclear power plants use uranium, a rare element.

(E) The writer reminds readers of a historical illustration.
(F) Alyssa concedes and rebuts a concern.

power excursion
a rapid increase in power level of a nuclear reactor

Petr Nad, 2011 / Used under license from Shutterstock.com

It is estimated that the Earth's supply of Uranium will last only thirty to sixty years, depending on how much is actually used in reactors ("Pros and Cons").

8 But is energy from fossil fuels really better than nuclear power? The burning of fossil fuels (including (G) coal, oil, and natural gas) is the most common method of energy production. Like nuclear, fossil fuels are nonrenewable. However, burning fossil fuels, for the time being, is a better option than using nuclear energy. It is true that using fossil fuels has a negative effect on the environment. In order to obtain fossil fuels, much damage is caused to the environment by drilling for oil or mining for coal. Also, burning fossil fuels produces gases that can aggravate respiratory conditions like asthma and emits greenhouse gases that damage the atmosphere. Moreover, particles emitted from smokestacks collect in clouds, causing acid rain (Sweet 25). With oil, spills can contaminate groundwater and surface water, creating risks to animals, plants, and humans.

9 Despite the fact that using fossil fuels involves many risks, it has some advantages over nuclear energy. Significantly, fossil fuels are much less expensive than uranium. Although it is still expensive to access fossil fuels, it is drastically cheaper than the cost of (H) nuclear energy. In addition, if large deposits of coal or oil are found, it will not be necessary to excavate in as many places to retrieve them. Although a larger area would be disturbed, fewer sites would be affected. Also, while fossil fuels are nonrenewable, they may be used wisely, conserving them until a better energy source can be established (Heron).

10 However, perhaps the biggest advantage of fossil fuel energy over nuclear energy lies in the possibility of progress to make current methods more environ-

mentally friendly. At this time, burning coal for power uses only one-third of its potential energy (Heron). If scientists study more efficient uses of the coal, this waste, as well as many health and environmental concerns, could be prevented. For example, burning coal can be made cleaner through electrostatic precipitators. Also known as "smokestack scrubbers," these filters can be used in smokestacks to prevent soot particles from getting into the air. As the soot-filled air passes through the smokestack, it goes through a set of wires that negatively charge the soot particles. As the air continues through the pipe, it passes through positively charged metal plates. The negatively charged soot particles, which are made up mostly of unburned carbon, "stick" to the positively charged plates, and the particle-free air continues out the smokestack. The stuck particles are then either manually scraped or automatically shaken off by the machine itself ("Static Electricity"). If more factories used electrostatic precipitators, a large amount of air pollution would be prevented.

11 Although it is not ideal, burning fossil fuels is still a better option than nuclear power until renewable energy sources such as wind, solar, and **geothermal** (I) power become more available. Clearly, society must continue to work toward greater conservation and use of renewable energy. As **stewards** of the Earth, all humans should be concerned about the environment. If people continue to use nuclear power, the risks related to accidents, sabotage, and radioactive waste will not only be their responsibility but will also impact their descendants for many generations.

Note: The Works Cited page is not shown. For examples, see MLA (pages 368–369) and APA (page 396).

(G) With a question, she turns to her own position, acknowledging its problems.

(H) Alyssa supports her position on fossil fuels by stressing its advantages and calling for improvements.

geothermal
heat produced from the earth

stewards
caretakers

(I) She restates her position and places it within a larger context of environmental changes.

Reading for Better Writing

Working by yourself or with a group, do the following:

1. Alyssa begins her essay by examining extensively an opposing position—support for nuclear energy. How effective is this strategy? How reliable is the evidence?

2. Review how Alyssa supports her position on energy from fossil fuels. How complete and compelling is this support?

3. Alyssa wrote her position paper prior to the BP oil spill in the Gulf of Mexico and the Fukushima Daiichi power-plant meltdown. How might acknowledging these environmental disasters change her essay?

4. Environmental issues tend to be hotly debated, with people of different positions using images and video footage to sway others to their position. The image on this page is a newspaper headline about the nuclear meltdown at Fukushima Daiichi. If Alyssa had used this image in her paper, would it have effectively supported her position in a specific way? Would it be part of an effective rebuttal of support for nuclear energy? Why or why not?

JustASC, 2011 / Used under license from Shutterstock.com

Make effective appeals. LO4

Sometimes, a writer takes a position in response to another writer, as shown in the following essays by Gary Steiner and Natalie Angier. Steiner, a professor of philosophy at Bucknell University and author of *Animals and the Moral Community,* advocates a pure vegan lifestyle in "Animal, Vegetable, Miserable" below. Angier's essay (pages 201–203), "Sorry, Vegans: Brussels Sprouts Like to Live, Too," responds in part to Steiner. Both pieces were published in 2009 in *The New York Times.* In these op-eds, Steiner and Angier demonstrate the position-taking strategies addressed earlier in this chapter: developing sound claims with reliable evidence, while also making concessions but rebutting opposing arguments. However, as discussed in the previous chapter on pages 186–187, a sound argument also involves using appropriate appeals to credibility, logic, and emotion, while avoiding a wide range of logical fallacies. As you read these opposing essays, study and evaluate these appeals and check the arguments for logical fallacies such as oversimplifying, either-or thinking, appeals to pity, and attacks against opponents.

Animal, Vegetable, Miserable

Survey • Question • Read • Recite • Review   **SQ3R**

LATELY more people have begun to express an interest in where the meat they eat comes from and how it was raised. Were the animals humanely treated? Did they have a good quality of life before the death that turned them into someone's dinner? (1) (A)

Some of these questions, which reach a fever pitch in the days leading up to Thanksgiving, pertain to the ways in which animals are treated. (Did your turkey get to live outdoors?) Others focus on the question of how eating the animals in question will affect the (2)

(A) The writer introduces the topic.

consumer's health and well-being. (Was it given hormones and antibiotics?)

3 None of these questions, however, make any consideration of whether it is wrong to kill animals for
(B) human consumption. And even when people ask this question, they almost always find a variety of resourceful answers that purport to justify the killing and consumption of animals in the name of human welfare. Strict ethical **vegans**, of which I am one, are customarily **excoriated** for equating our society's treatment of animals with mass murder. Can anyone seriously consider animal suffering even remotely comparable to human suffering? Those who answer with a resounding no typically argue in one of two ways.

4 Some suggest that human beings but not animals are made in God's image and hence stand in much
(C) closer proximity to the divine than any non-human animal; according to this line of thought, animals were made expressly for the sake of humans and may be used without scruple to satisfy their needs and desires. There is ample support in the Bible and in the writings of Christian thinkers like Augustine and Thomas Aquinas for this pointedly **anthropocentric** way of devaluing animals.

(B) He states the core issue and identifies his own position.
(C) He summarizes opposing positions and offers an example.

vegans
a vegetarian who will not eat or use any animal products, including milk, honey, and eggs

excoriated
belittled or denounced

anthropocentric
a view that sees human beings as the central figures of the universe

qualitatively
concerning quality

quantitatively
concerning numbers (facts, statistics, etc.)

iconoclastic
attacking

Treblinka
a Nazi extermination camp in Poland during World War II

5 Others argue that the human capacity for abstract thought makes us capable of suffering that both **qualitatively** and **quantitatively** exceeds the suffering of any non-human animal. Philosophers like Jeremy Bentham, who is famous for having based moral sta-
(D) tus not on linguistic or rational capacities but rather on the capacity to suffer, argue that because animals are incapable of abstract thought, they are imprisoned in an eternal present, have no sense of the extended future and hence cannot be said to have an interest in continued existence.

6 The most penetrating and **iconoclastic** response to this sort of reasoning came from the writer Isaac Bashevis Singer in his story "The Letter Writer," in which he called the slaughter of animals the "eternal **Treblinka**."

7 The story depicts an encounter between a man and a mouse. The man, Herman Gombiner, contemplates
(E) his place in the cosmic scheme of things and concludes that there is an essential connection between his own existence as "a child of God" and the "holy creature" scuffling about on the floor in front of him.

8 Surely, he reflects, the mouse has some capacity for thought; Gombiner even thinks that the mouse
(F) has the capacity to share love and gratitude with him. Not merely a means for the satisfaction of human desires, nor a mere nuisance to be exterminated, this tiny creature possesses the same dignity that any conscious being possesses. In the face of that inherent dignity, Gombiner concludes, the human practice of delivering animals to the table in the form of food is abhorrent and inexcusable.

9 Many of the people who denounce the ways in which we treat animals in the course of raising them for human consumption never stop to think about this profound contradiction. Instead, they make impassioned calls for more "humanely" raised meat. Many people soothe their consciences by purchasing
(G) only free-range fowl and eggs, blissfully ignorant that

(D) He offers a second example.
(E) He uses an anecdote to present a counter argument.
(F) Steiner states the story's theme and explains its relevance.
(G) He castigates "free-range" arguments.

"free range" has very little if any practical significance. Chickens may be labeled free-range even if they've never been outside or seen a speck of daylight in their entire lives. And that Thanksgiving turkey? Even if it

Tertman, 2011 / Used under license from Shutterstock.com

is raised "free range," it still lives a life of pain and confinement that ends with the butcher's knife.

10   How can intelligent people who purport to be deeply concerned with animal welfare and respectful of life turn a blind eye to such practices? And how can people continue to eat meat when they become aware that nearly 53 billion land animals are slaughtered ev-

(H) ery year for human consumption? The simple answer is that most people just don't care about the lives or fortunes of animals. If they did care, they would learn as much as possible about the ways in which our society systematically abuses animals, and they would

make what is at once a very simple and a very difficult choice: to forswear the consumption of animal prod- (I) ucts of all kinds.

     The easy part of this consists in seeing clearly   11 what ethics requires and then just plain doing it. The difficult part: You just haven't lived until you've tried to function as a strict vegan in a meat-crazed society. What were once the most straightforward activities become a constant ordeal. You might think that it's as simple as just removing meat, eggs and dairy products from your diet, but it goes a lot deeper than that.

     To be a really strict   12 vegan is to strive to avoid all animal products, and this includes (J) materials like leather, silk and wool, as well as a panoply of cosmetics and medications. The more you dig, the more you learn about products you would never stop to think might contain or involve animal products in their production—like wine and beer (isinglass, a kind of gelatin derived from fish bladders, is often used to "fine," or purify, these beverages), refined sugar (bone char is sometimes used to bleach it) or Band-Aids (animal products in the adhesive). Just last week I was told that those little comfort strips on most razor blades contain animal fat.

(I) He offers one acceptable solution.
(J) He defines and advocates a pure vegan lifestyle.

(H) He identifies his opponents' "real" reason for inaction as "not caring."

13   To go down this road is to stare headlong into an **abyss** that, to paraphrase Nietzsche, will ultimately stare back at you.

14   The challenges faced by a vegan don't end with the nuts and bolts of material existence. You face quite a few social difficulties as well, perhaps the chief one

(K) being how one should feel about spending time with people who are not vegans.

15   Is it O.K. to eat dinner with people who are eating meat? What do you say when a dining companion says, "I'm really a vegetarian—I don't eat red meat at home." (I've heard it lots of times, always without any prompting from me.) What do you do when someone starts to grill you (so to speak) about your vegan ethics during dinner? (Wise vegans always defer until food isn't around.) Or when someone starts to lodge accusations to the effect that you consider yourself morally superior to others, or that it is ridiculous to worry so much about animals when there is so much human suffering in the world? (Smile politely and ask them to pass the **seitan**.)

16   Let me be candid: By and large, meat-eaters are a self-righteous bunch. The number of vegans I know personally is . . . five. And I have been a vegan for almost 15 years, having been a vegetarian for almost 15 before that.

17   Five. I have lost more friends than this over arguments about animal ethics. One **lapidary** conclusion to be drawn here is that people take deadly seriously the **prerogative** to use animals as sources of satisfac-

tion. Not only for food, but as beasts of burden, as raw materials and as sources of captive entertainment—which is the way animals are used in zoos, circuses and the like.

18   These uses of animals are so institutionalized, so normalized in our society that it is difficult to find the critical distance needed to see them as the horrors that they are: so many forms of subjection, servitude and—in the case of killing animals for human consumption and other purposes—outright murder.

19   People who are ethical vegans believe that differences in intelligence between human and non-human animals have no moral significance whatsoever. The fact that my cat can't appreciate Schubert's late symphonies and can't perform **syllogistic logic** does not mean that I am entitled to use him as an organic toy, as if I were somehow not only morally superior to him but virtually entitled to treat him as a commodity with minuscule market value.

20   We have been trained by a history of thinking of which we are scarcely aware to view non-human animals as resources we are entitled to employ in whatever (L) ways we see fit in order to satisfy our needs and desires. Yes, there are animal welfare laws. But these laws have been formulated by, and are enforced by, people who proceed from the proposition that animals are fundamentally inferior to human beings. At best, these laws make living conditions for animals marginally better than they would be otherwise—right up to the point when we send them to the slaughterhouse.

21   Think about that when you're picking out your free-range turkey, which has absolutely nothing to be thankful for on Thanksgiving. All it ever had was a short and miserable life, thanks to us intelligent, compassionate humans.

(K) Steiner acknowledges the challenges of his position.

(L) He concludes by stating that the core problem is humans' belief that they are fundamentally superior to animals.

abyss
a deep, never-ending space

seitan
a protein-rich food used as a substitute for meat

lapidary
refined

prerogative
a right or power

syllogistic logic
a type of logic theorized by Aristotle

(A) Sorry, Vegans: Brussels Sprouts Like to Live, Too

Survey · Question · Read · Recite · Review **SQ3R**

1   I stopped eating pork about eight years ago, after a scientist happened to mention that the animal whose teeth most closely resemble our own is the pig. Un-

(B) able to shake the image of a perky little pig flashing me a brilliant George Clooney smile, I decided it was easier to forgo the Christmas ham. A couple of years later, I gave up on all mammalian meat, period. I still eat fish and poultry, however, and pour eggnog in my coffee. My dietary decisions are **arbitrary** and inconsistent, and when friends ask why I'm willing to try the duck but not the lamb, I don't have a good answer. Food choices are often like that: difficult to articulate yet strongly held. And lately, debates over food choices have flared with particular **vehemence**.

2   In his new book, *Eating Animals,* the novelist Jonathan Safran Foer describes his gradual transformation from omnivorous, oblivious slacker who "waffled among any number of diets" to "committed vegetarian." Last month, Gary Steiner, a philosopher

(C) at Bucknell University, argued on the Op-Ed page of *The New York Times* that people should strive to be "strict ethical vegans" like himself, avoiding all products derived from animals, including wool and silk. Killing animals for human food and finery is nothing less than "outright murder," he said, Isaac Bashevis Singer's "eternal Treblinka."

3   But before we cede the entire moral penthouse to "committed vegetarians" and "strong ethical vegans,"

(D) we might consider that plants no more aspire to being stir-fried in a wok than a hog aspires to being peppercorn-studded in my Christmas clay pot. This is not meant as a trite argument or a chuckled aside. Plants are lively and seek to keep it that way. The more that scientists learn about the complexity of plants—their keen sensitivity to the environment, the speed with which they react to changes in the environment, and the extraordinary number of tricks that plants will rally to fight off attackers and solicit help from afar—the more impressed researchers become, and the less easily we can dismiss plants as so much **fiberfill** backdrop, passive sunlight collectors on which deer, antelope and vegans can conveniently graze. It's time for a green revolution, a reseeding of our stubborn animal minds.

4   When plant biologists speak of their subjects, they use active verbs and vivid images. Plants "forage" for (E) resources like light and soil nutrients and "anticipate" rough spots and opportunities. By analyzing the ratio of red light and far red light falling on their leaves, for example, they can sense the presence of other **chlorophyllated** competitors nearby and try to grow the other way. Their roots ride the underground "**rhizosphere**" and engage in cross-cultural and **microbial** trade.

5   "Plants are not static or silly," said Monika Hilker of the Institute of Biology at the Free University of Berlin. "They respond to tactile cues, they recognize different wavelengths of light, they listen to chemical signals, they can even talk" through chemical signals.

(E) Angier explains animal-plant parallels.

(A) The title introduces the topic and sets a playful tone.
(B) Angier describes her position on meat eating as personal and arbitrary versus strict and ideological.
(C) She describes Steiner's position.
(D) She suggests his position (approves eating plants but disapproves eating meat) is logically inconsistent.

---

arbitrary
made without meaning

vehemence
eagerness or zeal

fiberfill
synthetic fibers used for filling pillows

chlorophyllated
green

rhizosphere
the area of soil around the roots of a plant

microbial
microorganism

Touch, sight, hearing, speech. "These are sensory **modalities** and abilities we normally think of as only being in animals," Dr. Hilker said.

6 Plants can't run away from a threat but they can stand their ground. "They are very good at avoiding getting eaten," said Linda Walling of the University of California, Riverside. "It's an unusual situation where insects can overcome those defenses." At the smallest nip to its leaves, specialized cells on the plant's surface release chemicals to irritate the predator or sticky goo to entrap it. Genes in the plant's DNA are activated to wage system-wide chemical warfare, the plant's version of an immune response. We need terpenes, alkaloids, phenolics—let's move.

7 "I'm amazed at how fast some of these things hap-
(F) pen," said Consuelo M. De Moraes of Pennsylvania State University. Dr. De Moraes and her colleagues did labeling experiments to clock a plant's systemic response time and found that, in less than 20 minutes from the moment the caterpillar had begun feeding on its leaves, the plant had plucked carbon from the air and forged defensive compounds from scratch.

8 Just because we humans can't hear them doesn't mean plants don't howl. Some of the compounds that plants generate in response to insect mastication—
(G) their feedback, you might say—are volatile chemicals that serve as cries for help. Such airborne alarm calls have been shown to attract both large predatory

insects like dragon flies, which delight in caterpillar meat, and tiny parasitic insects, which can infect a caterpillar and destroy it from within.

9 Enemies of the plant's enemies are not the only ones to tune into the emergency broadcast. "Some of these cues, some of these volatiles that are released (H) when a focal plant is damaged," said Richard Karban of the University of California, Davis, "cause other plants of the same species, or even of another species, to likewise become more resistant to herbivores."

10 Yes, it's best to nip trouble in the bud.

11 Dr. Hilker and her colleagues, as well as other research teams, have found that certain plants can sense when insect eggs have been deposited on their (I) leaves and will act immediately to rid themselves of the incubating menace. They may sprout carpets of tumorlike **neoplasms** to knock the eggs off, or secrete **ovicides** to kill them, or sound the S O S. Reporting in The Proceedings of the National Academy of Sciences, Dr. Hilker and her coworkers determined that when a female cabbage butterfly lays her eggs on a brussels sprout plant and attaches her treasures to the leaves with tiny dabs of glue, the vigilant vegetable detects the presence of a simple additive in the glue, benzyl cyanide. Cued by the additive, the plant swiftly alters the chemistry of its leaf surface to beckon female parasitic wasps. Spying the anchored bounty, the female wasps in turn inject their eggs inside, the gestating wasps feed on the **gestating** butterflies, and the plant's problem is solved.

12 Here's the lurid Edgar Allan Poetry of it: that benzyl cyanide tip-off had been donated to the female butterfly by the male during mating. "It's an **anti-aph-** (J) **rodisiac pheromone**, so that the female wouldn't mate anymore," Dr. Hilker said. "The male is trying to ensure his paternity, but he ends up endangering his own offspring."

13 Plants eavesdrop on one another **benignly** and **malignly.** As they described in *Science* and other journals, Dr. De Moraes and her colleagues have discovered

---

(F) She supports her assertions by quoting several experts.
(G) She compares plants and humans.

modalities
relating to different modes or manners

neoplasms
new growths

ovicides
substances that kills egg cells

gestating
pregnant

anti-aphrodisiac pheromone
a chemical that inhibits sexual desire

benignly
without the intention of harm

malignly
with the intention of harm

(H) Angier quotes an expert and playfully supports his opinion.
(I) She describes how plants communicate with insects.
(J) She playfully labels and describes the process.

that seedlings of the dodder plant, a parasitic weed related to morning glory, can detect volatile chemicals released by potential host plants like the tomato. The young dodder then grows inexorably toward the host, until it can encircle the victim's stem and begin sucking the life phloem right out of it. The parasite can even distinguish between the scents of healthier and weaker tomato plants and then head for the hale one.

14   "Even if you have quite a bit of knowledge about plants," Dr. De Moraes said, "it's still surprising to see how sophisticated they can be."

15   It's a small daily tragedy that we animals must kill
(K) to stay alive. Plants are the ethical **autotrophs** here, the ones that wrest their meals from the sun. Don't expect them to boast: they're too busy fighting to survive.

(K) In closing, Angier notes that to live, all animals must kill and eat something.

autotrophs
organisms that can nourish themselves through processes such as photosynthesis

Reading for Better Writing

Working by yourself or with a group, do the following:

1. On a sheet of paper, create two columns. In the left column, paraphrase Gary Steiner's core argument and list his supporting claims; and in the right column, paraphrase Natalie Angier's core argument and list her supporting claims. Explain how the positions are similar and different, and assess the strength of each writer's reasoning, taking into account the supporting claims and the evidence offered.

2. Describe each writer's voice and cite words or phrases exemplifying that voice. Then explain how each writer's voice colors his or her argument.

3. Examine each argument for logical fallacies such as either/or thinking (page 183), appeal to pity (page 183), and attack against the person (page 185). If you find examples, explain how they affect the writer's argument.

4. Imagine you are a page editor at *The New York Times*. In addition to the images on pages 199 and 203, what other visuals might you add to the articles to complement each writer's position? Explain.

Elena Elisseeva, 2011 / Used under license from Shutterstock.com

Write, revise, and edit a logical position paper. LO5

Writing Guidelines

Planning

1. **Select a debatable topic.** Review the list below and add topics as needed.
   - **Current Affairs:** Explore recent trends, new laws, and emerging controversies discussed in the news media, blogs, or online discussion groups.
   - **Burning Issues:** What issues related to family, work, education, recreation, technology, the environment, or popular culture do you care about?
   - **Dividing Lines:** What issues divide your communities? Religion, gender, politics, regionalism, nationalism? Choose a topic and freewrite to clarify your position.
   - **Fresh Fare:** Avoid tired issues unless you take a fresh perspective.

2. **Take stock.** Before you dig into your topic, assess your starting point. What is your current position on the topic? Why? What evidence do you have?

3. **Get inside the issue.** To take a defensible position, study the issue carefully:
   - Investigate all possible positions on the issue and research as needed.
   - Do firsthand research that produces current, relevant information.
   - In your research, carefully study visual information such as tables, graphs (e.g., pie graphs, bar graphs), photos, videos, and other multimedia texts for what they convey about the issue.
   - Write your position at the top of a page. Below it, set up "Pro" and "Con" columns. List arguments in each column.
   - Develop reasoning that supports your position and test it for the following: (a) no logical fallacies, such as slanted language, oversimplification, either/or thinking, straw-man and red-herring claims, appeals to pity, and personal attacks (see pages 182–185); and (b) an effective range of support: statistics, observations, expert testimony, comparisons, experiences, and analysis (see pages 180–181).

4. **Refine your position.** By now, you may have sharpened or radically changed your initial position on the topic. Before you organize and draft your essay, reflect on those changes. If it helps, use this formula:

   I believe this to be true about _____.

5. **Organize your argument and support.** Now you've committed yourself to a position. Before drafting, review these organizational options:
   - **Traditional Pattern:** Introduce the issue, state your position, support it, address and refute opposition, and restate your position.
   - **Blatant Confession:** Place your position statement in the first sentence.
   - **Delayed Gratification:** Describe various positions on the topic, compare and contrast them, and then take and defend your position.
   - **Changed Mind:** If your research changed your mind, explain how and why.
   - **Winning Over:** If readers oppose your position, address their concerns by anticipating and answering each objection or question.

Drafting

6. **Write your first draft.** Using freewriting and/or your notes, draft the paper.
   - **Opening:** Seize the reader's attention, possibly with a bold title—or raise concern for the issue with a dramatic story, a pointed example, a vivid picture, a thought-provoking question, or a personal confession. Supply background information that readers need to understand the issue.
   - **Development:** Deepen, clarify, and support your position statement, using solid logic and reliable support. Address opposing views fairly as part of a clear, well-reasoned argument that helps readers understand and accept your position. If appropriate, use graphs, visuals, and multimedia elements to deepen your ideas and advance your position.
   - **Closing:** End on a lively, thoughtful note that stresses your commitment. If appropriate, make a direct or indirect plea to readers to adopt your position.

Revising

7. Improve the ideas, organization, and voice.
Ask a classmate or someone from the college's writing center to read your position paper for the following:

Ideas: Does the writing effectively establish and defend a stand on a debatable issue? Is the position clearly stated and effectively qualified and refined? Do the reasoning and support help the reader understand and appreciate the position? If visuals are used, are they used effectively to deepen the thinking, not to distract or manipulate?

Organization: Does the opening effectively raise the issue? Does the middle offer a carefully sequenced development and defense of the position? Does the closing successfully drive home the position?

Voice: Is the voice thoughtful, measured, committed, and convincing?

Editing

8. Edit and proofread the essay by addressing these issues:

Words: Language is precise, concrete, and lively—no jargon, cliches, or insults.

Sentences: Constructions vary in length and flow smoothly.

Correctness: The copy includes no errors in spelling, usage, punctuation, grammar, or mechanics.

Design: The page design is correctly formatted and attractive; information is properly documented according to the required system (e.g., MLA, APA). Any graphics and visuals used are effectively integrated with the written text.

Publishing

9. Publish your essay. Submit your position paper according to your instructor's requirements. In addition, seek a forum for your position—with peers in a discussion group, with relatives, or online.

Critical-Thinking and Writing Activities

As directed by your instructor, complete the following critical-thinking and writing activities by yourself or with classmates.

1. Reflect on hot topics in your major—check textbooks, talk to professors or other experts, and review journals in the field. Then write a position paper on a controversial issue.

2. Review Alyssa Woudstra's essay, "Nuclear Is Not the Answer." Then research this or another energy-related topic and write an essay in which you take a clear, well-reasoned position on one or more key issues.

3. Review Gary Steiner's and Natalie Angier's essays on what we should or should not eat. Then research the topic and develop your own argument in which you address relevant issues that they raise, as well as other issues that you think are relevant. Seek to state your position clearly and support your claims with reliable evidence.

4. Draft or revise a position paper that addresses a controversial issue that exists within a community to which you belong (e.g., city, neighborhood, generation, race or ethnic group, gender, consumer group, online network) by respectfully describing opposing ideas and showing how each view is reasonable and acceptable.

Checklist: Learning Outcomes

Use the checklist below to assess what you have learned about taking a position in writing.

_____ I can read and evaluate a position paper for clarity and logic.

_____ I can develop sound claims with reliable evidence

_____ I can make concessions and rebut opposing arguments.

_____ I can make effective appeals to credibility, logic, and emotion while avoiding logical fallacies such as oversimplification, either/or thinking, straw-man and red herring claims, appeals to pity, and personal attacks.

_____ I can write, revise, and edit a well-reasoned position paper in a measured but compelling voice.

"Passion is often more effectual than force."
—Aesop

17

Persuading Readers to Act

Persuading people to do something is challenging, requiring that you convince them to believe you, to rethink their own perspectives, and to take a concrete step. In the end, you need to change people's minds in order to change their actions.

Writers achieve this goal with sound logic, reliable support, and fitting appeals. Every day, persuasive writing like this appears in newsletters, editorials, marketing documents, business proposals, academic journals, white papers, and traditional essays.

Because the form is so common, you can expect to read and write versions of it in college and in the workplace. As you read the essays in this chapter, carefully analyze how writers develop convincing appeals for action. Then when you write your own essay, try these same strategies.

Learning Outcomes

LO1 Know how to read an appeal for action.

LO2 Describe a debatable issue.

LO3 Make clear and rational claims.

LO4 Make transparent claims.

LO5 Use an informed and mature voice.

LO6 Write, revise, and edit an essay persuading readers to act.

Know how to read an appeal for action.

How should you read an argument that urges you to act on an issue? The instructions below offer helpful instructions.

Consider the rhetorical situation.

When reading an appeal to act, anticipate what the writer wants people to do, what audience he or she has in mind, and how the topic is treated.

Purpose: Whether in academics, the workplace, or public life, writers call for action because they believe change is needed. Something is not right. Something needs to be improved or fixed. The writer's goal is to convince readers to care about the issue strongly enough to take a concrete step.

Audience: The intended readers are people whom the writer believes need to be pressed to act. Readers may be unaware of the issue, may feel overwhelmed by it, may have an interest in not acting, or may not care enough about the issue to actually act. The writer thus educates and urges such readers.

Topic: In academics, the topics addressed might be related to a specific discipline (e.g., educational mentoring campaign, expanding an arts program), a political or social issue (e.g., shelter for abused women, Special Olympics program), or a general humanitarian concern (e.g., help for victims of an epidemic, a flood, or a war).

Look for convincing qualities.

When reading an appeal to act, look for the following:

Compelling Argument: The writer accurately describes the issue, convinces readers of its importance, and calls for a doable and effective action. The writer's claims are fact based and reasonable, not extreme, trivial, or unqualified (see pages 179–180).

Logical Argument: The argument is based on reliable evidence such as appropriate anecdotes, tests, experiments, analogies, and expert testimony (see pages 180–181); and the argument avoids logical fallacies

such as half-truths, unreliable testimonials, attacks against a person, and false analogies.

Mature Voice: The writing sounds informed and genuine; it includes no manipulative appeals, quarrelsome language, or demeaning accusations.

Checklist: Reading

✔ What is the issue, and what action is requested to address it?

✔ Who are the intended readers, and what capacity to act do they have?

✔ Are the writer's claims accurate, compelling, and logical?

✔ Is the argument's tone informed, genuine, and respectful?

✔ Is the writing convincing—does it move readers to do what the writer requests?

Describe a debatable issue.

Rebecca Pasok is an environmental studies major who wrote the following essay to persuade readers to support lifestyle choices and energy policies that do not require drilling for oil in the Arctic National Wildlife Refuge. As you read, assess whether she (1) objectively describes the issue, and (2) logically explains why the action that she proposes is needed.

Essay Outline

Introduction: Oil drilling could begin in ANWR's Area 1002.

1. *Claims for/against:* Drilling threatens wildlife like caribou.
2. *Claims for/against:* Drilling threatens native people.
3. *Claims for/against:* Drilling helps resolve long-term energy needs.

Closing: A long-term solution requires (1) energy-saving technologies and (2) ecological lifestyle choices.

To Drill or Not to Drill

Survey · Question · Read · Recite · Review **SQ3R**

1

(A) Known as "America's Last Frontier," the Arctic National Wildlife Refuge (ANWR) is located in the northeast corner of Alaska, right along the Beaufort Sea. President Dwight D. Eisenhower established the refuge in 1960, and today its 19 million acres make it one of the biggest refuges in the United States and home to a wide variety of wildlife such as eagles, wolves, moose, grizzly bears, polar bears, and caribou. During the last few years, however, the security of that home has been threatened by those who want to use one section of the ANWR to drill for oil. That section—named Area 1002—encompasses 1.5 million acres of pristine land near the coast.

2

(B) One of the strongest arguments against oil drilling anywhere in the refuge is that the environmental impact of drilling conflicts with the very purpose of the ANWR. The primary mandate for the ANWR, as laid out by the U.S. Fish and Wildlife Service that administers the refuge, is "to protect the wildlife and habitats of the area for the benefit of people now and in the future." The question then is whether drilling for oil supports, or is in conflict with, this mandate. President George W. Bush and others argue that oil drilling does not conflict with the mandate because new oil-drilling techniques cause only minimal damage to the environment. These techniques include drilling fewer wells, placing wells closer together, and building pipelines above ground so as not to disturb the animals (McCarthy).

3

Some environmental experts support the argument that the new techniques will not hurt wildlife. While these individuals acknowledge that some land disturbance will result, they argue that animals such as caribou will not suffer. One expert taking this position is Pat Valkenberg, a research coordinator with the Alaska Department of Fish and Game; he maintains that the caribou population is thriving and should continue to thrive. To support this point, Valkenberg notes that between 1997 and 2000, the caribou population actually grew from 19,700 to 27,128 (Petroleum News).

4

(C) Other experts challenge those statistics with information about the caribou's birthing patterns. These experts point to herds like the porcupine caribou that live in the ANWR and move along the coast of the Beaufort Sea in the United States and also into Canada. A majority of the females in this herd wear radio collars that have been tracked to Area 1002 during calving season. Experts who argue against drilling note that the calves born on ANWR's coastal plain have a greater chance of surviving than those that are born in the foothills, where many of their predators live (*U.S. Fish and Wildlife*). This difference in survival ratios, argue antidrilling experts, may not be accounted for in the statistics used by prodrilling advocates like Valkenberg.

(C) She counters the position with expert testimony for the other side.

(A) The opening provides background information before raising the controversial position.

(B) The writer starts with a strong argument against drilling but then maps out why others support it.

5 One specialist opposed to drilling is David Klein, a professor at the Institute of Arctic Biology at the University of Alaska–Fairbanks. Klein argues that if the oil industry opens up the ANWR for drilling, the number of caribou will likely decrease because the calving locations would change. He points out that oil-industry work in the Prudhoe oil field (also in Alaska) has already split up the Central Arctic herd of caribou, so it is likely that drilling in Area 1002 will similarly affect the porcupine herd (McCarthy).

6 But caribou are not the only wildlife that would be affected by drilling in Area 1002. Musk oxen, polar bears, and grizzly bears could be driven out of the refuge and possibly into regions where people live, thereby threatening both the animals' and people's safety. Clearly, the bottom line in this debate is that drilling in Area 1002 will destroy at least some of the **ecological integrity** that makes ANWR a natural treasure. Environmentalists say that "just as there is no way to be half-pregnant, there is no 'sensitive' way to drill in **(D)** a wilderness" (McCarthy). They are right.

7 However, oil drilling in ANWR will hurt more than the environment and wildlife; the drilling also **(E)** will hurt at least one of the two **Inuit tribes** living in Alaska—the Inupiat Eskimos and the Gwich'in Indians. The Inupiat is the larger group, and they favor drilling. Money generated by the oil industry, say the Inupiat, will help them improve a variety of tribal services such as education and health care. On the other hand, the Gwich'in tribe depends on the porcupine caribou for food. As a result, if oil drilling displaces such animals, the people will suffer. Not only do they need the caribou to survive, but they also need them to retain the tribe's dignity and way of life. In other words, while oil drilling in ANWR may give some residents more money, others clearly will pay a price.

8 So if oil drilling in ANWR would have so many negative effects, what is driving the argument for **(F)** drilling? Unfortunately, nothing more than a short-sighted, ill-informed effort to satisfy America's exces-

---

(D) The writer strongly states her thesis—that she agrees with opponents of drilling.
(E) By looking at effects on people, the writer expands her opposition.
(F) A question serves as a transition to a key counterargument.

ecological integrity
refers to an ecosystem's health in the face of pollution and other unnatural disturbances

Inuit tribes
native populations of northern Canada and parts of Greenland and Alaska

sive appetite for oil: To continue using too much, we want to produce more. But is drilling in the ANWR the answer to our consumption problem?

9   At best, getting more oil from Alaska is a shortsighted solution: ANWR's reserves are simply too small to provide a long-term solution. A 1998 study by the U.S. Geological Survey concluded that the total amount of accessible oil in the ANWR is 5.7 to 16 billion barrels, with an expected amount of 10.4 billion barrels (Arctic Power). While these figures are considered the official estimate, the National Resources Defense Council (a group of lawyers, scientists, and environmentalists) disagrees. It estimates the accessible amount to be 3.2 billion barrels—a resource the United States would use up in just six months! In the meantime, using the ANWR oil would do nothing to ease our dependence on Middle Eastern countries for oil. There has to be a better choice.

10   And there is. The question is not whether drilling
(G) should take place in the ANWR, but how to provide energy for everyone, now and in the future. A poll taken by the *Christian Science Monitor* shows that voters believe that the best option for Americans is to develop new technologies (Dillan). Finding new energy sources, they say, is more important than finding new oil reserves.

11   There are two main problems with relying primarily on oil for our energy: Oil supplies are limited, and oil use pollutes. Democratic Representative Rosa De-Lauro of Connecticut made this point well when she said the following:

12   "We need a serious energy policy in the United
(H) States. Drilling in the Arctic National Wildlife Refuge is not the solution. We should look to increase domestic production while balancing our desire for a cleaner environment. We must also look at ways to reduce our dependency on fossil fuels themselves, a smart and necessary step that will lead to a cleaner environment" (qtd. in Urban).

(G) The writer redirects the discussion to the root of the problem.
(H) A closing quotation focuses and supports the writer's objections.

While reducing our use of fossil fuels will not   13
be easy, it is possible if we do two things: (1) develop energy-saving technologies and (2) make lifestyle choices that conserve energy. Unlike the short-term (and shortsighted) solution of drilling in the ANWR, these strategies will help save the environment. In addition, the strategies will help people both now and in the future.

Note: The works-cited page is not shown.

Reading for Better Writing

Working by yourself or with a group, answer these questions:

1. The writer describes both positions on drilling before stating her opposition explicitly. Is this strategy effective?
2. The writer uses the testimony of experts extensively. Why?
3. What does the writer do to acknowledge, concede points to, and refute support for drilling?
4. Review pages 180–181 about types of support. Then trace the types of evidence provided in this essay. Evaluate the quality and completeness of the evidence.
5. Does the last paragraph offer an effective closing to the writer's argument? Why or why not?
6. Does Pasok objectively describe the issue and logically explain the need for action? Cite passages that support your answer.
7. Review the photos in this essay and explain how they affect your understanding of the text.

Make clear and rational claims. ___ LO3

Student writer Henry Veldboom, a mature student with children of his own, wrote this essay to call North American readers to reconsider what they value.

(A) Our Wealth: Where Is It Taking Us?

Survey · Question · Read · Recite · Review **SQ3R**

1   North America's wealth and the lifestyle it affords are known throughout the world. This knowledge has (B) created a belief that wealth and happiness are synonymous, which in turn has perpetuated the dreams of people around the globe who hope to achieve the same successes witnessed here in the West. Is there truth to the idea that wealth and happiness coexist? Ask North Americans if they would willingly trade life here for that in a struggling country and they would likely say "No." Their wealth has made their lives quite comfortable. Most would admit to enjoying the lifestyle such wealth allows; few would want to give it up. But what is this wealth really costing North Americans—especially children?

2   While North American wealth grew out of the capitalism that culminated in the nineteenth-century (C) Industrial Revolution, today's capitalism is a system largely based on consumerism—an attitude that values the incessant acquisition of goods in the belief that it is necessary and beneficial. The goal, then, of a modern capitalist economy is to produce many goods as cheaply as possible and have these goods purchased on a continual basis. The forces behind capitalism—business owners at the demand of stockholders—employ an ever-expanding array of marketing techniques to accomplish the goal of selling products. Expert on marketing George Barna defines marketing as the process of directing "goods and services from the producer to the consumer, to satisfy the needs and desires of the consumer and the goals of the producer" (41). On the receiving end of today's capitalism are consumers whose needs are in general self-serving and based on self-actualization. Corporations promote this way of thinking and capitalize on it through marketing techniques. Social commentator Benjamin Barber describes this modern interaction in the following way: "[This thinking] serves capitalist consumerism directly by nurturing a culture of **impetuous** consumption necessary to selling puerile goods in a developed world that has few genuine needs" (81).

3   Admittedly, deciphering genuine needs from superfluous wants is not an easy task. However, putting debates about materialism aside, people must consider (D) the results of their consumption. The 2008-2009 economic upheaval still lingers in people's minds despite the recent upward trend in the North American economy. When such financial turmoil happens, the typical response is to lay blame. Some people are quick to accuse corporations of causing the turmoil and governments of allowing corporations to operate as they do. Noted journalist and anti-establishment advocate Linda McQuaig comments on the shift in the 1970s that gave individuals more freedoms; in turn, corporations accommodated the lax attitudes of government to themselves and were "ensured freedom from their restraints on their profit-making" (22). Do North American corporations and governments share the responsibility to properly use wealth and direct the economy? Yes, they most certainly do. However, individuals must also examine their own fiscal responsibility. McQuaig addresses this issue as well, highlighting "the power and centrality of greed in our culture" (23). She raises a word that no one wants to be labeled with—greed. When people begin discussing their financial woes in relation to individual greed, the blame rests squarely on each member of society.

(A) Title: issue and central question
(B) Introduction: North American wealth and its real cost.
(C) Modern capitalism is based on harmful consumerism.

impetuous
impulsive; rash

(D) Consumers must consider the results of their consumption.

4   The behavior that has led to the current financial crisis is not only impacting adults but also putting (E) children at risk. Deceptive marketing tactics make use of psychological knowledge and **social patterning** research to convince consumers to purchase particu- (F) lar products. Adults who possess the mental capacity to discern motives and detect subversion are being effectively manipulated by cunning advertising tech- niques, resulting in massive debt loads, addiction, and bankruptcy. However, the greater concern with these marketing practices is that they are being aimed at children who have less ability to defend themselves. Psychiatrist Susan Linn describes the marketing aimed at children as "precisely targeted, refined by scientific method, and honed by child psychologists . . ." (5). It isn't the case that children are getting caught in marketing traps set for adults; rather, kids are being targeted. Linn remarks that developmental psychol- ogy which was once used solely for treating children's mental health is now used to determine "weaknesses" in children's thinking in order to exploit these weak- nesses (24). The weaknesses are due to children's brains not having reached full **cognitive development**, result- ing in unstable patterns of thinking in areas such as reasoning, memory, and problem solving (Weiten 47). At such a disadvantage, children are unable to with- stand the marketing ploys aimed at them.

5   Knowing that children are the targets of aggres- sive mass marketing is all the more serious when the (G) scope of the situation is considered. Much research has been done on purchasing patterns, and while the fact that North Americans spend large amounts of money on goods may not be surprising, when children are added to the equation the picture changes. Expert on consumerism, economics, and family studies Juliet Schor has done a considerable amount of convincing research in this area. She comments on the purchas- ing influence of children and notes that children aged four to twelve influenced an estimated $670 billion of adult purchasing in 2004 (23). Children having influ-

ence on such large amounts of money being spent catches the attention of producers who consequent- ly aim their marketing at kids in order to sell adult products. Schor also notes the results of a Nickel- odeon (an entertainment company) study that states when it comes to recognizing brands, "the average ten year old has memorized 300 to 400 brands" (25). Kids know the products and they know what they want; the dollar amount parents are spending in response to their children reflects this.

6   The effects of aggressive marketing and consum- erism on North American children are exhibited in a wide range of health problems. At first glance, the (H) relationship between consumerism and children's health may appear to be coincidental. However, much research shows a direct link between marketing to children and their health. Having done her own research and examined other studies, Juliet Schor

---

(H) Physical and mental health problems

social patterning
a repeated set of characteristics or behaviors pertaining to the same social group

cognitive development
a child's brain development, specifically for information processing and language learning

---

(E) People must examine how consumerism harms children.
(F) Marketing manipulation
(G) Influence on parental spending

concludes that "the more [children] buy into the commercial and materialist messages, the worse they feel about themselves, the more depressed they are, and the more they are beset by anxiety, headaches, stomach-aches, and boredom" (173). (On a related note, the time spent by children sitting in front of televisions and computers is an important factor in this outcome. These media are the prime vehicles for advertising and are contributing to sedentary lifestyles, which in turn cause health problems.) Materialism is having an effect not only on adults but also on youth. When children are asked what they aspire to be, the top answer is "to be rich" (37). The health of the minds and bodies of North American children is deteriorating as a result of consumerism and the new capitalism.

Having examined the current state of North American society in terms of the economic and personal health related to the new capitalism, one begins to see that society is in a situation that is neither beneficial nor sustainable. Changes must be made. If the response is to look for someone or something to blame, everyone must stop and take a look in the mirror. Changing habits and attitudes must start with the individual. While adopting a particular economic ideology is not the point, North Americans must take a hard look at their society and decide if this is how they want to live. If this society carries on unchanged, what future will its children have? North America has an abundance of wealth; the decision of where to go with it must be made: time is running out.

Note: The Works Cited pages is not shown. For sample pages, see MLA (pages 368–369) and APA (page 396).

(I) Conclusion: Individual consumers must change if society is to change.

Reading for Better Writing

Working by yourself or with a group, answer these questions:

1. In his title, Veldboom identifies the issue as wealth. How does he clarify and deepen the issue in the essay's opening paragraphs?

2. While acknowledging economic and social systems, Veldboom stresses individual values and responsibilities. How effective is this emphasis?

3. What action does the essay call for? Do you find the action practical and compelling? Why or why not?

4. Select three claims that Veldboom makes and explain why they are or are not (a) rational and (b) adequately supported.

Make transparent claims.

LO4

Dr. Martin Luther King, Jr., was a leader in the Civil Rights Movement during the 1950s and 1960s. On August 28, 1963, he delivered this persuasive speech to a crowd of 250,000 people gathered at the Lincoln Memorial in Washington, D.C. To appreciate its strong images and rhythmical language, read the speech aloud. Then assess the clarity and logic of its claims, looking specifically for half-truths (184), unreliable testimonials (184–185), personal attacks (185), and false analogies (185).

I Have a Dream

Survey • Question • Read • Recite • Review **SQ3R**

1   Five score years ago, a great American, in whose symbolic shadow we stand, signed the Emancipation **(A)** Proclamation. This momentous decree came as a great beacon light of hope to millions of Negro slaves who had been seared in the flames of withering injustice. It came as a joyous daybreak to end the long night of captivity.

2   But one hundred years later, we must face the tragic fact that the Negro is still not free. One hundred years later, the life of the Negro is still sadly crippled **(B)** by the manacles of segregation and the chains of discrimination. One hundred years later, the Negro lives on a lonely island of poverty in the midst of a vast ocean of material prosperity. One hundred years later, the Negro is still languishing in the corners of American society and finds himself an exile in his own land. So we have come here today to dramatize an appalling condition.

3   In a sense we have come to our nation's Capitol to cash a check. When the architects of our republic **(C)** wrote the magnificent words of the Constitution and the Declaration of Independence, they were signing a **promissory** note to which every American was to fall heir. This note was a promise that all men would be guaranteed the **unalienable** rights of life, liberty, and the pursuit of happiness.

4   It is obvious today that America has defaulted on this promissory note insofar as her citizens of color are concerned. Instead of honoring this sacred obligation, America has given the Negro people a bad check; a check which has come back marked "insufficient funds." But we refuse to believe that the bank of jus- **(D)** tice is bankrupt. We refuse to believe that there are insufficient funds in the great vaults of opportunity of this nation. So we have come to cash this check—a check that will give us upon demand the riches of freedom and the security of justice. We have also come to this hallowed spot to remind America of the fierce urgency of now. This is no time to engage in the luxury of cooling off or to take the tranquilizing drug of

(D) Repeated words and phrases create urgency.

(A) King starts with a tragic contrast.

(B) He uses figurative language to describe the present situation.

(C) An analogy clarifies the problem.

promissory
relating to a promise

unalienable
cannot be taken away

gradualism. Now is the time to make real the promises of Democracy. Now is the time to rise from the dark and desolate valley of segregation to the sunlit path of racial justice. Now is the time to open the doors of opportunity to all of God's children. Now is the time to lift our nation from the quicksands of racial injustice to the solid rock of brotherhood.

5   It would be fatal for the nation to overlook the urgency of the moment and to underestimate the determination of the Negro. This sweltering summer of the Negro's legitimate discontent will not pass until there is an invigorating autumn of freedom and equality. 1963 is not an end, but a beginning. Those who hope that the Negro needed to blow off steam and will now be content will have a rude awakening if the nation returns to business as usual. There will be neither rest nor tranquility in America until the Negro is granted his citizenship rights. The whirlwinds of revolt will continue to shake the foundations of our nation until the bright day of justice emerges.

6   But there is something I must say to my people who stand on the warm threshold which leads into the **(E)** palace of justice. In the process of gaining our rightful place we must not be guilty of wrongful deeds. Let us not seek to satisfy our thirst for freedom by drinking from the cup of bitterness and hatred. We must forever conduct our struggle on the high plane of dignity and discipline. We must not allow our creative protest to degenerate into physical violence. Again and again we must rise to the majestic heights of meeting physical force with soul force. The marvelous new militancy which has engulfed the Negro community must not lead us to a distrust of all white people, for many of our white brothers, as evidenced by their presence here today, have come to realize that their destiny is tied up with our destiny and their freedom is **inextricably** bound to our freedom. We cannot walk alone.

(E) King addresses specific audiences in turn.

---

inextricably
incapable of escaping or being undone

And as we talk, we must make the pledge that 7 we shall march ahead. We cannot turn back. There **(F)** are those who are asking the devotees of civil rights, "When will you be satisfied?" We can never be satisfied as long as the Negro is the victim of the unspeakable horrors of police brutality. We can never be satisfied as long as our bodies, heaving with the fatigue of travel, cannot gain lodging in the motels of the highways and the hotels of the cities. We cannot be satisfied as long as the Negro's basic mobility is from a smaller ghetto to a larger one. We can never be satisfied as long as a Negro in Mississippi cannot vote and a Negro in New York believes he has nothing for which to vote. No, no, we are not satisfied, and we will not be satisfied until justice rolls down like waters and righteousness like a mighty stream.

    I am not unmindful that some of you have come 8 here out of great trials and tribulations. Some of you **(G)** have come fresh from narrow jail cells. Some of you have come from areas where your quest for freedom left you battered by the storms of persecution and staggered by the winds of police brutality. You have been the veterans of creative suffering. Continue to work with the faith that unearned suffering is redemptive.

    Go back to Mississippi, go back to Alabama, go 9 back to South Carolina, go back to Georgia, go back to Louisiana, go back to the slums and ghettos of our northern cities, knowing that somehow this situation can and will be changed. Let us not wallow in the valley of despair.

    I say to you today, my friends, that in spite of the 10 difficulties and frustrations of the moment I still have a dream. It is a dream deeply rooted in the American dream.

    I have a dream that one day this nation will rise 11 up and live out the true meaning of its creed: "We hold these truths to be self-evident; that all men are created equal."

    I have a dream that one day on the red hills of 12 Georgia the sons of former slaves and the sons of for-

---

(F) He responds to the arguments of opponents.
(G) Appropriate emotional appeals are used in the context of suffering.

mer slave owners will be able to sit down together at the table of brotherhood.

13   I have a dream that the state of Mississippi, a desert state sweltering with the heat of injustice and op-
(H) pression, will be transformed into an oasis of freedom and justice.

14   I have a dream that my four little children will one day live in a nation where they will not be judged by the color of their skin but by the content of their character.

15   I have a dream today.

16   I have a dream that the state of Alabama, whose governor's lips are presently dripping with the words of **interposition** and **nullification**, will be transformed into a situation where little black boys and black girls will be able to join hands with little white boys and girls and walk together as sisters and brothers.

17   I have a dream today.

18   I have a dream that one day every valley shall be exalted, every hill and mountain shall be made low,
(I) the rough places will be made plain, and the crooked places will be made straight, and the glory of the Lord shall be revealed, and all flesh shall see it together.

19   This is our hope. This is the faith with which I return to the South. With this faith we will be able to hew out of the mountain of despair a stone of hope. With this faith we will be able to transform the jangling discords of our nation into a beautiful symphony of brotherhood. With this faith we will be able to work together, to pray together, to struggle together,

---

(H) The repetition of key phrases becomes a persuasive refrain.
(I) King's vision offers hope and motivates readers to change society.

to go to jail together, to stand up for freedom together, knowing that we will be free one day.

20   This will be the day when all God's children will be able to sing with new meaning.

> *My country 'tis of thee*
> *Sweet land of liberty,*   (J)
> *Of thee I sing,*
> *Land where my fathers died,*
> *Land of the pilgrims' pride,*
> *From every mountainside*
> *Let freedom ring.*

21   And if America is to be a great nation this must become true. So let freedom ring from the prodigious hilltops of New Hampshire. Let freedom ring from the mighty mountains of New York. Let freedom ring from the heightening Alleghenies of Pennsylvania!

22   Let freedom ring from the snow-capped Rockies of Colorado!

23   Let freedom ring from the curvaceous peaks of California!

24   But not only that; let freedom ring from Stone Mountain of Georgia!

25   Let freedom ring from Lookout Mountain of Tennessee!

26   Let freedom ring from every hill and molehill of Mississippi! From every mountainside, let freedom ring.

27   When we let freedom ring, when we let it ring from every village and every hamlet, from every state (K) and every city, we will be able to speed up that day when all of God's children, black men and white men, Jews and Gentiles, Protestants and Catholics, will be able to join hands and sing in the words of the old Negro spiritual, "Free at last! Free at last! Thank God almighty, we are free at last!"

(J) He appeals to ideals and to humanity's better nature, ending with a vision of a just society.
(K) The closing urges readers to work for a better future.

interposition
a doctrine that states a state can oppose a federal action it believes restricts its freedom

nullification
the refusal of a U.S. state to assist in enforcement of federal laws

Amy Nichole Harris, 2011 / Used under license from Shutterstock.com

Use an informed and mature voice.

LO5

Kofi Annan, the former Secretary General of the United Nations, wrote the essay below in order to urge readers worldwide to help address AIDS and famine in Africa. Read the essay carefully, noting the logic and tone of his claims. Then assess whether Annan's voice illustrates the quality described in LO5 above.

In Africa, AIDS Has a Woman's Face

Survey · Question · Read · Recite · Review **SQ3R**

1   A combination of famine and AIDS is threatening the backbone of Africa—the women who keep Afri-

(A) The title and introduction aim to create urgency about the issue.

exponentially
constantly

can societies going and whose work makes up the economic foundation of rural communities. For decades, we have known that the best way for Africa to thrive is to ensure that its women have the freedom, power, and knowledge to make decisions affecting their own lives and those of their families and communities. At the United Nations, we have always understood that our work for development depends on building a successful partnership with the African farmer and her husband.

2   Study after study has shown that there is no effective development strategy in which women do not play a central role. When women are fully involved, the benefits can be seen immediately: families are healthier; they are better fed; their income, savings and reinvestment go up. And, what is true of families is true of communities and, eventually, of whole countries.

3   But today, millions of African women are threatened by two simultaneous catastrophes: famine and AIDS. More than 30 million people are now at risk of starvation in southern Africa and the Horn of Africa. All of these predominantly agricultural societies are also battling serious AIDS epidemics. This is no coincidence: AIDS and famine are directly linked.

4   Because of AIDS, farming skills are being lost, agricultural development efforts are declining, rural livelihoods are disintegrating, productive capacity to work the land is dropping, and household earnings are shrinking—all while the cost of caring for the ill is rising **exponentially**. At the same time, H.I.V. infection and AIDS are spreading dramatically and disproportionately among women. A United Nations report released last month shows that women now make up 50 percent of those infected with H.I.V. worldwide—and in Africa that figure is now 59 percent. Today, AIDS has a woman's face.

5   AIDS has already caused immense suffering by killing almost 2.5 million Africans this year alone. It has left 11 million African children orphaned since

(B) Stressing the importance of women in African societies, Annan outlines the double catastrophe happening.

the epidemic began. Now it is attacking the capacity of these countries to resist famine by eroding those mechanisms that enable populations to fight back—the coping abilities provided by women.

6   In famines before the AIDS crisis, women proved more resilient than men. Their survival rate was higher, and their coping skills were stronger. Women were the ones who found alternative foods that could sustain their children in time of drought. Because droughts happened once a decade or so, women who had experienced previous droughts were able to pass on survival techniques to younger women. Women are the ones who nurture social networks that can help spread the burden in times of famine.

7   But today, as AIDS is eroding the health of Af-
(C) rica's women, it is eroding the skills, experience and networks that keep their families and communities going. Even before falling ill, a woman will often have to care for a sick husband, thereby reducing the time she can devote to planting, harvesting and marketing crops. When her husband dies, she is often deprived of credit, distribution networks or land rights. When she dies, the household will risk collapsing completely, leaving children to fend for themselves. The older ones, especially girls, will be taken out of school to work in the home or the farm. These girls, deprived of education and opportunities, will be even less able to protect themselves against AIDS.

8   Because this crisis is different from past famines,
(D) we must look beyond relief measures of the past. Merely shipping in food is not enough. Our effort will have to combine food assistance and new approaches to farming with treatment and prevention of H.I.V. and AIDS. It will require creating early-warning and analysis systems that monitor both H.I.V. infection rates and famine indicators. It will require new agricultural techniques, appropriate to a depleted work force. It will require a renewed effort to wipe out H.I.V.-related stigma and silence.

(C) Annan contrasts women's situation before and after the arrival of AIDS.
(D) He presses for a new combination of necessary, related actions.

It will require innovative, large-scale ways to care   9
for orphans, with specific measures that enable children in AIDS-affected communities to stay in school. Education and prevention are still the most powerful weapons against the spread of H.I.V. Above all, this new international effort must put women at the center of our strategy to fight AIDS.

Experience suggests that there is reason to hope.   10
The recent United Nations report shows that H.I.V. in-   (E)
fection rates in Uganda continue to decline. In South Africa, infection rates for women under 20 have started to decrease. In Zambia, H.I.V. rates show signs of dropping among women in urban areas and younger women in rural areas. In Ethiopia, infection levels have fallen among young women in the center of Addis Ababa.

We can and must build on those successes and   11
replicate them elsewhere. For that, we need leadership, partnership, and imagination from the international community and African governments. If we want to save Africa from two catastrophes, we would do well to focus on saving Africa's women.

(E) He points to hopeful signs and cases as a way of convincing readers that change can happen.

Reading for Better Writing

Working by yourself or with a group, answer these questions:

1. How does the writer introduce the topic and focus the essay? Explain.
2. What does Annan ask readers to do? Is his request clear and convincing? Why?
3. Choose a paragraph that you find particularly convincing and explain why.

Write, revise, and edit an essay persuading readers to act. LO6

Writing Guidelines

Planning

1. **Select a topic.** List issues about which you feel passionately such as community problems, international issues, disaster-relief efforts, educational outreach programs, environmental clean-up efforts, or social or political campaigns. Then choose a related topic that is debatable, significant, current, and manageable.

   Not Debatable
   Statistics on spending practices
   The existence of racism
   Recyclables are dumped in landfills

   Debatable
   The injustice of consumerism
   Solutions to racism
   Tax on paper/plastic grocery bags

2. **Choose and analyze your audience.** Think about who your readers are and why they might resist the change that you advocate.

3. **Narrow your focus and determine your purpose.** Should you focus on one aspect of the issue or all of it? What should you and can you try to change? How might you best organize your argument?

4. **Generate ideas and support.** Use prewriting strategies like those below to develop your thinking and gather support:

   - Set up "opposing viewpoints" columns in which you list arguments accepted by advocates of each position.
   - Research the issue to find current, reliable sources from multiple perspectives.
   - Research other calls to action on this issue, noting their appeals, supporting evidence, and success.

   - Brainstorm the range of actions that might be taken in response to the issue. For each action, explore how attractive and doable it might be for your readers.
   - Consider what outcomes or results you want.

5. **Organize your thinking.** Consider using the following strategies:

   - Make a sharp claim (like those below) that points toward action:

     On the issue of _____ , I believe _____ .
     Therefore, we must change _____ .

   - Review the evidence, and develop your line of reasoning by generating an outline or using a graphic organizer. (See pages 46–51.)

     Simple Outline: Introduction: the issue and initial claim
          Describing the issue and its importance: point 1, 2, and so on.
          Explaining possible actions and benefits: point 1, 2, and so on.
     Conclusion: call to specific action

Drafting

6. **Write your first draft.** As you write, remember your goal and specific readers:

   - **Opening:** Gain the readers' attention, raise the issue, help the readers care about it, and state your claim.
   - **Development:** Decide where to place your most persuasive supporting argument: first or last. Anticipate readers' questions and objections, and use appropriate logical and emotional appeals to overcome their resistance to change.
   - **Closing:** Restate your claim, summarize your support, and call your readers to act.
   - **Title:** Develop a thoughtful, energetic working title that stresses a vision or change. (For ideas, scan the titles of the sample essays in this chapter.)

Revising

7. Improve the ideas, organization, and voice.
Ask a classmate or someone from the college's writing center to read your call-to-action paper for the following:

Ideas: Does the writing prompt readers to change their thinking and behavior? Does the essay show effective reasoning, good support, and a clear call to action—without logical fallacies such as half-truths, unreliable testimonials, attacks against a person, and false analogies (see pages 182–185)?

Organization: Does the opening engagingly raise the issue? Does the middle carefully press the issue and the need for action? Does the closing successfully call for specific changes and actions?

Voice: Is the tone energetic but controlled, confident but reasonable? Does the writing inspire readers to join your cause and act?

Editing

8. Edit and proofread the essay by checking issues like these:

Words: Language is precise, concrete, and easily understood—no jargon, cliches, doublespeak, or loaded terms.

Sentences: Constructions flow smoothly and are varied in structure.

Correctness: The copy includes no errors in grammar, punctuation, usage, or spelling.

Design: The page design is correctly formatted and attractive; information is properly documented according to the required system (e.g., MLA, APA).

Publishing

9. Prepare and publish your final essay. Submit the essay to your instructor. If appropriate, solicit feedback from another audience—perhaps on a Web site, in the school newspaper, at a campus club, or from a community organization.

Critical-Thinking and Writing Activities

As directed by your instructor, complete the following critical-thinking and writing activities by yourself or with classmates.

1. The four essays in this chapter address significant social and ethical issues: wealth and poverty, health and famine, racial equality. List topics like these, choose one, narrow the focus to a specific issue, and then write an essay that persuades readers to do something related to the issue.

2. Choose an issue that is related to your major and requires change. Then write an essay in which you describe the issue and persuade readers to take the action that you recommend.

3. As a service project, visit an administrator at a local nonprofit agency (e.g., school, hospital, church, employment office, YMCA) and offer to write an editorial, news article, or letter in which you describe one of the agency's needs and persuade readers to offer their help.

4. What issues have come up in your job? Contemplate issues such as pay equity, equal opportunity, management policies, and unsafe work conditions. Then write a persuasive report to a decision maker or to fellow employees.

Checklist: Learning Outcomes

Use the checklist below to assess what you have learned about taking a position in writing.

____ I can understand and evaluate arguments that urge readers to act.

____ I objectively describe an issue and logically explain why action is needed.

____ I can make clear rational claims supported with reliable evidence.

____ I make transparent claims free of half-truths, unreliable testimonials, personal attacks, and false analogies.

____ I use an informed, mature voice.

____ I can write, revise, and edit an essay persuading readers to act.

"I believe that if you show people the problems and you show them solutions they will be moved to act."

—Bill Gates

18

Proposing a Solution

Proposals are prescriptions for change. As such, they challenge readers to care about a problem, accept a solution, and act on it. A strong proposal offers a logical, practical, and creative argument that leads toward positive change, whether it's helping immigrants acquire citizenship, defending against terrorism, or offering the poor compassion and meaningful support.

Proposal writers argue for such remedies in all areas of life. In your college courses, you'll be challenged to generate solutions to many difficult problems. In your community, you may participate in policy making and civic development. In the workplace, you may write proposals that justify expenditures, sell products, or troubleshoot problems. In each situation, you'll have to clearly explain the problem, offer a solution, argue for adopting it, and possibly also explain how to implement it.

Learning Outcomes

LO1 Understand how to read problem-solution essays.

LO2 Describe the problem and solution.

LO3 Analyze the solutions.

LO4 Analyze the problem.

LO5 Analyze a persuasive argument.

LO6 Write, revise, and edit a problem-solution essay.

Understand how to read problem-solution essays.

The instructions below will help you understand and use problem-solution logic.

Consider the rhetorical situation.

When reading problem-solution writing, think about its purpose, audience, and topic.

Purpose: Problem-solution writing aims to inform: to describe a problem accurately, to present workable solutions, and to explain the strengths and weaknesses of each. However, such writing also aims to persuade: to convince readers that a problem is urgent, that one solution is better than others, or that readers should implement it.

Audience: Potentially, writers could have four audiences: people responsible for the problem, decision makers with the power to adopt a solution, people affected by the problem, and a public who just want information about the problem. When reading the document, note whether it (1) offers all of its readers the information that they need and (2) communicates in language that they can understand and trust.

Topic: Clearly, problem-solution writing focuses on a problem, but it can be a problem broadly conceived—perhaps as a challenge or an opportunity. Across the college curriculum, such problems are typically discipline-related (e.g., dyslexia in Education, oil spills in Environmental Studies, agoraphobia in Psychology). In the workplace, problem-solution reasoning is used in proposals.

Consider the reasoning.

When reading problem-solution writing, look for the following:

Accurate Description: The writer correctly describes the problem, including relevant details regarding its history, causes, effects, dangers, costs, and direct or indirect impact on readers. The writing also describes all reasonable solutions, including details about their history, side effects, costs, successes, and failures.

Thorough Analysis: The writer carefully analyzes the problem, each solution, and why the recommended solution is the best choice. The writer supports all claims with reliable data and logical reasoning.

Rational Argument: The writer's claims and appeals for action are thoughtful, stated in objective terms, and presented in a measured, informed voice.

Checklist: Problem-Solution

- ✔ What is the problem, what is its history, and why should the problem be resolved?
- ✔ What is the solution, how does it resolve the problem, and with what side effects?
- ✔ What action does the writer call for, and is it effective, realistic, and cost effective?
- ✔ Are persuasive statements reasonable, well documented, and free of fallacies?

Describe the problem and solution.

Journalism major Renee Wielenga wrote and published "Dream Act . . ." as a newspaper article. She then revised the piece as an essay, but retained the problem-solution reasoning used in her original article. As you read the essay, assess whether her description of the problem and solution is accurate and free of fallacies.

Essay Outline

Introduction: (Problem) Students' dreams foiled by immigration laws; (Solution) Dream Act offers route to legal residency.

1. Bill's requirements for residency and citizenship
2. Bill's origin and increasing support
3. Bill's remaining impediments

Conclusion: The Dream Act warrants readers' support.

Dream Act May Help Local
(A) Student Fight for Residency

Survey · Question · Read · Recite · Review **SQ3R**

1

(B) Attending college, joining the military, creating a career path: these are dreams for most U.S. high school graduates. But for Maria Lopez, a senior at San Marshall High School who has lived in the U.S for seven years, there is only one legal option: return to Mexico. She is one of nearly 65,000 high school students each year who do not have the opportunity to pursue their dreams because they arrived in the U.S. illegally. Like many of these students, Maria is highly motivated, hard working, and excited to be involved in her high school. However, Maria's parents brought her to this country without going through the legal immigration process. As a result, by law she is an undocumented alien who has no method to achieve legal residency while living in the U.S.

2

(C) Currently, children like Maria have only one route to legal residency: go back to their country of birth, file the proper paperwork, and then return to the U.S. Unfortunately, attempts to return legally are often difficult, with roadblocks such as a ten-year restriction on re-entering the U.S. However, one piece of proposed federal legislation could help these young people pursue their dreams: The Development, Relief, and Education for Alien Minors Act (S. 729), better known as the Dream Act, is an amendment to the Illegal Immigration Reform and Immigrant Responsibility Act of 1996.

3

(D) The current version of this bill would grant eligible immigrant students six years of conditional residency during which they could earn full citizenship. To be eligible for conditional residency, a student must: (1) graduate from a U.S. high school or obtain a GED, (2) be of good moral character, (3) have arrived in the U.S. under the age of 16, (4) have proof of residence

in the U.S. for at least five consecutive years since the arrival date, and (5) be between the ages of 12 and 35 at the time of the bill's enactment. To gain full citizenship, the student must do one of the following during his or her residency: (1) complete at least two years of work toward a four-year college degree, (2) earn a two-year college degree, or (3) serve in the military for two years. If, within the six-year period, a student does not complete either the college requirement or the military-service requirement, the person would lose his or her temporary residency and be subject to deportation.

4

(E) While the Dream Act was first introduced in 2001, and its progress toward approval has been slow, the bill's popularity has grown each year since then. For example, in March 2009, the bill was re-introduced in the U.S. Senate by Richard Durbin (D-IL) and Richard Lugar (R-IN). Also at that time, Howard Berman (D-CA), Lincoln Diaz-Balart (R-FL), Lucille Roybal-Allard (D-CA), and a number of other legislators introduced the bill in the House of Representatives where the document is called the American Dream Act (H.R. 1751). In addition to these officials, many citizens such as Maria's guidance counselor, Ben Barry, favor the bill, believing that it would give immigrant students a chance to give back to the country that has given so much to them, and the bill would offer those students an opportunity to utilize their hard-earned education and talents.

5

(F) However, as of January 2010, the bill remains in the first step in the legislative process—a process in

(E) Bill's origin and increasing support
(F) Bill's remaining impediments

(A) Title: the problem and solution
(B) Introduction: (Problem) Students' dreams foiled by immigration laws
(C) (Solution) Dream Act offers route to legal residency.
(D) Bill's requirements for residency and citizenship

which bills go to committees or "mini congresses" that deliberate, investigate, and revise the bill before it is brought up for general debate in either the Senate or the House of Representatives. The disheartening fact, though, is that the majority of bills never make it out of these committees. Furthermore, supporters of Comprehensive Immigration Reform (CIR) are in favor of including the Dream Act as part of CIR, which could make the Dream Act subject to change yet again.

6   Given such debates, it might be a long time be-
(G) fore the bill becomes law, thereby dashing the dreams of nearly 65,000 high school students like Maria who can't wait another year because they may already be in deportation proceedings. We need to step up and educate our Representatives and Senators about the importance of passing the Dream Act on its own instead of including the bill along with CIR. We need to urge them to debate and approve the Dream Act now, thereby making Maria's dreams—and the dreams of thousands of students like her—a reality!

(G) Conclusion: The Dream Act warrants our support.

Reading for Better Writing

Working by yourself or with a group, answer these questions:

1. What problem does Wielenga address, and how does she get readers to care about it?

2. What solution does she propose, and how does she explain or assert its value?

3. In paragraph 6, Wielenga urges readers to promote her solution. Explain why you do or do not find her rationale for action convincing.

4. As noted in the introduction, Wielenga published an earlier form of this essay in a newspaper. Given its content and tone, explain why you think this version of the piece might be appropriate for a news article, an editorial, or both.

Analyze the solution.   LO3

In this essay, student writer Brian Ley defines agroterrorism, predicts that it could become a serious problem, determines that no single solution can solve it, and then proposes a multifaceted solution.

Preparing for Agroterror

Survey • Question • Read • Recite • Review   **SQ3R**

An al-Qaeda terrorist in Africa obtains a sample   *1* of fluid from a cow infected with foot-and-mouth dis- (A) ease, and he sends the fluid to an accomplice in a small, rural American town. This terrorist takes the sample around the country, stopping at several points to place small amounts of the fluid on objects that animals are likely to touch. When he is finished, he drives to the nearest airport and leaves the country unnoticed.

Cows, pigs, and sheep then come into contact with   *2* this highly contagious disease. Over the next few days, farmers see blisters on the feet and mouths of their animals. Thinking that the animals have a bacterial infection, the farmers administer antibiotics and wait

---

(A) The writer opens by illustrating the problem.

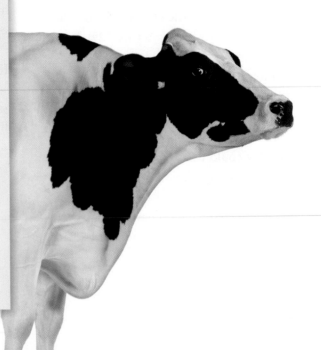

Eric Isselée, 2011 / Used under license from Shutterstock.com

for improvement. However, because antibiotics can't kill a virus, the animals get sicker. Meanwhile, the virus is spreading by means of wind and the movement of animals and humans. Within a few weeks, the virus is out of control.

3   While the story above is **hypothetical**, it is also very possible. People used to think of terrorists as men in ski masks blowing up embassies and taking hostages. But after the events of September 11, 2001, and the subsequent **anthrax** scares, it is clear that more kinds of terrorism are possible.

4   One type rarely considered is agroterrorism,
(B) which involves using diseases as weapons to attack a country's agriculture industry in order to attack the country itself. The agroterrorist's weapons of choice are those diseases that affect plants, animals, and even humans. Professor Peter Chalk of the RAND Corporation, an expert on transnational terrorism, believes that agroterrorism should be a huge concern for Americans because it has many advantages from a terrorist's point of view (37).

5   First of all, an attack on the agricultural sector of
(C) the United States would be quite easy. The diseases needed to kill large populations of animals can be obtained with little difficulty; the most devastating ones are ready for use in their natural form. These samples pose little risk to the terrorist because many of the diseases are harmless to humans.

6   In addition, doing agroterrorism is less risky in terms of getting caught and getting punished. Agroterrorism is hard to trace, especially because Americans have assumed that all animal epidemics are natural in origin and that American livestock contract such diseases only by accident. Consequences for those caught inflicting a disease on animals are also less severe than for terrorists who harm humans. In fact, because agroterrorism first affects the health of plants and animals rather than humans, terrorists using this strategy can even escape some guilt for their actions.

7   However, while agroterrorist diseases would have
(D) little direct effect on people's health, they would be devastating to the agricultural economy, in part because of the many different diseases that could be used in an attack. One of the most devastating is foot-and-mouth disease. This illness hurts all infected animals by impeding their weight gain, and it hurts dairy cows in particular by decreasing their milk production. Because the disease is highly contagious, all infected animals, along with any cloven-hoofed animals within about 50 miles of the infection site, must be killed.

8   While foot-and-mouth disease is not dangerous to humans, other animal diseases are. One of these is bovine spongiform encephalopathy, better known as mad-cow disease ("Mad Cow"). This illness is not easily spread, but a few cases in the United States would send people into a panic. Meat consumption would drop sharply, and the agricultural economy would be deeply shaken.

9   Another disease that could be used as a weapon is West Nile encephalitis. This virus can be spread by insects and can even cross species, affecting horses, birds, pigs, and humans. It is a fatal illness without a vaccination or a cure. These diseases are likely candidates for use in an agroterrorist attack (Smith 249).

10   The agricultural community is particularly susceptible to a terrorist attack. Unlike "typical" terrorist targets in metropolitan areas, farms do not have sophisticated security systems to protect against intruders. The average farmer's security system includes a mean dog and a shotgun: the dog for humans and the gun for animal pests. If terrorists wanted to infect a dairy, swine operation, or even a large-scale cattle-finishing operation, they would encounter few obstacles. The terrorists merely have to place a piece of

(B) He defines the problem and presents expert testimony.
(C) He analyzes why the problem could become serious.
(D) Using specific details, he outlines the problem's potential effects.

hypothetical
fictional

anthrax
a bacterial disease, often fatal, affecting the skin and lungs

Dmitrijs Bindemanis, 2011 / Used under license from Shutterstock.com

infected food in an area with livestock. This single action could start an epidemic.

11
(E) Agroterrorism is a threat that demands a response. Several actions can be taken to discourage terrorism as well as to deal with its consequences. One of the first steps is convincing all citizens—farmers and nonfarmers alike—that agroterrorism could happen, and that it could cause horrific consequences. Farmers must realize that they are susceptible to an attack even though they may live far from large metropolitan areas. Nonfarmers must realize how an attack could affect them. If nonfarmers know that an attack could create panic, drive up food prices, and possibly eliminate food sources, they will look out for suspicious activity and report it.

12 Preventive action on farms is needed to ensure the safety of the food supply. For example, the South Dakota Animal Industry Board recently published a newsletter outlining several precautions that farmers can take. Farms should have better security, especially in areas where animals are kept. These security measures include allowing only authorized persons to have access to farm buildings and animals and keeping all key farm buildings locked ("Precautions").

13 Farmers also need training to detect the diseases that terrorists might use and to know what actions can contain and decontaminate an infected area. For example, if a farmer discovers that cows have blisters on their tongues and noses, and that they are behaving abnormally, the owner should immediately call a veterinarian to assess the situation. Because the disease might be foot-and-mouth, no cattle should leave the farm until a diagnosis has been made.

14 In addition, public authorities need a plan for responding to an identified agroterrorism attack. For example, thousands of animals may have to be killed and disposed of—an action with significant environmental concerns. Moreover, public money should be used for continued research of the diseases that may be spread by agroterrorists. Vaccines and treatments may be produced that would stop diseases or limit them from becoming epidemic.

15
(F) Agroterrorism has not yet been used on a large scale anywhere on the globe. However, its use seems inevitable. The United States is a prime target for terrorism of this sort because the country has the largest, most efficiently raised food supply in the world. Destroying part of this supply would affect not only the United States but also all those countries with whom it trades. Because the United States is a prime target, it must act now to develop its defenses against agroterrorism. If the country waits until an attack happens, people may become ill, the overall economy could be damaged, and the agricultural economy may never recover.

Note: The Works Cited page is not shown. For sample pages, see MLA (pages 526–527) and APA (page 557).

(E) The closing stresses the problem's seriousness and calls for action.

Reading for Better Writing

Working by yourself or with a group, answer these questions:

1. This essay predicts that a problem may develop. Is the writer's prediction persuasive? Why or why not?

2. What tactics does the writer use to get readers concerned about the problem? Are these strategies successful?

3. The solution proposed is multifaceted. Briefly list who must do what. Is this solution persuasive? Is it workable? Does it get at root causes?

4. A strong proposal provides convincing evidence about both the problem and the solution. Trace the evidence used in this essay. Are the types of evidence convincing? Do any gaps need to be filled?

(E) The writer proposes a multifaceted solution.

Analyze the problem. LO4

In the essay below, David Blankenhorn argues that America is losing its understanding of and appreciation for fatherhood. To help readers understand that the problem does exist and must be resolved, he analyzes its history, causes, and effects.

Fatherless America

Survey · Question · Read · Recite · Review   SQ3R

1
(A)   The United States is becoming an increasingly fatherless society. A generation ago, an American child could reasonably expect to grow up with his or her father. Today, an American child can reasonably expect not to. Fatherlessness is now approaching a rough parity with fatherhood as a defining feature of American childhood.

2   This astonishing fact is reflected in many statistics, but here are the two most important. Tonight, about 40 percent of American children will go to sleep in homes in which their fathers do not live. Before they reach the age of eighteen, more than half of our nation's children are likely to spend at least a significant portion of their childhoods living apart from their fathers. Never before in this country have so many children been voluntarily abandoned by their fathers. Never before have so many children grown up without knowing what it means to have a father.

3   Fatherlessness is the most harmful demographic trend of this generation. It is the leading cause of declining child well-being in our society. It is also the engine driving our most urgent social problems, from crime to adolescent pregnancy to child abuse to domestic violence against women. Yet, despite its scale and social consequences, fatherlessness is a problem that is frequently ignored or denied. Especially within our elite discourse, it remains largely a problem with no name.

4   If this trend continues, fatherlessness is likely to change the shape of our society. Consider this prediction. After the year 2000, as people born after 1970 emerge as a large proportion of our working-age adult population, the United States will be a nation divided into two groups, separate and unequal. The two groups will work in the same economy, speak a common language, and remember the same national history. But they will live fundamentally divergent lives. One group will receive basic benefits—psychological, social, economic, educational, and moral—that are denied to the other group.

5   The primary fault line dividing the two groups will not be race, religion, class, education, or gender. It will be **patrimony**. One group will consist of those adults who grew up with the daily presence and provision of fathers. The other group will consist of those who did not. By the early years of the next [twenty-first] century, these two groups will be roughly the same size.

6   Surely a crisis of this scale merits a response. At a minimum, it requires a serious debate. Why is fatherhood declining? What can be done about it? Can our society find ways to invigorate effective fatherhood as a norm of male behavior? Yet, to date, the public discussion on this topic has been remarkably weak and defeatist. There is a prevailing belief that not much can—or even should—be done to reverse the trend.

7   When the crime rate jumps, politicians promise to do something about it. When the unemployment rate rises, task forces assemble to address the problem. As random shootings increase, public health officials worry about the **preponderance** of guns. But when it comes to the mass defection of men from family life, not much happens.

8   There is debate, even alarm, about specific social problems. Divorce. Out-of-wedlock childbearing. Children growing up in poverty. Youth violence. Unsafe neighborhoods. Domestic violence. The weakening of parental authority. But in these discussions, we

---

(A) Use this column to record your observations about the essay.

patrimony
a quality or characteristic that is inherited

preponderance
weight, force, influence, or number of something

seldom acknowledge the underlying phenomenon that binds together these otherwise **disparate** issues: the flight of males from their children's lives. In fact, we seem to go out of our way to avoid the connection between our most pressing social problems and the trend of fatherlessness.

9 We avoid this connection because, as a society, we are changing our minds about the role of men in family life. As a cultural idea, our inherited understanding of fatherhood is under siege. Men in general, and fathers in particular, are increasingly viewed as superfluous to family life: either as expendable or as part of the problem. Masculinity itself, understood as anything other than a rejection of what it has traditionally meant to be male, is typically treated with suspicion and even hostility in our cultural discourse. Consequently, our society is now manifestly unable to sustain, or even find reason to believe in, fatherhood as a distinctive domain of male activity.

10 The core question is simple: Does every child need a father? Increasingly, our society's answer is "no" or at least "not necessarily." Few idea shifts in this century are as consequential as this one. At stake is nothing less than what it means to be a man, who our children will be, and what kind of society we will become.

11 This [essay] is a criticism not simply of fatherlessness but of a culture of fatherlessness. For, in addition to losing fathers, we are losing something larger: our idea of fatherhood. Unlike earlier periods of father absence in our history, we now face more than a physical loss affecting some homes. We face a cultural loss affecting every home. For this reason, the most important absence our society must confront is not the absence of fathers but the absence of our belief in fathers.

12 In a larger sense, this [essay] is a cultural criticism because fatherhood, much more than motherhood, is a cultural invention. Its meaning for the individual man is shaped less by biology than by cultural script

disparate
separate or unalike

or story—a societal code that guides, and at times pressures, him into certain ways of acting and of understanding himself as a man.

13 Like motherhood, fatherhood is made up of both a biological and a social dimension. Yet in societies across the world, mothers are far more successful than fathers at fusing these two dimensions into a coherent parental identity. Is the nursing mother playing a biological or social role? Is she feeding or bonding? We can hardly separate the two, so seamlessly are they woven together.

14 But fatherhood is a different matter. A father makes his sole biological contribution at the moment of conception—nine months before the infant enters the world. Because social paternity is only indirectly linked to biological paternity, the connection between the two cannot be assumed. The phrase "to father a child" usually refers only to the act of insemination, not to the responsibility for raising a child. What fathers contribute to their offspring after conception is largely a matter of cultural devising.

15 Moreover, despite their other virtues, men are not ideally suited to responsible fatherhood. Although they certainly have the capacity for fathering, men are inclined to sexual promiscuity and paternal waywardness. Anthropologically, human fatherhood constitutes what might be termed a necessary problem. It is necessary because, in all societies, child well-being and societal success hinge largely upon a high level of paternal investment: the willingness of adult males

to devote energy and resources to the care of their offspring. It is a problem because adult males are frequently—indeed, increasingly—unwilling or unable to make that vital investment.

16 Because fatherhood is universally problematic in human societies, cultures must mobilize to devise and enforce the father role for men, coaxing and guiding them into fatherhood through a set of legal and extra-legal pressures that require them to maintain a close alliance with their children's mother and to invest in their children. Because men do not volunteer for fatherhood as much as they are conscripted into it by the surrounding culture, only an authoritative cultural story of fatherhood can fuse biological and social paternity into a coherent male identity.

17 For exactly this reason, Margaret Mead and others have observed that the supreme test of any civilization is whether it can socialize men by teaching them to be fathers—creating a culture in which men acknowledge their paternity and willingly nurture their offspring. Indeed, if we can equate the essence of the antisocial male with violence, we can equate the essence of the socialized male with being a good father. Thus, at the center of our most important cultural **imperative**, we find the fatherhood script: the story that describes what it ought to mean for a man to have a child.

18 Just as the fatherhood script advances the social goal of harnessing male behavior to collective needs, it also reflects an individual purpose. That purpose, in a word, is happiness. Anthropologists have long understood that the genius of an effective culture is its capacity to reconcile individual happiness with collective well-being. By situating individual lives within a social narrative, culture endows private behavior with larger meaning. By linking the self to moral purposes larger than the self, an effective culture tells us a story in which individual fulfillment transcends selfishness, and personal satisfaction transcends **narcissism**.

19 In this respect, our cultural script is not simply a set of imported moralisms, exterior to the individual and designed only to compel self-sacrifice. It is also a pathway—indeed, our only pathway—to what the founders of the American experiment called the pursuit of happiness.

20 The stakes on this issue could hardly be higher. Our society's conspicuous failure to sustain or create compelling norms of fatherhood amounts to a social and personal disaster. Today's story of fatherhood features one-dimensional characters, an unbelievable plot, and an unhappy ending. It reveals in our society both a failure of collective memory and a collapse of moral imagination. It undermines families, neglects children, causes or aggravates our worst social problems, and makes individual adult happiness—both male and female—harder to achieve.

21 Ultimately, this failure reflects nothing less than a culture gone awry: a culture increasingly unable to establish the boundaries, erect the sign-posts, and fashion the stories that can harmonize individual happiness with collective well-being. In short, it reflects a culture that increasingly fails to "**enculture**" individual men and women, mothers and fathers.

22 In personal terms, the end result of this process, the final residue from what David Gutmann calls the "**deculturation**" of paternity, is narcissism: a me-first egotism that is hostile not only to any societal goal or larger moral purpose but also to any save the most **puerile** understanding of personal happiness. In social terms, the primary results of decultured paternity are a decline in children's well-being and a rise in male violence, especially against women. In a larger sense, the most significant result is our society's steady fragmentation into atomized individuals, isolated from one another and estranged from the aspirations and

imperative
necessity

narcissism
an excessive love of oneself

enculture
create harmony between cultures

deculturation
a destruction of culture

puerile
relating to childhood

realities of common membership in a family, a community, a nation, bound by mutual commitment and shared memory.

23 [A good father] is a cultural model, or what Max Weber calls an ideal social type—an anthropomorphized composite of cultural ideas about the meaning of paternity. I call him the Good Family Man. As described by one of the fathers [I] interviewed . . . , a good family man "puts his family first."

24 A good society celebrates the ideal of the man who puts his family first. Because our society is now lurching in the opposite direction, I see the Good Family Man as the principal casualty of today's weakening fatherhood script. And because I cannot imagine a good society without him, I offer him as the protagonist in the stronger script that I believe is both necessary and possible.

Reading for Better Writing

Working by yourself or with a group, do the following:

1. In your own words, state the problem that Blankenhorn identifies and his proposed solution.

2. Choose five paragraphs and analyze their structure (e.g., topic sentence, supporting details, sentence structure, and transitions linking paragraphs). Then explain how these elements do or do not help present a clear message.

3. Working with a classmate, choose seven logical fallacies explained on pages 182–185. Then discuss why you believe that Blankenhorn's argument does or does not include these fallacies. Share your ideas with the class.

4. In paragraph 9, Blankenhorn makes the following claim: "Masculinity itself, understood as anything other than a rejection of what it has traditionally meant to be male, is typically treated with suspicion and even hostility in our cultural discourse." Explain what he means and why you find it a strong or weak claim.

5. Analyze three passages in which the writer uses data to support a point. Then explain why that use of data is or is not effective.

6. In paragraph 17, Blankenhorn says, "Margaret Mead and others have observed that the supreme test of any civilization is whether it can socialize men by teaching them to be fathers—creating a culture in which men acknowledge their paternity and willingly nurture their offspring." Explain what the quotation means and why it does or does not support the writer's thesis.

7. In paragraph 22, the writer says, "In personal terms, the end result of this process, the final residue from what David Gutmann calls the 'deculturation' of paternity, is narcissism." Define narcissism and explain how Blankenhorn's use of the term does or does not develop his argument.

Analyze a persuasive argument.

LO5

In the following essay, published in August 2009, Barbara Ehrenreich argues that whereas America's poor citizens sometimes loiter, trespass, or panhandle, most do these things because they're poor—not because they're criminals. In response to such behavior, she urges readers to show compassion and to act on behalf of the poor. Note how she supports her argument with *logical appeals* (186) linked to readers' *needs and values* (187).

Is It Now a Crime to Be Poor?

Survey · Question · Read · Recite · Review   SQ3R

It's too bad so many people are falling into poverty at a time when it's almost illegal to be poor. You won't

1

(A)

(A) As you read, highlight strategies and take marginal notes exploring how Ehrenreich raises the issue and calls for action.

be arrested for shopping in a Dollar Store, but if you are truly, deeply, in-the-streets poor, you're well advised not to engage in any of the biological necessities of life—like sitting, sleeping, lying down, or loitering. City officials boast that there is nothing discriminatory about the ordinances that afflict the destitute, most of which go back to the dawn of **gentrification** in the '80s and '90s. "If you're lying on a sidewalk, whether you're homeless or a millionaire, you're in violation of the ordinance," a city attorney in St. Petersburg, Fla., said in June, echoing Anatole France's immortal observation that "the law, in its majestic equality, forbids the rich as well as the poor to sleep under bridges."

2   In defiance of all reason and compassion, the criminalization of poverty has actually been intensifying as the recession generates ever more poverty. So concludes a new study from the National Law Center on Homelessness and Poverty, which found that the number of ordinances against the publicly poor has been rising since 2006, along with ticketing and arrests for more "neutral" infractions like jaywalking, littering or carrying an open container of alcohol. [*See Homes Not Handcuffs: The Criminalization of Homelessness in U.S. Cities.*]

3   The report lists America's 10 "meanest" cities—the largest of which are Honolulu, Los Angeles and San Francisco—but new contestants are springing up every day. The City Council in Grand Junction, Colo., has been considering a ban on begging, and at the end of June, Tempe, Ariz., carried out a four-day crackdown on the indigent. How do you know when someone is indigent? As a Las Vegas statute puts it, "An indigent person is a person whom a reasonable ordinary person would believe to be entitled to apply for or receive" public assistance.

4   That could be me before the blow-drying and eyeliner, and it's definitely Al Szekely at any time of day. A grizzled 62-year-old, he inhabits a wheelchair and is often found on G Street in Washington—the city that is ultimately responsible for the bullet he took in the spine in Fu Bai, Vietnam, in 1972. He had been enjoying the luxury of an indoor bed until last December, when the police swept through the shelter in the middle of the night looking for men with outstanding warrants.

5   It turned out that Mr. Szekely, who is an ordained minister and does not drink, do drugs or curse in front of ladies, did indeed have a warrant—for not appearing in court to face a charge of "criminal trespassing" (for sleeping on a sidewalk in a Washington suburb). So he was dragged out of the shelter and put in jail. "Can you imagine?" asked Eric Sheptock, the homeless advocate (himself a shelter resident) who introduced me to Mr. Szekely. "They arrested a homeless man in a shelter for being homeless."

6   The viciousness of the official **animus** toward the indigent can be breathtaking. A few years ago, a group called Food Not Bombs started handing out free veg-

Kuzma, 2011 / Used under license from Shutterstock.com

gentrification
the buying of and restoration of deteriorated urban houses by upper- and middle-class families

animus
strong dissatisfaction

an food to hungry people in public parks around the nation. A number of cities, led by Las Vegas, passed ordinances forbidding the sharing of food with the indigent in public places, and several members of the group were arrested. A federal judge just overturned the anti-sharing law in Orlando, Fla., but the city is appealing. And now Middletown, Conn., is cracking down on food sharing.

7   If poverty tends to criminalize people, it is also true that criminalization inexorably impoverishes them. Scott Lovell, another homeless man I interviewed in Washington, earned his record by committing a significant crime—by participating in the armed robbery of a steak house when he was 15. Although Mr. Lovell dresses and speaks more like a summer tourist from Ohio than a felon, his criminal record has made it extremely difficult for him to find a job.

8   For Al Szekely, the arrest for trespassing meant a further descent down the circles of hell. While in jail, he lost his slot in the shelter and now sleeps outside the Verizon Center sports arena, where the big problem, in addition to the security guards, is mosquitoes. His stick thin arms are covered with pink crusty sores, which he treats with a regimen of frantic scratching.

9   For the not-yet homeless, there are two main paths to criminalization—one involving debt, and the other skin color. Anyone of any color or pre-recession financial status can fall into debt, and although we pride ourselves on the abolition of debtors' prison, in at least one state, Texas, people who can't afford to pay their traffic fines may be made to "sit out their tickets" in jail.

10   Often the path to legal trouble begins when one of your creditors has a court issue a summons for you, which you fail to honor for one reason or another. (Maybe your address has changed or you never received it.) Now you're in contempt of court. Or suppose you miss a payment and, before you realize it, your car insurance lapses; then you're stopped for something like a broken headlight. Depending on the state, you may have your car impounded or face a steep fine—again, exposing you to a possible summons. "There's just no end to it once the cycle starts," said Robert Solomon of Yale Law School. "It just keeps accelerating."

11   By far the most reliable way to be criminalized by poverty is to have the wrong-color skin. Indignation runs high when a celebrity professor encounters racial profiling, but for decades whole communities have been effectively "profiled" for the suspicious combination of being both dark-skinned and poor, thanks to the "broken windows" or "zero tolerance" theory of policing popularized by Rudy Giuliani, when he was mayor of New York City, and his police chief William Bratton.

12   Flick a cigarette in a heavily patrolled community of color and you're littering; wear the wrong color T-shirt and you're displaying gang allegiance. Just strolling around in a dodgy neighborhood can mark you as a potential suspect, according to *Let's Get Free: A Hip-Hop Theory of Justice,* an eye-opening new book by Paul Butler, a former federal prosecutor in Washington. If you seem at all evasive, which I suppose is like looking "overly anxious" in an airport, Mr. Butler writes, the police "can force you to stop just to investigate why you don't want to talk to them." And don't get grumpy about it or you could be "resisting arrest."

13   There's no minimum age for being sucked into what the Children's Defense Fund calls "the cradle-to-prison pipeline." In New York City, a teenager caught in public housing without an ID—say, while visiting a friend or relative—can be charged with criminal trespassing and wind up in juvenile detention, Mishi Faruqee, the director of youth justice programs for the Children's Defense Fund of New York, told me. In just the past few months, a growing number of cities have taken to ticketing and sometimes handcuffing teenagers found on the streets during school hours.

14   In Los Angeles, the fine for truancy is $250; in Dallas, it can be as much as $500—crushing amounts for people living near the poverty level. According to the Los Angeles Bus Riders Union, an advocacy group, 12,000 students were ticketed for truancy in 2008.

15   Why does the Bus Riders Union care? Because it estimates that 80 percent of the "truants," especially those who are black or Latino, are merely late for school, thanks to the way that over-filled buses whiz by them without stopping. I met people in Los Angeles who told me they keep their children home if there's

the slightest chance of their being late. It's an ingenious anti-truancy policy that discourages parents from sending their youngsters to school.

16   The pattern is to curtail financing for services that might help the poor while ramping up law enforcement: starve school and public transportation budgets, then make truancy illegal. Shut down public housing, then make it a crime to be homeless. Be sure to harass street vendors when there are few other opportunities for employment. The experience of the poor, and especially poor minorities, comes to resemble that of a rat in a cage scrambling to avoid erratically administered electric shocks.

17   And if you should make the mistake of trying to escape via a brief marijuana-induced high, it's "gotcha" all over again, because that of course is illegal too. One result is our staggering level of incarceration, the highest in the world. Today the same number of Americans—2.3 million—reside in prison as in public housing.

18   Meanwhile, the public housing that remains has become ever more prisonlike, with residents subjected to drug testing and random police sweeps. The safety net, or what's left of it, has been transformed into a dragnet.

19   Some of the community organizers I've talked to around the country think they know why "zero tolerance" policing has ratcheted up since the recession began. Leonardo Vilchis of the Union de Vecinos, a community organization in Los Angeles, suspects that "poor people have become a source of revenue" for recession-starved cities, and that the police can always find a violation leading to a fine. If so, this is a singularly demented fund-raising strategy. At a Congressional hearing in June, the president of the National Association of Criminal Defense Lawyers testified about the pervasive "overcriminalization of crimes that are not a risk to public safety," like sleeping in a cardboard box or jumping turnstiles, which leads to expensively clogged courts and prisons.

20   A Pew Center study released in March found states spending a record $51.7 billion on corrections, an amount that the center judged, with an excess of moderation, to be "too much."

21   But will it be enough—the collision of rising prison populations that we can't afford and the criminalization of poverty—to force us to break the mad cycle of poverty and punishment? With the number of people in poverty increasing (some estimates suggest it's up to 45 million to 50 million, from 37 million in 2007) several states are beginning to ease up on the criminalization of poverty—for example, by sending drug offenders to treatment rather than jail, shortening probation and reducing the number of people locked up for technical violations like missed court appointments. But others are tightening the screws: not only increasing the number of "crimes" but also charging prisoners for their room and board—assuring that they'll be released with potentially criminalizing levels of debt.

22   Maybe we can't afford the measures that would begin to alleviate America's growing poverty—affordable housing, good schools, reliable public transportation and so forth. I would argue otherwise, but for now I'd be content with a consensus that, if we can't afford to truly help the poor, neither can we afford to go on tormenting them.

Reading for Better Writing

Working by yourself or with a group, answer these questions:

1. Note how Ehrenreich uses the title, opening sentence, and opening paragraph to introduce her topic and focus her argument. Are these strategies effective?

2. Identify two passages in which the writer makes a claim and then supports it by citing a study or an academic authority. Is this strategy convincing?

3. Cite two passages in which the writer uses an anecdote or illustration to support a claim. Do these strategies strengthen her argument?

4. Precisely what problem does the writer identify and what solution does she advocate?

5. How might Ehrenreich clarify her argument by displaying her supporting data in a graph or table? Explain.

Write, revise, and edit a problem-solution essay.

LO6

Writing Guidelines

Planning

1. **Select and narrow a topic.** Brainstorm possibilities from this list:

   People Problems: Consider generations—your own or a relative's. What problems face this generation? Why, and how can they be solved?

   College Problems: List problems faced by college students. In your major, what problems are experts trying to solve?

   Social Problems: What problems do our communities and country face? Where do you see suffering, injustice, inequity, waste, or harm?

   Workplace Problems: What job-related problems have you experienced or might you experience?

   Then test your topic:

   - Is the problem real, serious, and currently—or potentially—harmful?
   - Do you care about this problem and believe that it must be solved? Why?
   - Can you offer a workable solution—or should you focus on part of the problem?

2. **Identify and analyze your audience.** You could have four audiences: people responsible for the problem, decision makers with the power to deliver change, people affected by the problem, and a public that wants to learn about it.

   - What do readers know about the problem? What are their questions or concerns?
   - Why might they accept or resist change? What solution might they prefer?
   - What arguments and evidence would convince

them to acknowledge the problem, to care about it, and to take action?

3. **Probe the problem.** If helpful, use the graphic organizer on pages 50–51.

   - **Define the problem.** What is it, exactly? What are its parts or dimensions?
   - **Determine the problem's seriousness.** Why should it be fixed? Who is affected and how? What are its immediate, long-term, and potential effects?
   - **Analyze causes.** What are its root causes and contributing factors?
   - **Explore context.** What is the problem's background, history, and connection to other problems? What solutions have been tried in the past? Who, if anyone, benefits from the problem's existence?
   - **Think creatively.** Look at the problem from other perspectives—other states and countries, both genders, different races and ethnic groups, and so on.

4. **Choose the best solution.** List all imaginable solutions—both modest and radical fixes. Then evaluate the alternatives:

   - List criteria that any solution should meet.
   - List solutions and analyze their strengths, weaknesses, costs, and so on.
   - Choose the best solution and gather evidence supporting your choice.

Drafting

5. **Outline your proposal and complete a first draft.** Describe the problem, offer a solution, and defend it using strategies that fit your purpose and audience.

   - **The problem:** Inform and/or persuade readers about the problem by using appropriate background information, cause-effect analysis, examples, analogies, parallel cases, visuals, and expert testimony.
   - **The solution:** If necessary, first argue against alternative solutions. Then present your solution, stating what should happen, who should be involved, and why.
   - **The support:** Show how the solution solves the problem. Use facts and analysis to argue that

your solution is feasible and to address objections. If appropriate, use visuals such as photographs, drawings, or graphics to help readers grasp the nature and impact of the problem.

Revising

6. Improve the ideas, organization, and voice. Ask a classmate or someone from the college's writing center to read your paper for the following:

Ideas: Does the solution fit the problem? Is the proposal precise, well researched, and well reasoned—free from oversimplification and obfuscation?

Organization: Does the writing move convincingly from problem to solution, using fitting compare/contrast, cause/effect, and process structures?

Voice: Is the tone positive, confident, objective, and sensitive to opposing viewpoints—and appropriate to the problem's seriousness?

Editing

7. Edit and proofread the essay. Look for these issues:

Words: Words are precise, effectively defined, and clear.

Sentences: Sentences are smooth, energetic, and varied in structure.

Correctness: The copy has correct grammar, spelling, usage, and mechanics.

Design: The design includes proper formatting and documentation.

Publishing

8. Prepare and share your final essay. Submit your proposal to your instructor, but also consider sharing it with audiences who have a stake in solving the problem.

Critical-Thinking and Writing Activities

As directed by your instructor, complete the following critical-thinking and writing activities by yourself or with classmates.

1. "Preparing for Agroterror" predicts that a problem might develop. Thinking about current conditions and trends, forecast a problem, and write a proposal explaining how to prepare for or prevent it.

2. Review the section in chapter 15 about engaging the opposition (pages 185–186). Also review how David Blankenhorn engages his opposition in "Fatherless America." Then consider a persuasive piece that you are drafting or revising. How might you engage the opposition in a dialogue about your arguments? Revise your writing as needed.

3. Review the section in chapter 15 about "Identifying Logical Fallacies" (pages 182–185). Write a humorous problem/solution essay in which you make an argument that includes a number of obvious logical fallacies. Share your writing with the class.

4. What are some challenges facing the planet Earth and the human race in the foreseeable future? Find a focused challenge and write a proposal that addresses it.

Checklist: Learning-Outcomes

Use the checklist below to identify what you have learned from this chapter and what you should review.

____ I can read and evaluate problem-solution essays for clear information, logical claims, and reliable evidence.

____ I can describe a problem and solution accurately, avoiding the fallacies obfuscation (185), oversimplification (183), and slanted language (185).

____ I can objectively analyze each solution's strengths and weaknesses.

____ I can analyze a problem's history, causes, effects, and impact on my intended readers.

____ I can use logic (186), evidence (181–182) and appropriate appeals (186) to persuade readers.

____ I can write a rational, convincing problem-solution essay.

"He who knows only his own side of the case knows little of that."

—John Stuart Mill

19

Interview Report

An interview is a question-and-answer session with someone—an expert on a topic, a client, or a case-study subject—to gain insight into the topic and/or person. You might use what you learn as primary-source information, or you might use the interview as an entire piece of writing, such as an interview report.

Conducting a productive interview and writing a good report requires careful planning. Planning gives you background information and helps you develop questions that produce solid data, vivid details, and lively quotations—the qualities that engage readers and create memorable reading.

Learning Outcomes

LO1 Understand how to read and evaluate interview reports.

LO2 Ask evocative questions, listen carefully, and assimilate the answers.

LO3 Describe, summarize, paraphrase, and quote interviewees effectively.

LO4 Plan, schedule, and conduct an interview.

LO5 Write, revise, edit, and publish an interview report.

Understand how to read and evaluate interview reports.

LO1

The instructions below will help you read and evaluate interview reports.

Consider the rhetorical situation.

When reading an interview report, think about how the writer's purpose, audience, and topic influence the questions asked and the answers offered.

Purpose: A good writer interviews a person to get reliable, primary-source information that reveals the individual's insights, reflections, and feelings about the topic. The writer then uses that information respectfully to write a report with correct details and quotations, and accurate analysis of what the interviewee said and did.

Audience: Interview reports written within an organization (e.g., college or business) usually address topics important to the organization and are intended for readers within the organization. However, interview reports in magazines such as *People, Sports Illustrated,* or *Business Weekly* address topics that interest the publication's readers.

Topic: If the purpose for writing is to describe or analyze the interviewee, then the person interviewed is the topic. However, if the purpose is to gain the interviewee's insights or ideas about someone or something else, then the interviewee is a source for information about the topic. For example, in the report on pages 241–242, the mortuary business is the topic, and the mortician interviewed is a source.

Consider the interview process.

When reading interview reports, note how successful writers do the following:

Ask clear, relevant questions. Getting quality information depends on the art of interviewing—planning relevant questions, listening well, taking good notes, following up with sensible responses, and being open to surprises.

Respect the interviewee's ideas, feelings, and voice. Good writers seek to understand the interviewee's story, values, and personality. These interviewers listen much more than talk. They communicate their subject's words, ideas, and voice through accurate description, summaries, paraphrases, and quotations.

Analyze and synthesize the results. Analysis helps a writer understand pieces of information, and synthesis helps the person show how the pieces are related. A good writer does both in order to develop a unified essay with a meaningful theme.

Checklist: Reading Interviews

✔ Does the opening introduce the interview's setting, subject, and context?

✔ Are the questions clear and do they evoke interesting, meaningful information?

✔ Does the writer effectively use summaries, paraphrases, and quotations to communicate the person's ideas, feelings, and personality?

cozyta, 2011 / Used under license from Shutterstock.com

Ask evocative questions, listen carefully, and assimilate the answers. LO2

Because of a disturbing childhood experience, college student Benjamin Meyer toured a funeral home and interviewed the director. In the following essay, Benjamin reports on what he learned.

The Dead Business

Survey · Question · Read · Recite · Review   SQ3R

1   "You're going to tour a what?"

2   "A funeral home."

3   My friends were shocked. They laughed while describing scenes from *Night of the Living Dead* and *The Shining*.

(A)

4   But their stories didn't frighten me—I feared something else. When I was ten, my grandmother died, and my family drove to the funeral home to view the body. As we entered the place, I noticed the funeral director standing in the corner, looking like a too-eager-to-please salesman who'd made a deal he didn't deserve. The guy's thin-lipped smile seemed unnatural—almost glib. Like a ghoul in a business suit, he didn't seem to care that a stroke had stopped my grandmother's beating heart midway through the doxology that concluded the Sunday-evening church service. He didn't seem to care that she and I would share no more cookies, no more coloring books, no more Rook games, no more laughing, no more. I was ten, very sad, and he didn't seem to care.

5   Now a college student, I wanted to tour a different funeral home to work through my earlier experience. While I no longer feared ghouls, I was still nervous while driving to the Vander Ploeg Furniture Store/Funeral Home. I remembered the thin-lipped smile.

6   I walked inside not knowing what to expect. Suddenly, a man from behind a desk hopped out of his chair and said, "Hi, I'm Howard Beernink."

(B)

7   I looked at the tall, smiling guy, paused a moment, and glanced back at the door. His partner had stepped in front of the exit while scribbling on tags that dangled from Lazy Boy rockers. I realized that this interview was something I had to do . . . like getting a tetanus shot.

8   Howard led me into a room full of furniture where he found a soft, purple couch. We sat down, and he described how the business started.

(C)

9   In 1892, pioneers established the town of Sioux Center, Iowa. Winter storms and disease pummeled the tiny community, and soon residents needed someone to bury the dead. A funeral director wasn't available, but a furniture maker was. The furniture maker was the only person with the tools, hardwood, and knowledge to build coffins. As a result, the Vander Ploeg Furniture Store/Funeral Home was born.

(D)

10   Today, starting a funeral home isn't that easy. For example, a funeral home requires the services of an embalmer, and an embalmer must be certified by the state. To get a certificate, the person must complete two years of college, one year of embalming school, and one year of apprentice work. After that, the individual must pass a state exam every year to retain certification.

(E)

11   "But why a funeral home director?" I was baffled. Why would anyone embalm dead bodies for a living?

12   "Because it's a family business." Howard smiled as if he expected my question. "Vander Ploegs and Beerninks have run this place for generations. Today it's difficult to start a funeral home because there are so many of them with long histories and good reputations."

(A) The writer starts with background information that creates a personal theme.

(B) Freely using "I," the writer tells the story of his visit and interview.
(C) He describes the setting.
(D) He relates the early history of the business.
(E) The writer summarizes, paraphrases, and quotes from the interview.

13 After he answered the rest of my questions, Howard asked if I wanted to see the embalming room.

14 "Okay," I said, tentatively.

15 He led me through doors, down hallways, up a
(F) staircase, and into a well-lighted display room containing several coffins. Finally, we entered a small, cold room containing a row of cupboards, a large ceramic table, and a small machine that resembled a bottled-water cooler.

16 "We like to keep the room cold when we're not using it," Howard said.

17 "What is all this stuff?" I asked.

18 Howard described why embalming is done and what it involves. The purpose of embalming is to extend the period for viewing the body, and the process includes replacing body fluids with embalming fluid. He opened a cupboard, pulled out a bottle of fluid and said, "Here . . . smell."

19 "Smells like Pepto-Bismol," I replied.

20 After he embalms the body, Howard applies make-
(G) up so the face appears "more natural." He gets his cosmetics (common powders and tints) from the local Avon lady.

(F) He narrates what happened during the interview.
(G) The writer shares surprises and what he learned.

21 "But sometimes we also have to use this," Howard said, pulling out another bottle.

22 "Tissue builder?" I asked, squinting at the label.

23 "It's like silicon implants," he answered. "We inject it into sunken cheeks, like the cheeks of cancer victims."

24 When the body is ready for burial, the funeral director must show a price list to the family of the deceased. The Funeral Rule, adopted in 1984 by the Federal Trade Commission, requires that a price list be shown to the family before they see caskets, cement boxes, and vaults. The purpose of the Funeral Rule is to prevent unethical funeral directors from manipulating customers with comments like, "But that's a pauper's casket; you don't want to bury your mother in that. Bury her in this beauty over here." Unfortunately, only a third of the country's 22,000 funeral homes abide by the Funeral Rule.

25 "After showing customers where the caskets are, I step away so they can talk among themselves," said Howard. "It's unethical to bother the family at this difficult time."

26 Before burying a casket, Howard and his partner

pic4you © iStockphoto

place it in either a cement box or a vault. A cement box is a container that's neither sealed nor waterproofed, whereas a vault is both sealed and waterproofed. Howard explained, "Years ago, cemeteries began to sink and cave in on spots, so state authorities demanded containers. Containers make the cemetery look nicer."

27 After the tour, I asked Howard, "How has this job affected your life?"

28 He glanced at the ceiling, smiled, and said, "It's very fulfilling. My partner and I comfort people during a stressful time in their lives, and it strengthens our bond with them."

29 As I drove back to the college, I thought again
(H) about Howard's comment, and about my childhood fear. Howard was right. He doesn't exploit people. Instead, he comforts them and helps them move on. And while I still fear the pain of saying good-bye to someone I love, I don't fear funeral directors anymore. They're just people who provide services that a community needs.

(H) He ends the report with a strong quotation and personal reflection.

Reading for Better Writing

Working by yourself or with a group, answer these questions:

1. This report centers on the writer's own story, reflections, and needs. Discuss how these elements are woven into the report. Are they effective? Why or why not?

2. Examine the opening and the closing of the essay. Do they work well together? Do they effectively share a theme for the report? Explain.

3. Describe how the writer organizes the interview's results. Is the organization effective? Explain.

4. Look carefully at the writer's use of summary and paraphrase on the one hand and quotation on the other hand. Are the strategies effective? Explain.

Describe, summarize, paraphrase, and quote interviewees effectively. LO3

Jonathon Gatchouse, a senior correspondent for *Macleans Magazine,* wrote the following interview report on the Montreal-based rock band, Arcade Fire. As you read the piece, watch how he uses description, paraphrases, and quotations to help readers get to know the band members' personalities, music, and goals. (The article was published in *Macleans Magazine* in February 2011.)

Arcade Fire, on fame and putting it to good use

Survey · Question · Read · Recite · Review **SQ3R**

1 People in tuxedos fighting over hot dogs. That's the indelible image Win Butler and Régine Chassagne took home from their first trip to the Grammy Awards back in 2006. Their group, Arcade Fire, had received two nominations. One was for Best Alternative Album for their debut disc *Funeral*—a big-deal award handed out during the televised, evening portion of the ceremony. The other was a nod for a song that had shown up on HBO's *Six Feet Under,* in the decidedly less-prestigious Best Song Written for Motion Picture, Television, or Other Visual Media category, parcelled out hours before the real show begins. Not knowing any better, all seven members of the Montreal band dutifully took their seats inside an L.A. convention hall at 11 a.m., and spent the day politely applauding the winners of the best Hawaiian, polka and metal recordings. It was hot. It was boring. They didn't win. And there was no alcohol, food, or even water available.

2 Late in the afternoon, the famished crowd was finally herded across the street to the Staples Center, site of the evening festivities. Inside the rink, a huge lineup formed at the one open concession stand. Soon things turned ugly. "People were screaming," says

Butler. "Women in prom dresses were crying," Chassagne chimes in. Organizers told them they had to take their seats, and that no food would be allowed inside. Total chaos. "By the end there were people offering $50 for a hot dog," Butler says with a grin.

3   Sitting in a Montreal café, tucking into their quesadillas, the couple has every reason to laugh. When Arcade Fire returns to this year's Grammys on Feb. 13, they'll be performing for a worldwide television audience, earning both a dressing room and backstage catering. *The Suburbs,* their most recent disc, which debuted at No. 1 on the Billboard charts last August, is up for Album of the Year and Best Alternative Album. Their song "Ready to Start" snagged a Best Rock Performance nod. A couple of days later, they'll be in London, playing at the Brit Awards, where they're up for International Group and International Album of the Year. In late March, they'll also take the stage at the Junos in Toronto, where their six nominations have them tied with Drake. In April, there's a headlining date at the Coachella music festival in California. In June, a concert for 60,000 in London's Hyde Park. And in late July, a shared Moncton gig with U2, a band they became friendly with after opening their 2006 shows in Montreal and Toronto.

4   Already an international indie-rock success— *Funeral* and its follow-up *Neon Bible* are both approaching half-million-sold gold status in the U.S., and *The Suburbs* sold 156,000 copies there in just its first week—Arcade Fire hover at the threshold of the mainstream, uncharted territory for a band without the backing of a major label. (The group pay for, and own, all of their recordings, striking distribution deals with various partners.) Perhaps even a little weird, given their sprawling sound, which trips from fuzzy punk, to electronic new wave, to revival-tent sing-alongs. "Sometimes there's a little cultural moment for something that is different," says Butler. "But it mostly seems like an accident of history."

fidèle
faithful (French word)

Creole
a French-descended language of New Orleans and southern Lousiana

5   After lunch, and a quick trudge across the street through a fresh, deep snowfall, Chassagne and Butler join their bandmates—Richard Reed Parry, Tim Kingsbury, Jeremy Gara, Sarah Neufeld, and Win's younger brother Will—in a sun-filled room above a storefront for rehearsal. A week before the Grammys, the group still hasn't decided what song they want to play. "It's kind of subjective, since we don't really have a hit," says Butler. He discards his shoes and socks and starts tuning a guitar. Musically, Arcade Fire have always prided themselves in making it up as they go along—**fidèle** to the feeling, but not the rules. But there is a larger plan.

6   In the rehearsal room, as when they appear on stage, there are two drum kits. One kick drum bears the band's initials. The other, the Haitian coat of arms. Since 2005, the group has raised more than $1 million for development work in the Western hemisphere's poorest nation. Recently, Chassagne and Dominique Anglade, a Montreal businesswoman and childhood friend, formed their own charity, Kanpe (**Creole** for "stand up"). Working with Partners in Health, an international NGO, and Fonkoze, a Haitian micro-lending organization, Kanpe is set to launch a concerted attack on the roots of poverty in one island community, shepherding 300 families to economic and physical health. The budget for the three-year project is $2 million. The band has pledged to match every dollar raised, up to a million, from their own pockets. In March, in between award shows, they'll all travel together to Haiti to check out the work that has already begun, and get their own hands dirty.

7   Fame, even on the lower rungs, isn't always fun. For example, Butler, Chassagne and their cohorts have learned to be sparing with the details of their lives in Montreal, lest fans turn up on their doorsteps. But it can have a purpose. "Every time I think it's getting annoying, I say to myself, if people didn't know who you are, or what you do, then you wouldn't be able to raise all that money for Haiti," says Chassagne. "It's really all about doing something with it."

8   On the surface, at least, they seem like an unlikely pair. Edwin Farnham Butler III, 30, the lanky eldest son of a blue-blood New Englander and a Joni Mitchell-

style California musician, raised in Texas, and diminutive Régine Chassagne, the 33-year-old **Francophone** daughter of Haitian refugees who washed up on Montreal's south shore. On stage, he towers like an **Ent** with a guitar, and she flits from instrument to instrument like a **pixie**. But away from the music, he's the expansive story-teller, while she perches on the edge of the couch, arms and legs crossed tight.

9 They met at the McGill Faculty of Music in 2000. She was studying vocals and playing recorder in a medieval ensemble. He wasn't in s c h o o l—al-though he did study comparative Biblical Scripture for a time—just haunting the corridors, looking for a drummer for his then more-notional-than-actual band. Their paths crossed again at an art opening where Chassagne was singing with a jazz band. They got together a few nights later to play music and wrote a tune, "Headlights Look Like Diamonds," that ended up on Arcade Fire's first EP in 2003, the year they married. "It was a songwriting thing that turned into a date," Butler says. She snorts. "It wasn't a date. No way! I don't think it was."

10 The relationship has remained creative. Always together and always writing, they toss riffs and fragments back and forth. "We're each others' hard drives," says Chassagne. Music is intertwined with life. The ideas come while she's cleaning, or taking out the garbage. A drum kit dominates their living room. Parts of the latest album were recorded there, then handed off to the other band members for their input. Butler

Nikola Spasenoski, 2011 / Used under license from Shutterstock.com

says his wife "is music," melody and rhythm springing from her core. She praises his focus and perseverance; the ability to bring structure to their ideas.

11 The Butler brothers' musical pedigree stretches back two generations to their maternal grandfather, Alvino Rey, a big-band leader and pedal-steel guitar virtuoso who had a string of Top 10 hits in the 1940s. Win formed his first band as a student at Phillips Exeter Academy, the elite New Hampshire boarding school that counts George Plimpton, John Irving and Mark Zuckerberg among its other graduates. His first public performance was a cover of the "Cure's Just Like Heaven," at a school talent show. Music was the only career he ever gave serious consideration.

12 Chassagne taught herself to play piano at age four. Growing up in a close-knit household, song was always a part of daily life, but it was only after an un-

Francophone
a person who speaks French

Ent
a tree-like creature from J. R. R. Tolkien's *The Lord of the Rings*

pixie
a tiny fairy

dergrad degree in communications at Concordia, and her mother's untimely death, that she ever dared to breathe her dream of performing. Her parents had come to Montreal in the early 1970s, after meeting in the States. Régine's mother fled Haiti when she returned home from market one day to find her cousins and friends had been murdered. Her dad left after his father was taken away by the **Tonton Macoutes** and executed. (The price of refuge in America ended up being a tour of duty in Vietnam.) As new Canadians, both worked hard to establish themselves—he taught math, she worked as a secretary and at a daycare. But Haiti remained the country of all their imaginations. "Growing up, I never went there," says Chassagne. "It wasn't a possibility financially, and especially with my mom—she still had nightmares. She wanted to forget about it."

13   In the end, it was a Harvard physician who introduced Chassagne to her parents' homeland. She'd read a book about Paul Farmer, one of the founders of Partners in Health, and became fascinated by his quest to "cure the world." In October 2008, she and Win spent a couple of weeks on the island, touring PIH's clinics, and reconnecting with her roots. "Going there made me understand what was actually Haitian about my upbringing," says Chassagne. "I realized I was Haitian by osmosis."

Tonton Macoute
member of Haitian paramilitary force created by President "Papa Doc" Duvalier

14   Even before the trip, Arcade Fire had been raising money for Partners in Health, tacking on a charity surcharge—one dollar, one euro or one pound—to every ticket sold. The "biggest no-brainer thing we ever did," as Win calls it, has so far collected almost US 1 million. At shows, he gives a short spiel about the organization, and PIH volunteers are always on hand to pass out literature. "It's been kind of incredible," says Christine Hamann, the outreach coordinator for Partners in Health. "It amplifies everything we do." During the most recent tour, 5,500 fans signed up for its "Stand with Haiti" campaign.

15   The idea of Kanpe—an organization to fill in the gaps in the NGO network in Haiti—started with the 2008 visit. Paul Farmer had spoken of his frustration at returning TB and HIV patients to stable health, only to see them go back to the kind of impoverished conditions that gave rise to the illnesses in the first place. "It's like that Creole saying about washing your hands and drying them in the dirt," says Butler.

16   The earthquake just made it all the more pressing—and personal. The parents of Kanpe co-founder Dominique Anglade were crushed beneath the rubble of their Port-au-Prince home, the first confirmed Canadian casualties. In Montreal, the two exile families had been close friends, sharing birthday celebrations and summer camping trips. To date, Kanpe, which is still looking for corporate benefactors, has raised about $400,000. Half of it has come from the seven members of Arcade Fire.

17   Over the last few years, they've played on stage with David Bowie and Bruce Springsteen, appeared twice on *Saturday Night Live,* and entertained Obama's staff at one of the official 2008 inauguration balls. Just how much bigger the band can become is hard to predict. The music business isn't like it used to be (not that Arcade Fire ever aspired to be part of it anyway). "Radio is the wild card," says Butler. "That's what separates us and Coldplay—having radio hits. Reaching the people who just buy one or two albums a year."

18   They still control, or as Chassagne prefers to say, "direct" their own business, paying their way in the studio, on video shoots and the road. But there have

been small concessions to stardom, like the manager they share with Björk and Paul McCartney. Butler swears things haven't changed that much. "Our day-to-day life is identical, except for not sweating the electrical bill as much. We still have the same crap in our house; the old chairs, and the stool I fished out of the dumpster."

19   On tour, they occasionally forsake the hired car and take the subway, just to remind themselves of how absurd it has all become. Having Haiti top of mind is also a pretty fail-safe way of "keeping it real." "Now our lives are changing fast. Now our lives are changing fast. Hope that something pure can last," Butler sings on *The Suburbs'* track "We Used to Wait."

20   It's by a band that's trying to change the world, without letting it change them.

Reading for Better Writing

Working by yourself or with a group, answer these questions:

1. Describe how the writer gets his reader's attention, introduces his subject, and forecasts the focus of the essay. Then explain why this opening is or is not effective.

2. Identify each of the following: a descriptive paragraph, a summary, a paraphrase, and a quotation. Then explain what you learn from each passage and why the writing is or is not effective.

3. Review two or three songs by Arcade Fire and describe the music and lyrics. Then explain why this report does or does not help you understand and appreciate the music.

4. Review the photographs in this report and explain why they do or do not fit the tone and content of the writing.

Nikola Spasenoski, 2011 / Used under license from Shutterstock.com

Plan, schedule, and conduct an interview. LO4

Writing Guidelines

Planning

1. **Choose a topic and a person to interview.** If your purpose is to write about a specific person, choose someone intriguing. However, if your purpose is to use the interviewee as a resource, interview someone who is an authority or has special experience with the topic.

2. **Plan the interview.** As soon as possible, take care of the details:

   - Determine your goal—what you want the interview to accomplish and what information and insights you want to gather.
   - Choose a recording method (pen and paper, recorder) and a medium (face-to-face, telephone, e-mail, video conference).
   - Research the topic and interviewee and draft questions to evoke information.
   - Contact the interviewee and politely request an interview. Explain who you are, why you need the interview, and how you will use it. Schedule a time and place convenient for the interviewee. To record the interview, ask permission.
   - Gather and test tools and equipment: a notebook, pens, and perhaps recording equipment (tape, video, digital camera).

3. **Prepare questions.** Do the following to help you structure the interview:

   - Consider types of questions to ask—the five W's and H.
   - Understand open and closed questions. Closed questions ask for simple, factual answers; open questions ask for detailed explanations.
     - **Closed:** How many months did you spend in Vietnam?
     - **Open:** Can you describe your most vivid memory of Vietnam?
   - Avoid slanted questions that pressure a person to give a specific answer.
     - **Slanted:** Aren't you really angry that draft dodgers didn't do their duty?
     - **Neutral:** How do you feel about those who avoided the draft?
   - Think about specific topics to cover and write questions for each one. Start with simple questions that establish rapport and follow with key questions.
   - List questions on the left side of the page with room for notes on the right. Rehearse your questions, visualizing how the interview should go.

4. **Conduct the interview.** Arrive on time and be professional:

   - Introduce yourself, reminding the interviewee why you've come.
   - If you have permission to record the interview, set up equipment off to the side so that it doesn't interfere with the conversation. Take notes on key facts.
   - Listen actively by including nods and eye contact. Pay attention to the interviewee's body language.
   - Be flexible. If the person looks puzzled by a question, rephrase it or ask another. If the person avoids a question, politely rephrase it. Don't react negatively or forcefully invade the interviewee's private territory.
   - Ask one of these questions if an answer needs to be amplified:
     - **Clarifying:** "Do you mean this or that?"
     - **Explanatory:** "What do you mean by that?"
     - **Detailing:** "What happened exactly? Can you describe that?"
     - **Analytical:** "What were the causes? The outcomes?"
     - **Probing:** "What do you think that meant?"
     - **Comparative:** "Did that remind you of anything?"
     - **Contextual:** "What else was going on then? Who else was involved?"
     - **Summarizing:** "Overall, what was your response? What was the net effect?"
   - Listen "between the lines" for what the interviewee seems to want to say.
   - Give the interviewee a chance to add any final thoughts.

5. **Follow up.** As soon as possible, review your notes and fill in the blanks. By phone or in writing, clarify points and thank the interviewee.

Write, revise, edit, and publish an interview report.

_____ LO5

Drafting

6. Organize and draft the report. Shape the opening to seize interest, the middle to sustain interest, and the closing to reward interest:

- Analyze and interpret the interview results. Locate the heart or theme of your report, and then develop an outline supporting the theme.
- Start with background, along with a point that grabs readers' interest.
- Summarize and paraphrase material from the interview. (See pages 350–351.) Use quotations selectively to share the interviewee's voice or stress a point.
- If appropriate, weave your thoughts and reflections into the report.

Revising

7. Improve the ideas, organization, and voice. On your own or with help from a classmate or writing-center tutor, review these issues in your draft:

Ideas: Does the report supply complete, satisfying insights?

Organization: Does the draft have an engaging opening and closing?

Voice: Is the writing lively, fair, and respectful?

Editing

8. Edit and proofread. Review your report for precise _word choice, smooth sentences, correct grammar,_ and _reader-friendly design._ Make sure especially that quotations are integrated smoothly.

Publishing

9. Prepare a final copy. Submit a clean copy to your instructor (and perhaps the interviewee), but also look for ways to publish your report.

Critical-Thinking and Writing Activities

As directed by your instructor, complete the following activities.

1. Generate a list of people who understand the challenges and opportunities related to the career you want to pursue. Then select a person, interview her or him, and write a report.

2. "The Dead Business" recounts the writer's exploration of a topic that caused him discomfort and sadness. What similar issues affect you? Would an interview help you work through an issue? Write your own reflective interview report.

3. Do you know someone who has led a fascinating life? Someone who on the surface seems to have led an ordinary life? Someone serving others in inspiring ways? Interview that person and write his or her story in an extended interview report.

4. Is there a particular issue in your community that concerns you—a public debate, a college problem, a program being cut back? Who has insights into the issue? Who holds opposing views? Whose lives are affected? Who has the power to change things? Select one or more people to interview, and then write a report on the issue.

5. Read an interview report in a popular journal and analyze how the writer asks questions and uses the interviewee's answers. Then write a paper in which you explain why the writer's interview and report do or do not illustrate the standards discussed in this chapter.

Checklist: Learning Outcomes

Use the checklist below to assess and review what you have learned about reading and writing interview reports.

_____ I can read and evaluate interview reports for organization, details, clarity, and voice.

_____ I can ask evocative questions, listen carefully, and assimilate the answers.

_____ I can describe, summarize, paraphrase, and quote interviewees effectively.

_____ I can plan, schedule, and conduct an interview in an honest, professional manner.

_____ I can write an interview report that captures the writer's voice; includes correct quotes, summaries, and paraphrases; portrays the person accurately; and develops a unifying theme.

"A fact in science is not a mere fact,
but an instance."

— Bertrand Russell

20

Lab, Experiment, and Field Report

Good science writing is rooted in good science—the careful study of phenomena through observation and experiment. Social scientists seek to understand human behavior and societies, whereas natural scientists investigate the physical world.

As a student, you may be asked to read science articles and to conduct scientific research in a range of courses. In classes, you may write literature reviews to summarize and assess what research has been done on an issue. In labs and in the field, you may perform experiments, gather data, and interpret results, and then share your insights with others.

This chapter will help you put your science research into writing—and your good writing into science.

Learning Outcomes

LO1 Understand how to read and assess lab, experiment, and field reports.

LO2 Understand a lab report.

LO3 Understand an experiment report.

LO4 Understand a field report.

LO5 Write, revise, and edit a lab, experiment, or field report.

Understand how to read and assess lab, experiment, and field reports.

LO1

In order to read and do science writing effectively, you need to understand certain principles of science. Follow the guidelines below.

Consider the rhetorical situation.

When reading a scientific article (scholarly or popular), consider the rhetorical situation. When doing your own writing, perform a similar analysis.

Purpose: Typically, the goal is to report experimental and observational results. However, sometimes it is to summarize several studies on a topic so as to disseminate scientific knowledge to a broad audience.

Audience: Most readers are experts—scientists interested in the topic addressed, seeking to debate and build knowledge (typically in scholarly journals). Other readers may be laypeople—non-experts nevertheless interested in the topic (typically reading trade or popular magazines).

Topic: Scientists study phenomena, seeking to understand, for example, the cause-effect forces at work. Virtually any natural or social phenomenon is a potential topic.

Consider science-writing strategies.

Sound science writing depends on these principles: the **scientific method**, the **IMRAD format**, and careful **distinctions**.

The Scientific Method: Science focuses on measured observations aimed at understanding. Experiments are set up to test hypotheses about why things happen. However, experiments don't prove hypotheses correct: Experimental results can merely "agree with" or disprove a hypothesis. Overall, the method moves from observation to explanation as you do the following:

1. Observe something interesting (often while looking for something else).
2. Check whether other scientists have explained the same observation.
3. Summarize your observations and turn that generalization into a testable hypothesis—a working theory explaining the phenomenon.
4. Design research to test the hypothesis, paying attention to variables and controls.
5. Based on the results of your experiment, accept, reject, or modify your hypothesis.
6. Repeat steps 3 through 5 until you understand the phenomenon. Then write up your research so that others can respond to your work.

IMRAD Format: To model scientific thinking, lab and field reports include an *introduction* establishing the problem, a *methods* section detailing procedures, a *results* section providing the data, and a *discussion* that interprets the data: IMRAD.

Distinctions to Consider:

Distinguish facts from possibilities. Facts are data that is collected, and possibilities are interpretations of the data.

Distinguish experiments from studies. Experiments test hypotheses by manipulating variables. Studies observe what's there by counting, exampling, and so on. In this chapter, an experiment report is on 254–257, and a study report is on 257–259.

Understand a lab report.

L◯2

Student Coby Williams wrote the basic lab report below to describe a chemical compound and inform readers about its nature. Note how he introduces the topic, describes the procedure, and states the outcome.

Working with Hydrochloric Acid

Survey · Question · Read · Recite · Review SQ3R

Overview and Purpose

1 The goal in writing this report is to educate others on the dangers of using and storing hydrochloric acid in the lab (HCl) and in the home (muriatic acid). In addition, this report will list appropriate ways to protect against burns when using HCl as well as ways to dispose of it properly.

Characteristics

2 Hydrochloric acid (HCl), which is made from hydro- (A) gen gas and chlorine gas, is a clear, colorless to slightly yellow, fuming liquid with a sharp, irritating odor. HCl is a strong, highly corrosive acid, soluble in water and alcohol. Other characteristics include the following:

✓ The chemical reaction is $H2 + Cl2 = 2HCl$.
✓ Its molecular weight is 36.45.
✓ Its boiling point is 85°C.
✓ Its specific gravity is 1.16.

3 Hydrochloric acid is commercially known as muriatic acid, a substance used to manufacture dyes and plastics or to acidize (activate) petroleum wells. It is also used in the food processing of corn syrup and sodium glutamate and is an ingredient in many household and industrial cleaners.

Safety Procedures

4 Hydrochloric acid is highly corrosive and can severely burn skin. Whenever HCl is used, it must be handled according to the following precautions:

Storage

5
• Keep hydrochloric acid in tightly capped bottles back from the edge of the shelf or table.
• Keep bottles away from metals. Contact will corrode metals and could release hydrogen gas, which is highly explosive.

Protection

6
• Always wear safety glasses to protect your eyes. (B)
• Wear latex gloves and old clothes when using concentrated HCl—not short-sleeved shirts, shorts, or sandals.
• Do not breathe the fumes, which can cause fainting.
• If acid spills on skin or splashes in someone's eyes, rinse the area with water for five minutes.

(A) The writer identifies the chemical compound and states its nature.
(B) He organizes details in distinct categories.

Treat burns appropriately. In each case, get medical help immediately.

broukoid, 2011 / Used under license from Shutterstock.com

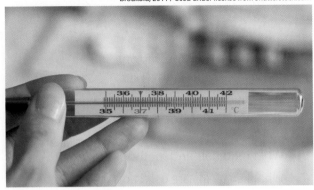

(C) Usage

7   In the lab, hydrochloric acid is either diluted or titrated.

- When diluting, always pour the acid into the water. Doing the reverse can cause boiling, splashing, and burning.
- When titrating, carefully measure the HCl needed. Then react the HCl with a sample that has a base such as sodium hydroxide to get an accurate measurement of the base in the sample.

8   **Disposal**

- To dispose of HCl, neutralize it by mixing the acid with a sodium-hydroxide solution. Flush the neutralized solution down the drain.
- If you spill HCl, cover the spill with baking soda. After the fizzing stops, sweep up the soda and flush it down the drain.

(C) Information is accurate and terms are precise.

Reading for Better Writing

Working by yourself or with a group, answer these questions:

1. Who would be the main audience for this type of report? What evidence can you point to that supports your answer?
2. List the strategies used to organize the report. Are these strategies effective? Explain.
3. How does this report demonstrate scientific thinking?

Understand an experiment report. ___ LO3

In this report, student writer Andrea Pizano shares the results of a lab experiment she completed to explore how different factors affect fermentation.

The Effects of Temperature and Inhibitors on the Fermentation Process for Ethanol

Survey · Question · Read · Recite · Review **SQ3R**

Andrea Pizano
January 29, 2008

Introduction

1   Alcoholic liquids were made and used for centuries before scientists fully understood the process by (A) which alcohol developed. An Egyptian papyrus dated 3500 B.C.E. mentions wine making, although production of alcoholic spirits like gin and brandy started only about a thousand years ago. From beverages such as beer and wine to fuel additives such as ethanol, alcohol has been used by people for recreation, religious rites, medical purposes, energy, and industry. Even today people are surprised to learn that it is ethanol—a by-product of yeast growth—that makes bread smell good. Studying the process by which alcohol is made can help make the process more efficient and successful.

(A) The opening creates context and explains concepts.

grafvision, 2011 / Used under license from Shutterstock.com

2   Generally, alcohol can be made by fermenting different types of sugars, including sucrose, glucose, and fructose. Fermentation is a process that creates heat and changes the properties of a substance through a leavening or fermenting agent. For the fermentation process to succeed, certain enzymes must function as catalysts. These enzymes are present in yeast, the fermenting agent. While useful as catalysts, these enzymes are sensitive to temperature changes and inhibitors.

3
(B) In this experiment, ethanol—a specific type of alcohol—was synthesized from sucrose in the presence of yeast. The effects of extreme temperatures and of inhibitors on the rate of fermentation were tested quantitatively. The factors below were tested, and the outcomes below were anticipated. First, extremely high temperatures denature enzymes. Therefore, fermentation in the sample was expected to stop. Second, extremely cool temperatures reduce the kinetic energy of molecules. Therefore, the reaction rate in the sample was expected to drastically slow. Third, sodium fluoride can inhibit one of the enzymes needed in the fermentation process. Therefore, the presence of sodium fluoride was expected to effectively stop the reaction. Fourth, normal fermentation usually delivers a maximum of up to 15% ethanol. Through distillation, a 95% concentration of ethanol can be obtained. However, the presence of concentrated ethanol kills the yeast cells and also acts as a negative feedback mechanism to the enzymes necessary for the fermentation process. Therefore, concentrated ethanol was expected to effectively stop the reaction.

Method

4
(C) To test each of these hypotheses, the following procedure was followed in this experiment:

1. 200 mg of yeast were mixed with 1.25 mL of warm water in a 5-mL round-bottomed, long-necked flask. The mixture was shaken until the yeast was well distributed.

2. 9 mg of disodium hydrogen phosphate, 1.30 g sucrose, and 3.75 mL warm water were added to the flask. This mixture was left for 15 minutes—until the fermentation was proceeding at a vigorous rate.

3. The fermentation mixture was then divided equally into 5 reaction tubes.
   - To tube 1, 1.0 mL of water was added.
   - To tube 2, 1.0 mL of 95% ethanol was added.
   - To tube 3, 1.0 mL of 0.5 M sodium fluoride solution was added.
   - To each of tubes 4 and 5, 1.0 mL of water was added.

4. The bubbles produced in a reaction tube filled *(D)* with water were counted. A septum was first fit over the neck of each reaction tube. Then some polyethylene tubing was connected from the septum to the water-filled reaction tube. In this way, the reaction rate could be quantitatively measured by counting the number of gas bubbles that were released into the water each minute for 5 minutes.

5. Test tube 4 was heated for 5 minutes in boiling water. Then it was cooled to room temperature, and the fermentation rate was measured as explained in step 4.

6. Test tube 5 was put on ice for 5 minutes, and then the fermentation rate was measured as explained in step 4, while the reaction tube was kept on ice to maintain the low temperature.

7. After the experiment was completed, the solutions were washed down the drain as waste.

(B) The writer describes the experiment and states her hypotheses.

(C) She details the procedure using numbered steps and precise terms.

(D) The writer uses passive voice to focus on the action and receiver—not the person doing the action.

Results

The reaction rates of the 5 reaction conditions are plotted on Figure 1 below.

(E)

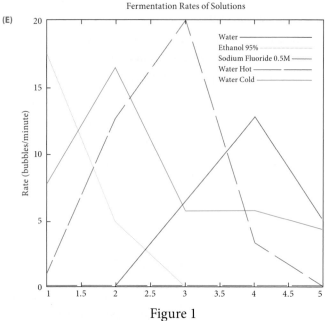

Figure 1

With the sample containing water at room temperature, the fermentation rate peaked at 13 bubbles/minute at minute 4. The fermentation rate of the sample with 95% ethanol started at 17 bubbles/minute, but within 2 minutes the rate quickly slowed to 5 bubbles/minute. By 3 minutes, the rate was 0 bubbles/minute. In the sample with sodium fluoride, the fermentation increased to 20 bubbles/minute after 3 minutes, but then quickly reached 0 bubbles/minute after 5 minutes. In the sample that was boiled, the fermentation rate was consistently 0 bubbles/minute. In the sample placed on ice, the fermentation rate increased to 17 bubbles/minute after 2 minutes, but then gradually slowed to 4 bubbles/minute after 5 minutes.

Discussion

Many different factors affect fermentation rates. For example, when ethanol concentration is very high, yeast usually dies. So when 95% ethanol is added to a fermenting sugar and yeast mixture, one would expect the fermentation rate to decline sharply. The experiment's data support this hypothesis. After 3 minutes, the fermentation had completely stopped.

In addition, sodium fluoride inhibits the action of a specific enzyme in yeast, an enzyme needed for the fermentation process. Therefore, when sodium fluoride is added to a fermenting mixture, one would expect a halted fermentation rate. However, the reaction rate initially increased to 20 bubbles/minute when sodium fluoride was added. This increase may have occurred because not all of the enzymes were inhibited at first. Perhaps the fermentation rate declined to 0 bubbles/minute only when the sodium fluoride became evenly distributed. This measurement occurred after 5 minutes.

Temperature is a third factor affecting fermentation. On the one hand, high temperatures denature many enzymes; therefore, when a fermenting mixture is placed in boiling water for 5 minutes, one would expect the fermentation rate to stop because no enzymes are present at that point to carry out the fermentation process. This hypothesis is supported by the data, as no fermentation occurred in the hot mixture. On the other hand, cold temperatures reduce the kinetic energy of molecules. As a result, the speed decreases, and the likelihood of the enzymes making contact with the substrate decreases exponentially in relation to the temperature. One would expect that the reaction rate would slow down drastically after the mixture has been cooled. This hypothesis is somewhat supported by the data. After an initial increase in the reaction rate to 17 bubbles/minute, the reaction rate slowed to 4 bubbles/minute after 5 minutes. A repeat of the experiment would be needed to clarify this result. Moreover, because the measuring method was somewhat unsophisticated (as indicated by the spikes in the line graph), perhaps a new experiment could be

---

(E) The results are summarized and displayed in a line graph.
(F) The writer interprets the results for each hypothesis.

(G) She explores possible explanations for unexpected results and suggests further research.

designed to measure fermentation-rate changes more sensitively.

10
(H) This experiment helped quantify the effects that various factors such as temperature, inhibitors, and high ethanol concentration have on fermentation rates. Even though the measuring apparatus was fairly basic, the experiment largely supported the hypotheses. Such data are helpful for determining methods of efficient and successful fermentation. Further research testing other factors and other inhibitors would add to this knowledge.

(H) The closing summarizes the experiment's value.

Reading for Better Writing

Working by yourself or with a group, answer these questions:

1. Where does the writer discuss the experiment's purpose and value? Are her efforts convincing?
2. In the "Method" section, which strategies does the writer use to ensure that the experiment can be repeated?
3. In the "Results" section, what is the relationship between the line graph and the paragraph?
4. In the "Discussion" section, the writer addresses results that did and did not support the hypotheses. Are her interpretations and conclusions sound? Explain your answer.

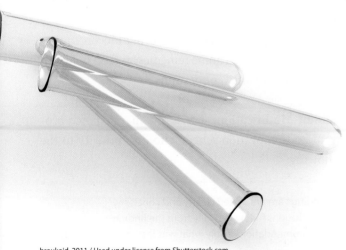

broukoid, 2011 / Used under license from Shutterstock.com

Understand a field report.
LO4

In the following workplace field report, a team of writers investigates the causes and effects of cockroach infestation in an apartment complex. In the study, they use their findings to recommend solutions.

Sommerville Development Corporation

Survey · Question · Read · Recite · Review **SQ3R**

Date: September 20, 2011

To: Bert Richardson, VP of Tenant Relations

From: Hue Nguyen, Cherryhill Complex Manager
             Sandra Kao, Building Superintendent
             Roger Primgarr, Tenant Relations
             Juan Alexander, Tenant Representative

Subject: **Investigation of Cockroach Infestation at** (A)
             5690 Cherryhill

During the month of July 2011, 26 tenants of the 400-unit building at 5690 Cherryhill informed the building superintendent that they had found cockroaches in their units. On August 8, the management-tenant committee authorized us to investigate these questions:

1. How extensive is the cockroach infestation?
2. How can the cockroach population best be controlled?

We monitored this problem from August 9 to September 8, 2011. This report contains a summary, an overview of our research methods and findings, conclusions, and recommendations.

(A) The subject line functions as a title.
(B) The opening clarifies the study's purpose and goals.

SUMMARY

3
(C) The 5690 Cherryhill building has a moderate infestation of German cockroaches. Only an integrated control program can manage this infestation. Pesticide fumigations address only the symptoms, not the causes. We recommend that Sommerville adopt a comprehensive program that includes (1) education, (2) cooperation, (3) habitat modification, (4) treatment, and (5) ongoing monitoring.

RESEARCH METHODS AND FINDINGS

Overview of Research

4
(D) We researched the problem in the following ways:

1. Contacted the Department of Agriculture, the Ecology Action Center, and Ecological Agriculture Projects.

2. Consulted three exterminators.

3. Inspected the 5690 Cherryhill building, from ground to roof.

4. Placed pheromone traps in all units to monitor the cockroach population.

The Cockroach Population

5
(E) Pheromone traps revealed German cockroaches, a common variety. Of the 400 units, 112 units (28 percent) showed roaches. Based on the numbers, the infestation is rated as moderate.

The German Cockroach

6
Research shows that these roaches thrive in apartment buildings.

- Populations thrive when food, water, shelter, and migration routes are available. They prefer dark, humid conditions near food sources.
- The cockroach seeks shelter in spaces that allow its back and underside to remain in constant contact with a solid surface.

(C) The summary focuses on outcomes.
(D) Research methods are described.
(E) Results are categorized logically.

Methods of Control

7
(F) Sources we consulted stressed the need for an integrated program of cockroach control involving sanitation, habitat modification, and nontoxic treatments that attack causes. Here are the facts:

- The German cockroach is immune to many chemicals.
- Roaches detect most pesticides before direct contact.
- Spot-spraying simply causes roaches to move to unsprayed units.
- Habitat modification through (1) eliminating food and water sources, (2) caulking cracks and crevices, (3) lowering humidity, and (4) increasing light and airflow makes life difficult for cockroaches.

CONCLUSIONS

8
Based on our findings, we conclude the following:

1. (G) A single method of treatment, especially chemical, will be ineffective.

2. A comprehensive program of sanitation, habitat modification, and nontoxic treatments will eliminate the German cockroach.

RECOMMENDATIONS

9
(H) We recommend that Sommerville Development adopt an Integrated Program of Cockroach Prevention and Control for its 5690 Cherryhill building. Management would assign the following tasks to appropriate personnel:

Education: (1) Give tenants information on sanitation, prevention, and home remedies; and (2) hold tenant meetings to answer questions.
10

Habitat Modification: Revise the maintenance program and renovation schedule to give priority to the following:
11

(F) Findings are presented clearly and concisely.
(G) Conclusions follow logically from the findings.
(H) Recommendations apply what was learned in the study.

- Apply residual insecticides before sealing cracks.
- Caulk cracks and crevices (baseboards, cupboards, pipes, sinks). Insert steel wool in large cavities (plumbing, electrical columns).
- Repair leaking pipes and faucets. Insulate pipes to eliminate condensation.
- Schedule weekly cleaning of common garbage areas.

12 **Treatment:** In addition to improving sanitation and prevention through education, attack the roach population through these methods:

- Use home remedies, traps, and hotels.
- Use borax or boric acid powder formulations as residual, relatively nontoxic pesticides.
- Use chemical controls on an emergency basis.
- Ensure safety by arranging for a Health Department representative to make unannounced visits to the building.

Monitoring: Monitor the cockroach population in 13 the following ways:

1. Every six months, use traps to check on activity in all units.
2. Keep good records on the degree of occurrence, population density, and control methods used.

We believe that this comprehensive program will solve 14 the cockroach problem. We recommend that Sommerville adopt this program for 5690 Cherryhill and consider implementing it in all its buildings. (I)

(I) The closing stresses the value and benefits of the study.

Reading for Better Writing

Working by yourself or with a group, answer these questions:

1. Examine the report's format and organizational strategies. How is this workplace report similar to and different from the other lab and experiment reports in this chapter?
2. Describe the tone of the report. What does this tone accomplish?
3. This report depends extensively on cause/effect thinking. Where do the writers use cause/effect thinking, and how effective is it?

Write, revise, and edit a lab, experiment, or field report.

— LO5

Writing Guidelines

Planning

1. **Review the lab manual and any handouts.** In most science courses, studies and experiments are assigned through textbooks, manuals, and handouts. Study those materials to understand what you must do and why. Read background information on the topic in textbooks and other sources.

2. **Use a field or lab notebook.** Accurate, complete record keeping is crucial to doing good scientific research. Use the notebook to plan research, record what you do, collect data, make drawings, and reflect on results. For each notebook entry, record the date and your goal.

3. **Plan and complete your study or experiment.** Do the following:
   - Develop your key research questions. If you are conducting an experiment (not just a study), then state your hypotheses and design procedures for testing them.
   - Gather the proper tools, equipment, and materials required.
   - Carefully conduct your tests and perform your observations.
   - Take copious notes, being especially careful to record data accurately, clearly, and completely. If helpful, use a data-collection sheet.

Drafting

4. **Relying on your notebook, draft the report.** Study the data. Were results expected or unexpected? Which factors could explain those results? What further research might be necessary? Then draft the report in the sequence outlined below:
   - **Methods:** Explain what you did to study the topic or test the hypothesis. Supply essential details, factors, and explanations. Be so clear that someone else could repeat the steps you took.

   - **Results:** Using two strategies, present the data you collected. First, share data in graphical forms—as tables, line charts, bar graphs, photographs, and so on. While the correct design of graphics and the proper presentation of statistical data are beyond the scope of this book, follow this basic rule: Make your graphic independent of the written text by giving it a descriptive title, clear headings and labels, units of measurement, and footnotes. Readers should be able to study your graphics and see the "story" of your study. Second, draw attention to the major observations and key trends available in the data. However, do not interpret the data in your results or give your reactions to them.

   - **Discussion:** Interpret the results by relating the data to your original questions and hypotheses, offering conclusions, and supporting each conclusion with details. Essentially, answer the question, "What does it all mean?" Explain which hypotheses were supported, and why. Also explore unexpected results, and suggest possible explanations. Conclude by reemphasizing the value of what you learned.

   - **Introduction:** Once you have mapped out the methods, results, and discussion, write an introduction that creates a framework for the report. Explain why you undertook the study, provide background information and any needed definitions, and raise your key questions and/or hypotheses.

   - **Summary or abstract:** If required, write a summary of your study's purpose, methods, results, and conclusions. An abstract is a one-paragraph summary that allows readers to (1) get the report in a nutshell and (2) determine whether or not to read the study.

   - **Title:** Develop a precise title that captures the "story" of your study. Worry less about the length of the title and more about its clarity.

   - **Front and end matter:** If required, add a title page, references page, and appendixes.

Revising

5. **Improve the ideas, organization, and voice.** Review your report, or ask a classmate or some-

one from the college's writing center to check the following:

Ideas: Does the report provide scientifically sound conclusions about accurate data related to a clear hypothesis or issue?

Organization: Is the traditional IMRAD structure followed effectively?

Voice: Is the tone objective and informed, but also inquisitive?

Editing

6. Edit and proofread the essay by checking for these conventions of science writing:

Words: The language is precise (not ambiguous), specific (not vague), and concise (not wordy); technical terms are defined as needed.

Sentences: Constructions flow smoothly, using the passive voice when needed to focus on the action and the receiver, not the actor. (See page 72.)

Correctness: The copy includes no errors in spelling, usage, punctuation, grammar, or mechanics. The writing follows the disciplinary conventions for capitalization, abbreviations, numbers, and symbols.

Design: The page design is correctly formatted and attractive, including presentation of graphics; information is properly documented.

Publishing

7. Prepare and share your report. Submit a polished report to your instructor. Also consider writing a relevant article, editorial, or blog post on the topic.

Critical-Thinking and Writing Activities

As directed by your instructor, complete the following critical-thinking and writing activities by yourself or with classmates.

1. Guided by your instructor, develop a hypothesis about a technological or social change (e.g., cell phone habits, online gaming, reality TV shows). Then develop a simple, manageable experiment to test your hypothesis.

2. The field report objectively researches the problem of cockroach infestation. Which campus or community problems could you research in a similar manner? Develop a research plan, get approval from your instructor, and complete your study.

3. In a popular science magazine such as *Nature* or *National Geographic,* read an article about a topic that interests you. Then read an article on the same topic in a scholarly science journal (available typically through your library's databases). Compare and contrast the two articles in terms of purpose, audience, content, and style.

Checklist: Learning Outcomes

Use the checklist below to assess what you have learned about science writing.

_____ I can read and evaluate science reports for logic and clarity.

_____ I understand how a lab report introduces its topic, describes a process or procedure, and states the outcomes.

_____ I understand how an experiment report introduces a problem, presents and tests hypotheses, and analyzes outcomes.

_____ I understand how a field report introduces its topic, reports on what was found and sampled, and analyzes the results.

_____ I can write, revise, and edit a lab, experiment, or field report.

"The only impeccable writers are those who never wrote."

—William Hazlitt

21

Analyzing
the Arts

In one way or another, people respond to the arts. Audiences may applaud a dancer, gripe about a film, or praise a poet. Often writers respond more precisely, by analyzing one actor's performance while criticizing another's, or by praising a film's script but questioning camera angles or lighting.

Because the arts are complex, writing about them requires careful listening, reading, and/or viewing. For example, you might analyze a film or play in terms of the acting, the casting, or the directing. Similarly, you might analyze a poem or story by looking at its form, its diction, or the insights it provides. This chapter includes model essays, guidelines, and literary terms to help you respond to and analyze a variety of art forms.

Learning Outcomes

LO1 Evaluate literature and arts-specific writing.

LO2 Analyze a short story.

LO3 Analyze a poem.

LO4 Analyze a film.

LO5 Understand and use literary terms.

LO6 Write an arts-specific analysis.

Evaluate literature and arts-specific writing. LO1

The instructions below will help you read about and respond to the arts.

Consider the rhetorical situation.

To understand art analyses, think about the writer's purpose, audience, and topic.

Purpose: Most writers aim to analyze an artwork: to describe its features, to explain how it impacts an audience, and to understand its essential qualities. However, writers reviewing an artwork focus more on its strengths and weaknesses.

Audience: In college, the primary audience for writing about the arts is students and instructors; off campus, art stories and reviews are written for any community members interested in art events, art-related issues, or reading books.

Topic: The topic might be one artwork (e.g., a sculpture, novel, or film), multiple works created by the same artist (e.g., a series of poems or paintings), a group performance (e.g., a play, an opera, or a symphony), an individual performance (e.g., a pianist, an actor, or a dancer), or critical approaches to an art.

Understand terms used to write about the arts.

As you read, note the terms used to address specific art forms; three examples follow:

Plays and Films: To describe characters, writers use terms such as *antago-*nist, *protagonist*, or *tragic hero*; to discuss plots, they use words like *exposition*, *rising action*, and *denouement*; or to describe a setting, they might use *stage picture*, *proscenium arch*, or *thrust stage*.

Stories and Novels: Writers might describe diction with terms like *archaic*, *colloquial*, or *slang*; describe nuanced language as *antithetical*, *hyperbolic*, or *understated*; or describe style with terms such as *genre*, *satire*, or *melodrama*.

Poetry: Writers describe word sounds with terms like *assonance*, *consonance*, or *alliteration*; they describe rhythmic effects with words such as *iambic*, *pyrrhic*, or *quatrain*; and they refer to visual allusions as *symbols*, *images*, or *motifs*. (For definitions of terms like these, see the lists on page 273.)

Checklist: Analyzing the Arts

- ✔ Does the writer understand the elements of the art form, what distinguishes a quality artwork, and how to assess those qualities?
- ✔ Does the essay explore nuances such as ironies, motifs, symbols, or allusions?
- ✔ Does the essay have a clear thesis supported by relevant evidence?
- ✔ Is the tone informed, respectful, and honest?

Analyze a short story.

In the essay below, student writer Anya Terekhina analyzes Flannery O'Connor's short story "Good Country People." Note how Terekhina focuses on the story's characters, plot, symbols, and diction.

"Good Country People": Broken Body, Broken Soul

Survey • Question • Read • Recite • Review **SQ3R**

1
(A)
Flannery O'Connor's short stories are filled with characters who are bizarre, freakish, devious, and sometimes even murderous. Every short story, according to O'Connor in *Mystery and Manners: Occasional Prose,* should be "long in depth" and meaning (94). To achieve this, O'Connor develops characters with heavily symbolic attributes and flaws, and "it is clearly evident that boldly outlined inner compulsions are reinforced dramatically by a mutilated exterior self" (Muller 22). In "Good Country People," Joy-Hulga is a typical O'Connor character—grotesque yet real. Her realness comes from her many flaws and, ironically, her flaws are a self-constructed set of illusions. Throughout the story, O'Connor carefully links Joy-Hulga's physical impairments with deeper handicaps of the soul; then, at the closing, she strips Hulga of these physical flaws while helping her realize that her corresponding beliefs are flawed as well.

2
O'Connor first introduces her character as Joy Hopewell, a name of optimism. However, we soon understand that her chosen name, Hulga, is more fitting. The new name distresses her mother, Mrs. Hopewell, who is "certain that she [Joy] had thought and thought until she had hit upon the ugliest name in any language" (O'Connor 1943). Hulga has connotations of "hull = hulk = huge = ugly" (Grimshaw 51), and all of these are accurate descriptions of her. Far from having a sweet temperament, Hulga stomps and sulks around the farm, "constant outrage . . . [purging] every expression from her face" (1942).

3
(B)
Although Hulga's demeanor could be blamed on her physical impairments, she devises her own rationalizations for behaving as she does. Ironically, each rationale is symbolized by one of her physical disabilities, yet she doesn't recognize the handicaps for what they imply.

4
One of Hulga's many ailments is her weak heart, which will likely limit her life span. Hulga blames this affliction for keeping her on the Hopewell farm, making it plain that "if it had not been for this condition, she would be far from these red hills and good country people" (1944). Having a Ph.D. in philosophy, Hulga claims to want work as a university professor, lecturing to people at her intellectual level. Hulga's weak heart functions as more than a dream-crusher; it "symbolizes her emotional detachment—and inability to love anyone or anything" (Oliver 233). She exhibits no compassion or love for anything, not even "dogs or cats or birds or flowers or nature or nice young men" (1944–45).

5
Hulga also suffers from poor vision. Without her eyeglasses, she is helpless. Strangely though, her icy blue eyes have a "look of someone who has achieved blindness by an act of will and means to keep it" (1942). Her self-induced blindness symbolizes her blindness to reality. She is indeed intelligent, but she has packed her brain full of ideas and thoughts that only obscure common sense, let alone truth. Because of Hulga's extensive education and her focus on philosophical reasoning, she considers herself superior to everyone around her. For example, she yells at her mother, "Woman! . . . Do you ever look inside and see what you are not? God!" (1944).

6
Hulga's last and most noticeable physical impairment is her missing leg, which was "literally blasted off" (1944) in a hunting accident when she was ten years old. In *Mystery and Manners,* O'Connor stresses that the wooden leg operates interdependently at a lit-

---

(A) The writer provides background for understanding the characters in O'Connor's stories.

(B) The writer begins listing the protagonist's physical disabilities and explains how each one symbolizes a deeper problem in her soul.

eral and a symbolic level, which means "the wooden leg continues to accumulate meaning" throughout the story (99). Hulga's biggest physical handicap symbolizes her deepest affliction: her belief in nothing.

7
(C) Hulga's philosophical studies did focus on the study of nothing, particularly on the arguments of the French philosopher Nicolas Malebranche. O'Connor describes Hulga as believing "in nothing but her own belief in nothing" (*Mystery* 99). Over time, Hulga's belief in nothing develops into more than just academic study. Her nihilism becomes her religion—suitable for a woman who considers herself superior and despises platitudes. As she explains to Manley Pointer, "We are all damned . . . but some of us have taken off our blindfolds and see that there's nothing to see. It's a kind of salvation" (1952). Hulga's religious terms suggest that she uses faith in nothingness to find the meaning that she can't find elsewhere.

8
(D) Hulga's nihilism is symbolized by her wooden leg, which is the only thing she tends to with care: "She took care of it as someone else would his soul, in private and almost with her own eyes turned away" (1953). This limb is wooden and corresponds to Hulga's wooden soul. Whereas she believes she worships Nothing, what she actually worships is an "artificial leg and an artificial belief" (Oliver 235).

9
Not realizing that her false leg and false religion cripple her both physically and spiritually, Hulga considers seducing Manley Pointer, the Bible salesman. She delightfully imagines that she will have to help him deal with his subsequent remorse, and then she will instruct him into a "deeper understanding of life" (1950). Of course, her intellectual blindness keeps her from realizing that her superiority is only an illusion.

Instead, she views Manley as "a vulnerable innocent, a naïve Fundamentalist, and she wishes to seduce him to prove that her sophisticated textbook nihilism is superior to his simpleminded faith" (Di Renzo 76).

10
In classic O'Connor fashion, the characters and situation reverse dramatically at the end of the story. Hulga and Manley are alone in a hayloft and begin embracing. At first, Hulga is pleased with her reaction to kissing as it aligns well with Malebranche's teachings: "it was an unexceptional experience and all a matter of the mind's control" (1951). Soon, however, she realizes that she is enjoying the first human connection of her life. At this point, the innocent Bible salesman has already stripped Hulga of her first physical impairment: her weak heart.

11
(E) Hulga hardly notices when Manley takes advantage of her next impairment: "when her glasses got in his way, he took them off of her and slipped them into his pocket" (1952). With her heart opened and her intellectual perspective fuzzy, Hulga swiftly descends into what she despises—platitudes. Hulga and Manley exchange cliched mumblings of love, and this leads Manley to ask if he can remove her artificial leg. After brief hesitation, Hulga agrees because she feels he has

---

(C) She points out the root of the protagonist's problems: her lack of belief in anything.

(D) The writer demonstrates how the protagonist's flaws lead her to make distorted judgments.

(E) She revisits the protagonist's physical disabilities, showing how the Bible salesman exploits each one.

touched and understood a central truth inside her. She considers it a complete surrender, "like losing her own life and finding it again, miraculously, in his" (1953).

12   As soon as the artificial leg is off, Manley whips out one of his Bibles, which is hollow. Inside are whiskey, obscene playing cards, and contraceptives. In only moments, Hulga loses control: As each of her physical handicaps is exploited, pieces of her world view crumble, leaving her confused and weak.

13   In an ironic reversal, Hulga becomes the naïf and
(F)   Manley becomes the cynic. Hulga pleads in disbelief, "Aren't you . . . just good country people?" (1954). She knows that she has reverted to her mother's platitudes: "If the language is more sophisticated than any at Mrs. Hopewell's command, it is no less trite, and the smug self-deception underlying it . . . is, if anything, greater" (Asals 105). Manley assumes a startling, haughty air, exclaiming, "'I hope you don't think . . . that I believe in that crap! I may sell Bibles but I know which end is up and I wasn't born yesterday and I know where I'm going!'" (1954). Although they exchange roles, both characters use cliches to express their immature, yet authentic, worldviews.

14   Manley runs off with Hulga's wooden leg, leaving her vulnerable and dependent, two things she previously despised. But "Hulga's artificial self—her mental fantasy of her own perfection—has gone out the door with her artificial limb. She is stuck in the hayloft with her actual self, her body, her physical and emotional incompleteness" (Di Renzo 79).

15   In one brief morning of delusional seduction,
(G)   Hulga learns more about herself and her world than she learned in all her years of university. Forced to acknowledge her physical, emotional, and spiritual disabilities, Hulga begins to realize what she is not—neither a wise intellectual for whom there is hope, nor "good country people" who merely *hope well*.

Note: The Works Cited page is not shown. For sample pages, see MLA (pages 368–369) and APA (page 396).

(F) The writer reflects on the change in both characters.
(G) She explains how the protagonist finally acknowledges the truth about herself.

Reading for Better Writing

Working by yourself or with a group, answer these questions:

1. In her opening paragraph, Terekhina cites Flannery O'Connor's view that every short story should be "long in depth" and meaning. Does Terekhina adequately explore that depth and meaning? Why?

2. In her second paragraph, Terekhina analyzes Hulga Hopewell's first name; in the last paragraph, she comments on the last name. Does Terekhina's attention to names help you understand Hulga's character and the story's themes? How?

3. A writer's thesis is a type of "contract" that he or she makes with readers, spelling out what the essay will do. Review Terekhina's thesis (last sentence, first paragraph) and assess how effectively she fulfills that contract. Cite supporting details.

4. Flannery O'Connor has received strong acclaim for her clearly developed, complex characters. Does Terekhina adequately explore that complexity? Explain.

5. Many praise O'Connor for the challenging philosophical or ethical questions raised in her fiction. What questions does Terekhina identify in "Good Country People," and does she effectively discuss them?

6. What does Terekhina say about the story's plot, symbols, and diction? Does she effectively analyze these elements? Why?

Analyze a poem. LO3

In the essay on pages 268–270, student writer Sherry Van Egdom analyzes the form and meaning of the poem below, "Let Evening Come," by American poet Jane Kenyon. Born in 1947 and raised on a farm near Ann Arbor, Michigan, Kenyon settled in New Hampshire at Eagle Pond Farm after she married fellow poet Donald Hall. During her life, Kenyon struggled with her faith, with depression, and with cancer. At the time of her death in 1995 from leukemia, she was the poet laureate of New Hampshire.

Before you read the student writer's analysis, read the poem aloud to enjoy its sounds, rhythm, images, diction, and comparisons. Then read the piece again to grasp more fully how the poem is structured, what it expresses, and how its ideas might relate to your life. Finally, read Van Egdom's analysis and answer the questions that follow it.

Let Evening Come

Let the light of late afternoon
shine through chinks in the barn, moving
up the bales as the sun moves down.

Let the crickets take up chafing
as a woman takes up her needles
and her yarn. Let evening come.

Let dew collect on the hoe abandoned
in long grass. Let the stars appear
and the moon disclose her silver horn.

Let the fox go back to its sandy den.
Let the wind die down. Let the shed
go black inside. Let evening come.

To the bottle in the ditch, to the scoop
in the oats, to air in the lung
let evening come.

Let it come, as it will, and don't
be afraid. God does not leave us
comfortless, so let evening come.

"Let Evening Come": An Invitation to the Inevitable

Survey • Question • Read • Recite • Review

1
(A) The work of American poet Jane Kenyon is influenced primarily by the circumstances and experiences of her own life. She writes carefully crafted, deceptively simple poems that connect both to her own life and to the lives of her readers. Growing out of her rural roots and her struggles with illness, Kenyon's poetry speaks in a still voice of the ordinary things in life in order to wrestle with issues of faith and mortality (Timmerman 163). *(B)* One of these poems is "Let Evening Come." In this poem, the poet takes the reader on a journey into the night, but she points to hope in the face of that darkness.

2
That movement toward darkness is captured in the stanza form and in the progression of stanzas. Each three-line stanza offers a self-contained moment in the progress of transition from day to night. The first stanza positions the reader in a simple farm setting. *(C)* Late afternoon fades into evening without the rumble of highways or the gleam of city lights to distract one's senses from nature, the peace emphasized by the alliteration of "l" in "Let the light of late afternoon." As the sun sinks lower on the horizon, light seeps through cracks in the barn wall, moving up the bales of hay. In the second stanza, the crickets get busy with their nighttime noises. Next, a forgotten farm hoe becomes covered with dew drops, and the silvery stars and moon appear in the sky. In the fourth stanza, complete blackness arrives as a fox returns to *(D)* its empty den and the silent wind rests at close of day. The alliteration of "d" in "den" and "die down" gives a sinking, settling feeling (Timmerman 176). In the

---

(A) The writer introduces the poet and her poetry.
(B) Narrowing her focus to the specific poem, the writer states her thesis.
(C) She begins her analysis by explaining the stanza structure and progression.
(D) The writer shows attention to the poem's fine details and to secondary sources on the poem.

fifth stanza, a bottle and scoop keep still, untouched in their respective places, while sleep comes upon the human body. In the final stanza, Kenyon encourages readers to meet this emerging world of darkness without fear.

3 Within this stanza progression, the journey into the night is intensified by strong images, figures of speech, and symbols. The natural rhythm of work and rest on the farm is symbolized by the light that rises and falls in the first stanza (Timmerman 175). The simile comparing the crickets taking up their song **(E)** to a woman picking up her knitting suggests a homespun energy and conviction. The moon revealing her "silver horn" implies that the moon does not instantly appear with brightness and beauty but rather reveals her majesty slowly as the night comes on. The den, the wind, and the shed in stanza four stress a kind of internal, hidden darkness. Then stanza five focuses on connected objects: the thoughtlessly discarded bottle resting in the ditch, oats and the scoop for feeding, human lungs and the air that fills them. Kenyon mentions the air in the lung *after* the bottle, ditch, scoop,

and oats in order to picture humanity taking its position among the established natural rhythm of the farm (Harris 31).

The refrain, "let evening come," is a powerful part 4 of the poem's journey toward darkness, though critics interpret the line differently. Judith Harris suggests that it symbolizes an acceptance of the inevitable: Darkness will envelop the world, and night will surely **(F)** come, just as mortality will certainly take its toll in time. This acceptance, in turn, acts as a release from the confinement of one's pain and trials in life. Rather than wrestle with something that cannot be beaten or worry about things that must be left undone, Kenyon advises herself and her readers to let go (31). Night intrudes upon the work and events of the day, perhaps leaving them undone just as death might cut a life short and leave it seemingly unfinished.

By contrast, John Timmerman argues that "let" is 5 used twelve times in a supplicatory, prayer-like manner (176). The final two lines, in turn, act as a benediction upon the supplications. The comfort of God is as inevitable as the evening, so cling to faith and hope and let evening come. Although the Comforter

---

(E) She advances her reading of the poem by exploring images, comparisons, and symbols: the poem's "imaginative logic."

(F) The writer compares possible interpretations of a central, repeated statement in the poem.

Dudarev Mikhail, 2011 / Used under license from Shutterstock.com

is mentioned only in the last two lines, that statement of faith encourages readers to find a spiritual comfort in spite of the coming of the night.

6 (G) When asked how she came to write "Let Evening Come," Jane Kenyon replied that it was a redemptive poem given to her by the Holy Ghost. When there could be *nothing*—a great darkness and despair, there is a great *mystery* of love, kindness, and beauty (Moyers 238). In the poem's calm journey into the night, Kenyon confronts darkness and suffering with a certain enduring beauty and hope (Timmerman 161). Death will come, but there remains divine comfort. "Let Evening Come" encourages readers to release their grip on the temporary and pay attention to the Comforter who reveals Himself both day *and* night.

Note: The Works Cited page is not shown. For sample pages, see MLA (pages 368–369) and APA (page 396).

(G) In her conclusion, the writer offers the poet's explanation of the poem's origin and then expands on the thesis.

Reading for Better Writing

Working by yourself or with a group, answer these questions:

1. Review the opening and closing paragraphs of the essay. How do they create a framework for the writer's analysis of the poem?

2. On which elements of the poem does the writer focus? Does this approach make sense for her analysis? Explain.

3. In her essay, the writer refers to the poet's life and to ideas from secondary sources. Do these references work well with her analysis? Why or why not?

4. Read the essay "Four Ways to Talk About Literature" on pages 206–207. Which approach does the student writer use to analyze Kenyon's poem? Does this approach make sense? How might another approach interpret the poem differently?

Analyze a film.
LO4

In the film review below, David Schaap analyzes Stephen Spielberg's film *War of the Worlds* by asking key questions about the filmmaker's strategies and their effects.

Terror on the Silver Screen: Who Are the Aliens?

Survey · Question · Read · Recite · Review **SQ3R**

1 (A) In Steven Spielberg's 2005 movie *War of the Worlds,* Ray Ferrier and his two children flee their New Jersey home in a stolen minivan. To escape outer-space aliens who are destroying houses and killing people from their enormous three-legged machines, this father, son, and daughter lurch through scene after scene of 9/11-type destruction. At one point, the daughter surveys the violence, panics, and shrieks, "Is it the terrorists?"

2 (B) The girl's question nudges the audience to ask the same question, "Are the aliens terrorists?" That would make sense. Often filmmakers will play off members of the audience's real-life emotions to give them a sensational imaginary experience as well as a glimpse at their real world. In this case, by suggesting that the aliens' imaginary attack resembles Al Qaeda's 9/11 attack, Spielberg could be doing two things: (1) heightening fear of the alien characters and (2) suggesting a political theme.

3 (C) But is Spielberg's *War of the Worlds* this type of film? First, does the film inspire fear by suggesting that the aliens' attack is similar to Al Qaeda's attack? And second, does the film's alien attack represent a future terrorist invasion of the United States?

(A) The writer introduces the filmmaker and film; he then describes a pivotal scene.
(B) He cites an important quotation and explores its significance.
(C) Two questions focus the writer's analysis.

4 The answer to the first question is yes. Spielberg
(D) inspires fear of his outer-space aliens by emphasizing their resemblance to 9/11 terrorists. In a series of scenes, he shows a crashed airliner like the ones used on 9/11, a wall covered with posters of missing loved ones, and mobs of ash- and dust-covered characters like those escaping the collapsing World Trade Center. Because the film takes place in the United States, viewers subconsciously further fear the aliens' violence.

5 However, do the aliens invading the United States
(E) represent Al Qaeda fighters? Not really. The aliens are Spielberg's universal stand-in for whatever strikes fear into viewers' hearts. This film does not examine the political, psychological, or cultural roots of any problem. The film's focus is on the effect of violence, not the identity of the perpetrators. *War of the Worlds* is about terror, not terrorists.

(D) He answers the first question and offers supporting details.
(E) He answers the second question by explaining the film's focus.

Reading for Better Writing

Working by yourself or with a group, answer these questions:

1. Where in this analysis does the writer share his thesis?
2. Explain how the writer prepares the reader for his focus. In your explanation, include details or quotations from the analysis.
3. Is the writer's method of development effective? Explain.

red-feniks, 2011 / Used under license from Shutterstock.com

Understand and use literary terms. LO5

Your analysis of novels, poems, plays, and films will be deeper and more sophisticated if you understand the most common literary terms.

Allusion is a reference to a person, a place, or an event in history or literature.

Analogy is a comparison of two or more similar objects, suggesting that if they are alike in certain respects, they will probably be alike in other ways, too.

Anecdote is a short summary of an interesting or humorous, often biographical incident or event.

Antagonist is the person or thing actively working against the protagonist, or hero.

Climax is the turning point, an intense moment characterized by a key event.

Conflict is the problem or struggle in a story that triggers the action. There are five basic types of conflict:

Person versus person: One character in a story is in conflict with one or more of the other characters.

Person versus society: A character is in conflict with some element of society: the school, the law, the accepted way of doing things, and so on.

Person versus self: A character faces conflicting inner choices.

Person versus nature: A character is in conflict with some natural happening: a snowstorm, an avalanche, the bitter cold, or any other element of nature.

Person versus fate: A character must battle what seems to be an uncontrollable problem. Whenever the conflict is a strange or unbelievable coincidence, the conflict can be attributed to fate.

Denouement is the outcome of a play or story. See *Resolution*.

Diction is an author's choice of words based on their correctness or effectiveness.

Archaic words are old-fashioned and no longer sound natural when used, such as "I believe thee not" for "I don't believe you."

Colloquialism is an expression that is usually accepted in informal situations and certain locations, as in "He really grinds my beans."

Heightened language uses vocabulary and sentence constructions that produce a stylized effect unlike that of standard speech or writing, as in much poetry and poetic prose.

Profanity is language that shows disrespect for someone or something regarded as sacred.

Slang is the everyday language used by group members among themselves.

Trite expressions lack depth or originality, or are overworked or not worth mentioning.

Vulgarity is language that is generally considered common, crude, gross, and, at times, offensive. It is sometimes used in fiction, plays, and films to add realism.

Exposition is the introductory section of a story or play. Typically, the setting, main characters, and themes are introduced, and the action is initiated.

Falling action is the action of a play or story that follows the climax and shows the characters dealing with the climactic event or decision.

Figure of speech is a literary device used to create a special effect or to describe something in a fresh way. The box that follows describes common figures of speech.

Antithesis is an opposition, or contrast, of ideas.
"It was the best of times, it was the worst of times, it was the age of wisdom, it was the age of foolishness . . ."
— Charles Dickens, *A Tale of Two Cities*

Hyperbole (hi-pur´ ba-lee) is an extreme exaggeration or overstatement.
"I have seen this river so wide it had only one bank."
—Mark Twain, *Life on the Mississippi*

Metaphor is a comparison of two unlike things in which no word of comparison (*as* or *like*) is used: "Life is a banquet."

Metonymy (ma-ton´a-mee) is the substituting of one term for another that is closely related to it, but not a literal restatement.
"Friends, Romans, countrymen, lend me your ears." (The request is for the *attention* of those assembled, not literally their *ears*.)

Personification is a device in which the author speaks of or describes an animal, object, or idea as if it were a person: "The rock stubbornly refused to move."

Simile is a comparison of two unlike things in which *like* or *as* is used.
"She stood in front of the altar, shaking like a freshly caught trout."
—Maya Angelou, *I Know Why the Caged Bird Sings*

Understatement is stating an idea with restraint, often for humorous effect. Mark Twain described Aunt Polly as being "prejudiced against snakes." (Because she hated snakes, this way of saying so is *understatement*.)

Genre refers to a category or type of literature based on its style, form, and content. The mystery novel is a literary genre.

Imagery refers to words or phrases that a writer uses to appeal to the reader's senses.
"The sky was dark and gloomy, the air was damp and raw, the streets were wet and sloppy."
—Charles Dickens, *The Pickwick Paper*

Irony is a deliberate discrepancy in meaning or in the way something is understood. There are three kinds of irony:

Dramatic irony, in which the reader or the audience sees a character's mistakes or misunderstandings, but the character does not.

Verbal irony, in which the writer says one thing and means another

Irony of situation, in which there is a great difference between the purpose of a particular action and the result.

Mood is the feeling that a piece of literature arouses in the reader: *happiness, sadness, peacefulness, anxiety,* and so forth.

Paradox is a statement that seems contrary to common sense yet may, in fact, be true: "The coach considered this a good loss."

Plot is the action or sequence of events in a story. It is usually a series of related incidents that build upon one another as the story develops. There are five basic elements in a plot line: *exposition, rising action, climax, falling action,* and *resolution.*

Point of view is the vantage point from which the story unfolds.

In the **first-person** point of view, the story is told by one of the characters: "I stepped into the darkened room and felt myself go cold."

In the **third-person** point of view, the story is told by someone outside the story: "He stepped into the darkened room and felt himself go cold."

Third-person narrations can be *omniscient,* meaning that the narrator has access to the thoughts of all the characters, or *limited,* meaning that the narrator focuses on the inner life of one central character.

Protagonist is the main character of the story.

Resolution (or *denouement*) is the portion of the play or story in which the problem is solved. The resolution comes after the climax and falling action and is intended to bring the story to a satisfactory end.

Rising action is the series of conflicts or struggles that build a story or play to a fulfilling climax.

Satire is a literary tone used to ridicule or make fun of human vice or weakness, often with the intent of correcting, or changing, the subject of the satiric attack.

Setting is the time and place in which the action of a literary work occurs.

Structure is the form or organization a writer uses for her or his literary work. A great number of possible forms are used regularly in literature: parable, fable, romance, satire, and so on.

Style refers to how the author uses words, phrases, and sentences to form his or her ideas. Style is also thought of as the qualities that distinguish one writer's work from the work of others.

Symbol is a person, a place, a thing, or an event used to represent something else. For example, the dove is a symbol of peace.

Theme is the statement about life that a particular work shares with readers. In stories written for children, the theme is often spelled out clearly at the end. In more complex literature, the theme will be implied, not stated.

Tone is the overall feeling, or effect, created by a writer's use of words. This feeling may be serious, mock-serious, humorous, satiric, and so on.

Poetry Terms

Alliteration is the repetition of initial consonant sounds in words such as "rough and ready."

Assonance is the repetition of vowel sounds without the repetition of consonants.

Blank verse is an unrhymed form of poetry. Each line normally consists of ten syllables in which every other syllable, beginning with the second, is stressed.

Consonance is the repetition of consonant sounds."
"... and high school girls with clear-skin smiles ..."
—Janis Ian, "At Seventeen"

Foot is the smallest repeated pattern of stressed and unstressed syllables in a poetic line. (See **Verse.**)

Iambic: an unstressed followed by a stressed syllable (re-peat´)

Anapestic: two unstressed followed by a stressed syllable (in-ter-rupt´)

Trochaic: a stressed followed by an unstressed syllable (old´-er)

Dactylic: a stressed followed by two unstressed syllables (o´-pen-ly)

Spondaic: two stressed syllables (heart´-break´)

Pyrrhic: two unstressed syllables (Pyrrhic seldom appears by itself.)

Onomatopoeia is the use of a word whose sound suggests its meaning, as in *clang* and *buzz*.

Refrain is the repetition of a line or phrase of a poem at regular intervals, especially at the end of each stanza. A song's refrain may be called the *chorus*.

Rhythm is the ordered or free occurrences of sound in poetry. Ordered or regular rhythm is called *meter*. Free occurrence of sound is called *free verse*.

Stanza is a division of poetry named for the number of lines it contains:

Couplet: two-line stanza
Triplet: three-line stanza
Quatrain: four-line stanza
Quintet: five-line stanza
Sestet: six-line stanza
Septet: seven-line stanza
Octave: eight-line stanza

Verse is a metric line of poetry. It is named according to the kind and number of feet composing it. (See **Foot.**)

Monometer: one foot
Dimeter: two feet
Trimeter: three feet
Tetrameter: four feet
Pentameter: five feet
Hexameter: six feet
Heptameter: seven feet
Octometer: eight feet

Write an arts-specific analysis.

LO6

Writing Guidelines

Planning

1. **Select a topic.** Choose an art form and artwork with which you are familiar or you are willing to learn about.

2. **Understand the work.** Experience it thoughtfully (two or three times, if possible), looking carefully at its content, form, and overall effect.
   - For plays and films, examine the plot, props, setting, characters, dialogue, lighting, costumes, sound effects, music, acting, and directing.
   - For novels and short stories, focus on point of view, plot, setting, characters, style, diction, symbols, and theme. (See pages 271–273.)
   - For poems, examine diction, tone, sound patterns, figures of speech (e.g., metaphors), symbolism, irony, structure, genre, and theme. (See page 273.)
   - For music, focus on harmonic and rhythmic qualities, dynamics, melodic lines, lyrics, and interpretation.

3. **Develop a focus and approach.** Take notes on what you experience, using the list above to guide you. Seek to understand the whole work before you analyze the parts, exploring your ideas and digging deeply through freewriting and annotating. Select a dimension of the work as a focus, considering what approach to analyzing that element might work. (See "Four Ways to Talk About Literature" on pages 134–135.)

4. **Organize your thoughts.** Review the notes that you took as you analyzed the work. What key insights has your analysis led you to see? Make a key insight your thesis, and then organize supporting points logically in an outline.

Drafting

5. **Write the first draft.**

   Opening: Use ideas like the following to gain your readers' attention, identify your topic, narrow the focus, and state your thesis:
   - Summarize your subject briefly. Include the title, the author or artist, and the literary form or performance.
     Example: In her poem "Let Evening Come," Jane Kenyon points to hope in the face of death.
   - Start with a quotation from the work and then comment on its importance.
   - Explain the artist's purpose and how well she or he achieves it.
   - Open with a general statement about the artist's style or aesthetic process.
     Example: The work of American poet Jane Kenyon is influenced primarily by the circumstances and experiences of her own life.
   - Begin with a general statement about the plot or performance.
     Example: In Stephen Spielberg's movie *War of the Worlds,* Ray Ferrier and his two children flee from their New Jersey home in a stolen minivan.
   - Assert your thesis. State the key insight about the work that your analysis has revealed—the insight your essay will seek to support.

   Middle: Develop or support your focus by following this pattern:
   - State the main points, relating them clearly to the focus of your essay.
   - Support each main point with specific details or direct quotations.
   - Explain how these details prove your point.

   Conclusion: Tie key points together and assert your thesis or evaluation in a fresh way, leaving readers with a sense of the larger significance of your analysis.

Revising

6. **Improve the ideas, organization, and voice.** Review your draft for its overall content and tone. Ask a classmate or writing-center tutor for help, if appropriate.

   Ideas: Does the essay show clear and deep insight into specific elements of the text, artwork, or performance? Is that insight effectively developed with specific references to the work itself?

Organization: Does the opening effectively engage the reader, introduce the text or artwork, and focus attention on an element or issue? Does the middle carefully work through a "reading" of the work? Does the conclusion reaffirm the insight into the work and expand the reader's understanding?

Voice: Does the tone convey a controlled, measured interest in the text or artwork? Is the analytical attitude confident but reasonable?

Editing

7. Edit and proofread the essay by checking issues like these:

Words: Language, especially the terminology, is precise and clear.

Sentences: Constructions flow smoothly and are varied in length and structure; quotations are effectively integrated into sentence syntax.

Correctness: The copy includes no errors in spelling, usage, punctuation, grammar, or mechanics.

Design: The page design is correctly formatted and attractive; references are properly documented according to the required system (e.g., MLA).

Publishing

8. Publish your essay. Submit your essay to your instructor, but consider other ways of sharing your insights about this work or artist—blogging, submitting a review to a periodical (print or online), or leading classmates in a discussion (e.g., book club, post-performance meeting, exhibition tour).

Critical-Thinking and Writing Activities

As directed by your instructor, complete the following activities.

1. Get a copy of "Good Country People," read the story, write your own analysis, and share the essay with your class.
2. Review "Let Evening Come" and write your own analysis of the poem. Read your essay to the class and discuss how its style and content compare with that of the essay on pages 268–270.
3. Choose a film and watch it critically, preferably twice. Then find two reviews of the film, note their theses and supporting evidence, and write an essay in which you evaluate why the reviews are (or are not) informed, insightful, and fair.
4. Attend a concert with classmates. Afterward, discuss the style of the music, the performance of the singer or group, and the content of the lyrics.
5. Visit an art gallery and examine an exhibit that engages you. Describe what you find appealing or intriguing and explain why.

Checklist: Learning Outcomes

Use the checklist below to assess and review what you have learned about reading and writing about the arts.

_____ I can read and evaluate writing about literature and the arts for clarity, reasoning, and insight.

_____ I can critically analyze a short story, including its character, plot, setting, dialogue, symbols, and themes.

_____ I can critically analyze a poem, including its rhythms, rhymes, symbols, images, and ideas.

_____ I can analyze a film by addressing relevant issues, looking for appropriate qualities, and using reasonable criteria.

_____ I can use arts-related terminology to describe, analyze, and critique artwork.

_____ I can write an analysis that has an insightful thesis, clear reasoning, and relevant supporting evidence from the work.

"Many ideas grow better when transplanted into
another mind than in the one where they sprang up."
—Oliver Wendell Holmes

22

Workplace Writing

One thing you already know about writing in college life is that you have to do a lot of writing in your courses—and it has to be good. By writing well, you make a positive impression in the classroom. But did you know that life outside the classroom also requires lots of writing?

This chapter will help you write work-related documents. Sample letters and memos will help you communicate effectively with people ranging from the registrar to scholarship committees. The sample application essay and résumés will help you apply for a job, a program, or an internship. In addition, the e-mail writing instructions will help you take care of business with other readers, no matter where in the world they might be.

Learning Outcomes

LO1 Write effective memos and e-mail.

LO2 Write effective business letters.

LO3 Write an effective application essay.

LO4 Write effective résumés.

Write effective memos and e-mail. LO1

Writing Memos

A memorandum is a written message sent from one person to one or more other people within the same organization. As such, a memo is less formal than a letter. A memo can vary in length from a sentence or two to a four- or five-page report, and a memo can be delivered in person, dropped in a mailbox, or sent via e-mail.

Memos are written to create a flow of information within an organization—asking and answering questions, describing procedures and policies, or reminding people about appointments and meetings. Here are some guidelines:

- Write memos only when necessary, and only to those people who need them.
- Distribute them through the appropriate media—mail, fax, bulletin boards, kiosk, intranet, or e-mail.
- Make your subject line precise (a brief summary) so that the topic is clear and the memo is easy to file.
- Get to the point: (1) state the subject, (2) give necessary details, and (3) state the response you want.

Writing E-Mail

With e-mail, people can correspond through computer networks around the globe. E-mail allows you to do the following:

- Send, forward, and receive many messages quickly and efficiently, making it ideal for group projects and other forms of collaboration.
- Set up mailing lists (specific groups of e-mail addresses) so that you can easily send the same message to several people at the same time.
- Organize messages in "folders" for later reference, and reply to messages.

Tip for e-mail

Revise and edit messages for clarity and correctness before sending them. Confusing sentences, grammatical errors, and typos limit your ability to communicate on a computer screen just as they do on paper.

Use e-mail responsibly. Sooner or later you will send e-mail to the wrong person, or a reader will forward your message to another person without your permission. Keep these possibilities in mind at all times, and never write anything that would embarrass you if the wrong party received it.

Make messages easy to read and understand. (1) Provide a clear, complete subject line so readers can scan it and decide whether to read or delete the message. (2) Type short paragraphs.

Checklist: Workplace Writing

- ✔ The **ideas** are clear accurate, and address the readers' needs.
- ✔ The **organization** is logical, with an informative opening, fully-developed middle, and appropriate closing.
- ✔ The **voice** is informed and courteous.
- ✔ The **words** are precise and clear; personal pronouns (especially "you") convey a caring tone.
- ✔ The **sentences** are clear, easily read, and linked with transitions.
- ✔ **Correct** punctuation, mechanics, and usage are used.
- ✔ The page **design** is attractive and fits the message's form and content.

ostill, 2011 / Used under license from Shutterstock.com

Memo

Date: September 24, 2011

To: All Users of the Bascom Hill Writing Lab

From: Kerri Kelley, Coordinator

Subject: New Hours/New Equipment for Writing Lab

Beginning October 1, the Bascom Hill Writing Lab will expand its weekend hours as follows: Fridays, 7:00 a.m.–11:00 p.m.; Saturdays, 8:00 A.M.–11:00 p.m.

Also, six additional computers will be installed next week, making it easier to get computer time. We hope these changes will help meet the increased demand for time and assistance we've experienced this fall. Remember, it's still a good idea to sign up in advance. To reserve time, call the lab at 462-7722 or leave your request at bhill@madwis.edu.

Finally, long-range planners, mark your calendars. The lab will be closed on Thanksgiving Day morning and open from 1:00 p.m. to 11:00 p.m. We will also be closed on Christmas and New Year's Day. We will post our semester-break hours sometime next month.

E-Mail

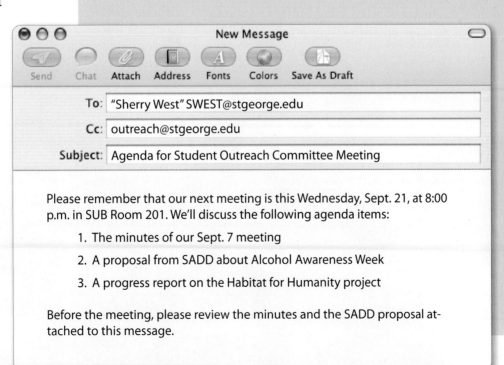

New Message

Send   Chat   Attach   Address   Fonts   Colors   Save As Draft

To: "Sherry West" SWEST@stgeorge.edu

Cc: outreach@stgeorge.edu

Subject: Agenda for Student Outreach Committee Meeting

Please remember that our next meeting is this Wednesday, Sept. 21, at 8:00 p.m. in SUB Room 201. We'll discuss the following agenda items:

1. The minutes of our Sept. 7 meeting
2. A proposal from SADD about Alcohol Awareness Week
3. A progress report on the Habitat for Humanity project

Before the meeting, please review the minutes and the SADD proposal attached to this message.

Write effective business letters. _____ LO2

Business letters do many things—for example, share ideas, promote products, or ask for help. Putting a message in writing gives you time to think about, organize, and edit what you want to say. In addition, a written message serves as a record of important details for both the sender and the recipient.

Parts of the Business Letter

Heading The heading gives the writer's complete address, either in the letterhead (company stationery) or typed out, followed by the date.

Inside Address The inside address gives the reader's name and address.

- If you're not sure which person to address or how to spell someone's name, you could call the company or check their Web site for the information.
- If the person's title is a single word, place it after the name and a comma (Mary Johnson, President). A longer title goes on a separate line.

Salutation The salutation begins with Dear and ends with a colon, not a comma.

- Use *Mr.* or *Ms.* plus the person's last name, unless you are well acquainted. Do not guess at *Miss* or *Mrs.*

- If you can't get the person's name, replace the salutation with *Dear* or *Attention* followed by the title of an appropriate reader. (*Examples:* Dear Dean of Students: or Attention: Personnel Manager)

  Note: See pages 89–90 for a complete list of "unbiased" ways to refer to an individual or a particular group.

Body The body should consist of single-spaced paragraphs with double-spacing between paragraphs. (Do not indent the paragraphs.)

- If the body goes to a second page, put the reader's name at the top left, the number 2 in the center, and the date at the right margin.

Complimentary Closing For the complimentary closing, use *Sincerely, Yours sincerely,* or *Yours truly* followed by a comma; use *Best wishes* if you know the person well.

Signature The signature includes the writer's name both handwritten and typed.

Initials When someone types the letter for the writer, that person's initials appear (in lowercase) after the writer's initials (in capitals) and a colon.

Enclosure If a document (brochure, form, résumé, or other form) is enclosed with the letter, the word *Enclosure* or *Encl.* appears below the initials.

Copies If a copy of the letter is sent elsewhere, type *cc:* beneath the enclosure line, followed by the person's or department's name.

Informative Letter

Heading

Box 143
Balliole College
Eugene, OR 97440-5125
August 29, 2011

Four to Seven Spaces

Inside Address

Ms. Ada Overlie
Ogg Hall, Room 222
Balliole College
Eugene, OR 97440-0222

Double Space

Salutation

Dear Ms. Overlie:

Double Space

As the president of the Earth Care Club, I welcome you to Balliole Community College. I hope the year will be a great learning experience both inside and outside the classroom.

Double Space

Body

That learning experience is the reason I'm writing—to encourage you to join the Earth Care Club. As a member, you could participate in the educational and action-oriented mission of the club. The club has most recently been involved in the following:

- Organizing a reduce, reuse, recycle program on campus
- Promoting cloth rather than plastic bag use among students
- Giving input to the college administration on landscaping, renovating, and building for energy efficiency
- Putting together the annual Earth Day celebration

Double Space

Which environmental concerns and activities would you like to focus on? Bring them with you to the Earth Care Club. Simply complete the enclosed form and return it by September 9. Then watch the campus news for details on our first meeting.

Double Space

Yours sincerely,

Dave Wetland   **Four Spaces**

Complimentary Closing and Signature

Dave Wetland
President

Double Space

Initials Enclosure Copies

DW:kr
Encl. membership form
cc: Esther du Toit, membership committee

Letter of Application

Your letter of application (or cover letter) introduces you to an employer and often highlights information on an accompanying résumé. Your goal in writing this letter is to convince the employer to invite you for an interview.

Ogg Hall, Room 222
Balliole College
Eugene, OR 97440-0222
September 2, 2011

Address a specific person, if possible.

Professor Edward Mahaffy
Greenhouse Coordinator
Balliole College
Eugene, OR 97440-0316

Dear Professor Mahaffy:

State the desired position and your chief qualification

I recently talked with Ms. Sierra Arbor in the Financial Aid Office about work-study jobs for 2011–2012. She told me about the Greenhouse Assistant position and gave me a job description. As a full-time Balliole student, I'm writing to apply for this position. I believe that my experience qualifies me for the job.

Focus on how your skills meet the reader's needs.

As you can see from my résumé, I spent two summers working in a raspberry operation, doing basic plant care and carrying out quality-control lab tests on the fruit. Also, as I was growing up, I learned a great deal by helping with a large farm garden. In high school and college, I studied botany. Because of my interest in this field, I'm enrolled in the Environmental Studies program at Balliole.

Request an interview and thank the reader.

I am available for an interview. You may phone me any time at 341-3611 (and leave a message on my machine) or e-mail me at dvrl@balliole.edu. Thank you for considering my application.

Yours sincerely,

Ada Overlie

Ada Overlie

Encl. résumé

Recommendation-Request Letter

When you apply for a job or program, it helps to present references or recommendations to show your fitness for the position. To get the support you need from people familiar with your work (instructors and employers), you need to ask for that support. You can do so in person or by phone, but a courteous and clear letter or e-mail message makes your request official and helps the person complete the recommendation effectively. Here is a suggested outline:

Situation: Remind the reader of your relationship to him or her; then ask the person to write a recommendation or to serve as a reference for you.

Explanation: Describe the work you did for the reader and the type of job, position, or program for which you are applying.

Action: Explain what form the recommendation should take, to whom it should be addressed, and where and when it needs to be sent.

2456 Charles Street
Lexington, KY 40588-8321
March 19, 2011

Dr. Rosa Perez
271 University Boulevard
University of Kentucky
Lexington, KY 40506-1440

Dear Dr. Perez:

The Situation

As we discussed on the phone, I would appreciate your writing a recommendation letter for me. You know the quality of my academic work, my qualities as a person, and my potential for working in the medical field.

The Explanation

As my professor for Biology 201 and 202, you are familiar with my grades and work habits. As my adviser, you know my career plans and understand whether I have the qualities needed to succeed in the medical profession. I am asking you for your recommendation because I am applying for summer employment with the Lexington Ambulance Service. I recently received my Emergency Medical Technician (Basic) license to prepare for such work.

The Action

Please send your letter to Rick Falk, EMT Coordinator, at the University Placement Office by April 8. Thank you for your help. Let me know if you need any other information (phone 231-6700; e-mail jnwllms@ukentucky.edu).

Yours sincerely,

Jon Williams

Jon Williams

Write an effective application essay. — LO2

For some applications, you may be asked to submit an essay, a personal statement, or a response paper. For example, you might be applying for admission to an academic program (social work, engineering, optometry school) or for an internship, a scholarship, or a research grant. Whatever the situation, what you write and how well you write it will be important factors in the success of your application.

Below is a model application essay. Jessy Jezowski wrote this essay as part of her application to a college social work program.

Tip for an application essay

Understand what you are being asked to write and why. How does the essay fit into the entire application? Who will read your essay? What will they look for?

Focus on the instructions for writing the essay. What type of question is it? What topics are you asked to write about? What hints do the directions give about possible organization, emphasis, style, length, and method of submitting the essay?

Be honest with yourself and your readers. Don't try to write only what you think readers want to hear.

Think about your purpose and audience:

- What do you want to gain (internship, scholarship, job interview), and how could your writing help you gain it?

- Who are your readers? What do they know about you? What should they know?

Develop your essay using the following organization (if the instructions allow for it):

- An introduction with a fresh, interesting opening statement and a clear focus or theme

- A body that develops the focus or theme clearly and concisely—with some details and examples—in a way appropriate to the instructions

- A conclusion that stresses a positive point and looks forward to participating in the program, internship, organization, or position

Write in a style that is personal but professional. Use words that fit the subject and the readers. Avoid cliches, and balance generalizations with concrete examples and details.

Refine your first draft into a polished piece. First, get feedback from another student or, if appropriate, a professor, and revise the essay. Second, edit the final version thoroughly: You don't want typos, incorrect names, and grammar errors to derail your application.

Application Essay

February 28, 2010

Jessy Jezowski

Personal Statement

1

(A)

While growing up in Chicago, I would see people hanging out on street corners, by grocery stores, and in parks—with no home and barely any belongings. Poverty and its related problems are all around us, and yet most people walk by them with blinders on. I have found myself quick to assume that someone else will help the poor man on the corner, the woman trapped in an abusive relationship, or the teenager struggling with an eating disorder. But I know in my heart that all members of society are responsible to and for each other. Social welfare issues affect every member of society— including me.

(A) The opening provides a clear focus for the essay.

2
(B) Because these issues are serious and difficult to solve, I wish to major in social work and eventually become a social worker. In the major, I want to gain the knowledge, skills, and attitudes that will make me part of the solution, not part of the problem. By studying social work institutions, the practices of social work, and the theory and history behind social work, I hope to learn how to help people help themselves. When that pregnant teenager comes to me, I want to have strong, practical advice—and be part of an effective social work agency that can help implement that advice.

3
(C) I am especially interested at this point in working with families and teenagers, in either a community counseling or school setting. Two experiences have created this interest. First, a woman in my church who works for an adoption agency, Ms. Lesage, has modeled for me what it means to care for individuals and families within a community and around the world. Second, I was involved in a peer counseling program in high school. As counselors, we received training in interpersonal relationships and the nature of helping. In a concrete way, I experienced the complex challenges of helping others.

4
(D) I believe strongly in the value of all people and am interested in the well-being of others. As a social worker, I would strive to make society better (for individuals, families, and communities) by serving those in need, whatever their problems.

(B) The writer demonstrates knowledge of the field and explains what she hopes to learn.
(C) Two concrete examples help back up her general statements.
(D) The conclusion summarizes her goals for the future.

Write effective résumés. LO2

A strong résumé isn't generic—a ho-hum fill-in-the-blanker. Rather, it's a vivid word picture of your skills, knowledge, and past responsibilities. It says exactly who you are by providing the kind of information that follows.

Personal Data: name, address, phone number, e-mail address (enough for the reader to identify you and reach you easily).

Job Objective: the type of position you want and the type of organization for which you want to work.

Skills Summary: the key qualities and skills you bring to a position, listed with supporting details. Here are some skill areas that you might consider for your own résumé:

Communication	Management (people, money, other resources)
Organization	Working with people, counseling, training
Problem solving	Sales, marketing, public relations
Computer	Languages

Experience: positions you've held (where and when), and your specific duties and your accomplishments.

Education: degrees, courses, and special projects.

Other Experiences: volunteer work, awards, achievements, tutoring jobs, extra-curricular activities (related to your job objective), licenses, and certifications.

Tip for résumé writing

Design each résumé to fit the particular job.

Be specific—use numbers, dates, and names.

Present information first that is the most impressive and/or most important to the job for which you are applying. This guideline will help you determine whether to put your experience or your education first.

Use everyday language and short, concise phrases.

Be parallel—list similar items using similar structures.

Use boldface type, underlining, white space, and indentations to make your résumé more readable.

Get someone else's reaction; then revise and proofread.

Print Résumé

Some employers request that applications be sent to a postal service address. In these cases, submit a print résumé.

Ada Overlie

Home	**School**
451 Wiser Lake Road	Ogg Hall, Room 222
Ferndale, WA 98248-8941	Balliole College
(360) 354-5916	Eugene, OR 97440-0222
	Phone: (503) 341-3611
	E-mail: dvrl@balliole.edu

Present contact information and employment objectives.

Job Objective: Part-time assistant in a nursery or greenhouse.

Feature skills with appropriate headings and lists.

Skills Summary:

Horticultural Skills: Familiar with garden planting, care, and harvesting practices—planning, timing, companion planting, fertilizing.

Lab Skills: Familiar with procedures for taking fruit samples, pureeing them, checking for foreign objects, and testing sugar content.

List work and education chronologically, from most to least current.

Experience:

Summers 2009 and 2010: Lab Technician.
Mayberry Farms and Processing Plant, Ferndale, WA.
Worked in Quality Control testing raspberries to make sure they met company standards.

Summers 2007 and 2008: Camp Counselor.
Emerald Lake Summer Camp, Hillsboro, WA.
Supervised 12-year-olds in many camp activities, including nature hikes in which we identified plants and trees.

Format for paper only; boldface, underlining, bulleted or indented lists, two columns.

Education:

August 2010 to present: Balliole College, Eugene, OR.
Environmental Studies and Communication major.
Courses completed and in progress include Environmental Studies and General Botany. First semester GPA 3.7.

August 2006 to June 2010: Ferndale High School, Ferndale, WA.
Courses included Biology, Agriculture, U.S. Government, and Economics.
Special Projects: Completed research papers on clean-water legislation and organic farming practices.

Offer references.

References available upon request.

Digital Résumé

To find employees, companies often use computer programs to search electronic résumés for keywords (especially nouns) found in job descriptions or ads. Anticipating such a search, Jonathan Greenlind identified keywords and inserted them into his job description and résumé.

Present contact information and employment objective.

Jonathan L. Greenlind
806 5th Avenue
Waterloo, Iowa 50701
Telephone: 319.268.6955
E-mail: grnlnd@aol.com

List skills, experiences, and education using many keywords.

OBJECTIVE
Position as hydraulics supervisor that calls for hydraulics expertise, technical skills, mechanical knowledge, reliability, and enthusiasm

SKILLS
Operation and repair specialist in main and auxiliary power systems, subsystems, landing gears, brakes and pneumatic systems, hydraulic motors, reservoirs, actuators, pumps and cylinders from six types of hydraulic systems
Dependable, resourceful, strong leader, team worker

Format for e-mail:
- one column
- bullets
- simple sans serif typeface
- flush-left margin
- no italics, boldface, or underlining
- ASCII or RTF text (readable by all computers)

EXPERIENCE
Aviatioulics Technician
United States Navy (2007–present)
· Repair, test, and maintain basic hydraulics, distribution systems, and aircraft structural hydraulics systems
· Manufacture low-, medium-, and high-pressure rubber and Teflon hydraulic hoses, and aluminum stainless-steel tubing
· Perform preflight, postflight, and other periodic aircraft inspections
· Operate ground-support equipment
· Supervise personnel

Aircraft Mechanic
Sioux Falls International Airport (2005–2007)
Sioux Falls, South Dakota
· Performed fueling, engine overhauls, minor repairs, and tire and oil changes of various aircraft

EDUCATION
· United States Navy (2007–2011)
· Certificate in Hydraulic Technical School "A", GPA 3.8/4.0
· Certificate in Hydraulic, Pneumatic Test Stand School, GPA 3.9/4.0
· Courses in Corrosion Control, Hydraulic Tube Bender, Aviation Structural Mechanics
· Equivalent of 10 semester hours in Hydraulic Systems Maintenance and Structural Repair

Offer references.

References available upon request.

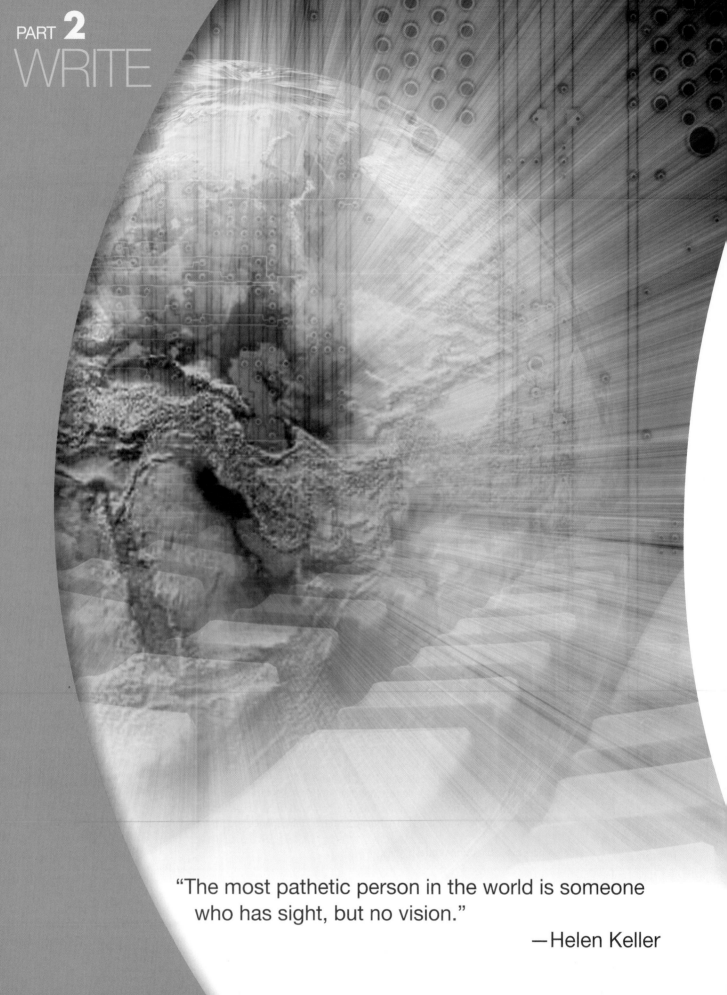

"The most pathetic person in the world is someone who has sight, but no vision."

—Helen Keller

23

Web Writing

A strong Web site depends on well-written, well-organized, and well-designed content. Above all, Web content should be concise, focused, and visually appealing. After all, people don't read Web sites so much as they scan them, so information should be presented in short chunks of text. For that reason, Web pages should be brief, designed to minimize scrolling and maximize the use of available screen space.

This chapter addresses the rhetorical fundamentals of creating a strong Web site, developing strong Web pages, and using writing venues such as OWLs, blogs, MUDs, MOOs, and social networking sites.

Learning Outcomes

LO1 Understand Web page elements.

LO2 Develop a Web site.

LO3 Analyze a Web site.

LO4 Understand other writing venues.

LO5 Develop a blog.

LO6 Learn about and contribute to a wiki.

Understand Web page elements. — LO1

To design an effective Web site and develop dynamic Web pages, you need to start with a basic understanding of Web page elements and functions. Because Web pages use the same elements as printed pages, many of the same design principles apply. However, unlike printed pages, Web pages are fluid (flowing their contents to match screen and browser settings), and they can include both elements and functions, as shown and discussed below and on the pages that follow.

Page Elements

On the Web, page elements are defined primarily by purpose—headings, body text, image, and so forth. Before designing a Web page, it helps to understand the purpose of those elements.

1. Headings (also called headers) come in six levels and are used to separate different sections and subsections of Web documents. Heading 1 is the largest; heading 6 is the smallest. All are bold black serif font by default.

2. Body text is organized into chunks, called paragraphs, which are separated by white space. Unlike printed text, paragraphs on the Web do not generally have a first-line indentation. By default, body text is a black serif font roughly the same size as a heading level 4 (though not bold).

3. Preformatted text is "monospaced"; it displays all characters at the same width, like typewriter font. It is used primarily to show mathematical formulas, computer code, and the like.

4. Lists can be formatted in three types: Ordered lists are numbered, unordered lists are bulleted, and definition lists present pairs of information—usually terms alongside their definitions, which are indented. Because readers can scan them quickly, lists are an efficient way to present information.

5. Images can include photographs, clip art, graphs, line drawings, cartoon figures, icons, and animations. These can make a page much slower to display, so use them judiciously. Always be sure you have the legal right to use any images that you include in your pages. (See "Copyright violations," page 356.)

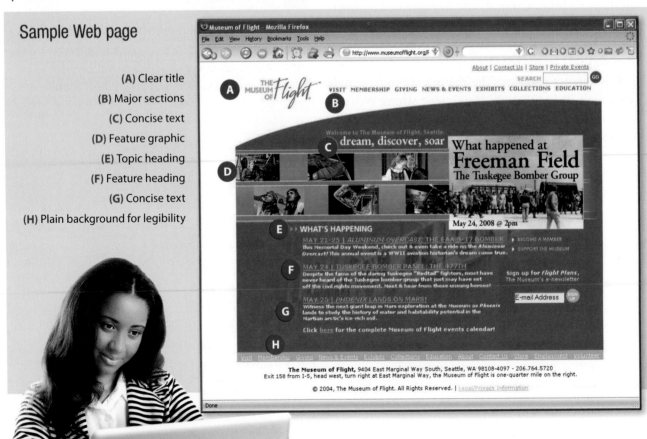

Sample Web page

(A) Clear title
(B) Major sections
(C) Concise text
(D) Feature graphic
(E) Topic heading
(F) Feature heading
(G) Concise text
(H) Plain background for legibility

6. Background color for a Web page is white by default (medium gray in older browsers), which makes the standard headings and text easily legible.

7. Tables are a common tool for Web page layout. Simply put, tables are grids made up of rows and columns. By creating a table with no visible borders, a Web designer can gain some control over where elements appear on a page.

fyi As seen on the previous page, not all Web pages have black serif font on a white background. However, because Web browsers are designed to flow content to suit each computer screen, changing the default styles can be problematic. It helps to keep the following tips in mind:

Simple is best. Simple pages display the fastest and have the least chance of breaking. The more graphics you add, the longer a page takes to load. The more you change the default font settings, the more complicated the code becomes and the greater the chance of computer error.

Different computers display things differently. Not every computer has the same font styles installed, and colors look different on different monitors. Always check your work on many different systems.

The user is king (or queen). No matter which font style and size you choose, the reader can change how things display on her or his machine. So focus on useful content and clear organization instead of struggling to control graphic design.

Page Functions

Web page functions set electronic pages apart from printed pages. On the Web, readers can browse pages in almost any order, send and receive e-mail, send messages and files, post messages, and join live "chat" sessions. In short, readers can interact with Web pages in ways they cannot with printed pages. Like Web page elements, Web page functions should serve your site's purpose.

1. Hyperlinks are strings of specially formatted text that enable readers to jump to another spot on the Web. Internal hyperlinks (links for short) take you to another section of the same Web page or to another page on the same site. External links lead to pages on other Web sites. "Mail to" links allow readers to address e-mail to recipients, such as a professor or a classmate.

2. Menus offer structured lists of links that operate like a Web site's table of contents. Menus are typically presented in a column or row at the edge of a Web page. Good Web sites include a standard site menu on every page so readers don't get lost.

3. Forms enable the host of a Web site to interact with the site's readers. Web forms can be used for questionnaires, surveys, complaints and service requests, job applications, or suggestion boxes.

Develop a Web site.

Regardless of the purpose, topic, and audience of your Web site, you can develop it by following the steps outlined on the next four pages.

Get focused.

Create an overview of the project—the purpose, the audience, and the topic. The questions below will help you get focused and develop fitting content for the site.

1. What is the primary purpose of the Web site? Am I creating a library of documents that my audience will reference? Am I going to present information and announcements about myself or my organization? Am I trying to promote a specific product or service?

2. Who is the site's audience? Which people will seek out this site? Why? What do they need? How often will they visit the site, and how often should it be updated? How comfortable is my audience with using computers and Web sites? What level of formality is appropriate for the language? Which graphics, colors, and design will appeal to them?

3. What is the site's central topic? What do I already know about the topic? What do I need to learn, and where can I find the information? How will I demonstrate that the information is credible and reliable? What will my audience want to know about the topic? How can I divide the information into brief segments?

What visual elements would help present my message? Which other Web sites address this topic? Should my Web site link to them?

Establish your central message.

After you've made decisions about your purpose, audience, and topic, write out the main idea you want to communicate. You might call this the theme or "mission statement" of your Web site.

> The purpose of this Web site is to inform fellow students and the general public about current research into hybrid-vehicle transportation.

To help you stay on target with your project, post this mission statement in plain sight. Note, too, that you might modify your goal as the site develops, or add secondary goals for the site.

Create a site map.

As you gather content for your site, create a site map. Web sites can be as simple as an elementary school bulletin board or as complex as a United States federal government site. Here are four principles to keep in mind:

1. No one will read your entire site. People curl up with books, not Web sites. If your audience is not asking for content, don't provide it.

2. Your site will have many small audiences—not one big audience. A site's audience may include anyone with a computer, an Internet connection, and an interest in your site's topic. Keep all potential readers in mind.

3. Web sites are not linear. A single "home page" or "splash page" introduces the site, which branches out like tree limbs into pages with varied content. Web sites "conclude" whenever the reader quits reading.

4. You may need to build the site in phases. You can add pages to a Web site after it has been published, so be careful that your site's organization does not limit future additions.

Study similar sites.

Learn from successful sites, especially sites that serve a similar purpose—a campus club site, a department site, a personal job-search site. How do similar sites use elements: headings, body text, preformatted text, background color, lists, images, and tables? How do the sites use functions—links, menus, and forms? The seven traits (see page 293) can also supply helpful benchmarks for evaluating sites.

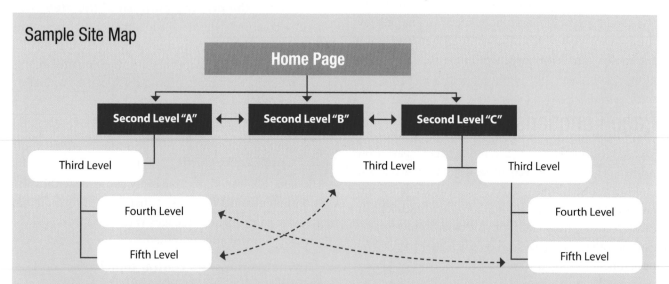

Sample Site Map

A map for a simple site might include only four items—a home page, page "A," page "B," and page "C" (as shown in green and red on the diagram). Users can "jump" between any of the secondary-level pages or back to the home page.

A more complex Web site typically needs more levels (as shown in white on the diagram). Likewise, its menu will offer more navigation choices. Related pages might be connected with links (as represented by the dotted lines).

1. **Ideas:** Does the site present clear ideas and information?
2. **Organization:** Is the content carefully and clearly structured?
3. **Voice:** Is the tone fitting for the audience?
4. **Words:** Is the language understandable? Is the wording concise?
5. **Sentences:** Are the sentences easy to read and generally short?
6. **Correctness:** Does the site avoid distracting errors?
7. **Design:** Are the pages user-friendly? Is the site easy to navigate?

Gather and prioritize content.

Brainstorm and research the actual content, with the goal of creating an outline for your site. How many topics will the site address? How wide will your coverage of a topic be? How deep? Your outline can also be used to create the Web site's table of contents. Based on your research, discussions with others, and the deadlines for the project, select the content, features, and functions your site will offer.

Think about support materials.

List the documents (brochures, artworks, instructions, poems, reports) that will be presented on your site and note whether they will be displayed as Web pages, made available for readers to download, or both. Construct a grid to keep track of how documents will be used.

List graphics that could make your pages more visual and informative and could help readers grasp the meaning of complex data or processes. Photographs may help "put a face" on your organization. Logos and icons will help brand your pages. Review the list below for electronic files that may be appropriate to your topic, audience, and purpose. (Remember: Use only graphics that are legally available. See the discussion of copyright on page 356.)

Images	Audio	Video
charts	music	animations
drawings	sound effects	film clips
graphs	spoken text	presentations
photographs		Web casts

Design and develop individual pages.

When you create individual pages for your site, consider both the design and the content—specifically, how to make the two work well together.

Design Principles

Most Web pages—and the pages of most other publications—are designed on grids. Look at any newspaper or magazine page, and you should be able to draw horizontal and vertical lines denoting columns and rows of content. Some rows may span multiple columns, and some columns may overrun several rows.

Another fundamental design concept is balance. You might balance light elements with dark ones, text with images, and so forth. The balance of your page design should be driven by the purpose of your Web site, its audience, and its topic.

Web sites may contain a variety of pages—each tailored to different purposes, audiences, and topics—to present some combination of informational and promotional content. Use each page's purpose to guide decisions about which elements and functions to include.

jordeangjelovik, 2011 / Used under license from Shutterstock.com

Drafting Principles

1. **Identify the site.** Working from your mission statement, write a brief introduction informing visitors about the site's purpose.
2. **Provide clear links.** Create links for your pages, using clear descriptors such as "Original Poetry." (Avoid phrases such as "Click here for poetry.") If necessary, add a descriptive sentence to further identify the link. Let visitors know precisely where each link will take them.
3. **Introduce each page.** Search sites may deliver some visitors to a page other than your home page. Give each page a brief introduction that clearly identifies it. Also, remember to provide a link back to your home page.
4. **Title each page.** Atop the browser window is a title bar where the current page should be identified. This title is used in browser bookmarks, search engine listings, and the like, so be sure to give every page on your Web site a descriptive title.
5. **Keep pages uncluttered.** Dense text is even more difficult to read on screen than on paper, so use short paragraphs when you can. Add headings to identify sections, and include visuals to help break up the text.
6. **Save the page as HTML.** To be viewed in a Web browser, your pages must be formatted in Hypertext Markup Language (HTML). Your word processor may have a "Save as HTML" or "Save as Web page" option. Many HTML editing programs are also available on the Web.

Test, refine, and post your site.

Most Web sites are developed through the combined efforts of writers, graphic designers, and programmers. In such an environment, many content and layout ideas might be considered, rejected, and reformulated to produce and launch the site. Of course, the audience ultimately decides a Web site's success or failure. For that reason, test and refine your site before posting it.

1. **Check the site yourself.** Open your home page from your Web browser. Does the site make sense? Can you navigate it easily?

2. **Get peer review.** Ask classmates—both experienced and inexperienced with the Web site's topic and with Internet searching—to use your site. Watch them navigate it, and take notes about any confusion they have.

3. **Check the text.** Reread all the text on your site. Trim wherever possible (the shorter, the better online), and check all spelling and punctuation.

4. **Check the graphics.** Do images load properly? Do they load quickly? Are menus and page headings in the same place on every page?

5. **Provide a feedback link.** Provide your e-mail address on the site, inviting visitors to contact you with any comments after the site goes "live."

6. **Post the site.** Upload the site to your hosting space. (Check your host's instructions for doing so.) Add the posting date to each page, and update it each time you change a page.

7. **Check for universality.** View the site on several different types of computers, using different browsers. Does the layout display well on all of them? Make any needed changes.

8. **Announce the site.** Advertise your site in e-mails. Submit it to search sites. Consider joining a "Web ring" of similar sites to draw more traffic. Let your professors, classmates, friends, and family know about your site.

9. **Monitor the site.** After a site has been launched, its success may be measured by the amount of traffic it receives, feedback submitted by users, and any use of resources or services. (Check with your host for ways to measure traffic.)

10. **Make adjustments and updates.** A Web site should be a living thing. Update the content when possible to keep it fresh, and make any adjustments needed to adapt to changing technologies.

Insight: Avoid using any features and functions that do not support your overall purpose for writing. If you find yourself distracted by the many bells and whistles of the Web, remember that it's better to have a simple Web site that presents information clearly and effectively than a complex site that does not.

Analyze a Web site.   LO3

On the next two pages, you'll find sample pages from student and academic Web sites. Study each model for insights about what makes for strong Web content and design.

Student-Designed Web site

The following Web site was developed by undergraduate students from a Southwestern U.S. university who were studying abroad. Southwest Sojourners is a multiuser site with blogs and chat rooms that allow students to keep in touch with one another and with friends and family back home.

Purpose: This site is a gathering place for undergraduate students studying abroad. It describes itself as a "home away from home" for such students. The tone is light, conversational, and inviting, as befitting the purpose of connecting these students to one another and to the important people in their lives.

Audience: The site is meant for students, friends, and family members. By providing straight news, individualized blogs, and chat rooms and e-mail options, the site allows users to be as passive or as active as they wish. Membership is required for active participation, and members must "sign" a user's agreement before posting material.

Format: The golden background and sun icon visually convey the Southwestern theme, while the minimalist format makes the site easy to navigate. A large four-item toolbar on the left directs users to the linked pages, and brief text on the right gives a clear indication of what lies at the end of each link.

SOUTHWEST SOJOURNERS

Welcome to Southwest Sojourners! This site is meant to be a home away from home for students from southwestern U.S. universities who are studying abroad. If you are such a student—or a friend or family member of such a student—this is the spot for you! Lurk, if you like, or log in and join the conversation.

Sojourners News

These pages are updated regularly with information about special events on this site—and in reality.

Click here for a list of students who are blogging about their studies abroad.

Student Blogs

For members only: Join the conversation with students in England, Germany, Italy, India, Japan—and elsewhere!

Chat Rooms

Membership is free, but we do need a little information and a digital signature on our posting agreement.

Log In!

Contact the Webmaster at: Webmaster@southsojourn.edu.
Site design: Mikayla Evans and Griffin Jenson

site launched: 29 January 2008
last updated: 29 July 2011

Academic Web site

The Massachusetts Institute of Technology's Space Nanotechnology Laboratory Web site is an academic research site. It contains information about a specialized laboratory in the MIT Kavli Institute for Astrophysics and Space Research.

Purpose: This site aims to inform a very specific audience about a team of professors, graduate research assistants, and staff and their work to develop nanotechnology for space exploration. The site features the laboratory's creation of the "MIT Nanoruler," a device capable of measuring to the billionth of a meter. The site also provides pages that outline the laboratory's mission, history, people, projects, and facilities.

Audience: This Web site addresses "a consortium of microfabrication facilities with shared interests." In addition to providing articles of interest to this group, the site includes a list of available positions for professionals and students who may wish to join the laboratory. A sponsors page shows that the audience also includes funding agencies such as NASA and the National Science Foundation.

Format: The top of the home page announces the site and university, using iconic images of waveforms and a satellite to convey its central focus. Beneath this masthead, the page features the laboratory's current great achievement: "Home of the MIT Nanoruler" and "Read more about the Nanoruler." A selection of photos highlights work in the lab, and to the left, a list of pages makes navigation transparent.

Understand other writing venues.

LO4

The Internet is a complex construct made up of much more than Web pages. Other writing venues on the Net are described below, with writing tips for each.

OWLs Your university or college probably has a writing lab where you can seek help with your writing assignments. It might also have a Web-based OWL (online writing lab) where you can access help. OWLs post answers to questions you may have about writing, and they often allow you to e-mail or send an instant message (see the next page) to a writing tutor. Before contacting an OWL tutor, carefully read any instructions posted on the site.
Example: Purdue University OWL, owl.english.purdue.edu

MUDs, MOOs, and MUSHes Some instructors hold classes or deliver lectures online in a MUD (multiuser dimension), a text-based "world" that people can share. (MOOs and MUSHes are variants of MUDs.) MUDs have virtual rooms to explore and virtual objects to examine and handle. To use a MUD, you must learn the text commands for interacting with it. Most MUDs require software

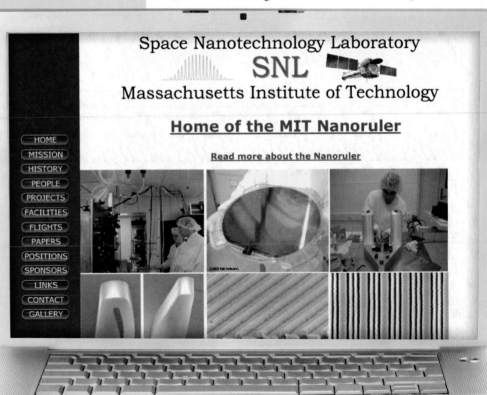

Courtesy of Space Nanotechnology Laboratory, Massachusetts Institute of Technology. andersphoto, 2011 / Used under license from Shutterstock.com

for a telnet connection, but some are accessible via telnet-enabled Web pages.
Example: Diversity University MOO, www.marshall.edu/commdis/moo

Message Boards Many Web sites have forms that allow visitors to post messages for public display. The messages and any replies are usually listed together so that readers can follow the message "thread."

Mailing Lists Mailing lists allow users to send and receive text messages within a specific group of people interested in a particular subject. The software that maintains a mailing list is called a "list server." Some mailing lists are excellent resources of specialized information.
Example: QUANTUMTEACHING-NMC <MTEACHING-NMC@LISTS.MAINE.EDU>

Chat Servers A chat server provides a place on the Net where you can type a message that other people will see instantly. Those people can then respond with text messages of their own. Some teachers and tutors may use a chat room to confer with students or to hold a class discussion online. Although some chat servers require special software, many are available as Web pages.
Example: Yahoo! Chat, chat.yahoo.com

Instant Messaging Services Instant messaging (IM) services allow you to send a text message instantaneously to friends and colleagues who use the same software. Most IMs also allow users to send computer files to one another. (Just be careful not to pass on a computer virus this way.)
Example: ICQ, Web.icq.com

Blogs A blog (short for "Web log") is basically just an online journal posted to a Web page. In effect, it is a one-person message board (see above). For many people, blogging is more convenient than creating a Web page of their own, because it involves no design issues and requires no uploading of files. For more on blogs, see the material that follows on pages 297–298.

Wikis Wikis are shared spaces in which many contributors can add content. Think of wikis as communal blogs, allowing online discussions, collaborative creation of content, versioning of material, and quick response to changing conditions. For more on wikis, see page 299.

Develop a blog.

Blogs (short for "Web logs") have exploded in popularity. Some blogs have risen to the level of daily newspapers in terms of number of readers, number of contributors, level of journalism, and coverage of breaking news. Most blogs, though, publish the work of a single owner, often a person just like you. Blogging presents unique opportunities and challenges for writers.

Analyze the blogging situation.

As with all forms of communication, when you are blogging, you need to think about the communication situation.

- What **subject** will you address? Breaking news, interviews, reviews, fiction?
- Who is your **audience**? Others in your field of study, friends, fans?
- What is your **purpose**? To inform, persuade, entertain, organize, rally, advertise?

Choose blogging software.

Many different blogging programs exist, such as Wordpress and Typepad. Check out reviews of different types online to decide which platform provides you the functionality that you seek. Also check with friends and professors to find their recommendations.

Decide on a broadcast schedule.

If your blog is rarely updated, you'll have difficulty getting people to return to it. If it is updated too often, the impact of any specific blog post will be diminished. Decide how often you want to post on your blog, and choose times when you can catch most of your readers.

Write blog posts.

Create blog posts keeping your subject, audience, and purpose in mind. Though blogging allows you to publish instantly, use the writing process to do your best work. Take the time to review, revise, and edit your work before posting it publicly. If you discover a mistake afterward, be sure to correct the mistake and repost the page. Also remember the following tips.

1. Connect with readers: Use an inviting tone that welcomes readers to understand and use the information you provide.

2. Create a strong heading: Use keywords that will interest readers and will catch the attention of search engines. Create intriguing questions or plays on words.

3. Use an eye-catching visual: A photo or an illustration near the top of the blog post will draw readers to the story. Often such an image will be posted as a thumbnail when you link to your post on other social media.

4. Include other media: Embed videos, podcasts, charts, graphs, surveys, and other types of media that help you make your point and help readers deeply engage with your content.

5. Link to other sites: Connect your content to other materials that your reader will appreciate. Links not only enrich your blog but also inspire other sites to link to you.

6. Tag your post: Most blogging software allows you to tag each post to indicate its subject or post type. That way, if you are doing a series of movie reviews, readers can find and read the whole series rather than having to sort through individual postings.

7. Spread the word: When you post a new blog entry, send out an announcement on other social media that you use. Most blogging software allows for you to connect your blog to these other services to coordinate announcements.

8. Monitor and respond to comments: Before approving a comment from another person, make sure it is not posted by a spam bot (a program that automatically posts comments). Also, make sure that the comment is not inflammatory or otherwise problematic. Then write a polite response, engaging the reader in conversation.

Create a community.

Blogging is just the beginning of a conversation between you and your readers. Read other people's blogs and politely comment on their material. If you find a blogger whom you really appreciate, ask the person to write a guest post for your blog—and offer to do the same. Or you might interview the other person as a part of your blog.

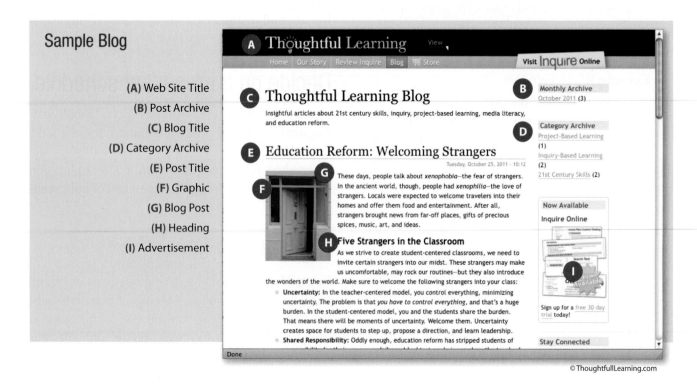

Sample Blog

(A) Web Site Title
(B) Post Archive
(C) Blog Title
(D) Category Archive
(E) Post Title
(F) Graphic
(G) Blog Post
(H) Heading
(I) Advertisement

© ThoughtfullLearning.com

Contribute to a wiki. LO6

A wiki (the Hawaiian word for "fast") provides an on-line collaborative space in which many contributors work together to write, edit, illustrate, and otherwise produce something in common. You are no doubt familiar with the most famous wiki—the Wikipedia® site, which has millions of articles and contributors from around the world. Other wikis focus on specific areas of specialty, from astronomy to zoology.

Consider uses.

Because wikis are built to be collaborative, they offer many possibilities for uses.

Discussion group: A wiki provides a digital meeting room in which people in many different locations can interact, brainstorm thoughts, share links to resources, and make decisions. In addition, the wiki functions as a diligent secretary, recording the contributions of all members of the group.

Collaborative project developer: A wiki also functions as a gathering point for developing the pieces of a collaborative project. Different group members take on different assignments—whether writing, editing, designing, illustrating, videoing, or other tasks. Members can work in sequence (one after another) or simultaneously. When all are satisfied, the result can be published to a public Web site.

Living document platform: As open-ended platforms, wikis allow a project to continuously evolve. Often previous contributors depart and new ones arrive. In this way, wikis work well for developing encyclopedias, dictionaries, manuals, project "bibles," progress reports, and other collaborative reference works that are never actually "finished."

Find and join a wiki.

Often, your first experience contributing to a wiki will relate to a specific class. You can also seek out public wikis in your area of interest and create an account, providing a username and password.

Every wiki has different ground rules, and you need to understand them and follow them or you may be blocked from contributing. Also, every wiki has a certain culture of collaboration. For example, in some wikis, only those who have been assigned to edit certain text are expected to touch it, while in other wikis, anyone can make changes. To fit in, abide by the existing culture.

Write and edit responsibly.

You have learned the art of conversations—what to say and what not to say in person. Follow the same sort of guidelines as you work on a wiki. Don't share your own personal information or anyone else's. Respect other people's ideas, opinions, and emotions. Don't let the computer interface fool you—there are real people collaborating with you, and anything you post will be recorded for all to see.

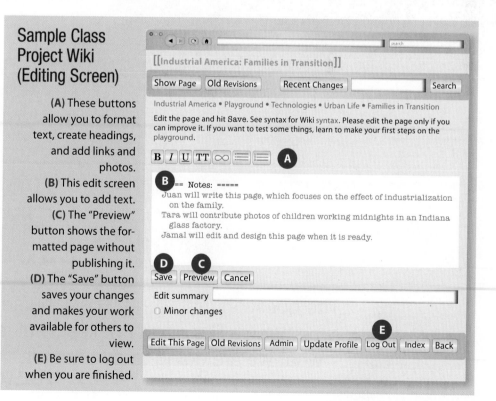

Sample Class Project Wiki (Editing Screen)

(A) These buttons allow you to format text, create headings, and add links and photos.
(B) This edit screen allows you to add text.
(C) The "Preview" button shows the formatted page without publishing it.
(D) The "Save" button saves your changes and makes your work available for others to view.
(E) Be sure to log out when you are finished.

"The question that we must ask ourselves is not whether we like or do not like what is going on, but what we are going to do about it."

—Winston Churchill

24

Assessment

There is nothing more disheartening than sitting down to take a test for which you're not prepared. The results are predictable—and they're not pretty. Conversely, there is nothing more exhilarating than walking out of a classroom after nailing a test. This is especially true in a college setting, where tests count for so much and second chances and extra credit are rare.

Many of the writing skills that you've already developed should serve you well in taking essay tests. Read the instructions for an essay test carefully, identify the professor's specific assignment (e.g., describe, analyze, classify, persuade), plan your answer, and write a clear focused response.

This chapter will help you write better essay answers. As a bonus, it suggests a variety of other helpful ways to answer objective questions.

Learning Outcomes

LO1 Prepare for exams.

LO2 Analyze and answer essay questions.

LO3 Analyze and answer objective questions.

Prepare for exams.

Do you consider yourself a "bad" test taker? Do you know the material, yet somehow perform poorly on tests? Do you feel overwhelmed by all the information you have to cover when studying for a test? Does even the thought of studying so much material make you nervous? What you need is a positive mental attitude—and good study habits. Together they can make the difference between "spacing" during a test and "acing" an exam.

Perform daily reviews.

Why daily? Begin your reviews on the first day of class; if you miss a day, dust yourself off and keep going. Daily reviews are especially good because you tend to forget new information rapidly. Reviewing while the material is fresh in your mind helps to move it from your short-term memory into your long-term memory.

How much time? Even spending five or ten minutes on your review before or after each class will pay big dividends. Depending on the day's class, you may read through (or talk through) your notes, look over the headings in a reading assignment, skim any summaries you have, or put information into graphic organizers.

What to Do

- Put "Daily review of . . ." on your "To Do" list, calendar, or date book.
- Use the buddy system. Make a pact with a classmate and review together.
- Put your subconscious to work by reviewing material before you go to sleep.

Perform weekly reviews.

Why weekly? More than anything else, repetition helps anchor memory. You can cram a lot of data into your brain the night before an exam, but a day or two later you won't remember much of anything. And when final exam time comes, you'll have to learn the material all over again.

How much time? Plan to spend about one hour per week for each class. (This review can take place either by yourself or with a study group.) Remember that repetition is the single most important factor in learning anything.

What to Do

- Make mind maps and flash cards of important information.
- Practice answering review questions by saying them aloud and by writing out short answers.
- Test your understanding of a subject by teaching or explaining it to someone else.
- Organize a study group.
- Create mnemonics. (See page 303–304.)

Forming a study group.

A study group can keep you interested in a subject, force you to keep up with class work, and increase your retention of study material. Group energy can be more powerful than individual energy. You will hear other points of view and other ways to approach a subject that you may never have thought of on your own. If you use a chat room, you can meet via a computer. To get started, follow these guidelines.

1. **Find five to six people.**
   - Consider people who seem highly motivated and collaborative.
   - Ask your instructor to inform the class about the opportunity.
2. **Consider a chat room.**
   - Check first with your instructor and student services about the availability of chat rooms on your campus network.
   - Go to any search engine (Yahoo!, Google, Excite, and so on) and enter the term "chat room." For example, Yahoo! provides both private and public chat rooms ("clubs") free of charge.
3. **Arrange a time and place.**
   - Plan one session. (It may become obvious at the first meeting that your group won't work out.)
   - Agree on a time limit for the initial session.

- Choose somebody in the group to keep everyone on task (or rotate this duty) and agree to accept any prodding and nudging with good humor.

4. **Set realistic goals and decide on a plan of action.**
   - Discuss what the group needs to accomplish and what your goals are.
   - Agree to practice "people skills" (listening, observing, cooperating, responding, and clarifying).
   - Decide which parts of the coursework you will review (lectures? labs? texts? exam questions?).

5. **Evaluate at the end of the first session.**
   - Honestly and tactfully discuss any problems that arose.
   - Ask who wants to continue.
   - Choose a time (and place) for your next session.
   - Determine an agenda for the next session.
   - Exchange necessary information such as phone numbers, e-mail addresses, chat room passwords, and so forth.

Using mnemonics and other memory guides.

Mnemonics is the art of improving memory by using key words, formulas, or other aids to create "file tabs" in your brain that help you pull out hard-to-remember information.

Acronyms Use the first letter in each word to form a new word. Everyone learns a few acronyms during their school years, but feel free to make up your own.

HOMES (the Great Lakes—**H**uron, **O**ntario, **M**ichigan, **E**rie, **S**uperior)

Acrostics Form a phrase or silly sentence in which the first letter of each word helps you remember the items in a series.

Zoe **C**ooks **C**howder **I**n **P**ink **P**ots **I**n **M**iami. (essential minerals—**z**inc, **c**alcium, **c**hromium, **i**ron, **p**otassium, **p**hosphorus, **i**odine, **m**agnesium)

Categories Organize your information into categories for easier recall.

Types of joints in body

immovable: skull sutures, teeth in sockets . . . slightly movable: between vertebrae, junction at front of pelvis . . . freely movable: shoulder, elbow, hip, knee, ankle . . .

Peg words Create a chain of associations with objects in a room, a sequence of events, or a pattern with which you are familiar (such as the player positions on a baseball diamond).

To remember a sequence of Civil War battles, you might "peg" them to the positions on a baseball field—for example, Shiloh to home plate (think of the "high" and "low" balls); the Battle of Bull Run to the pitcher's mound (think of the pitcher's battle for no runs); and so on.

Rhymes Make up rhymes or puns.

Brown v. Board of Education / ended public-school segregation.

Analyze and answer essay questions.

LO2

Your instructors expect you to include all the right information, and they expect you to organize it in a clear, well-thought-out way. In addition, they expect you to evaluate, synthesize, predict, analyze, and write a worthwhile answer.

Look for key words.

Key words help you define your task. Pay special attention to them when you read questions. Key words tell you how to present all the information you'll need to write an essay answer.

Following is a list of key terms, along with a definition and an example of how each is used. Studying these terms carefully is the first step in writing worthwhile answers to essay questions.

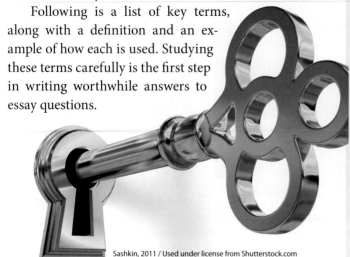

Sashkin, 2011 / Used under license from Shutterstock.com

Quick Guide: Key Words

Analyze To analyze is to break down a larger problem or situation into separate parts of relationships.

Analyze the major difficulties found at urban housing projects.

Classify To classify is to place persons or things (especially animals and plants) together in a group because they share similar characteristics. Science uses a special classification or group order: phylum, class, order, family, genus, species, and variety.

Classify three kinds of trees found in the rainforests of Costa Rica.

Compare To compare is to use examples to show how things are similar and different, placing the greater emphasis on similarities.

Compare the vegetation in the rainforests of Puerto Rico with the vegetation in the rainforests of Costa Rica.

Contrast To contrast is to use examples to show how things are different in one or more important ways.

Contrast the views of George Washington and Harry S Truman regarding the involvement of the United States in world affairs.

Compare and contrast To compare and contrast is to use examples that show the major similarities and differences between two things (or people, events, ideas, and so forth). In other words, two things are used to clarify each other.

Compare and contrast people-centered leadership with task-centered leadership.

Define To define is to give the meaning for a term. Generally, defining involves identifying the class to which a term belongs and explaining how it differs from other things in that class.

Define the term "emotional intelligence" as it pertains to humans.

Describe To describe is to give a detailed sketch or impression of a topic.

Describe how the Euro tunnel (the Chunnel) was built.

Diagram To diagram is to explain with lines or pictures—a flowchart, map, or other graphic device. Generally, a diagram will label the important points or parts.

Diagram the parts of a DNA molecule.

Discuss To discuss is to review an issue from all sides. A discussion answer must be carefully organized to stay on track.

Discuss how Rosa Parks's refusal to move to the back of the bus affected the civil rights movement.

Evaluate To evaluate is to make a value judgment by giving the pluses and minuses along with supporting evidence.

Evaluate the efforts of midsized cities to improve public transportation services.

Explain To explain is to bring out into the open, to make clear, and to analyze. This term is similar to *discuss* but places more emphasis on cause/effect relationships or step-by-step sequences.

Explain the effects of global warming on a coastal city like New Orleans.

Justify To justify is to tell why a position or point of view is good or right. A justification should be mostly positive—that is, the advantages are stressed over the disadvantages.

Justify the use of antilock brakes in automobiles.

Outline To outline is to organize a set of facts or ideas by listing main points and subpoints. A good outline shows at a glance how topics or ideas fit together or relate to one another.

Outline the events that caused the United States to enter World War II.

Prove To prove is to bring out the truth by giving evidence to back up a point.

Prove that Atticus Finch in *To Kill a Mockingbird* provided an adequate defense for his client.

Review To review is to reexamine or to summarize the key characteristics or major points of the topic. Generally speaking, a review presents material in the order in which it happened or in decreasing order of importance.

Review the events since 1976 that have led to the current hip-hop culture.

State To state is to present a concise statement of a position, fact, or point of view.

State your reasons for voting in the last national election.

Summarize To summarize is to present the main points of an issue in a shortened form. Details, illustrations, and examples are usually omitted.

Summarize the primary responsibilities of a school in a democracy.

Trace To trace is to present—in a step-by-step sequence—a series of facts that are somehow related. Usually the facts are presented in chronological order.

Trace the events that led to the fall of the Union of Soviet Socialist Republics.

Plan and write the essay-test answer.

In addition to a basic understanding of the key words, you must understand the process of writing the essay answer.

1. **Reread the question several times.** (Pay special attention to any key words used in the question.)

2. **Rephrase the question into a topic sentence/thesis statement** with a clear point.

   Question: Explain why public housing was built in Chicago in the 1960s.

   Thesis statement: Public housing was built in Chicago because of the Great Migration, the name given to the movement of African Americans from the South to the North.

3. **Outline the main points you plan to cover in your answer.** Time will probably not allow you to include all supporting details in your outline.

4. **Write your essay (or paragraph).** Begin with your thesis statement (or topic sentence). Add whatever background information may be needed, and then follow your outline, writing as clearly as possible.

One-Paragraph Answer

If you feel that only one paragraph is needed to answer the question, use the main points of your outline as supporting details for your thesis statement.

> **Question:** Explain why public housing was built in Chicago in the 1960s.

(A) Public housing was built in Chicago because of the Great Migration, the name given to the movement of African Americans from the South to the North. The mechanical cotton picker, introduced in the 1920s, replaced field hands in the cotton fields of the South. At that time Chicago's factories and stockyards were hiring workers. In addition, Jim Crow laws caused hardships and provided reasons for African Americans to move north. Finally, some African Americans **(B)** had family and relatives in Chicago who had migrated earlier and who, it was thought, could provide a home base for the new migrants until they could get work and housing. According to the U.S. Census Reports, there were 109,000 African Americans in Chicago in 1920. By 1960, there were more than 800,000. However, this increase in population could have been handled except that the public wanted to keep the African Americans in the Black Belt, an area in South Chicago. Reluctant lending agencies and realtors made it possible for speculators to operate. Speculators increased the cost of houses by 75 percent. All of these factors led to a housing shortage for African Americans, which **(C)** public housing filled.

(A) Topic sentence
(B) Supporting details
(C) Conclusion

SeanPavonePhoto, 2011 / Used under license from Shutterstock.com

Multi-Paragraph Answer

If the question is too complex to be handled in one paragraph, your opening paragraph should include your thesis statement and any essential background information. Begin your second paragraph by rephrasing one of the main points from your outline into a suitable topic sentence. Support this topic sentence with examples, reasons, or other appropriate details. Handle additional paragraphs in the same manner. If time permits, add a summary or concluding paragraph to bring all of your thoughts to a logical close.

> **Question:** Explain the advantages and disadvantages of wind energy.
>
> **Thesis:** Wind energy has an equal number of advantages and disadvantages.

> Outline
> I. Advantages of wind energy
>   A. Renewable
>   B. Economical
>   C. Nonpolluting
> II. Disadvantages of wind energy
>   A. Intermittent
>   B. Unsightly
>   C. A danger to some wildlife

1 Wind energy has an equal number of advantages and disadvantages. It is renewable, economical, and **(A)** nonpolluting; but it is also intermittent, unsightly, and a danger to the bird population.

2 Wind energy is renewable. No matter how much wind energy is used today, there will still be a supply tomorrow. As evidence indicates that wind energy was used to propel boats along the Nile River about 5000 B.C.E., it can be said that wind is an eternal, renewable resource.

3 Wind energy is economical. The fuel (wind) is free, but the initial cost for wind turbines is higher than for fossil-fueled generators. However, wind energy costs do not include fuel purchases and only minimal op-

---

(A) The introductory paragraph sets up the essay's organization.

erating expenses. Wind power reduces the amount of foreign oil the United States imports and reduces health and environmental costs caused by pollution. Is it possible to sell excess power? The Public Utilities Regulatory Policy Act of 1978 (PURPA) states that a local electric company must buy any excess power produced by a qualifying individual. This act encourages the use of wind power.

4

(B) Wind energy does not pollute. Whether one wind turbine is used by an individual or a wind farm supplies energy to many people, no air pollutants or greenhouse gases are emitted. California reports that 2.5 billion pounds of carbon dioxide and 15 million pounds of other pollutants have not entered the air thanks to wind energy.

5

How unfortunate is it that wind energy is intermittent? If a wind does not blow, there is little or no electrical power. One way to resolve this dilemma is to store the energy that wind produces in batteries. The word *intermittent* also refers to the fact that wind power is not always available at the places where it is most needed. Often the sites that offer the greatest winds are located in remote locations far from the cities that demand great electrical power.

6

(C) Are wind turbines unsightly? A home-sized wind machine rises about 30 feet with rotors between 8 and 25 feet in diameter. The largest machine in Hawaii stands about 20 stories high with rotors a little longer than the length of a football field. This machine supplies electricity to 1,400 homes. Does a single wind turbine upset the aesthetics of a community as much as a wind farm? The old adage "Beauty is in the eye of the beholder" holds up wherever wind turbines rotate. If ongoing electrical costs are almost nil, that wind turbine may look beautiful.

7

(D) How serious is the issue of bird safety? The main questions are these: (1) Why do birds come near wind turbines? (2) What, if any, are the effects of wind development on bird popu-

lations? (3) What can be done to lessen the problem? If even one bird of a protected species is killed, the Endangered Species Act has been violated. If wind turbines kill migratory birds, the Migratory Bird Treaty Act has been violated. As a result, many countries and agencies are studying the problem carefully.

The advantages of wind energy seem to outweigh the disadvantages. The wind-energy industry has been growing steadily in the United States and around the world. The new wind turbines are reliable and efficient. People's attitudes toward wind energy are mostly positive. Many manufacturers and government agencies are now cooperating to expand wind energy, making it the fastest-growing source of electricity in the world.

8

(E)

(E) The ending summarizes the writer's assignment and offers additional details.

Reading for Better Writing

Working by yourself or with a group, answer these questions:

1. How does the writer provide a clear focus and logical organization in the essay answer? How soon are the focus and organization provided? What advantages does this approach offer the writer? The reader?

2. How do the sentences used to introduce the advantages differ from the sentences used to introduce the disadvantages? How does this technique aid the reader?

3. Why must the paragraphs in the body contain specific facts and examples? Which facts and examples does this writer use?

(B) Each paragraph follows a point in the outline.
(C) Specific details explain the main point.
(D) Questions help the reader understand the issue.

Quick Guide: Writing Under Pressure

Make sure you are ready for the test both mentally and physically.

- **Carefully listen to or read the instructions.**
  1. How much time do you have to complete the test?
  2. Do all the essay questions count equally?
  3. Can you use any aids, such as a dictionary or handbook?
  4. Are there any corrections, changes, or additions to the test?
- **Begin the test immediately and watch the time.** Don't spend so much time answering one question that you run out of time before answering the others.
- **Read all the essay questions carefully,** paying special attention to the key words. (See pages 304–305.)
- **Ask the instructor for clarification** if you don't understand something.
- **Rephrase each question into a controlling idea for your essay answer.** (This idea becomes your thesis statement.)
- **Think before you write.** Jot down all the important information and work it into a brief outline. Do this on the back of the test sheet or on a piece of scrap paper.
- **Use a logical pattern of organization and a strong topic sentence for each paragraph.** Tie points together with clear, logical transitions.
- **Write concisely,** but don't use abbreviations or nonstandard language.
- **Be efficient.** Write about those areas of the subject of which you are most certain first; then work on other areas as time permits.
- **Keep your test paper neat and use reasonable margins.** Neatness is always important, and readability is a must, especially on an essay exam.
- **Revise and proofread.** Read through your essay as carefully and completely as time permits.

Analyze and answer objective questions.

LO3

Even though objective tests are generally straightforward and clear, following are some tips can help you avoid making foolish mistakes.

True/False Test

- Read the entire question before answering. Often the first half of a statement will be true or false, while the second half is just the opposite. For an answer to be true, the entire statement must be true.
- Read each word and number. Pay special attention to names, dates, and numbers that are similar and could be easily confused.
- Beware of true/false statements that contain words such as *all, every, always,* and *never.* Very often these statements will be false.
- Watch for statements that contain more than one negative word. Remember: Two negatives make a positive. (*Example:* It is unlikely ice will not melt when the temperature rises above 32 degrees F.)

Matching Test

- Read through both lists quickly before you begin answering. Note any descriptions that are similar and pay special attention to the differences.
- When matching a word to a word, determine the part of speech of each word. If the word is a verb, for example, match it with another verb.
- When matching a word to a phrase, read the phrase first and look for the word it describes.
- Cross out each answer as you find it—unless you are told that the answer can be used more than once.
- Use capital letters rather than lowercase letters because they are less likely to be misread by the person correcting the test.

Multiple-Choice Test

- Read the directions to determine whether you are looking for the correct answer or the best answer. Also, check whether some questions can have two (or more) correct answers.
- Read the first part of the question, checking for negative words such as *not, never, except,* and *unless.*
- Try to answer the question in your mind before looking at the choices.
- Read all the choices before selecting your answer. This step is especially important on tests in which you must select the best answer, or on tests where one of your choices is a combination of two or more answers. (*Example:* d. Both a and b / e. All of the above / f. None of the above)

VIPDesignUSA, 2011 / Used under license from Shutterstock.com

Tip for coping with test anxiety

Consider the following advice:

Study smart. Use a variety of study and memory techniques to help you see your coursework from several different angles.

Review with others. Join a study group and prepare with the members. Also, ask a classmate or family member to put you to the test.

Prepare yourself both physically and mentally. Get a good night's sleep and eat a healthful, light meal before the test (doughnuts and coffee are not a healthful, light meal).

Get some exercise. Aerobic exercise (running, swimming, walking, aerobics) is a great way to relieve stress, and exercise has been proven to help you think more quickly and more clearly.

Hit the shower. Hot water is relaxing, cold water is stimulating, and warm water is soothing. Take your pick.

Get to class early . . . but not too early! Hurrying increases anxiety, but so does waiting.

Relax. Take a few deep breaths, close your eyes, and think positive thoughts. The more relaxed you are, the better your memory will serve you.

Glance through the entire test. Then plan your time, and pace yourself accordingly. You don't want to discover with only 5 minutes of class time left that the last question is an essay that counts for 50 percent of your grade.

Begin by filling in all the answers you know. This process relieves anxiety and helps to trigger answers for other questions that you may not know immediately. Also, jot down important facts and formulas that you know you will need later on.

Don't panic. If other people start handing in their papers long before you are finished, don't worry. They may have given up or rushed through the exam. The best students often finish last.

Bottom Line

The better you prepare for a test—mentally and physically—the less likely you'll be to suffer serious test anxiety.

"Life is either a daring adventure or nothing at all."
—Helen Keller.

25

Planning Your Research Project

In 1978, Ben Cohen and Jerry Greenfield pooled $8,000 of their own money and borrowed another $4,000 to open a small ice-cream shop in Burlington, Vermont. From that small start, Ben and Jerry's Ice Cream has grown into a highly profitable multinational business known for its innovations and social conscience. (In 2000, Unilever, an Anglo-Dutch corporation, bought Ben and Jerry's for $326 million dollars.)

From a distance, it would seem that Cohen and Greenfield have approached this "project" with a **joie de vivre** that should be the envy of everyone. They've developed an irresistible line of ice cream, created a wonderful work environment, committed millions to good causes, and on and on. What's not to like about Ben and Jerry's?

So what does this story have to tell you about your own research projects? (1) Start with topics that truly interest you; this is the only way you can do meaningful work. (2) Learn as much as you can about each topic. You can't guess in a research paper; you have to know what you're talking about. (3) Take a few risks by approaching each topic in a new or unusual way. (4) And give yourself plenty of time. Quality research can't be rushed.

This chapter will help you initiate such meaningful research projects, beginning with understanding the nature of college-level research.

Learning Outcomes

LO1 Understand academic research.

LO2 Initiate the process.

LO3 Develop a research plan.

LO4 Consider possible resources and sites.

LO5 Understand sources.

joie de vivre
French for "joy of life," a quality in people who live life to its fullest

Understand academic research.

Take ownership of each research project by exploring a topic or an angle that truly interests you and compels you to get started. Your main goal is to become thoroughly knowledgeable about your topic and share your findings in a thoughtful way. The traditional **research paper** is a fairly long essay (5 to 15 pages), complete with a thesis statement, supporting evidence, integrated sources, and documentation. Research can also be presented in a field report, on a Web site, or in a multimedia presentation.

Your instructors, peers, and the academic community in general will be your main audience. However, you may also have a more specific audience in mind—smokers, Floridians, fellow immigrants, and so on. The expected voice in most research projects is formal or semiformal. Always try to maintain a thoughtful, confident tone throughout your writing. Generally, you should avoid the pronouns "I" and "you" in an effort to remain objective and academic. Unfortunately though, avoiding "I" and "you" can result in the overuse of the pronoun "one," so watch for that problem as well.

fyi Some instructors encourage students to connect research with personal experience, meaning that you can, at times, use the pronouns "I" and "you." But be careful to keep the focus where it belongs—on the topic. The best research writing always centers on compelling ideas and information about the topic.

Research involves many steps.

The research process involves getting started, planning, conducting research, and developing the results. While research generally follows these steps, you should understand that the process is dynamic and recursive, meaning that it can be full of twists and turns, detours and side trips. For example, during your research, you may discover information that will

change your mind about the topic or about the thesis statement you developed earlier. The flowchart below shows you the different tasks related to research.

A Research Flowchart

Getting Started
- Review the assignment.
- Consider your resources.
- Choose a subject.

List or cluster your current ideas and opinions.	Talk with others to learn opposing opinions.	Conduct preliminary research in reference works.

Planning Your Research
Narrow the topic, form a research question or working thesis, develop a research plan, and select keyword searching terms.

Conducting Research

Conduct Primary Research	**Take Careful Notes**	**Conduct Secondary Research**
Observe, interview, survey, or experiment.	Reflect in your research journal.	Check books, articles, and Web sites.
Analyze primary documents and artifacts.	Create and add to a working bibliography.	Search catalogs, indexes, databases, and the Internet.

- Evaluate and take notes from sources.
- Summarize, paraphrase, and quote.

Organizing and Drafting
- Answer your research question or refine your thesis.
- Develop an outline.
- Write the research paper, integrating and documenting sources.

Initiate the process.

To get started, you need to do four things: (1) understand the assignment, (2) select a topic, (3) build research questions, and (4) develop a working thesis. Your research project will only be as good as the planning that you put into it, so attend to each step with care.

Understand the assignment.

The first important step in a research project is to thoroughly review the assignment. Take some initial

research paper
a fairly long essay (5–15 pages), complete with thesis statement, supporting evidence, integrated sources, and careful documentation

notes about it; record key words, options, restrictions, and requirements. Finally, write down any questions you still have about the project, find answers, and proceed.

Select a topic.

Author Joyce Carol Oates says, "As soon as you connect with your true subject, you will write." Your goal at the outset of a research project is to find your "true subject," an appropriate topic you sincerely want to explore and write about.

Making It Manageable

In most cases, your instructor will establish a general subject area to get you started. Your job is to select a specific, manageable topic related to that subject. A topic is "manageable" when you can learn about it in a reasonable amount of time. (You may have to carry out some cursory research in order to select a topic.)

General Subject	Area of Interest	Manageable Topic
urban social problems	the homeless	increase in homeless families
World War II legislation & initiatives	the Marshall Plan	the Plan's impact on the new world order
alternative energy	new generation of vehicles	hybrid-electric vehicles

Build research questions.

Generating research questions helps you find meaningful information and ideas about your topic. These questions sharpen your research goal, and the answers become the focus of your writing. Create questions by following the guidelines below.

Needing to Know

List questions about your topic—both simple and complex—to discover what you need to know about it. Keep listing until you land on the **main question** you want to answer—the main issue you need to address. Then brainstorm **supporting questions** that you must research in order to adequately answer the main question.

Main Question:

Should consumers embrace hybrid-electric vehicles?

Supporting Questions (*Who? What? When? Where? Why? How?*):

Who has developed hybrid-electric cars?
What is a hybrid-electric car?
When were they developed?
Where are they currently in use?
Why are hybrids is use?
How do they work?

Checklist: Main Question

- ✔ Is the question too narrow, too broad, or just about right for a research paper?
- ✔ Is the question too easy or too hard to answer?
- ✔ Am I committed to answering this question? Does it interest me?
- ✔ Will I be able to find enough information about it within a reasonable amount of time?
- ✔ Will the question and answers interest the reader?

Develop a working thesis.

A **working thesis** offers a preliminary answer to your main research question. An effective working thesis keeps you focused during your research, helping you decide whether to read a particular book or just skim it, fully explore a Web site or quickly surf through it. When forming your working thesis, don't settle for a simple statement of fact about your topic; instead, form a statement that demands to be proved or that requires thoughtful explanation. The quick guide on the next page includes a formula for writing this statement.

working thesis
a preliminary answer to
your main research question, the focus of your research

Quick Guide: Working Thesis

Formula:

a limited topic + a tentative claim, statement, or hypothesis = a working thesis

Samples:

Hybrid-electric cars offer consumers a reasonable alternative to gas-only cars.

The sharp increase in homeless families will force city planners to rethink their social service policies.

The Marshall Plan benefited Europe and the United States in three significant ways.

Use the following checklist to evaluate your working thesis.

Checklist: Working Thesis

✔ Does my working thesis focus on a single, limited topic?

✔ Is it stated clearly and directly?

✔ Does it provide a preliminary answer to my main research question?

✔ Do I have access to information that supports it?

✔ Does my working thesis meet the requirements of the assignment?

fyi Remember that your working thesis is set in sand, not stone. Your thinking on it might change as you research the topic because different sources may push you in new directions. Such changes show that you are truly engaged in your research. For more help with developing and refining a thesis, see page 44.

Library of Congress classification
a system of classification used in most academic and research libraries

databases
a collection of data

Develop a research plan.

 LO3

As you develop your research plan, consider what you already know about your topic. You can find this out by freewriting, clustering, or talking about your topic. (See pages 37–38.) Push yourself to gather as many of your own thoughts and feelings about the topic as you can before you conduct any "outside" research. Once you determine what you already know, then you can decide what you still need to find out. You should also figure out what resources can help you develop your research questions and working thesis.

Choose research methods.

Do you need more background information? Is primary research a possibility? What other types of research are you interested in? The following information will answer your questions about planning your research.

Background Research

Take these steps to find information about central concepts and key terms related to your topic.

- Use the **Library of Congress** subject headings to find keywords for searching the library catalog, periodical **databases**, and the Internet (page 320).
- Conduct a preliminary search of the library catalog, journal databases, and the Internet to confirm that strong resources on your topic exist.
- Use specialized reference works to find background information, definitions, facts, and statistics (page 327).

Primary Research

If at all possible, conduct primary research about your topic. Primary research is firsthand research in which you carry out interviews, observe the topic in action, and so on in order to develop your distinctive approach to the topic.

- Use interviews (238–249) and surveys (pages 323–324) to get key information from experts and others.

- Conduct observations or experiments (pages 250–261) to obtain hard data.
- Analyze original documents or **artifacts**.

Library Research

With the help of a librarian or research specialist, search for important library resources. As you probably know, the library contains a wide variety of useful materials.

- Use scholarly books to get in-depth, reliable material (pages 326–327).
- Refer to periodical articles (print or electronic) to get current, reliable information (pages 328–329). Select from news sources, popular magazines, scholarly journals, and trade journals.
- Consider other resources, such as recorded interviews, pamphlets, marketing studies, or various government publications.

Internet Research

The Internet serves as an incredible resource that you can access at your fingertips. Use the following information to help you plan effective Internet searches.

- Use tools, such as search engines and subject guides, that will lead you to quality resources (pages 331–337).
- Select reputable Web sites that librarians, instructors, or other experts recommend (page 332).
- Test Web sites for reliability (pages 337–340).

Sketch out tentative deadlines for completing each phase of your work: getting started, conducting research, drafting, and so on. Generally, you should spend about half your time on research and planning and half on writing. For some projects, you may have to formalize your planning in the form of a proposal, which shows your instructor that your plan is workable within the constraints of the assignment.

Consider possible resources and sites. LO4

When researching your topic, be sure to use a wide range of quality resources, as opposed to relying exclusively on information, substantial or not, from a few Web sites. (Your instructor may establish guidelines for the number and type of resources you should consult.) As you review your researching options, consider which resources will give you the best information about your topic. A sociology paper on airport behavior may require personal, direct research; a business paper on the evolution of subprime mortgage loans may best be researched in business publications, government reports, journals, newspapers, and so on.

Consider information resources.

The sources of information available to you are almost unlimited, from interviewing someone to referring to bibliographies, from reviewing journal articles to studying graphics. Listed here are the common sources of information.

Type of Resource	Examples
Personal, primary resources	Memories, diaries, journals, logs, experiments, tests, observations, interviews, surveys
Reference works (print and electronic)	Dictionaries, thesauruses, encyclopedias, almanacs, yearbooks, atlases, directories, guides, handbooks, indexes, abstracts, catalogs, bibliographies
Books (print and electronic)	Nonfiction, how-to, biographies, fiction, trade books, scholarly and scientific studies
Periodicals and news sources	Print newspapers, magazines, and journals; broadcast news and news magazines; online magazines, news sources, and discussion groups
Audiovisual, digital, and multimedia resources	Graphics (tables, graphs, charts, maps, drawings, photos), audiotapes, CD's, videos, DVD's, Web pages, online databases
Government publications	Guides, programs, forms, legislation, regulations, reports, records, statistics
Business and nonprofit publications	Correspondence, reports, newsletters, pamphlets, brochures, ads, catalogs, instructions, handbooks, manuals, policies and procedures, seminar and training materials

artifact
any object made or modified by a human culture and later discovered

Consider information sites.

Where do you go to find the resources that you need? Consider the information sites listed below, remembering that many resources may be available in different forms in different locations. For example, a journal article may be available in a library or in an electronic database.

Information Location	Specific Sites
People	Experts (knowledge area, skill, occupation)
	Population segments or individuals (with representative or unusual experiences)
Libraries	General: public, college, online
	Specialized: legal, medical, government, business
Computer resources	Computers: software, CD-ROM's
	Networks: Internet and other online services (e-mail, limited-access databases, discussion groups, MUDs, chat rooms, Web sites, blogs, YouTube, image banks, wikis); intranets
Mass media	Radio (AM and FM), television (network, public, cable, satellite), print (newspapers, magazines, journals)
Testing, training, meeting, and observation sites	Plants, facilities, field sites, laboratories, research centers, universities, think tanks, conventions, conferences, seminars, museums, galleries, historical sites
Municipal, state, and federal government offices	Elected officials, representatives, offices and agencies, Government Printing Office, and Web sites (GPO, www.gpoaccess.gov)
Business and nonprofit publications	Computer databases, company files, desktop reference materials, bulletin boards (physical and electronic), company and department Web sites, departments and offices, associations, professional organizations, consulting, training, and business information services

primary sources
original sources that give firsthand information about a topic

secondary sources
sources that are at least once removed from the original; sources that provide secondhand information

tertiary sources
sources that provide thirdhand information, such as wikis; discouraged for college research projects

Understand sources. LO5

Information sources can be primary, secondary, or tertiary. Depending on your assignment, you may be required to use primary and/or secondary sources, but rarely tertiary.

The Sources

Primary sources are original sources, which means they give firsthand information on a topic. These sources (such as diaries, people, or events) inform you directly about the topic, rather than through other people's explanations or interpretations. The most common forms of primary research are observations, interviews, surveys, experiments, and analyses of original documents and artifacts.

Secondary sources present secondhand information on your topic—information at least once removed from the original. This information has been compiled, summarized, analyzed, synthesized, interpreted, or evaluated by someone studying primary sources. Journal articles, documentaries, and nonfiction books are typical examples of such secondary sources.

Tertiary sources present thirdhand information on your topic. They are essentially reports of reports of research and, therefore, are distant from the original information. Examples of tertiary sources would include some articles in popular magazines and entries in Wikipedia. Aside from giving you ideas for focusing your topic and for conducting further research, tertiary sources should generally not be used in college research projects and should not appear in workscited or reference lists.

The next column lists possible primary and secondary sources for a research project exploring hybrid car technology and its viability. *Note:* Whether a source is primary or secondary depends on what you are studying. For example, if you were studying U.S. *attitudes* toward hybrid cars, a newspaper editorial or a TV roundtable discussion would be a primary source. However, if you were studying hybrid technology itself, the same newspaper editorial or TV roundtable would be a secondary source.

Hybrid Car Technology

Primary Sources
- E-mail interview with automotive engineer
- Fuel-efficiency legislation
- Test-drive of a car at a dealership
- Published statistics about hybrid car sales

Secondary Sources
- Journal article discussing the development of hybrid car technology
- Newspaper editorial on fossil fuels
- TV news roundtable discussion of hybrid car advantages and disadvantages
- Promotional literature for a specific hybrid car

Critical-Thinking and Writing Activities

As directed by your instructor, complete the following critical-thinking and writing activities by yourself or with classmates.

1. Examine a research paper that you wrote in the past (e.g., in high school). What features of that paper are consistent with a college-level approach to research writing? What would you have to change to improve the thinking, level, and approach of the paper?

2. From the broad list of research subjects below, select one and (a) brainstorm a list of related topics, (b) select and refine a topic, (c) list key research questions, (d) formulate a working thesis, and (e) develop a list of possible resources (primary, secondary, and tertiary) for the topic.

   Subjects: *museums, organic foods, department stores, the entertainment industry, third-world struggles, comedy, wealth, mental illness, forests*

3. Using what you have learned in this chapter, develop a research plan that identifies a topic of interest to you, clarifies the value of the research, zeros in on specific research questions and a working thesis, maps out research methods, and establishes a workable schedule.

Checklist: Learning Outcomes

Use the checklist below to assess what you have learned about planning a research project, as well as to measure what you have done to plan a specific project.

_____ I understand the nature of academic research in terms of its purpose, audience, and context.

_____ I understand the research process and have initiated the process through analyzing the assignment, developing a manageable topic, brainstorming research questions, and articulating a working thesis.

_____ I have developed a research plan that includes consideration of background research, primary research, library research, and Internet research.

_____ As part of my planning, I have considered the range of information resources available as well as sites where resources can be found.

_____ I understand differences between primary, secondary, and tertiary sources, and I know which types make sense for my project.

"Basic research is what I am doing
when I don't know what I am doing."
—Wernher von Braun

26

Doing Your Research

Merriam-Webster's Collegiate Dictionary thinks it's pretty clever. A person who consults it to find the origin of the word **research** learns that it comes from the Middle French *recercher,* which means "to go about seeking"—after which *Webster's* promises "more at SEARCH."

In looking up *search,* one learns that the word comes from the Late Latin *circare,* which means "to go about" and which comes from the Latin *circum,* which means "round about." Then *Webster's* indicates there is "more at CIRCUM-."

Circum-, it turns out, comes from the Latin *circus,* which means "circle," and, yes, there's "more at CIRCLE." *Circle* comes from *circus,* of course, but it is also from (or akin to) the Greek *krikos,* which means "ring" and which is akin to the Old English *hring,* and—you guessed it—there's "more at RING."

So, you see, the clever editors of *Merriam-Webster's Collegiate Dictionary* are not content simply to provide you the etymology of *research.* They want you to research *research.* They want you "to go about seeking," to go "round about" in "circles" that feel like "circuses" and are all about "rings." They don't just define *research* for you—they give you a quick sampler of doing it.

In this chapter, you'll learn how research is about searching and re-searching and going about in circles—circles that will nevertheless lead you, through whatever tangents and side trips, to the knowledge you are seeking.

Learning Outcomes

LO1   Learn keyword searching.

LO2   Conduct primary research.

LO3   Do library research.

LO4   Use books.

LO5   Find periodical articles.

LO6   Understand the Internet.

LO7   Find reliable free-Web information.

LO8   Evaluate online sources.

Learn keyword searching. —— LO1

Keyword searching can help you find solid information in electronic library catalogs, online databases that index periodical articles (LexisNexis, EBSCOhost), print indexes to periodical publications, Internet resources, print books, and e-books. If you need additional help, consult with an information specialist in your library.

Navigate the search.

Keywords give you compass points for navigating the vast sea of information ahead of you. To plot the best course, choose the best keywords.

Begin brainstorming a list of possible keywords—topics, titles, and names—based on your current knowledge and background reading. **Then consult the Library of Congress subject headings** to find the keywords librarians use when classifying materials. Topic entries like the one in the next column contain keywords to use, along with narrower, related, and/or broader terms. When you are conducting subject searches of catalogs and databases, these are the terms that will get the best results.

Boolean operators
words or symbols used when searching research databases and that describe the relationship between various words or phrases in a search

Topic	**Immigrants** (*May Subd Geog*)
Tips	Here are entered works on foreign-born persons who enter a country intending to become permanent residents or citizens. This heading may be locally subdivided by names of places where immigrants settle. For works discussing emigrants from a particular place, an additional heading is assigned to designate the nationality of origin of the emigrant group and the place to which they have immigrated, e.g., Chinese—United States: American—Foreign countries.

"Used for"	UF Emigrants
	        Foreign-born population
	        Foreign population

"Broader term"	BT Persons
"Related term"	RT Aliens

"Narrower term"	NT Children of immigrants
	        Social work with immigrants
	        Teenage immigrants
	        Women immigrants

Subtopic	— Employment USE Alien labor
Recommended keywords	— Housing (*May Subd Geog*) — — Great Britain — Legal status, laws, etc. USE Emigration and immigration law

Employing Keyword Search Strategies

The goal of a keyword search is to find quality sources of information. To realize the best sources, employ these strategies:

Keyword Strategy

- **Get to know the database.** Look for answers to these questions: What material does the database contain? What time frames? What are you searching—authors, titles, subjects, full text? What are the search rules? How can you narrow the search?
- **Use a shotgun approach.** Start with the most likely keyword. If you have no "hits," choose a related term. Once you get some hits, check the citations for clues regarding which words to use as you continue searching.
- **Use Boolean operators to refine your search.** When you combine keywords with **Boolean operators**—such as those in the next column—you will obtain better results.

Narrowing a Search ▶ and, +, not, –

Use when one term gives you too many hits, especially irrelevant ones.

buffalo **and** bison *or* buffalo + bison	Searches for citations containing both keywords
buffalo **not** water *or* buffalo -water	Searches for "buffalo" but not "water," so that you eliminate material on water buffalo

Expanding a Search ▶ or

Combine a term providing few hits with a related word

buffalo **or** bison	Searches for citations containing either term

Specifying a Phrase ▶ quotation marks

Indicate that you wish to search for the exact phrase enclosed

"reclamation project"	Searches for the exact phrase "reclamation project"

Sequencing Operations ▶ parentheses

Indicate that the operation should be performed before other operations in the search string

(buffalo or bison) and ranching	Searches first for citations containing either "buffalo" or "bison" before checking the resulting citations for "ranching"

Finding Variations ▶ wild card symbols

Depending on the database, symbols such as $, ?, or # can find variations of a word

ethic# ethic$	Searches for terms like *ethics* and *ethical*

Conduct primary research.

LO2

When published sources can't give you the information that you need, consider conducting primary research. Primary research gives you direct, hands-on access to your topic, providing information precisely tailored to your needs. Such research takes time, however. It also requires special skills like designing surveys or analyzing statistics and original documents. The following quick guide is an overview of research methods. Choose those that best suit your project.

Eric Isselée, 2011 / Used under license from Shutterstock.com

Quick Guide: Primary Research Methods

Surveys • Surveys and **questionnaires** gather written responses you can review, tabulate, and analyze. These research tools pull together varied information—from simple facts to personal opinions and attitudes.

Interviews • Interviews involve consulting two types of people. First, you can interview experts for their insights on your topic. Second, you can interview people whose direct experiences with the topic give you their personal insights. (See pages 000-000 for more about interviews.)

Observations • **Observations, inspections,** and **field research** require you to examine and analyze people, places, events, and so on. Whether you rely simply on your five senses or use scientific techniques, observing provides insights into the present state of your subject. (See page 252 for more on field reports.)

Experiments • Experiments test hypotheses—predictions about why things do what they do—to arrive at conclusions that can be accepted and acted upon. Such testing often explores cause-effect relationships. (See page 252 for more on lab reports.)

Analysis • Analysis of documents and artifacts involves studying original reports, statistics, legislation, literature, artwork, and historical records. Such analysis provides unique, close-up interpretations of your topic.

Student Model

Student writer Cho Lang created the following paper survey to determine how many athletes at her college used training supplements, how, and why. She also created a Web-based version of the survey, asking athletes to sign on anonymously to complete it.

Confidential Survey

My name is Cho Lang, and I'm conducting research about the use of training supplements. I'd like to hear from you, Alfred University's athletes. Please answer the questions below by circling or writing out your responses. Return your survey to me, care of the Dept. of Psychology, through campus mail by Friday, April 5. Your responses will remain confidential. **(A)**

1. Circle your gender.   **(B)**
   Male   Female

2. Circle your year.
   Freshman   Sophomore   Junior   Senior

3. List the sports that you play.

4. Are you presently using a training supplement?
   Yes   No
   Note: If you circled "no," you may turn in your survey at this point.

5. Describe your supplement use (type, amount, and frequency).   **(C)**

6. Who supervises your use of this training supplement?
   Coach   Trainer   Self   Others

7. How long have you used it?
   Less than 1 month   1–12 months   12+ months

8. How many pounds have you gained while using this supplement?   **(D)**

9. How much has your athletic performance improved?
   None   1   2   3   4   5   Greatly

10. Circle any side effects you've experienced.
    Dehydration   Nausea   Diarrhea

Thank you for taking the time to complete this confidential survey. Please return it by Friday, April 5, to Cho Lang, care of the Dept. of Psychology, through campus mail.

(A) The introduction includes the essential information about the survey.
(B) The survey begins with clear, basic questions.
(C) The survey asks an open-ended question.
(D) The survey covers the topic thoroughly.

Writing Guidelines

Conducting Surveys

Your goal is to create a survey or questionnaire that collects facts and opinions from a target audience about your topic. To get valid information, follow these guidelines:

1. **Find a focus.** Define the writing situation. What is your specific topic? What is the purpose of your survey (what do you want to find out)? Who is the audience for your survey?

2. **Create effective questions.** Phrase questions so that they can be easily understood. Use neutral language to avoid skewing results. Use **closed questions** (e.g., rating, multiple choice, yes/no) to generate data that can be charted and quantified. Use **open-ended questions** (e.g., fill-in-the-blank, write-in answers) to bring in a wider variety of complex data.

3. **Draft your survey.** Whether you present your survey on paper or online, organize it so that it's easy to complete.

> **Opening:** State who you are and why you need the information. Explain how to complete the survey and when and where to return it.
>
> **Middle:** Provide the questions. Guide the reader with numbers, instructions, and headings. Begin with basic, closed questions and progress to complex, open-ended questions. Move in a logical order from topic to topic.
>
> **Ending:** Thank the respondent for taking the survey and remind the person when and where to return it.

4. **Revise your survey.** Ask a friend or classmate to take your survey and help you revise it, if necessary, before publishing it. Take the survey yourself. Note questions that should be added or reworded or removed, parts that should be reorganized, places in which the voice should be more neutral, and instructions that should be clearer. After revising, try out your survey with a small test group, and revise again.

5. **Edit your survey.** Check sentences, words, letters, and each punctuation mark. Make certain your survey is error free before publishing it.

6. **Conduct your survey.** Distribute the survey to a clearly defined group that won't prejudice the sample (random or cross section). Encourage the target group to respond, aiming for 10 percent response if at all possible. Tabulate responses carefully and objectively. To develop statistically valid results, you may need expert help. Check with your instructor.

Laurence Gough, 2011 / Used under license from Shutterstock.com

survey/questionnaire
a set of questions created for the purpose of gathering information from respondents about a specific topic

observation
noting information received in person through the senses

inspection
the purposeful analysis of a site or situation in order to understand it

field research
an on-site scientific study conducted for the purpose of attaining raw data

closed questions
questions that can be answered with a simple fact or with a *yes* or a *no*

open-ended questions
questions that require elaborate answers

Do library research.

The library door is your gateway to information. Inside, the college library holds a wide range of research resources, from books to periodicals, from reference librarians to electronic databases.

Making the Library Work

To improve your ability to succeed at all your research assignments, become familiar with your college library system. Take advantage of tours and orientation sessions to learn its physical layout, resources, and services. Check your library's Web site for policies, tutorials, and research tools.

Knowing Where to Go

The college library offers four basic resources for your research projects.

Librarians are information experts who manage the library's materials and guide you to resources. They also can help you perform online searches.

Collections are the materials housed within the library, including books and electronic materials, periodicals, reference materials, and special collections.

Research tools are the systems and services to help you find what you need. They include online catalogs, print indexes and **subscription databases**, and Internet access to other libraries and online references.

Special services are additional options to help you complete research, including interlibrary loan, "hold" and "reserve" services, the reference desk, photocopies, CD burners, scanners, and presentation software.

Catalog Searches

Library materials are cataloged so that they are easy to find. In most college libraries, books, videos, and other holdings are cataloged in an electronic database. To find material, use book titles, author names, and related keyword searching. (See pages 320–321.)

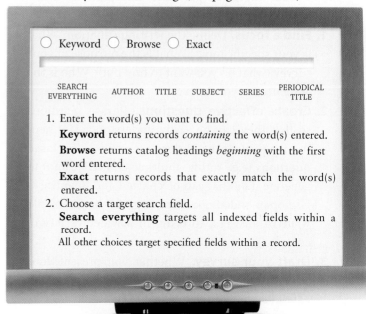

When you find a citation for a book or other resource (see below), the result will likely provide the author or editor's name, the title and subtitle, publisher and copyright date, descriptive information, subject headings (crucial list of topics), call number, and location. Use that information to determine whether the resource is worth exploring further and to figure out other avenues of research. *Note:* A number of items appearing in blue underlined type provide links to related books and other resources in the catalog.

Cudworth, Erika, 1966–

Title: Environment and Society

Publisher: London; New York: Routledge, 2003.

Physical descript.: xii, 232 p.: ill.; 24 cm.

Subjects: Human ecology [65 rec.]

      Nature—Effect of human being on [15 rec.]

      Environmental protection [25 rec.]

Call number: GF 41 .C83 2003

---

collections
the materials housed within a library

subscription databases
online services that, for a fee, provide access to hundreds of thousands of articles

Locating by Call Numbers

Library of Congress (LC) **call numbers** combine letters and numbers to specify a resource's broad subject area, topic, and authorship or title. Finding a book, DVD, or other item involves combining both the alphabetical and the numerical order.

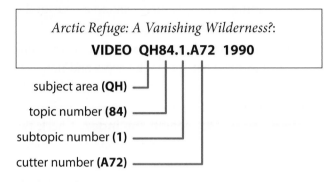

Arctic Refuge: A Vanishing Wilderness?:

VIDEO QH84.1.A72 1990

subject area **(QH)**

topic number **(84)**

subtopic number **(1)**

cutter number **(A72)**

To find the example resource in the library, first note the tab VIDEO. Although not part of the call number, this locator will send you to a specific area of the library. Once there, follow the parts of the call number one at a time:

1. Find the section on natural history containing videos with the "QH" designation.

2. Follow the numbers until you reach "84."

3. Within the "84" items, find those with the subtopic "1."

4. Use the cutter number "A72" to locate the resource alphabetically with "A" and numerically with "72."

Note: In the LC system, pay careful attention to the arrangement of subject area letters, topic numbers, and subtopic numbers: Q98 comes before QH84; QH84 before QH8245; QH84.A72 before QH84.1.A72.

Classification Systems

The **LC classification system** combines letters and numbers. The **Dewey decimal system,** which is used in some libraries, uses numbers only. Here is a list of the subject classes for both the LC and Dewey systems.

Category	LC	Dewey Decimal
General Works	A	000–999
Philosophy	B	100–199
Psychology		150–159
Religion		200–299
History: Auxiliary Sciences	C	910–929
History: General and Old World	D	930–999
History: American	E–F	970–979
Geography	G	910–919
Anthropology		571–573
Recreation		700–799
Social Sciences	H	300–399
Political Science	J	320–329
Law	K	340–349
Education	L	370–379
Music	M	780–789
Fine Arts	N	700–799
Language	P	800–899
Literature		400–499
Science	Q	500–599
Medicine	R	610–619
Agriculture	S	630–639
Technology	T	600–699
Military Science	U	355–359, 623
Naval Science	V	359, 623
Bibliography and Library Science	Z	010–019 020–029

Library of Congress call numbers
a set of numbers and letters specifying the subject area, topic, and authorship or title of a book

Use books. LO4

Your college library contains a range of books, from scholarly studies and reference works to trade books and biographies.

When you find a helpful book, browse nearby shelves for more books. If your library subscribes to an e-book service such as NetLibrary, you can conduct electronic searches, browse or check out promising books, and read them online.

Unfortunately, for most research projects, you simply don't have time to read an entire book, and rarely do the entire contents relate to your topic. Instead, use the strategy outlined in the next column to refine your research effort.

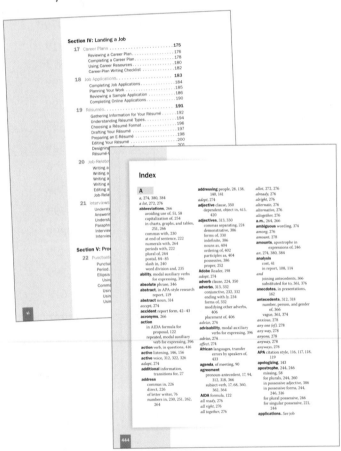

Research Strategy

- **Check out front and back information.** The title and copyright pages give the book's full title and subtitle; the author's name; and publication information, including publication date and Library of Congress subject headings. The back may contain a note on the author's credentials and other publications.

- **Scan the table of contents.** Examine the contents page to see what the book covers and how it is organized. Ask yourself which chapters are relevant to your project.

- **Using key words, search the index.** Check the index for coverage and page locations of the topics most closely related to your project. Are there plenty of pages, or just a few? Are these pages concentrated or scattered throughout the book?

- **Skim the foreword, preface, or introduction.** Skimming the opening materials will often indicate the book's perspective, explain its origin, and preview its contents.

- **Check appendixes, glossaries, or bibliographies.** These special sections may be good sources of tables, graphics, definitions, statistics, and clues for further research.

- **Carefully read appropriate chapters and sections.** Think through the material you've read and take good notes. (See pages 347–348.) Follow references to authors and other works to do further research on the topic. Study footnotes and endnotes for insights and leads.

appendixes
sections (in a book) that provide additional or background information

glossaries
lists of important terms and their definitions

bibliographies
lists of works that cover a particular subject

Quick Guide:
Informational Reference Resources

Encyclopedias supply facts and overviews for topics arranged alphabetically. General encyclopedias, such as *Encyclopedia Britannica* or *Collier's Encyclopedia*, cover many fields of knowledge. Specialized encyclopedias, such as *McGraw-Hill Encyclopedia of Science and Technology* and the *Encyclopedia of American Film Comedy*, focus on a single topic.

Almanacs, **yearbooks**, **and statistical resources**, normally published annually, contain diverse facts. *The World Almanac and Book of Facts* presents information on politics, history, religion, business, social programs, education, and sports. *Statistical Abstract of the United States* provides data on population, geography, politics, employment, business, science, and industry.

Vocabulary resources supply information on languages. General dictionaries, such as *The American Heritage College Dictionary*, supply definitions and histories for a whole range of words. Specialized dictionaries, such as the *Dictionary of Engineering* or *The New Harvard Dictionary of Music*, define words common to a field, topic, or group. Bilingual dictionaries translate words from one language to another.

Biographical resources supply information about people. General biographies, such as *Who's Who in America*, cover a broad range of people. Other biographies, such as the *Dictionary of Scientific Biography* or *World Artists 1980-1990*, focus on people from a specific group.

Directories supply contact information for people, groups, and organizations: *The National Directory of Addresses and Telephone Numbers*, *USPS ZIP Code Lookup and Address Information* (online), *Official Congressional Directory*.

Reference Works as Research Tools

Guides and handbooks help readers explore specific topics: *The Handbook of North American Indians*, *A Guide to Prairie Fauna*.

Indexes point you to useful resources. Some indexes are general, such as *Readers' Guide to Periodical Literature*; others are more specific, such as *Environment Index* or *Business Periodicals Index*. (Many are now available online in databases your library subscribes to.)

Bibliographies list resources on a specific topic. A good current bibliography can be used as an example when you compile your own bibliography on a topic.

Abstracts, like indexes, direct you to articles on a particular topic. But abstracts also summarize those materials so you learn whether a resource is relevant before you invest time in locating and reading it. Abstracts are usually organized into subject areas: Computer Abstracts, Environmental Abstracts, Social Work Abstracts. They are incorporated in many online subscription databases.

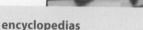

encyclopedias
reference works filled with articles written about a variety of topics

almanacs/yearbooks
regularly published references that chronicle the major events of a specific time period

directories
references that provide contact information for people, groups, and organizations

indexes
searchable lists of resources on various topics

abstracts
summaries of resources; a collection of summaries in a specific subject area

Find periodical articles. LO5

Periodicals are publications or broadcasts produced at regular intervals (daily, weekly, monthly, quarterly). Although some periodicals are broad in their subject matter and audience, as a rule they focus on a narrow range of topics geared toward a particular audience.

There are basically three forms of periodical publications. **Daily newspapers and newscasts** provide up-to-date information on current events, opinions, and trends—from politics to natural disasters (*Wall Street Journal, USA Today, The NewsHour*). **Weekly and monthly magazines and newscasts** generally provide more in-depth information on a wide range of topics (*Time, Newsweek, 60 Minutes*). Finally, **journals**, generally published quarterly, provide specialized scholarly information for a narrowly focused audience (*English Journal*).

Online Databases

If your library subscribes to EBSCOhost, Lexis-Nexis, or another database service, use keyword searching (see pages 320–321) to find citations on your topic. You might start with the general version of such databases, such as EBSCOhost's Academic Search Elite, which provides access to more than 4,100 scholarly publications covering all disciplines.

Basic Search

The example (**Sample 1 on next page**) shows an EBSCOhost search screen for a search on hybrid electric cars. Notice how limiters, expanders, and other advanced features help you find the highest-quality materials.

Making the Advanced Search

A more focused research strategy involves turning to specialized databases, which are available for virtually every discipline and are often an option within search services such as EBSCOhost (for example, Business Source Elite, PsycINFO, ERIC) and Lexis-Nexis (for example, Legal, Medical, and Business databases). If a basic search turns up little, turn to specialized databases, seeking help from a librarian if necessary.

Citation Lists

Your database search should generate lists of citations, brief descriptions of articles that were flagged through keywords in titles, subject terms, abstracts, and so on. For example, a search focused on hybrid electric cars leads to the results shown (**Sample 2 on the next page**). At this point, study the results and do the following:

- Refine the search by narrowing or expanding it.
- Mark specific citations for "capture" or further study.
- Re-sort the results.
- Follow links in a specific citation to further information.

Identifying Information

By studying citations (especially abstracts), you can determine if the article is relevant to your research, is available in an electronic version, and is available as a periodical. To develop your working bibliography (see page 346), you should also "capture" the article's identifying details by using the save, print, or e-mail

function, or by recording the periodical's title, the issue and date, and the article's title and page numbers.

Full-Text Articles

When citations indicate that you have promising articles, access those articles efficiently, preferably through a direct link in the citation to an electronic copy. From there you can print, save, or e-mail the article. If the article is not available electronically, track down a print version.

Check the online citation to see if your library has the article. If necessary, check your library's inventory of periodicals held; this list should be available online and/or in print. Examine especially closely the issues and dates available, the form (print or microfilm), and the location (bound or current shelves).

To get the article, follow your library's procedure. You may have to submit a request slip so that a librarian can get the periodical, or you may be able to get it yourself in the current, bound, or microfilm collection. If the article is not available online or in your library, use interlibrary loan.

Sample 1: Online Database

(A) Keyword field and database list
(B) Limiters available
(C) Expanders available

fyi Particularly if you need articles published before 1985, you may need to go to the *Readers' Guide to Periodical Literature* or another print index. While databases are converting pre-1985 articles to digital form (for example, the JSTOR database), many excellent periodical articles are available only in print. To use the *Readers' Guide*, consult a librarian.

© Courtesy of EBSCOhost.com

Sample 2: Online Database Citation List

(A) Folder feature for "capturing" citations
(B) "Sort" options
(C) Numbered citations including titles, authors, journal information, length, location notes
(D) Narrowed subject links

Understand the Internet.

LO6

If you're familiar with the Internet, you already understand the basics of searching this medium. However, the following information may help you do quality research on the Net.

The **Internet** is a worldwide network of connected local computers and computer networks that allows computers to share information with one another. Your college's network likely gives you access to the library, local resources, and the Internet.

How the Network Works

The **World Wide Web** provides access to much of the material on the Internet. Millions of Web pages are available because of **hypertext links** that connect them.

These links appear as clickable icons or highlighted Web addresses. A **Web site** is a group of related **Web pages** posted by the same sponsor or organization. A **home page** is a Web site's "entry" page. A **Web browser** such as Safari, Internet Explorer, or Firefox gives you access to Web resources through a variety of tools, such as directories and search engines. (Directories and **search engines** are special Web sites that provide a searchable listing of many services on the Web.)

Distinguish between the **deep Web** and the free Web. The deep Web includes material not generally accessible with popular search engines, such as all the scholarly research available through your library's subscription databases. The free Web offers less reliable information.

Understanding Internet Addresses

An Internet address is called a uniform resource locator (**URL**). The address includes the protocol indicating how the computer file should be accessed—often *http:* or *ftp:* (followed by a double slash); a domain name—often beginning with *www;* and additional path information (following a single slash) to access other pages within a site.

> http://www.nrcs.usda.gov/news/

Internet
a worldwide network of connected computers that allows a sharing of information

World Wide Web
the collection of Web sites on the Internet accessible to Web browsers and search engines

hypertext link
a clickable bit of text that connects the user to another location on the Web

Web site
a group of related Web pages posted by the same sponsor or organization

Web page
a page viewable as a single unit on a Web site

Web browser
a program that provides access to Web resources through a variety of tools

deep Web
Internet materials not accessible via popular search engines but available through a library's subscription databases

URL
the uniform resource locator; the Web address telling the browser how to access a certain file

Sample Web Page

(A) Title bar
(B) Navigation bar
(C) Graphic link
(D) Status bar
(E) Text links

The **domain name** is a key part of the address because it indicates what type of organization created the site and gives you clues about its goal or purpose—to educate, inform, persuade, sell, and/or entertain. Most sites combine a primary purpose with secondary ones.

Sample Domain Names

.com   a commercial organization or business

.gov   a government organization—federal, state, or local

.edu   an educational institution

.org   a nonprofit organization

.net   an organization that is part of the Internet's infrastructure

.mil   a military site

.biz   a business site

.info   any site primarily providing information

International addresses generally include national abbreviations (for example, Canada = .ca). This clue helps you determine the origin of the information and communicate more sensitively on the Internet.

Saving Internet Information

Accurately saving Internet addresses and material is an essential part of good research. Moreover, you may want to revisit sites and embed URLs in your research writing. Save Internet information through these methods:

Bookmark: Your browser can save a site's address through a "bookmark" or "favorites" function on your menu bar.

Printout: If a document looks promising, print a hard copy of it. Remember to write down all details needed for citing the source. (Although many details will automatically print with the document, some could be missing.)

Save or download: To keep an electronic copy of material, save the document to a specific drive on your computer. Beware of large files with many graphics: They take up a lot of space. To save just the text, highlight it, copy it, and then paste it into a word-processing program.

E-mail: If you're not at your own computer, you can e-mail the document's URL to your e-mail address through copy and paste.

Volodymyr Vasylkiv, 2011 / Used under license from Shutterstock.com

Find reliable free-Web information. LO7

Because the Internet contains so much information of varying reliability, you need to become familiar with search tools that locate information you can trust. The key is knowing which search tool to use in which research situation. It's also important to proceed with caution.

Adhere to your assignment's restrictions on using Web sites (number and type). In fact, some instructors may not allow Web resources for specific projects, limiting you to print sources and scholarly articles available in subscription databases.

When you are using Web resources, make sure the sites are sponsored by legitimate, recognizable organizations: government agencies, nonprofit groups, and educational institutions. For most projects, avoid relying on personal, commercial, and special-interest sites, as well as chat rooms, blogs, and news groups. Test the quality and reliability of online information by using the benchmarks outlined on page 338.

Avoid developing your paper by simply copying and pasting together chunks of Web pages. By doing so, you not only fail to engage your sources meaningfully, but you also commit plagiarism. For more on plagiarism, see pages 354–355.

domain name
the name of a site, including the extension after the dot (.), which indicates what type of organization created the site

bookmark
a digital tag that allows the user to easily return to a favorite site

Reliable Web Sites

Your library may sponsor a Web site that gives you access to quality Internet resources. For example, it may provide tutorials on using the Internet, guides to Internet resources in different disciplines, links to on-line document collections (Project Gutenberg, Etext Archives, New Bartleby Digital Library, and so on), or connections to other virtual resources (virtual libraries, subscription databases, search engines, directories, government documents, and online reference works). If your library provides access to the global catalog WorldCat, click on the "Internet" limiter to search for information recommended by librarians.

Finding other useful Web sites can be as easy as typing in a URL. If you don't have the exact URL, sometimes you can guess it, especially for an organization (company, government agency, or nonprofit group). Of course, you can also search for the Web site, checking the URLs that are presented to make sure you select the actual site you seek, not a copycat.

You can also find useful sites by following links provided on other useful sites. If you come across a helpful link (often highlighted in blue), click on the link to visit that new page. Note that the link may take you to another site.

Your browser keeps a record of the pages you visit. Click the back arrow to go back one page or the forward arrow to move ahead again. Clicking the right mouse button on these arrows shows a list of recently visited pages.

Subject Trees

A **subject tree**, sometimes called a subject guide or directory, lists Web sites that have been organized into categories by experts who have reviewed those sites. Use subject trees or directories if you need to narrow a broad topic or if you want sites that have been evaluated (quality over quantity).

How does a subject tree work? Essentially, it allows you to select from a broad range of subjects or "branches." With each topic choice, you narrow your selection until you arrive at a list of Web sites, or you can keyword-search a limited number of Web sites.

Check whether your library subscribes to a service such as NetFirst, a database in which subject experts have cataloged Internet resources by topic. Here are some other common subject directories that you can likely access at your library:

> **WWW Virtual Library** • http://vlib.org/Overview.html
> **Argus** • http://www.clearinghouse.net
> **Google Directory** • http://www.google.com/dirhp
> **LookSmart** • http://looksmart.com
> **LookSmart** • http://looksmart.com
> **Internet Public Library** • http://www.ipl2.org

Tip To get the best results from your search, avoid these problems: misspelling keywords; using vague or broad keywords (education or business); incorrectly combining Boolean operators; or shortening keywords too much.

---

subject tree
a listing of Web sites, arranged by experts

Examine the subject-tree search explained below and on the next page. Afterward, conduct your own search using a subject tree available through your library.

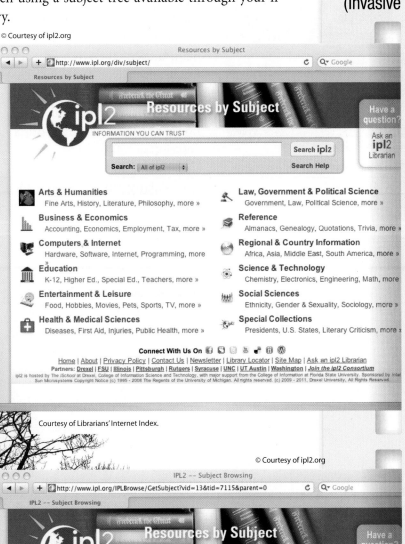

Subject-Tree Search (Invasive Plant Species)

Step 1: Select an appropriate broad category. Study the subject tree to the left provided by the Internet Public Library (ipl2). To find reviewed Web sites containing information on invasive plant species, you could select from this start page a range of categories, depending on the angle you want to explore: Business and Economics, Health and Medical Sciences, Science and Technology, and so on. Each of these starting points will lead to a different listing of relevant sites. Another option would be to use the keyword search feature shown.

Step 2: Choose a fitting subcategory. If you chose Science and Technology, the subcategories shown in the sidebar would appear. At this point, you would again have several choices: to select Agriculture and Aquaculture, to follow Environmental Sciences and Ecology, and so on. Each choice might lead to a distinct set of Web sites.

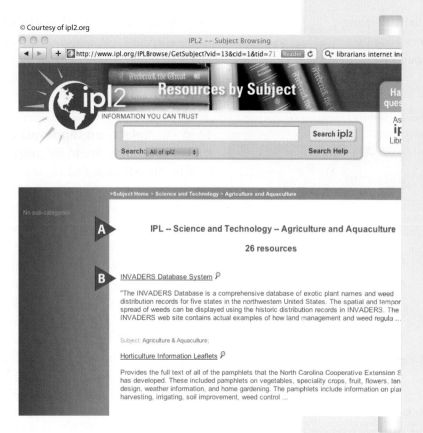

IPL2 -- Subject Browsing

http://www.ipl.org/IPLBrowse/GetSubject?vid=13&cid=1&tid=71   Reader   C   Q▾ librarians internet in

ipl2

Resources by Subject

INFORMATION YOU CAN TRUST

Search: All of ipl2

Search ipl2

Search Help

Ha
que

As
ip
Libr

>Subject Home > Science and Technology > Agriculture and Aquaculture

No sub-categories

A

IPL -- Science and Technology -- Agriculture and Aquaculture

26 resources

B

INVADERS Database System

"The INVADERS Database is a comprehensive database of exotic plant names and weed
distribution records for five states in the northwestern United States. The spatial and tempor
spread of weeds can be displayed using the historic distribution records in INVADERS. The
INVADERS web site contains actual examples of how land management and weed regula ...

Subject: Agriculture & Aquaculture;

Horticulture Information Leaflets

Provides the full text of all of the pamphlets that the North Carolina Cooperative Extension S
has developed. These included pamphlets on vegetables, speciality crops, fruit, flowers, lan
design, weather information, and home gardening. The pamphlets include information on plan
harvesting, irrigating, soil improvement, weed control ...

Step 3: Work toward a listing of Web sites. As you work down through narrower branches of the tree, you will see listings of relevant Web sites in the main area of the window. Such sites, remember, have all been reviewed in terms of quality, though you still need to evaluate what you find. In the citation for a site, study the site title and the description of information available. Visit the site and notice its Web address (particularly the domain name). Use that information to determine the site's relevance to your research.

(A) Site title and link
(B) Site description, and types of content

Visiting, Exploring, and Evaluating

Look through the listing of recommended sites. Once you have identified a promising site, follow the links provided. Study and evaluate the site by asking questions such as these:

1. Who authored or sponsored the site? What is the author's or sponsor's perspective on the topic? Why did the author post these pages? What can you find out about the author through a broader Internet search?

2. What content does the site offer? What depth of information is available?

3. Does the Web site function as a primary, secondary, or tertiary source?

4. What external links does the site offer? Might these links take you to additional resources that are relevant and reliable?

Insight: Careful investigation and evaluation of Web sites is even more important when you use search engines like those discussed on the next page. Use the resource evaluation guidelines on page 338 for Web pages that you find through either subject directories or search engines. Always proceed with caution, making sure that your research writing does not rely on unstable, shallow Web pages.

Search and Metasearch

Unlike a subject directory, which provides a list crafted with human input, a search engine provides a list generated automatically by scouring millions of Web sites. Not all search engines are the same. Some search citations of Internet materials, whereas others conduct full-text searches. Choose a search engine that covers a large portion of the Internet, offers quality indexing, and provides high-powered search capabilities.

Basic **search engines** search millions of Web pages, and they include engines such as Alta Vista, AllTheWeb, Google, HotBot, Vivisimo, and Yahoo. (The URL for each of these is the engine name, without spaces, followed by <.com>.)

Metasearch tools search several basic search engines at once, and they include sites such as Ask, Dog Pile, Ixquick, and Northern Light. (The URL for each of these is the engine name, without spaces, followed by <.com>.)

fyi Deep-Web tools check Internet databases and other sources not accessible to basic search engines. One excellent deep-Web tool is Complete Planet at www.completeplanet.com.

© Courtesy of Google.com

Reprinted by permission of Google.

Basic Web Search
(Toyota Hybrid Electric Cars)

Step 1: Begin the search with precise terms. Using Boolean operators and quotation marks, you might begin with the search terms "Wisconsin" and "invasive plant species." The more precise your terms are, the better your results will be.

Step 2: Study the results and refine your search. The results of the initial search appear here. At this point, you can click one of the resulting Web links, click a sponsored link, follow links on the right to related topics, or narrow or broaden your search.

Refinement through search questions with drop-down lists

(A) Results: sponsored sites (primarily advertising)

(B) Results: other Web pages

search engines
sites that search other Web sites using key words

metasearch tools
sites that search other search engines

Understanding the Uses and Limits of Wikipedia

You likely recognize the screen below—an article from Wikipedia. From its beginning in 2001 to today, a large population of volunteer writers and editors has made Wikipedia a top-ten Internet-traffic site. But is Wikipedia acceptable for college-level research? Put simply, Wikipedia is a controversial resource for academic research.

Know Wikipedia's strengths.

Because of its wiki nature, Wikipedia offers researchers a number of advantages.

- **Consensus Model of Knowledge:** Articles represent a collaborative agreement about a topic—a topical knowledge base that is fair and fairly comprehensive. Generally, articles improve over time, offering "open-source" knowledge.
- **Currency of Information:** Because they are Web based, articles are regularly monitored and updated—a distinct advantage over print encyclopedias.
- **Breadth of Information:** With its size and global community, Wikipedia offers articles on a wide range of topics—especially strong in pop culture, current events, computer, and science topics.
- **Links:** Articles are linked throughout so that readers can pursue associated topics, sources, recommended reading, and related categories.

Understand Wikipedia's standards for truth.

Wikipedia applies a different standard of truth than more traditional sources of information. In his revealing article, "Wikipedia and the Meaning of Truth," Simson L. Garfinkle provides an explanation. (See pages 119–123 for the complete essay.)

Screen Features

1 Semi-protected article icon
2 History tab
3 Discussion page
4 Title
5 Introduction
6 Links
7 Wikipedia's search field
8 Wikipedia's menus
9 Contents Menu
10 Essential facts

Source: Wikipedia

Know Wikipedia's weaknesses.

In some ways, Wikipedia's strengths are closely related to its weaknesses for college-level research. Consider these issues:

- **Popularity Model of Knowledge:** The dynamics of popularity can lead to bias, imbalance, and errors. In some ways, this approach minimizes the value of training, education, and expertise while promoting a kind of democracy of knowledge.

- **Anonymity of Authorship:** Wikipedia allows contributors to remain anonymous. Researchers thus have little way of checking credentials and credibility.

- **Variable Quality of Content:** While many well-established articles are quite stable, balanced, and comprehensive, other articles can be partial, driven by a biased perspective, erroneous, and poorly sourced.

- **Variable Coverage:** Wikipedia's strength in some content areas is matched by gaps and incompleteness in other content areas.

- **Vulnerability to Vandalism:** Wikipedia has a number of processes in place to limit people from harming articles with misinformation, with the result that most vandalism is corrected within hours, but some errors have persisted for months.

- **Tertiary Nature of Information:** For most research projects, Wikipedia articles function as tertiary sources—reports of reports of research. As such, Wikipedia articles are not substantial enough for academic projects.

Use Wikipedia cautiously.

Based on Wikipedia's strengths and weaknesses, follow these guidelines:

1. **Respect your assignment.** Instructors may give you varied instruction about using Wikipedia. Respect their guidelines.

2. **Verify Wikipedia information.** If you use information from Wikipedia, also use other more traditional sources to verify that information.

3. **Use Wikipedia as a semi-authoritative reference source.** Generally, the more academic your research assignment, the less you should rely on Wikipedia articles, which are essentially sources of basic and background information.

4. **Use Wikipedia as one starting point.** From a Wikipedia article, you can learn what is considered "open-source" knowledge on your topic, gather ideas for developing a topic, find links to related topics and other resources, and begin to build a bibliography.

5. **Study individual articles to get a sense of their reliability.** When you find a Wikipedia article relevant to your research project, check the article for quality and stability. Use the evaluation criteria on the following pages, but also check the article's history, its discussion page, any tags or icons indicating the article's state, and the "what links here" link in the toolbox at the left of the screen.

Evaluate online sources.
 LO8

The Internet contains a wealth of information, but much of it is not suitable for a research report. The information may be incorrect, biased, outdated, plagiarized, or otherwise unreliable. These pages discuss issues to watch for.

Assignment Restrictions

Before engaging any Web resources, carefully review your assignment and note any restrictions on what type of sources may be used. If Web resources are allowed, abide by the number or percentage indicated in the assignment.

Author/Organization

When using Web resources, make sure the sites are sponsored by legitimate, recognizable organizations: government agencies, nonprofit groups, and educational institutions. For most projects, avoid relying on personal or special-interest sites, as well as chat rooms, blogs, news groups, or wikis. (These sources may help you explore a topic, but they do not provide scholarly material suitable for most research reports.)

Balance or Bias

Be aware of the purpose of a site or an article. Editorials and reviews, for example, express the point of view of a given author but are not sources for unbiased information. Unless your purpose is to show the author's point of view or point out two sides of an argument, avoid sources that show a bias toward or against a specific region, country, political party, industry, gender, race, ethnic group, or religion. Also, avoid sites that promote a specific cause, product, service, or belief.

Quality of Information

Test the quality of information on a site. Note whether the information is current (when was it posted/updated last), and check it against other sources for corroboration. Also, favor sites with a depth of information and those that show they truly engage their topic rather than treat it superficially.

Quality of Writing and Design

Avoid sites that show sloppy editing and poor design. These surface flaws can reveal a lack of scholarly rigor or serious commitment on the part of the site's creators.

Checklist: Evaluation

Use this checklist to assess the reliability of Web sources. The more items you check off, the more reliable the source is.

Assignment Restrictions

✔ Does the source fit with the type and number allowed in the assignment?

Author/Organization

✔ Is the person or organization behind the site reliable?

✔ Is contact information for the person or organization provided?

✔ Is the site well known and well connected in the field?

✔ Does the site have a clear "About Us" page and mission statement?

Balance or Bias

✔ Is the material on the site balanced and unbiased?

✔ Does the site avoid unfair and inflammatory language?

✔ Does the site avoid pushing a particular product, cause, service, or belief?

✔ Does the site provide ample support for its claims?

✔ Does the site avoid logical fallacies and twisted statistics? (See pages 182–185.)

Quality of Information

✔ Is the material current?

✔ Is the Web site often updated?

✔ Is the Web site information-rich?

✔ Is the information backed up by other reputable print and online sources?

Quality of Writing and Design

✔ Is the text free of errors in punctuation, spelling, and grammar?

✔ Is the site effectively and clearly designed?

Sample Evaluations

Reliable

Assignment Restrictions
- The site below would be appropriate for most assignments about the life and work of William Faulkner, as long as free-Web sources are allowed.

Author/ Organization
- This site is sponsored by the University of Mississippi, a scholarly source for information, and the article's author, Dr. John B. Padgett, is an authority on Faulkner.

Balance or Bias
- The site clearly extols Faulkner as a great writer but does not shy from showing his shortcomings. The claims are fair and amply supported, without logical fallacies.

Quality of Information
- The Web site is current, often updated, and information-rich. It is also connected to many other Faulkner resources available on the Web.

Quality of Writing and Design
- The site is well designed, with easy navigation, readable text, informative headings, helpful photos, and strong links. The text is well written and well edited.

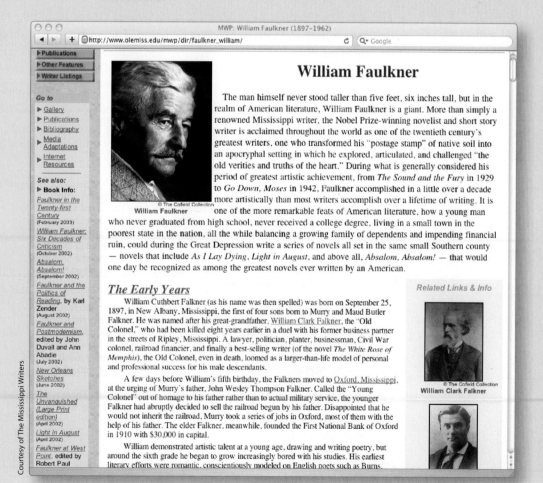

Sample Evaluations

Unreliable

Assignment Restrictions
- As a blog, the made-up Web site below would not be appropriate for an assignment about the life and work of William Faulkner. A site such as this should be recognized as reflective only of the writer's opinion, not of reliable information or fact.

Author/Organization
- There is no author or organization listed for this Web site. The domain name—myviewsonliterature.wordpress.com—shows that this is a personal opinion blog. Its lack of connection to other Web sites shows it represents an isolated opinion.

Balance or Bias
- This blog post shows a strong bias against William Faulkner. The few facts cited inadequately support the writer's main point, and logical fallacies are apparent. The tone of the post is unscholarly, with inflammatory language.

Quality of Information
- Though this Web site is frequently updated, the blog post does not represent current scholarship about William Faulkner. The Web site is information-poor and is not backed up by any reputable print or online sources.

Quality of Writing and Design
- The site has an amateurish design and numerous errors, including the persistent misspelling of William Faulkner's name. The writing is slipshod and the editing is poor.

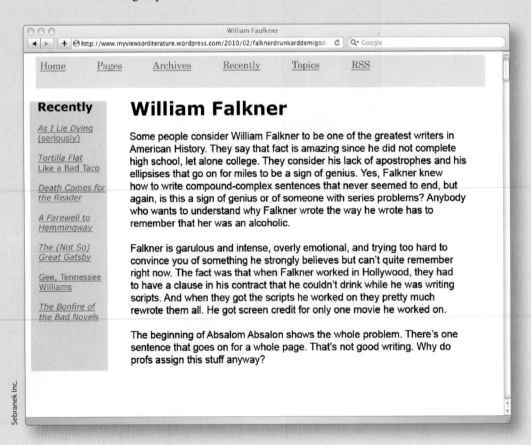

Critical-Thinking and Writing Activities

As directed by your instructor, complete the following critical-thinking and writing activities by yourself or with classmates.

1. Focus on a research project that you are doing now. How might primary research and library research (scholarly books and journal articles) strengthen your writing? Why not do all your research on the free Web using Google and resources like Wikipedia? What blend of primary research, library research, and/or free-Web research might this project require?

2. By working with your library's Web site and its orientation tools, identify where you can physically and/or electronically locate books, reference resources, and journals. Similarly, explore your library's handouts and Web site for information about Internet research. What services, support, and access does the library provide? Now use what you have discovered to conduct research for your current project.

3. Indicate which section of the library would house the following items: (a) *JAMA*, the *Journal of the American Medical Association*, (b) *Places Rated Almanac*, and (c) *Principles of Corporate Finance*, a book.

4. Brainstorm issues related to food production, consumption, or culture. Choosing one focused topic, use your library's catalog and journal database tools to track down print books and periodical articles. Assess the nature, breadth, and depth of what you find. Then do a free-Web search of the topic, comparing the results.

5. Using the variety of Internet search methods outlined in this chapter, work with some classmates to search the free Web for information on a controversial topic, event, person, or place. Carefully analyze and evaluate the range of Web information you find—the quality, perspective, depth, and reliability. Create a report on your findings for the rest of the class.

Checklist: Learning Outcomes

Use the checklist below to assess what you have learned about planning a research project, as well as to measure what you have done to plan a specific project.

____ I have generated keywords for my project and know how to use them.

____ I understand methods of primary research and have chosen accordingly for my project.

____ I am familiar with my library's research tools and holdings.

____ I have learned to use online catalogs to find books, and I understand how to use scholarly and trade books for my project.

____ I have learned to use the library's periodical databases, and I have tracked down periodical articles for my project.

____ I understand the strengths and limitations of the Internet for college-level research.

____ I have learned to find reliable resources on the free Web, and have done so for my current project.

____ I can and have effectively evaluated online sources for credibility and reliability.

Alexander Motrenko, 2011 / Used under license from Shutterstock.com

"The outcome of any serious research can only
be to make two questions grow where only
one grew before."

—Thorstein Veblen

27

Working with Your Sources

What does it mean to speak from authority? It doesn't come from a mere title. Titles can be withdrawn as easily as awarded. Instead, authority comes from familiarity with a topic. You probably know someone you trust to advise about family issues, someone you consult for mechanical problems, someone who can help with a difficult subject in your coursework. Each of these people is an authority based on knowledge of a subject.

When you write a report, you need to become an authority on your chosen topic. You must gain a broad knowledge of the information available, evaluate it for trustworthiness and applicability, and effectively incorporate it into your writing—with proper credit. This chapter will help you with those things, so that your reader will recognize your authority.

Learning Outcomes

LO1 Evaluate your sources.

LO2 Create a working bibliography.

LO3 Take notes effectively.

LO4 Summarize, paraphrase, and quote.

Evaluate your sources. LO1

Sources of information can be rated for depth and reliability based on their authorship, length, topic treatment, documentation, method of publication, distance from primary sources, and so on. Remember that credible sources boost your own credibility; sources that are not credible, destroy it.

Rate sources.

Don't automatically use sources simply because they support your opinion; conversely, don't reject sources simply because they disagree with your perspective. Instead, base your selection of information on reliable, thoughtful criteria.

From Good to Bad

Use this table to target sources that fit your project's goals, to assess the quality of the sources, and to build a strong bibliography. The table is organized according to the depth and reliability of different sources, with "10" being the deepest and most reliable, and "0" being the thinnest, most unreliable.

10 Scholarly Books and Articles: largely based on careful research; written by experts for experts; address topics in depth; involve peer review and careful editing; offer stable discussion of topic

9 Trade Books and Journal Articles: largely based on careful research; written by experts for educated general audience; sample periodicals: *The Atlantic, Scientific American, Nature, Orion*

8 Government Resources: books, reports, Web pages, guides, statistics developed by experts at government agencies; provided as service to citizens; relatively objective; sample source: *Statistical Abstract of the United States*

7 Reviewed Official Online Documents: Internet resources posted by legitimate institutions—colleges and universities, research institutes, service organizations; although offering a particular perspective, sources tend to be balanced

6 Reference Works and Textbooks: provide general and specialized information; carefully researched, reviewed, and edited; lack depth for focused research (e.g., general encyclopedia entry)

5 News and Topical Stories from Quality Sources: provide current-affairs coverage (print and online), introduction-level articles of interest to general public; may lack depth and length; sample sources: the *Washington Post*, the *New York Times*; *Time, Psychology Today*; NPR's *All Things Considered*

4 Popular Magazine Stories: short, introductory articles often distant from primary sources and without documentation; heavy advertising; sample sources: *Glamour, Seventeen, Reader's Digest*

3 Business and Nonprofit Publications: pamphlets, reports, news releases, brochures, manuals; range from informative to sales-focused

2 List Server Discussions, Usenet Postings, Blog Articles, Talk Radio Discussions: highly open, fluid, undocumented, untested exchanges and publications; unstable resource

1 Unregulated Web Material: personal sites, joke sites, chat rooms, special-interest sites, advertising and junk e-mail (spam); no review process, little accountability, biased presentation

0 Tabloid Articles (print and Web): contain exaggerated and untrue stories written to titillate and exploit; sample source: the *National Enquirer*, the *Weekly World News*

Test print and online source reliability.

When assessing the credibility of a source, consider the author and his or her perspective (or bias), and consider the source's timeliness and accuracy. The benchmarks in the quick guide on the next page apply to both print and online sources; note, however, the additional tests concerning sources on the Web, as well as the discussion on pages 337–340 concerning how to evaluate Web sites.

Quick Guide: Reliability Test

Credible Author

Is the author an expert on this topic? What are her or his credentials, and can you confirm them? For example, an automotive engineer would be an expert on hybrid-vehicle technology, whereas a celebrity in a commercial would not.

> **Web test:** Is an author indicated? If so, are the author's credentials noted and contact information offered (for example, an e-mail address)?

Reliable Publication

Has the source been published by a scholarly press, a peer-reviewed professional journal, a quality trade-book publisher, or a trusted news source? Did you find this resource through a reliable search tool?

> **Web test:** Which individual or group posted this page? Is the site rated by a subject directory or library organization? How stable is the site—has it been around for a while and is the material current, well-documented, and readily accessible? Check the site's home page, and read "About Us" pages and mission statements.

Unbiased Discussion

While all sources come from a specific perspective and represent specific commitments, a biased source may be pushing an agenda in an unfair, unbalanced, incomplete manner. Watch for bias toward a certain region, country, political party, industry, gender, race, ethnic group, or religion. Be alert to connections among authors, financial backers, and the points of view shared. For example, if an author has functioned as a consultant to or a lobbyist for a particular industry or group (oil, animal rights), his or her allegiances may lead to a biased presentation of an issue.

> **Web test:** Is the online document one-sided? Is the site nonprofit (.org), government (.gov), commercial (.com), educational (.edu), business (.biz), informational (.info), network-related (.net), or military (.mil)? Is the site U.S. or international? Is this organization pushing a cause, product, service, or belief? How do advertising or special interests affect the site? You might suspect, for example, the scientific claims of a site sponsored by a pro-smoking organization.

Current Information

A five-year-old book on computers may be outdated, but a forty-year-old book on Abraham Lincoln could still be the best source. Given what you need, is this source's discussion up-to-date?

> **Web test:** When was the material originally posted and last updated? Are links live or dead?

Accurate Information

Bad research design, poor reporting, and sloppy documentation can lead to inaccurate information. Check the source for factual errors, statistical flaws, and conclusions that don't add up.

> **Web test:** Is the site information-rich or -poor—filled with helpful, factual materials or fluffy with thin, unsubstantiated opinions? Can you trace and confirm sources by following links or conducting your own search?

Full, Logical Support

Is the discussion of the topic reasonable, balanced, and complete? Are claims backed up with quality evidence? Does the source avoid faulty assumptions, twisted statistical analysis, logical fallacies, and unfair persuasion tactics? (See pages 182–184 for help.)

> **Web test:** Does the Web page offer well-supported claims and helpful links to additional information?

Quality Writing and Design

Is the source well written? Is it free of sarcasm, derogatory terms, cliches, catch phrases, mindless slogans, grammar slips, and spelling errors?

> **Web test:** Are words neutral ("conservative perspective") or emotionally charged ("fascist agenda")? Are pages well designed—with clear rather than flashy, distracting multimedia elements? Is the site easy to navigate?

Positive Relationship with Other Sources

Does the source disagree with other sources? If yes, is the disagreement about the facts themselves or about how to interpret the facts? Which source seems more credible?

> **Web test:** Is the site's information logically consistent with print sources? Do other reputable sites offer links to this site?

To evaluate visual resources, ask yourself the following types of questions: Is the graphic informative or merely decorative? Is the graphic manipulative in any way? What does it include or exclude? Is it well designed? And is it the product of a reliable source?

Create a working bibliography. LO2

A **working bibliography** lists sources that you have used and/or intend to use. Compiling this list helps you track your research, develop your final bibliography, and avoid plagiarism.

Building a Bibliography

Use note cards (see below), a small notebook, or a computer for your work. Research software such as TakeNote, EndNote, or Bookends Pro may prove helpful.

Include identifying information.

The explanations that follow tell you which details to include for each type of source you use. You may find it helpful later to record bibliographic details in the format of the documentation system you are expected to use—MLA or APA (pages 370–397). Also give each source a code number or letter.

Sample Working Bibliography Entries

Books: author, title and subtitle, publication details (place, publisher, date), call number

> #2
>
> Howells, Coral Ann.
>
> Alice Munro. Contemporary World Writers. Manchester and New York: Manchester UP, 1998.
>
> PS 8576.U57 Z7 1998
>
> Book provides good introduction to Alice Munro's fiction, chapters arranged by Munro's works; contains intro, conclusion, and bibliography; 1998 date means author doesn't cover Munro's recent fiction

Periodicals: author, article title, journal name, publication information (volume, number, date), page numbers, method of access (stacks, current periodical, database)

> #5
>
> Valdes, Marcela. "Some Stories Have to Be Told by Me: A Literary History of Alice Munro." Virginia Quarterly Review 82.3 (Summer 2006): 82-90.
>
> EBSCOhost Academic Search Premier http://web.ebscohost.com
>
> Article offers good introduction to Munro's life, her roots in Ontario, her writing career, and the key features of her stories

Online sources: author (if available), document title, site sponsor, database name, publication or posting date, access date, other publication information, URL

> #3
>
> "Alice Munro." Athabasca University Centre for Language and Literature: Canadian Writers. Updated 31 January 2011. Accessed 17 April 2011.
>
> http://www.athabascau.ca/writers/munro.html
>
> Site offers good introduction to Munro's writing, along with links to bibliography and other resources

Primary or field research: date conducted, name and/or descriptive title of person interviewed, place observed, survey conducted, document analyzed

> #4
>
> Thacker, Robert. E-mail interview. 7 March 2011.
>
> rthacker@mdu.edu
>
> Author of critical biography on Munro, Alice Munro: Writing Her Lives, offered really helpful insights into her creative process, especially useful for story "Carried Away"

Take notes effectively. LO3

Accurate, thoughtful notes serve as the foundation for your research writing. A good note-taking system should help you (1) work efficiently, (2) glean key information from sources, (3) engage sources critically and reflectively, and (4) record summaries, quotations, and paraphrases. Effective notes separate source material from your own ideas, which, in turn, helps you to avoid unintentional plagiarism.

Select a system.

When taking notes, think carefully about the information that you record. Each idea should clearly relate to or enhance your understanding of the topic. What you shouldn't do is simply collect quotations to plunk in your paper, gather a lot of disconnected facts and details, or create extensive notes for every source.

Four note-taking systems are outlined in this section. Choose the system that works best for your project, or combine elements to develop your own system. Be aware that one note-taking style may work better than another, depending on the discipline. For example, in a literature class, the copy-and-annotating method works especially well.

System 1: Paper or electronic note cards . . .

Using paper note cards is the traditional method of note taking; however, note-taking software is now available with most word-processing programs and with programs like TakeNote, EndNote Plus, and Bookends Pro. Here's how a note-card system works:

1. Establish one set of cards (3 × 5 inches, if paper) for your bibliography.
2. On a second set of cards (4 × 6 inches, if paper), take notes on sources:
   - Record one point from one source per card.
   - Clarify the source: List the author's last name, a shortened title, or a code from the matching bibliography card. Include a page number.
   - Provide a topic or heading: Called a slug, the topic helps you categorize and order information.
   - Label the note as a summary, paraphrase, or quotation of the original.
   - Distinguish between the source's information and your own thoughts.

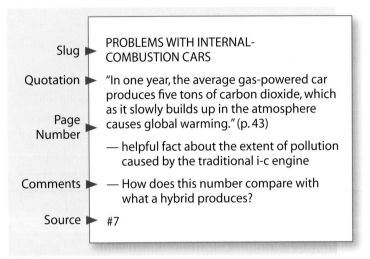

Pros & Cons: Although note cards can be initially tedious and time consuming, they are very helpful for categorizing and organizing material for an outline and a first draft.

System 2: Copy (or save) and annotate . . .

The copy-and-**annotate** method involves working with photocopies, print versions, or digital texts of sources:

1. Selectively photocopy, print, or save important sources. Copy carefully, making sure you have full pages, including the page numbers.
2. As needed, add identifying information on the copy—author, publication details, and date. Each page should be easy to identify and trace. When working with books, simply copy the title and copyright pages and keep them with the rest of your notes.
3. As you read, mark up the copy and highlight key statements. In the margins or digital file, record your ideas:
   - Ask questions. Insert a "?" in the margin, or write out the question.
   - Make connections. Draw arrows to link ideas, or make notes like "see page 36."

> **working bibliography**
> a list of sources that you have read and/or intend to use in your research
>
> **annotate**
> underline or highlight important passages in a text and make notes in the margins

- Add asides. Record what you think and feel while reading.
- Define terms. Note important words that you need to understand.
- Create a marginal index. Write key words to identify themes and main parts.

Pros & Cons: Even though organizing the various pages for drafting can be inconvenient, copying, printing, or saving gives you an accurate record of your sources. And annotating, when approached with more care than mere skimming and highlighting, encourages critical thinking.

System 3: The computer notebook or research log . . .

The computer notebook or research log method involves taking notes on a computer or on sheets of paper. Here's how it works:

1. Establish a central location for your notes—a notebook, a file folder, a binder, or an electronic folder.
2. Take notes one source at a time, making sure to identify the source fully. Number your note pages.
3. Using your initials or some other symbol, distinguish your own thoughts from source material.
4. Use codes in your notes to identify which information in the notes relates to which topic in your outline. Then, under each topic in the outline, write the page number in your notes where that information is recorded. With a notebook or log, you may be able to rearrange your notes into an outline by using copy and paste—but don't lose source information in the process!

Pros & Cons: Taking notes in this way feels natural, although using them to outline and draft may require some time-consuming paper shuffling.

System 4: The double-entry notebook . . .

The double-entry notebook involves parallel note taking—notes from sources beside your own brainstorming, reaction, and reflection. Using a notebook or the columns feature of your word-processing program, do the following:

1. Divide pages vertically.
2. In the left column, record bibliographic information and take notes on sources.
3. In the right column, write your responses. Think about what the source is saying, why the point is important, whether you agree with it, and how the point relates to other ideas and other sources.

Pros & Cons: Although organizing the double-entry notes for drafting may be challenging, this method creates accurate source records and directly engages the researcher with the material.

Bibliographic Info and Notes	Responses
Cudworth, Erika. *Environment and Society*. Routledge Introductions to Environment Series. London and New York: Routledge, 2003.	I've actually had a fair bit of personal experience with animals—the horses, ducks, dogs, and cats on our hobby farm. Will this chapter make trouble for my thinking?
Ch. 6 "Society, Culture and Nature—Human Relations with Animals"	
Chapter looks at how social scientists have understood, historically, the relationship between people and animals (158).	Yes, what really are the connections and differences between people and animals? Is it a different level of intelligence? Is there something more basic or fundamental? Are we afraid to see ourselves as animals, as creatures?
The word "animal" is itself a problem when we remember that people too are animals, but the distinction is often sharply made by people themselves (159)	
"In everyday life, people interact with animals continually" (159). Author gives many common examples.	Many examples—pets, food, TV programs, zoos—apply to me. Hadn't thought about how much my life is integrated with animal life! What does that integration look like? What does it mean for me, for the animals?

Summarize, paraphrase, and quote.

— LO4

As you work with sources, decide what to put in your notes and how to record it—as a summary, a paraphrase, or a quotation. The passage below comes from an article on GM's development of fuel-cell technology. On the following pages, note how the researchers **summarize**, **paraphrase**, and **quote** material. Then practice the same strategies in your own source notes.

Source Passage

From Burns, L. D., McCormick, J. B., and Borroni-Bird, C. E. "Vehicle of Change." *Scientific American* 287:4 (October 2002): 10 pp.

When Karl Benz rolled his Patent Motorcar out of the barn in 1886, he literally set the wheels of change in motion. The advent of the automobile led to dramatic alterations in people's way of life as well as the global economy—transformations that no one expected at the time. The ever increasing availability of economical personal transportation remade the world into a more accessible place while spawning a complex industrial infrastructure that shaped modern society.

Now another revolution could be sparked by automotive technology: one fueled by hydrogen rather than petroleum. Fuel cells—which cleave hydrogen atoms into protons and electrons that drive electric motors while emitting nothing worse than water vapor—could make the automobile much more environmentally friendly. Not only could cars become cleaner, they could also become safer, more comfortable, more personalized—and even perhaps less expensive. Further, these fuel-cell vehicles could be instrumental in motivating a shift toward a "greener" energy economy based on hydrogen. As that occurs, energy use and production could change significantly. Thus, hydrogen fuel-cell cars and trucks could help ensure a future in which personal mobility—the freedom to travel independently—could be sustained indefinitely, without compromising the environment or depleting the earth's natural resources.

A confluence of factors makes the big change seem increasingly likely. For one, the petroleum-fueled internal-combustion engine (ICE), as highly refined, reliable, and economical as it is, is finally reaching its limits. Despite steady improvements, today's ICE vehicles are only 20 to 25 percent efficient in converting the energy content of fuels into drive-wheel power. And although the U.S. auto industry has cut exhaust emissions substantially since the unregulated 1960s—hydrocarbons dropped by 99 percent, carbon monoxide by 96 percent, and nitrogen oxides by 95 percent—the continued production of carbon dioxide causes concern because of its potential to change the planet's climate.

summarize
to condense in your own words the main points in a passage

paraphrase
to put a whole passage in your own words

quotation
a word-for-word statement or passage from an original source

Summarize.

Summarizing condenses in your own words the main points in a passage. Summarize when the source provides relevant ideas and information on your topic.

1. Reread the passage, jotting down a few key words.
2. State the main point in your own words. Add key supporting points, leaving out examples, details, and long explanations. Be objective: Don't mix your reactions with the summary.
3. Check your summary against the original, making sure that you use quotation marks around any exact phrases you borrow.

Sample Summary:

While the introduction of the car in the late nineteenth century has led to dramatic changes in society and world economics, another dramatic change is now taking place in the shift from gas engines to hydrogen technologies. Fuel cells may make the car "greener," and perhaps even safer, cheaper, and more comfortable. These automotive changes will affect the energy industry by making it more environmentally friendly; as a result, people will continue to enjoy mobility while transportation moves to renewable energy. One factor leading to this technological shift is that the internal-combustion engine has reached the limits of its efficiency, potential, and development—while remaining problematic with respect to emissions, climate change, and health.

fyi For instruction on effectively integrating quotations, paraphrases, and summaries into your writing, see pages 357–359.

Paraphrase.

Paraphrasing puts a whole passage in your own words. Paraphrase passages that present key points, explanations, or arguments that are useful to your project. Follow these steps:

1. Quickly review the entire passage for a sense of the whole, and then reread it sentence by sentence.
   - State the ideas in your own words.
   - Edit for clarity, but don't change the meaning.
   - Put directly borrowed phrases in quotation marks.
2. Check your paraphrase against the original for accurate tone and meaning.

Sample Paraphrase:

The passage below paraphrases the second paragraph in the source passage on page 349.

Automobile technology may be delivering another radical economic and social change through the shift from gasoline to hydrogen fuel. By breaking hydrogen into protons and electrons so that the electrons run an electric motor with water vapor as the only the by-product, fuel cells could make the car a "green" machine. But this technology could also increase the automobile's safety, comfort, personal tailoring, and affordability. Moreover, this shift to fuel-cell engines in automobiles could lead to dramatic environmentally friendly changes in the broader energy industry, an industry that will be tied to hydrogen rather than to fossil fuels. The result of this shift will be radical changes in the way we use and produce energy. In other words, the shift to clean technology and hydrogen-powered vehicles could maintain society's valued mobility while preserving the environment and earth's natural resources.

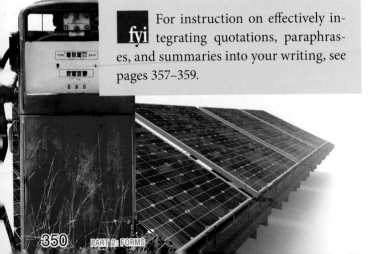

Quote.

Quoting records statements or phrases from an original source word for word. Quote nuggets only—statements that are well phrased or authoritative:

1. Note the quotation's context—how it fits in the author's discussion.

2. Copy the passage word for word, enclosing it in quotation marks and checking its accuracy.

3. If you omit words, note that omission with an ellipsis. If you change any word for grammatical reasons, enclose it in brackets. (See page 437).

Sample Quotations:

This sentence captures the authors' main claim about the benefits and future of fuel-cell technology.

"[H]ydrogen fuel-cell cars and trucks could help ensure a future in which personal mobility . . . could be sustained indefinitely, without compromising the environment or depleting the earth's natural resources."

This quotation offers a well-phrased statement about the essential problem.

"[T]he petroleum-fueled internal-combustion engine (ICE), as highly refined, reliable, and economical as it is, is finally reaching its limits."

INSIGHT Careful note taking helps prevent unintentional plagiarism. Plagiarism—using source material without giving credit—is treated more fully elsewhere (pages 354–355). But at the planning stage, you can prevent this problem by (1) maintaining an accurate working bibliography, (2) distinguishing source material from your own ideas in your notes, (3) paraphrasing, summarizing, and quoting source material selectively and accurately, and (4) clearly identifying the source of the information, including material gleaned from the Internet.

Critical-Thinking and Writing Activities

As directed by your instructor, complete the following critical-thinking and writing activities by yourself or with classmates.

1. What note-taking practices have you used for research projects in the past? Compare and contrast your practices with the guidelines outlined in this chapter: what do you plan to change?

2. Using the rating scale on page 344, find three sources on the same topic: one from a source near the top of the scale, one from the middle, and one near the bottom. Compare and contrast the types of information found in each resource, as well as the depth and reliability.

3. For your current research project, carry out the following tasks based on the results of your primary, library, and free-Web research:

   • Shape your list of resources into a working bibliography. Then add a commentary to the bibliography explaining why you believe this list to represent good, balanced research.

   • Using the instructions on evaluating sources (pages 344–345), assess the quality and reliability of three of your sources. Summarize your comparative assessment in a paragraph.

   • Summarize a passage from one of your key sources. Then choose a portion of the passage and paraphrase it. Finally, record a significant statement in the passage as a direct quotation.

Checklist: Learning Outcomes

Use the checklist below to assess what you have learned about working with sources, as well as to measure what you have accomplished on a specific project.

____ I have carefully evaluated all my sources for credible authorship, reliable publication, unbiased discussion, information currency, information accuracy, logical support, quality writing and design.

____ I have created and maintained an accurate working bibliography.

____ I have effectively taken notes from my sources using a note-taking system.

____ In my source notes, I have effectively summarized, paraphrased, and quoted relevant passages.

"Facts are stubborn things; and whatever may be our wishes, our inclinations, or the dictates of our passion, they cannot alter the state of facts and evidence."
—John Adams

28

Writing a Research Paper

In 1960, the famed **paleontologist** Louis Leakey sent his young secretary on a four-month expedition to Tanzania to observe chimpanzees in the wild. Jane Goodall was not a trained scientist, but she was a keen observer, patient and meticulous and gentle. She did something naturalists had never thought of doing. She sat still and let the animals come to her. The first chimpanzee who approached she named David Greybeard—not Specimen TZ196001. And she took extensive notes, created detailed drawings, and learned more about wild chimpanzees in four months than humanity had learned since the dawn of time.

Then Jane came back to civilization. She had so much to report, but no one would listen to a twenty-something woman with no scientific degree who lived with chimps in the wild. At Leakey's request, Jane enrolled at Cambridge and by 1965 received her Ph.D. She did her paper chase and became Dr. Jane Goodall and wrote up her findings and changed the world.

The point is this: You can do all the research you want, but until you put it into a documented form that others in your field can read and respond to, your discoveries make no impact. You have to do the paper chase. You have to document.

Writing your research paper is the culmination of your discovery process. It's the chance for you to share your discoveries and change minds. This chapter will guide you through the process.

Learning Outcomes

LO1 Avoid plagiarism.

LO2 Avoid other source abuses.

LO3 Use sources well.

LO4 Write a research paper.

LO5 Follow a model.

paleontologist
a scientist who studies life forms that lived in past geologic time

Avoid plagiarism. LO1

The road to **plagiarism** may be paved with the best intentions—or the worst. Either way, the result is a serious academic offense. As you write your research paper, do everything you can to stay off that road! Start by studying your school's and your instructor's guidelines on plagiarism and other academic offenses. Then study the following pages.

What is plagiarism?

Plagiarism is using someone else's words, ideas, or images (what's called intellectual property) so that they appear to be your own. When you plagiarize, you use source material—whether published in print or online—without acknowledging the source. In this sense, plagiarism refers to a range of thefts: submitting a paper you didn't write (even if you bought it), pasting source material into your paper and passing off that content as your own, using exact quotations without quotation marks and **documentation**, and summarizing and paraphrasing material without documentation. And plagiarism is more than "word theft." The rules also apply to images, tables, graphs, charts, maps, music, videos, and so on.

What makes it wrong?

Plagiarism is stealing, and colleges punish it as such. It may result in a failing grade for the assignment or course, a note on your **academic transcript** (often seen by potential employers), and possibly even expulsion.

Aside from the punitive aspects, plagiarism short-circuits dialogue within a discipline. It discounts the work of other thinkers, disrespects writers and readers, insults instructors, and damages the reputation of colleges.

plagiarism
presenting someone else's work or ideas as one's own

documentation
crediting sources of information through in-text citations or references and a list of works cited or references

academic transcript
the permanent record of educational achievement and activity

working bibliography
list of the sources that you have used and/or intend to use in your research

Also consider what plagiarism does to you. It prevents you from learning the skills you need to have as a scholar. It also demonstrates to others around you that you are not a serious thinker, that you aren't to be trusted, relied upon, or listened to. In short, it damages your reputation, a key component to your success academically and professionally.

What does it look like?

Plagiarism can take on a number of forms. Read the passage below and then review the four types of plagiarism that follow, noting how each misuses the source.

> What makes Munro's characters so enthralling is their inconsistency; like real people, at one moment they declare they will cover the house in new siding, at the next, they vomit on their way to the hospital. They fight against and seek refuge in the people they love. The technique that Munro has forged to get at such contradictions is a sort of pointillism, the setting of one bright scene against another, with little regard for chronology.
>
> Excerpt taken from page 87 of "Some Stories Have to Be Told by Me: A Literary History of Alice Munro," by Marcela Valdes, published in the *Virginia Quarterly Review* 82.3 (Summer 2006).

1. **Submitting another writer's paper** is the most blatant form of plagiarism. Whether the paper was written by another student, was downloaded and reformatted from the Internet, or was purchased from a "paper mill," the result is still plagiarism. Remember that though it may seem easy to plagiarize material from the Internet, it's equally easy for professors to use Internet tools to discover plagiarism.

2. **Pasting material into your paper and passing it off as your own** is another form of plagiarism. In the example below, the boldface material is plagiarized from the original article, masquerading as the writer's own idea.

> Life typically unfolds mysteriously for Munro's characters, with unexplained events and choices. **Like real people, at one moment they declare they will cover the house in new siding, at the next, they vomit on their way to the hospital.**

3. **Using material without quotation marks and citation** is another form of plagiarism. Whether you use a paragraph or a phrase, if you use the exact wording of a source, you must enclose the material in quotation marks and provide a source citation. The lack of quotation marks makes the boldface material plagiarized.

> What makes Munro's characters so typically human is that **they fight against and seek refuge in the people they love (Valdes 87).**

4. **Failing to cite a source for summarized or paraphrased ideas** is another form of plagiarism. Even if borrowed information has been re-worded, the source must be acknowledged. In the following example, the writer correctly summarizes the passage's ideas but offers no citation.

> **For the reader, the characters in Munro's stories are interesting because they are so changeable. Munro shows these changes by using a method of placing scenes side by side for contrast, without worrying about the chronological connections.**

How do I avoid it?

Of course, some types of plagiarism may happen by accident, perhaps through sloppy note taking or inexpert use of punctuation. Plagiarism is like speeding— regardless of whether the infraction was purposeful or accidental, it carries the same consequences.

Preventing plagiarism begins the moment you get an assignment. Essentially, prevention requires commitment and diligence throughout the process. Begin, of course, by pledging never to plagiarize, no matter how easy the Internet may make it. Also follow the rules established by your college and your professor.

Avoiding Plagiarism Strategy

- **As you research,** take orderly notes and maintain an accurate working bibliography. Make sure to carefully summarize, paraphrase, and quote material. (see pages 349–351.)

- **As you write,** carefully credit all material that is quoted, summarized, or paraphrased from another source. For quoted material, use quotation marks. For summaries and paraphrases, signal where borrowed material begins by using a phrase like "As Valdes notes, many of Munro's characters exhibit . . ."; then signal where the material ends by providing the source citation.

- **After you write,** compile a complete, accurate works-cited or reference list with full source information for all borrowed material in your writing.

Avoid other source abuses. LO2

Plagiarism, though the most serious offense, is not the only source abuse to avoid when writing a paper with documented research. The information that follows covers source abuses that are subtly deceptive or make for poor research writing.

Eight to Eliminate

Avoid these eight documentation pitfalls in your writing. The examples reference the excerpt on the previous page.

1. **Using sources inaccurately:** When you get a quotation wrong, botch a summary, paraphrase poorly, or misstate a statistic, you misrepresent the original. Example: In this quotation, the writer carelessly uses several wrong words that change the meaning, and also adds two words that are not in the original.

> As Marcela Valdes explains, "[w]hat makes Munro's characters so **appalling** is their **consistency. . . .** They fight against and seek **refuse** in the people **they say** they love" (87).

2. **Using source material out of context:** By ripping a statement out of its **context** and forcing it into yours, you can make a source seem to say something that it didn't really say. *Example:* This writer uses part of a statement to say the opposite of the original.

> According to Marcela Valdes, while Munro's characters are interesting, Munro's weakness as a fiction writer is that she shows "little regard for chronology" (87).

3. **Overusing source material:** When your paper reads like a string of references, especially quotations, your own thinking disappears. Example: The writer takes the source passage, chops it up, and splices it together.

> Anyone who has read her stories knows that "[w]hat makes Munro's characters so enthralling is their inconsistency." That is to say, "like real people, at one moment they declare they will cover the house in new siding, at the next, they vomit on their way to the hospital." Moreover, "[t]hey fight against and seek refuge in the people they love." This method "that Munro has forged to get at such contradictions is a sort of pointillism," meaning "the setting of one bright scene against another, with little regard for chronology" (Valdes 87).

4. **"Plunking" quotations:** You "plunk" quotations into your paper by failing both to introduce them to the reader and to provide a follow-up. The discussion becomes choppy and disconnected. Example: The writer interrupts the flow of ideas with a quotation "out of the blue." In addition, the quotation hangs at the end of a paragraph with no follow-up.

> Typically, characters such as Del Jordan, Louisa Doud, and Almeda Roth experience a crisis through contact with particular men. "They fight against and seek refuge in the people they love" (Valdes 87).

context
the set of circumstances in which a statement is made; the text and other factors that surround a specific statement and are crucial to understanding it

5. **Using "blanket" citations:** Blanket citations make the reader guess where borrowed material begins and ends. For example, if you place a parenthetical citation at the end of a paragraph, does that citation cover the whole paragraph or just the final sentence?

6. **Relying heavily on one source:** If your writing is dominated by one source, the reader may doubt the depth and integrity of your research. Instead, your writing should show your reliance on a balanced diversity of sources.

7. **Failing to match in-text citations to bibliographic entries:** All in-text citations must clearly refer to accurate entries in the works-cited, reference, or endnote pages. Mismatching occurs when (a) an in-text citation refers to a source not listed in the bibliography or (b) a bibliographic entry is never referenced in the paper itself.

8. **Violating copyrights:** When you copy, distribute, and/or post in whole or in part any intellectual property without permission from or payment to the copyright holder, you commit a copyright infringement, especially when you profit from this use. To avoid copyright violations in your research projects, follow the strategies below.

Avoiding Copyright Violations Strategy

- **Observe fair use guidelines:** Quote small portions of a document for limited purposes, such as education or research. Avoid copying large portions for your own gain.
- **Understand what's in the public domain:** You need not obtain permission to copy and use public domain materials—primarily documents created by the government, but also some material posted on the Internet as part of the "copy left" movement.
- **Observe intellectual property and copyright laws:** First, know your college's policies on copying documents. Second, realize that copyright protects the expression of ideas in a range of materials—writings, videos, songs, photographs, drawings, computer software, and so on. Always obtain permission to copy and distribute copyrighted materials.
- **Avoid changing a source** (e.g., a photo) without permission of the creator or copyright holder.

Use sources well.

After you've found good sources and taken good notes on them, you want to use that research effectively in your writing. Specifically, you want to show (1) what information you are borrowing and (2) where you got it. By doing so, you create credibility. This section shows you how to develop credibility by integrating and documenting sources so as to avoid plagiarism and other abuses. (Note: For a full treatment of documentation, see pages 370–397.)

Integrate sources.

Source material—whether summary, paraphrase, or quotation—should be integrated smoothly into your discussion. To do so, you should focus on what you want to say, not on all the sources you've collected. Use sources to deepen and develop your point, provide evidence for your argument, give authority to your position, illustrate your point, or address a counterargument.

Managing Your Sources

Failure to manage your sources will result in those sources determining the course and character of your work. Here's a pattern you can follow to make sure you control your sources, rather than letting them control you:

> **Source Management Pattern**
> **1.** State and explain your idea, creating context for the source.
> **2.** Identify and introduce the source, linking it to your discussion.
> **3.** Summarize, paraphrase, or quote the source.
> **4.** Provide a citation in an appropriate spot.
> **5.** Comment on the source by explaining, expanding on, or refuting it.
> **6.** When appropriate, refer again to a source to further develop the ideas it contains.
> (Review the keyed model that follows.)

> The motivation and urgency to cre- *1* ate and improve hybrid-electric technology comes from a range of complex forces. Some of these forces are economic, others environmental, and still others social. In *2* "Societal Lifestyle Costs of Cars with Alternative Fuels/Engines," Joan Ogden, Robert Williams, and Eric Larson argue that "[c]ontinued reliance on current transporta- *3* tion fuels and technologies poses serious oil supply insecurity, climate change, and urban air pollution risks" (7). Because of the nonre- *4* newable nature of fossil fuels as well as their *5* negative side effects, the transportation industry is confronted with making the most radical changes since the introduction of the internal-combustion automobile more than *6* 100 years ago. Hybrid-electric vehicles are one response to this pressure.

Incorporating Quotations

Be especially careful with quotations, which can overwhelm your own thinking and create a choppy flow. Use restraint. Include only quotations that are key statements by authorities, well-phrased claims and conclusions, or passages that require word-by-word analysis and interpretation. Quotations—especially long ones—need to pull their weight, so generally paraphrase or summarize source material instead.

When you do use quotations, work them into your writing as smoothly as possible, paying attention to style, punctuation, and syntax. Use enough of the quotation to make your point without changing the meaning of the original. Place quotation marks around key phrases taken from the source.

> Ogden, Williams, and Larson also conclude that the hydrogen fuel-cell vehicle is "a strong candidate for becoming the Car of the Future," given the trend toward "tighter environmental constraints" and the "intense efforts underway" by automakers to develop commercially viable versions of such vehicles (25).

Document sources.

Just as you need to integrate source material carefully into your writing, so you must also carefully document where that source material comes from. The reader should recognize which material is yours and which is not.

Identifying the Start

Sources need to be introduced. It's the introduction that signals an encounter with ideas and facts from someone other than you, the writer.

First Reference: For the first reference to a source, use an attributive statement that indicates some of the following: author's name and credentials, title of the source, nature of the study or research, and helpful background.

> **Joan Ogden, Robert Williams, and Eric Larson, members of the Princeton Environmental Institute, explain** that modest improvements in energy efficiency and emissions reductions will not be enough over the next century because of anticipated transportation increases (7).

Subsequent References: For subsequent references to a source, use a simplified **attributive phrase**, such as the author's last name or a shortened version of the title.

> **Ogden, Williams, and Larson go on to argue** that "effectively addressing environmental and oil supply concerns will probably require radical changes in automotive engine/fuel technologies" (7).

Other References: In some situations, such as quoting straightforward facts, simply skip the attributive phrase. The parenthetical citation supplies sufficient attribution.

> Various types of transportation are by far the main consumers of oil (three-fourths of world oil imports); moreover, these same technologies are responsible for one-fourth of all greenhouse gas sources (Ogden, Williams, and Larson 7).

The verb you use to introduce source material is key. Use fitting verbs, such as those in the table below. Normally, use the present tense. (Use the past tense only to stress the previous time frame of a source.)

> In their 2004 study, "Societal Lifecycle Costs of Cars with Alternative Fuels/Engines," Ogden, Williams, and Larson present a method for comparing and contrasting alternatives to internal-combustion engines. Earlier, these authors made preliminary steps . . .

Quick Guide: Introductory Verbs:

accepts	declares	points out
acknowledges	defends	praises
adds	denies	proposes
affirms	describes	refutes
argues	disagrees	rejects
asserts	discusses	reminds
believes	emphasizes	responds
cautions	enumerates	shares
claims	explains	shows
compares	highlights	states
concludes	identifies	stresses
confirms	insists	suggests
considers	interprets	supports
contradicts	lists	urges
contrasts	maintains	verifies
criticizes	outlines	warns

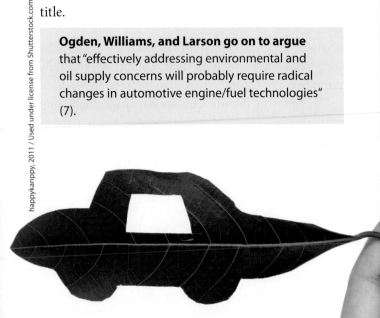

happykanppy, 2011 / Used under license from Shutterstock.com

attributive phrase
a group of words that indicates the source of an idea or a quotation

Identifying the End

Quotations and Ideas: Closing quotation marks and a citation, as shown in the following example, indicate the end of a source quotation. Generally, place the citation immediately after any quotation, paraphrase, or summary. However, you may also place the citation early in the sentence or at the end if the parenthetical note is obviously obtrusive. When you discuss several details from a page in a source, use an attributive phrase at the beginning of your discussion and a single citation at the end.

> As the "Lifestyle Costs" study concludes, when greenhouse gases, air pollution, and oil insecurity are factored into the analysis, alternative-fuel vehicles "offer lower LCCs than typical new cars" (Ogden, Williams, and Larson 25).

Longer Quotations: If a quotation is longer than four typed lines, set it off from the main text. Generally, introduce the quotation with a complete sentence and a colon. Indent the quotation one inch (10 spaces) and double-space it, but don't put quotation marks around it. Put the citation outside the final punctuation mark.

> Toward the end of the study, Ogden, Williams, and Larson argue that changes to the fuel delivery system must be factored into planning:
>
> > In charting a course to the Car of the Future, societal LCC comparisons should be complemented by considerations of fuel infrastructure requirements. Because fuel infrastructure changes are costly, the number of major changes made over time should be minimized. The bifurcated strategy advanced here—of focusing on the H2FCV for the long term and advanced liquid hydrocarbon-fueled ICEVs and ICE/HEVs for the near term—would reduce the number of such infrastructure changes to one (an eventual shift to H2). (25)

Changing Quotations: You may shorten or change a quotation so that it fits more smoothly into your sentence—but don't alter the original meaning. Use an **ellipsis** within square brackets [. . .] to indicate that you have omitted words from the original. An ellipsis is three periods with spaces between them.

> In their projections of where fuel-cell vehicles are heading, Ogden, Williams, and Larson discuss GM's AUTOnomy vehicle, with its "radical redesign of the entire car. [. . .] In these cars, steering, braking, and other vehicle systems are controlled electronically rather than mechanically" (24).

Using Brackets: Use square brackets to indicate a clarification, to change a pronoun or verb tense, or to switch around uppercase and lowercase.

> As Ogden, Williams, and Larson explain, "[e]ven if such barriers [the high cost of fuel cells and the lack of an H2 fuel infrastructure] can be overcome, decades would be required before this embryonic technology could make major contributions in reducing the major externalities that characterize today's cars" (25).

ellipsis
a set of three periods with one space preceding and following each period; a punctuation mark that indicates deletion of material

OlgaLis, 2011 / Used under license from Shutterstock.com

Write a research paper.

LO4

Writing Guidelines

Your research may generate a mass of notes, printouts, photocopies, electronic files, and more. Your goal is to move from this mass to a coherent structure for the paper you need to write. If you have systematically taken good notes, you are well on the way. Follow the guidelines below to move toward order.

1. **Review your research materials.** Is the information complete or at least sufficient for the project? Is the information reliable and accurate? How do different pieces of evidence connect to each other? What patterns do you see? By reviewing your research once, twice, and even three times, you'll begin to see your research paper taking shape before you.

2. **Revisit your research questions and working thesis.** Has research changed your perspective and position? Revise your thesis accordingly. A solid thesis gives you a road map for writing your paper.

3. **Organize your work effectively.** Reread the assignment, which may suggest a pattern of organization, such as comparison-contrast. If not, use a pattern of organization suggested by your thesis and support. Turn key ideas into main headings and arrange support and evidence under each. After categorizing information, decide on the best sequence for your ideas. The following quick guide explains some common organizational patterns available to you.

Quick Guide: Organizational Patterns:

Argumentation asserts and supports a claim, counters opposition, and reasserts the claim.

Cause-effect explores the factors that lead to an event and the consequences that result from it.

Chronological order puts items in a time sequence.

Classification groups details based on common traits or qualities.

Comparison-contrast shows similarities and differences between two subjects.

Description orders details in terms of spatial relationships.

Explanation clarifies how something works by breaking the object or phenomenon into parts or phases and showing how they work together.

Order of importance arranges items from most to least or least to most important.

Problem-solution states a problem, explores its causes and effects, and presents solutions.

Question-answer moves back and forth from questions to answers in a sequence that logically clarifies a topic.

4. **Develop your first draft.** As you write your paper, your main goal is to develop and support your ideas, referring to sources but not being dominated by them. Your second goal is to respect sources by integrating them naturally and accurately, with correct documentation. (Review pages 357–359 to understand how to use source material.) Make sure to indicate the source of all borrowed ideas and quotations as you develop the following parts:

Opening. Start by saying something interesting or surprising to gain your reader's attention. Then establish common ground with your reader and the topic, and identify a specific issue or challenge. Finally, offer your thesis.

Middle. Develop your thesis by presenting each main point, expanding upon the points logically, including evidence such as facts and examples, and analyzing each issue. Think of each main point as a conversation you are having with your reader, in which you share the most interesting, amazing, and salient aspects of each point. Don't try to cram everything you have learned into the draft.

Closing. Review or tie together important points in your paper, reinforce your thesis, and draw a conclusion. In closing, expand the scope of your text by connecting the topic of the paper to the reader's experience or to life in general.

5. **Revise your first draft.** Ask a peer to read your first draft and indicate any parts that could be improved. Reread your draft as well, and use the following questions to help you revise it.

Checklist: Revising

- ✔ Is my thesis clear?
- ✔ Do I support the thesis with strong main points?
- ✔ Do I support the main points with evidence and analysis?
- ✔ Have I used an organizational plan that fits the assignment, my topic, and purpose?
- ✔ Do the main points appear in the best order?
- ✔ Are the paragraphs (and the sentences within them) in the best order?
- ✔ Is my writing voice objective and scholarly, focused on the topic?
- ✔ Is my writing voice knowledgeable and engaging?
- ✔ Have I selected strong words and correctly used topic-specific terms?
- ✔ Do my sentences read smoothly?

6. **Edit your paper.** Once you have finished making large-scale improvements to your paper, it's time to edit your work and create a works-cited or reference section. Use the following questions to help you edit your work.

Checklist: Editing

- ✔ Have I correctly punctuated sentences and abbreviations?
- ✔ Have I used correct capitalization with proper nouns?
- ✔ Have I double-checked the spelling of all specialized words, authors' names, and titles?
- ✔ Have I watched for easily confused words (*there, their, they're*)?
- ✔ Have I carefully checked the format of each in-text citation or reference? (See pages 374–380.)
- ✔ Have I carefully checked the format of each entry in my works-cited or reference section? (See pages 379–380.)

7. **Design your paper.** The two major documentation styles (MLA and APA) have strict requirements for the final presentation of a research report. Make certain that your paper follows the appropriate style and abides by any guidelines your instructor may have provided.

fyi The paper on the following pages shows MLA format and documentation. For more on both MLA and APA systems, see the following chapter, pages 370–397.)

Follow a model. LO5

Stevie Jeung wrote the following research paper for an American Studies course focusing on crime and punishment in America. The paper examines cultural perceptions of a condemned prisoner's last meal. Because this paper focuses on a humanities topic, Jeung used MLA style for format and documentation. As you read her paper, study her reasoning, her use of sources, and her documentation practices.

Jeung 1

Stevie Jeung **(A)**

Professor Sasha Abramsky

American Studies 101D

17 February 2008

"I Did *Not* Get My Spaghetti-O's": **(B)**

Death Row Consumption in the Popular Media

Jesus Christ: Roast lamb, matzo, wine; around AD 30. Perry Smith and Richard Hickock: **(C)** Identical meals of shrimp, French fries, garlic bread, ice cream and strawberries with whipped cream; 1965. Timothy McVeigh: Two pints of Ben & Jerry's mint chocolate chip ice cream: 2001. Tony Soprano: Holsten's onion rings; 2007. Karl Chamberlein: final meal yet to be consumed; 15 days from now.

While executions historically demand a certain degree of morbid curiosity, the last meals of **(D)** the condemned seem to stimulate heightened interest. Indeed, a prisoner's final feast has almost become an event in its own right, not only for the prisoner, but for the prison staff and the public. Web sites, novels, movies, television shows, newspapers, and even cookbooks report, dissect, criticize, and speculate regarding last meals real and imagined. When confronted with the **(E)** ultimate consumption of dying people in so many areas of our popular media, the truth becomes alarmingly clear: This is odd behavior. There must be some reason that we institutionally allow our most hated and feared prisoners to choose and enjoy their final meal before we execute them, and there must be some reason that we like to watch and reproduce the event in popular culture.

The last meal appears in almost every major arena of public entertainment. In *The Green* **(F)** *Mile,* a motion picture based on Stephen King's novel of the same name, protagonist John Coffey is wrongfully executed in a heartbreaking, dramatic scene, but not before careful thought about his last meal: "Meatloaf be nice. Mashed taters with gravy. Okra, maybe. I's not picky." Prisoners

---

(A) The heading (in MLA format) supplies identifying details.
(B) The title (centered) indicates the paper's topic and theme.
(C) The writer opens with a chronological catalog of executed people and last suppers.

(D) The intro zeros in on the topic, focuses on what is odd or difficult to explain, and announces a search for explanations.
(E) The analysis focuses on specific examples in film and television.
(F) Because the film title is identified in the sentence, an in-text citation isn't needed.

are also served their last meals on the small screen. Take, for example, FOX's network TV show, *Prison Break,* in which Lincoln Burrows is served his last blueberry pancakes ("Sleight of Hand"). In fact, on an episode of *The Simpsons,* a staple of American television, Homer eats Hans Moleman's last meal of lobster tail and raspberry tort just before Hans is executed, protesting, "But he ate my last meal!" ("Springfield Connection"). Clearly, this animated man **(G)** did not think it right to be executed without enjoying his final choice of cuisine. Of course, his expression of outrage is followed by, "Are you really allowed to execute people in local jail?" reminding us that *The Simpsons,* however rich with American icons, is not real. Regardless of actual death row ceremony, the Americans who produce and consume these works of fiction expect that a special meal accompanies execution.

Compulsory inclusion of a last meal in fictional executions is one thing, but our fascination does not stop there. Where convicts are executed, the state documents and even publishes **(H)** details of the last meal and last words before they administer capital punishment. Until recently, Texas, the number one execution state, posted prisoners' last meals on their Justice Department's Web site ("Death Row"). They discontinued this practice for unclear reasons, **(I)** but the archived lists from 2003 and earlier are still readily available, and the department continues to publish names, execution dates, case records, and even pictures of the dead and soon-to-be-dead (like Karl Chamberlain, mentioned above). Oklahoma, ranked third among execution states, takes a more voyeuristic approach: "the local newspaper [prints] a blow-by-blow account. Time of injection. Facial expressions. Final meal requests" ("Artist"). While this might seems like a gruesome practice on the state's part, the public does not shy away. In fact, commercial reproduction of this information proves that it's not just reporting; it's entertainment.

It is evident not only that people read this stuff, but that they actually use available **(J)** execution and last-meal information to create and market their own masterpieces of morbid exposition. It becomes at once blatantly, amusingly, and disgustingly clear when you stumble across Web sites like *Last Suppers: Famous Final Meals from Death Row, Meals to Die For,* and **(K)** *Dead Man Eating,* which faithfully posts the last meal (along with "the skinny" on the day's events and case details) of every person executed in the United States since 2002. The most

---

(G) A direct quotation is placed within quotation marks.
(H) The analysis turns to real executions and state practices.
(I) An in-text citation uses a shortened title and no page number for a government Web page.

(J) The writer explores the presence of "last supper" interest on the Web, using concrete details and examples.
(K) Free-Web resources (fitting the cultural focus of the essay) function as primary sources showing society's fascination with last meals. The sources are all clearly identified.

shocking part is that the *Dead Man Eating* Web site also sells t-shirts, coffee mugs, and even thong underwear, all of which read "Dead Man Eating: looking for a killer meal?" and feature a crude drawing of a dead man hanging with an ice cream cone in his hand. A more tasteful, if just as morbid, strategy is to publish a "last meal" cookbook or coffee table book. A quick search for "last meal" on Amazon.com yields at least four such books (along with Snoop Dogg's album entitled *Tha Last Meal*). According to its description, one of the books, *Last Suppers: Famous Final Meals from Death Row,* both lists the gritty details of last meals and uses the public's "appetite" for this last-minute courtesy to comment on the death penalty. The book *Meals to Die For* comes from Brian D. Price, a former inmate who personally cooked eleven years' worth of final meals for Texas death row inmates. It reveals recipes, pictures, and even hand-written last-meal requests he received during his incarceration. The last things that our allegedly deadliest murderers eat, then, are not only published for the public, but published *again* with extra details for *sale* to the public. This doubly-consuming public just eats this stuff up. **(L)**

The more closely we look at it, the more bizarre this cycle of consumption and death appears: a man kills, he eats, we kill him, and then we eat it up. Where does it really begin, though? The "last meal" has a symbolic and ritualistic significance since, well, Jesus and the Last Supper (Peck). At some point, between Jesus and today's American mega-prisons, we began to recognize the last meal as a ritual of institutionalized execution. **(M)**

Since the early nineteenth century, Americans have been fascinated with not just execution, but the ritual of a condemned criminal's last day. A large crowd would turn up to hear the death warrant, sermon, and last words before a hood was slipped over the offender's head and he or she was hanged by the neck. Still more people read the details of the execution as it was published, and "if the offender could not or would not utter any memorable last words, the publisher had no compunction against compositing them" (Atwell 8). The 1840s brought the **(N)** American death penalty's first decline in a trend of fluctuating popularity that would continue to the present day, but wherever there was a spectacle, there was an audience. As the death penalty remained popular in the South, so did reporting the last days of convicts in gross detail.

Each of the states that employ capital punishment uses its own set of rules and procedures.

(L) The analysis draws conclusions from the examples discussed.

(M) With a question, the writer explores possible origins of the phenomenon, and offers a chronological survey.

(N) As the analysis deepens, Jeung refers to scholarly sources, using direct quotation when appropriate and in-text citations noting author and page number.

Some states enforce a price limit, while Texas limits a last meal to the things accessible by the regular prison kitchen staff. In 1995, the Federal Government administered its first execution since 1969. Timothy McVeigh's execution prompted development of a 56-page "Execution Protocol," "meant to ensure that all executions are carried out 'in an efficient and humane manner.'" This document clearly outlines a last meal choice as a scheduled step in the execution process: "At least seven days prior to the execution, the warden or designee will contact the condemned individual to arrange for his/her last meal," and "The condemned individual will be served a final meal at a time determined by the warden" between twelve and three hours prior to the execution (qtd. in Fritsch). In Texas, the meal would be ready at 3:45 p.m. and delivered at 4 p.m., two hours before lethal injection. This last tray of food, which would become very public following the execution, was covered in paper "for privacy" (Price). Although an inmate could request anything, he or she often received something different: "The local newspaper would always say they got 24 tacos and 12 enchiladas, but they would actually get four tacos and two enchiladas" ("Confessions"). After all of this procedure, the report sensationalizes the last meal, much as early publications sensationalized the last words.

So why does the state even allow a last meal? Bob Greene argues that "inviting" prisoners to choose a last meal is "hypocritical and insulting to the memory of the victims" because, he poignantly argues, murderers take that foresight and choice from their victims. Perhaps, Tony Karon of *TIME* suggests, the prisoners accept a last bit of freedom and humanity to make up for the "grim act of violence of the state" that is about to occur. Especially considering that prisoners don't always get what they ask for, this seems unlikely. Daniel LaChance notices that although execution practices have historically moved toward anonymity and bureaucracy, the last meal and final speech have incongruently been sustained. His recent paper, "Last Words, Last Meals, and Last Stands: Agency and Individuality in the Modern Execution Process," argues that in giving the prisoners choice in their final meals and words, the state portrays them as autonomous agents who have chosen their deeds and accepted their fates. In other words, the prison system denies a prisoner individuality until his or her last day of life in order to feel righteousness in executing him or her (LaChance). As Sasha Abramsky points out, in the midst of a vengeful prison system this makes perfect sense. It is much more satisfying to exact revenge on a person than on a number. In fact, despite the moves toward more humane

(O)

(P)

(Q)

(R)

(O) The analysis compares and contrasts the capital-punishment practices of different government bodies (federal, states).
(P) The citation indicates that the source was quoted in another source.

(Q) A "why" question pushes forward the analysis; to answer the question, Jeung fluently uses a variety of different sources.
(R) Disagreeing with one source's explanation, the writer turns to another source.

and less painful execution, the state can treat mentally ill patients with antipsychotics so that they're "sane enough to be executed" ("Confessions"). Clearly, the "ideal candidate" is an irredeemable individual, sane enough both to feel and participate in the death. In other words, if candidates can choose the last thing they eat, they must have chosen to murder, in which case they deserve to die. Furthermore, resemblance to the biblical Last Supper might justify vengeful treatment in the name of religion, especially for prison staff like Oscar Dees, who believed that God intended him to punish criminals. This powerful, righteous moral logic is published and extended to the public, creating a sense of justice that maintains support for the death penalty. As in *Cool Hand Luke*, this public spectacle of punishment and revenge is a self-serving institution of the prison system itself.

(S)

The public, however, has its own incentives for gobbling it all up, so to speak. Revenge is probably one of them, as is pure, unabashed voyeurism. American people tend to take the idea of the last meal to heart, though, and somehow make it their own. Many visitors to the *Dead Man Eating* Web site and message boards all over the internet do this by submitting their own "last meal requests," as if they were going to die tomorrow. Apparently, then, this fixation on the last meal is not limited to intrusive consumption of execution records; it extends to the public and their own final food choices. In fact, the subject of hypothetical last meals has given this icon of criminality and death a fresh, not-so-morbid vantage point. James L. Dickerson's book, *Last Suppers: If the world ended tomorrow, what would be your last meal?* asks popular celebrities and political figures to divulge their last meal of choice. Bill Clinton, for instance, would like to enjoy chicken enchiladas before his hypothetical death (117), and professional football coach Mike Ditka (22) fancies pigs in a blanket. *My Last Supper,* by Melanie Dunea, asks the same of chefs.

(T)

(U)

Still others forego the macabre enjoyment and the distant speculation and use the vivid image of eating for the last time to protest the death penalty through art. Photographer Jacquelyn C. Black organizes pictures of inmates and their meals in a book entitled *Last Meal*, in which she also includes statistics. According to the publisher's description, for example, 10 of the 12 states without the death penalty have homicide rates below the national average. University of Oklahoma professor Julie Green paints a series of dinner plates, each depicting

(V)

(S) The writer analyzes the moral psychology of the execution rituals, including the last meal.

(T) Jeung turns her attention to the motivations of the public in its obsession with last meals and other execution details.

(U) The writer summarizes sources.

(V) The writer turns to artistic renderings of last meals, works that make political statements.

what was on the last plate of a particular inmate. Reading about the executions in the newspaper "humanized death row" for her and struck her as an invasion of privacy ("Artist"). Whether they seek revenge or redemption, Americans see the last meal as a symbol in the life-or-death of justice, on death row and in their living rooms. **(W)**

The final episode of *The Sopranos* illustrates the place of "The Last Supper," generally speaking, in the American psyche. Mob leader Tony Soprano sits down at Holsten's diner in New Jersey and tension builds around him as the other characters bustle about in their respective scenes. The viewer gets the distinct feeling that they are preparing to kill Tony, who looks nervous, as though he knows that his criminal career is about to end in execution. Tony's family arrives at the diner and as he offers a basket of onion rings around the table, and before we find out whether or not he dies, the scene cuts to black ("Made in America"). The end. No more Tony, no more *Sopranos*. This could just be another cliffhanger, but many fans see it as Tony's "Last Supper," and "If Holsten's onion rings—round, crunchy, and, according to one influential diner, the best in the state—didn't symbolize communion wafers, as some viewers of the final scene of *The Sopranos* have theorized, they do now" (Hyman). The point is that the subsequent pilgrimage to Holsten's taken by many fans of the show proves one of two things. Either a) the mega-hit show *did* intend to showcase a symbolic "last meal" for its main character, or b) all of these people are making it up. Either case gives powerful support to the idea that this last ritual of consumption is popularly recognized as the appropriate ending to a life, whether fictional, criminal, or biblical. **(X)**

The interplay between the public, the media, and the criminal justice system gives the last meal a unique importance to each. The criminal system perpetuates the tradition in its own interest and uses the media to lend righteousness to its questionable and somewhat manipulative actions, but the media and the public interact to derive much greater religious, social, emotional, and political meaning, thus creating a pervasive and lasting icon which permeates popular culture and popular perception. Thomas J. Grasso, executed by lethal injection in Oklahoma (1995), seemed to appreciate the significance of a last meal in the public eye when he gave his last speech: "I did not get my Spaghetti-O's, I got spaghetti. I want the press to know this" ("Last Words").

(W) Exploring an example from television, the writer pulls together the strands of her analysis.

(X) In her conclusion, the writer answers her original questions and offers a final quotation that drives home her point and harkens back to her title.

Works Cited (A)

Abramsky, Sasha. *American Furies: Crime, Punishment, and Vengeance in the Age of Mass Imprisonment*. Boston: Beacon Press, 2007. Print.

"Artist serves 'Last Supper' on plates." *Lawrence Journal*. 29 Oct. 2006. Web. 5 Feb. 2008.

Atwell, Mary Welek. *Evolving Standards of Decency: Popular Culture and Capital Punishment*. New York: Peter Lang, 2004. Print.

"Confessions of a Death Row Chef." *The Observer*. 14 March 2004. Web. 5 Feb. 2008. (B)

"Death Row Information." *Texas Department of Criminal Justice*. 7 Nov 2007. Web. 5 Feb. 2008.

Dickerson, James L. *Last Suppers: If the world ended tomorrow, what would be your last meal?* USA: Citadel, 2004. Print.

Fritsch, Jane. "Word for Word/Execution Protocol; Please Order Your Last Meal Seven Days in Advance." *The New York Times*. 22 April 2001. Web. 5 Feb. 2008. (C)

The Green Mile. Dir. Frank Darabont. Perf. Tom Hanks, Michael Clarke Duncan, David Morse, and Bonnie Hunt. Castle Rock, 1999. Film.

Greene, Bob. "They didn't get to choose their last meals." *Jewish World Review*. 12 June 2001. Web. 5 Feb. 2008.

Hyman, Vicki. "Chewing Over Tony's Last Meal." *The Star Ledger*. 23 June 2007. Web. 5 Feb. 2008.

Karon, Tony. "Why We're Fascinated by Death Row Cuisine." *TIME*. 10 August 2000. Web. 5 Feb. 2008.

LaChance, Daniel. "Last Words, Last Meals, and Last Stands: Agency and Individuality in the Modern Execution Process." *Law & Social Inquiry* 32 (2007): 701-724. JSTOR. Web. 5 Feb. 2008. (D)

(A) The list of works cited begins on a separate page and includes the title, header, and page number.

(B) The paper's bibliography lists a range of scholarly books, trade books, scholarly articles, popular articles, and Web sites on the topic.

(C) Sources are listed in alphabetical order by author (or by title if no author is given) and identified by medium.

(D) Quotation marks and italics are properly used with titles, as are punctuation and abbreviations.

"Last Words on Death Row." *CNN: The Best of Court TV.* 31 Dec. 2007. Web. 5 Feb. 2008. **(E)**

"Made in America." *The Sopranos.* Dir. David Chase. HBO. 10 June 2007. Television.

Peck, John. "Last Meals." *Tuscon Weekly.* 5 Jan. 2006. Print. 5 Feb. 2008.

Price, Brian D. *Meals to Die For.* USA: Dyna-Paige Corporation, 2001. Print. **(F)**

"Sleight of Hand." *Prison Break.* Dir. Dwight Little. Fox Network. 7 Nov. 2005. Television.

"The Springfield Connection." *The Simpsons.* Dir. Mark Kirkland. Fox Network. 7 May 1995.

   Television.

(E) Items are double-spaced throughout. Second and subsequent lines are indented (hanging indent).

(F) Each entry provides complete identifying information, properly formatted.

Reading for Better Writing

Working by yourself or with a group, do the following:

1. How did reading Jeung's paper on last meals contribute to your understanding of crime and punishment?

2. What types of evidence does Jeung use in her paper? Where has she gotten her evidence? Are her resources reliable?

3. How does Jeung distinguish her own thinking from source material? Why are these strategies necessary?

Critical-Thinking and Writing Activities

As directed by your instructor, complete the following critical-thinking and writing activities.

1. With some classmates, debate the seriousness of plagiarism and the use of tools such as Turnitin.com.

2. Closely examine one of your most recent research papers. Have you followed this chapter's guidelines for treating sources in a research paper? How might the paper be strengthened?

Checklist: Learning Outcomes

Use the checklist below to assess what you have learned about writing a research paper, as well as to measure what you have accomplished on a specific project.

_____ I know what constitutes plagiarism and how to avoid it.

_____ I understand and can avoid other source abuses, such as inaccurate use of sources, taking sources out of context, overusing source material, dropping in quotations, and over-reliance on a single source.

_____ I effectively use sources in my research writing by smoothly integrating them and correctly documenting them.

_____ I have written, revised, and edited a quality research paper.

_____ I have learned helpful strategies from the student model in the chapter.

"The palest ink is better than the best memory."

—Chinese Proverb

29

MLA and APA Styles

In research papers, it is commonly said, "You are commanded to borrow but forbidden to steal." To borrow ideas while avoiding plagiarism (see pages 354-355), you must not only mention the sources you borrow from but also document them completely and accurately. You must follow to the last dot the format and documentation conventions required for your paper.

The two styles most frequently used in college have been developed by the Modern Language Association (MLA) and the American Psychological Association (APA). Whereas MLA is used most frequently in the Humanities, APA is typically used in the Social Sciences—with each system reflecting the specific concerns of the disciplines involved. The systems are similar, however, in that both require (1) parenthetical citations within the body of the paper and (2) a final listing of all resources cited in the paper.

In this chapter, we provide you with instructions for using those two styles to format your research paper pages and to document your sources within the text of your paper and at its end. To best illuminate the rationale of each style, we compare them side by side throughout the chapter. In those few cases where one style calls for an item not covered by the other (as in MLA's standard for short verse citations, a source not likely to be used in APA), we have called out that information in a separate box.

As anyone who has studied a foreign tongue can attest, one's native language is revealed in a brand-new way by comparison. Contrast makes things clear. That has been our goal in presenting MLA and APA styles side by side in this chapter.

Learning Outcomes

LO1 Learn the basics of MLA and APA styles.

LO2 Understand in-text citations.

LO3 List books and other nonperiodical documents.

LO4 List print periodical articles.

LO5 List online sources.

LO6 List other sources.

LO7 Follow format guidelines for MLA and APA.

Learn the basics of
MLA and APA style. LO1

While the rest of this chapter details in-text citations, works-cited and reference entries, and format issues, this page and the next answer frequently asked questions regarding MLA and APA style.

Is a separate title page required?

MLA **No** (unless your instructor requires one). On the first page of a research paper, type your name, your instructor's name, the course name and number, and the date, one below the other. The title comes next, centered. Then simply begin the text on the next line.

APA **Yes.** Include your paper's title, your name, and the name of your school on three separate lines, double-spaced, centered, and beginning approximately one-third of the way down from the top of the page. Place the running head (an abbreviated title) in the upper right corner, and the page number 1 in the upper right.

Is an abstract required?

MLA **No.** An abstract (a summary of your research paper) is not an MLA requirement.

APA **Usually.** An APA-style abstract is a paragraph summarizing your research paper. It is 150 to 250 words long. (See page 390.) Place your abstract on a new page and label it "Abstract" (centered); place the running head in the upper right corner, and the page number 2 in the upper right.

Is the research paper double-spaced?

MLA **Yes.** Double-space everything, even tables, captions, long quotations, or works-cited entries.

APA **Yes.** Double-space all text lines, titles, headings, quotations, captions, and references.

Are page numbers required?

MLA **Yes.** Pages should be numbered consecutively in the upper right corner, one-half inch from the top and flush with the right margin (one inch). Your last name should precede the page number.

APA **Yes.** Page numbers appear at the top right margin, above the first line of text; but do not include your name. Instead, place the running head in the upper right corner.

What about longer quotations?

MLA Do not use quotation marks. (1) Indent verse quotations of more than three lines one inch (ten spaces). Each line of a poem or play begins a new line of the quotation. (2) When quoting prose that needs more than four typed lines, indent each line one inch (ten spaces) from the left margin. (3) To quote two or more paragraphs, further indent the first line of each paragraph a quarter-inch (three spaces). However, if the first sentence quoted does not begin a paragraph, do not indent it; use the additional indent only on the first lines of the successive paragraphs.

APA Type quotations of 40 or more words in block style (all lines flush left) one-half inch (five spaces) in from the left margin. Indent the first lines of any additional paragraphs in the long quotation one-half inch (five spaces) in from the margin set for the quotation.

Is an appendix required?

MLA **No.** In MLA style, tables and illustrations are placed as close as possible to the related text.

APA **Maybe.** While tables and figures already appear on separate pages, one or more appendices may also be used to supplement the text of the paper.

How wide should the margins be?

MLA Top, bottom, left, and right margins should be one inch (except for page numbering). Do not justify lines, but rather leave the right margin ragged with no word breaks at the ends of lines.

APA Leave a margin of at least one inch on all four sides. Do not justify lines, but rather leave the right margin ragged with no word breaks at the ends of lines.

Are references placed in the text?

MLA **Yes.** Indicate only page numbers parenthetically if you identify the author in your text. Give the author's last name in a parenthetical reference if it is not mentioned in the text.

Example, author identified in the text:

Galuszka notes that minorities have limited opportunities for training in this field (9).

Example, author cited in parentheses:

Minorities currently have limited opportunities for training in this field (Galuszka 9).

APA **Yes.** Include the author's last name and the year, separated by a comma; for quotations, add the page number after a comma and "p."

Example without quotation:

Game-design training opportunities are limited for minorities (Galuszka, 2009).

Example with quotation:

"Few historically Black colleges and universities offer much in the way of computer gaming" (Galuszka, 2009, p. 9).

Is a list of sources used in the paper required?

MLA **Yes.** Full citations for all sources used (e.g., books, periodicals) are placed in an alphabetized list labeled "Works Cited" at the end of the paper, providing full publication details for each work cited in the report. Hanging indentation is required for the entries in this works-cited list.

Example:

Galuszka, Peter. "Getting into the Game." *Diverse: Issues in Higher Education* 19 Mar. 2009: 9–10. Print.

APA **Yes.** Full citations for all sources used (books, periodicals, and so on) are placed in an alphabetized list labeled "References" at the end of the paper, providing full publication details for each work referenced in the report. Hanging indentation is the standard format.

Example:

Galuszka, P. (2009, March 19). Getting into the game. *Diverse: Issues in Higher Education, 26*(3), 9-10.

What about headings?

MLA MLA style does not specify a particular format for headings within the text; normally, headings are used only for separate sections of the paper ("Works Cited" or "Notes," for example).

APA Headings, like an outline, show the organization of your APA paper and the importance of each topic. All topics of equal importance should have headings of the same level, or style. Below are the various levels of headings used in APA papers.

Level 1:	**Centered, Boldface, Uppercase and Lowercase Heading**
Level 2:	**Flush Left, Boldface, Uppercase and Lowercase Heading**
Level 3:	**Indented, boldface, lowercase paragraph heading ending with a period.**
Level 4:	***Indented, boldface, italicized, lowercase paragraph heading ending with a period.***

Are reference markers needed if I submit my paper electronically?

MLA **Yes.** Number (in brackets) each paragraph at its beginning, followed by a space before starting the text.

APA **No.** APA style does not call for reference markers, but double-check with your instructor or publisher about acceptable file formats for any tables or figures.

Are there any other special instructions?

Always ask whether your school, department, or instructor has special requirements that may take precedence over the guidelines listed here.

Understand in-text citations.

As a general rule, keep citations brief and integrate them smoothly into your writing. When paraphrasing or summarizing, make it clear where your borrowing begins and ends. Use stylistic cues to distinguish the source's thoughts ("Kalmbach points out . . . ," "Some critics argue . . . ") from your own ("I believe . . . ," "It seems obvious, however . . ."). See page 357 for more on integrating sources. Make sure each in-text citation clearly points to an entry in your list of sources. The identifying information (usually the author's last name) must be the word or words by which the entry is alphabetized in that list. When using a shortened title of a work, begin with the word by which the work is alphabetized in your list of sources (e.g., "Egyptian, Classical," for "Egyptian, Classical, and Middle Eastern Art"). When including a parenthetical citation at the end of a sentence, place it before the end punctuation. (See page 373.)

MLA Note When citing inclusive page numbers larger than ninety-nine, MLA calls for giving only the two digits of the second number (*Augustyn* 113–14; not *Augustyn* 113–114).

Note: The following pages illustrate the most common citation forms. Refer to this information as you build your draft.

One Author: A Complete Work

MLA You do not need an in-text citation if you identify the author in your text. (This is the preferred way of citing a complete work.) Do not offer page numbers when citing complete works, articles in alphabetized encyclopedias, one-page articles, and unpaginated sources.

> In *No Need for Hunger,* Robert Spitzer recommends that the U.S. government develop a new foreign policy to help Third World countries overcome poverty and hunger.

However, you must give the author's last name in an in-text citation if it is not mentioned in the text.

> *No Need for Hunger* recommends that the U.S. government develop a new foreign policy to help Third World countries overcome poverty and hunger (Spitzer).

When a source is listed in your works-cited page with an editor, a translator, a speaker, or an artist, instead of the author, use that person's name in your citation.

APA The correct form for a parenthetical reference to a single source by a single author is parenthesis, last name, comma, space, year of publication, parenthesis.

> . . . in this way, the public began to connect certain childhood vaccinations with an autism epidemic (Baker, 2008).

If the author is identified in your text, include the year in parentheses immediately after.

> Dohman (2009) argues that parents of affected children . . .

One Author: Part of a Work

MLA List the necessary page numbers in parentheses if you borrow words or ideas from a particular source. Leave a space between the author's last name and the page reference. No abbreviation or punctuation is needed. (The first example below identifies the author in text, the second in parentheses.)

> Bullough writes that genetic engineering was dubbed "eugenics" by a cousin of Darwin's, Sir Francis Galton, in 1885 (5).
>
> Genetic engineering was dubbed "eugenics" by a cousin of Darwin's, Sir Francis Galton, in 1885 (Bullough 5).

APA When you cite a specific part of a source, give the page, paragraph, or chapter, using the appropriate abbreviation (*p.* or *pp., para.*) or word (*chapter*). Always give the page number for a direct quotation.

> …while a variety of political and scientific forces were at work in the developing crisis, it was parents who pressed the case "that autism had become epidemic and that vaccines were its cause" (Baker, 2008, p. 251).

Two or More Works by the Same Author(s)

MLA In addition to the author's last name(s) and page number(s), include a shortened version of the work's title when you cite two or more works by the same author(s).

> Wallerstein and Blakeslee claim that divorce creates an enduring identity for children of the marriage (*Unexpected Legacy* 62).
>
> They are intensely lonely despite active social lives (Wallerstein and Blakeslee, *Second Chances* 51).

APA If the same author has published two or more articles in the same year, avoid confusion by placing a small letter *a* after the year for the first work listed in the reference list, *b* after the year for the next one, and so on. Alphabetize by title.

> **Parenthetical Citation:**
> Reefs harbor life forms heretofore unknown (Milius, 2001a, 2001b).
>
> **References:**
> Milius, D. (2001a). Another world hides inside coral reefs. *Science News, 160*(16), 244.
>
> Milius, D. (2001b). Unknown squids—with elbows—tease science. *Science News, 160*(24), 390.

Works by Authors with the Same Last Name

MLA When citing different sources by authors with the same last name, it is best to use the authors' full names in the text to avoid confusion. If circumstances call for parenthetical references, add each author's first initial. If first initials are the same, use each author's full name.

> Some critics think *Titus Andronicus* too abysmally melodramatic to be a work of Shakespeare (A. Parker 73). Others suggest that Shakespeare meant it as black comedy (D. Parker 486).

APA When citing different sources by authors with the same last name, add the authors' initials to avoid confusion, even if the publication dates are different.

> While J. D. Wallace (2005) argued that privatizing social security would benefit only the wealthiest citizens, others such as E. S. Wallace (2006) supported greater control for individuals.

Works by Multiple Authors

MLA When citing a work by **two or three authors,** give the last names of every author in the same order that they appear in the works-cited section. (The correct order of the authors' names can be found on the title page of the book.)

> Students learned more than a full year's Spanish in ten days using the complete supermemory method (Ostrander and Schroeder 51).

When citing a work by **four or more authors,** give the first author's last name as it appears in the works-cited section, followed by "et al." (meaning "and others").

> Communication on the job is more than talking; it is "inseparable from your total behavior" (Culligan et al. 111).

APA When citing from **two to five authors,** all must be mentioned in the first text citation. The last two authors' names are always separated by a comma and an ampersand (&) when enclosed in parentheses.

> Love changes not just who we are, but who we can become, as well (Lewis, Amini, & Lannon, 2000).

Subsequently, for works with **two authors,** *list both in every citation.* For works with **three to five authors,** *list all only the first time;* after that, use only the name of the first author followed by "et al.," like this:

> These discoveries lead to the hypothesis that love actually alters the brain's structure (Lewis et al., 2000).

If your source has **six or more authors,** refer to the work by the first author's name followed by "et al.," both for the first reference in the text and all references after that. However, be sure to list all the authors (up to seven) in your references list.

> According to a recent study, post-traumatic stress disorder (PTSD) continues to dominate the lives of Vietnam veterans, though in modified forms (Trembley et al., 2008).

A Work Authored by an Agency, a Committee, or an Organization

MLA If a book or other work was written by an organization such as an agency, a committee, or a task force, it is said to have a corporate author. If the corporate name is long, include it in the text (rather than in parentheses) to avoid disrupting the flow of your writing. After the full name has been used at least once, use a shortened form of the name (common abbreviations are acceptable) in subsequent references. For example, *Task Force* may be used for *Task Force on Education for Economic Growth.*

> The thesis of the Task Force's report is that economic success depends on our ability to improve large-scale education and training as quickly as possible (113–14).

APA Treat the name of the group as if it were the last name of the author. If the name is long and easily abbreviated, provide the abbreviation in square brackets.

> A problem for many veterans continues to be heightened sensitivity to noise (National Institute of Mental Health [NIMH], 2005).

Use the abbreviation without brackets in subsequent references.

> In addition, veterans suffering from PTSD continue to have difficulty discussing their experiences (NIMH, 2005).

A Work with No Author Indicated

MLA When there is no author listed, give the title or a shortened version of the title as it appears in the works-cited section.

> Statistics indicate that drinking water can make up 20 percent of a person's total exposure to lead (*Information* 572).

APA If your source lists no author, treat the first few words of the title (capitalized normally) as you would an author's last name. A title of an article or a chapter belongs in quotation marks; the titles of books or reports should be italicized.

> …including a guide to low-stress postures ("How to Do It," 2001).

Two or More Works Included in One Citation

To cite multiple works within a single parenthetical reference, separate the references with a semicolon.

MLA The following example refers to a work by Albala and another by Lewis.

> In Medieval Europe, Latin translations of the works of Rhazes, a Persian scholar, were a primary source of medical knowledge (Albala 22; Lewis 266).

APA Remember to include the year of publication. Place the citations in alphabetical order, just as they would be ordered in the reference list:

> Others report near-death experiences (Rommer, 2000; Sabom, 1998).

MLA: A Series of Citations from a Single Work

If no confusion is possible, it is not necessary to name a source repeatedly when making multiple parenthetical references to that source in a single paragraph. If all references are to the same page, identify that page in a parenthetical note after the last reference. If the references are to different pages within the same work, you need identify the work only once, and then use a parenthetical note with page number alone for the subsequent references.

> Domesticating science meant not only spreading scientific knowledge, but also promoting it as a topic of public conversation (Heilbron 2). One way to enhance its charm was by depicting cherubic putti as "angelic research assistants" in book illustrations (5).

A Work Referred to in Another Work

MLA If you must cite an indirect source—that is, information from a source that is quoted from another source—use the abbreviation *qtd. in* (quoted in) before the indirect source in your reference.

> Paton improved the conditions in Diepkloof (a prison) by "removing all the more obvious aids to detention. The dormitories [were] open at night: the great barred gate [was] gone" (qtd. in Callan xviii).

APA If you need to cite a source that you have found referred to in another source (a "secondary" source), mention the original source in your text. Then, in your parenthetical citation, cite the secondary source, using the words "as cited in."

> ...theorem given by Ullman (as cited in Hoffman, 1998).

A Work in an Anthology or a Collection

MLA When citing an entire work that is part of an anthology or a collection, a work identified by author in your list of works cited, treat the citation as you would for any other complete work.

> In "The Canadian Postmodern," Linda Hutcheon offers a clear analysis of the self-reflexive nature of contemporary Canadian fiction.

Similarly, if you are citing particular pages of such a work, follow the directions for citing part of a work.

> According to Hutcheon, "postmodernism seems to designate cultural practices that are fundamentally self-reflexive, in other words, art that is self-consciously artifice" (18).

An entry from a **reference work** such as an encyclopedia or a dictionary should be cited similarly to a work from an anthology or a collection. For a dictionary definition, include the abbreviation *def.* followed by the particular entry designation.

> This message becomes a juggernaut in the truest sense, a belief that "elicits blind devotion or sacrifice" ("Juggernaut," def. 1).

While many such entries are identified only by title (as above), some reference works include an author's name for each entry (as below). Others may identify the entry author by initials, with a list of full names elsewhere in the work.

> The decisions of the International Court of Justice are "based on principles of international law and cannot be appealed" (Pranger).

See pages 380–387 for guidelines on formatting these entries in your works-cited list.

APA When citing an article or a chapter in an anthology or a collection, use the authors' names for the specific article, not the names of the anthology's editors. (Similarly, the article should be listed by its authors' names in the reference section.)

> Phonological changes can be understood from a variationist perspective (Guy, 2005).

A Sacred Text or Famous Literary Work

Sacred texts and famous literary works are published in many different editions. For that reason, when you are referring to specific sections of the work, it is best to identify parts, chapters, or other divisions instead of (or in addition to) your version's page numbers. Note that books of the Bible and other well-known literary works may be abbreviated, if no confusion is possible.

MLA: Quoting Verse

Do not use page numbers when referencing classic verse plays and poems. Instead, cite them by division (act, scene, canto, book, part) and line, using Arabic numerals for the various divisions unless your instructor prefers Roman numerals. Use periods to separate the various numbers.

> In the first act, Hamlet comments, "How weary, stale, flat and unprofitable, / Seem to me all the uses of this world" (1.2.133-34).

A slash, with a space on each side, shows where each new line of verse begins. If you are citing lines only, use the word *line* or *lines* in your first reference and numbers only in additional references.

> At the beginning of the sestet in Robert Frost's "Design," the speaker asks this pointed question: "What had that flower to do with being white, / The wayside blue and innocent heal-all?" (lines 9–10).

See page 372 for instructions for verse quotations of more than three lines.

MLA If using page numbers, list them first, followed by an abbreviation for the type of division and the division number.

> The more important a person's role in society—the more apparent power an individual has—the more that person is a slave to the forces of history (Tolstoy 690; bk. 9, ch. 1).

> As Shakespeare's famous Danish prince observes, "One may smile, and smile, and be a villain" (*Ham.* 1.5.104).

APA The original date of publication may be unavailable or not pertinent. In such cases, use your edition's year of translation (for example, *trans. 2003*) or indicate your edition's year of publication (*2003 version*).

> An interesting literary case of such dysfunctional family behavior can be found in Franz Kafka's *The Metamorphosis,* where it becomes the commandment of family duty for Gregor's parents and sister to swallow their disgust and endure him (trans. 1972, part 3).

> "Generations come and generations go, but the earth remains forever" (*The New International Version Study Bible,* 1985 version, Eccles. 1.4).

Citing Internet Sources

MLA The current (seventh edition) *MLA Handbook* discourages use of Internet addresses, or URLs, as they can so easily change with time. Ideally, you should refer to an entire Web site by its title, or to a specific article on a site by its author; then, include full reference information in your works-cited list. A URL should be listed in your document or in your works-cited list only when the reader probably cannot locate the source without it, or if your instructor requires it. If that is the case, enclose the address in brackets:

> <www.thecollegewriter.com/4e>

APA As with print sources, cite an electronic source by the author (or by shortened title if the author is unknown) and the publication date (not the date you accessed the source). If citing a specific part of the source, use an appropriate abbreviation: *p.* for page and *para.* for paragraph.

> One study compared and contrasted the use of Web and touch screen transaction log files in a hospital setting (Nicholas, Huntington, & Williams, 2001).

Whenever possible, cite a Web site by its author and posting date. In addition, refer to a specific page or document rather than to a home page or a menu page. If you are referring to a specific part of a Web page that does not have page numbers, direct your reader, if possible, with a section heading and a paragraph number.

> According to the National Multiple Sclerosis Society (2003, "Complexities" section, para. 2), understanding of MS could not begin until scientists began to research nerve transmission in the 1920s.

APA: Personal Communications

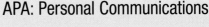

If for APA papers you do the kind of personal research recommended elsewhere in *COMP*, you may have to cite personal communications that have provided you with some of your knowledge. Personal communications may include personal letters, phone calls, memos, and so forth. Because they are not published in a permanent form, APA style does not place them among the citations in your reference list. Instead, cite them only in the text of your paper in parentheses, like this:

> …according to M. T. Cann (personal communication, April 1, 2009).

> …by today (M. T. Cann, personal communication, April 1, 2009).

Quick Guide: MLA Works Cited

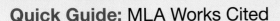

The works-cited section lists only the sources you have cited in your text. Begin your list on the page after the text and continue numbering each page. Format your works-cited pages using these guidelines and page 389.

1. Type the page number in the upper right corner, one-half inch from the top of the page, with your last name before it.

2. Center the title *Works Cited* (not in italics or underlined) one inch from the top; then double-space before the first entry.

3. Begin each entry flush with the left margin. If the entry runs more than one line, indent additional lines one-half inch (five spaces) or use the hanging indent function on your computer.

4. End each element of the entry with a period. (Elements are separated by periods in most cases unless only a space is sufficient.) Use a single space after all punctuation.

5. Double-space lines within each entry and between entries.

6. List each entry alphabetically by the author's last name. If there is no author, use the first word of the title (disregard *A*, *An*, or *The* as the first word). If there are multiple authors, alphabetize them according to which author is listed first in the publication.

7. The *MLA Handbook*, Seventh Edition, requires that each source be identified as *Print*, *Web*, or other (such as *Television* or *DVD*). For print sources, this information is included after the publisher and date. For Web publications, include *Web*. after the date of publication or updating of the site, and before the date you accessed the site.

8. A basic entry for a book follows:

> Black, Naomi. *Virginia Woolf as Feminist*. Ithaca: Cornell UP, 2004. Print.

9. A basic entry for a journal or magazine follows:

> Stelmach, Kathryn. "From Text to Tableau: Ekphrastic Enchantment in *Mrs. Dalloway* and *To the Lighthouse*." *Studies in the Novel* 38.3 (Fall 2006): 304-26. Print.

10. A basic entry for an online source is given below. Note that the URL is included only if the reader probably cannot locate the source without it, or when your instructor requires it.

> Clarke, S. N. "Virginia Woolf (1882-1941): A Short Biography." *Virginia Woolf Society of Great Britain*. 2000. Web. 12 Mar. 2012.

Quick Guide: APA References

The reference section lists all the sources you have cited in your text (with the exception of personal communications such as phone calls and e-mails). Begin your reference list on a new page after the last page of your paper. Number each reference page, continuing the numbering from the text. Then format your reference list by following the guidelines below.

1. Type the running head in the upper left corner and the page number in the upper right corner, approximately one-half inch from the top of the page.

2. Center the title, *References*, approximately one inch from the top; then double-space before the first entry.

3. Begin each entry flush with the left margin. If the entry runs more than one line, indent additional lines approximately one-half inch (five to seven spaces), using a hanging indent.

4. Adhere to the following conventions about spacing, capitalization, and italics:
   - Double-space between all lines on the reference page.
   - Use one space following each word and punctuation mark.
   - With book and article titles, capitalize only the first letter of the title (and subtitle) and proper nouns.

Example: *The impact of the cold war on Asia.*

(Note that this capitalization practice differs from the presentation of titles in the body of the essay.)
   - Use italics for titles of books and periodicals, not underlining.

5. List each entry alphabetically by the last name of the author, or, if no author is given, by the title (disregarding *A, An,* or *The*). For works with multiple authors, use the first author listed in the publication.

6. Follow these conventions with respect to abbreviations:
   - With authors' names, generally shorten first and middle names to initials, leaving a space after the period. For a work with more than one author, use an ampersand (&) before the last author's name.
   - For publisher locations, use the full city name plus the two-letter U.S. Postal Service abbreviation for the state. For international publishers, include a spelled-out province and country name.
   - Spell out "Press" or "Books" in full, but omit unnecessary terms like "Publishers," "Company," or "Inc."

List books and other nonperiodical documents.

LO3

MLA In MLA style, a works-cited entry for a book or similar document follows this general form.

Author's last name, first name. *Title.* Place of publication: publisher, year published. Medium ("Print").

Publishers' Names: Publishers' names should be shortened by omitting articles (*A, An, The*), business abbreviations (*Co., Inc.*), and descriptive words (*Books, Press*). For publishing houses that consist of the names of more than one person, cite only the first of the surnames. Abbreviate University Press as UP. Also use standard abbreviations whenever possible (*Assn., Acad.*). In addition, use the following abbreviations in place of any information you cannot supply:

n.p.   *No place of publication given*
n.p.   *No publisher given*
n.d.   *No date of publication given*
n. pag. *No pagination given*

APA In APA style, a reference-list entry for a book or similar document follows this general form.

Author, A. (year). *Title.* Location: Publisher.

A Book by One Author

MLA The example below demonstrates the most basic book entry.

> Green, Christopher. *Picasso: Architecture and Vertigo.* New Haven: Yale UP, 2005. Print.

APA Capitalize only the first word of the title and the first word of any subtitle, along with proper nouns and initialisms.

> Kuriansky, J. (2007). *Beyond bullets and bombs: Grassroots peacebuilding between Israelis and Palestinians.* Westport, CT: Praeger Press.

Two or More Books by the Same Author

MLA List the books alphabetically according to title. After the first entry, substitute three hyphens for the author's name.

> Dershowitz, Alan M. *Rights from Wrongs.* New York: Basic, 2005. Print.
> - - - . *Supreme Injustice: How the High Court Hijacked Election 2000.* Oxford: Oxford UP, 2001. Print.

APA Arrange multiple works by the same author in chronological order, earliest first.

> Sacks, O. (1995). *An anthropologist on Mars: Seven paradoxical tales.* New York, NY: Alfred A. Knopf.
> Sacks, O. (2007). *Musicophilia: Tales of music and the brain.* New York, NY: Alfred A. Knopf.

A Work by Two or More Authors

MLA For **two or three authors,** list them all, in title-page order, reversing only the first author's name.

> Bystydzienski, Jill M., and Estelle P. Resnik. *Women in Cross-Cultural Transitions.* Bloomington: Phi Delta Kappa Educational Foundation, 1994. Print.

For **four or more authors,** list only the first, followed by "et al."

> Schulte-Peevers, Andrea, et al. *Germany.* Victoria: Lonely Planet, 2000. Print.

APA List **up to seven authors** by last name and first initial, separating them by commas, with an ampersand (&) before the last.

> Hooyman, N., & Kramer, B. (2006). *Living through loss: Interventions across the life span.* New York, NY: Columbia University Press.

For **eight or more authors,** list the first six followed by an ellipsis, and then the last.

A Work Authored by an Agency, a Committee, or an Organization

MLA & **APA** Treat the organization as the author.

An Anonymous Book

MLA If no author or editor is listed, begin the entry with the title.

> *Chase's Calendar of Events 2002.* Chicago: Contemporary, 2002. Print.

APA If an author is listed as "Anonymous," treat it as the author's name. Otherwise, put the title in the author's spot.

> *Publication manual of the American Psychological Association* (5th ed.). (2001). Washington, DC: American Psychological Association.

A Single Work from an Anthology

MLA Place the title of the single work in quotation marks before the title of the complete work. (*Note:* Some large single works, such as complete plays, may call for italics instead.)

> Mitchell, Joseph. "The Bottom of the Harbor." *American Sea Writing.* Ed. Peter Neill. New York: Lib. of America, 2000. 584-608. Print.

APA Start with information about the individual work, followed by details about the collection in which it appears, including the page span. When editors' names come in the middle of an entry, follow the usual order: initial first, surname last. Note the placement of Eds. in parentheses in the following example.

> Guy, G. R. (2005). Variationist approaches to phonological change. In B. D. Joseph & R. D. Janda (Eds.), *The handbook of historical linguistics* (pp. 369-400). Malden, MA: Blackwell.

MLA: Citing Multiple Works or a Complete Anthology

To avoid unnecessary repetition when citing two or more entries from a larger collection, you may cite the collection once with complete publication information (see Rothfield, below). The individual entries (see Becker and Cuno, below) can then be cross-referenced by listing the author, title of the piece, editor of the collection, and page numbers.

> Becker, Carol. "The Brooklyn Controversy: A View from the Bridge." Rothfield 15-21.
>
> Cuno, James. "Sensation and the Ethics of Funding Exhibitions." Rothfield 162-170.
>
> Rothfield, Lawrence, ed. *Unsettling Sensation: Arts-Policy Lessons from the Brooklyn Museum of Art Controversy.* New Brunswick: Rutgers UP, 2001. Print. Rutgers Series on the Public Life of the Arts.

If you cite a **complete anthology,** begin the entry with the editor(s).

> Neill, Peter, ed. *American Sea Writing.* New York: Lib. of America, 2000. Print.
>
> Smith, Rochelle, and Sharon L. Jones, eds. *The Prentice Hall Anthology of African American Literature.* Upper Saddle River: Prentice, 2000. Print.

One Volume of a Multivolume Work

MLA Include the volume number after the title of the complete work.

> Cooke, Jacob Ernest, and Milton M. Klein, eds. *North America in Colonial Times.* Vol. 2. New York: Scribner's, 1998. Print.

If you cite two or more volumes of a multivolume work, give the total number of volumes in the work. Offer specific references to volume and page numbers in the parenthetical reference in your text, like this: (8: 112–114).

> Salzman, Jack, David Lionel Smith, and Cornel West. *Encyclopedia of African-American Culture and History.* 5 vols. New York: Simon, 1996. Print.

APA Indicate the volume in parentheses after the work's title.

> Salzman, J., Smith, D. L., & West, C. (Eds.). (1996). *Encyclopedia of African-American culture and history* (Vol. 4). New York, NY: Simon & Schuster Macmillan.

When a work is part of a larger series or collection, make a two-part title with the series and the particular volume you are citing.

> The Associated Press. (1995). *Twentieth-century America: Vol. 8. The crisis of national confidence: 1974-1980.* Danbury, CT: Grolier Educational Corp.

A Chapter, an Introduction, a Preface, a Foreword, or an Afterword

MLA To cite a chapter from a book, list the chapter title in quotation marks after the author's name. For an introduction, preface, foreword, or afterword, identify the part by type, with no quotation marks or underlining. Next, identify the author of the work, using the word "by." (If the book's author and the part's author are the same person, give just the last name after "by.") For a book that gives cover credit to an editor instead of an author, identify the editor as usual. Finally, list any page numbers for the part cited.

> Proulx, Annie. Introduction. *Dance of the Happy Shades*. By Alice Munro. Toronto: Penguin Canada, 2005. Print.

APA List the chapter title after the date of publication, followed by a period or appropriate end punctuation. Use "In" before the book title, and follow the book title with the inclusive page numbers of the chapter.

> Tattersall, I. (2002). How did we achieve humanity? In *The monkey in the mirror* (pp. 138-168). New York, NY: Harcourt.

A Group Author as Publisher

MLA List the unabbreviated group name as author, omitting any initial article (*A, An, The*), then again as publisher, abbreviated as usual.

> Amnesty International. *Maze of Injustice: The Failure to Protect Indigenous Women from Sexual Violence in the USA*. London: Amnesty Intl., 2007. Print.

APA When the author is also the publisher, simply put *Author* in the spot where you would list the publisher's name.

> Amnesty International. (2007). *Maze of injustice: The failure to protect indigenous women from sexual violence in the USA*. London England: Author.

If the publication is a brochure, identify it as such in brackets after the title.

List print periodic articles. LO4

MLA The general form for a periodical entry in MLA format follows.

> Author's last name, first name. "Article Title." *Periodical Title Series* number or name. Volume.issue. [separated by period but no space]. Publication date: page numbers. Medium (Print).

APA The general form for a periodical entry in APA format follows. If the periodical does not use volume and issue numbers, include some other designation with the year, such as the month and day, the month, or a season.

> Author, A. (year). Article title. *Periodical Title, volume number* (issue number if paginated by issue), page numbers.

An Article in a Magazine or Scholarly Journal

MLA For a scholarly journal, list the volume number immediately after the journal title, followed by a period and the issue number, and then the date of publication (in parentheses). For a magazine, do not include volume and issue number. End with the page numbers of the article followed by the medium of publication (Print).

> Sanchez, Melissa E. "Seduction and Service in *The Tempest*." *Studies in Philology* 105.1 (Winter 2008): 50-82. Print.
>
> "Feeding the Hungry." *Economist* (2004): 74. Print.

Note: For a scholarly journal, if no volume number exists, list the issue number alone.

APA List author and year as for a book reference. (For a magazine, also include other date elements, as the month and day or the season.) In the article's title, lowercase all but the first word, proper nouns, acronyms, initialisms, and the first word of any subtitle. Capitalize the journal's title normally and italicize it. Italicize the volume number and place the issue number in parentheses, without italics. Provide inclusive page numbers.

Weintraub, B. (2007, October). Unusual suspects. *Psychology Today, 40*(5), 80-87.

Tomatoes target toughest cancer. (2002, February). *Prevention, 54*(2), 53.

Benson, P., Karlof, K. L., & Siperstein, G. N. (2008). Maternal involvement in the education of young children with autism spectrum disorders. *Autism: The International Journal of Research & Practice, 12*(1), 47-63.

Note: Do not include an issue number for a journal that continues pagination from issue to issue.

A Newspaper Article

MLA Cite the edition of a major daily newspaper (if given) after the date (1 May 1995, Midwest ed.: 1). If a local paper's name does not include the city of publication, add it in brackets (not italicized) after the name.

Segal, Jeff, and Lauren Silva. "Case of Art Imitating Life?" *Wall Street Journal* 3 March 2008, Eastern ed.: C9. Print.

Swiech, Paul. "Human Service Agencies: 'It's Going to Take a Miracle.'" *Pantagraph* [Bloomington, IL] 30 June 2009: B7. Print.

To cite an article in a lettered section of the newspaper, list the section and the page number. (For example, A4 would refer to page 4 in section A of the newspaper.) If the sections are numbered, however, use a comma after the year (or the edition); then indicate the section and follow it with a colon, the page number (sec. 1:20), and the medium of publication you used. An unsigned newspaper article follows the same format:

"Bombs—Real and Threatened—Keep Northern Ireland Edgy." *Chicago Tribune* 6 Dec. 2001, sec. 1: 20. Print.

If an article is an unsigned editorial, put *Editorial* (no italics) and a period after the title.

"Hospital Power." Editorial. *Bangor Daily News* 14 Sept. 2004: A6. Print.

To identify a letter to the editor, put *Letter* (no italics) and a period after the author's name.

Sory, Forrest. Letter. *Discover* July 2001: 10. Print.

APA For newspaper articles, include the full publication date, year first followed by a comma, the month (spelled out) and the day. Identify the article's location in the newspaper using page numbers and section letters, as appropriate. If the article is a letter to the editor, identify it as such in brackets following the title. For newspapers, use *p.* or *pp.* before the page numbers; if the article is not on continuous pages, give all the page numbers, separated by commas.

Schmitt, E., & Shanker, T. (2008, March 18). U.S. adapts cold-war idea to fight terrorists. *The New York Times*, pp. 1A, 14A-15A.

Benderoff, E. (2008, March 14). Facebook sites face scrutiny for March Madness pools. *Chicago Tribune*, pp. 2C-3C.

An Abstract

An abstract is a summary of a work.

MLA To cite an abstract, first give the publication information for the original work (if any); then list the publication information for the abstract itself. Add the term *Abstract* and a period between these if the journal title does not include that word. If the journal identifies abstracts by item number, include the word *item* followed by the number. (Add the section identifier [A, B, or C] for those volumes of *Dissertation Abstracts [DA]* and *Dissertation Abstracts International [DAI]* that have one.) If no item number exists, list the page number(s).

Faber, A. J. "Examining Remarried Couples Through a Bowenian Family System Lens." *Journal of Divorce and Remarriage* 40.4 (2004): 121-33. *Social Work Abstracts* 40 (2004): item 1298. Print.

APA When referencing an abstract published separately from an article, provide publication details of the article followed by information about where the abstract was published.

Shlipak, M. G., Simon, J. A., Grady, O., Lin, F., Wenger, N. K., & Furberg, C. D. (2001, September). Renal insufficiency and cardiovascular events in postmenopausal women with coronary heart disease. *Journal of the American College of Cardiology, 38,* 705-711. Abstract retrieved from *Geriatrics,* 2001, *56*(12), Abstract No. 5645351.

List online sources.

The general form for an online entry in MLA style is given below.

MLA Start with the same elements given for a print source.

> Author's last name, first name. Title of Work (in italics or quotation marks). *Web Site Title* (if different from title of work). Version or edition used. Publisher or sponsor (or n.p. if none identified). Publication date (or n.d.). Medium (Web). Date of access.

Include a URL only if your reader needs it to locate the source (or if your instructor requires it). See "Using URLs" below for instructions.

APA Whenever possible, use the final, archival version of an electronic resource (often called the version of record), as opposed to a prepublished version. In the reference entry for an electronic source, start with the same elements in the same order given for a print or other fixed-media resource (author, title, and so on). Then add the most reliable electronic retrieval information that will (a) clarify what version of the source you used and (b) help your reader find the source.

DOI: If possible, use the electronic document's digital object identifier (DOI). The DOI will usually be published at the beginning of the article or be available in the article's citation.

> Author, A. A. (year). Title of article. *Title of Periodical, volume number* (issue number), pages. doi: code

URL: If a DOI is not available, give the URL (without a period at the end). Use the home or menu-page URL for subscription-only databases and online reference works.

> Author, A. A. (year). Title of article. *Title of Periodical, volume number* (issue number), pages. Retrieved from URL

Retrieval Date: If the content of the document is stable (e.g., archival copy or copy of record with DOI), do not include a retrieval date in your reference entry. However, if the content is likely to change or be updated, then offer a retrieval date.

> Author, A. A. (year). *Title of document.* Retrieved date from website: URL

Using URLs

MLA and APA documentation styles differ slightly in how they treat URLs (Internet addresses).

MLA If you need to include a URL, place it immediately following the date of access, a period, and a space. The URL should be enclosed in angle brackets and end with a period. Give the complete address, including http, for the work you are citing.

> MacLeod, Donald. "Shake-Up for Academic Publishing." *Guardian Unlimited.* Guardian News and Media Ltd., 10 Nov. 2008. Web. 6 Jan. 2009. <http://www.guardian.co.uk/Archive/>.

> "Fort Frederica." *National Parks Service.* U.S. Department of the Interior, n.d. Web. 27 Feb. 2009. <http://home.nps.gov/fofr/forteachers/curriculummaterials.htm>.

If the URL must be divided between two lines, break it only **after** a **single** or **double slash.** Do not add a hyphen.

APA When necessary, break a URL **before** a **slash** or **other punctuation mark.** Do not underline or italicize the URL, place it in angle brackets, or end it with a period.

An Undated Online Item

MLA List "n.d." in place of the missing date.

> Booth, Philip. "Robert Frost's Prime Directive." *Poets.org.* Academy of American Poets, n.d. Web. 1 Oct. 2009.

APA List "(n.d.)" in place of the missing date.

> National Institute of Allergy and Infectious Diseases. (n.d.). *Antimicrobial (drug) resistance.* Retrieved June 19, 2008, from http://www3.niaid.nih.gov/topics/AntimicrobialResistance/default.htm

A Home Page

MLA If a nonperiodical publication has no title, identify it with a descriptor such as *Home page, Intro-*

duction, or *Online posting* (using no italics or quotation marks). You may add the name of the publication's creator or editor after the overall site title, if appropriate.

> Wheaton, Wil. Home page. *Wil Wheaton dot Net.* n.p., 31 May 2006. Web. 19 Mar. 2009.

APA Whenever possible, cite a Web site by its author and posting date. In addition, refer to a specific page or document rather than to a home page or a menu page.

An Entry in an Online Reference Work

Unless the author of the entry is identified, begin with the entry name.

MLA Place the entry name in quotation marks.

> "Eakins, Thomas." *Britannica Online Encyclopedia.* Encyclopedia Britannica, 2008. Web. 26 Sept. 2008.

APA Use the word "In" to identify the larger source.

> Agonism. (2008). In *Encyclopaedia Britannica.* Retrieved March 18, 2008, from http://search .eb.com

An Electronic Book

MLA Include publication information for the original print version if available. Follow the date of publication with the electronic information.

> Simon, Julian L. *The Ultimate Resource II: People, Materials, and Environment.* College Park: U of Maryland, 1996. U of Maryland Libraries. Web. 9 Apr. 2009.

APA Provide the DOI (see page 264) if one exists. Otherwise, use the phrase "Retrieved from" to introduce the URL.

> Bittlestone, R. (2005). *Odysseus unbound.* doi: 10.2277/0521853575
>
> Kafka, F. (2002). *Metamorphosis.* D. Wylie (Trans.). Retrieved from http://www.gutenberg.org /etext/5200

MLA: Online Multimedia

For online postings of photographs, videos, sound recordings, works of art, and so on, follow the examples on pages 358–386. In place of the original medium of publication, however, include the title of the database or Web site (italicized), followed by the medium (Web) and the date of access, as for other online entries.

> Brumfield, William Craft. *Church of Saint Nicholas Mokryi.* 1996. Prints and Photographs Div., Lib. of Cong. *Brumfield Photograph Collection.* Web. 9 May 2009.
>
> *Sita Sings the Blues.* Prod. Nina Paley. 2008. *Internet Archive.* Web. 5 June 2008.

List other sources. LO6

A Television or Radio Program

MLA Include the medium (Television or Radio) at the end of the citation, followed by a period.

> "U.S. Health Care Gets Boost from Charity." *60 Minutes.* CBS. WBBM, Chicago. 28 Feb. 2008. Television.

APA Indicate the episode by writers, if possible. Then follow with the airing date, the episode title, and the type of series in brackets. Add the producer(s) as you would the editors(s) of a print medium, and complete the entry with details about the series itself.

> Berger, Cynthia. (Writer). (2001, December 19). Feederwatch [Radio series program]. In D. Byrd & J. Block (Producers), *Earth & Sky.* Austin, TX: The Production Block.

A Motion Picture or Performance

MLA The director, distributor, and year of release follow the title. Other information may be included if pertinent. End with the medium, in this case *Film*, followed by a period.

> *Atonement*. Dir. Joe Wright. Perf. James McAvoy, Keira Knightley. Universal Pictures, 2007. Film.

Treat a **performance** as you would a film, but add its location and date.

> *Chanticleer: An Orchestra of Voices*. Young Auditorium, Whitewater, WI. 23 Feb. 2003. Performance.

APA Give the name and function of the director, producer, or both.

> Cohn, J., & Cohn, E. (Directors). (2007). *No country for old men* [Motion picture]. United States: Miramax Films.

A Video Recording or an Audio Recording

MLA Cite a filmstrip, slide program, videocassette, or DVD as you do a film; include the medium of publication last, followed by a period.

> *Monet: Shadow & Light*. Devine Productions, 1999. Videocassette.

If you are citing a specific song on a musical recording, place its title in quotation marks before the title of the recording.

> Bernstein, Leonard. "Maria." *West Side Story*. Columbia, 1995. CD.

APA Begin the entry with the speaker's or writer's name, not the producer. Indicate the type of recording in brackets.

> Kim, E. (Author, speaker). (2000). *Ten thousand sorrows* [CD]. New York, NY: Random House.

For a **music recording,** give the name and function of the originators or primary contributors. Indicate the recording medium in brackets immediately following the title.

> ARS Femina Ensemble. (1998). *Musica de la puebla de Los Angeles: Music by women of baroque Mexico, Cuba, & Europe* [CD]. Louisville, KY: Nannerl Recordings.

A Lecture, Speech, Reading, or Dissertation

MLA Provide the speaker's name, the title of the presentation (if known) in quotation marks, the meeting and the sponsoring organization, the location, and the date. End with an appropriate descriptive label such as *Address, Lecture,* or *Reading.*

> Annan, Kofi. "Acceptance of Nobel Peace Prize." Oslo City Hall, Oslo, Norw. 10 Dec. 2001. Speech.

APA For an unpublished paper presented at a meeting, indicate when the paper was presented, at what meeting, in what location.

> Lycan, W. (2002, June). *The plurality of consciousness*. Paper presented at the meeting of the Society for Philosophy and Psychology, New York, NY.

For an unpublished doctoral dissertation, place the dissertation's title in italics, even though the work is unpublished. Indicate the school at which the writer completed the dissertation.

> Roberts, W. (2001). *Crime amidst suburban wealth* (Unpublished doctoral dissertation). Bowling Green State University, Bowling Green, OH.

Big Pants Production, 2011 / Used under license from Shutterstock.com

Follow format guidelines for MLA and APA. LO7

While pages 370–387 describe some of the key features of MLA and APA formats, the sample pages that follow show you these formats.

MLA Format at a Glance

You can find a complete model in MLA style, Stevie Jeung's "'I Did *Not* Get My Spaghetti-O's': Death Row Consumption in the Popular Media," at the end of chapter 28 (pages 362–369). Below, however, are the basic rules for formatting the first page, middle pages, and the works-cited page in MLA format.

MLA Paper (Excerpt)

The heading (in MLA format) supplies identifying details.

The title (centered) indicates the paper's topic and theme.

The writer opens with a chronological catalog of executed people and last suppers.

The intro zeros in on the topic, focuses on what is odd or difficult to explain, and announces a search for explanations.

The analysis focuses on specific examples in film and television.

Jeung 1

Stevie Jeung

Professor Sasha Abramsky

American Studies 101D

17 February 2008

"I Did *Not* Get My Spaghetti-O's":

Death Row Consumption in the Popular Media

Jesus Christ: Roast lamb, matzo, wine; around AD 30. Perry Smith and Richard Hickock: Identical meals of shrimp, French fries, garlic bread, ice cream and strawberries with whipped cream; 1965. Timothy McVeigh: Two pints of Ben & Jerry's mint chocolate chip ice cream: 2001. Tony Soprano: Holsten's onion rings; 2007. Karl Chamberlein: final meal yet to be consumed; 15 days from now.

While executions historically demand a certain degree of morbid curiosity, the last meals of the condemned seem to stimulate heightened interest. Indeed, a prisoner's final feast has almost become an event in its own right, not only for the prisoner, but for the prison staff and the public. Web sites, novels, movies, television shows, newspapers, and even cookbooks report, dissect, criticize, and speculate regarding last meals real and imagined. When confronted with the ultimate consumption of dying people in so many areas of our popular media, the truth becomes alarmingly clear: This is odd behavior. There must be some reason that we institutionally allow our most hated and feared prisoners to choose and enjoy their final meal before we execute them, and there must be some reason that we like to watch and reproduce the event in popular culture. . . .

MLA Works-Cited List

The list of works cited begins on a separate page and includes the title, header, and page number.

The paper's bibliography lists a range of scholarly books, trade books, scholarly articles, popular articles, and Web sites on the topic.

Sources are listed in alphabetical order by author (or by title if no author is given) and identified by medium.

Quotation marks and italics are properly used with titles, as are punctuation and abbreviations.

Works Cited

Abramsky, Sasha. *American Furies: Crime, Punishment, and Vengeance in the Age of Mass Imprisonment.* Boston: Beacon Press, 2007. Print.

"Artist serves 'Last Supper' on plates." *Lawrence Journal.* 29 Oct. 2006. Web. 5 Feb. 2008.

Atwell, Mary Welek. *Evolving Standards of Decency: Popular Culture and Capital Punishment.* New York: Peter Lang, 2004. Print.

"Confessions of a Death Row Chef." *The Observer.* 14 March 2004. Web. 5 Feb. 2008.

"Death Row Information." *Texas Department of Criminal Justice.* 7 Nov. 2007. Web. 5 Feb. 2008.

Dickerson, James L. *Last Suppers: If the world ended tomorrow, what would be your last meal?* New York: Citadel, 2004. Print.

Fritsch, Jane. "Word for Word/Execution Protocol; Please Order Your Last Meal Seven Days in Advance." *The New York Times.* 22 April 2001. Web. 5 Feb. 2008.

The Green Mile. Dir. Frank Darabont. Perf. Tom Hanks, Michael Clarke Duncan, David Morse, and Bonnie Hunt. Castle Rock, 1999. Film.

Greene, Bob. "They didn't get to choose their last meals." *Jewish World Review.* 12 June 2001. Web. 5 Feb. 2008.

Hyman, Vicki. "Chewing Over Tony's Last Meal." *The Star Ledger.* 23 June 2007. Web. 5 Feb. 2008.

Karon, Tony. "Why We're Fascinated by Death Row Cuisine." *TIME.* 10 August 2000. Web. 5 Feb. 2008.

LaChance, Daniel. "Last Words, Last Meals, and Last Stands: Agency and Individuality in the Modern Execution Process." *Law & Social Inquiry* 32 (2007): 701-724. JSTOR. Web. 5 Feb. 2008.

"Last Words on Death Row." *CNN: The Best of Court TV.* 31 Dec. 2007. Web. 5 Feb. 2008.

"Made in America." *The Sopranos.* Dir. David Chase. HBO. 10 June 2007. Television.

Peck, John. "Last Meals." *Tucson Weekly.* 5 Jan. 2006. Print. 5 Feb. 2008.

Price, Brian D. *Meals to Die For.* San Antonio: Dyna-Paige Corporation, 2001. Print.

"Sleight of Hand." *Prison Break.* Dir. Dwight Little. Fox Network. 7 Nov. 2005. Television.

"The Springfield Connection." *The Simpsons.* Dir. Mark Kirkland. Fox Network. 7 May 1995. Television.

APA Research Report: Format, Documentation, and Structure

Student writers Thomas I. DeJong and Adam B. Smit wrote the following research paper based on an experiment that they conducted in a psychology course.

You can use the paper to study how a research report based on experimentation structures and builds a discussion, how sources are used and integrated into social-science research writing, and how format and documentation practices work in APA style.

APA Title Page

Place manuscript page headers one-half inch from the top. Put five spaces between the page header and the page number.

Full title, authors, and school name are centered on the page, typed in uppercase and lowercase.

Running on Empty:

The Effects of Food Deprivation on

Concentration and Perseverance

Thomas I. DeJong and Adam B. Smit

Dordt College

APA Abstract

The abstract summarizes the problem, participants, hypotheses, methods used, results, and conclusions.

Abstract

This study examined the effects of short-term food deprivation on two cognitive abilities—concentration and perseverance. Undergraduate students (N-51) were tested on both a concentration task and a perseverance task after one of three levels of food deprivation: none, 12 hours, or 24 hours. We predicted that food deprivation would impair both concentration scores and perseverance time. Food deprivation had no significant effect on concentration scores, which is consistent with recent research on the effects of food deprivation (Green et al., 1995; Green et al., 1997). However, participants in the 12-hour deprivation group spent significantly less time on the perseverance task than those in both the control and 24-hour deprivation groups, suggesting that short-term deprivation may affect some aspects of cognition and not others.

APA Paper

Running on Empty: The Effects of Food Deprivation
on Concentration and Perseverance

Many things interrupt people's ability to focus on a task: distractions, headaches, noisy environments, and even psychological disorders. To some extent, people can control the environmental factors that make it difficult to focus. However, what about internal factors, such as an empty stomach? Can people increase their ability to focus simply by eating regularly?

One theory that prompted research on how food intake affects the average person was the glucostatic theory. Several researchers in the 1940s and 1950s suggested that the brain regulates food intake in order to maintain a blood-glucose set point. The idea was that people become hungry when their blood-glucose levels drop significantly below their set point and that they become satisfied after eating, when their blood-glucose levels return to that set point. This theory seemed logical because glucose is the brain's primary fuel (Pinel, 2000). The earliest investigation of the general effects of food deprivation found that long-term food deprivation (36 hours and longer) was associated with sluggishness, depression, irritability, reduced heart rate, and inability to concentrate (Keys, Brozek, Henschel, Mickelsen, & Taylor, 1950). Another study found that fasting for several days produced muscular weakness, irritability, and apathy or depression (Kollar, Slater, Palmer, Docter, & Mandell, 1964). Since that time, research has focused mainly on how nutrition affects cognition. However, as Green, Elliman, and Rogers (1995) point out, the effects of food deprivation on cognition have received comparatively less attention in recent years.

The relatively sparse research on food deprivation has left room for further research. First, much of the research has focused either on chronic starvation at one end of the continuum or on missing a single meal at the other end (Green et al., 1995). Second, some of the findings have been contradictory. One study found that skipping breakfast impairs certain aspects of cognition, such as problem-solving abilities (Pollitt, Lewis, Garza, & Shulman, 1983). However, other research by M. W. Green, N. A. Elliman, and P. J. Rogers (1995, 1997) has found that food deprivation ranging from missing a single meal to 24 hours without eating does not significantly impair cognition. Third, not all groups of people have been sufficiently studied. Studies have been done on 9–11 year-olds (Pollitt et al., 1983), obese subjects (Crumpton, Wine, & Drenick, 1966), college-age men and women (Green et al., 1995, 1996, 1997), and middle-age males (Kollar et al., 1964). Fourth, not all cognitive aspects have been studied. In 1995 Green, Elliman, and Rogers studied sustained attention, simple reaction time, and immediate memory; in 1996 they studied attentional bias; and in 1997 they studied simple reaction time, two-finger tapping, recognition memory, and free recall. In 1983, another study focused on reaction time and accuracy, intelligence quotient, and problem solving (Pollitt et al.).

Center the title one inch from the top. Double-space throughout.

The introduction states the topic and the main questions to be explored.

The researchers supply background information by discussing past research on the topic.

Extensive referencing establishes support for the discussion.

The researchers explain how their study will add to past research on the topic.

Clear transitions guide readers through the researchers' reasoning.

According to some researchers, most of the results so far indicate that cognitive function is not affected significantly by short-term fasting (Green et al., 1995, p. 246). However, this conclusion seems premature due to the relative lack of research on cognitive functions such as concentration and perseverance. To date, no study has tested perseverance, despite its importance in cognitive functioning. In fact, perseverance may be a better indicator than achievement tests in assessing growth in learning and thinking abilities, as perseverance helps in solving complex problems (Costa, 1984). Another study also recognized that perseverance, better learning techniques, and effort are cognitions worth studying (D'Agostino, 1996). Testing as many aspects of cognition as possible is key because the nature of the task is important when interpreting the link between food deprivation and cognitive performance (Smith & Kendrick, 1992). Therefore, the current study helps us understand how short-term food deprivation affects concentration on and perseverance with a difficult task. Specifically, participants deprived of food for 24 hours were expected to perform worse on a concentration test and a perseverance task than those deprived for 12 hours, who in turn were predicted to perform worse than those who were not deprived of food.

Method

Participants

Participants included 51 undergraduate-student volunteers (32 females, 19 males), some of whom received a small amount of extra credit in a college course. The mean college grade point average (GPA) was 3.19. Potential participants were excluded if they were dieting, menstruating, or taking special medication. Those who were struggling with or had struggled with an eating disorder were excluded, as were potential participants addicted to nicotine or caffeine.

Materials

Concentration speed and accuracy were measured using an online numbers-matching test (www.psychtests.com/tests/iq/concentration.html) that consisted of 26 lines of 25 numbers each. In 6 minutes, participants were required to find pairs of numbers in each line that added up to 10. Scores were calculated as the percentage of correctly identified pairs out of a possible 120. Perseverance was measured with a puzzle that contained five octagons—each of which included a stencil of a specific object (such as an animal or a flower). The octagons were to be placed on top of each other in a specific way to make the silhouette of a rabbit. However, three of the shapes were slightly altered so that the task was impossible. Perseverance scores were calculated as the number of minutes that a participant spent on the puzzle task before giving up.

Procedure

At an initial meeting, participants gave informed consent. Each consent form contained an assigned identification number and requested the participant's GPA.

The researchers support their decision to focus on concentration and perseverance.

The researchers state their initial hypotheses.

Headings and subheadings show the paper's organization.

The experiment's method is described, using the terms and acronyms of the discipline.

Passive voice is used to emphasize the experiment, not the researchers; otherwise, active voice is used.

Students were then informed that they would be notified by e-mail and telephone about their assignment to one of the three experimental groups. Next, students were given an instruction sheet. These written instructions, which we also read aloud, explained the experimental conditions, clarified guidelines for the food deprivation period, and specified the time and location of testing.

Participants were randomly assigned to one of these conditions using a matched-triplets design based on the GPAs collected at the initial meeting. This design was used to control individual differences in cognitive ability. Two days after the initial meeting, participants were informed of their group assignment and its condition and reminded that, if they were in a food-deprived group, they should not eat anything after 10 a.m. the next day. Participants from the control group were tested at 7:30 p.m. in a designated computer lab on the day the deprivation started. Those in the 12-hour group were tested at 10 p.m. on that same day. Those in the 24-hour group were tested at 10:40 a.m. on the following day.

At their assigned time, participants arrived at a computer lab for testing. Each participant was given written testing instructions, which were also read aloud. The online concentration test had already been loaded on the computers for participants before they arrived for testing, so shortly after they arrived they proceeded to complete the test. Immediately after all participants had completed the test and their scores were recorded, participants were each given the silhouette puzzle and instructed how to proceed. In addition, they were told that (1) they would have an unlimited amount of time to complete the task, and (2) they were not to tell any other participant whether they had completed the puzzle or simply given up. This procedure was followed to prevent the group influence of some participants seeing others give up. Any participant still working on the puzzle after 40 minutes was stopped to keep the time of the study manageable. Immediately after each participant stopped working on the puzzle, he/she gave demographic information and completed a few manipulation-check items. We then debriefed and dismissed each participant outside of the lab.

Results

Perseverance data from one control-group participant were eliminated because she had to leave the session early. Concentration data from another control-group participant were dropped because he did not complete the test correctly. Three manipulation-check questions indicated that each participant correctly perceived his or her deprivation condition and had followed the rules for it. The average concentration score was 77.78 (SD = 14.21), which was very good considering that anything over 50 percent is labeled "good" or "above average." The average time spent on the puzzle was 24.00 minutes (SD = 10.16), with a maximum of 40 minutes allowed.

We predicted that participants in the 24-hour deprivation group would perform worse on the concentration test and the perseverance task than those in the 12-

---

The experiment is laid out step by step, with time transitions like "then" and "next."

Attention is shown to the control features.

The writers summarize their findings, including problems encountered.

hour group, who in turn would perform worse than those in the control group. A one-way analysis of variance (ANOVA) showed no significant effect of deprivation condition on concentration, $F(2,46) = 1.06$, $p = .36$ (see Figure 1). Another one-way ANOVA indicated a significant effect of deprivation condition on perseverance time, $F(2,47) = 7.41$, $p < .05$. Post-hoc Tukey tests indicated that the 12-hour deprivation group ($M = 17.79$, $SD = 7.84$) spent significantly less time on the perseverance task than either the control group ($M = 26.80$, $SD = 6.20$) or the 24-hour group ($M = 28.75$, $SD = 12.11$), with no significant difference between the latter two groups (see Figure 2). No significant effect was found for gender either generally or with specific deprivation conditions, $Fs < 1.00$. Unexpectedly, food deprivation had no significant effect on concentration scores. Overall, we found support for our hypothesis

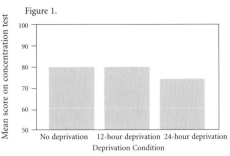

Figure 1.

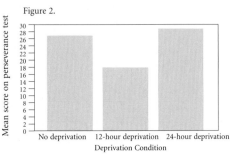

Figure 2.

that 12 hours of food deprivation would significantly impair perseverance when compared to no deprivation. Unexpectedly, 24 hours of food deprivation did not significantly affect perseverance relative to the control group. Also unexpectedly, food deprivation did not significantly affect concentration scores.

Discussion

The purpose of this study was to test how different levels of food deprivation affect concentration on and perseverance with difficult tasks. We predicted that the longer people had been deprived of food, the lower they would score on the concentration task, and the less time they would spend on the perseverance task. In this study, those deprived of food did give up more quickly on the puzzle, but only in the 12-hour group. Thus, the hypothesis was partially supported for the perseverance task. However, concentration was found to be unaffected by food deprivation, and thus the hypothesis was not supported for that task.

The findings of this study are consistent with those of Green et al. (1995), where short-term food deprivation did not affect some aspects of cognition, including attentional focus. Taken together, these findings suggest that concentration is not significantly impaired by short-term food deprivation. The findings on perseverance, however, are not as easily explained. We surmise that the participants in the 12-hour group gave up more quickly on the perseverance task because of their hunger produced by the food deprivation. But why, then, did those in the 24-hour group fail to yield the same effect? We postulate that this result can be explained by the concept of "learned industriousness," wherein participants who perform one difficult task do better on a subsequent task than the participants who never took the initial task (Eisenberger & Leonard, 1980; Hickman, Stromme, & Lippman, 1998). Because participants had successfully completed 24 hours of fasting already, their tendency to persevere had already been increased, if only temporarily. Another possible explanation is that the motivational state of a participant may be a significant determinant of behavior under testing (Saugstad, 1967). This idea may also explain the short perseverance times in the 12-hour group: because these participants took the tests at 10 p.m., a prime time of the night for conducting business and socializing on a college campus, they may have been less motivated to take the time to work on the puzzle.

Research on food deprivation and cognition could continue in several directions. First, other aspects of cognition may be affected by short-term food deprivation, such as reading comprehension or motivation. With respect to this latter topic, some students in this study reported decreased motivation to complete the tasks because of a desire to eat immediately after the testing. In addition, the time of day when the respective groups took the tests may have influenced the results: those in the 24-hour group took the tests in the morning and may have been fresher and more relaxed than those in the 12-hour group, who took the tests at night. Perhaps, then, the motivation level of food-deprived participants could be effectively tested. Second, longer-term food deprivation periods, such as those experienced by people fasting for religious reasons, could be explored. It is possible that cognitive function fluctuates over the duration of deprivation. Studies could ask how long a person can remain focused despite a lack of nutrition. Third, and perhaps most fascinating, studies could explore how food deprivation affects learned industriousness. As stated above, one possible explanation for the better perseverance times in the 24-hour group could be that they spontaneously improved their perseverance faculties by simply forcing themselves not to eat for 24 hours. Therefore, research could study how food deprivation affects the acquisition of perseverance.

The conclusion summarizes the outcomes, stresses the experiment's value, and anticipates further advances on the topic.

In conclusion, the results of this study provide some fascinating insights into the cognitive and physiological effects of skipping meals. Contrary to what we predicted, a person may indeed be very capable of concentrating after not eating for many hours. On the other hand, if one is taking a long test or working long hours at a tedious task that requires perseverance, one may be hindered by not eating for a short time, as shown by the 12-hour group's performance on the perseverance task. Many people—students, working mothers, and those interested in fasting, to mention a few—have to deal with short-term food deprivation, intentional or unintentional. This research and other research to follow will contribute to knowledge of the disadvantages—and possible advantages—of skipping meals. The mixed results of this study suggest that we have much more to learn about short-term food deprivation.

References

Costa, A. L. (1984). Thinking: How do we know students are getting better at it? *Roeper Review, 6* (4), 197–199.

Crumpton, E., Wine, D. B., & Drenick, E. J. (1966). Starvation: Stress or satisfaction? *Journal of the American Medical Association, 196* (5), 394–396.

D'Agostino, C. A. F. (1996). Testing a social-cognitive model of achievement motivation. *Dissertation Abstracts International Section A: Humanities & Social Sciences, 57,* 1985.

Eisenberger, R., & Leonard, J. M. (1980). Effects of conceptual task difficulty on generalized persistence. *American Journal of Psychology, 93* (2), 285–298.

Green, M. W., Elliman, N. A., & Rogers, P. J. (1995). Lack of effect of short-term fasting on cognitive function. *Journal of Psychiatric Research, 29* (3), 245–253.

Green, M. W., Elliman, N. A., & Rogers, P. J. (1996). Hunger, caloric preloading, and the selective processing of food and body shape words. *British Journal of Clinical Psychology, 35,* 143–151.

Green, M. W., Elliman, N. A., & Rogers, P. J. (1997). The study effects of food deprivation and incentive motivation on blood glucose levels and cognitive function. *Psychopharmacology, 134,* 88–94.

Hickman, K. L., Stromme, C., & Lippman, L. G. (1998). Learned industriousness: Replication in principle. *Journal of General Psychology, 125* (3), 213–217.

Keys, A., Brozek, J., Henschel, A., Mickelsen, O., & Taylor, H. L. (1950). *The biology of human starvation* (Vol. 2). Minneapolis, MN: University of Minnesota Press.

Kollar, E. J., Slater, G. R., Palmer, J. O., Docter, R. F., & Mandell, A. J. (1964). Measurement of stress in fasting man. *Archives of General Psychology, 11,* 113–125.

Pinel, J. P. (2000). *Biopsychology* (4th ed.). Boston, MA: Allyn and Bacon.

Pollitt, E., Lewis, N. L., Garza, C., & Shulman, R. J. (1982–1983). Fasting and cognitive function. *Journal of Psychiatric Research, 17* (2), 169–174.

Saugstad, P. (1967). Effect of food deprivation on perception-cognition: A comment [Comment on the article by David L. Wolitzky]. *Psychological Bulletin, 68* (5), 345–346.

Smith, A. P., & Kendrick, A. M. (1992). Meals and performance. In A. P. Smith & D. M. Jones (Eds.), *Handbook of human performance: Vol. 2, Health and performance* (pp. 1–23). San Diego, CA: Academic Press.

Smith, A. P., Kendrick, A. M., & Maben, A. L. (1992). Effects of breakfast and caffeine on performance and mood in the late morning and after lunch. *Neuropsychobiology, 26* (4), 198–204.

All works referred to in the paper appear on the reference page, listed alphabetically by author (or title).

Each entry follows APA guidelines for listing authors, dates, titles, and publishing information.

Capitalization, punctuation, and hanging indentation are consistent with APA format.

Reading for Better Writing

Working by yourself or with a group, answer these questions:

1. Before you read Thomas and Adam's paper, what were your expectations about food deprivation's effects on concentration and perseverance? Did the paper confirm or confound your expectations?

2. Did you find the report interesting? Why or why not?

3. What types of evidence did Thomas and Adam use in their paper? Where did they obtain their evidence?

4. How did Thomas and Adam distinguish their own ideas from their sources' ideas? Was it necessary for them to do, and if so, why?

5. Could the results of Thomas and Adam's research be applied to other situations? In other words, how might particular groups interpret these findings?

Critical-Thinking and Writing Activities

As directed by your instructor, complete the following critical-thinking and writing activities.

1. The MLA and APA systems involve many rules about format and documentation. To make sense of these rules, compare and contrast the essential logic of each system.

2. Create MLA works-cited entries for the following publications:

   - An article in the May 27, 2002, issue (vol. 145, no. 11) of *Fortune* magazine by Joseph Nocera: "Return of the Raider" (pages 97–114)

   - Ernest Hemingway's novel *A Farewell to Arms*, published in 1986 by Collier Books, located in New York City

   - The Web page "Aruba," part of *The 2008 World Factbook*, sponsored by the Central Intelligence Agency. No author or publication date is listed. The site was last accessed March 8, 2011, at http://www.cia.gov/library/publications/the-world-factbook/ index.html.

3. Create references list entries in correct APA style for the following sources:

   - An article in the October 2001 issue (vol. 29, no. 2) of *Learning & Leading with Technology* magazine by Bob Albrecht and Paul Davis titled "The Metric Backpack" (pages 29–31, 55)

   - The book *The Playful World: How Technology Is Transforming Our Imagination,* by Mark Pesce, published in 2000 by Ballantine Books, located in New York City

   - A Web page by Roger Fouts called "Frequently Asked Questions," part of the *Chimpanzee and Human Communication Institute* site, sponsored by Central Washington University; no publication date; site accessed May 8, 2011, at http://www.cwu.edu/~cwuchci/quanda.html.

4. Compare and contrast the sample MLA paper at the end of chapter 28 (pages 362–369) with the sample APA paper in this chapter (pages 390–396). Aside from issues of format and documentation, how do the research essay (MLA model) and the research report (APA model) compare in terms of focus, organization, voice, and treatment of sources?

Checklist: Learning Outcomes

Use the checklist below to assess how well you now understand and can use MLA and APA styles.

_____ I understand the basics of MLA and APA styles.

_____ I understand how to do in-text citation with each style.

_____ In the works-cited or references list, I can correctly list books and other nonperiodical documents.

_____ In the works-cited or references list, I can correctly list a range of periodical articles.

_____ In the works-cited or references list, I can correctly list online sources.

_____ In the works-cited or references list, I can correctly list primary, personal, and multimedia sources.

_____ I can format my paper according to the guidelines of MLA or APA.

30
Grammar

Grammar is the study of the structure and features of the language, consisting of rules and standards that are to be followed to produce acceptable writing and speaking. Parts of speech refers to the eight different categories that indicate how words are used in the English language—as nouns, pronouns, verbs, adjectives, adverbs, prepositions, conjunctions, or interjections.

Learning Outcomes

LO1 Noun
LO2 Pronoun
LO3 Verb
LO4 Adjective
LO5 Adverb
LO6 Preposition
LO7 Conjunction
LO8 Interjection

Noun
LO1

A **noun** is a word that names something: a person, a place, a thing, or an idea.

Toni Morrison/author	*Lone Star*/film
Renaissance/era	UC-Davis/university
A Congress of Wonders/book	

Classes of Nouns

All nouns are either **proper nouns** or **common nouns**. Nouns may also be classified as *individual* or *collective*, or *concrete* or *abstract*.

Proper Nouns — A proper noun, which is always capitalized, names a specific person, place, thing, or idea.

Rembrandt, Bertrand Russell	person
Stratford-upon-Avon, Tower of London	places
The Night Watch, Rosetta stone	things
New Deal, Christianity	ideas

Common Nouns — A common noun is a general name for a person, a place, a thing, or an idea. Common nouns are not capitalized.

optimist, instructor	person
cafeteria, park	places
computer, chair	things
freedom, love	ideas

Collective Nouns — A collective noun names a group or a unit.

family • audience • crowd • committee • team • class

Concrete Nouns — A concrete noun names a thing that is tangible (can be seen, touched, heard, smelled, or tasted).

child • the White Stripes • gym • village • microwave oven • pizza

Skyline, 2011 / Used under license from Shutterstock.com

Abstract Nouns

Abstract Nouns — An abstract noun names an idea, a condition, or a feeling—in other words, something that cannot be seen, touched, heard, smelled, or tasted.

> beauty • Jungian psychology • anxiety • agoraphobia • trust

Forms of Nouns

Nouns are grouped according to their *number, gender,* and *case.*

Number of Nouns — Number indicates whether a noun is singular or plural. A singular noun refers to one person, place, thing, or idea. A plural noun refers to more than one person, place, thing, or idea.

> Singular:
> student • laboratory • lecture • note • grade result
>
> Plural:
> students • laboratories • lectures • notes • grade results

Gender of Nouns — Gender indicates whether a noun is masculine, feminine, neuter, or indefinite.

Masculine	father • king • brother • men • colt • rooster
Feminine	mother • queen • sister • women • filly • hen
Neuter (without gender)	notebook • monitor • car • printer
Indefinite (masculine or feminine)	professor • customer • children • doctor • people

Case of Nouns — The case of a noun tells what role the noun plays in a sentence. There are three cases: *nominative, possessive,* and *objective.*

Nominative: A noun in the nominative case is used as a subject. The subject of a sentence tells who or what the sentence is about.

> **Dean Henning** manages the College of Arts and Communication.

Note: A noun is also in the nominative case when it is used as a predicate noun (or predicate nominative). A predicate noun follows a linking verb, usually a form of the be verb (such as *am, is, are, was, were, be, being, been*), and repeats or renames the subject.

> Ms. Yokum is the **person** to talk to about the college's impact in our community.

Possessive: A noun in the possessive case shows possession or ownership. In this form, it acts as an adjective.

> Our **president's** willingness to discuss concerns with students has boosted campus morale.

Objective: A noun in the objective case serves as an object of the preposition, a direct object, an indirect object, or an object complement.

> To survive, institutions of higher **learning** sometimes cut **budgets** in spite of **protests** from **students** and **instructors**.
> (*Learning* is the object of the preposition *of*, *protests* is the object of the preposition *in spite of*, *budgets* is the direct object of the verb *cut*, and *students* and *instructors* are the objects of the preposition *from*.)

A Closer Look: Direct and Indirect Objects

A **direct object** is a noun (or pronoun) that identifies what or who receives the action of the verb.

> Budget cutbacks reduced class **choices**.
> (*Choices* is the direct object of the active verb *reduced*.)

An **indirect object** is a noun (or pronoun) that identifies the person *to whom* or *for whom* something is done, or the thing *to which* or *for which* something is done. An indirect object is always accompanied by a direct object.

> Recent budget cuts have given **students** fewer class choices. (*Choices* is the direct object of *have given; students* is the indirect object.)

ESL Note: Not every transitive verb is followed by both a direct object and an indirect object. Both can, however, follow *give, send, show, tell, teach, find, sell, ask, offer, pay, pass,* and *hand.*

Pronoun

A pronoun is a word that is used in place of a noun. Most pronouns have an antecedent. An antecedent is the noun or pronoun that the pronoun refers to or replaces. Most pronouns have antecedents, but not all do. (See "Indefinite Pronouns" on page 401.)

Sample Pronouns:
Roger was the most interesting 10-year-old I ever taught. **He** was a good thinker and thus a good writer. **I** remember **his** paragraph about the cowboy hat **he** received from **his** grandparents. **It** was "too new looking." The brim was not rolled properly. But the hat's imperfections were not the main idea in Roger's writing. No, the main idea was how **he** was fixing the hat **himself** by wearing it when **he** showered.

Sample Antecedents:
As the wellness **counselor** checked *her* chart, several **students** *who* were waiting *their* turns shifted uncomfortably.
   (*Counselor* is the antecedent of *her; students* is the antecedent of *who* and *their.*)

Note: Each pronoun must agree with its antecedent in number, person, and gender. (See page 421.)

Classes of Pronouns

There are several classes of pronouns: *personal, reflexive and intensive, relative, indefinite, interrogative, demonstrative,* and *reciprocal.*

Quick Guide: Classes of Pronouns

Personal	I, me, my, mine / we, us, our, ours / you, your, yours / they, them, their, theirs / he, him, his, she, her, hers, it, its
Reflexive and Intensive	myself, yourself, himself, herself, itself, ourselves, yourselves, themselves
Relative	who, whose, whom, which, that
Indefinite	all, another, any, anybody, anyone, anything, both, each, each one, either, everybody, everyone, everything, few, many, most, much, neither, nobody, none, no one, nothing, one, other, several, some, somebody, someone, something, such
Interrogative	who, whose, whom, which, what
Demonstrative	this, that, these, those
Reciprocal	each other, one another

Personal Pronouns — A **personal pronoun** refers to a specific person or thing.

Marge started **her** car; **she** drove the antique convertible to *Monterey,* where **she** hoped to sell **it** at an auction.

Reflexive Pronouns — A **reflexive pronoun** is formed by adding *-self* or *-selves* to a personal pronoun. A reflexive pronoun can act as a direct object or an indirect object of a verb, an object of a preposition, or a predicate nominative.

> Charles loves **himself**.
>   ┈┈┈┈┈┈┈ direct object of **loves**
>
> Charles gives **himself** A's for fashion sense
>   ┈┈┈┈┈┈┈ indirect object of **gives**
>
> Charles smiles at **himself** in store windows.
>   ┈┈┈┈┈┈┈ object of preposition **at**
>
> Charles can be **himself** anywhere.
>   ┈┈┈┈┈┈┈ predicate nominative

Intensive Pronouns — An **intensive pronoun** intensifies, or emphasizes, the noun or pronoun it refers to.

> Leo **himself** taught his children to invest their lives in others.
>
> The lesson was sometimes painful—but they learned it **themselves**.

Relative Pronouns — A **relative pronoun** relates an adjective dependent (relative) clause to the noun or pronoun it modifies. (The noun is italicized in each example below; the relative pronoun is in bold.)

> *Freshmen* **who** believe they have a lot to learn are absolutely right.
>
> Just navigating this *campus*, **which** is huge, can be challenging.

Indefinite Pronouns — An **indefinite pronoun** refers to unnamed or unknown people, places, or things.

> **Everyone** seemed amused when I was searching for my classroom in the student center.
>   (The antecedent of *everyone* is unnamed.)
>
> **Nothing** is more unnerving than rushing at the last minute into the wrong room for the wrong class.
>   (The antecedent of *nothing* is unknown.)

Most indefinite pronouns are singular, so when they are used as subjects, they should have singular verbs. (See pages 418–420.)

Interrogative Pronouns — An **interrogative pronoun** asks a question.

> So **which** will it be—highlighting and attaching a campus map to the inside of your backpack, or being lost and late for the first two weeks?

Note: When an interrogative pronoun modifies a noun, it functions as an adjective.

Demonstrative Pronouns — A **demonstrative pronoun** points out people, places, or things.

> We advise **this**: Bring along as many maps and schedules as you need.
>
> **Those** are useful tools. **That** is the solution.

Note: When a demonstrative pronoun modifies a noun, it functions as an adjective.

Forms of Personal Pronouns

The **form** of a personal pronoun indicates its *number* (singular or plural), its *person* (first, second, or third), its *case* (nominative, possessive, or objective), and its *gender* (masculine, feminine, neuter, or indefinite).

Number of Pronouns — A personal pronoun is either singular *(I, you, he, she, it)* or plural *(we, you, they)*.

> **He** should have a budget and stick to it. (singular)
>
> **We** can help new students learn about budgeting. (plural)

Person of Pronouns — The person of a pronoun indicates whether the person is speaking (first person), is spoken to (second person), or is spoken about (third person).

First person is used to name the speaker(s).

> **I** know **I** need to handle **my** stress in a healthful way, especially during exam week; **my** usual chips-and-doughnuts binge isn't helping.
>   (singular)
>
> **We** all decided to bike to the tennis court.
>   (plural)

Second person is used to name the person(s) spoken to.

> Maria, **you** grab the rackets, okay?
>   (singular)
>
> John and Tanya, can **you** find the water bottles?
>   (plural)

Third person is used to name the person(s) or thing(s) spoken about.

> Today's students are interested in wellness issues. **They** are concerned about **their** health, fitness, and nutrition.
>   (plural)
>
> Maria practices yoga and feels **she** is calmer for **her** choice.
>   (singular)
>
> One of the advantages of regular exercise is that **it** raises one's energy level.
>   (singular)

Case of Pronouns

The case of each pronoun tells what role it plays in a sentence. There are three cases: *nominative*, *possessive*, and *objective*.

Nominative: A pronoun in the nominative case is used as a subject. The following are nominative forms: *I, you, he, she, it, we, they.*

> **He** found an old map in the trunk.
>
> My friend and **I** went biking. (not *me*)

A pronoun is also in the nominative case when it is used as a predicate nominative, following a linking verb (*am, is, are, was, were, seems*) and renaming the subject.

> It was **he** who discovered electricity. (not *him*)

Possessive: A pronoun in the possessive case shows possession or ownership: *my, mine, our, ours, his, her, hers, their, theirs, its, your, yours.* A possessive pronoun before a noun acts as an adjective: *your coat.*

> That coat is **hers**. | This coat is **mine**. | **Your** coat is lost.

Objective: A pronoun in the objective case can be used as the direct object, indirect object, object of a preposition, or object complement: *me, you, him, her, it, us, them.*

> Professor Adler hired **her**.
>   (*Her* is the direct object of the verb *hired*.)
>
> He showed Mary and **me** the language lab.
>   (*Me* is the indirect object of the verb *showed*.)
>
> He introduced the three of **us**—Mary, Shavonn, and **me**—to the faculty.
>   (*Us* is the object of the preposition *of*; *me* is part of the appositive renaming *us*.)

Gender of Pronouns

The gender of a pronoun indicates whether the pronoun is masculine, feminine, neuter, or indefinite.

Masculine	he, him, his
Feminine	she, her, hers
Neuter (without gender)	it, its
Indefinite (masculine or feminine)	they, them, their

Quick Guide: Number, Person, and Case of Personal Pronouns

	Nominative Case	Possessive Case	Objective Case
First Person Singular	I	my, mine	me
Second Person Singular	you	your, yours	you
Third Person Singular	he, she, it	his, her, hers, its	him, her, it
First Person Plural	we	our, ours	us
Second Person Plural	you	your, yours	you
Third Person Plural	they	their, theirs	them

Verb

LO3

A verb shows action *(pondered, grins)*, links words *(is, seemed)*, or accompanies another action verb as an auxiliary or helping verb *(can, does)*.

> Harry **honked** the horn. (shows action)

> Harry **is** impatient. (links words)

> Harry **was** honking the truck's horn.
> (accompanies the verb *honking*)

Classes of Verbs

Verbs are classified as action, auxiliary (helping), or linking (state of being).

Action Verbs: Transitive and Intransitive
— As its name implies, an action verb shows action. Some action verbs are *transitive;* others are *intransitive.* (The term *action* does not always refer to a physical activity.)

> Rain **splashed** the windshield. (transitive verb)

> Josie **drove** off the road. (intransitive verb)

Transitive: Transitive verbs have direct objects that receive the action.

> The health-care industry **employs** more than 7 million **workers** in the United States.
> (*Workers* is the direct object of the action verb *employs*.)

Intransitive: Intransitive verbs communicate action that is complete in itself. They do not need an object to receive the action.

> My new college roommate **smiles** and **laughs** a lot.

Note: Some verbs can be either transitive or intransitive.

> Ms. Hull **teaches** physiology and microbiology.
> (transitive)

> She **teaches** well. (intransitive)

Auxiliary (Helping) Verbs
— Auxiliary verbs (helping verbs) help to form some of the *tenses,* the *mood,* and the *voice* of the main verb. (See pages 404–405.)

Auxiliary Verbs				
is	were	can	shall	must
am	be	could	should	have
are	being	will	may	has
was	been	would	might	did

ESL Note: "Be" auxiliary verbs are always followed by either a verb ending in *ing* or a past participle.

Linking (State of Being) Verbs
— A linking verb is a special form of intransitive verb that links the subject of a sentence to a noun, a pronoun, or an adjective in the predicate.

> The streets **are** flooded. (adjective)

> The streets **are** rivers! (noun)

Common Linking Verbs				
am	be	been	is	were
are	become	being	was	

Additional Linking Verbs				
appear	look	sound	remain	taste
feel	seem	grow	smell	

Note: The verbs listed as "additional linking verbs" above function as linking verbs when they do not show actual action. An adjective usually follows these linking verbs.

> The sky **looked** ominous. (adjective)

> My little brother **grew** frightened. (adjective)

Note: When these same words are used as action verbs, an adverb or a direct object may follow them.

> I **looked** carefully at him. (adverb)

> My little brother **grew** corn for a science project.
> (direct object)

Forms of Verbs

A verb's form differs depending on its *number* (singular, plural), *person* (first, second, third), *tense* (present, past, future, present perfect, past perfect, future perfect), *voice* (active, passive), and *mood* (indicative, imperative, subjunctive).

Number of a Verb — Number indicates whether a verb is singular or plural. The verb and its subject both must be singular, or they both must be plural. (See "Subject-Verb Agreement," pages 418–420.)

> My college **enrolls** high schoolers in summer programs. (singular)

> Many colleges **enroll** high schoolers in summer courses. (plural)

Person of a Verb — Person indicates whether the subject of the verb is *first, second,* or *third person.* The verb and its subject must be in the same person. Verbs usually have a different form only in **third person singular of the present tense**.

	1st Person	2nd Person	3rd Person
Singular	I think	you think	he/she/it thinks
Plural	we think	you think	they think

Tense of a Verb — Tense indicates the time of an action or state of being. There are three basic *tenses* (past, present, and future) and three verbal *aspects* (progressive, perfect, and perfect progressive).

Present tense: This tense expresses action happening at the present time or regularly.

> In the United States, more than 75 percent of workers **hold** service jobs.

Present progressive tense: This tense also expresses action that is happening continually, in an ongoing fashion at the present time, but it is formed by combining *am, are,* or *is* and the present participle (ending in *ing*) of the main verb.

> More women than ever before **are working** outside the home.

Present perfect tense: This tense expresses action that began in the past and has recently been completed or that continues up to the present time.

> My sister **has taken** four years of swimming lessons.

Present perfect progressive tense: This tense also expresses an action that began in the past but stresses the continuing nature of the action. Like the present progressive tense, it is formed by combining auxiliary verbs (*have been* or *has been*) and present participles.

> She **has been taking** them since she was six years old.

Past tense: This tense expresses action that was completed at a particular time in the past.

> A hundred years ago, more than 75 percent of laborers **worked** in agriculture.

Past progressive tense: This tense expresses past action that continued over time. It is formed by combining *was* or *were* with the present participle of the main verb.

> In 1900, my great-grandparents **were farming**.

Past perfect tense: This tense expresses an action in the past that was completed at a specific time before another past action occurred.

> By the time we sat down for dinner, my cousins **had eaten** all the olives.

Past perfect progressive tense: This tense expresses a past action but stresses the continuing nature of the action. It is formed by using *had been* along with the present participle.

> They **had been eating** the olives all afternoon.

Future tense: This tense expresses action that will take place in the future.

> Next summer I **will work** as a lifeguard.

Future progressive tense: This tense expresses an action that will be continuous in the future.

> I **will be working** for the park district at North Beach.

Future perfect tense: This tense expresses future action that will be completed by a specific time.

> By 10:00 p.m., I **will have completed** my research project.

Future perfect progressive tense: This tense also expresses future action that will be completed by a specific time but (as with other perfect progressive tenses) stresses the action's continuous nature. It is formed using *will have been* along with the present participle.

> I **will have been researching** the project for three weeks by the time it's due.

Voice of a Verb — Voice indicates whether the subject is acting or being acted upon.

Active voice: This voice indicates that the subject of the verb is performing the action.

> People **update** their résumés on a regular basis.
> (The subject, *people*, is acting; *résumés* is the direct object.)

Passive voice: This voice indicates that the subject of the verb is being acted upon or is receiving the action. A passive verb is formed by combining a *be* verb with a past participle.

> Your résumé **should be updated** on a regular basis.
> (The subject, *résumé*, is receiving the action.)

Quick Guide: Using Active Voice

Generally, use active voice rather than passive voice for more direct, energetic writing. To change your passive sentences to active ones, do the following: First, find the noun that is doing the action and make it the subject. Then find the word that had been the subject and use it as the direct object.

> **Passive:** The winning goal **was scored** by Eva.
> (The subject, *goal*, is not acting.)
>
> **Active:** Eva **scored** the winning goal.
> (The subject, *Eva*, is acting.)

Note: When you want to emphasize the receiver more than the doer—or when the doer is unknown—use the passive voice. (Much technical and scientific writing regularly uses the passive voice.)

Mood of a Verb — The mood of a verb indicates the tone or attitude with which a statement is made.

Indicative mood: This mood is the most common, is used to state a fact or to ask a question.

> **Can** any theme **capture** the essence of the complex 1960s culture? President John F. Kennedy's directive [to the right] **represents** one ideal popular during that decade.

Imperative mood: This mood is used to give a command. (The subject of an imperative sentence is *you*, which is usually understood and not stated in the sentence.)

> **Ask** not what your country can do for you—**ask** what you can do for your country. —John F. Kennedy

Subjunctive mood: This mood is used to express a wish, an impossibility or unlikely condition, or a necessity. The subjunctive mood is often used with *if* or *that*. The verb forms below create an atypical subject-verb agreement, forming the subjunctive mood.

> If I **were** rich, I would travel for the rest of my life.
> (a wish)

> If each of your brain cells **were** one person, there would be enough people to populate 25 planets.
> (an impossibility)

> The English Department requires that every student **pass** a proficiency test.
> (a necessity)

Verbals — A verbal is a word that is made from a verb, but it functions as a noun, an adjective, or an adverb. There are three types of verbals: *gerunds, infinitives,* and *participles.*

Gerund: A **gerund** ends in *ing* and is used as a noun.

> **Waking** each morning is the first challenge. (subject)

> I start **moving** at about seven o'clock. (direct object)

> I work at **jump-starting** my weary system.
> (object of the preposition)

> As Woody Allen once said, "Eighty percent of life is **showing up**." (predicate nominative)

Infinitive: An **infinitive** is *to* and the base form of the verb. The infinitive may be used as a noun, an adjective, or an adverb.

To succeed is not easy. (noun)

That is the most important thing **to remember**. (adjective)

Students are wise **to work** hard. (adverb)

ESL Note: It can be difficult to know whether a gerund or an infinitive should follow a verb. It's helpful to become familiar with lists of specific verbs that can be followed by one but not the other.

Participle: A **present participle** ends in *ing* and functions as an adjective. A **past participle** ends in *ed* (or another past tense form) and also functions as an adjective.

The **studying** students were annoyed by the **partying** ones.

The students **playing** loud music were **annoying**. (These participles function as adjectives: *studying*, *partying*, *playing*, and *annoying* students. Notice, however, that *playing* has a direct object: *music*. All three types of verbals may have direct objects. See "Verbal Phrase" on page 414.)

Quick Guide: Using Verbals

Make sure that you use verbals correctly; look carefully at the examples below.

Verbal: **Diving** is a popular Olympic sport.
(*Diving* is a gerund used as a subject.)

Diving gracefully, the Olympian hoped to get high marks.
(*Diving* is a participle modifying *Olympian*.)

Verb: The next competitor was **diving** in the practice pool.
(Here, *diving* is a verb, not a verbal.)

Irregular Verbs

Irregular verbs can often be confusing. That's because the past tense and past participle of irregular verbs are formed by changing the word itself, not merely by adding *d* or *ed*. The following list contains the most troublesome irregular verbs.

Common Irregular Verbs and Their Principal Parts

Present Tense	Past Tense	Past Participle
am, be	was, were	been
arise	arose	arisen
awake	awoke, awaked	awoken, awaked
beat	beat	beaten
become	became	become
begin	began	begun
bite	bit	bitten, bit
blow	blew	blown
break	broke	broken
bring	brought	brought
build	built	built
burn	burnt, burned	burnt, burned
burst	burst	burst
buy	bought	bought
catch	caught	caught
choose	chose	chosen
come	came	come
cost	cost	cost
cut	cut	cut
dig	dug	dug
dive	dived, dove	dived
do	did	done
draw	drew	drawn
dream	dreamed, dreamt	dreamed, dreamt
drink	drank	drunk
drive	drove	driven
eat	ate	eaten

Present Tense	Past Tense	Past Participle
fall	fell	fallen
feel	felt	felt
fight	fought	fought
find	found	found
flee	fled	fled
fly	flew	flown
forget	forgot	forgotten, forgot
freeze	froze	frozen
get	got	gotten
give	gave	given
go	went	gone
grow	grew	grown
hang (execute)	hanged	hanged
hang (suspend)	hung	hung
have	had	had
hear	heard	heard
hide	hid	hidden
hit	hit	hit
keep	kept	kept
know	knew	known
lay	laid	laid
lead	led	led
leave	left	left
lend	lent	lent
let	let	let
lie (deceive)	lied	lied
lie (recline)	lay	lain
make	made	made
mean	meant	meant
meet	met	met
pay	paid	paid
prove	proved	proved, proven
put	put	put
read	read	read
ride	rode	ridden
ring	rang	rung

Present Tense	Past Tense	Past Participle
rise	rose	risen
run	ran	run
see	saw	seen
set	set	set
shake	shook	shaken
shine (light)	shone	shone
shine (polish)	shined	shined
show	showed	shown
shrink	shrank	shrunk
sing	sang	sung
sink	sank	sunk
sit	sat	sat
sleep	slept	slept
speak	spoke	spoken
spend	spent	spent
spring	sprang	sprung
stand	stood	stood
steal	stole	stolen
strike	struck	struck, stricken
strive	strove	striven
swear	swore	sworn
swim	swam	swum
swing	swung	swung
take	took	taken
teach	taught	taught
tear	tore	torn
tell	told	told
think	thought	thought
throw	threw	thrown
wake	woke, waked	woken, waked
wear	wore	worn
weave	wove	woven
wind	wound	wound
wring	wrung	wrung
write	wrote	written

Adjective _____ LO4

An adjective describes or modifies a noun or pronoun. The articles *a*, *an*, and *the* are adjectives.

> Advertising is **a big** and **powerful** industry.
> (*A*, *big*, and *powerful* modify the noun *industry*.)

Note: Many demonstrative, indefinite, and interrogative forms may be used as either adjectives or pronouns (*that*, *these*, *many*, *some*, *whose*, and so on). These words are adjectives if they come before a noun and modify it; they are pronouns if they stand alone.

> **Some** advertisements are less than truthful.
> (*Some* modifies *advertisements* and is an adjective.)

> **Many** cause us to chuckle at their outrageous claims.
> (*Many* stands alone; it is a pronoun and replaces the noun *advertisements*.)

Proper Adjectives — Proper adjectives are created from proper nouns and are capitalized.

> **English** has been influenced by advertising slogans.
> (proper noun)

> The **English** language is constantly changing.
> (proper adjective)

Predicate Adjectives — A predicate adjective follows a form of the *be* verb (or other linking verb) and describes the subject. (See "Linking (State of Being) Verbs" on page 403.)

> At its best, advertising is **useful;** at its worst, **deceptive**.
> (*Useful* and *deceptive* modify the noun *advertising*.)

Forms of Adjectives — Adjectives have three forms: *positive*, *comparative*, and *superlative*.

The **positive form** is the adjective in its regular form. It describes a noun or a pronoun without comparing it to anyone or anything else.

> Joysport walking shoes are **strong** and **comfortable**.

The **comparative form** (*-er*, *more*, or *less*) compares two things. (*More* and *less* are used generally with adjectives of two or more syllables.)

> Air soles make Mile Eaters **stronger** and **more comfortable** than Joysports.

The **superlative form** (*-est*, *most*, or *least*) compares three or more things. (*Most* and *least* are used most often with adjectives of two or more syllables.)

> My old Canvas Wonders are the **strongest, most comfortable** shoes of all!

Adverb _____ LO5

An adverb describes or modifies a verb, an adjective, another adverb, or a whole sentence. An adverb answers questions such as *how*, *when*, *where*, *why*, *how often*, or *how much*.

> The temperature fell **sharply**.
> (*Sharply* modifies the verb *fell*.)

> The temperature was **quite** low.
> (*Quite* modifies the adjective *low*.)

> The temperature dropped **very quickly**.
> (*Very* modifies the adverb *quickly*, which modifies the verb *dropped*.)

> **Unfortunately,** the temperature stayed cool.
> (*Unfortunately* modifies the whole sentence.)

Types of Adverbs — Adverbs can be grouped in four ways: *time*, *place*, *manner*, and *degree*.

Time: These adverbs tell *when*, *how often*, and *how long*.

today, yesterday
daily, weekly
briefly, eternally

Place: These adverbs tell *where*, *to where*, and *from where*.

here, there
nearby, beyond
backward, forward

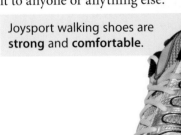

Manner: These adverbs often end in *ly* and tell *how* something is done.

precisely
regularly
regally
well

Degree: These adverbs tell *how much* or *how little*.

substantially	partly
greatly	too
entirely	

Forms of Adverbs — Adverbs have three forms: *positive*, *comparative*, and *superlative*.

The **positive form** is the adverb in its regular form. It describes a verb, an adjective, or another adverb without comparing it to anyone or anything else.

> With Joysport shoes, you'll walk **fast**. They support your feet **well**.

The **comparative form** (*-er*, *more*, or *less*) compares two things. (*More* and *less* are used generally with adverbs of two or more syllables.)

> Wear Jockos instead of Joysports, and you'll walk **faster**. Jockos' special soles support your feet **better** than the Joysports do.

The **superlative form** (*-est*, *most*, or *least*) compares three or more things. (*Most* and *least* are used most often with adverbs of two or more syllables.)

> Really, I walk **fastest** wearing my old Canvas Wonders. They seem to support my feet, my knees, and my pocketbook **best** of all.

Quick Guide: Regular and Irregular Adverbs

	Regular	Irregular
Positive	fast effectively	well badly
Comparative	faster more effectively	better worse
Superlative	fastest most effectively	best worst

Preposition

A preposition is a word (or group of words) that shows the relationship between its object (a noun or pronoun following the preposition) and another word in the sentence.

> **Regarding** your reasons **for** going **to** college, do they all hinge **on** getting a good job **after** graduation?
> (In this sentence, *reasons, going, college, getting,* and *graduation* are objects of their preceding prepositions *regarding, for, to, on,* and *after.*)

Prepositions

aboard	down	outside
about	down from	outside of
above	during	over
according to	except	over to
across	except for	owing to
across from	excepting	past
after	for	prior to
against	from	regarding
along	from among	round
alongside	from between	save
alongside of	from under	since
along with	in	subsequent to
amid	in addition to	through
among	in behalf of	throughout
apart from	in front of	till
around	in place of	to
as far as	in regard to	together with
aside from	inside	toward
at	inside of	under
away from	in spite of	underneath
back of	instead of	until
because of	into	unto
before	like	up
behind	near	upon
below	near to	up to
beneath	notwithstanding	with
beside	of	within
besides	off	without
between	on	
beyond	on account of	
but	on behalf of	
by	onto	
by means of	on top of	
concerning	opposite	
considering	out	
despite	out of	

ESL Note: Prepositions often pair up with a verb and become part of an idiom, a slang expression, or a two-word verb.

Prepositional Phrases — A prepositional phrase includes the preposition, the object of the preposition, and the modifiers of the object. A prepositional phrase may function as an adverb or an adjective.

> A broader knowledge **of the world** is one benefit **of higher education.**
> (The two phrases function as adjectives modifying the nouns *knowledge* and *benefit* respectively.)
>
> He placed the flower **in the window.**
> (The phrase functions as an adverb modifying the verb *placed.*)

Conjunction LO7

A conjunction connects individual words or groups of words.

> **When** we came back to Paris, it was clear **and** cold **and** lovely. —Ernest Hemingway

Coordinating Conjunctions — Coordinating conjunctions usually connect a word to a word, a phrase to a phrase, or a clause to a clause. The words, phrases, or clauses joined by a coordinating conjunction are equal in importance or are of the same type.

> Civilization is a race between education **and** catastrophe. —H. G. Wells

Correlative Conjunctions — Correlative conjunctions are a type of coordinating conjunction used in pairs.

> There are two inadvisable ways to think: **either** believe everything **or** doubt everything.

Subordinating Conjunctions — Subordinating conjunctions connect two clauses that are not equally important. A subordinating conjunction connects a dependent clause to an independent clause. The conjunction is part of the dependent clause.

> Experience is the worst teacher; it gives the test **before** it presents the lesson.
> (The clause *before it presents the lesson* is dependent. It connects to the independent clause *it gives the test.*)

Note: Relative pronouns can also connect clauses. (See "Relative Pronouns" on page 401.)

Conjunctions

Coordinating	
	and, but, or, nor, for, so, yet
Correlative	
	either, or; neither, nor; not only, but (but also); both, and; whether, or
Subordinating	
	after, although, as, as if, as long as, because, before, even though, if, in order that, provided that, since, so that, than, that, though, unless, until, when, whenever, where, while

Interjection LO8

An interjection communicates strong emotion or surprise (*oh, ouch, hey,* and so on). Punctuation (often a comma or an exclamation point) is used to set off an interjection.

> **Hey! Wait! Well,** so much for catching the bus.

 A Closer Look: Parts of Speech

Noun — A noun is a word that names something: a person, a place, a thing, or an idea.

Toni Morrison/author	*Lone Star*/film
UC–Davis/university	Renaissance/era
A Congress of Wonders/book	

Pronoun — A pronoun is a word used in place of a noun.

| I | my | that | themselves | which |
| it | ours | they | everybody | you |

Verb — A verb is a word that expresses action, links words, or acts as an auxiliary verb to the main verb.

| are | break | drag | fly | run | sit | was |
| bite | catch | eat | is | see | tear | were |

Adjective — An adjective describes or modifies a noun or pronoun. (The articles *a, an,* and *the* are adjectives.)

The carbonated drink went down easy on **that hot, dry** day. (*The* and *carbonated* modify *drink; that, hot,* and *dry* modify *day.*)

Adverb — An adverb describes or modifies a verb, an adjective, another adverb, or a whole sentence. An adverb generally answers questions such as *how, when, where, how often,* or *how much.*

greatly	precisely	regularly	there
here	today	partly	quickly
slowly	yesterday	nearly	loudly

Preposition — A preposition is a word (or group of words) that shows the relationship between its object (a noun or pronoun that follows the preposition) and another word in the sentence. Prepositions introduce prepositional phrases, which are modifiers.

| across | for | with | out | to | of |

Conjunction — A conjunction connects individual words or groups of words.

| and | because | but | for | or | since | so | yet |

Interjection — An interjection is a word that communicates strong emotion or surprise. Punctuation (often a comma or an exclamation point) is used to set off an interjection from the rest of the sentence.

Stop! No! What, am I invisible?

31
Sentences

A **sentence** is made up of at least a subject (sometimes understood) and a verb and expresses a complete thought. Sentences can make statements, ask questions, give commands, or express feelings.

> The Web delivers the universe in a box.

Learning Outcomes

LO1 Subjects and Predicates
LO2 Phrases
LO3 Clauses
LO4 Sentence Variety

Subjects and Predicates
LO1

Sentences have two main parts: a **subject** and a **predicate**.

> Technology frustrates many people.

Note: In the sentence above, *technology* is the subject—the sentence talks about technology. *Frustrates many people* is the complete predicate—it tells what the subject is doing.

The Subject

The **subject** names the person or thing either performing the action, receiving the action, or being described or renamed. The subject is most often a noun or a pronoun.

> **Technology** is an integral part of almost every business.

> **Manufacturers** need technology to compete in the world market.

> **They** could not go far without it.

A verbal phrase or a noun dependent clause may also function as a subject.

> **To survive without technology** is difficult.
>   (infinitive phrase)

> **Downloading information from the Web** is easy.
>   (gerund phrase)

> **That the information age would arrive** was inevitable. (noun dependent clause)

Note: To determine the subject of a sentence, ask yourself *who* or *what* performs or receives the action or is described. In most sentences, the subject comes before the verb; however, in many questions and some other instances, that order is reversed.

ESL Note: Some languages permit the omission of a subject in a sentence; English does not. A subject must be included in every sentence. (The only exception is an "understood subject," which is discussed on page 413.)

Simple Subject

— A **simple subject** is the subject without the words that describe or modify it.

> Thirty years ago, reasonably well-trained **mechanics** could fix any car on the road.

Complete Subject

— A **complete subject** is the simple subject and the words that describe or modify it.

> Thirty years ago, **reasonably well-trained mechanics** could fix any car on the road.

Compound Subject

— A **compound subject** is composed of two or more simple subjects joined by a conjunction and sharing the same predicate(s).

> Today, **mechanics** and **technicians** would need to master a half million manual pages to fix every car on the road.
>
> ---
>
> **Dealerships** and their service **departments** must sometimes explain that situation to the customers.

Understood Subject

— Sometimes a subject is **understood**. This means it is not stated in the sentence, but a reader clearly understands what the subject is. An understood subject occurs in a command (imperative sentence).

> **(You)** Park on this side of the street.
>   (The subject *you* is understood.)
>
> ---
>
> Put the CD player in the trunk.

Delayed Subject

— In sentences that begin with *There is, There was,* or *Here is,* the subject follows the verb.

> There are 70,000 **fans** in the stadium.
>   (The subject is *fans; are* is the verb. *There* is an expletive, an empty word.)
>
> ---
>
> Here is a **problem** for stadium security.
>   (*Problem* is the subject. *Here* is an adverb.)

The subject is also delayed in questions.

> Where was the **event**? (*Event* is the subject.)
>
> ---
>
> Was **Dave Matthews** playing?
>   (*Dave Matthews* is the subject.)

The Predicate (Verb)

The **predicate**, which contains the verb, is the part of the sentence that either tells what the subject is doing, tells what is being done to the subject, or describes or renames the subject.

> Students **need technical skills as well as basic academic skills**.

Simple Predicate

— A **simple predicate** is the complete verb without the words that describe or modify it. (The complete verb can consist of more that one word.)

> Today's workplace **requires** employees to have a range of skills.

Complete Predicate

— A **complete predicate** is the verb, all the words that modify or explain it, and any objects or complements.

> Today's workplace **requires employees to have a range of skills**.

Compound Predicate

— A **compound predicate** is composed of two or more verbs, all the words that modify or explain them, and any objects or complements.

> Engineers **analyze problems** and **calculate solutions**.

Direct Object

— A **direct object** is the part of the predicate that receives the action of an active transitive verb. A direct object makes the meaning of the verb complete.

> Marcos visited several **campuses**.
>   (The direct object *campuses* receives the action of the verb *visited* by answering the question "Marcos visited what?")

Note: A direct object may be compound.

> A counselor explained the academic **programs** and the application **process**.

Indirect Object

Indirect Object — An **indirect object** is the word(s) that tells *to whom/to what* or *for whom/for what* something is done. A sentence must have a direct object before it can have an indirect object.

> I wrote **them** a note.

Quick Guide: Indirect Object

Use these questions to find an indirect object:

What is the verb? ·········· *showed*

Showed what? ············ *school* (direct object)

Showed school ·········· *children* (indirect object) to whom?

> I showed our **children** my new school.

Note: An indirect object may be compound.

> I gave the **instructor** and a few **classmates** my e-mail address.

Phrases ———————— LO2

A **phrase** is a group of related words that functions as a single part of speech. A phrase lacks a subject, a predicate, or both. There are three phrases in the following sentence:

> Examples **of technology can be found in ancient civilizations.**

of technology
: (prepositional phrase that functions as an adjective; no subject or predicate)

can be found
: (verb phrase—all of the words of the verb; no subject)

in ancient civilizations
: (prepositional phrase that functions as an adverb; no subject or predicate)

Types of Phrases

There are several types of phrases: *verb, verbal, prepositional, appositive,* and *absolute.*

Verb Phrase — A **verb phrase** consists of a main verb and its helping verbs.

> Students, worried about exams, **have camped** at the library all week.

Verbal Phrase — A **verbal phrase** is a phrase that expands on one of the three types of verbals: *gerund, infinitive,* or *participle.*

Gerund Phrase: A gerund phrase consists of a gerund and its modifiers and objects. The whole phrase functions as a noun.

> **Becoming a marine biologist** is Rashanda's dream.
> (The gerund phrase is used as the subject of the sentence.)

> She has acquainted herself with the various methods for **collecting sea-life samples.**
> (The gerund phrase is the object of the preposition *for.*)

Infinitive Phrase: An infinitive phrase consists of an infinitive and its modifiers and objects. The whole phrase functions as a noun, an adjective, or an adverb.

> **To dream** is the first step in any endeavor.
> (The infinitive phrase functions as a noun used as the subject.)

> Remember **to make a plan to realize your dream.**
> (The infinitive phrase *to make a plan* functions as a noun used as a direct object; *to realize your dream* functions as an adjective modifying *plan.*)

> Finally, apply all of your talents and skills **to achieve your goals.**
> (The infinitive phrase functions as an adverb modifying *apply.*)

Participial Phrase: A participial phrase consists of a present or past participle (a verb form ending in *ing* or *ed*) and its modifiers. The phrase functions as an adjective.

Doing poorly in biology, Theo signed up for a tutor.
(The participial phrase modifies the noun *Theo*.)

Some students **frustrated by difficult course work** don't seek help.
(The participial phrase modifies the noun *students*.)

A Closer Look:
Functions of Verbal Phrases

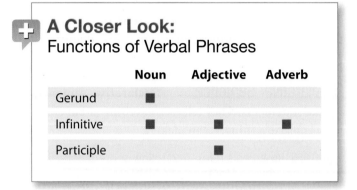

	Noun	Adjective	Adverb
Gerund	■		
Infinitive	■	■	■
Participle		■	

Prepositional Phrase — A **prepositional phrase**
is a group of words beginning with a preposition and ending with its object, a noun or a pronoun. Prepositional phrases are used mainly as adjectives and adverbs. See page 409 for a list of prepositions.

Denying the existence **of exam week** hasn't worked **for anyone** yet.
(The prepositional phrase *of exam week* is used as an adjective modifying the noun *existence; for anyone* is used as an adverb modifying the verb *has worked*.)

Test days still dawn and GPAs still plummet for **the unprepared student.**
(The prepositional phrase *for the unprepared student* is used as an adverb modifying the verbs *dawn* and *plummet*.)

ESL Note: Do not mistake the following adverbs for nouns and incorrectly use them as objects of prepositions: *here, there, everywhere.*

Appositive Phrase — An **appositive phrase,** which
follows a noun or a pronoun and renames it, consists of a noun and its modifiers. An appositive adds new information about the noun or pronoun it follows.

The Olympic-size pool, **a prized addition to the physical education building,** gets plenty of use.
(The appositive phrase renames *pool*.)

Absolute Phrase — An **absolute phrase** consists of
a noun and a participle (plus the participle's object, if there is one, and any modifiers). It usually modifies the entire sentence.

Their enthusiasm sometimes waning, the students who cannot swim are required to take lessons.
(The noun *enthusiasm* is modified by the present participle *waning*; the entire phrase modifies *students*.)

Note: Phrases can add valuable information to sentences, but some phrases add nothing but "fat" to your writing. For a list of phrases to avoid, see page 88.

Clauses _____ LO3

A **clause** is a group of related words that has both a subject and a verb.

Independent/Dependent Clauses — An **independent clause** contains at least one subject and one verb,
presents a complete thought, and can stand alone as a sentence; a **dependent clause** (also called a subordinate clause) does not present a complete thought and cannot stand alone (make sense) as a sentence.

Though airplanes are twentieth-century inventions (dependent clause), people have always dreamed of flying (independent clause).

Types of Clauses

There are three basic types of dependent, or subordinate, clauses: *adverb, adjective,* and *noun.* These dependent clauses are combined with independent clauses to form complex and compound-complex sentences.

Adverb Clause — An **adverb clause** is used like an
adverb to modify a verb, an adjective, or an adverb. All adverb clauses begin with subordinating conjunctions.

Because Orville won a coin toss, he got to fly the power-driven air machine first.
(The adverb clause modifies the verb *got*.)

Adjective Clause

Adjective Clause — An **adjective clause** is used like an adjective to modify a noun or a pronoun. Adjective clauses begin with relative pronouns *(which, that, who)*.

> The men **who invented the first airplane** were brothers, Orville and Wilbur Wright.
> (The adjective clause modifies the noun *men*. *Who* is the subject of the adjective clause.)

> The first flight, **which took place December 17, 1903,** was made by Orville.
> (The adjective clause modifies the noun *flight*. *Which* is the subject of the adjective clause.)

Noun Clause

Noun Clause — A **noun clause** is used in place of a noun. Noun clauses can appear as subjects, as direct or indirect objects, as predicate nominatives, or as objects of prepositions. Noun clauses can also play a role in the independent clause. They are introduced by subordinating words such as *what, that, when, why, how, whatever, who, whom, whoever,* and *whomever*.

> He wants to know **what made modern aviation possible.**
> (The noun clause functions as the object of the infinitive.)

> **Whoever invents an airplane with vertical takeoff ability** will be a hero.
> (The noun clause functions as the subject.)

Note: If you can replace a whole clause with the pronoun *something* or *someone*, it is a noun clause.

Sentence Variety

LO4

A sentence can be classified according to the kind of statement it makes and according to the way it is constructed.

Kinds of Sentences

Sentences can make five basic kinds of statements: *declarative, interrogative, imperative, exclamatory,* or *conditional*.

Declarative Sentence — **Declarative sentences** make statements. They tell us something about a person, a place, a thing, or an idea.

> In 1955, Rosa Parks refused to follow segregation rules on a bus in Montgomery, Alabama.

Interrogative Sentence — **Interrogative sentences** ask questions.

> Do you think Ms. Parks knew she was making history?

> Would you have had the courage to do what she did?

Imperative Sentence — **Imperative sentences** give commands. They often contain an understood subject *(you)*.

> Read chapters 6 through 10 for tomorrow.

ESL Note: Imperative sentences with an understood subject are the only sentences in which it is acceptable to have no subjects stated.

Exclamatory Sentence — **Exclamatory sentences** communicate strong emotion or surprise. They are punctuated with exclamation points.

> I simply can't keep up with these long reading assignments!

> Oh my gosh, you scared me!

Conditional Sentence

Conditional sentences express two circumstances. One of the circumstances depends on the other circumstance. The words *if*, *when*, or *unless* are often used in the dependent clause in conditional sentences.

> **If** you practice a few study-reading techniques, college reading loads will be manageable.
>
> **When** I manage my time, it seems I have more of it.
>
> Don't ask me to help you **unless** you are willing to do the reading first.

Structure of Sentences

A sentence may be *simple, compound, complex,* or *compound-complex,* depending on how the independent and dependent clauses are combined.

Simple Sentence

A **simple sentence** contains one independent clause. The independent clause may have compound subjects and verbs, and it may also contain phrases.

> My **back aches**.
> (single subject: *back*; single verb: *aches*)
>
> My **teeth** and my **eyes hurt**.
> (compound subject: *teeth* and *eyes*; single verb: *hurt*)
>
> My **memory** and my **logic come** and **go**.
> (compound subject: *memory* and *logic*; compound verb: *come* and *go*)
>
> **I must need** a **vacation**.
> (single subject: *I*; single verb: *must need*; direct object: *vacation*)

Compound Sentence

A **compound sentence** consists of two independent clauses. The clauses must be joined by a semicolon, by a comma and a coordinating conjunction (*and, but, or, nor, so, for, yet*), or by a semicolon followed by a conjunctive adverb (*besides, however, instead, meanwhile, then, therefore*) and a comma.

> I take good care of myself**;** I get enough sleep.
>
> I had eight hours of sleep**, so** why am I so exhausted?
>
> I still feel fatigued**; therefore,** I must need more exercise.

Complex Sentence

A **complex sentence** contains one independent clause (in bold) and one or more dependent clauses (underlined).

> When I can, **I get eight hours of sleep**.
> (dependent clause; independent clause)
>
> When I get up on time, and if someone hasn't used up all the milk, **I eat breakfast**.
> (two dependent clauses; independent clause)

When the dependent clause comes before the independent clause, use a comma.

Compound-Complex Sentence

A **compound-complex sentence** contains two or more independent clauses (in bold type) and one or more dependent clauses (underlined).

> If I'm not in a hurry, **I take leisurely walks, and I try to spot some wildlife**.
> (dependent clause; two independent clauses)
>
> **I saw a hawk** when I was walking, and **other smaller birds were chasing it**.
> (independent clause, dependent clause; independent clause)

Stephen Mcsweeny, 2011 / Used under license from Shutterstock.com

32
Sentence Errors

This chapter will help you familiarize yourself with common sentence errors, so that you will know what to watch for when editing your writing. Remember, sentence errors can derail the meaning of your writing, so be careful to avoid them.

Learning Outcomes

LO1 Subject-Verb Agreement

LO2 Pronoun-Antecedent Agreement

LO3 Shifts in Sentence Construction

LO4 Fragments, Comma Splices, and Run-Ons

LO5 Misplaced and Dangling Modifiers

LO6 Ambiguous Wording

LO7 Nonstandard Language

Subject-Verb Agreement
LO1

The subject and verb of any clause must agree in both *person* and *number*. *Person* indicates whether the subject of the verb is *first*, *second*, or *third* person. *Number* indicates whether the subject and verb are *singular* or *plural*.

	Singular	Plural
First Person	I think	we think
Second Person	you think	you think
Third Person	he/she/it thinks	they think

Agreement in Number — A verb must agree in number (singular or plural) with its subject.

The **student was** rewarded for her hard work.
(Both the subject *student* and the verb *was* are singular; they agree in number.)

Note: Do not be confused by phrases that come between the subject and the verb. Such phrases may begin with words like *in addition to, as well as,* or *together with*.

The **instructor**, as well as the students, is expected to attend the orientation.
(*Instructor*, not *students*, is the subject.)

Compound Subjects — **Compound subjects** connected with *and* usually require a plural verb.

Dedication and creativity are trademarks of successful students.

Note: If a compound subject joined by *and* is thought of as a unit, use a singular verb.

Macaroni and cheese is always available in the cafeteria.

Brooke Becker, 2011 / Used under license from Shutterstock.com

Delayed Subjects

Delayed subjects occur when the verb comes *before* the subject in a sentence. In these inverted sentences, the true (delayed) subject must still agree with the verb.

> There **are** many nontraditional **students** on our campus. Here **is** the **syllabus** you need.
> (*Students* and *syllabus* are the subjects of these sentences, not the adverbs *there* and *here*.)

Note: Using an inverted sentence, on occasion, will lend variety to your writing style. Simply remember to make the delayed subjects agree with the verbs.

> However, included among the list's topmost items **was "revise research paper."**
> (Because the true subject here is singular—one item—the singular verb *was* is correct.)

Titles as Subjects

When the subject of a sentence is the title of a work of art, literature, or music, the verb should be singular. This is also true of a word (or phrase) being used as a word (or phrase).

> *Lyrical Ballads* **was published** in 1798 by two of England's greatest poets, Wordsworth and Coleridge.
> (Even though the title of the book, *Lyrical Ballads*, is plural in form, it is still a single title being used as the subject, correctly taking the singular verb *was*.)

> **"Over-the-counter drugs" is** a phrase that means nonprescription medications.
> (Even though the phrase is plural in form, it is still a single phrase being used as the subject, correctly taking the singular verb *is*.)

Singular Subjects with *Or* or *Nor*

Singular subjects joined by *or* or *nor* take a singular verb.

> Neither a **textbook** nor a **notebook is required** for this class.

Note: When the subject nearer a present-tense verb is the singular pronoun *I* or *you,* the correct singular verb does not end in *s.*

> Neither **Marcus** nor **I feel** (not *feels*) right about this.

> Either **Rosa** or **you have** (not *has*) to take notes for me.

> Either **you** or **Rosa has** to take notes for me.

Singular/Plural Subjects

When one of the subjects joined by *or* or *nor* is singular and one is plural, the verb must agree with the subject nearer the verb.

> Neither the **professor** nor her **students were** in the lab.
> (The plural subject *students* is nearer the verb; therefore, the plural verb *were* agrees with *students*.)

> Neither the **students** nor the **professor was** in the lab.
> (The singular subject *professor* is nearer the verb; therefore, the singular verb *was* is used to agree with *professor*.)

Collective Nouns

Generally, **collective nouns** (*faculty, pair, crew, assembly, congress, species, crowd, army, team, committee,* and so on) take a singular verb. However, if you want to emphasize differences among individuals in the group or are referring to the group as individuals, you can use a plural verb.

> My lab **team takes** its work very seriously.
> (*Team* refers to the group as a unit; it requires a singular verb, *takes*.)

> The **team assume** separate responsibilities for each study they undertake.
> (In this example, *team* refers to individuals within the group; it requires a plural verb, *assume*.)

Note: Collective nouns such as (the) *police, poor, elderly,* and *young* use plural verbs.

> The police direct traffic here between 7:00 and 9:00 a.m.

Plural Nouns with Singular Meaning

Some nouns that are plural in form but singular in meaning take a singular verb: *mumps, measles, news, mathematics, economics, robotics,* and so on.

> **Economics is** sometimes called "the dismal science."

> The economic **news is** not very good.

Note: The most common exceptions are *scissors, trousers, tidings,* and *pliers.*

> The **scissors are** missing again.

> **Are** these **trousers** prewashed?

With Linking Verbs — When a sentence contains a linking verb (usually a form of *be*)—and a noun or pronoun comes before and after that verb—the verb must agree with the subject, not the predicate nominative (the noun or pronoun coming after the verb).

> The cause of his problem **was** poor study habits.
> (*Cause* requires a singular verb, even though the predicate nominative, *habits*, is plural.)
>
> ---
>
> His poor study habits **were** the cause of his problem.
> (*Habits* requires a plural verb, even though the predicate nominative, *cause*, is singular.)

Nouns Showing Measurement, Time, and Money — Mathematical phrases and phrases that name a period of time, a unit of measurement, or an amount of money take a singular verb.

> Three and three **is** six.
>
> ---
>
> Eight pages **is** a long paper on this topic.
>
> ---
>
> In my opinion, two dollars **is** a high price for a cup of coffee.

Relative Pronouns — When a **relative pronoun** (*who, which, that*) is used as the subject of a dependent clause, the number of the verb is determined by that pronoun's antecedent. (The *antecedent* is the word to which the pronoun refers.)

> This is one of the **books that are** required for English class.
> (The relative pronoun *that* requires the plural verb *are* because its antecedent is *books*, not the word *one*. To test this type of sentence for agreement, read the *of* phrase first: *Of the books that are* . . .)

Note: Generally, the antecedent is the nearest noun or pronoun to the relative pronoun and is often the object of a preposition. Sometimes, however, the antecedent is not the nearest noun or pronoun, especially in sentences with the phrase "the only one of."

> Dr. Graciosa wondered why Claire was the only **one** of her students **who was** not attending lectures regularly.
> (In this case, the addition of the modifiers *the only* changes the meaning of the sentence. The antecedent of *who* is *one*, not *students*. Only one student was not attending.)

Indefinite Pronoun with Singular Verb — Many indefinite pronouns (*someone, somebody, something; anyone, anybody, anything; no one, nobody, nothing; everyone, everybody, everything; each, either, neither, one, this*) serving as subjects require a singular verb.

> **Everybody is** welcome to attend the chancellor's reception.
>
> ---
>
> **No one was** sent an invitation.

Note: Although it may seem to indicate more than one, *each* is a singular pronoun and requires a singular verb. Do not be confused by words or phrases that come between the indefinite pronoun and the verb.

> **Each** of the new students **is** (not *are*) **encouraged** to attend the reception.

Indefinite Pronoun with Plural Verb — Some indefinite pronouns (*both, few, many, most,* and *several*) are plural; they require a plural verb.

> **Few are** offered the opportunity to study abroad.
>
> ---
>
> **Most take** advantage of opportunities closer to home.

Indefinite Pronoun or Quantity Word with Singular/Plural Verb — Some indefinite pronouns or quantity words (*all, any, most, part, half, none,* and *some*) may be either singular or plural, depending on the nouns they refer to. Look inside the prepositional phrase to see what the antecedent is.

> **Some** of the students **were** missing.
> (*Students*, the noun that *some* refers to, is plural; therefore, the pronoun *some* is considered plural, and the plural verb *were* is used to agree with it.)
>
> ---
>
> **Most** of the lecture **was** over by the time we arrived.
> (Because *lecture* is singular, *most* is also singular, requiring the singular verb *was*.)

Pronoun–Antecedent Agreement

LO2

A pronoun must agree in number, person, and gender (sex) with its *antecedent*. The antecedent is the word to which the pronoun refers.

> **Yoshi** brought **his** laptop and e-book to school.
> (The pronoun *his* refers to the antecedent *Yoshi*. Both the pronoun and its antecedent are singular, third person, and masculine; therefore, the pronoun is said to agree with its antecedent.)

Singular Pronoun

— Use a singular pronoun to refer to such antecedents as *each, either, neither, one, anyone, anybody, everyone, everybody, somebody, another, nobody,* and *a person.*

> **Each** of the maintenance vehicles has **their** doors locked at night. (Incorrect)

> **Each** of the maintenance vehicles has **its** doors locked at night. (Correct: Both *Each* and *its* are singular.)

> **Somebody** left **his or her** (not *their*) vehicle unlocked. (Correct)

Plural Pronoun

— When a plural pronoun (*they, their*) is mistakenly used with a singular indefinite pronoun (such as *everyone* or *everybody*), you may correct the sentence by replacing *their* or *they* with optional pronouns (*her* or *his* or *he* or *she*), or make the antecedent plural.

> **Everyone** must learn to wait **their** turn. (Incorrect)

> **Everyone** must learn to wait **her or his** turn. (Correct: Optional pronouns *her* or *his* are used.)

> **People** must learn to wait **their** turns. (Correct: The singular antecedent, *Everyone*, is changed to the plural antecedent, *People*.)

Two or More Antecedents

— When two or more antecedents are joined by *and*, they are considered plural.

> **Tomas** and **Jamal** are finishing **their** assignments.

When two or more singular antecedents are joined by *or* or *nor*, they are considered singular.

> **Connie** or **Shavonn** left **her** headset in the library.

Note: If one of the antecedents is masculine and one feminine, the pronouns should likewise be masculine and feminine.

> Is **Ahmad** or **Phyllis** bringing **his or her** laptop?

Note: If one of the antecedents joined by *or* or *nor* is singular and one is plural, the pronoun is made to agree with the nearer antecedent.

> Neither **Ravi** nor **his friends** want to spend **their** time studying.

> Neither **his friends** nor **Ravi** wants to spend **his** time studying.

Shifts in Sentence Construction

LO3

A shift is an improper change in structure midway through a sentence. The following examples will help you identify and fix several different kinds of shifts.

Shift in Person

— **Shift in person** is mixing first, second, or third person within a sentence.

> **Shift:** **One** may get spring fever unless **you** live in California or Florida.
> (The sentence shifts from third person, *one*, to second person, *you*.)
>
> **Corrected:** **You** may get spring fever unless **you** live in California or Florida.
> (Stays in second person)
>
> **Corrected:** **People** may get spring fever unless **they** live in California or Florida.
> (*People*, a third person plural noun, requires a third person plural pronoun, *they*.)

Shift in Tense

— **Shift in tense** is using more than one tense in a sentence when only one is needed.

> **Shift:** Sheila **looked** at nine apartments in one weekend before she **had chosen** one.
> (Tense shifts from past to past perfect for no reason.)
>
> **Corrected:** Sheila **looked** at nine apartments in one weekend before she **chose** one.
> (Tense stays in past.)

Shift in Voice

Shift in voice is mixing active with passive voice. Usually, a sentence beginning in active voice should remain so to the end.

Shift:	As you look (active voice) for just the right place, many interesting apartments **will probably be seen.** (passive voice)
Corrected:	As you look (active voice) for just the right place, **you will probably see** (active voice) many interesting apartments.

Unparallel Construction

Unparallel construction occurs when the kind of words or phrases being used shifts or changes in the middle of a sentence.

Shift:	In my hometown, people pass the time shooting pool, pitching horseshoes, and at softball games. (Sentence shifts from a series of gerund phrases, *shooting pool* and *pitching horseshoes*, to the prepositional phrase *at softball games*.)
Parallel:	In my hometown, people pass the time **shooting pool, pitching horseshoes, and playing softball.** (Now all three activities are gerund phrases—they are consistent, or parallel.)

Fragments, Comma Splices, and Run-Ons L○4

Except in a few special situations, you should use complete sentences when you write. By definition, a complete sentence expresses a complete thought. However, a sentence may actually contain several ideas, not just one. The trick is getting those ideas to work together to form a clear, interesting sentence that expresses your exact meaning. Among the most common sentence errors that writers make are fragments, comma splices, and run-ons.

Fragments

A **fragment** is a phrase or dependent clause used as a sentence. It is not a sentence, however, because a phrase lacks a subject, a verb, or some other essential part, and a dependent clause must be connected to an independent clause to complete its meaning.

Fragment:	Pete gunned the engine. Forgetting that the boat was hooked to the truck. (This is a sentence followed by a fragment. This error can be corrected by combining the fragment with the sentence.)
Corrected:	Pete gunned the engine**,** forgetting that the boat was hooked to the truck.

Fragment:	Even though my best friend had a little boy last year. (This clause does not convey a complete thought. We need to know what is happening despite the birth of the little boy.)
Corrected:	Even though my best friend had a little boy last year, **I do not comprehend the full meaning of "motherhood."**

Comma Splices

A **comma splice** is a mistake made when two independent clauses are connected ("spliced") with only a comma. The comma is not enough: A period, semicolon, or conjunction is needed.

Splice:	People say that being a stay-at-home mom or dad is an important job, their actions tell a different story.
Corrected:	People say that being a stay-at-home mom or dad is an important job, **but** their actions tell a different story. (The coordinating conjunction *but,* added after the comma, corrects the splice.)
Corrected:	People say that being a stay-at-home mom or dad is an important job**;** their actions tell a different story. (A semicolon—rather than just a comma—makes the sentence correct.)
Corrected:	People say that being a stay-at-home mom or dad is an important job. **Their** actions tell a different story. (A period creates two sentences and corrects the splice.)

Run-Ons

Run-Ons — A **run-on sentence** is actually two sentences (two independent clauses) joined without adequate punctuation or a connecting word.

> ***Run-on:*** The Alamo holds a special place in American history it was the site of an important battle between the United States and Mexico.
>
> **Corrected:** **The Alamo holds a special place in American history because it was the site of an important battle between the United States and Mexico.**
> (A subordinating conjunction is added to fix the run-on by making the second clause dependent.)

> ***Run-on:*** Antonio de Santa Anna, the president of Mexico who once held a funeral for his amputated leg, is the same Santa Anna who stormed the Alamo he led his troops to victory over the Texan rebels defending that fort. Two famous American frontiersmen died they were James Bowie and Davy Crockett. Santa Anna enjoyed fame, power, and respect among his followers. He died in 1876 he was poor, blind, and ignored.
>
> **Corrected:** Antonio de Santa Anna, the president of Mexico who once held a funeral for his amputated leg, is the same Santa Anna who stormed the Alamo. He led his troops to victory over the Texan rebels defending that fort. Two famous American frontiersmen were killed in the battle; they were James Bowie and Davy Crockett. Santa Anna enjoyed fame, power, and respect among his followers. When he died in 1876, he was poor, blind, and ignored.

The writer corrected the run-on sentences in the paragraph above by adding punctuation and making one sentence a dependent clause. The writer makes further improvements in the paragraph below by revising one sentence and by combining two sets of short sentences into one stronger sentence.

> **Improved**
>
> Antonio de Santa Anna, the president of Mexico who once held a funeral for his amputated leg, is the same Santa Anna who stormed the Alamo. He led his troops to victory over Texan rebels defending that fort. Two famous American frontiersmen, **James Bowie and Davy Crockett, were killed in the battle**. Santa Anna enjoyed fame, power, and respect among his followers; **but when** he died in 1876, he was poor, blind, and ignored.

Misplaced and Dangling Modifiers LO5

Writing is thinking. Before you can write clearly, you must think clearly. Nothing is more frustrating for the reader than having to reread writing just to understand its basic meaning. Look carefully at the common errors that follow. Then use this section as a checklist when you revise. Always avoid leaving misplaced or dangling modifiers in your finished work.

Misplaced Modifiers

Misplaced Modifiers — **Misplaced modifiers** are descriptive words or phrases so separated from what they are describing that the reader is confused.

> ***Misplaced:*** The neighbor's dog has nearly been barking nonstop for two hours.
> (*Nearly* been barking?)
>
> **Corrected:** The neighbor's dog has been barking nonstop **for nearly two hours**.
> (Watch your placement of *only, just, nearly, barely*, and so on.)

> ***Misplaced:*** The commercial advertised an assortment of combs for active people with unbreakable teeth.
> (*People* with unbreakable teeth?)
>
> **Corrected:** The commercial advertised an assortment of combs **with unbreakable teeth for active people**.
> (*Combs* with unbreakable teeth)

> ***Misplaced:*** The pool staff gave large beach towels to the students marked with chlorine-resistant ID numbers.
> (*Students* marked with chlorine-resistant ID numbers?)
>
> **Corrected:** The pool staff gave large beach towels **marked with chlorine-resistant ID numbers to the students**.
> (*Towels* marked with chlorine-resistant ID numbers)

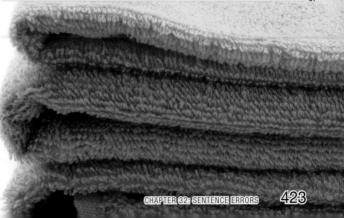

Dangling Modifiers

Dangling Modifiers — **Dangling modifiers** are descriptive phrases that tell about a subject that isn't stated in the sentence. These often occur as participial phrases containing *ing* or *ed* words.

Dangling:	After standing in line all afternoon, the manager informed us that all the tickets had been sold. (It sounds as if the manager has been *standing in line all afternoon.*)
Corrected:	**After we had stood in line all afternoon,** the manager informed us that all the tickets had been sold.
Dangling:	After living in the house for one month, the electrician recommended we update all the wiring. (It sounds as if the electrician has been *living in the house.*)
Corrected:	After living in the house for one month, **we hired an electrician, who recommended we update all the wiring.**

Ambiguous Wording — LO6

Sloppy sentences confuse readers. No one should have to wonder, "What does this writer mean?" When you revise and edit, check for indefinite pronoun references, incomplete comparisons, and unclear wording.

Indefinite Pronoun References

Indefinite Pronoun References — An **indefinite reference** is a problem caused by careless use of pronouns. There must always be a word or phrase nearby (its antecedent) that a pronoun clearly replaces.

Indefinite:	When Tonya attempted to put her dictionary on the shelf, it fell to the floor. (The pronoun *it* could refer to either the dictionary or the shelf since both are singular nouns.)
Corrected:	When Tonya attempted to put her dictionary on the shelf, **the shelf** fell to the floor.
Indefinite:	Juanita reminded Kerri that she needed to photocopy her résumé before going to her interview. (Who *needed to photocopy her résumé*— Juanita or Kerri?)
Corrected:	Juanita reminded Kerri **to photocopy her résumé before going to her interview.**

Incomplete Comparisons

Incomplete Comparisons — **Incomplete comparisons**—leaving out words that show exactly what is being compared to what—can confuse readers.

Incomplete:	After completing our lab experiment, we concluded that helium is lighter. (*Lighter* than what?)
Corrected:	After completing our lab experiment, we concluded that helium is lighter **than oxygen.**

Unclear Wording

Unclear Wording — One type of ambiguous writing is wording that has two or more possible meanings due to an unclear reference to something elsewhere in the sentence.

Unclear:	I couldn't believe that my sister bought a cat with all those allergy problems. (Who has the *allergy problems*—the cat or the sister?)
Corrected:	I couldn't believe that my sister, **who is very allergic, bought a cat.**
Unclear:	Dao intended to wash the car when he finished his homework, but he never did. (It is unclear which he *never did*—wash the car or finish his homework.)
Corrected:	Dao intended to wash the car when he finished his homework, **but he never did manage to wash the car.**

Nonstandard Language — LO7

Nonstandard language is language that does not conform to the standards set by schools, media, and public institutions. It is often acceptable in everyday conversation and in fictional writing but seldom is used in formal speech or other forms of writing.

Colloquial Language

Colloquial Language — **Colloquial language** is wording used in informal conversation that is unacceptable in formal writing.

Colloquial:	Hey, wait up! Cal wants to go with.
Standard:	Hey, wait! Cal wants to go with us.

Double Preposition — The use of certain **double prepositions**—*off of, off to, from off*—is unacceptable.

Double Preposition:	Pick up the dirty clothes from off the floor.
Standard:	Pick up the dirty clothes **from the floor.**

Substitution — Avoid substituting *and* for *to.*

Substitution:	Try and get to class on time.
Standard:	**Try to** get to class on time.

Avoid substituting *of* for *have* when combining with *could, would, should,* or *might.*

Substitution:	I should of studied for that exam.
Standard:	**I should have** studied for that exam.

Double Negative — A **double negative** is a sentence that contains two negative words used to express a single negative idea. Double negatives are unacceptable in academic writing.

Double Negative:	After paying for essentials, I haven't got no money left.
Standard:	**I haven't got** any money left. / **I have no** money left.

Slang — Avoid the use of **slang** or any "in" words in formal writing.

Slang:	The way the stadium roof opened was way cool.
Standard:	The way the stadium roof opened **was remarkable.**

Quick Guide: Avoiding Sentence Problems

Does every subject agree with its verb? (See pages 418–420.)

- In person and number?
- When a word or phrase comes between the subject and the verb?
- When the subject is delayed?
- When the subject is a title?
- When a compound subject is connected with *or*?
- When the subject is a collective noun (*faculty, team,* or *crowd*)?
- When the subject is a relative pronoun (*who, which, that*)?
- When the subject is an indefinite pronoun (*everyone, anybody,* or *many*)?

Does every pronoun agree with its antecedent? (See page 421.)

- When the pronoun is a singular indefinite pronoun such as *each, either,* or *another*?
- When two antecedents are joined with *and*?
- When two antecedents are joined with *or*?

Did you unintentionally create inappropriate shifts? (See pages 421–422.)

- In person?
- In tense?
- From active voice to passive voice?
- In another unparallel construction?

Are all your sentences complete? (See pages 422–423.)

- Have you used sentence fragments?
- Are some sentences "spliced" or run together?

Did you use any misplaced modifiers or ambiguous wording? (See pages 423–424.)

- Have you used misplaced or dangling modifiers?
- Have you used incomplete comparisons or indefinite references?

Did you use any nonstandard language? (See pages 424–425.)

- Have you used slang or colloquial language?
- Have you used double negatives or double prepositions?

33
Punctuation

This chapter will help you use correct punctuation. Applying these rules will make your writing clearer and easier to follow.

Learning Outcomes

LO1 Period

LO2 Ellipsis

LO3 Question Mark

LO4 Comma

LO5 Semicolon

LO6 Colon

LO7 Hyphen

LO8 Dash

LO9 Quotation Marks

LO10 Italics (Underlining)

LO11 Parentheses

LO12 Diagonal

LO13 Brackets

LO14 Exclamation Point

LO15 Apostrophe

Period ————————— LO1

After Sentences — Use a **period** to end a sentence that makes a statement, requests something, or gives a mild command.

Statement:	By 2010, women made up 56 percent of undergraduate students and 59 percent of graduate students**.**
Request:	Please read the instructions carefully**.**
Mild command:	If your topic sentence isn't clear, rewrite it**.**
Indirect question:	The professor asked if we had completed the test**.**

Note: It is not necessary to place a period after a statement that has parentheses around it and is part of another sentence.

Think about joining a club (**the student affairs office has a list of organizations**) for fun and for leadership experience.

After Initials and Abbreviations — Use a period after an initial and some abbreviations.

Mr.	Mrs.	B.C.E.	Ph.D.	Sen. Russ Feingold
Jr.	Sr.	D.D.S.	U.S.	Booker T. Washington
Dr.	M.A.	p.m.	B.A.	A. A. Milne

Some abbreviations (such as *pm*) also can be written without periods. Use no spacing in abbreviations except when providing a person's initials.

When an abbreviation is the last word in a sentence, use only one period at the end of the sentence.

Mikhail eyed each door until he found the name Rosa Lopez, **Ph.D.**

As Decimal Points — Use a period as a decimal point.

The government spends approximately **$15.5** million each year just to process student loan forms.

Ellipsis

To Show Omitted Words — Use an **ellipsis** (three periods) to show that one or more words have been omitted in a quotation. When typing, leave one space before and after each period.

> (Original) We the people of the United States, in order to form a more perfect Union, establish justice, insure domestic tranquility, provide for the common defense, promote the general welfare, and secure the blessings of liberty to ourselves and our posterity, do ordain and establish this Constitution for the United States of America.
> —Preamble, U.S. Constitution

> (Quotation) "We the people . . . in order to form a more perfect Union . . . establish this Constitution for the United States of America."

Note: Omit internal punctuation (a comma, a semicolon, a colon, or a dash) on either side of the ellipsis marks unless it is needed for clarity.

To Use After Sentences — If words from a quotation are omitted at the end of a sentence, place the ellipsis after the period or other end punctuation.

> (Quotation) "Five score years ago, a great American, in whose symbolic shadow we stand, signed the Emancipation Proclamation. . . . But one hundred years later, we must face the tragic fact that the Negro is still not free."
> —Martin Luther King, Jr., "I Have a Dream"

The first word of a sentence following a period and an ellipsis may be capitalized, even though it was not capitalized in the original.

> (Quotation) "Five score years ago, a great American . . . signed the Emancipation Proclamation. . . . One hundred years later, . . . the Negro is still not free."

Note: If the quoted material forms a complete sentence (even if it was not in the original), use a period, then an ellipsis.

> (Original) I am tired; my heart is sick and sad. From where the sun now stands I will fight no more forever.
> —Chief Joseph of the Nez Percé

> (Quotation) "I am tired. . . . I will fight no more forever."

To Show Pauses — Use an ellipsis to indicate a pause or to show unfinished thoughts.

> Listen . . . did you hear that?

> I can't figure out . . . this number doesn't . . . just how do I apply the equation in this case?

Question Mark

After Direct Questions — Use a **question mark** at the end of a direct question.

> What can I know? What ought I to do? What may I hope?
> —Immanuel Kant

> Since when do you have to agree with people to defend them from injustice?
> —Lillian Hellman

Not After Indirect Questions — No question mark is used after an indirect question.

> After listening to Edgar sing, Mr. Noteworthy asked him if he had ever had formal voice training.

Note: When a single-word question like *how, when,* or *why* is woven into the flow of a sentence, capitalization and special punctuation are not usually required.

> The questions we need to address at our next board meeting are not *why* or *whether*, but *how* and *when*.

After Quotations That Are Questions — When a question ends with a quotation that is also a question, use only one question mark, and place it within the quotation marks. (Also see page 435.)

> Do you often ask yourself, "What should I be?"

To Show Uncertainty — Use a question mark within parentheses to show uncertainty about a word or phrase within a sentence.

> This July will be the 34th (?) anniversary of the first moon walk.

Note: Do *not* use a question mark in this manner for formal writing.

For Questions in Parentheses or Dashes

— A question within parentheses—or a question set off by dashes—is punctuated with a question mark unless the sentence ends with a question mark.

> You must consult your handbook (**what choice do you have?**) when you need to know a punctuation rule.
>
> ---
>
> Should I use your charge card (you have one, don't you), or should I pay cash?
>
> ---
>
> Maybe somewhere in the pasts of these humbled people, there were cases of bad mothering or absent fathering or emotional neglect—w**hat family surviving the '50s was exempt?**—but I couldn't believe these human errors brought the physical changes in Frank.
>
> —Mary Kay Blakely, *Wake Me When It's Over*

Comma
4

Between Independent Clauses

— Use a **comma** between independent clauses that are joined by a coordinating conjunction (*and, but, or, nor, for, yet, so*).

> Heath Ledger completed his brilliant portrayal as the Joker in *The Dark Knight,* **but** he died before the film was released.

Note: Do not confuse a compound verb with a compound sentence.

> Ledger's Joker became instantly iconic and won him the Oscar for best supporting actor. (compound verb)
>
> ---
>
> His death resulted from the abuse of prescription drugs, but it was ruled an accident. (compound sentence)

Between Items in a Series

— Use commas to separate individual words, phrases, or clauses in a series. (A series contains at least three items.)

> Many college students must balance studying with **taking care of a family, working a job, getting exercise, and finding time to relax.**

Note: Do *not* use commas when all the items in a series are connected with *or*, *nor*, or *and*.

> Hmm . . . should I study **or** do laundry **or** go out?

To Separate Adjectives

— Use commas to separate adjectives that *equally* modify the same noun. Notice in the examples below that no comma separates the last adjective from the noun.

> You should exercise regularly and follow a **sensible, healthful** diet.
>
> ---
>
> A good diet is one that includes lots of **high-protein, low-fat** foods.

Quick Guide: To Determine Equal Modifiers

To determine whether the adjectives in a sentence modify a noun *equally*, use these two tests.

1. Reverse the order of the adjectives; if the sentence is clear, the adjectives modify equally. (In the example below, *hot* and *crowded* can be reversed, and the sentence is still clear; *short* and *coffee* cannot.)

   > Matt was tired of working in the **hot, crowded** lab and decided to take a **short coffee** break.

2. Insert *and* between the adjectives; if the sentence reads well, use a comma when *and* is omitted. (The word *and* can be inserted between *hot* and *crowded*, but *and* does not make sense between *short* and *coffee*.)

Feng Yu, 2011 / Used under license from Shutterstock.com

To Set Off Nonrestrictive Appositives — A specific kind of explanatory word or phrase called an appositive identifies or renames a preceding noun or pronoun.

> Albert Einstein, **the famous mathematician and physicist,** developed the theory of relativity.

Note: Do *not* use commas with *restrictive appositives.* A restrictive appositive is essential to the basic meaning of the sentence.

> The famous mathematician and physicist **Albert Einstein** developed the theory of relativity.

To Set Off Adverb Dependent Clauses — Use a comma after most introductory dependent clauses functioning as adverbs.

> **Although Charlemagne was a great patron of learning,** he never learned to write properly. (adverb dependent clause)

You may use a comma if the adverb dependent clause following the independent clause is not essential. Adverb clauses beginning with *even though, although, while,* or another conjunction expressing a contrast are usually not needed to complete the meaning of a sentence.

> Charlemagne never learned to write properly, **even though he continued to practice.** (adverb dependent clause)

Note: A comma is *not* used if the dependent clause following the independent clause is needed to complete the meaning of the sentence.

> Maybe Charlemagne didn't learn **because he had an empire to run.**

After Introductory Phrases — Use a comma after introductory phrases.

> **In spite of his practicing,** Charlemagne's handwriting remained poor.

Note: A comma is usually omitted if the phrase follows an independent clause.

> Charlemagne's handwriting remained poor **in spite of his practicing.**

Also Note: You may omit the comma after a short (four or fewer words) introductory phrase unless it is needed to ensure clarity.

> **At 6:00 a.m.** he would rise and practice his penmanship.

To Set Off Transitional Expressions — Use a comma to set off conjunctive adverbs and transitional phrases. (See page 431.)

> Handwriting is not, **as a matter of fact,** easy to improve upon later in life; **however,** it can be done if you are determined enough.

Note: If a transitional expression blends smoothly with the rest of the sentence, it does not need to be set off. *Example:* If you are in fact coming, I'll see you there.

A Closer Look:
Nonrestrictive and Restrictive Clauses and Phrases

Use Commas with Nonrestrictive Clauses and Phrases — Use commas to enclose **nonrestrictive** (unnecessary) phrases or dependent (adjective) clauses. A nonrestrictive phrase or dependent clause adds information that is not necessary to the basic meaning of the sentence. For example, if the clause or phrase (in **boldface**) were left out of the two examples below, the meaning of the sentences would remain clear. Therefore, commas are used to set off the nonrestrictive information.

> The locker rooms in Swain Hall, **which were painted and updated last summer,** give professors a place to shower. (nonrestrictive clause)
>
> Work-study programs, **offered on many campuses,** give students the opportunity to earn tuition money. (nonrestrictive phrase)

Don't Use Commas with Restrictive Clauses and Phrases — Do *not* use commas to set off **restrictive** (necessary) adjective clauses and phrases. A restrictive clause or phrase adds information that the reader needs to understand the sentence. For example, if the adjective clause and phrase (in **boldface**) were dropped from the examples that follow, the meaning would be unclear.

Only the professors **who run at noon** use the locker rooms in Swain Hall to shower. (restrictive clause)

Using tuition money **earned through work-study programs** is the only way some students can afford to go to college. (restrictive phrase)

Using "That" or "Which" — Use *that* to introduce restrictive (necessary) adjective clauses; use *which* to introduce nonrestrictive (unnecessary) adjective clauses. When the two words are used in this way, the reader can quickly distinguish the necessary information from the unnecessary.

Campus jobs **that are funded by the university** are awarded to students only. (restrictive)

The cafeteria**, which is run by an independent contractor,** can hire nonstudents. (nonrestrictive)

Note: Clauses beginning with *who* can be either restrictive or nonrestrictive.

Students **who pay for their own education** are highly motivated. (restrictive)

The admissions counselor**, who has studied student records,** said that many returning students earn high GPAs in spite of demanding family obligations. (nonrestrictive)

To Set Off Items in Addresses and Dates — Use commas to set off items in an address and the year in a date.

Send your letter to **1600 Pennsylvania Avenue, Washington, DC 20006, before January 1, 2009, or** send an e-mail to president@whitehouse.gov.

Note: No comma is placed between the state and ZIP code. Also, no comma separates the items if only the month and year are given: January 2009.

To Set Off Dialogue — Use commas to set off the words of the speaker from the rest of the sentence.

"Never be afraid to ask for help," advised Ms. Kane.

"With the evidence that we now have," Professor Thom said, **"many scientists believe there is life on Mars."**

To Separate Nouns of Direct Address — Use a comma to separate a noun of direct address from the rest of the sentence.

Jamie, would you please stop whistling while I'm trying to work?

To Separate Interjections — Use a comma to separate a mild interjection from the rest of the sentence.

Okay, so now what do I do?

Note: Exclamation points are used after strong interjections: Wow! You're kidding!

To Set Off Interruptions — Use commas to set off a word, phrase, or clause that interrupts the movement of a sentence. Such expressions usually can be identified through the following tests: (1) They may be omitted without changing the meaning of a sentence; and (2) they may be placed nearly anywhere in the sentence without changing its meaning.

For me, **well,** it was just a good job gone!
—Langston Hughes, "A Good Job Gone"

Lela, **as a general rule,** always comes to class ready for a pop quiz.

To Separate Numbers — Use commas to separate a series of numbers to distinguish hundreds, thousands, millions, and so on.

Do you know how to write the amount **$2,025** on a check?

25,000   973,240   18,620,197

To Enclose Explanatory Words — Use commas to enclose an explanatory word or phrase.

Time management**, according to many professionals,** is such an important skill that it should be taught in college.

To Separate Contrasted Elements — Use commas to separate contrasted elements within a sentence.

We work to become, **not to acquire.**   —Eugene Delacroix

Where all think alike, **no one thinks very much.**
—Walter Lippmann

Before Tags
— Use commas before tags, which are short statements or questions at the ends of sentences.

> You studied for the test, **right?**

To Enclose Titles or Initials
— Use commas to enclose a title or initials and given names that follow a surname.

> Until Martin, **Sr.,** was 15, he never had more than three months of schooling in any one year.
> —Ed Clayton, *Martin Luther King: The Peaceful Warrior*

> The genealogical files included the names Sanders, **L. H.,** and Sanders, **Lucy Hale.**

Note: Some style manuals no longer require commas around titles.

For Clarity or Emphasis
— Use a comma for clarity or for emphasis. There will be times when none of the traditional rules call for a comma, but one will be needed to prevent misreading or to emphasize an important idea.

> What she does, does matter to us. (clarity)

> It may be those who do most, dream most. (emphasis)
> —Stephen Leacock

Quick Guide: Avoid Overusing Commas

The commas (in **red**) below are used incorrectly. Do *not* use a comma between the subject and its verb or the verb and its object.

> Current periodicals on the subject of psychology, are available at nearly all bookstores.

> I think she should read, *Psychology Today.*

Do *not* use a comma before an indirect quotation.

> My roommate said, that she doesn't understand the notes I took.

Semicolon

To Join Two Independent Clauses
— Use a **semicolon** to join two or more closely related independent clauses that are not connected with a coordinating conjunction. In other words, each of the clauses could stand alone as a separate sentence.

> I was thrown out of college for cheating on the metaphysics exam; I looked into the soul of the boy next to me.
> —Woody Allen

Before Conjunctive Adverbs
— Use a semicolon before a conjunctive adverb when the word clarifies the relationship between two independent clauses in a compound sentence. A comma often follows the conjunctive adverb. Common conjunctive adverbs include *also, besides, however, instead, meanwhile, then,* and *therefore.*

> Many college freshmen are on their own for the first time; **however,** others are already independent and even have families.

Before Transitional Phrases
— Use a semicolon before a transitional phrase when the phrase clarifies the relationship between two independent clauses in a compound sentence. A comma usually follows the transitional phrase.

> Pablo was born in the Andes; **as a result,** he loves mountains.

Transitional Phrases

after all	in addition
as a matter of fact	in conclusion
as a result	in fact
at any rate	in other words
at the same time	in the first place
even so	on the contrary
for example	on the other hand
for instance	

To Separate Independent Clauses Containing Commas — Use a semicolon to separate independent clauses that contain internal commas, even when the independent clauses are connected by a coordinating conjunction.

> Your MP3 player, computer, bike, and other valuables are expensive to replace; so include these items in your homeowner's insurance policy and remember to use the locks on your door, bike, and storage area.

To Separate Items in a Series That Contains Commas — Use a semicolon to separate items in a series that already contain commas.

> My favorite foods are pizza with pepperoni, onions, and olives; peanut butter and banana sandwiches; and liver with bacon, peppers, and onions.

Colon
LO6

After Salutations — Use a **colon** after the salutation of a business letter.

> Dear Mr. Spielberg: Dear Professor Higgins:
> Dear Members:

Between Numbers Indicating Time or Ratios — Use a colon between the hours, minutes, and seconds of a number indicating time.

> 8:30 p.m.   9:45 a.m.   10:24:55

Use a colon between two numbers in a ratio.

> The ratio of computers to students is 1:20. (one to twenty)

For Emphasis — Use a colon to emphasize a word, a phrase, a clause, or a sentence that explains or adds impact to the main clause.

> I have one goal for myself: to become the first person in my family to graduate from college.

To Distinguish Parts of Publications — Use a colon between a title and a subtitle, volume and page, and chapter and verse.

> *Ron Brown: An Uncommon Life*   *Britannica* 4: 211
> Psalm 23:1–6

To Introduce Quotations — Use a colon to introduce a quotation following a complete sentence.

> John Locke is credited with this prescription for a good life: "A sound mind in a sound body."

> Lou Gottlieb, however, offered this version: "A sound mind or a sound body—take your pick."

To Introduce a List — Use a colon to introduce a list following a complete sentence.

> A college student needs a number of things to succeed: basic skills, creativity, and determination.

Quick Guide: Avoid Colon Errors

Do *not* use a colon between a verb and its object or complement.

> Dave likes: comfortable space and time to think. (Incorrect)

> Dave likes two things: comfortable space and time to think. (Correct)

Hyphen
LO7

In Compound Words — Use a **hyphen** to make some compound words.

> great-great-grandfather (noun)   starry-eyed (adjective)
>
> three-year-old (adjective)
>
> mother-in-law (noun)

Writers sometimes combine words in new and unexpected ways. Such combinations are usually hyphenated.

> And they pried pieces of **baked-too-fast** sunshine cake from the roofs of their mouths and looked once more into the boy's eyes.
>
> —Toni Morrison, *Song of Solomon*

Note: Consult a dictionary to find how it lists a particular compound word. Some compound words (*living room*) do not use a hyphen and are written separately. Some are written solid (*bedroom*). Some do not use a hyphen when the word is a noun (*ice cream*) but do use a hyphen when it is a verb or an adjective (*ice-cream sundae*).

To Join Letters and Words — Use a hyphen to join a capital letter or a lowercase letter to a noun or a participle.

T-shirt	U-turn	V-shaped	x-ray

To Join Words in Compound Numbers — Use a hyphen to join the words in compound numbers from twenty-one to ninety-nine when it is necessary to write them out. (See page 444.)

Forty-two people found seats in the cramped classroom.

Between Numbers in Fractions — Use a hyphen between the numerator and the denominator of a fraction, but not when one or both of these elements are already hyphenated.

four-tenths   five-sixteenths
seven thirty-seconds (7/32)

In a Special Series — Use a hyphen when two or more words have a common element that is omitted in all but the last term.

We have cedar posts in **four-**, **six-**, and **eight-**inch widths.

To Create New Words — Use a hyphen to form new words beginning with the prefixes *self, ex, all,* and *half.* Also use a hyphen to join any prefix to a proper noun, a proper adjective, or the official name of an office.

post-Depression	mid-May	ex-mayor

To Prevent Confusion — Use a hyphen with prefixes or suffixes to avoid confusion or awkward spelling.

re-cover (not *recover*) the sofa

shell-like (not *shelllike*) shape

To Join Numbers — Use a hyphen to join numbers indicating a range, a score, or a vote.

Students study **30-40** hours a week.

The final score was **84-82**.

To Divide Words — Use a hyphen to divide a word between syllables at the end of a line of print.

Guidelines for Word Division

1. Leave enough of the word at the end of the line to identify the word.
2. Never divide a one-syllable word: **rained, skills, through.**
3. Avoid dividing a word of five or fewer letters: **paper, study, July.**
4. Never divide a one-letter syllable from the rest of the word: **omit-ted,** not **o-mitted.**
5. Always divide a compound word between its basic units: **sister-in-law,** not **sis-ter-in-law.**
6. Never divide abbreviations or contractions: **shouldn't,** not **should-n't.**
7. When a vowel is a syllable by itself, divide the word after the vowel: **epi-sode,** not **ep-isode.**
8. Avoid dividing a numeral: **1,000,000,** not **1,000,-000.**
9. Avoid dividing the last word in a paragraph.
10. Never divide the last word in more than two lines in a row.
11. Check a dictionary for acceptable word divisions.

To Form Adjectives — Use a hyphen to join two or more words that serve as a single-thought adjective before a noun.

In real life I am a large, **big-boned** woman with rough, **man-working** hands.
—Alice Walker, "Everyday Use"

Most single-thought adjectives are not hyphenated when they come after the noun. (Check the dictionary to be sure.)

In real life, I am large and **big boned**.

Note: When the first of these words is an adverb ending in *ly,* do not use a hyphen. Also, do not use a hyphen when a number or a letter is the final element in a single-thought adjective.

fresh**ly** painted barn

grade **A** milk (letter is the final element)

Dash LO8

To Set Off Nonessential Elements — Use a **dash** to set off nonessential elements—explanations, examples, or definitions—when you want to emphasize them.

> Near the semester's end—**and this is not always due to poor planning**—some students may find themselves in academic trouble.

> The term *caveat emptor*—**let the buyer beware**—is especially appropriate to Internet shopping.

Note: A dash is indicated by two hyphens--with no spacing before or after--in typewriter-generated material. Don't use a single hyphen when a dash (two hyphens) is required.

To Set Off an Introductory Series — Use a dash to set off an introductory series from the clause that explains the series.

> **Cereal, coffee, and Facebook**—without these I can't get going in the morning.

To Show Missing Text — Use a dash to show that words or letters are missing.

> **Mr. —** won't let us marry.　　　—Alice Walker, *The Color Purple*

To Show Interrupted Speech — Use a dash (or an ellipsis) to show interrupted or faltering speech in dialogue. (Also see page 427.)

> Well, **I—ah—had** this terrible case of the flu, **and— then—ah—the** library closed because of that flash flood, **and—well—the** high humidity jammed my printer.
> 　　　　　　　　　　　　　　　　—Excuse No. 101

> "If you *think* you can—"
> "Oh, I *know*—"
> "Don't interrupt!"

For Emphasis — Use a dash in place of a colon to introduce or to emphasize a word, a series, a phrase, or a clause.

> **Jogging**—that's what he lives for.

> **Life is like a grindstone**—whether it grinds you down or polishes you up depends on what you're made of.

> **This is how the world moves**—not like an arrow, but a boomerang.
> 　　　　　　　　　　　　　　　　—Ralph Ellison

Quotation Marks LO9

To Punctuate Titles — Use **quotation marks** to punctuate some titles. (Also see page 436.)

> "Two Friends" (short story)
> "New Car Designs" (newspaper article)
> "Sparks" (song)
> "Multiculturalism and the Language Battle" (lecture title)
> "The New Admissions Game" (magazine article)
> "Reflections on Advertising" (chapter in a book)
> "Blink" (television episode from *Doctor Who*)
> "Annabel Lee" (short poem)

For Special Words — Use quotation marks (1) to show that a word is being discussed as a word, (2) to indicate that a word or phrase is directly quoted, (3) to indicate that a word is slang, or (4) to point out that a word is being used in a humorous or ironic way.

> A commentary on the times is that the word **"honesty"** is now preceded by **"old-fashioned."**

> She said she was **"incensed."**

> I drank a Dixie and ate bar peanuts and asked the bartender where I could hear **"chanky-chank,"** as Cajuns call their music.
> 　　　　　　—William Least Heat-Moon, *Blue Highways*

> In an attempt to be popular, he works very hard at being **"cute."**

Note: A word used as a word can also be set off with italics.

Placement of Periods or Commas — Always place periods and commas inside quotation marks.

> "Dr. Slaughter wants you to have liquids, Will," Mama said anxiously. "He said not to give you any solid food tonight."
>
> —Olive Ann Burns, *Cold Sassy Tree*

Placement of Exclamation Points or Question Marks — Place an exclamation point or a question mark inside quotation marks when it punctuates both the main sentence and the quotation or just the quotation; place it outside when it punctuates the main sentence.

> Do you often ask yourself, "What should I be?"

> I almost croaked when he asked, "That won't be a problem, will it?"

> Did he really say, "Finish this by tomorrow"?

Placement of Semicolons or Colons — Always place semicolons or colons outside quotation marks.

> I just read "Computers and Creativity"; I now have some different ideas about the role of computers in the arts.

+ A Closer Look:
Marking Quoted Material

For Direct Quotations — Use quotation marks before and after a direct quotation—a person's exact words.

> Sitting in my one-room apartment, I remember Mom saying, **"Don't go to the party with him."**

Note: Do *not* use quotation marks for *indirect* quotations.

> I remember Mom saying **that I should not date him**.
>   (These are not the speaker's exact words.)

For Quoted Passages — Use quotation marks before and after a quoted passage. Any word that is not part of the original quotation must be placed inside brackets.

> (Original) First of all, it must accept responsibility for providing shelter for the homeless.
>
> ────────────────
>
> (Quotation) "First of all, it **[the federal government]** must accept responsibility for providing shelter for the homeless."

Note: If you quote only part of the original passage, be sure to construct a sentence that is both accurate and grammatically correct.

> The report goes on to say that the federal government **"must accept responsibility for providing shelter for the homeless."**

For Long Quotations — If more than one paragraph is quoted, quotation marks are placed before each paragraph and at the end of the last paragraph (**Example A**). Quotations that are five or more lines (MLA style) or forty words or more (APA style) are usually set off from the text by indenting ten spaces from the left margin (a style called "block form"). Do not use quotation marks before or after a block-form quotation (**Example B**), except in cases where quotation marks appear in the original passage (**Example C**).

Example A

Example B

Example C

For Quoting Quotations — Use single quotation marks to punctuate quoted material within a quotation.

> "I was lucky," said Jane. "The proctor announced, **'Put your pencils down,'** just as I was filling in the last answer."

Italics (Underlining) __LO10__

In Handwritten and Printed Material — **Italics** is a printer's term for a style of type that is slightly slanted. In this sentence, the word *happiness* is printed in italics. In material that is handwritten or typed on a machine that cannot print in italics, underline each word or letter that should be in italics.

> In <u>The Road to Memphis</u>, racism is a contagious disease. (typed or handwritten)

> Mildred Taylor's *The Road to Memphis* exposes racism. (printed)

In Titles — Use italics to indicate the titles of magazines, newspapers, books, pamphlets, full-length plays, films, videos, radio and television programs, book-length poems, ballets, operas, lengthy musical compositions, CDs, paintings and sculptures, legal cases, Web sites, and the names of ships and aircraft. (Also see page 434.)

The Week (magazine)	*New York Times* (newspaper)
The Lost Symbol (book)	*Yankee Tavern* (play)
Enola Gay (airplane)	*The Fame* (album)
ACLU v. State of Ohio (legal case)	*Billy the Kid* (ballet)
Avatar (film)	*The Thinker* (sculpture)
CSI (television program)	*GeoCities* (Web site)
College Loans (pamphlet)	

When one title appears within another title, punctuate as follows:

> I read an article entitled "The Making of *Up*." (title of movie in an article title)

> He wants to watch *Inside the* New York Times on PBS tonight. (title of newspaper in title of TV program)

For Key Terms — Italics are often used for a key term in a discussion or for a technical term, especially when it is accompanied by its definition. Italicize the term the first time it is used. Thereafter, put the term in roman type.

> This flower has a ***zygomorphic*** (bilateral symmetry) structure.

For Foreign Words and Scientific Names — Use italics for foreign words that have not been adopted into the English language; italics are also used to denote scientific names.

> Say ***arrivederci*** to your fears and try new activities. (foreign word)

> The voyageurs discovered the shy ***Castor canadensis***, or North American beaver. (scientific name)

Parentheses __LO11__

To Enclose Explanatory or Supplementary Material — Use **parentheses** to enclose explanatory or supplementary material that interrupts the normal sentence structure.

> The RA **(resident assistant)** became my best friend.

To Set Off Numbers in a List — Use parentheses to set off numbers used with a series of words or phrases.

> Dr. Beck told us **(1)** plan ahead, **(2)** stay flexible, and **(3)** follow through.

For Parenthetical Sentences — When using a full "sentence" within another sentence, do not capitalize it or use a period inside the parentheses.

> Your friend doesn't have the assignment **(he was just thinking about calling you)**, so you'll have to make a few more calls.

When the parenthetical sentence comes after the main sentence, capitalize and punctuate it the same way you would any other complete sentence.

> But Mom doesn't say boo to Dad; she's always sweet to him. **(Actually she's sort of sweet to everybody.)**
> —Norma Fox Mazer, *Up on Fong Mountain*

To Set Off References — Use parentheses to set off references to authors, titles, pages, and years.

> The statistics are alarming **(see page 9)** and demand action.

Note: For unavoidable parentheses within parentheses use brackets, (. . . [. . .] . . .). Avoid overuse of parentheses by using commas instead.

Diagonal

To Form Fractions or Show Choices — Use a **diagonal** (also called a *slash*) to form a fraction. Also place a diagonal between two words to indicate that either is acceptable.

> My **walking/running** shoe size is **5 1/2**; my dress shoes are **6 1/2**.

When Quoting Poetry — When quoting poetry, use a diagonal (with one space before and after) to show where each line ends in the actual poem.

> A dryness is upon the house **/** My father loved and tended. **/** Beyond his firm and sculptured door **/** His light and lease have ended.
> —Gwendolyn Brooks, "In Honor of David Anderson Brooks, My Father"

Brackets

With Words That Clarify — Use **brackets** before and after words that are added to clarify what another person has said or written.

> "They'd **[the sweat bees]** get into your mouth, ears, eyes, nose. You'd feel them all over you."
> —Marilyn Johnson and Sasha Nyary, "Roosevelts in the Amazon"

Note: The brackets indicate that the words *the sweat bees* are not part of the original quotation but were added for clarification. (See page 435.)

Around Comments by Someone Other Than the Author — Place brackets around comments that have been added by someone other than the author or speaker.

> "In conclusion, *docendo discimus*. Let the school year begin!" **[Huh?]**

Around Editorial Corrections — Place brackets around an editorial correction or addition.

> "Brooklyn alone has 8 percent of lead poisoning **[victims]** nationwide," said Marjorie Moore.
> —Donna Actie, student writer

Around the Word *Sic* — Brackets should be placed around the word sic (Latin for "so" or "thus") in quoted material; the word indicates that an error appearing in the quoted material was made by the original speaker or writer.

> "There is a higher principal **[sic]** at stake here: Is the school administration aware of the situation?"

Exclamation Point

To Express Strong Feeling — Use an **exclamation point** to express strong feeling. It may be placed at the end of a sentence (or an elliptical expression that stands for a sentence). Use exclamation points sparingly.

> "That's not the point," said Wangero. "These are all pieces of dresses Grandma used to wear. She did all this stitching by hand. **Imagine!**"
> —Alice Walker, "Everyday Use"

> Su-su-something's crawling up the back of my neck**!**
> —Mark Twain, *Roughing It*

> She was on tiptoe, stretching for an orange, when they heard, **"HEY YOU!"**
> —Beverley Naidoo, *Journey to Jo'burg*

Apostrophe
_____ LO15

In Contractions
Use an **apostrophe** to show that one or more letters have been left out of two words joined to form a contraction.

don't	o is left out
she'd	woul is left out
it's	i is left out

Note: An apostrophe is also used to show that one or more numerals or letters have been left out of numbers or words.

class of '02	20 is left out
good mornin'	g is left out

To Form Plurals
Use an apostrophe and an *s* to form the plural of a letter, a number, a sign, or a word discussed as a word.

A .... A's   8 .... 8's   + ... +'s
You use too many **and's** in your writing.

Note: If two apostrophes are called for in the same word, omit the second one.

Follow closely the do's and **don'ts** (not **don't's**) on the checklist.

To Form Singular Possessives
The possessive form of singular nouns is usually made by adding an apostrophe and an *s*.

Spock's ears   my **computer's** memory

Note: When a singular noun of more than one syllable ends with an *s* or a *z* sound, the possessive may be formed by adding just an apostrophe—or an apostrophe and an *s*.

When the singular noun is a one-syllable word, however, the possessive is usually formed by adding both an apostrophe and an s.

Dallas' sports teams *or* **Dallas's** sports teams
    (two-syllable word)

Kiss's last concert   my **boss's** generosity
    (one-syllable words)

To Form Plural Possessives
The possessive form of plural nouns ending in *s* is made by adding just an apostrophe.

the **Joneses'** great-grandfather

bosses' offices

Note: For plural nouns not ending in *s*, add an apostrophe and *s*.

women's health issues

children's program

To Determine Ownership
You will punctuate possessives correctly if you remember that the word that comes immediately before the apostrophe is the owner.

girl's guitar (*girl* is the owner)
girls' guitar (*girls* are the owners)

boss's office (*boss* is the owner)
bosses' office (*bosses* are the owners)

To Show Shared Possession
When possession is shared by more than one noun, use the possessive form for the last noun in the series.

Jason, Kamil, and **Elana's** sound system
    (All three own the same system.)

Jason's, Kamil's, and **Elana's** sound systems
    (Each owns a separate system.)

In Compound Nouns
The possessive of a compound noun is formed by placing the possessive ending after the last word.

his **mother-in-law's** name (singular)
the **secretary of state's** career (singular)

their **mothers-in-law's** names (plural)
the **secretaries of state's** careers (plural)

With Indefinite Pronouns — The possessive form of an indefinite pronoun is made by adding an apostrophe and an *s* to the pronoun. (See page 401.)

everybody's grades

no one's mistake

one's choice

In expressions using *else*, add the apostrophe and *s* after the last word.

anyone else's

somebody else's

To Show Time or Amount — Use an apostrophe and an *s* with an adjective that is part of an expression indicating time or amount.

yesterday's news

a **day's** wage

a **month's** pay

Quick Guide: Punctuation Marks

Do *not* use a colon between a verb and its object or complement.

´ (é)	Accent, acute	(ä)	Dieresis
` (è)	Accent, grave	. . .	Ellipsis
< >	Angle brackets	!	Exclamation point
'	Apostrophe	-	Hyphen
*	Asterisk	.....	Leaders
{ }	Braces	¶	Paragraph
[ ]	Brackets	( )	Parentheses
^	Caret	.	Period
ç	Cedilla	?	Question mark
^ (â)	Circumflex	" "	Quotation marks
:	Colon	§	Section
,	Comma	;	Semicolon
†	Dagger	˜ (ñ)	Tilde
—	Dash	____	Underscore
/	Diagonal/slash		

34

Mechanics

This chapter focuses on the mechanical part of the English language. Learning and applying these rules will help you tune up your writing and keep it running smoothly.

Learning Outcomes

LO1 Capitalization

LO2 Plurals

LO3 Numbers

LO4 Abbreviations

LO5 Acronyms and Initialisms

LO6 Basic Spelling Rules

Capitalization
LO1

Proper Nouns and Adjectives — **Capitalize** all proper nouns and all proper adjectives (adjectives derived from proper nouns). The chart below provides a quick overview of capitalization rules. The pages following explain specific or special uses of capitalization.

Quick Guide: Capitalization at a Glance

Days of the week......... **Sunday, Monday, Tuesday**

Months ....**June, July, August**

Holidays, holy days . **Thanksgiving, Easter, Hanukkah**

Periods, events in history . . **Middle Ages, World War I**

Special events....................... **Tate Memorial Dedication Ceremony**

Political parties..... **Republican Party, Socialist Party**

Official documents.................. **the Declaration of Independence**

Trade names .... **Oscar Mayer hot dogs, Pontiac Firebird**

Formal epithets .... **Alexander the Great**

Official titles .... **Mayor John Spitzer, Senator Feinstein**

Official state nicknames .... **the Badger State, the Aloha State**

Geographical names

Planets, heavenly bodies ..... **Jupiter, the Milky Way**

Continents .... **Australia, South America**

Countries .... **Ireland, Grenada, Sri Lanka**

States, provinces .... **Ohio, Utah, Nova Scotia**

Cities, towns, villages ....**El Paso, Burlington, Wonewoc**

Streets, roads, highways .....**Park Avenue, Route 66, Interstate 90**

Sections of the United States and the world .... **the Southwest, the Far East**

Landforms .... **the Rocky Mountains, the Kalahari Desert**

Bodies of water .... **the Nile River, Lake Superior, Bee Creek**

Public areas .... **Central Park, Yellowstone National Park**

First Words

Capitalize the first word in every sentence and the first word in a full-sentence direct quotation. (Also see page 435.)

> **Attending** the orientation for new students is a good idea.

> Max suggested, "**Let's** take the guided tour of the campus first."

Sentences in Parentheses

Capitalize the first word in a sentence that is enclosed in parentheses if that sentence is not contained within another complete sentence.

> The bookstore has the software. (**Now** all I need is the computer.)

Note: Do *not* capitalize a sentence that is enclosed in parentheses and is located in the middle of another sentence. (Also see page 436.)

> Your college will probably offer everything (**this** includes general access to a computer) that you'll need for a successful year.

Sentences Following Colons

Capitalize a complete sentence that follows a colon when that sentence is a formal statement, a quotation, or a sentence that you want to emphasize. (Also see page 432.)

> Sydney Harris had this to say about computers: "**The** real danger is not that computers will begin to think like people, but that people will begin to think like computers."

Salutation and Complimentary Closing

In a letter, capitalize the first and all major words of the salutation. Capitalize only the first word of the complimentary closing.

> **Dear Personnel Director:**   **Sincerely** yours,

Sections of the Country

Words that indicate sections of the country are proper nouns and should be capitalized; words that simply indicate direction are not proper nouns.

> Many businesses move to the **South**. (section of the country)

> They move **south** to cut fuel costs and other expenses. (direction)

Languages, Ethnic Groups, Nationalities, and Religions

Capitalize languages, ethnic groups, nationalities, and religions.

African	**American**	**Latino**
Navajo	**French**	**Islam**

Nouns that refer to the Supreme Being and holy books are capitalized.

God	**Allah**	**Jehovah**
the **Koran**	**Exodus**	the **Bible**

Titles

Capitalize the first word of a title, the last word, and every word in between except articles (*a, an, the*), short prepositions, *to* in an infinitive, and coordinating conjunctions. Follow this rule for titles of books, newspapers, magazines, poems, plays, songs, articles, films, works of art, and stories.

> *Going to Meet the Man* | *Chicago Tribune*
> "Nothing Gold Can Stay" | "Jobs in the Cyber Arena"
> *A Midsummer Night's Dream* | *The War of the Roses*

Note: When citing titles in a bibliography, check the style manual you've been asked to follow. For example, in APA style, only the first word of a title is capitalized.

Organizations

Capitalize the name of an organization or a team and its members.

> **American Indian Movement** | **Democratic Party**
> **Tampa Bay Buccaneers** | **Tucson Drama Club**

Abbreviations

Capitalize abbreviations of titles and organizations. (Some other abbreviations are also capitalized. See pages 446–448.) (Also see page 426.)

> **M.D.** | **Ph.D.** | **NAACP** | **C.E.** | **B.C.E.** | **GPA**

Letters

Capitalize letters used to indicate a form or shape.

> **U**-turn | **I**-beam | **S**-curve | **V**-shaped | **T**-shirt

Words Used as Names

Capitalize words like *father, mother, uncle, senator,* and *professor* when they are parts of titles that include a personal name or when they are substituted for proper nouns (especially in direct address). (Also see page 430.)

> Hello, **Senator** Feingold. (*Senator* is part of the name.)
> Our **senator** is an environmentalist.

> Who was your chemistry **professor** last quarter?
> I had **Professor** Williams for Chemistry 101.

Note: To test whether a word is being substituted for a proper noun, simply read the sentence with a proper noun in place of the word. If the proper noun fits in the sentence, the word being tested should be capitalized. Usually the word is not capitalized if it follows a possessive—*my, his, our, your,* and so on.

> Did **Dad (Brad)** pack the stereo in the trailer?
> (Brad works in this sentence.)

> Did your **dad (Brad)** pack the stereo in the trailer?
>
> (*Brad* does not work in this sentence; the word *dad* follows the possessive *your*.)

Titles of Courses

Words such as *technology, history,* and *science* are proper nouns when they are included in the titles of specific courses; they are common nouns when they name a field of study.

> Who teaches **Art History 202**? (title of a specific course)

> Professor Bunker loves teaching **history.** (a field of study)

Note: The words *freshman, sophomore, junior,* and *senior* are not capitalized unless they are part of an official title.

> The **seniors** who maintained high GPAs were honored at the **Mount Mary Senior Honors Banquet.**

Internet and E-Mail

The words *Internet* and *World Wide Web* are always capitalized because they are considered proper nouns. When your writing includes a Web address (URL), capitalize any letters that the site's owner does (on printed materials or on the site itself). Not only is it respectful to reprint a Web address exactly as it appears elsewhere, but, in fact, some Web addresses are case-sensitive and must be entered into a browser's address bar exactly as presented.

> When doing research on the **Internet**, be sure to record each site's **Web** address (**URL**) and each contact's **e-mail** address.

Note: Some people include capital letters in their e-mail addresses to make certain features evident. Although e-mail addresses are not case-sensitive, repeat each letter in print just as its owner uses it.

A Closer Look:
Avoid Capitalization Errors

Do not capitalize any of the following:

- A prefix attached to a proper noun
- Seasons of the year
- Words used to indicate direction or position
- Common nouns and titles that appear near, but are not part of, a proper noun

Capitalize	Do Not Capitalize
American	un-American
January, February	winter, spring
The South is quite conservative.	Turn south at the stop sign.
Duluth City College	a Duluth college
Chancellor John Bohm	John Bohm, our chancellor
President Obama	the president of the United States
Earth (the planet)	earthmover
Internet	e-mail

Plurals

LO2

Nouns Ending in a Consonant — Some nouns remain unchanged when used as **plurals** (*species, moose, halibut,* and so on), but the plurals of most nouns are formed by adding an *s* to the singular form.

> dorm—dorms   credit—credits
> midterm—midterms

The plurals of nouns ending in *sh, ch, x, s,* and *z* are made by adding *es* to the singular form.

lunch—lunches	wish—wishes
class—classes	

Nouns Ending in *y* — The plurals of common nouns that end in *y* (preceded by a consonant) are formed by changing the *y* to *i* and adding *es*.

dormitory—dormitories	sorority—sororities
duty—duties	

The plurals of common nouns that end in *y* (preceded by a vowel) are formed by adding only an *s*.

attorney—attorneys	monkey—monkeys
toy—toys	

The plurals of all proper nouns ending in *y* (whether preceded by a consonant or a vowel) are formed by adding an *s*.

the three Kathys	the five Faheys

Nouns Ending in *o* — The plurals of words ending in *o* (preceded by a vowel) are formed by adding an *s*.

radio—radios	cameo—cameos
studio—studios	

The plurals of most nouns ending in *o* (preceded by a consonant) are formed by adding *es*.

echo—echoes	hero—heroes
tomato—tomatoes	

Musical terms always form plurals by adding an *s;* check a dictionary for other words of this type.

alto—altos	banjo—banjos
solo—solos	piano—pianos

Nouns Ending in *f* or *fe* — The plurals of nouns that end in *f* or *fe* are formed in one of two ways: If the final *f* sound is still heard in the plural form of the word, simply add *s*; if the final sound is a *v* sound, change the *f* to *ve* and add an *s*.

Plural ends with *f* sound:	
roof—roofs	chief—chiefs

Plural ends with *v* sound:	
wife—wives	loaf—loaves

Note: The plurals of some nouns that end in *f* or *fe* can be formed by either adding *s* or changing the *f* to *ve* and adding an *s*.

Plural ends with either sound:
hoof—hoofs, hooves

Irregular Spelling — Many foreign words (as well as some of English origin) form a plural by taking on an irregular spelling; others are now acceptable with the commonly used *s* or *es* ending. Take time to check a dictionary.

child—children	goose—geese
syllabus—syllabi, syllabuses	datum—data
radius—radii, radiuses	alumnus—alumni

Words Discussed as Words — The plurals of symbols, letters, figures, and words discussed as words are formed by adding an apostrophe and an *s*.

Many colleges have now added **A/B's** and **B/C's** as standard grades.

Note: You can choose to omit the apostrophe when the omission does not cause confusion.

YMCA's or YMCAs	**CD's or CDs**

Nouns Ending in *ful* — The plurals of nouns that end with *ful* are formed by adding an *s* at the end of the word.

three teaspoonfuls	two tankfuls

Compound Nouns — The plurals of compound nouns are usually formed by adding an *s* or an *es* to the important word in the compound. (Also see pages 432–433.)

brothers-in-law	maids of honor
secretaries of state	

Collective Nouns
— Collective nouns do not change in form when they are used as plurals.

> class (a unit—singular form)
>
> class (individual members—plural form)

Because the spelling of the collective noun does not change, it is often the pronoun used in place of the collective noun that indicates whether the noun is singular or plural. Use a singular pronoun (**its**) to show that the collective noun is singular. Use a plural pronoun (**their**) to show that the collective noun is plural.

> The class needs to change its motto.
> (The writer is thinking of the group as a unit.)
>
> The class brainstormed with their professor.
> (The writer is thinking of the group as individuals.)

ESL Note: To determine whether a plural requires the article *the*, you must first determine whether it is definite or indefinite. Definite plurals use *the*, whereas indefinite plurals do not require any article. (See page 455.)

Numbers
 LO3

Numerals or Words
— **Numbers** from one to one hundred are usually written as words; numbers 101 and greater are usually written as numerals. (APA style uses numerals for numbers 10 and higher.) Hyphenate numbers written as two words if less than one hundred.

> two | seven | ten | twenty-five | 106 | 1,079

The same rule applies to the use of ordinal numbers.

> second | tenth | twenty-fifth | ninety-eighth
> 106th | 333rd

If numbers greater than 101 are used infrequently in a piece of writing, you may spell out those that can be written in one or two words.

> two hundred | fifty thousand | six billion

You may use a combination of numerals and words for very large numbers.

> 1.5 million | 3 billion to 3.2 billion | 6 trillion

Numbers being compared or contrasted should be kept in the same style.

> 8 to 11 years old *or* eight to eleven years old

Particular decades may be spelled out or written as numerals.

> the '80s and '90s *or* the eighties and nineties

Numerals Only
— Use numerals for the following forms: decimals, percentages, pages, chapters (and other parts of a book), addresses, dates, telephone numbers, identification numbers, and statistics.

26.2	8 percent	chapter 7
pages 287–289	Highway 36	(212) 555–1234
398-55-0000	a vote of 23 to 4	May 8, 2007

Note: Abbreviations and symbols are often used in charts, graphs, footnotes, and so forth, but typically they are not used in texts.

> He is five feet one inch tall and ten years old.

> She walked three and one-half miles to work through twelve inches of snow.

However, abbreviations and symbols may be used in scientific, mathematical, statistical, and technical texts (APA style).

> Between 20% and 23% of the cultures yielded positive results.

> Your 245B model requires 220V.

Always use numerals with abbreviations and symbols.

> 5'4" | 8% | 10 in. | 3 tbsp. | 6 lb. 8 oz. | 90°F

Use numerals after the name of local branches of labor unions.

> The Office and Professional Employees International Union, Local 8

Hyphenated Numbers — Hyphens are used to form compound modifiers indicating measurement. They are also used for inclusive numbers and written-out fractions.

a **three-mile** trip	the **2001–2005** presidential term
a **2,500-mile** road trip	**one-sixth** of the pie
a **thirteen-foot** clearance	**three-eighths** of the book

Time and Money — If time is expressed with an abbreviation, use numerals; if it is expressed in words, spell out the number.

4:00 a.m. *or* **four** o'clock (not 4 o'clock)

the **5:15** p.m. train

a **seven o'clock** wake-up call

If money is expressed with a symbol, use numerals; if the currency is expressed in words, spell out the number.

$20 *or* **twenty** dollars (not 20 dollars)

Abbreviations of time and of money may be used in text.

The concert begins at **7:00** p.m., and tickets cost **$30**.

Words Only — Use words to express numbers that begin a sentence.

Fourteen students "forgot" their assignments.

Three hundred contest entries were received.

Note: Change the sentence structure if this rule creates a clumsy construction.

Six hundred thirty-nine students are new to the campus this fall. (Clumsy)

This fall, **639** students are new to the campus. (Better)

Use words for numbers that precede a compound modifier that includes a numeral. (If the compound modifier uses a spelled-out number, use numerals in front of it.)

She sold **twenty 35-millimeter** cameras in one day.

The chef prepared **24 eight-ounce** filets.

Use words for the names of numbered streets of one hundred or less.

Ninth Avenue

123 Forty-fourth Street

Use words for the names of buildings if that name is also its address.

One Thousand State Street | **Two Fifty Park Avenue**

Use words for references to particular centuries.

the twenty-first century | **the fourth century B.C.E.**

Abbreviations LO4

An **abbreviation** is the shortened form of a word or a phrase. These abbreviations are always acceptable in both formal and informal writing:

Mr. Mrs. Ms. Dr. Jr. a.m. (A.M.) p.m. (P.M.)

Note: In formal writing, do not abbreviate the names of states, countries, months, days, units of measure, or courses of study. Do not abbreviate the words *Street, Road, Avenue, Company,* and similar words when they are part of a proper name. Also, do not use signs or symbols (%, &, #, @) in place of words. (The dollar sign, however, is appropriate when numerals are used to express an amount of money. See page 445.)

Also Note: When abbreviations are called for (in charts, lists, bibliographies, notes, and indexes, for example), standard abbreviations are preferred. Reserve the postal abbreviations for ZIP code addresses.

Correspondence Abbreviations

States/Territories

	Standard	Postal
Alabama	Ala.	AL
Alaska	Alaska	AK
Arizona	Ariz.	AZ
Arkansas	Ark.	AR
California	Cal.	CA
Colorado	Colo.	CO
Connecticut	Conn.	CT
Delaware	Del.	DE
District of Columbia	D.C.	DC
Florida	Fla.	FL
Georgia	Ga.	GA
Guam	Guam	GU
Hawaii	Hawaii	HI
Idaho	Idaho	ID
Illinois	Ill.	IL
Indiana	Ind.	IN
Iowa	Ia.	IA
Kansas	Kans.	KS
Kentucky	Ky.	KY
Louisiana	La.	LA
Maine	Me.	ME
Maryland	Md.	MD
Massachusetts	Mass.	MA
Michigan	Mich.	MI
Minnesota	Minn.	MN
Mississippi	Miss.	MS
Missouri	Mo.	MO
Montana	Mont.	MT
Nebraska	Neb.	NE
Nevada	Nev.	NV
New Hampshire	N.H.	NH
New Jersey	N.J.	NJ
New Mexico	N. Mex.	NM
New York	N.Y.	NY
North Carolina	N.C.	NC
North Dakota	N. Dak.	ND
Ohio	Ohio	OH
Oklahoma	Okla.	OK
Oregon	Ore.	OR
Pennsylvania	Pa.	PA
Puerto Rico	P.R.	PR
Rhode Island	R.I.	RI
South Carolina	S.C.	SC
South Dakota	S. Dak.	SD
Tennessee	Tenn.	TN
Texas	Tex.	TX
Utah	Utah	UT
Vermont	Vt.	VT
Virginia	Va.	VA
Virgin Islands	V.I.	VI
Washington	Wash.	WA
West Virginia	W. Va.	WV
Wisconsin	Wis.	WI
Wyoming	Wyo.	WY

Canadian Provinces

	Standard	Postal
Alberta	Alta.	AB
British Columbia	B.C.	BC
Manitoba	Man.	MB
New Brunswick	N.B.	NB
Newfoundland	N.F.	NL
Northwest Territories	N.W.T.	NT
Nova Scotia	N.S.	NS
Nunavut		NU
Ontario	Ont.	ON
Prince Edward Island	P.E.I.	PE
Quebec	Que.	QC
Saskatchewan	Sask.	SK
Yukon Territory	Y.T.	YT

Address Abbreviations

	Standard	Postal
Apartment	Apt.	APT
Avenue	Ave.	AVE
Boulevard	Blvd.	BLVD
Circle	Cir.	CIR
Court	Ct.	CT
Drive	Dr.	DR
East	E.	E
Expressway	Expy.	EXPY
Freeway	Frwy.	FWY
Heights	Hts.	HTS
Highway	Hwy.	HWY
Hospital	Hosp.	HOSP
Junction	Junc.	JCT
Lake	L.	LK
Lakes	Ls.	LKS
Lane	Ln.	LN
Meadows	Mdws.	MDWS
North	N.	N
Palms	Palms	PLMS
Park	Pk.	PK
Parkway	Pky.	PKY
Place	Pl.	PL
Plaza	Plaza	PLZ
Post Office Box	P.O. Box	PO BOX
Ridge	Rdg.	RDG
River	R.	RV
Road	Rd.	RD
Room	Rm.	RM
Rural	R.	R
Rural Route	R.R.	RR
Shore	Sh.	SH
South	S.	S
Square	Sq.	SQ
Station	Sta.	STA
Street	St.	ST
Suite	Ste.	STE
Terrace	Ter.	TER
Turnpike	Tpke.	TPKE
Union	Un.	UN
View	View.	VW
Village	Vil.	VLG
West	W.	W

Common Abbreviations

abr. abridged, abridgment

AC, ac alternating current, air-conditioning

ack. acknowledgment

AM amplitude modulation

A.M., a.m. before noon (Latin *ante meridiem*)

AP advanced placement

ASAP as soon as possible

avg., av. average

B.A. bachelor of arts degree

BBB Better Business Bureau

B.C.E. before common era

bibliog. bibliography

biog. biographer, biographical, biography

B.S. bachelor of science degree

C 1. Celsius 2. centigrade 3. coulomb

c. 1. *circa* (about) 2. cup(s)

cc 1. cubic centimeter 2. carbon copy 3. community college

CDT, C.D.T. central daylight time

C.E. common era

CEEB College Entrance Examination Board

chap. chapter(s)

cm centimeter(s)

c/o care of

COD, c.o.d. 1. cash on delivery 2. collect on delivery

co-op cooperative

CST, C.S.T. central standard time

cu 1. cubic 2. cumulative

D.A. district attorney

d.b.a., d/b/a doing business as

DC, dc direct current

dec. deceased

dept. department

disc. discount

DST, D.S.T. daylight saving time

dup. duplicate

ed. edition, editor

EDT, E.D.T. eastern daylight time

e.g. for example (Latin *exempli gratia*)

EST, E.S.T. eastern standard time

etc. and so forth (Latin *et cetera*)

F Fahrenheit, French, Friday

FM frequency modulation

F.O.B., f.o.b. free on board

FYI for your information

g 1. gravity 2. gram(s)

gal. gallon(s)

gds. goods

gloss. glossary

GNP gross national product

GPA grade point average

hdqrs. headquarters

HIV human immunodeficiency virus

hp horsepower

Hz hertz

ibid. in the same place (Latin *ibidem*)

id. the same (Latin *idem*)

i.e. that is (Latin *id est*)

illus. illustration

inc. incorporated

IQ, I.Q. intelligence quotient

IRS Internal Revenue Service

ISBN International Standard Book Number

JP, J.P. justice of the peace

K 1. kelvin (temperature unit) 2. Kelvin (temperature scale)

kc kilocycle(s)

kg kilogram(s)

km kilometer(s)

kn knot(s)

kw kilowatt(s)

L liter(s), lake

lat. latitude

l.c. lowercase

lit. literary, literature

log logarithm, logic

long. longitude

Ltd., ltd. limited

m meter(s)

M.A. master of arts degree

man. manual

Mc, mc megacycle

MC master of ceremonies

M.D. doctor of medicine (Latin *medicinae doctor*)

mdse. merchandise

MDT, M.D.T. mountain daylight time

mfg. manufacture, manufacturing

mg milligram(s)

mi. 1. mile(s) **2.** mill(s) (monetary unit)

misc. miscellaneous

mL milliliter(s)

mm millimeter(s)

mpg, m.p.g. miles per gallon

mph, m.p.h. miles per hour

MS 1. manuscript **2.** multiple sclerosis

Ms. title of courtesy for a woman

M.S. master of science degree

MST, M.S.T. mountain standard time

NE northeast

neg. negative

N.S.F., n.s.f. not sufficient funds

NW northwest

oz, oz. ounce(s)

PA public-address system

pct. percent

pd. paid

PDT, P.D.T. Pacific daylight time

PFC, Pfc. private first class

pg., p. page

Ph.D. doctor of philosophy

P.M., p.m. after noon (Latin *post meridiem*)

POW, P.O.W. prisoner of war

pp. pages

ppd. 1. postpaid **2.** prepaid

PR, P.R. public relations

PSAT Preliminary Scholastic Aptitude Test

psi, p.s.i. pounds per square inch

PST, P.S.T. Pacific standard time

PTA, P.T.A. Parent-Teacher Association

R.A. residence assistant

RF radio frequency

R.P.M., rpm revolutions per minute

R.S.V.P., r.s.v.p. please reply (French *répondez s'il vous plaît*)

SAT Scholastic Aptitude Test

SE southeast

SOS 1. international distress signal **2.** any call for help

Sr. 1. senior (after surname) **2.** sister (religious)

SRO, S.R.O. standing room only

std. standard

SW southwest

syn. synonymous, synonym

tbs., tbsp. tablespoon(s)

TM trademark

UHF, uhf ultrahigh frequency

v 1. physics: velocity **2.** volume

V electricity: volt

VA Veterans Administration

VHF, vhf very high frequency

VIP informal: very important person

vol. 1. volume **2.** volunteer

vs. versus, verse

W 1. electricity: watt(s) **2.** physics: (also w) work **3.** west

whse., whs. warehouse

whsle. wholesale

wkly. weekly

w/o without

wt. weight

www World Wide Web

Acronyms and Initialisms

L○5

Acronyms — An **acronym** is a word formed from the first (or first few) letters of words in a set phrase. Even though acronyms are abbreviations, they require no periods.

radar	radio detecting and ranging
CARE	Cooperative for Assistance and Relief Everywhere
NASA	National Aeronautics and Space Administration
VISTA	Volunteers in Service to America
FICA	Federal Insurance Contributions Act

Initialisms — An **initialism** is similar to an acronym except that the initials used to form this abbreviation are pronounced individually.

CIA	Central Intelligence Agency
FBI	Federal Bureau of Investigation
FHA	Federal Housing Administration

Common Acronyms and Initialisms

AIDS	acquired immune deficiency syndrome
APR	annual percentage rate
CAD	computer-aided design
CAM	computer-aided manufacturing
CETA	Comprehensive Employment and Training Act
FAA	Federal Aviation Administration
FCC	Federal Communications Commission
FDA	Food and Drug Administration
FDIC	Federal Deposit Insurance Corporation
FEMA	Federal Emergency Management Agency
FHA	Federal Housing Administration
FTC	Federal Trade Commission
IRS	Internal Revenue Service
MADD	Mothers Against Drunk Driving
NAFTA	North American Free Trade Agreement
NATO	North Atlantic Treaty Organization

OEO	Office of Economic Opportunity
ORV	off-road vehicle
OSHA	Occupational Safety and Health Administration
PAC	political action committee
PIN	personal identification number
POP	point of purchase
PSA	public service announcement
REA	Rural Electrification Administration
RICO	Racketeer Influenced and Corrupt Organizations (Act)
ROTC	Reserve Officers' Training Corps
SADD	Students Against Destructive Decisions
SASE	self-addressed stamped envelope
SPOT	satellite positioning and tracking
SSA	Social Security Administration
SUV	sport-utility vehicle
SWAT	Special Weapons and Tactics
TDD	telecommunications device for the deaf
TMJ	temporomandibular joint
TVA	Tennessee Valley Authority
VA	Veterans Administration
WHO	World Health Organization

Basic Spelling Rules LO6

Write *i* Before *e* — Write *i* before *e* except after *c*, or when sounded like *a* as in *neighbor* and *weigh*.

believe	relief	receive	eight

Note: This sentence contains eight exceptions:

Neither sheik dared leisurely seize either weird species of financiers.

Words with Consonant Endings — When a one-syllable word (*bat*) ends in a consonant (*t*) preceded by one vowel (*a*), double the final consonant before adding a suffix that begins with a vowel (*batting*).

sum—**summary**	god—**goddess**

Note: When a multisyllable word (*control*) ends in a consonant (*l*) preceded by one vowel (*o*), the accent is on the last syllable (*con trol´*), and the suffix begins with a vowel (*ing*)—the same rule holds true: Double the final consonant (*controlling*).

prefer—**preferred**	begin—**beginning**
forget—**forgettable**	admit—**admittance**

Words with a Final Silent *e* — If a word ends with a silent *e*, drop the *e* before adding a suffix that begins with a vowel. Do *not* drop the *e* when the suffix begins with a consonant.

state—**stating**—**statement**	use—**using**—**useful**
nine—**ninety**—**nineteen**	like—**liking**—**likeness**

Note: Exceptions are **judgment, truly, argument, ninth**.

Words Ending in *y* — When *y* is the last letter in a word and the *y* is preceded by a consonant, change the *y* to *i* before adding any suffix except those beginning with *i*.

fry—**fries, frying**	hurry—**hurried, hurrying**
lady—**ladies**	ply—**pliable**
happy—**happiness**	beauty—**beautiful**

Note: When forming the plural of a word that ends with a *y* that is preceded by a vowel, add *s*.

toy—**toys**	play—**plays**	monkey—**monkeys**

TIP: Never trust your spelling to even the best spell checker. Carefully proofread and use a dictionary for words you know your spell checker does not cover.

marekuliasz, 2011 / Used under license from Shutterstock.com

Quick Guide: Steps to Becoming a Better Speller

1. **Be patient.** Becoming a good speller takes time.

2. **Check the correct pronunciation of each word you are attempting to spell.**
   Knowing the correct pronunciation of each word can help you to remember its spelling.

3. **Note the meaning and history of each word as you are checking the dictionary for the pronunciation.**
   Knowing the meaning and history of a word provides you with a better notion of how the word is properly used, and it can help you remember the word's spelling.

4. **Before you close the dictionary, practice spelling the word.**
   You can do so by looking away from the page and trying to "see" the word in your "mind's eye." Write the word on a piece of paper. Check the spelling in the dictionary and repeat the process until you are able to spell the word correctly.

5. **Learn some spelling rules.**
   The four rules in this handbook (page 449) are four of the most useful—although there are others.

6. **Make a list of the words that you misspell.**
   Select the first ten words and practice spelling them.
   First: Read each word carefully; then write it on a piece of paper. Look at the written word to see that it's spelled correctly. Repeat the process for those words that you misspelled.
   Then: Ask someone to read the words to you so you can write them again. Then check for misspellings. Repeat both steps with your next ten words.

7. **Write often.**
   As noted educator Frank Smith said, *"There is little point in learning to spell if you have little intention of writing."*

Commonly Misspelled Words

The commonly misspelled words that follow are hyphenated to show where they would logically be broken at the end of a line.

A

ab-bre-vi-ate
abrupt
ab-scess
ab-sence
ab-so-lute (-ly)
ab-sorb-ent
ab-surd
abun-dance
ac-a-dem-ic
ac-cede
ac-cel-er-ate
ac-cept (-ance)
ac-ces-si-ble
ac-ces-so-ry
ac-ci-den-tal-ly
ac-com-mo-date
ac-com-pa-ny
ac-com-plice
ac-com-plish
ac-cor-dance
ac-cord-ing
ac-count
ac-crued
ac-cu-mu-late
ac-cu-rate
ac-cus-tom (-ed)
ache
achieve (-ment)
ac-knowl-edge
ac-quaint-ance
ac-qui-esce
ac-quired
ac-tu-al
adapt
ad-di-tion (-al)
ad-dress
ad-e-quate
ad-journed
ad-just-ment
ad-mi-ra-ble
ad-mis-si-ble
ad-mit-tance
ad-van-ta-geous
ad-ver-tise-ment
ad-ver-tis-ing
ad-vice (n.)
ad-vis-able
ad-vise (v.)
ad-vis-er
ae-ri-al
af-fect
af-fi-da-vit
a-gainst
ag-gra-vate

ag-gres-sion
a-gree-able
a-gree-ment
aisle
al-co-hol
a-lign-ment
al-ley
al-lot-ted
al-low-ance
all right
al-most
al-ready
al-though
al-to-geth-er
a-lu-mi-num
al-um-nus
al-ways
am-a-teur
a-mend-ment
a-mong
a-mount
a-nal-y-sis
an-a-lyze
an-cient
an-ec-dote
an-es-thet-ic
an-gle
an-ni-hi-late
an-ni-ver-sa-ry
an-nounce
an-noy-ance
an-nu-al
a-noint
a-non-y-mous
an-swer
ant-arc-tic
an-tic-i-pate
anx-i-ety
anx-ious
a-part-ment
a-pol-o-gize
ap-pa-ra-tus
ap-par-ent (-ly)
ap-peal
ap-pear-ance
ap-pe-tite
ap-pli-ance
ap-pli-ca-ble
ap-pli-ca-tion
ap-point-ment
ap-prais-al
ap-pre-ci-ate
ap-proach
ap-pro-pri-ate
ap-prov-al
ap-prox-i-mate-ly

ap-ti-tude
ar-chi-tect
arc-tic
ar-gu-ment
a-rith-me-tic
a-rouse
ar-range-ment
ar-riv-al
ar-ti-cle
ar-ti-fi-cial
as-cend
as-cer-tain
as-i-nine
as-sas-sin
as-sess (-ment)
as-sign-ment
as-sist-ance
as-so-ci-ate
as-so-ci-a-tion
as-sume
as-sur-ance
as-ter-isk
ath-lete
ath-let-ic
at-tach
at-tack (-ed)
at-tempt
at-tend-ance
at-ten-tion
at-ti-tude
at-tor-ney
at-trac-tive
au-di-ble
au-di-ence
au-dit
au-thor-i-ty
au-to-mo-bile
au-tumn
aux-il-ia-ry
a-vail-a-ble
av-er-age
aw-ful
aw-ful-ly
awk-ward

B

bac-ca-lau-re-ate
bach-e-lor
bag-gage
bal-ance
bal-loon
bal-lot
ba-nan-a
ban-dage
bank-rupt

bar-gain
bar-rel
base-ment
ba-sis
bat-tery
beau-ti-ful
beau-ty
be-com-ing
beg-gar
be-gin-ning
be-hav-ior
be-ing
be-lief
be-lieve
ben-e-fi-cial
ben-e-fit (-ed)
be-tween
bi-cy-cle
bis-cuit
bliz-zard
book-keep-er
bought
bouil-lon
bound-a-ry
break-fast
breath (n.)
breathe (v.)
brief
bril-liant
Brit-ain
bro-chure
brought
bruise
bud-get
bul-le-tin
buoy-ant
bu-reau
bur-glar
bury
busi-ness
busy

C

caf-e-te-ria
caf-feine
cal-en-dar
cam-paign
can-celed
can-di-date
can-is-ter
ca-noe
ca-pac-i-ty
cap-i-tal
cap-i-tol
cap-tain
car-bu-ret-or
ca-reer
car-i-ca-ture
car-riage
cash-ier
cas-se-role
cas-u-al-ty

cat-a-log
ca-tas-tro-phe
caught
cav-al-ry
cel-e-bra-tion
cem-e-ter-y
cen-sus
cen-tu-ry
cer-tain
cer-tif-i-cate
ces-sa-tion
chal-lenge
chan-cel-lor
change-a-ble
char-ac-ter (-is-tic)
chauf-feur
chief
chim-ney
choc-o-late
choice
choose
Chris-tian
cir-cuit
cir-cu-lar
cir-cum-stance
civ-i-li-za-tion
cli-en-tele
cli-mate
climb
clothes
coach
co-coa
co-er-cion
col-lar
col-lat-er-al
col-lege
col-le-giate
col-lo-qui-al
colo-nel
col-or
co-los-sal
col-umn
com-e-dy
com-ing
com-mence
com-mer-cial
com-mis-sion
com-mit
com-mit-ment
com-mit-ted
com-mit-tee
com-mu-ni-cate
com-mu-ni-ty
com-par-a-tive
com-par-i-son
com-pel
com-pe-tent
com-pe-ti-tion
com-pet-i-tive-ly
com-plain
com-ple-ment
com-plete-ly
com-plex-ion

com-pli-ment
com-pro-mise
con-cede
con-ceive
con-cern-ing
con-cert
con-ces-sion
con-clude
con-crete
con-curred
con-cur-rence
con-demn
con-de-scend
con-di-tion
con-fer-ence
con-ferred
con-fi-dence
con-fi-den-tial
con-grat-u-late
con-science
con-sci-en-tious
con-scious
con-sen-sus
con-se-quence
con-ser-va-tive
con-sid-er-ably
con-sign-ment
con-sis-tent
con-sti-tu-tion
con-tempt-ible
con-tin-u-al-ly
con-tin-ue
con-tin-u-ous
con-trol
con-tro-ver-sy
con-ven-ience
con-vince
cool-ly
co-op-er-ate
cor-dial
cor-po-ra-tion
cor-re-late
cor-re-spond
cor-re-spond-
    ence
cor-rob-o-rate
cough
coun-cil
coun-sel
coun-ter-feit
coun-try
cour-age
cou-ra-geous
cour-te-ous
cour-te-sy
cous-in
cov-er-age
cred-i-tor
cri-sis
crit-i-cism
crit-i-cize
cru-el
cu-ri-os-i-ty

cu-ri-ous
cur-rent
cur-ric-u-lum
cus-tom
cus-tom-ary
cus-tom-er
cyl-in-der

D

dai-ly
dair-y
dealt
debt-or
de-ceased
de-ceit-ful
de-ceive
de-cid-ed
de-ci-sion
dec-la-ra-tion
dec-o-rate
de-duct-i-ble
de-fend-ant
de-fense
de-ferred
def-i-cit
def-i-nite (-ly)
def-i-ni-tion
del-e-gate
de-li-cious
de-pend-ent
de-pos-i-tor
de-pot
de-scend
de-scribe
de-scrip-tion
de-sert
de-serve
de-sign
de-sir-able
de-sir-ous
de-spair
des-per-ate
de-spise
des-sert
de-te-ri-o-rate
de-ter-mine
de-vel-op
de-vel-op-ment
de-vice
de-vise
di-a-mond
di-a-phragm
di-ar-rhe-a
dic-tio-nary
dif-fer-ence
dif-fer-ent
dif-fi-cul-ty
di-lap-i-dat-ed
di-lem-ma
din-ing
di-plo-ma
di-rec-tor

dis-agree-able
dis-ap-pear
dis-ap-point
dis-ap-prove
dis-as-trous
dis-ci-pline
dis-cov-er
dis-crep-an-cy
dis-cuss
dis-cus-sion
dis-ease
dis-sat-is-fied
dis-si-pate
dis-tin-guish
dis-trib-ute
di-vide
di-vis-i-ble
di-vi-sion
doc-tor
doesn't
dom-i-nant
dor-mi-to-ry
doubt
drudg-ery
du-pli-cate
dye-ing
dy-ing

E

ea-ger-ly
ear-nest
eco-nom-i-cal
econ-o-my
ec-sta-sy
e-di-tion
ef-fer-ves-cent
ef-fi-ca-cy
ef-fi-cien-cy
eighth
ei-ther
e-lab-o-rate
e-lec-tric-i-ty
el-e-phant
el-i-gi-ble
e-lim-i-nate
el-lipse
em-bar-rass
e-mer-gen-cy
em-i-nent
em-pha-size
em-ploy-ee
em-ploy-ment
e-mul-sion
en-close
en-cour-age
en-deav-or
en-dorse-ment
en-gi-neer
En-glish
e-nor-mous
e-nough
en-ter-prise

en-ter-tain
en-thu-si-as-tic
en-tire-ly
en-trance
en-vel-op (v.)
en-ve-lope (n.)
en-vi-ron-ment
equip-ment
equipped
e-quiv-a-lent
es-pe-cial-ly
es-sen-tial
es-tab-lish
es-teemed
et-i-quette
ev-i-dence
ex-ag-ger-ate
ex-ceed
ex-cel-lent
ex-cept
ex-cep-tion-al-ly
ex-ces-sive
ex-cite
ex-ec-u-tive
ex-er-cise
ex-haust (-ed)
ex-hi-bi-tion
ex-hil-a-ra-tion
ex-is-tence
ex-or-bi-tant
ex-pect
ex-pe-di-tion
ex-pend-i-ture
ex-pen-sive
ex-pe-ri-ence
ex-plain
ex-pla-na-tion
ex-pres-sion
ex-qui-site
ex-ten-sion
ex-tinct
ex-traor-di-nar-y
ex-treme-ly

F

fa-cil-i-ties
fal-la-cy
fa-mil-iar
fa-mous
fas-ci-nate
fash-ion
fa-tigue (-d)
fau-cet
fa-vor-ite
fea-si-ble
fea-ture
Feb-ru-ar-y
fed-er-al
fem-i-nine
fer-tile
fic-ti-tious
field

fierce
fi-ery
fi-nal-ly
fi-nan-cial-ly
fo-li-age
for-ci-ble
for-eign
for-feit
for-go
for-mal-ly
for-mer-ly
for-tu-nate
for-ty
for-ward
foun-tain
fourth
frag-ile
fran-ti-cal-ly
freight
friend
ful-fill
fun-da-men-tal
fur-ther-more
fu-tile

G

gad-get
gan-grene
ga-rage
gas-o-line
gauge
ge-ne-al-o-gy
gen-er-al-ly
gen-er-ous
ge-nius
gen-u-ine
ge-og-ra-phy
ghet-to
ghost
glo-ri-ous
gnaw
go-ril-la
gov-ern-ment
gov-er-nor
gra-cious
grad-u-a-tion
gram-mar
grate-ful
grat-i-tude
grease
grief
griev-ous
gro-cery
grudge
grue-some
guar-an-tee
guard
guard-i-an
guer-ril-la
guess
guid-ance
guide

guilty
gym-na-si-um
gyp-sy
gy-ro-scope

H

hab-i-tat
ham-mer
hand-ker-chief
han-dle (-d)
hand-some
hap-haz-ard
hap-pen
hap-pi-ness
ha-rass
har-bor
hast-i-ly
hav-ing
haz-ard-ous
height
hem-or-rhage
hes-i-tate
hin-drance
his-to-ry
hoarse
hol-i-day
hon-or
hop-ing
hop-ping
horde
hor-ri-ble
hos-pi-tal
hu-mor-ous
hur-ried-ly
hy-drau-lic
hy-giene

I

i-am-bic
i-ci-cle
i-den-ti-cal
id-io-syn-cra-sy
il-leg-i-ble
il-lit-er-ate
il-lus-trate
im-ag-i-nary
im-ag-i-na-tive
im-ag-ine
im-i-ta-tion
im-me-di-ate-ly
im-mense
im-mi-grant
im-mor-tal
im-pa-tient
im-per-a-tive
im-por-tance
im-pos-si-ble
im-promp-tu
im-prove-ment
in-al-ien-able
in-ci-den-tal-ly

in-con-ve-nience
in-cred-i-ble
in-curred
in-def-i-nite-ly
in-del-ible
in-de-pend-ence
in-de-pend-ent
in-dict-ment
in-dis-pens-able
in-di-vid-u-al
in-duce-ment
in-dus-tri-al
in-dus-tri-ous
in-ev-i-ta-ble
in-fe-ri-or
in-ferred
in-fi-nite
in-flam-ma-ble
in-flu-en-tial
in-ge-nious
in-gen-u-ous
in-im-i-ta-ble
in-i-tial
ini-ti-a-tion
in-no-cence
in-no-cent
in-oc-u-la-tion
in-quir-y
in-stal-la-tion
in-stance
in-stead
in-sti-tute
in-struc-tor
in-sur-ance
in-tel-lec-tu-al
in-tel-li-gence
in-ten-tion
in-ter-cede
in-ter-est-ing
in-ter-fere
in-ter-mit-tent
in-ter-pret (-ed)
in-ter-rupt
in-ter-view
in-ti-mate
in-va-lid
in-ves-ti-gate
in-ves-tor
in-vi-ta-tion
ir-i-des-cent
ir-rel-e-vant
ir-re-sis-ti-ble
ir-rev-er-ent
ir-ri-gate
is-land
is-sue
i-tem-ized
i-tin-er-ar-y

J

jan-i-tor
jeal-ous (-y)

jeop-ar-dize
jew-el-ry
jour-nal
jour-ney
judg-ment
jus-tice
jus-ti-fi-able

K

kitch-en
knowl-edge
knuck-le

L

la-bel
lab-o-ra-to-ry
lac-quer
lan-guage
laugh
laun-dry
law-yer
league
lec-ture
le-gal
leg-i-ble
leg-is-la-ture
le-git-i-mate
lei-sure
length
let-ter-head
li-a-bil-i-ty
li-a-ble
li-ai-son
lib-er-al
li-brar-y
li-cense
lieu-ten-ant
light-ning
lik-able
like-ly
lin-eage
liq-ue-fy
liq-uid
lis-ten
lit-er-ary
lit-er-a-ture
live-li-hood
log-a-rithm
lone-li-ness
loose
lose
los-ing
lov-able
love-ly
lun-cheon
lux-u-ry

M

ma-chine
mag-a-zine

mag-nif-i-cent
main-tain
main-te-nance
ma-jor-i-ty
mak-ing
man-age-ment
ma-neu-ver
man-u-al
man-u-fac-ture
man-u-script
mar-riage
mar-shal
ma-te-ri-al
math-e-mat-ics
max-i-mum
may-or
mean-ness
meant
mea-sure
med-i-cine
me-di-eval
me-di-o-cre
me-di-um
mem-o-ran-dum
men-us
mer-chan-dise
mer-it
mes-sage
mile-age
mil-lion-aire
min-i-a-ture
min-i-mum
min-ute
mir-ror
mis-cel-la-neous
mis-chief
mis-chie-vous
mis-er-a-ble
mis-ery
mis-sile
mis-sion-ary
mis-spell
mois-ture
mol-e-cule
mo-men-tous
mo-not-o-nous
mon-u-ment
mort-gage
mu-nic-i-pal
mus-cle
mu-si-cian
mus-tache
mys-te-ri-ous

N

na-ive
nat-u-ral-ly
nec-es-sary
ne-ces-si-ty
neg-li-gi-ble
ne-go-ti-ate
neigh-bor-hood

nev-er-the-less
nick-el
niece
nine-teenth
nine-ty
no-tice-able
no-to-ri-ety
nu-cle-ar
nui-sance

O

o-be-di-ence
o-bey
o-blige
ob-sta-cle
oc-ca-sion
oc-ca-sion-al-ly
oc-cu-pant
oc-cur
oc-curred
oc-cur-rence
of-fense
of-fi-cial
of-ten
o-mis-sion
o-mit-ted
op-er-ate
o-pin-ion
op-po-nent
op-por-tu-ni-ty
op-po-site
op-ti-mism
or-di-nance
or-di-nar-i-ly
orig-i-nal
out-ra-geous

P

pag-eant
pam-phlet
par-a-dise
para-graph
par-al-lel
par-a-lyze
pa-ren-the-ses
pa-ren-the-sis
par-lia-ment
par-tial
par-tic-i-pant
par-tic-i-pate
par-tic-u-lar-ly
pas-time
pa-tience
pa-tron-age
pe-cu-liar
per-ceive
per-haps
per-il
per-ma-nent
per-mis-si-ble
per-pen-dic-u-lar

per-se-ver-ance
per-sis-tent
per-son-al (-ly)
per-son-nel
per-spi-ra-tion
per-suade
phase
phe-nom-e-non
phi-los-o-phy
phy-si-cian
piece
planned
pla-teau
plau-si-ble
play-wright
pleas-ant
plea-sure
pneu-mo-nia
pol-i-ti-cian
pos-sess
pos-ses-sion
pos-si-ble
prac-ti-cal-ly
prai-rie
pre-cede
pre-ce-dence
pre-ced-ing
pre-cious
pre-cise-ly
pre-ci-sion
pre-de-ces-sor
pref-er-a-ble
pref-er-ence
pre-ferred
prej-u-dice
pre-lim-i-nar-y
pre-mi-um
prep-a-ra-tion
pres-ence
prev-a-lent
pre-vi-ous
prim-i-tive
prin-ci-pal
prin-ci-ple
pri-or-i-ty
pris-on-er
priv-i-lege
prob-a-bly
pro-ce-dure
pro-ceed
pro-fes-sor
prom-i-nent
pro-nounce
pro-nun-ci-a-tion
pro-pa-gan-da
pros-e-cute
pro-tein
psy-chol-o-gy
pub-lic-ly
pump-kin
pur-chase
pur-sue
pur-su-ing

pur-suit

Q

qual-i-fied
qual-i-ty
quan-ti-ty
quar-ter
ques-tion-naire
quite
quo-tient

R

raise
rap-port
re-al-ize
re-al-ly
re-cede
re-ceipt
re-ceive
re-ceived
rec-i-pe
re-cip-i-ent
rec-og-ni-tion
rec-og-nize
rec-om-mend
re-cur-rence
ref-er-ence
re-ferred
reg-is-tra-tion
re-hearse
reign
re-im-burse
rel-e-vant
re-lieve
re-li-gious
re-mem-ber
re-mem-brance
rem-i-nisce
ren-dez-vous
re-new-al
rep-e-ti-tion
rep-re-sen-ta-tive
req-ui-si-tion
res-er-voir
re-sis-tance
re-spect-a-bly
re-spect-ful-ly
re-spec-tive-ly
re-spon-si-bil-i-ty
res-tau-rant
rheu-ma-tism
rhyme
rhythm
ri-dic-u-lous
route

S

sac-ri-le-gious
safe-ty
sal-a-ry

sand-wich
sat-is-fac-to-ry
Sat-ur-day
scarce-ly
scene
scen-er-y
sched-ule
schol-ar-ship
sci-ence
scis-sors
sec-re-tary
seize
sen-si-ble
sen-tence
sen-ti-nel
sep-a-rate
ser-geant
sev-er-al
se-vere-ly
shep-herd
sher-iff
shin-ing
siege
sig-nif-i-cance
sim-i-lar
si-mul-ta-ne-ous
since
sin-cere-ly
ski-ing
sol-dier
sol-emn
so-phis-ti-cat-ed
soph-o-more
so-ror-i-ty
source
sou-ve-nir
spa-ghet-ti
spe-cif-ic
spec-i-men
speech
sphere
spon-sor
spon-ta-ne-ous
sta-tion-ary
sta-tion-ery
sta-tis-tic
stat-ue
stat-ure
stat-ute
stom-ach
stopped
straight
strat-e-gy
strength
stretched
study-ing
sub-si-dize
sub-stan-tial
sub-sti-tute
sub-tle
suc-ceed
suc-cess

suf-fi-cient
sum-ma-rize
su-per-fi-cial
su-per-in-tend-
  ent
su-pe-ri-or-i-ty
su-per-sede
sup-ple-ment
sup-pose
sure-ly
sur-prise
sur-veil-lance
sur-vey
sus-cep-ti-ble
sus-pi-cious
sus-te-nance
syl-la-ble
sym-met-ri-cal
sym-pa-thy
sym-pho-ny
symp-tom
syn-chro-nous

T

tar-iff
tech-nique
tele-gram
tem-per-a-ment
tem-per-a-ture
tem-po-rary
ten-den-cy
ten-ta-tive
ter-res-tri-al
ter-ri-ble
ter-ri-to-ry
the-ater
their
there-fore
thief
thor-ough (-ly)
though
through-out
tired
to-bac-co
to-geth-er
to-mor-row
tongue
to-night
touch
tour-na-ment
tour-ni-quet
to-ward
trag-e-dy
trai-tor
tran-quil-iz-er
trans-ferred
trea-sur-er
tru-ly
Tues-day
tu-i-tion
typ-i-cal
typ-ing

U

unan-i-mous
un-con-scious
un-doubt-ed-ly
un-for-tu-nate-ly
unique
u-ni-son
uni-ver-si-ty
un-nec-es-sary
un-prec-e-dent-ed
un-til
up-per
ur-gent
us-able
use-ful
using
usu-al-ly
u-ten-sil
u-til-ize

V

va-can-cies
va-ca-tion
vac-u-um
vague
valu-able
va-ri-ety
var-i-ous
veg-e-ta-ble
ve-hi-cle
veil
ve-loc-i-ty
ven-geance
vi-cin-i-ty
view
vig-i-lance
vil-lain
vi-o-lence
vis-i-bil-i-ty
vis-i-ble
vis-i-tor
voice
vol-ume
vol-un-tary
vol-un-teer

W

wan-der
war-rant
weath-er
Wednes-day
weird
wel-come
wel-fare
where
wheth-er
which
whole
whol-ly
whose
width
wom-en
worth-while
wor-thy
wreck-age
wres-tler
writ-ing
writ-ten
wrought

Y

yel-low
yes-ter-day
yield

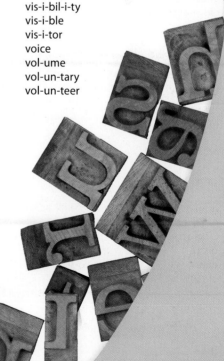

35

Multilingual and ESL Guidelines

Learning Outcomes

LO1 Parts of Speech

LO2 Sentence Basics

LO3 Sentence Problems

LO4 Numbers, Word Parts, and Idioms

Parts of Speech — LO1

Noun

Nouns are words that name people, places, and things. The information tells how to use nouns correctly.

Count Nouns — Count nouns refer to things that can be counted. They can have *a, an, the,* or *one* in front of them. One or more adjectives can come between the articles *a, an, the,* or *one* and the singular count noun.

> an apple, one orange, a plum, a purple plum

Count nouns can be singular, as in the examples above, or plural, as in the examples below.

> plums, apples, oranges

Note: When count nouns are plural, they can have the article *the*, a number, or a demonstrative adjective in front of them. (See pages 455 and 456.)

> I used **the** plums to make a pie.
>
> He placed **five** apples on my desk.
>
> **These** oranges are so juicy!

The *number* of a noun refers to whether it names a single thing *(book)*, in which case its number is *singular*, or whether it names more than one thing *(books)*, in which case the number of the noun is *plural*.

Note: There are different ways in which the plural form of nouns is created. For more information, see pages 442–444.

Noncount Nouns — Noncount nouns refer to things that cannot be counted. Do not use *a, an,* or *one* in front of them. They have no plural form, so they always take a singular verb. Some nouns that end in *s* are not plural; they are noncount nouns.

> fruit, furniture, rain, thunder, advice, mathematics, news

Abstract nouns name ideas or conditions rather than people, places, or objects. Many abstract nouns are noncount nouns.

> The students had **fun** at the party. Good **health** is a wonderful gift.

Collective nouns name a whole category or group and are often noncount nouns.

> homework, furniture, money

Note: The parts or components of a group or category named by a noncount noun are often count nouns. For example, *report* and *assignment* are count nouns that are parts of the collective, noncount noun *homework*.

Two-Way Nouns

— Some nouns can be used as either count or noncount nouns, depending on what they refer to.

> I would like a **glass** of water. (count noun)

> **Glass** is used to make windows. (noncount noun)

Articles and Other Noun Markers

Use articles and other noun markers or modifiers to give more information about nouns.

Specific Articles

— Use articles and other noun markers or modifiers to give more information about nouns. The **specific** (or **definite**) **article** *the* is used to refer to a specific noun.

> I found **the** book I misplaced yesterday.

Indefinite Articles and Indefinite Adjectives

—
Use the **indefinite article** *a* or *an* to refer to a nonspecific noun. Use *an* before singular nouns beginning with the vowels *a, e, i, o,* and *u*. Use *a* before nouns beginning with all other letters of the alphabet, the consonants. Exceptions do occur: *a* unit; *a* university.

> I always take **an** apple to work.

> It is good to have **a** book with you when you travel.

Indefinite adjectives can also mark nonspecific nouns—*all, any, each, either, every, few, many, more, most, neither, several, some* (for singular and plural count nouns); *all, any, more, most, much, some* (for noncount nouns).

> **Every** student is encouraged to register early.

> **Most** classes fill quickly.

Quick Guide: Determining Whether to Use Articles

Listed below are a number of guidelines to help you determine whether to use an article and which one to use.

Use *a* or *an* with singular count nouns that do not refer to one specific item.	A **zebra** has black and white stripes. An **apple** is good for you.
Do not use *a* or *an* with plural count nouns.	**Zebras** have black and white stripes. **Apples** are good for you.
Do not use *a* or *an* with noncount nouns.	**Homework** needs to be done promptly.
Use *the* with singular count nouns that refer to one specific item.	**The apple** you gave me was delicious.
Use *the* with plural count nouns.	**The zebras** at Brookfield Zoo were healthy.
Use *the* with noncount nouns.	**The money** from my uncle is a gift.
Do not use *the* with most singular proper nouns. **Note:** There are many exceptions: *the* Sahara Desert, *the* University of Minnesota, *the* Fourth of July.	Mother Theresa loved the poor and downcast.
Use *the* with plural nouns.	the Joneses (both Mr. and Mrs. Jones), **the Rocky Mountains, the United States**

Possessive Adjectives — The possessive case of nouns and pronouns can be used as adjectives to mark nouns.

> **Possessive Nouns:** *Tanya's, father's, store's*
> The car is **Tanya's**, not her **father's**.
>
> ---
>
> **Possessive Pronouns:** *my, your, his, her, its, our*
> **My** hat is purple.

Demonstrative Adjectives — Demonstrative pronouns can be used as adjectives to mark nouns.

> **Demonstrative adjectives:** *this, that, these, those* (for singular and plural count nouns); *this, that* (for noncount nouns)
> **Those** chairs are lovely. Where did you buy **that** furniture?

Quantifiers — **Expressions of quantity and measure** are often used with nouns. Below are some of these expressions and guidelines for using them.

The following expressions of quantity can be used with count nouns: *each, every, both, a couple of, a few, several, many, a number of.*

> We enjoyed **both** concerts we attended. **A couple of** songs performed were familiar to us.

Use a number to indicate a specific quantity of a continuum.

> I saw **fifteen** cardinals in the park.

To indicate a specific quantity of a noncount noun, use *a* + quantity (such as *bag, bottle, bowl, carton, glass,* or *piece*) + *of* + noun.

> I bought **a carton of milk, a head of lettuce, a piece of cheese,** and **a bag of flour** at the grocery store.

The following expressions can be used with noncount nouns: *a little, much, a great deal of.*

> We had **much** wind and **a little** rain as the storm passed through yesterday.

The following expressions of quantity can be used with both count and noncount nouns: *no/not any, some, a lot of, lots of, plenty of, most, all, this, that.*

> I would like **some** apples *(count noun)* and **some** rice *(noncount noun),* please.

Verb

As the main part of the predicate, a verb conveys much of a sentence's meaning. Using verb tenses and forms correctly ensures that your readers will understand your sentences as you intend them to. For a more thorough review of verbs, see pages 403–407.

Progressive (Continuous) Tenses — Progressive or continuous tense verbs express action in progress (see page 404).

To form the **present progressive** tense, use the helping verb *am, is,* or *are* with the *ing* form of the main verb.

> He **is washing** the car right now.
>
> ---
>
> Kent and Chen **are studying** for a test.

To form the **past progressive** tense, use the helping verb *was* or *were* with the *ing* form of the main verb.

> Yesterday he **was working** in the garden all day.
>
> ---
>
> Julia and Juan **were watching** a movie.

To form the future progressive tense, use *will* or a phrase that indicates the future, the helping verb *be,* and the *ing* form of the main verb.

> Next week he **will be painting** the house.
>
> ---
>
> He **plans to be painting** the house soon.

> **Note** that some verbs are generally not used in the progressive tenses, such as the following groups of frequently used verbs:
> - Verbs that express thoughts, attitudes, and desires: *know, understand, want, prefer*
> - Verbs that describe appearances: *seem, resemble*
> - Verbs that indicate possession: *belong, have, own, possess*
> - Verbs that signify inclusion: *contain, hold*
>
> > **Correct:** Kala **knows** how to ride a motorcycle.
> >
> > **Incorrect:** Kala is **knowing** how to ride a motorcycle.

Objects and Complements of Verbs

Active transitive verbs take objects. These can be direct objects, indirect objects, or object complements. Linking verbs take subject complements—predicate nominatives or predicate adjectives—that rename or describe the subject.

Infinitives as Objects — Infinitives can follow
many verbs, including these: *agree, appear, attempt, consent, decide, demand, deserve, endeavor, fail, hesitate, hope, intend, need, offer, plan, prepare, promise, refuse, seem, tend, volunteer, wish.* (See page 406 for more on infinitives.)

> He **promised to bring** some samples.

The following verbs are among those that can be followed by a noun or pronoun plus the infinitive: *ask, beg, choose, expect, intend, need, prepare, promise, want.*

> I **expect you to be** there on time.

Note: Except in the passive voice, the following verbs must have a noun or pronoun before the infinitive: *advise, allow, appoint, authorize, cause, challenge, command, convince, encourage, forbid, force, hire, instruct, invite, order, permit, remind, require, select, teach, tell, tempt, trust.*

> I will **authorize Emily to use** my credit card.

Unmarked infinitives (no *to*) can follow these verbs: *have, help, let, make.*

> These glasses **help me see** the board.

Gerunds as Objects — Gerunds can follow these
verbs: *admit, avoid, consider, deny, discuss, dislike, enjoy, finish, imagine, miss, postpone, quit, recall, recommend, regret.* (Also see page 405.)

> I **recommended hiring** Ian for the job.

Here *hiring* is the direct object of the active verb *recommended*, and *Ian* is the object of the gerund.

Infinitives or Gerunds as Objects — Either **gerunds** or **infinitives** can follow these verbs: *begin, continue, hate, like, love, prefer, remember, start, stop, try.*

> I **hate having** cold feet. I **hate to have** cold feet.
> (In either form, the verbal phrase is the direct object of the verb *hate*.)

Note: Sometimes the meaning of a sentence will change depending on whether you use a gerund or an infinitive.

> I **stopped to smoke.** (I *stopped* weeding the garden to *smoke* a cigarette.)

> I **stopped smoking.** (I no longer smoke.)

Common Modal Auxiliary Verbs — **Modal auxiliary verbs** are a kind of auxiliary verb. (See page 403.) They help the main verb express meaning. Modals are sometimes grouped with other helping or auxiliary verbs.

Modal verbs must be followed by the base form of a verb without *to* (not by a gerund or an infinitive). Also, modal verbs do not change form; they are always used as they appear in the following chart.

Modal	Expresses	Sample Sentence
can	ability	I can program a VCR.
could	ability	I could babysit Tuesday.
	possibility	He could be sick.
might	possibility	I might be early.
may,	possibility	I may sleep late Saturday.
might	request	May I be excused?
must	strong need	I must study more.
have to	strong need	I have to (have got to) exercise.
ought to	feeling of duty	I ought to (should) help Dad.
should	advisabillity	She should retire.
	expectation	I should have caught that train.
shall	intent	Shall I stay longer?
will	intent	I will visit my grandma soon.
would	intent	I would live to regret my offer.
	repeated action	He would walk in the meadow.
would + you	polite request	Would you help me?
could + you	polite request	Could you type this letter?
will + you	polite request	Will you give me a ride?
can + you	polite request	Can you make supper tonight?

Common Two-Word Verbs

— This chart lists some common verbs in which two words—a verb and a preposition—work together to express a specific action. A noun or pronoun is often inserted between the parts of the two-word verb when it is used in a sentence: *break it down, call it off.*

break down	to take apart or fall apart
call off	cancel
call up	make a phone call
clear out	leave a place quickly
cross out	draw a line through
do over	repeat
figure out	find a solution
fill in/out	complete a form or an application
fill up	fill a container or tank
find out	discover
get in	enter a vehicle or building
get out of	leave a car, a house, or a situation
get over	recover from a sickness or a problem
give back	return something
give in/up	surrender or quit
hand in	give homework to a teacher
hand out	give someone something
hang up	put down a phone receiver
leave out	omit or don't use
let in/out	allow someone or something to enter or go out
look up	find information
mix up	confuse
pay back	return money or a favor
pick out	choose
point out	call attention to
put away	return something to its proper place
put down	place something on a table, the floor, and so on.
put off	delay doing something
shut off	turn off a machine or light
take part	participate
talk over	discuss
think over	consider carefully
try on	put on clothing to see if it fits
turn down	lower the volume
turn up	raise the volume
write down	write on a piece of paper

Spelling Guidelines for Verb Forms

The same spelling rules that apply when adding a suffix to other words apply to verbs as well. Most verbs need a suffix to indicate tense or form. The third-person singular form of a verb, for example, usually ends in *s*, but it can also end in *es*. Formation of *ing* and *ed* forms of verbs and verbals needs careful attention, too. Consult the rules below to determine which spelling is correct for each verb. (For general spelling guidelines, see page 449.)

fyi There may be exceptions to these rules when forming the past tense of irregular verbs because the verbs are formed by changing the word itself, not merely by adding *d* or *ed*. (See the chart of irregular verbs on page 406.)

Past Tense: Adding *ed*

Add *ed* . . .

- When a verb ends with two consonants:

  touch—**touched**   ask—**asked**   pass—**passed**

- When a verb ends with a consonant preceded by two vowels:

  heal—**healed**   gain—**gained**

- When a verb ends in *y* preceded by a vowel:

  annoy—**annoyed**   flay—**flayed**

- When a multisyllable verb's last syllable is not stressed (even when the last syllable ends with a consonant preceded by a vowel):

  budget—**budgeted**   enter—**entered**
  interpret—**interpreted**

Change *y* to *i* and add *ed* when a verb ends in a consonant followed by *y*:

  liquefy—**liquefied**   worry—**worried**

Double the final consonant and add *ed* . . .

- When a verb has one syllable and ends with a consonant preceded by a vowel:

  wrap—**wrapped**   drop—**dropped**

- When a multisyllable verb's last syllable (ending in a consonant preceded by a vowel) is stressed:

admit—admitted   confer—conferred
abut—abutted

Past Tense: Adding *d*
Add *d*...

- When a verb ends with *e*:

chime—**chimed**   tape—**taped**

- When a verb ends with *ie*:

tie—**tied**   die—**died**   lie—**lied**

Present Tense: Adding *s* or *es*
Add *es*...

n When a verb ends in *ch, sh, s, x,* or *z*:

watch—**watches**   fix—**fixes**

- To *do* and *go*:

do—**does**   go—**goes**

Change *y* to *i* and add *es* when the verb ends in a consonant followed by *y*:

liquefy—**liquefies**   quantify—**quantifies**

Add *s* to most other verbs, including those already ending in *e* and those that end in a vowel followed by *y*:

write—**writes**   buy—**buys**

Present Tense: Adding *ing*
Drop the *e* and add *ing* when the verb ends in *e*:

drive—**driving**   rise—**rising**

Double the final consonant and add *ing*...

- When a verb has one syllable and ends with a consonant preceded by a single vowel:

wrap—**wrapping**   sit—**sitting**

- When a multisyllable verb's last syllable (ending in a consonant preceded by a single vowel) is stressed:

forget—**forgetting**   begin—**beginning**
abut—**abutting**

Change *ie* to *y* and add *ing* when a verb ends with *ie*:

tie—**tying**   die—**dying**   lie—**lying**

Add *ing*...

- When a verb ends with two consonants:

touch—**touching**   ask—**asking**   pass—**passing**

- When a verb ends with a consonant preceded by two vowels:

heal—**healing**   gain—**gaining**

- When a verb ends in *y*:

buy—**buying**   study—**studying**   cry—**crying**

- When a multisyllable verb's last syllable is not stressed (even when the last syllable ends with a consonant preceded by a vowel):

budget—**budgeting**   enter—**entering**
interpret—**interpreting**

Note: Never trust your spelling to even the best computer spell checker. Carefully proofread. Use a dictionary for questionable words your spell checker may miss.

Adjective

Placing Adjectives
You probably know that an adjective often comes before the noun it modifies. When several adjectives are used in a row to modify a single noun, it is important to arrange the adjectives in the well-established sequence used in English writing and speaking. The following list shows the usual order of adjectives. (Also see page 428.)

First, place...

1. articles .... **a, an, the**
   demonstrative adjectives .... **that, those**
   possessives .... **my, her, Misha's**

Then place words that . . .

2. indicate time .... **first, next, final**
3. tell how many .... **one, few, some**
4. evaluate .... **beautiful, dignified, graceful**
5. tell what size .... **big, small, short, tall**
6. tell what shape .... **round, square**
7. describe a condition .... **messy, clean, dark**
8. tell what age .... **old, young, new, antique**
9. tell what color .... **blue, red, yellow**
10. tell what nationality .... **English, Chinese, Mexican**
11. tell what religion .... **Buddhist, Jewish, Protestant**
12. tell what material .... **satin, velvet, wooden**

Finally, place nouns . . .

13. used as adjectives .... **computer [monitor], spice [rack]**

my second try (1 + 2 + noun)

gorgeous young white swans (4 + 8 + 9 + noun)

Present and Past Participles as Adjectives

Both the **present participle** and the **past participle** can be used as adjectives. (Also see page 406.) Exercise care in choosing whether to use the present participle or the past participle. A participle can come either before a noun or after a linking verb.

A **present participle** used as an adjective should describe a person or thing that is causing a feeling or situation.

His **annoying** comments made me angry.

A **past participle** should describe a person or thing that experiences a feeling or situation.

He was **annoyed** because he had to wait so long.

Note: Within each of the following pairs, the present (*ing* form) and past (*ed* form) participles have different meanings.

annoying/annoyed	boring/bored
confusing/confused	depressing/depressed
exciting/excited	exhausting/exhausted
fascinating/fascinated	surprising/surprised

Nouns as Adjectives

Nouns sometimes function as adjectives by modifying another noun. When a noun is used as an adjective, it is always singular.

Many European cities have **rose** gardens.

Marta recently joined a **book** club.

 Tip Try to avoid using more than two nouns as adjectives for another noun. These "noun compounds" can get confusing. Prepositional phrases may get the meaning across better than long noun strings.

Correct: Omar is a **crew** member in the restaurant kitchen during **second** shift.

Not correct: Omar is a **second-shift restaurant kitchen crew** member.

Adverb
Placing Adverbs

Consider the following guidelines for placing adverbs correctly. See pages 408–409 for more information about adverbs.

Place adverbs that tell how often (*frequently, seldom, never, always, sometimes*) after a helping (auxiliary) verb and before the main verb. In a sentence without a helping verb, adverbs that tell how often are placed before an action verb but after a linking verb.

The salesclerk will **usually** help me.

Place adverbs that tell when (*yesterday, now, at five o'clock*) at the end of a sentence.

Auntie El came home **yesterday**.

Adverbs that tell where (*upside-down, around, downstairs*) usually follow the verb they modify. Many prepositional phrases (*at the beach, under the stairs, below the water*) function as adverbs that tell where.

We waited **on the porch**.

Adverbs that tell how (*quickly, slowly, loudly*) can be placed either at the beginning, in the middle, or at the end of a sentence—but not between a verb and its direct object.

Softly he called my name. He **softly** called my name. He called my name **softly**.

Place adverbs that modify adjectives directly before the adjective.

That is a **most** unusual dress.

Adverbs that modify clauses are most often placed in front of the clause, but they can also go inside or at the end of the clause.

Fortunately, we were not involved in the accident. We were not involved, **fortunately,** in the accident. We were not involved in the accident, **fortunately.**

Note: Adverbs that are used with verbs that have direct objects must *not* be placed between the verb and its object.

> **Correct:** Luis **usually** catches the most fish.
> **Usually,** Luis catches the most fish.
>
> **Incorrect:** Luis **catches usually** the most fish.

Preposition

A **preposition** combines with a noun to form a prepositional phrase, which acts as a modifier—an adverb or an adjective. See page 409 for a list of common prepositions and for more information about prepositions.

Using *In, On, At,* and *By*

In, on, at, and *by* are four common prepositions that refer to time and place. Here are some examples of how these prepositions are used in each case.

To show time

in part of a day:	*in* the afternoon
in a year or month:	*in* 2008, *in* April
in a period of time:	completed *in* an hour
by a specific time or date:	*by* noon, *by* the fifth of May
at a specific time of day or night:	*at* 3:30 this afternoon

To show place

at a meeting place or location:	*at* school, *at* the park
at the edge of something:	standing *at* the bar
at the corner of something:	turning *at* the intersection
at a target:	throwing a dart *at* the target
on a surface:	left *on* the floor
on an electronic medium:	*on* the Internet, *on* television
in an enclosed space:	*in* the box, *in* the room
in a geographic location:	*in* New York City, *in* Germany
in a print medium:	*in* a journal
by a landmark:	*by* the fountain

> **Tip** Do not insert a preposition between a transitive verb and its direct object. Intransitive verbs, however, are often followed by a prepositional phrase (a phrase that begins with a preposition).
>
> I **cooked** hot dogs on the grill. (transitive verb)
>
> I **ate** in the park. (intransitive verb)

Phrasal Prepositions

Some prepositional phrases begin with more than one preposition. These **phrasal prepositions** are commonly used in both written and spoken communication. A list of common phrasal prepositions follows:

according to	because of	in case of	on the side of
across from	by way of	in spite of	up to
along with	except for	instead of	with respect to

Sentence Basics

Simple sentences in the English language follow the five basic patterns shown below. (See pages 412–417 for more information.)

Subject + Verb

```
 ┌─S─┐┌─V─┐
Naomie winked.
```

Some verbs like *winked* are intransitive. Intransitive verbs do not need a direct object to express a complete thought. (See page 403.)

Subject + Verb + Direct Object

```
 ┌S┐┌V┐┌DO┐
Harris grinds his teeth.
```

Some verbs like *grinds* are transitive. Transitive verbs *do* need a direct object to express a complete thought. (See page 403.)

Subject + Verb + Indirect Object + Direct Object

```
 ┌S┐ ┌V┐ ┌IO┐ ┌DO┐
Elena offered her friend an anchovy.
```

The direct object names who or what receives the action; the indirect object names to whom or for whom the action was done.

Subject + Verb + Direct Object + Object Complement

```
 ┌───S───┐┌V┐┌DO┐┌──OC──┐
The chancellor named Ravi the outstanding
student of 2010.
```

The object complement renames or describes the direct object.

Subject + Linking Verb + Predicate Nominative (or Predicate Adjective)

```
 ┌S┐LV┌───── PN ─────┐
Paula is a computer programmer.
 ┌S┐LV┌──PA──┐
Paula is very intelligent.
```

A linking verb connects the subject to the predicate noun or predicate adjective. The predicate noun renames the subject; the predicate adjective describes the subject.

Inverted Order

In the previous sentence patterns, the subject comes before the verb. In a few types of sentences, such as those below, the subject comes after the verb.

```
LV┌S┐┌PN┐
Is Larisa a poet?
    (A question)
   LV ┌─S─┐
There was a meeting.
    (A sentence beginning with "there")
```

Sentence Problems

This section looks at potential trouble spots and sentence problems. For more information about English sentences, their parts, and how to construct them, see pages 412–417 in the handbook. Pages 418–425 cover the types of problems and errors found in English writing. The guide to avoiding sentence problems found on page 425 is an excellent editing tool.

Double Negatives

When making a sentence negative, use *not* or another negative adverb (*never, rarely, hardly, seldom,* and so on), but not both. Using both results in a double negative (see page 425).

Subject–Verb Agreement

Be sure the subject and verb in every clause agree in person and number. (See pages 418–420.)

> The **student was** rewarded for her hard work.
>
> The **students were** rewarded for their hard work.
>
> The **instructor**, as well as the students, **is** expected to attend the orientation.
>
> The **students**, as well as the instructor, **are** expected to attend the orientation.

Omitted Words

Do not omit subjects or the expletives *there* or *here*. In all English clauses and sentences (except imperatives in which the subject *you* is understood), there must be a subject.

Correct:	Your mother was very quiet; **she** seemed to be upset.
Not correct:	Your mother was very quiet; seemed to be upset.
Correct:	**There** is not much time left.
Not correct:	Not much time left.

Repeated Words

Do not repeat the subject of a clause or sentence.

Correct:	The doctor prescribed an antibiotic.
Not correct:	The doctor, **she** prescribed an antibiotic.

Do not repeat an object in an adjective dependent clause.

Correct:	I forgot the flowers that I intended to give to my hosts.
Not correct:	I forgot the flowers that I intended to give them to my hosts.

Note: Sometimes the relative pronoun that begins the adjective dependent clause is omitted but understood.

I forgot the flowers I intended to give to my hosts. (The relative pronoun *that* is omitted.)

Conditional Sentences

Conditional sentences express a situation requiring that a condition be met in order to be true. Selecting the correct verb tense for use in the two clauses of a conditional sentence can be problematic. Following, you will find an explanation of the three types of conditional sentences and the verb tenses that are needed to form them.

1. **Factual conditionals:** The conditional clause begins with *if, when, whenever,* or a similar expression. Furthermore, the verbs in the conditional clause and the main clause should be in the same tense.

Whenever we **had** time, we **took** a break and **went** for a swim.

2. **Predictive conditionals** express future conditions and possible results. The conditional clause begins with *if* or *unless* and has a present tense verb. The main clause uses a modal (*will, can, should, may, might*) plus the base form of the verb.

Unless we **find** a better deal, we **will buy** this sound system.

3. **Hypothetical past conditionals** describe a situation that is unlikely to happen or that is contrary to fact. To describe situations in the past, the verb in the conditional clause is in the past perfect tense, and the verb in the main clause is formed from *would have, could have,* or *might have* plus the past participle.

If we **had started out** earlier, we **would have arrived** on time.

Note: If the hypothetical situation is a present or future one, the verb in the conditional clause is in the past tense, and the verb in the main clause is formed from *would, could,* or *might* plus the base form of the verb.

If we **bought** groceries once a week, we **would** not **have** to go to the store so often.

Quoted and Reported Speech

Quoted speech is the use of exact words from another source in your own writing; you must enclose these words in quotation marks. It is also possible to report nearly exact words without quotation marks. This is called **reported speech,** or indirect quotation. (See pages 434–435 for a review of the use of quotation marks.)

Direct quotation:	Felicia said, "Don't worry about tomorrow."
Indirect quotation:	Felicia said that you don't have to worry about tomorrow.

In the case of a question, when a direct quotation is changed to an indirect quotation, the question mark is not needed.

Direct quotation:	Ahmad asked, "Which of you will give me a hand?"
Indirect quotation:	Ahmad asked which of us would give him a hand.

Notice how pronouns are often changed in indirect quotations.

> **Direct quotation:** My friends said, "You're crazy."
>
> **Indirect quotation:** My friends said that I was crazy.

Note: In academic writing, the use of another source's spoken or written words in one's own writing without proper acknowledgment is called *plagiarism*. Plagiarism is severely penalized in academic situations. (See pages 354–355.)

Numbers, Word Parts, and Idioms
LO4

Numbers

As a multilingual/ESL learner, you may be accustomed to a way of writing numbers that is different than the way it is done in North America. Become familiar with the North American conventions for writing numbers. Pages 444–445 show you how numbers are written and punctuated in both word and numeral form.

Using Punctuation with Numerals

Note that the **period** is used to express percentages (5.5%, 75.9%) and the **comma** is used to organize large numbers into units (7,000; 23,100; 231,990,000). Commas are not used, however, in writing the year (2011). (Also see page 430.)

Cardinal Numbers

Cardinal numbers are used when counting a number of parts or objects. Cardinal numbers can be used as nouns (she counted to **ten**), pronouns (I invited many guests, but only **three** came), or adjectives (there are **ten** boys here).

Write out in words the numbers one through one hundred. Numbers 101 and greater are often written as numerals. (See page 444.)

Ordinal Numbers

Ordinal numbers show place or succession in a series: the fourth row, the twenty-first century, the tenth time, and so on. Ordinal numbers are used to talk about the parts into which a whole can be divided, such as a fourth or a tenth, and as the denominator in fractions, such as one-fourth or three-fifths. Written fractions can also be used as nouns (I gave him **four-fifths**) or as adjectives (a **four-fifths** majority).

Note: See the list below for names and symbols of the first twenty-five ordinal numbers. Consult a college dictionary for a complete list of cardinal and ordinal numbers.

First	1st	Fourteenth	14th
Second	2nd	Fifteenth	15th
Third	3rd	Sixteenth	16th
Fourth	4th	Seventeenth	17th
Fifth	5th	Eighteenth	18th
Sixth	6th	Nineteenth	19th
Seventh	7th	Twentieth	20th
Eighth	8th	Twenty-first	21st
Ninth	9th	Twenty-second	22nd
Tenth	10th	Twenty-third	23rd
Eleventh	11th	Twenty-fourth	24th
Twelfth	12th	Twenty-fifth	25th
Thirteenth	13th		

Prefixes, Suffixes, and Roots

Following is a list of many common word parts and their meanings. Learning them can help you determine the meaning of unfamiliar words as you come across them in your reading. For instance, if you know that *hemi* means "half," you can conclude that *hemisphere* means "half of a sphere."

Quick Guide: Prefixes, Suffixes, and Roots

Prefixes	Meaning
a, an	not, without
anti, ant	against
co, con, com	together, with
di	two, twice
dis, dif	apart, away
ex, e, ec, ef	out
hemi, semi	half
il, ir, in, im	not
inter	between
intra	within
multi	many
non	not
ob, of, op, oc	toward, against
per	throughout
post	after
super, supr	above, more
trans, tra	across, beyond
tri	three
uni	one

Suffixes	Meaning
able, ible	able, can do
age	act of, state of
al	relating to
ate	cause, make
en	made of
ence, ency	action, quality
esis, osis	action, process
ice	condition, quality
ile	relating to
ish	resembling
ment	act of, state of
ology	study, theory
ous	full of, having
sion, tion	act of, state of
some	like, tending to
tude	state of
ward	in the direction of

Roots	Meaning
acu	sharp
am, amor	love, liking
anthrop	man
aster, astr	star
auto	self
biblio	book
bio	life
capit, capt	head
chron	time
cit	to call, start
cred	believe
dem	people
dict	say, speak
erg	work
fid, feder	faith, trust
fract, frag	break
graph, gram	write, written
ject	throw
log, ology	word, study, speech
man	hand
micro	small
mit, miss	send
nom	law, order
onym	name
path, pathy	feeling, suffering
rupt	break
scrib, script	write
spec, spect, spic	look
tele	far
tempo	time
tox	poison
vac	empty
ver, veri	true
zo	animal

Idioms

Idioms are phrases that are used in a special way. An idiom can't be understood just by knowing the meaning of each word in the phrase. It must be learned as a whole. For example, the idiom to *bury the hatchet* means to "settle an argument," even though the individual words in the phrase mean something much different. These pages list some of the common idioms in American English.

a bad apple

One troublemaker on a team may be called **a bad apple**. *(a bad influence)*

an axe to grind

Mom has **an axe to grind** with the owners of the dog that dug up her flower garden. *(a problem to settle)*

as the crow flies

She lives only two miles from here **as the crow flies**. *(in a straight line)*

beat around the bush

Dad said, "Where were you? Don't **beat around the bush**." *(avoid getting to the point)*

benefit of the doubt

Ms. Hy gave Henri the **benefit of the doubt** when he explained why he fell asleep in class. *(another chance)*

beyond the shadow of a doubt

Salvatore won the 50-yard dash **beyond the shadow of a doubt**. *(for certain)*

blew my top

When my money got stolen, I **blew my top**. *(showed great anger)*

bone to pick

Nick had a **bone to pick** with Adrian when he learned they both liked the same girl. *(problem to settle)*

break the ice

Shanta was the first to **break the ice** in the room full of new students. *(start a conversation)*

burn the midnight oil

Carmen had to **burn the midnight oil** the day before the big test. *(work late into the night)*

chomping at the bit

Dwayne was **chomping at the bit** when it was his turn to bat. *(eager, excited)*

cold shoulder

Alicia always gives me the **cold shoulder** after our disagreements. *(ignores me)*

cry wolf

If you **cry wolf** too often, no one will come when you really need help. *(say you are in trouble when you aren't)*

drop in the bucket

My donation was a **drop in the bucket**. *(a small amount compared with what's needed)*

face the music

José had to **face the music** when he got caught cheating on the test. *(deal with the punishment)*

flew off the handle

Tramayne **flew off the handle** when he saw his little brother playing with matches. *(became very angry)*

floating on air

Teresa was **floating on air** when she read the letter. *(feeling very happy)*

food for thought

The coach gave us some **food for thought** when she said that winning isn't everything. *(something to think about)*

get down to business

In five minutes you need to **get down to business** on this assignment. (*start working*)

get the upper hand

The other team will **get the upper hand** if we don't play better in the second half. (*probably win*)

go overboard

The teacher told us not to **go overboard** with fancy lettering on our posters. (*do too much*)

hit the ceiling

Rosa **hit the ceiling** when she saw her sister painting the television. (*was very angry*)

hit the hay

Patrice **hit the hay** early because she was tired. (*went to bed*)

in a nutshell

In a nutshell, Coach Roby told us to play our best. (*to summarize*)

in the nick of time

Zong grabbed his little brother's hand **in the nick of time** before he touched the hot pan. (*just in time*)

in the same boat

My friend and I are **in the same boat** when it comes to doing Saturday chores. (*have the same problem*)

iron out

Jamil and his brother were told to **iron out** their differences about cleaning their room. (*solve, work out*)

it stands to reason

It stands to reason that if you keep lifting weights, you will get stronger. (*it makes sense*)

knuckle down

Grandpa told me to **knuckle down** at school if I want to be a doctor. (*work hard*)

learn the ropes

Being new in school, I knew it would take some time to **learn the ropes**. (*get to know how things are done*)

let's face it

"**Let's face it!**" said Mr. Sills. "You're a better long-distance runner than you are a sprinter." (*let's admit it*)

let the cat out of the bag

Tia **let the cat out of the bag** and got her sister in trouble. (*told a secret*)

lose face

If I strike out again, I will **lose face**. (*be embarrassed*)

nose to the grindstone

If I keep my **nose to the grindstone**, I will finish my homework in one hour. (*working hard*)

on cloud nine

Walking home from the party, I was **on cloud nine**. (*feeling very happy*)

on pins and needles

I was **on pins and needles** as I waited to see the doctor. (*feeling nervous*)

over and above

Over and above the assigned reading, I read two library books. (*in addition to*)

put his foot in his mouth

Chivas **put his foot in his mouth** when he called his teacher by the wrong name. (*said something embarrassing*)

put your best foot forward

Grandpa said that whenever you do something, you should **put your best foot forward**. (*do the best that you can do*)

rock the boat

The coach said, "Don't **rock the boat** if you want to stay on the team." (*cause trouble*)

rude awakening

I had a **rude awakening** when I saw the letter *F* at the top of my Spanish quiz. (*sudden, unpleasant surprise*)

save face

> Grant tried to **save face** when he said he was sorry for making fun of me in class. (*fix an embarrassing situation*)

see eye to eye

> My sister and I finally **see eye to eye** about who gets to use the phone first after school. (*are in agreement*)

sight unseen

> Grandma bought the television **sight unseen**. (*without seeing it first*)

take a dim view

> My brother will **take a dim view** if I don't help him at the store. (*disapprove*)

take it with a grain of salt

> If my sister tells you she has no homework, **take it with a grain of salt**. (*don't believe everything you're told*)

take the bull by the horns

> This team needs to **take the bull by the horns** to win the game. (*take control*)

through thick and thin

> Max and I will be friends **through thick and thin**. (*in good times and in bad times*)

time flies

> When you're having fun, **time flies**. (*time passes quickly*)

time to kill

> We had **time to kill** before the ballpark gates would open. (*extra time*)

under the weather

> I was feeling **under the weather**, so I didn't go to school. (*sick*)

word of mouth

> We found out who the new teacher was by **word of mouth**. (*talking to other people*)

Note: Like idioms, collocations are groups of words that often appear together. They may help you identify different senses of a word; for example, *old* means slightly different things in these collocations: *old man, old friends.* You will find sentence construction easier if you check for collocations.

Help for Speakers of European Languages

Advice	DO NOT Write . . .	DO Write . . .
Do not omit the subject, *it* as a subject, or *there* with delayed subjects (pages 413, 462).	Are thousands of books in the library. Is okay to talk.	There are thousands of books in the library. It is okay to talk.
Avoid using *the* with certain generalizations and singular proper nouns (page 455).	I excel at the physics. The Professor Smith marks grammar errors.	I excel at physics. Professor Smith marks grammar errors.
Learn to use progressive verb tenses (page 456).	I still work on my term paper.	I am working on my term paper.
Learn whether to use a gerund or an infinitive after a verb (page 457).	The students need finishing their projects. The professors finished to grade the papers.	The students need to finish their projects. The professors finished grading the papers.
Avoid placing adverbs between verbs and direct objects (pages 460–461).	I wrote very quickly the first draft.	I wrote the first draft very quickly.
Do not use *which* to refer to people.	I am one of the students which sing in the choir.	I am one of the students who sing in the choir.

Help for Speakers of African and Caribbean Languages

Advice	DO NOT Write . . .	DO Write . . .
Avoid double subjects (page 463).	The professor she gave us an assignment.	The professor gave us an assignment.
Use plural nouns after plural numbers (page 456).	The class has two professor.	The class has two professors.
Use the correct form of the *be* verb (page 403).	The union be having a blood drive. We be going.	The union is having a blood drive. We are going.
Make subjects and verbs agree in number (pages 418–420).	She have her own notes. They finishes on time.	She has her own notes. They finish on time.
Use past tense verbs correctly (page 404).	When the semester began, I study hard.	When the semester began, I studied hard.
Study the rules for article use (page 455).	I need to buy computer. Entrance exam is required.	I need to buy a computer. An entrance exam is required.

Help for Speakers of East Asian Languages

Advice	DO NOT Write . . .	DO Write . . .
Use plural forms of nouns (page 456).	I have three difficult class.	I have three difficult classes.
Learn to use adjectival forms (pages 459–460).	He is a very intelligence professor.	He is a very intelligent professor.
Use the objective case of pronouns (page 402).	The tutor helps I with homework.	The tutor helps me with homework.
Include a subject (or *there*) (pages 413, 462).	Is good to be here. Are many parts.	It is good to be here. There are many parts.

Advice	DO NOT Write . . .	DO Write . . .
Study subject–verb agreement (pages 418–420).	The course have a long reading list.	The course has a long reading list.
Study past tenses (page 404).	We study yesterday. At first, I don't get it.	We studied yesterday. At first, I didn't get it.
Use articles—*a, an,* and *the* (pages 454–455).	I want to be nurse.	I want to be a nurse.
Study conjunction use (page 410).	Though she studies, but she struggles.	Though she studies, she struggles.
Learn whether to use a gerund or an infinitive (page 457).	The students need helping each other study.	The students need to help each other study.

Help for Speakers of Middle Eastern Languages

Advice	DO NOT Write . . .	DO Write . . .
Study pronoun gender and case (page 402).	My mother works hard at his job. Give she credit.	My mother works hard at her job. Give her credit.
Don't include a pronoun after a relative clause (pages 416, 462).	The study space that I share with two others it is too small.	The study space that I share with two others is too small.
Place most subjects before the verb (page 462).	Received the freshmen the assignment.	The freshmen received the assignment.
Don't overuse progressive verb tenses (page 456).	I am needing a nap. I am wanting food.	I need a nap. I want food.
Use the definite article *the* correctly (page 454).	Union is closed during the July.	The union is closed during July.

Credits

Professional models

Page 6: Dan Heath, Why Change Is So Hard: Self-Control Is Exhaustible, Fast Company, June 2, 2010. Copyright 2010 Mansueto Ventures LLC. All rights reserved.

Page 59: *From Of Human Bondage* by W. Somerset Maugham

Page 105: Elizabeth Fuller, "When Dreams Take Flight" From The New York Times, November 25, 2009. Copyright 2009 The New York Times/Daily Beast Company LLC. All rights reserved. Used by permission and protected by the Copyright Laws of the United States. The printing, copying, redistribution, or retransmission of the Material without the express written permission is prohibited.

Page 107: "The Muscle Mystique" (pp. 80-84) from HIGH TIDE IN TUCSON: ESSAYS FROM NOW OR NEVER by BARBARA KINGSOLVER

Page 118: Essay, "Daft or Deft," by David Schelhaas. Reprinted by permission of the author.

Page 119: Simson L. Garfinkel, "Wikipedia and the Meaning of Truth," November/December 2008. Reprinted by permission.

Page 132: Steward Brand, "Four Sides to Every Story" From The New York Times, December 15, 2009. Copyright 2009 The New York Times/Daily Beast Company LLC. All rights reserved. Used by permission and protected by the Copyright Laws of the United States. The printing, copying, redistribution, or retransmission of the Material without the express written permission is prohibited.

Page 134: John Van Rys, "Four Ways to Talk About Literature." Reprinted by permission of the author.

Page 143: Gerald L. Early, "The End of Race as We Know It" from The Chronicle Review, October 10, 2008.

Page 147: Verne Meyer, "Instructions." Reprinted by permission of the author.

Page 155: Gelareh Asayesh, "Shrouded in Contradiction." Copyright 2001. Gelareh Asayesh. First appeared in The New York Times Magazine, November 2, 2001. Reprinted by permission of the author.

Page 157: Shankar Vedantam, "Shades of Prejudice." Reprinted by permission of SLL/Sterling Lord Literistic, Inc. Copyright January 18, 2010 by Shankar Vedantam.

Page 169: Mary Brophy Marcus, "If You Let Me Play…" from U.S. NEWS & WORLD REPORT, October 27, 1997. Copyright 1997 U.S. News & World Report, L.P. Reprinted with permission.

Page 172: Steven Pinker, "Mind Over Mass Media" From The New York Times, June 11, 2010. Copyright 2010 The New York Times/Daily Beast Company LLC. All rights reserved. Used by permission and protected by the Copyright Laws of the United States. The printing, copying, redistribution, or retransmission of the Material without the express written permission is prohibited.

Page 197: Gary Steiner, "Animal, Vegetable, Miserable" From The New York Times, November 22, 2009. Copyright 2009 The New York Times/Daily Beast Company LLC. All rights reserved. Used by permission and protected by the Copyright Laws of the United States. The printing, copying, redistribution, or retransmission of the Material without the express written permission is prohibited.

Page 201: Natalie Angier, "Sorry Vegans: Brussels Sprouts Like to Live, Too" From The New York Times, November 22, 2009. Copyright 2009 The New York Times/Daily Beast Company LLC. All rights reserved. Used by permission and protected by the Copyright Laws of the United States. The printing, copying, redistribution, or retransmission of the Material without the express written permission is prohibited.

Page 215 Martin Luther King Jr., "I Have a Dream" Copyright 1963 Dr. Martin Luther King Jr; copyright renewed 1991 Coretta Scott King. Reprinted by arrangement with The Heirs to the Estate of Martin Luther King Jr., c/o Writers House as agent for proprietor New York, NY.

Page 218: Kofi A. Annan, "In Africa, AIDS Has a Woman's Face" From The New York Times, December 29, 2002. Copyright 2002 The New York Times/Daily Beast Company LLC. All rights reserved. Used by permission and protected by the Copyright Laws of the United States. The printing, copying, redistribution, or retransmission of the Material without the express written permission is prohibited.

Page 229: David Blankenhorn, "Fatherless America," from FATHERLESS AMERICA: Confronting Our Most Urgent Social Problems, 1995, pp 1-5. Copyright 1996 David Blankenhorn. Reprinted by permission of Basic Books, a member of Perseus BooksGroup

Page 232: Barbara Ehrenreich, "Is It Now a Crime to Be Poor?" from The New York Times, August 8, 2009. Reprinted by permission of Internation Creative Management, Inc. Copyright 2009 by Barbara Ehrenreich

Page 243: *Profile: Their main act: Arcade Fire doesn't chase fame,* by Jonathon Gatehouse. Maclean's, February 21, 2011. Reprinted by permission of Maclean's.

Page 268: Jane Kenyon, "Let Evening Come" from Collected Poems. Copyright 2005 by The Estate of Jane Kenyon. Reprinted by permission of Graywolf Press, Minneapolis, Minnesota. www.graywolfpress.com

Student models

Page 57: David Zupp, "Seeing the Light" (excerpt)

Page 58: Paula Treick, "My Obsession" (excerpt)

Page 60: Jessica Tan Haken, "Four Temperaments" (excerpt)

Page 100: Robert Minto, "The Entomology of Village Life"

Page 103: Teresa Zsuffa, "Spare Change"

Page 115: Shon Bogar, "Economic Disparities Fuel Human Trafficking"

Page 117: Mary Beth Bruins, "The Gullible Family"

Page 129: Kathleen Kropp, "Latin American Music: A Diverse and Unifying Force"

Page 141: Kerri Mertz, "Wayward Cells"

Page 153: Rachel De Smith, "Sethe in Beloved and Orleanna in Poisonwood Bible: Isolation, Children, and Getting Out"

Page 165: Sarah Hanley, "Adrenaline Junkies"

Page 166: Brittany Korver, "Dutch Discord"

Page 191: Aleah Stenberg, "Ah, the Power of Women"

Page 194: Alyssa Woudstra, "Nuclear is Not the Answer"

Page 209: Rebecca Pasok, "To Drill or Not To Drill"

Page 212: Henry Veldboom, "Our Wealth: Where Is It Taking Us?"

Page 225: Renee Wielenga, "Dream Act May Help Local Student Fight for Residence"

Page 226: Brian VanderLey, "Preparing for AgroTerror"

Page 241: Benjamin Meyer, "The Dead Business"

Page 253: Coby Williams, "Working with Hydrochlorc Acid"

Page 254: Andrea Van Wyk "The Effects of Temperature and Inhibitors on the Fermentation Process for Ethanol"

Page 268: Sherry Van Egdom, "'Let Evening Come': An Invitation to the Inevitable"

Page 270: David Schaap, "Terror on the Silver Screen: Who are the Aliens?"

Page 362: Stevie Jeung, "I Did Not Get My Spaghetti-O's: Death Row Consumption in the Popular Media"

Page 390: Thomas I. DeJong and Adam B. Smit, "Running on Empty: The Effects of Food Deprivation on Concentration and Perseverance"

Index

G

Gender, 90
  Noun, 399
  Pronoun, 402, 421
Gender references, 90, 280
Generalization, 184
Genre, 134, 272
Gerund, 405, 406, 412, 414, 415, 457
Gerund phrase, 412, 414, 415
Grammar, 91, 345, 398–411
Graphic organizers, 46, 49, 50–51
  Cause/effect, 50
  Classification, 48, 51
  Cluster, 16, 38
  Comparison, 50
  Comparison/contrast, 49, 50
  Definition, 51
  Line Diagram, 49
  Persuasion, 50
  Problem/solution web, 51
  Process analysis, 50
  Venn diagram, 50
Graphics 7, 10, 34, 49, 124, 125, 147,
    164, 181, 190, 204–205, 236–237,
    292–295, 298, 315, 346
Groups, study, 302–303
Guidelines for writing,
  About literature and the
    arts, 274–275
  Analysis of a process, 148–149
  Application essay, 284–285
  Cause-effect essay, 174–175
    Thesis, 45
  Classification essay, 136–137
    Thesis, 46
  Comparison-contrast essay, 160–161
    Thesis, 45
  Definition essay, 124–125
    Thesis, 46
  Description essay, 110–111
  Description and reflection essay,
    110–111
  Editing, 25–26
  Freewriting, 37
  Interview report, 248–249
  Lab reports. *See* Lab, experiment,
    and field reports.
  Letter, 185
  Literary analysis, 274–275
  Narration essay, 110–111
    Thesis, 45

Paraphrases, 41, 350
Peer review, 77–78
Personal narrative, 00–00
  Thesis, 45
Personal reflection, 110–111
Persuasion, 220–221
  Thesis, 46
Position paper, 204–205
  Thesis, 46
Problem/solution essay, 000–000
  Thesis, 46
Process writing, 148–149
  Thesis, 46
Proposing a solution, 236–237
  Thesis, 46
Reflective essay, 110–111
Research papers, 360–361
Résumé, 285
Revising, 21–24
Summaries, 350
Guides, as research tool, 315, 327, 344

H

Half-truths, 184
Handbooks, as research tool, 327
Heading, business letter, 280, 281
Helping (auxiliary) verb, 403, 457
Heptameter, 273
Hexameter, 273
Hyperbole, 272
Hyphen, 432–433, 439

I

Iambic, 273
Ideas, generating, 16–18, 36–38, 110,
    124, 148, 160, 174, 204, 220, 236,
    248, 274, 291, 313
Idioms, 410, 466–468
Illustration. *See* Anecdote.
  Paragraph, 58
Imagery, 272
Imperative mood, 405
Imperative sentence, 85, 148, 405, 416,
    462
Incomplete comparison, 84, 424
Inconsistent construction, 421–422
Indefinite gender, 400, 401, 421
Indefinite pronoun, 401
  Agreement with antecedent, 421
  Unclear reference, 424

Independent clause, 415, 417, 428, 429,
    431
  Punctuation of, 428–429, 431
Index,
  As research tool, 315, 320, 324, 326,
    327, 332–333
Indicative mood, 405
Indirect object, 399, 413, 462
Indirect question, 426, 427
Indirect quotation, 463–464
Inductive reasoning, 12, 182
Infinitive, 83, 406, 414, 415
  Complement used as, 457
  Phrase, 83, 414, 457
Information,
  Avoiding other source abuses,
    355–356
  Avoiding plagiarism, 354–355
  Collecting, 38–41, 318–341
  Evaluation of, 305, 337–340,
    344–345
  Letter, 281
  Searching for, 314–315, 315–316,
    318–341
  Services, 315–316
  Sites, 331–334
  Sources, primary and secondary, 40,
    314, 316–317, 321–323 386–387
Initialisms, 448–449
Initials, 280, 348, 375, 426, 431, 448
Inside address, 280
Inspections, as primary research, 323
Instant messaging, 297
Intensive pronoun, 400, 401
Interjection, 410, 411, 430
Internet, 288–299, 330–340
  Capitalization, 442
  Source documentation, 378–379,
    385–386
  Source note, 346
  Terms, 296–297
  Using for research, 312, 315, 316,
    330–340
  Writing venue, 288–299
Interpret, 34
Interrogative,
  Pronoun, 400, 401
  Sentence, 416
Interrupted speech, 434
Interruption, punctuation of, 430, 434
Interview,
  Conducting an, 322, 248

LO1 Analyzing Your Purpose

Your writing purpose will depend upon the circumstances. In college, you will often write for an assignment. At work, you will write to meet a business need. In personal writing, your purpose may be more casual. In each case, purpose tends to fall into one of the following categories:

- **To analyze:** Analysis means considering a body of information and coming to a conclusion. In school, this makes analysis a great tool for learning. In business, analysis is useful for problem solving.
- **To entertain:** Sometimes your purpose may be simply to amuse an audience. Yet entertainment may also analyze, explain, inform, or persuade.
- **To explain:** Explanation presents the connection between facts. It may be organized by cause and effect, comparison and contrast, or chronological order.
- **To inform:** Some writing is simply intended to present information, leaving readers to draw their own conclusions. You may receive informational writing assignments to further your own knowledge.
- **To persuade:** Often writing serves the purpose of arguing for a position, usually with a call to action.

Identify the purpose that best suits your writing situation.

LO2 Analyzing Your Topic

Typically you will be given a general subject to write about. You will then need to choose a specific topic and research it before writing. Use the following process:

1. **Cluster** or **brainstorm** for topic ideas within the subject area, and then choose one to write about.
2. **Freewrite** to determine what you already know about your chosen topic and what you need to learn.
3. **Research** to fill in the gaps in your understanding. Remember to document your sources for credit in your writing.

Use this process to focus on a specific topic for your writing.

LO3 Analyzing Your Audience

To write effectively, you need to adapt to your readers. The following questions can help you to analyze your audience:

- What do they already know about your topic?
- How interested are they in the topic?
- What is their attitude toward the topic?
- What do they expect from you in this writing?

Answer these questions to identify your audience.

Glossary Terms

cluster
generating or focusing ideas by writing words in circles, with lines to show their relationships (See page 38.)

brainstorm
generating ideas by freely listing everything that comes to mind, without judgment (See page 38.)

freewrite
spontaneously writing in journal style as a means of generating or identifying ideas (See page 37.)

Glossary Terms

blog
short for "Web log," an online journal

microblog
a Web service that hosts publicly viewable text messages

wiki
named after the Hawaiian word for "quick," a Web site created and edited by community

LO4 Analyzing Your Audience

Purpose, topic, and *audience* together point to the form your writing should take.

General Forms

- **Analysis** draws a conclusion from a body of information.
- **Argumentation** makes a case for a particular way of thinking.
- **Cause-effect** presents the result or results of one or more causes.
- **Comparison-contrast** evaluates how things are alike and different.
- **Description** depicts a person, place, or thing. It is used in many other forms of writing.
- **Narration** reveals events, often chronologically.
- **Persuasion** asks readers to adopt a way of thinking and act upon it.
- **Reflection** reveals the writer's reflections on a topic.
- **Report** presents knowledge assembled about a particular topic.

Workplace Forms

Besides the general forms, workplace writing may involve...

- **Correspondence:** Business letters and memos must be written in a concise, professional style.
- **Résumé:** This job-application document presents the writer's skills and achievements.

Web Forms

Besides the general forms, Web forms may involve...

- **Blogs:** Blog writing calls for short sentences and paragraphs with graphics for quick reading.
- **Microblogs:** Social media requires careful writing to pack the most meaning in the fewest characters.
- **Wikis:** Wikis and other cooperative projects require precise planning, writing, and editing.

Choose the appropriate form for your writing situation.

LO1 Developing an Argument

When you are writing to argue a point, you start by making up your own mind about the issue. That requires research and thought. Don't make up your mind right away. Instead, read, view, discuss, and think.

As your thinking develops, consider two different approaches to building an argument, depending on your reader's likely reaction.

Neutral Reader

Introduction: Get the reader's attention and lead to your claim.

1. Provide strong support.
2. Provide additional support.
3. Answer an objection.
4. Give your strongest support.

Conclusion: Call the reader to act.

Resistant Reader

Introduction: Get the reader's attention and lead to your claim.

1. Answer objection 1.
2. Answer objection 2.
3. Answer objection 3.
4. Give strongest support.

Conclusion: Call the reader to act.

LO2 Making and Qualifying a Claim

A claim is a debatable statement drawn from logical thought and reliable evidence. A strong claim is **arguable, defendable, responsible, understandable,** and **interesting**. A strong claim also is not a fact (something that can be easily demonstrated) or a personal opinion (something that cannot be argued).

Fact: The world population has passed 7 billion.

Opinion: I dislike crowded cities.

Claim: As world population increases, urban planners will need to innovate new solutions to address crowding.

LO3 Supporting Your Claims

After stating a strong claim, you need to support it using effective evidence. Different types of evidence provide different support.

- Observations and anecdotes personalize the information.
- Statistics quantify information.
- Tests and experiments provide scientific evidence.
- Graphics present a lot of information in a visual fashion.
- Analogies explain a topic by comparing it to something familiar.
- Expert testimony gives evidence from the point of view of experts.
- Illustrations and demonstrations show a concept.
- Analyses use thought patterns such as comparison, process, classification, and cause-effect.
- Predictions offer insight into possible outcomes or consequences.

LO4 Engaging the Opposition

Not all readers will agree with you, but if you can anticipate their objections, you can respond to them. You can overcome an objection (rebuttal) or can admit that it is true (concession).

Glossary Terms

argument
a series of statements building logically on each other to reach a conclusion; a claim that is supported with evidence

claim
a debatable statement that should be arguable, defendable, responsible, understandable, and interesting

anecdote
a brief story that demonstrates an idea

analogy
comparing something unfamiliar with something familiar

Glossary Terms

assertion
a claim

sentiment
feeling, emotion

herring
a stinky fish dragged across a trail to throw off scent hounds

generalization
applying a specific case to many cases

hypothesis
an educated guess

contrary
against; opposite

testimony
a person's statement about an issue

LO5 Identifying and Avoiding Logical Fallacies

Fallacies are false arguments—fuzzy, dishonest, or incomplete thinking. They come in many varieties.

Distorting the Issue

- **Bare assertion:** Saying, "That's just the way it is"
- **Begging the question:** Assuming the conclusion as a premise
- **Complex question:** Phrasing a question so it cannot be answered
- **Either/or thinking:** Reducing many options to two extremes
- **Oversimplification:** Reducing complexity to simplicity
- **Straw man:** Attacking a position the opposition does not take

Sabotaging the Argument

- **Appeal to pity:** Manipulating the reader through strong emotion
- **Appeal to popular sentiment:** Connecting to something beloved
- **Bandwagoning:** Arguing that the popular position must be true
- **Misuse of humor:** Making a joke to dismiss an opposing point
- **Red herring:** Distracting the reader using a shocking diversion
- **Threatening:** Bullying the reader into agreement

Drawing Faulty Conclusions

- **Appeal to ignorance:** Arguing based on the lack of evidence
- **Broad generalization:** Jumping to a conclusion
- **False cause:** Identifying an incorrect reason for something
- **Slippery slope:** Saying one small step will start an unstoppable chain of events

Misusing Evidence

- **Attacking the person:** Focusing on the opponent, not the argument
- **False analogy:** Equating two dissimilar things
- **Half-truths:** Presenting only part of the story
- **Hypothesis contrary to fact:** Arguing "if only . . ."
- **Impressing with numbers:** Dazzling readers with many statistics
- **Unreliable testimony:** Quoting an untrustworthy source

Misusing Language

- **Obfuscation:** Using complicated language to confuse
- **Ambiguity:** Using statements that point two different directions
- **Slanted language:** Using biased terms to skew an argument

LO1 Understanding Plagiarism

Plagiarism is taking credit for other people's work. It is a type of stealing. It usually takes one of the following forms.

1. **Submitting another writer's paper as if it were your own**
2. **Pasting material into your paper and passing it off as yours**
3. **Using exact words without quotation marks and citation**
4. **Summarizing or paraphrasing ideas without citing their source**

Take care to avoid plagiarism. Plagiarism can damage your reputation and hurt your academic career.

LO2 Avoiding Plagiarism

The best way to avoid plagiarism is simply to be careful at each stage of the writing process. Specifically...

1. **As you research, take orderly notes.**
   - Keep a bibliographic record of each source you take notes from.
   - Use quotation marks for exact words of sources.
   - Keep your own thoughts and comments distinct from source material.
   - Consider keeping photocopies or printouts of original material for accurate reference.

2. **As you write, credit all material you quote, summarize, or paraphrase from another source.**
   - Include a clear pointer to the appropriate source for each instance of borrowed material. (Most often this will be a parenthetical citation.)
   - Use textual cues to signal where your thinking ends and a summary or paraphrase begins.
   - Signal the end each summary or paraphrase with a parenthetical citation or a clear textual cue.
   - Use quotation marks to show exact words borrowed. (See pages 359 and 372 for exceptions involving multi-line quotations.)

3. **After you write, compile an accurate list of sources with publication details for each.**
   - For MLA style, compile a "Works Cited" list.
   - For APA style, compile a "References" list.
   - Make sure each in-text citation points to an entry on your list.

Use these strategies to give credit where it is due in your writing.

Glossary Terms

plagiarism
accidentally or intentionally presenting someone else's work as if it were your own

paraphrase
restating an idea in different words

bibliographic record
a list of sources used during research

citation
a reference in text to the source of an idea or information

MLA
the Modern Language Association, which publishes a report and documentation style used in the humanities

APA
the American Psychological Association, which publishes a report and documentation style used in psychology and some other fields

Glossary Terms

in-text citation
a reference in the body of a text to the specific source of borrowed information

fair use
the legal right to use small portions of a copyrighted material for education or research, but not for other gain

copyright
law protecting the ownership of created works

public domain
works whose copyright has expired, or which were never in copyright (such as government materials)

intellectual property
writing, music, and other works belonging to a creator or other copyright holder

creator guidelines
instructions from a work's creator, defining whether that work may be reproduced, modified, and/or incorporated into other works

LO3 Avoiding Other Source Abuses

Be sure to understand and avoid these eight other misuses of sources materials.

1. **Using sources inaccurately**
   Take care to represent sources exactly as you find them. This includes:
   - quoting word for word
   - summarizing and paraphrasing correctly
   - stating statistics and facts accurately
   - In other words, don't misrepresent the original.

2. **Using source material out of context**
   Words taken out of context can seem to mean something different from their original intent. Use each source in keeping with its original meaning.

3. **Overusing source material**
   Your writing should reflect your own thoughts. The purpose of sources is to support those thoughts, giving specific details and showing your knowledge of the subject. Don't let your paper read like a string of quotations.

4. **"Plunking" quotations**
   To avoid "plunking," apply the following strategies:
   - Introduce the concept first, in your own voice.
   - Present a quotation that illustrates that concept.
   - Comment on the idea contained in the quotation.

   These three steps will help to incorporate the quotation into your overall message.

5. **Using "blanket" citations**
   Don't make the reader guess where borrowed material begins and ends. Include clear cues instead.

6. **Relying heavily on one source**
   Unless you are specifically reviewing a single source, your writing should reference a wide range of sources to show the depth of your research.

7. **Failing to match in-text citations to bibliographic entries**
   Every reference in your text must point to a specific bibliographic entry, and every bibliographic entry must be referred to in your text.

8. **Violating copyrights**
   Understand lawful copyright use. (See page 356.)
   - Follow fair use guidelines.
   - Understand what's in the public domain.
   - Observe intellectual property and copyright law.
   - Follow creator guidelines on adapting graphics, sound recordings, and so on.

L◯1 Analyzing the Situation

Writing is communication, and it has the same basic parts as any other communication situation: subject, audience, and purpose. As you get started, ask yourself questions about each part.

- **Subject:** What do I want to say about my subject?
- **Audience:** Who is my reader? What does the person know already about this subject? What does the person need to know?
- **Purpose:** Why am I writing—to explain, to persuade, to entertain?

L◯2 Understanding the Assignment

Most writing you do in college relates to an assignment. Consider the options (what the assignment allows) and the restrictions (what the assignment requires). Read the assignment carefully and watch for key terms like these:

Analyze: Break down.	**Contrast:** Show differences.	**Interpret:** Put in your words.
Apply: Use information.	**Define:** Give the meaning.	**Persuade:** Convince.
Argue: Logically explain.	**Describe:** Show in detail.	**Reflect:** Think thoroughly.
Classify: Make categories.	**Evaluate:** Rate the worth.	**Summarize:** State briefly.
Compare: Show similarities.	**Explain:** Tell how it works.	**Synthesize:** Create something.

L◯3 Selecting a Topic

Often writing assignments have a broad subject and you need to select a specific topic and focus. Review your notes and journal for possible topics, or use freewriting, clustering, or listing. Choose a topic that meets the assignment's requirements, fits the length of the document you are to write, and genuinely interests you.

L◯4 Gathering Details

Begin your research process, finding out the information you need to know to write well about your subject. Follow these steps:

- **Discover what you know** through freewriting and directed writing: describe, compare, associate, analyze, argue, apply.
- **Ask questions** about the value, history, function, and description of the topic. Think about problems, policies, and concepts.
- **Identify possible sources** including original documents and experiences (primary) and information others have gathered (secondary).
- **Conduct** your research looking for a variety of reliable sources.

L◯5 Form Your Thesis Statement

During your research, you should write a preliminary thesis statement. Use this basic formula:

a limited topic		a specific focus		an effective thesis
wind power	**+**	viable energy for plains states	**=**	Wind power provides a viable energy source in the plains states.

Glossary Terms

purpose
reason for writing

options
what the assignment allows

restrictions
what the assignment requires

thesis statement
a sentence that captures a specific focus for writing

Glossary Terms

order of location
arranging details according to their position—front to back, top to bottom, left to right

chronological order
arranging details according to a time sequence—first, next, then, afterward

parallel
using the same grammatical form for similar parts (e.g., a list of nouns, a list of phrases, a list of clauses)

LO6 Develop Your Ideas

Your working thesis statement can guide the development of the rest of your writing. Here are common methods of development:

- **Argument:** Use a series of statements to build toward a point.
- **Cause-effect:** Explore reasons and results of the topic.
- **Classification:** Break the topic into groups or categories.
- **Comparison:** Show the similarities and differences of two topics.
- **Definition:** Explore the meaning of a term.
- **Descriptive:** Provide sensory details, often by order of location.
- **Narrative:** Tell a story, often in chronological order.
- **Persuading:** Convince the reader of an opinion or to take action.
- **Process:** Tell how to do something or how something works.
- **Problem-solution:** Explain a problem and propose a solution.

LO7 Develop a Plan

You can develop a plan for your writing by using an outline. Here's how to make two types of outlines

- **Topic Outline:** Write your thesis statement in full, but state each main point and key detail as a word or phrase. Try to keep items parallel.
- **Sentence outline:** Write your thesis statement and each main point as a sentence.

You can also use a graphic organizer to gather your thoughts. Choose the type that best fits your thesis and method of development.

Process Analysis

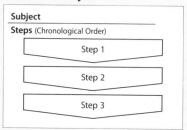

Problem/Solution

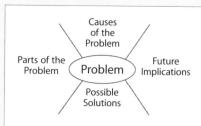

Definition

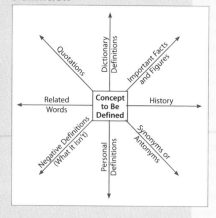

Classification

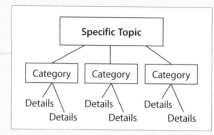

Persuasion

Comparison

Comparison/Contrast (Venn Diagram)

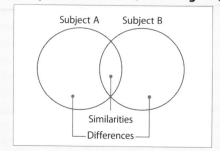

Cause-Effect

LO1 Framing a Working Thesis

A thesis is the main idea that you develop and support in your piece of writing. You can think of a thesis as following this pattern:

limited or manageable topic	**+**	tentative claim or statement about the topic	**=**	Working thesis statement

So what's your point? What thesis do you want to develop and support in your writing? Follow the steps below to do your initial thesis thinking.

- **My limited, manageable topic:** Describe the topic as precisely as possible, paying careful attention to the key terms that identify the topic. Explore why the topic matters and what interests you most about it.
- **Possible claims or statements that I could make, develop, and support in my writing:** Brainstorm as many ideas as come to you based upon your thinking through, reading about, and discussing the topic.
- **My working thesis:** Based on your brainstorming, what is the main idea that you wish to develop in your essay? Write out that idea as a single sentence following the formula above.

LO2 Strengthening Your Thesis

Taking your working thesis and strengthening it requires that you deepen your own thinking about the topic and the claim you are making. Getting there might involve more reading, discussing, and reflecting. However, you can start by understanding the differences between poor and strong theses and exploring ways to sharpen a thesis.

Poor vs. Strong Working Theses

A poor thesis is a simple statement of fact that can be easily checked, an opinion that cannot really be debated, a vague statement, a broad generalization, or an illogical conclusion.

> Many auto manufacturers are developing hybrid vehicles. [statement of fact]
>
> *The fact that many celebrities are buying hybrid vehicles is really cool.* [statement of opinion]

A strong thesis demonstrates clarity of thought and higher level thinking skills—analytical patterns such as compare/contrast, argumentative patterns such as problem/solution.

> *The hybrid car is part of a family of vehicles that combine two or more sources of power to create motion.* [analysis]
>
> *Hybrid cars are a positive step forward from the average internal-combustion car, but they won't have a large enough environmental impact.* [argument]

Glossary Terms

thesis statement
a sentence or set of sentences that sums up the central idea of a piece of writing

working thesis
a preliminary answer to your main research questions, the focus of your research

Test these theses: Are the theses below poor or strong? Somewhere between? Assess each thesis, giving reasons for your judgment.

1. Wind farms are ugly and must be banned across the state.
2. The mortgage crisis in America can be resolved in the long term by changes in two areas: regulation of more conservative, less risky lending practices; and better education in personal finance in schools.
3. Arcade Fire didn't deserve the Grammy for Best Album because their sound isn't mainstream enough and the group hasn't even had a number 1 hit song.

Your working thesis: How does the working thesis you drafted measure up? Identify its strengths and weaknesses.

LO3 Sharpening and Deepening Your Thesis

If your thesis needs work, how can you sharpen it and deepen it? Here are some ways:

1. **Test your logic.** Does the idea at the heart of your thesis hold water? Does it avoid faulty cause-effect thinking, either-or thinking, bandwagon mentality, and so on? Weed out the weak thinking to give room for your good thinking to grow.

2. **Use richer, clearer terms.** Test your working thesis for vague, broad, or inappropriate terms or concepts. While plain English is always a good choice, use terms in your thesis that have rich meanings, that are respected in discussions of your topic, and that refine your original thinking.

3. **Introduce qualifying terms where needed.** With qualifying terms such as "normally," "often," and "usually," as well as with phrases that limit the reach of your thesis, you are paradoxically not weakening your thesis but making it more reasonable and thoughtful.

4. **Stress your idea through opposition.** You can deepen your working thesis by adding opposition (usually phrased in a dependent clause) in order to emphasize your own idea through contrast.

5. **Get at the "so what?" of your idea.** Why does your claim matter—practically, intellectually, personally? Building a "so what?" answer into your thesis, often through a "because" clause, can lend a sense of urgency and significance to your idea.

Practice Sharpening: Using the strategies explained to the right, take the working thesis below and strengthen it.

> Popular music bridges gaps between different types of people.

Sharpening Your Own Thesis: Now deepen and strengthen your own thesis. Test out possible changes.

Original Thesis: In Alice Munro's "An Ounce of Cure," infatuation messes with the narrator's head so her life gets turned upside down.

Revised Thesis: While Alice Munro's "An Ounce of Cure" tells a simple story of infatuation leading to confusion and trouble, the story is more importantly about the "plots of life"—the ways in which the narrator experiences life as a competing set of stories (romance, fairy tale, farce), none of which does justice to the complexity of real life.

Thesis Checklist

Does your thesis pass the test? Check it against these questions:

✔ Does my thesis focus on a single, limited topic?

✔ Is my thesis stated in a clear, direct sentence?

✔ Does my thesis convey my best thinking about the topic?

✔ Does my thesis get at some complexity about the topic?

✔ Do I have enough good information to develop and support this thesis?

✔ Does my thesis direct me to write a paper that meets all assignment requirements?

LO1 Revising for Clarity

When you revise for clarity, you focus on the ideas in your writing and how those ideas are organized. Check for the following:

- **Complete thinking:** Make sure that you answer the audience's main questions about the topic—the 5 W's and H. Check that your details are specific and complete.
- **Clear thesis:** Revise your thesis statement to make it clearly state your topic and the focus of your writing.
- **Strong opening:** Your opening paragraph needs to get the reader's attention, provide any necessary background, and lead to your thesis statement. If the opening falls short in any of these ways, revise it.
- **Organized middle:** The middle paragraphs should follow a clear pattern of organization (chronological, importance, classification, and so on). Transition words and phrases should connect the details.
- **Strong closing:** The closing paragraph should effectively summarize the writing, providing the reader with something to think about.

LO2 Revising for Voice

Voice reveals what you feel about all aspects of the communication situation. Make sure your voice fits the following:

- **Topic:** Show your interest and knowledge.
- **Audience:** Connect to your reader.
- **Purpose:** Show your reason for writing (persuade/explain).
- **Medium:** Use the accepted style for the type of writing.
- **Self:** Use a voice that reflects well on you, the writer.

LO3 Using an Academic Style

College writing requires an academic style that is different from writing in social media. Use the following tips.

- **Avoid personal pronouns** (*I, we, you*) in most academic writing. In a personal piece such as a narrative, these words are okay.
- **Avoid jargon and define technical terms** so that your writing can be understood by a broad audience.
- **Use a formal voice,** with a serious tone, careful word choice, longer sentences, correct grammar, and no slang.
- **Remove excess modifiers** such as *mostly, often, likely, really, truly.*
- **Use active voice** for most sentences. The subject of the sentence should be performing the action of the verb.
- **Use passive voice** to be tactful, to stress what is acted upon, or if the actor is unknown or unimportant.

Glossary Terms

thesis statement
a sentence that names the topic and provides the specific focus of writing

chronological
ordered by time

classification
ordered by category

voice
the way writing "sounds," revealing the writer's feelings about all parts of the communication situation

medium
the form that communication takes (e.g., essay, e-mail, phone call)

personal pronouns
words such as *I, me, you, your, he, it* that take the place of nouns and other pronouns

jargon
words known only by insiders

active voice
construction in which the subject of the sentence performs the action of the verb

passive voice
construction in which the subject of the sentence receives the action of the verb

Glossary Terms

topic sentence
a sentence that names the topic and focus of a paragraph

body sentence
a sentence that gives details that support the topic sentence of the paragraph

transition
a word, phrase, or clause that shows the connection between details

closing sentence
the sentence that sums up the paragraph

LO4 Addressing Paragraph Issues

Paragraphs are the building blocks of essays, so when you revise, you need to make sure these blocks are solid. Check the following issues:

Topic Sentence

Make sure that each of your middle paragraphs has a clear topic sentence. The topic sentence most often comes first in a paragraph, but it can also come in the center or at the end to create specific effects. Use this formula.

a limited topic		a specific focus		an effective topic sentence
consumer confidence	+	24-hour media bombards consumers	=	The 24-hour news cycle bombards consumers with bad economic news and erodes consumer confidence.

Body Sentences

Make sure that every sentence in a paragraph supports the topic sentence (unity) and smoothens the flow of ideas (coherence). Smooth the flow by using effective repetition of words and clear transitions. Here are some common transition words, by category:

- **Location:** above, across, against, around, along, among, behind, below, beneath, beside, between, beyond, by, down, in front of, in back of, inside, into on top of, onto, outside, throughout, under
- **Time:** about, after, afterward, as soon as, during, finally, first, last, later, meanwhile, next, then
- **Compare/contrast:** also, although, as, but, even though, in the same way, likewise, on the one hand, on the other hand, however, similarly, yet
- **Emphasis:** again, for this reason, in fact, particularly, to repeat, to emphasize
- **Summarize:** all in all, as a result, finally, in conclusion, in summary, therefore, to sum up
- **Add information:** additionally, again, along with, also, as well, and, another, besides, for example, for instance, in addition
- **Clarify:** for instance, in other words, put another way, that is

Variety of Details

Your writing will be vivid and interesting if you support your main point through a variety of details. Consider using details such as the following:

facts	anecdotes	analyses	sensations
statistics	quotations	explanations	comparisons
examples	definitions	summaries	analogies

Closing Sentence

Not all paragraphs have a closing sentence, but if you do include a closing sentence, make sure that it effectively sums the paragraph in an interesting way.

Use the checklists on this card to edit for punctuation, mechanics, usage, and grammar. For more information about any topic, see the index to this book and check out pages in the handbook section.

LO1 Editing for Punctuation

Have I used . . .

____ 1. **periods** after sentences other than questions?

____ 2. **question** marks after direct questions?

____ 3. **commas** between the clauses of a compound sentence?

____ 4. **commas** between items in a series?

____ 5. **commas** after introductory words?

____ 6. **commas** to separate equal adjectives?

____ 7. **commas** to separate nonrestrictive phrases and clauses?

____ 8. **hyphens** to join numbers indicating a range?

____ 9. **quotation marks** around direct quotations and titles of short works?

____ 10. **end quotation** marks following periods and commas and preceding other punctuation marks.

____ 11. **italics** for titles of long works?

____ 12. **apostrophes** to indicate missing letters in contractions?

____ 13. **apostrophes** to form possessives (but not possessive pronouns)?

LO2 Editing for Mechanics

Have I . . .

____ 1. **capitalized** first words in sentences and full quotations?

____ 2. **capitalized** proper nouns and adjectives?

____ 3. **capitalized** languages, ethnic groups, nationalities, and religions?

____ 4. **capitalized** the first and last word of titles and other words except articles (*a, an, the*), short prepositions, *to* in an infinitive, and coordinating conjunctions (*and, but, or, nor, for, so, yet*)?

____ 5. **formed plurals** by adding an *s* after most singular nouns and adding *es* after those ending in *sh, ch, x, s,* or *z*?

____ 6. **formed plurals** of compound nouns by adding an *s* or *es* to the most important word in the compound?

____ 7. **spelled out numbers** from one to one hundred?

____ 8. **used numerals** for decimals, percentages, pages, chapters, addresses, dates, statistics, numbers with abbreviations, and phone and identification numbers.

____ 9. **checked spelling** using a spell checker and dictionary.

LO3 Editing for Grammar

Do all my . . .

____ 1. **pronouns** have clear antecedents?

____ 2. **pronouns** use the right case (nominative, possessive, objective)?

____ 3. **verbs** have a consistent tense and correct form?

____ 4. **adjectives** and **adverbs** have the right form (positive, comparative, superlative)?

Glossary Terms

equal adjectives
adjectives that equally modify a noun and so can be reversed in order and still make sense

nonrestrictive
not needed for the basic understanding of the sentence

infinitive
to plus the base form of a verb; a phrase that can function as a noun, adjective, or adverb

nominative
case of a word used as a subject or a predicate noun

possessive
case of a word used to show ownership

objective
case of a word used as a direct or indirect object or as the object of a preposition

positive
the base form of an adjective or adverb

comparative
an adjective or adverb that compares something to one other thing

superlative
an adjective or adverb that compares something to two or more things

Glossary Terms

usage
using the correct word

relative pronoun
pronoun that introduces a relative clause; *who, whom, which, that*

indefinite pronoun
pronoun that does not refer to a specific person, place, thing, or idea; *all, another, any, anybody* and so on

antecedent
the word that a pronoun renames or replaces

person
for pronouns, the one speaking (first person), the one being spoken to (second person), or the one being spoken about (third person)

tense
for verbs, the time of an action or state of being; past, present, future

voice
whether the subject of a sentence is doing the action of the verb or is being acted upon by the verb

compound sentence
two or more independent clauses (sentences) joined by a comma and a coordinating conjunction

parallel
similar parts of sentences being expressed in similar grammatical form

LO4 Editing for Usage

Have I used . . .

____ 1. **a** (the article) before consonants and **an** before vowels?

____ 2. **accept** to mean "to receive" and **except** to mean "other than"?

____ 3. **affect** to mean "to influence" and **effect** to mean "the result"?

____ 4. **among** for more than two things and **between** for two things?

____ 5. **bring** for movement toward me and **take** for movement away?

____ 6. **can** for ability and **may** for permission?

____ 7. **cent** for "penny," **sent** for past tense of "send," and **scent** for "odor"?

____ 8. **desert** for "abandon" or "dry place"; **dessert** for a sweet food?

____ 9. **discrete** for "separate" and **discreet** for "modest" or "wise"?

____ 10. **fewer** for countable things and **less** for measurable things?

____ 11. **for** to mean "because" or "meant for" and **four** to mean **4**?

____ 12. **good** as an adjective and **well** as an adverb or as "healthy"?

____ 13. **its** as possessive of "it" and **it's** as a contraction of "it is" or "it has"?

____ 14. **passed** as a verb and **past** as a noun, adjective, or preposition?

____ 15. **poor** as "needy/bad"; **pore** as "hole/to study"; and **pour** as "to flow"?

____ 16. **quiet** as "hushed"; **quit** as "stop"; and **quite** as "very"?

____ 17. **sight** as "something seen"; **cite** as "quote"; and **site** as "location"?

____ 18. **than** for comparing and **then** to tell when?

____ 19. **threw** for past of "throw" and **through** for passing within?

____ 20. **to** as a preposition or in an infinitive; **too** as "also; and **two** as 2?

____ 21. **waist** as a person's middle and **waste** as refuse?

____ 22. **wait** to mean "await" and **weight** to mean measure of mass?

____ 23. **who** as a subject and **whom** as an object?

____ 24. **whose** as a possessive and **who's** as a contraction?

____ 25. **your** as a possessive and **you're** as a contraction?

LO5 Editing for Sentence Errors

Do all of my . . .

____ 1. **subjects and verbs** agree in number (singular/plural)?

____ 2. **compound subjects** joined with and have plural verbs?

____ 3. **compound subjects** joined with or have verbs that match the last subject?

____ 4. **indefinite pronouns subjects** agree with their verbs?

____ 5. **pronouns and antecedents** agree in number and gender?

____ 6. **sentences have consistent person** (first, second, or third)?

____ 7. **sentences have consistent tense** (past, present, or future)?

____ 8. **sentences have consistent voice** (active or passive)?

____ 9. **series have parallel structure** (all nouns, all phrases, all clauses)?

____ 10. **sentences** have a subject and verb and express a complete thought?

____ 11. **compound sentences** have a comma and a coordinating conjunction (or a semicolon) joining the two independent clauses?

____ 12. **modifiers** clearly connect to a nearby word in the sentence?

____ 13. **sentences** avoid ambiguous meanings?

____ 14. **comparisons** clearly show the two things being compared?

____ 15. **conventions** conform to the rules of standard English?

LO1 Editing for Word Choice

When you check the word-choice of your writing, watch for the following issues:

1. Make nouns specific. Avoid using modifiers to prop up a general noun.
2. Make verbs specific, showing instead of telling. Limit your use of "be" verbs, and prefer active verbs to passive verbs.
   Passive: The song was played well by the band.
   Active: The band played the song well.

General			Specific
Person	woman	actress	Meryl Streep
Place	school	university	Notre Dame
Thing	book	novel	*Pride and Prejudice*
Idea	theory	scientific theory	relativity

3. Avoid jargon (insider language) and **cliches** (worn-out expressions).
   Jargon: That drama is a Nielson nonstarter.
   Cliche: That drama jumped the shark.
   Clear: The writing, acting, and premise doom that drama.
4. Replace biased words, which do not show respect for differences in ethnicity, gender, or ability.

LO2 Creating Sentence Variety

Effective sentences provide variety to readers in the following ways:

- **Openings:** Start some sentences with the subject and other sentences with phrases or clauses.
- **Lengths:** Use medium-length sentences for most material. Create short sentence for impact. Use long sentences for complex ideas.
- **Kinds:** Use statements to give information, questions to engage the reader, commands to call readers to act, and conditionals to show how one situation depends on another.
- **Types:** Use simple sentences for straightforward information, compound sentences to connect ideas equally, and complex sentences to show a special relationship between ideas.
- **Arrangement:** Place the main point at the beginning (loose), in the middle (cumulative), or at the end (periodic) of the sentence.

LO3 Sentence Combining and Expanding

1. Combine short choppy sentences by creating a compound or complex sentence.
   Choppy: The pizza arrived. Everybody ate.
   Compound: The pizza arrived, so everybody ate.
   Complex: After the pizza arrived, everybody ate.
2. Expand say-nothing sentences by answering one or more of the 5 W's and H and inserting your responses.
   Say-nothing: They ate.
   Expanded: Devon, Jackson, and Tiresa devoured the pepperoni pizza.

Glossary Terms

passive
construction in which the subject of the sentence is being acted upon by the verb

active
construction in which the subject of the sentence is doing the action of the verb

jargon
an expression understood by only a small group

cliche
a wornt-out expression

bias
an expression that betrays a prejudice

compound sentence
two sentences (independent clauses) joined by a coordinating conjunction or a semicolon

complex sentence
a sentence (independent clause) joined to a group of words with a subject and verb but that can't stand alone (subordinate or relative clause)

Glossary Terms

parallel structure
using similar grammatical structures for similar parts of a sentence

series
a list of three or more items

nominalization
a strong verb turned into a noun and paired with a weak verb

expletive
the construction "here is," "there is," or "it is" at the beginning of a sentence

LO4 Editing for Problem Sentences

When editing sentences, watch for the following common problems, and implement the solutions to the right.

Sentence Problems	Solutions
Short, Choppy	Combine or expand any short, choppy sentences; use the examples and guidelines on pages 82–83.
Flat, Predictable	Rewrite any sentences that sound predictable and uninteresting by varying their structure and expanding them with modifying words, phrases, and clauses.
Incorrect	Look carefully for fragments, run-ons, and comma splices and correct them.
Unclear	Edit any sentences that contain unclear wording, misplaced modifiers, dangling modifiers, or incomplete comparisons.
Unacceptable	Change sentences that include nonstandard language, double negatives, or unparallel construction.
Unnatural	Rewrite sentences that contain jargon, cliches, or flowery language.

LO5 Creating Parallel Sentences

Create effective rhythm in sentences by making sure that similar parts have a similar grammatical structure (e.g., a series of nouns, a list of prepositional phrases, a contrast between two gerund phrases).

1. Keep elements in a series parallel (a series of words, phrases, or clauses).
2. Use both parts of correlative conjunctions (either, or; neither, nor; not only, but also; as, so; whether, or; both, and).
3. Keep compound elements parallel (whether compound subjects, compound predicates, compound objects, compound sentences).
4. Keep comparisons parallel (using the same units of measure—for example, not mixing hours and days or kilometers and miles).

LO6 Removing Poor Construction

As you edit, watch for the following poor sentence constructions and rework the sentences to improve them:

1. **Remove nominalizations:** A nominalization occurs when a strong verb is converted to a noun and paired with a weak verb. Liberate the verb to make the sentence energetic.
   Sluggish: I give a recommendation that we have a discussion about this.
   Energetic: I recommend that we discuss this.
2. **Get rid of expletives:** Sentences that begin with "there is," "here is," or "it is" begin with expletives—constructions that make the sentence sluggish. Rework such sentences to remove the expletives.
   Sluggish: It is clear that there is an error in this HTML code.
   Energetic: This HTML code contains an error.
3. **Remove negative constructions:** Negative words state something that is not rather than something that is. Make language positive and direct.
   Negative: I have not failed to pay my share of the rent and have not avoided doing my share of the housework.
   Positive: I pay my share of the rent and do my share of the housework.

LO1 Understanding Primary, Secondary, and Tertiary Sources

Not all sources are created equal. Consider these three types:

- **Primary sources** are firsthand information such as diaries, interviews, surveys, experiments, and events you observe. They provide unfiltered information for your research.
- **Secondary sources** are secondhand reports such as journal articles, documentaries, encyclopedia entries, and nonfiction books. They add expert authority to your research but may also contain bias.
- **Tertiary sources** (such as Wikipedia) are based on secondary sources and add a level of distance and possible distortion. *Do not include tertiary sources in college research.*

LO2 Conducting Primary Research

- **Surveys** and **questionnaires** can help gather responses from a variety of people.
- **Interviews** (personal, by phone, or by mail or e-mail) allow you to ask questions of an expert.
- **Observations, inspections,** and **field research** give you personal experience with a subject.
- **Experiments** test your hypotheses (educated predictions) about a subject.
- **Analysis** of documents and artifacts involves studying and evaluating original reports, statistics, literature, artworks, and historical documents.

Survey Tips

- Focus your survey to suit your topic.
- Phrase questions to be easily understood.
- Use neutral language to not skew results.
- Use *closed questions* to gather chartable data.
- Use *open-ended questions* for more complex responses.

Interview Tips

- Prepare and review your questions beforehand.
- Ask open-ended questions to gain rich answers.
- Take notes or record the interview for accuracy.
- Thank the person interviewed.

Analysis Tips

- Choose documents specific to your topic.
- Guide your examination with research questions.
- Consider the document or artifact in its own context.

Glossary Terms

survey/questionnaire
a set of questions created to gather information from respondents about a specific topic

observation
information gained in person through the senses

inspection
the purposeful analysis of a site or situation

field research
on-site scientific study to gather raw data

closed question
a question answerable with a *yes*, a *no*, or a simple fact

open-ended question
a question requiring an answer that explains or expands upon the topic

Glossary Terms

forum/message board
an Internet site where members can post messages to discuss a topic

mailing list (e-mail)
a program that sends messages to a set of e-mail addresses

RSS feed
a program that converts forum or blog posts to a file for easy access by "RSS reader" software or by e-mail

LO3 Conducting Secondary Research

Secondary research involves information published in one medium or another.

Library Research

Your college library exists to help your research succeed.

- **Librarians** are information experts who manage the library's materials and guide you to resources. They can also help with online searches.
- **Collections** are materials housed in the library: books, periodicals, reference publications, electronic recordings, and special collections.
- **Research tools** include the library catalog, print indexes, subscription databases of information, and Internet access to other sources.
- **Special services** are options including interlibrary loans, services to "hold" or "reserve" materials, photocopiers, audio players, and so on.

See pages 324–325 for guidelines to searching library catalogs.

Internet Research

The Internet connects computers together around the world, allowing them to share information.

- **World Wide Web:** Much—but not all—of the Net is available on the Web. Many organizations host Web sites to make information available by browser search.
- **Deep Web:** Some Internet materials are available only by subscription or by special Internet connection. Your library has access to many.
- **E-Mail:** Experts on a subject can often be reached by e-mail to answer questions or verify information.
- **Forums, message boards, mailing lists,** and **RSS** feeds provide access to people discussing your topic.

LO4 Finding Reliable Information

Electronic publishing and on-demand printing have led to an explosion of information. Evaluating reliability is essential.

- **Scholarly publications**, whether journals or books, are peer reviewed and generally trustworthy.
- **Domain name extensions** tell the type of Web site: *.edu* and *.gov* are educational and government sites; *.com* and *.biz* are commercial; *.org* is often nonprofit.
- **Credentials** such as degrees and official positions can help to verify authority.
- **Date** of publication indicates how timely a source is.
- **Balance** of views shows depth of thought in a source.
- **Comments** help to rate a source's value.

LO1 Asking for Feedback in a Writing Workshop

When you revise, the feedback of a reader can make a huge difference. Follow these tips to get a helpful response.

- **Choose the right reader.** Find someone who is not familiar with your paper but also isn't completely unfamiliar with your topic. Choose someone who will be honest but also who wants you to succeed.
- **Share the original assignment.** Your reviewer can't help much without knowing what the paper is supposed to do.
- **Share your own goal for the paper.** Say what you are trying to accomplish.
- **Focus the feedback.** Tell the person what depth of criticism you want (e.g., a quick proofread or suggestions for rewriting). If you are stuck in one area or are worried especially about one part, tell your reader.
- **Tell how you want the feedback.** If you want the person to mark up your paper, say so. If you want a conversation, say so.
- **Give the reader space.** Don't hover. Tell the person to let you know when he or she is ready to respond.
- **Focus on the writing, not on your emotions.** Don't feel threatened or defensive about the feedback. Listen and glean what you can.
- **Thank the reader.** Just as it's tough to receive a critique, it's tough to give one, and if the person helped you, let her or him know that.

LO2 Providing Feedback in a Writing Workshop

When someone asks you to read and respond to a paper, take the responsibility seriously. Use these tips to provide a helpful critique.

- **Ask about the paper.** Find out what the original assignment is, when it is due, what level of feedback the person wants, what concerns the person has, and whether you can mark up the paper.
- **Read the whole paper once before responding.** You can jot a few notes and first impressions on another piece of paper, but don't make up your mind about anything until you read the paper at least once more.
- **Record your comments.** If possible, annotate the paper. Point out positives as well as negatives.
- **Start with the positive.** Doing so lets the person know you are trying to help and creates a sense of teamwork.
- **Focus on the work.** Talk about the words, sentences, paragraphs, and ideas, not about the writer. Use *you* and *your* positively if at all.
- **Focus on solutions rather than problems.** Doing so is the difference between constructive and destructive criticism. Don't say, "this is all mixed up" but "if we rearrange these details, this part would be clearer."
- **Be honest but tactful.** Tell the truth in a way the person can benefit. Read the writer's face, tone, and body language for cues of how he or she is receiving the response.
- **Be specific.** General comments like "this is really good" or "this isn't very good" don't help. Tell why something works or doesn't.
- **Step back.** Let the writer decide how to proceed.

Glossary Terms

feedback
response to writing

proofread
a close read at the final stages of a writing project, focusing on specific issues of punctuation, mechanics, usage, and grammar

critique
an evaluation of what is working and what needs to work better in a piece of writing

annotate
write notes on

constructive criticism
honest feedback intended to improve a piece of writing

destructive criticism
dishonest feedback or honest feedback intended to discourage or mock the writer

tactful
providing truthful criticism in a way that the person can receive and use it

Glossary Terms

writing center
a service offered by colleges and universities to help students improve their writing

tutoring
work with a tutor or mentor who can help an individual writer improve

style manual
guide to the writing style expected within a particular field of study

workshop
event providing concentrated writing practice

OWL
online writing lab

LO3 Understanding the Writing Center

Most colleges and universities have a writing center to assist students with improving their papers. Here are common features of many writing centers.

- **One-on-one tutoring:** You can usually make an appointment to take your writing to the writing center and sit down with a tutor, who will read your work and give you advice.
- **Style manuals and support:** Most writing centers offer style manuals (MLA, APA, CMS, and so on) as well as knowledgeable staff to answer your questions about these styles.
- **Workshops:** Often, writing centers offer free or paid workshops to provide a focused experience to improve your writing.
- **Jobs:** Writing centers often need skilled student writers who can mentor and tutor other writers. If you are interested in such a position, ask for qualifications and an application.
- **Online support:** In addition to offering tutoring sessions online, many writing centers also are active through social media such as forums, blogs, microblogs, message boards, and wikis. Some schools offer online writing labs that provide all kinds of support (such as Purdue's famous OWL) to students and the public, alike.

LO4 Understanding the Writer's Role and the Advisor's Role

A successful session at the writing center depends on knowing what you are supposed to do. In addition to following the advice provided on the front of this card, check the quick guide below:

Writer's Role	Mentor's Role
Be respectful	Make you feel at home
Be ready to work	Discuss your needs
Decide on a topic	Help you choose a topic
Know your purpose and audience	Discuss your purpose and audience
Embrace the best ideas	Help you generate ideas
Consider other points of view; stretch your own perspective	Help you develop your logic
Do the research	Help you understand how to research your material
Share your writing	Read your draft
Recognize and fix problems	Identify problems in organization, logic, expression, and format
Learn important principles	Teach ways to correct weaknesses
Correct all errors	Help you with grammar, usage, diction, vocabulary, and mechanics

LO1 Understanding Page Design

Design elements help make text easy to read and concepts easy to grasp. In general, follow these guidelines…

Formatting

- Use clean white paper.
- Set one-inch margins on all sides.

For research reports, also use the appropriate style guidelines (such as MLA or APA).

Typography

Use…

- **Serif** type in 10- or 12-point size for the body text. (Serif letters, like this text, have "tails" at top and bottom.)
- **Sans serif** type for headings. (Sans serif letters, like this text, have no "tails.") Also use a larger size—such as 18 point for the paper title and 14 point for other headings.

Spacing

Avoid…

- **Orphans**: An orphan is a single line of a new paragraph at the bottom of a page.
- **Widows:** A widow is a single word or line at the top of a page, from a previous paragraph.
- **Tombstones:** A tombstone is a heading alone at the bottom of a page.

Graphic devices

Use…

- **Lists,** like those on this page, to make parallel information quickly scannable.
- **Bulleted** lists show that items are equivalent.
1. **Numbered** lists indicate a sequence or hierarchy.
- **Illustrations** and **diagrams** to picture information.

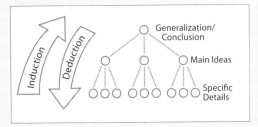

- **Tables** and **charts** to present numbers and other facts in an easily grasped form.

	Singular	Plural
First Person	I am	we are
Second Person	you are	you are
Third Person	he, she, it is	they are

LO2 Using MLA Paper Format

For an MLA paper, follow the example layout below.

Hughey 1

Katie Hughey
Professor E. K. Trump
Political Science 350
17 April 2008

centered
An American Hybrid:
double spaced,
paragraph indent

The Art Museum as Public-Private Institution

The American art museum suffers from a multiple personality disorder. It is a strange hybrid, both public and private in nature, and beholden to a constituency so varied in its interests that the function of the museum has become increasingly difficult to discern. Much of the confusion surrounding the nature and proper function of the art museum in the United States has to do with the unique form that arts patronage has taken in this country. There is a primary difficulty facing funding of the arts in America—namely, the fact that the benefits of art and art museums are not easily stated in the simple utilitarian terms that justify expenditures on things like roads and a police force. For this reason, cultural patronage has largely been a private venture. The first American museums were born of the private collections of robber barons, organized as not-for-profit corporations, and placed under the control of private boards of trustees. Only subsequently were municipal governments asked to contribute by way of funding construction costs for new buildings and providing maintenance expenses.

The involvement of the government in the funding of art museums raises several questions that serve to highlight the confusing hybrid nature of this uniquely American cultural institution. First, why do governments fund museums at all? The short answer involves the educational benefits conferred on the public by art museums. But once a municipality has taken on the task of paying for a public service that happens to be provided by an autonomous private institution, the real question becomes one of control. Who exactly "owns" the museum? If the stated goal of the museum enterprise is public in nature, while the works hanging on the walls and the programs offered by the museum are supported mainly by private funds, to whom is the museum accountable? Is it appropriate, for example, for a museum . . .

Hughey 10

double spaced,
hanging indent

centered
Works Cited

Becker, Carol. "The Brooklyn Controversy: A View from the Bridge." Rothfield 15-21.

Bowie, David. *BowieNet.* Davidbowie.com, n.d. Web. 5 April 2008.

Cuno, James. "Sensation and the Ethics of Funding Exhibitions." Rothfield 162-70.

Edelson, Gilbert. "Some Sensational Reflections." Rothfield 171-80.

Edelstein, Teri. "Sensational or Status Quo: Museums and Public Perception." Rothfield 104-14.

Fraser, Andrea. "A Sensation Chronicle." *Social Text* 19.2 (2001): 127-56. Print.

Halle, David, et al. "The Attitude of the Audience for 'Sensation' and of the General Public Toward Controversial Works of Art." Rothfield 134-52.

Levine, Peter. "Lessons from the Brooklyn Museum Controversy." *Philosophy and Public Policy Quarterly* 20.2-3 (2000): n. pag. Web. 7 April 2008.

Meyer, Karl. *The Art Museum: Power, Money, Ethics.* New York: Morrow, 1979. Print.

Presser, Stephen. "Reasons We Shouldn't Be Here: Things We Cannot Say." Rothfield 52-71.

Ross, David. "An All-Too-Predictable Sensation." Rothfield 96-103.

Rothfield, Lawrence, ed. *Unsettling Sensation: Arts-Policy Lessons from the Brooklyn Museum of Art Controversy.* New Brunswick: Rutgers UP, 2001. Print. Rutgers Ser. on the Public Life of the Arts.

Schuster, J. Mark. "Who Should Pay (for the Arts and Culture)? Who Should Decide? And What Difference Should It Make?" Rothfield 72-89.

Smolensky, Eugene. "Municipal Financing of the U.S. Fine Arts Museum: A Historical Rationale." *Journal of Economic History* 46.3 (1986): 757-68. Print.

Stántó, András. "Don't Shoot the Messenger: Why the Art World and the Press Don't Get Along." Rothfield 181-98.

Steinfels, Margaret. "Virgins No More." *Commonweal* 19 May 2000: 23-24. Print.

Strauss, David. "The False Promise of Free Speech." Rothfield 44-51.

MLA and APA Format: Use 1-inch margins on all sides. Set page numbers, and APA running head, 1/2 inch from top.

LO3 Using APA Paper Format

For an APA paper, follow the example layout below.

Running head: OUR ROOTS GO BACK TO ROANOKE   1

centered
Our Roots Go Back to Roanoke:
Investigating the Link between
the Lost Colony and the Lumbee People of North Carolina
Renee Danielle Singh
University of California Davis

OUR ROOTS GO BACK TO ROANOKE   3

centered
Our Roots Go Back to Roanoke:
Investigating the Link between the Lost Colony
and the Lumbee People of North Carolina

double spaced,
paragraph indent

Introduction: Something is Terribly Wrong

Consider the following narrative, which features historical information from Kupperman (1984, 1985), Miller (2002), Oberg (1994), and Quinn (1985):

Imagine yourself sailing across the warm waters of the Atlantic. It is a time before airplanes and automobiles, and our nation, which someday will lie just a few miles ahead of you, is still called the "New World." You are on your way to an island off the coast of what will one day be called North at

OUR ROOTS GO BACK TO ROANOKE   2

centered
Abstract

double-spaced,
no paragraph
indent

While remaining something of a mystery, the disappearance in the late sixteenth century of a group of colonists from Roanoke Island off North Carolina is likely related to the mystery of the ancestry of the North Carolina's Native American Lumbee tribe. Using evidence from the parallel example of the Catawba Indians, as well as evidence related to baldcypress tree rings, historical analysis, immunology, genetic studies, and linguistic patterns, one can tentatively conclude that the lost colonists were perhaps captured by, intermarried with, and were absorbed by the sixteenth-century ancestors of the Lumbee. This conclusion points to the need for further study, as the Lumbee People's status as Native American is currently contested and needs to be resolved for them to be recognized by the federal government.

OUR ROOTS GO BACK TO ROANOKE   12

double spaced,
hanging indent

centered
References

Beltrane, T., & McQueen, D. V. (1979). Urban and rural Indian drinking patterns: The special case of the Lumbee. *International Journal of the Addictions, 14*(4), 533-548.

Blu, K. I. (1980). *The Lumbee problem: The making of an American Indian people.* Cambridge: Cambridge University Press.

Bryant, A., Goins, R. T., Bell, R., Herrell, R., Manson, S. M., & Buchwald, D. (2004). Health differences among Lumbee Indians using public and private sources of care. *Journal of Rural Health, 20*(3), 231-236.

While the writing process always involves the same steps, details may change from task to task and writer to writer.

1. Starting

- **Consider the assignment:** The assignment itself may tell you exactly how to proceed. (E.g. *Write one page about your thoughts* on "The Secret Sharer.")
- **Cluster or web:** To find a focus, consider clustering words around a central idea.

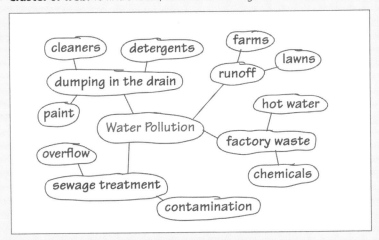

- **List:** A simple list of thoughts can often get you going.
- **Freewrite:** In *Writing without Teachers,* Peter Elbow argues that not only is freewriting good for starting, it can also apply to drafting and revising. Your writing becomes more focused and polished with each pass.
- **Talk:** Sometimes discussing an assignment with someone—thinking out loud—can get ideas moving. Similarly, imagining a listener can keep writing going.

2. Planning

- **Schedule:** Publishing companies schedule backward from a due date. You can, too. For big projects, mark a calendar with each step, counting backward from final edit, to leave enough time for each step.
- **Form a thesis statement:** This defines your aim, like the destination of a journey. But your goal may shift along the way, as you learn more about the topic.
- **Know your subject:** Do your research before you begin writing. Consider what you already know, then go looking for information to expand on that and fill in any gaps. *Take careful notes to avoid source abuses.*
- **List or outline:** Whether casual or formal, a map of points you plan to make, in order, along with critical supporting points, can help with the next step: drafting.

3. Drafting

- **Draft freely:** Turn off the critical part of your brain and focus on ideas.
- **Use your plan or outline as a guide:** But feel free to deviate from it as new ideas arise.
- **Look away from the monitor:** Don't let your computer's spelling and grammar suggestions distract you at this stage. Just write.
- **Imagine your reader:** One way to avoid getting stuck is to write as if you were speaking out loud to a friendly reader. Remember, you can always revise later.

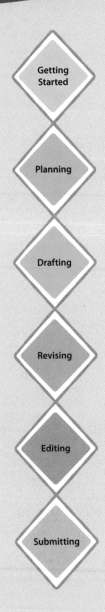

Getting Started

Planning

Drafting

Revising

Editing

Submitting

Getting Started

Planning

Drafting

Revising

Editing

Submitting

4. Revising

- **Take a break:** Avoid revising immediately after drafting. Turn your mind to something else for a while, then come back with a fresh perspective.
- **Get a second opinion:** Even professional writers have editors. Use the university writing center or ask a peer to read your writing and to point out what works well and what they find confusing or missing.
- **Revise more than once:**
  - *Revise once for general organization.* Rearrange parts as necessary to make the overall order of ideas flow smoothly.
  - *Revise again for details* and to fill in any unclear sections. Fine-tune your message from beginning to end.
- **Don't settle for "close enough":** The revising step is the time to turn on the critical part of the brain that you turned off during drafting.

5. Editing

- **Take a break again:** As with revising, editing requires a fresh perspective. So let your writing sit for a while.
- **Edit more than once:**
  - *Edit once for style,* making sure that sentences flow smoothly, that transitions carry the reader from idea to idea, and that every word is exactly what you mean to say. (Your computer dictionary and thesaurus can help.)
  - *Edit again for correctness,* checking spelling, grammar, punctuation, and word usage, to make sure no careless error distracts from your message.
- **Use proofreading strategies:**
  - *Use your computer spellchecker and grammar checker.* These will catch many careless errors (but not problems like their instead of there.)
  - *Proofread out loud.* Often, pronouncing each word as you check it helps to catch any errors.
  - *Proofread from back to front.* If it helps, start with the last word of your document and move toward the front to check each word out of context.
- **Ask for help:** Again, professional authors have proofreaders. And studies show that even college professors make more mistakes in spelling and grammar when writing about difficult topics. So don't be afraid to ask someone to check your work.

6. Publishing

In our electronic age, writing often finds publication in more than one venue. So after you prepare a clean final copy to hand in to your professor, keep another copy for publication in an online journal, blog, or message board.

LO1 Using Evidence to Support an Argument

A position statement is only as strong as the support for it. Use different types of support to achieve different effects in your arguments.

Support	Use to ...	Example
Analogies	connect what is known to what is unknown	Lobbyists create a false reality around legislators, much as groupies do around a rock band.
Analyses	break a topic into parts and examine their connection	Lobbyists use the private citizen's right to free speech to benefit organizations and corporations.
Anecdotes	demonstrate an idea through a story	Jack Abramoff went to prison for his lobbying practices and now is calling for Beltway reform.
Facts	ground arguments in what is not debatable	Past attempts to reform lobbying rules have failed in part due to lobbyists, themselves.
Demonstrations	show how to do something or how something works	As political action committees demonstrate, ingenious minds find ways around regulation.
Illustrations	show what you mean, providing a clear example	If a group spends $10 million on lobbying, it expects to gain $10 million worth of influence.
Graphics	represent data in a graphic way to show relationships	2008 $3.30 Billion 2009 $3.49 Billion 2010 $3.51 Billion
Logic	build support through premises, inferences, and conclusions	Paying a member of Congress for influence is illegal, but paying someone else to influence the member is standard practice.
Predictions	connect current conditions with the future	If lobbying reform passes, citizens' trust of government would be strengthened.
Quotations	let experts and others speak for themselves	*Time* magazine dubbed Jack Abramoff the "man who bought Washington."
Sensations	make arguments vivid through sights, sounds, smells and so on	Once deals were made in the blue cigar smoke of back rooms. Now they are made over mai tais on bright beaches in the Bahamas.
Statistics	quantify information, telling how much or how long	Last year, Google spent over $6 million and Facebook over $1 million to lobby Congress.

Glossary Terms

analogy
comparison between something unknown and something known

analysis
use of comparison, definition, classification, and similar strategies to closely study something

anecdote
a brief story that makes a point

demonstration
performance showing how something works

logic
a series of statements used to reach a conclusion

sensation
sights, sounds, aromas, tastes, and touch experiences (weight, texture, heat, position)

statistics
factual information that uses measurements to quantify something

Glossary Terms

credibility
believability

tone
the quality of writing that reveals the author's feeling about the topic

logic
a series of statements used to reach a conclusion

logical fallacies
fuzzy or false forms of reasoning

premise
statement taken as "given" within a logical argument

inference
statement drawn from previous premises or inferences

conclusion
final statement derived from an argument

countering
overcoming an objection by solving the problem or showing it doesn't matter

conceding
recognizing an objection as valid before moving on

LO2 Creating Effective Appeals

Aristotle identified three types of appeals that you can make in a rhetorical argument to convince your audience.

Appeal to Credibility

The reader's first question is whether you are a reliable source of information. To appeal to credibility, do the following.

- **Be thoroughly honest,** not falsifying data, ignoring facts, or failing to document sources.
- **Make realistic claims** and support them with facts.
- **Use a reasonable tone,** showing your serious commitment to the topic but avoiding overly emotional language.
- **Treat the subject and the reader respectfully** and avoid shortcuts in thinking.

Appeal to Logic

Build your argument carefully, avoiding logical fallacies, which only weaken your position.

- **Start with reliable premises** that readers will readily accept.
- **Derive inferences from premises,** showing each step of your argument.
- **Draw careful conclusions,** which can become premises for additional arguments.
- **Recognize objections** and address them by countering or conceding them.
- **Appeal to Needs**

Think about what your reader needs, wants, and values. Instead of showing how your position benefits you, show how it benefits the reader.

Study Abraham Maslow's hierarchy of human needs (below and to the left). Lower levels in this pyramid need to be satisfied before upper levels become important. Decide which needs on this pyramid you wish to appeal to, and show how your position helps the reader with this need.

morality, creativity, problem solving

self-esteem, respect, achievement, confidence

friendship, family, acceptance

health, property, security, employment

air, water, food, clothing, shelter, sleep

Need	Topic/Action	Appeal
to improve the world	helping others	to values and social obligation
to achieve	being good at something	to self-fulfillment, status
to achieve	getting recognition	to appreciation
to belong	being part of a group	to group identity, acceptance
to survive	avoiding threats	to safety, security
to survive	having necessities	to physical needs

LO1 APA Documentation

APA documentation involves two parts: (1) an in-text citation within your text whenever you incorporate a source and (2) a matching bibliographic entry in a "References" page at the end of your text. In the example below, "Pollitzer et al." and "(1967)" tell the reader that

- the borrowed material came from a source written by a group of authors including Pollitzer and others.
- the source material was published in 1967.
- full source details are in the references list under "Pollitzer et al."

1. In-Text Citation in the Body of the Writing

> As Pollitzer et al. explain (1967), in 1962 the Catawba opted to terminate their reservation status, thus relinquishing all forms of federal recognition.

2. Matching References Entry at the End of the Paper

> Pollitzer, W. S., Phelps, D. S., Waggoner, R. E., & Leyshon, W. C. (1967). Catawba Indians: morphology, genetics, and history. *American Journal of Physical Anthropology, 26*(1), 5-14.

LO2 The Basics: In-Text Citation

In APA, in-text citations generally follow these guidelines:

1. Refer to the author, date of publication, and page number (when citing a specific part) by using one of these methods:
   Last name and publication year in parentheses:

> Game-design training opportunities are limited for minorities (Galuszka, 2009).

   Name cited in sentence, publication year in parentheses (page number included in this example):

> Baker notes it was parents who pressed the case "that autism had become epidemic and that vaccines were its cause" (2008, p. 251).

2. Present and punctuate citations according to these rules:
   - Clearly indicate where cited material begins and ends.
   - List authors in text by last name only.
   - Include the publication date in parentheses.
   - Give any page numbers as numerals, not words.
   - In parentheses, separate author name, date, and any page numbers with commas.
   - Use *p.* for a page number and *pp.* for multiple pages.

Glossary Terms

APA
the American Psychological Association, which publishes a manuscript style for the "soft" sciences

documentation
notations in text, pointing to outside sources of information

references list
in APA style, a list of all sources referred to in a paper or article

in-text citation
a reference within the body of an article to an entry in a matching references list

Glossary Terms

doi
digital object identifier, intended to en-sure an electronic source can be found even if its online location changes

Ed., Eds.
abbreviation *for editor* and *editors*

periodical
a journal or magazine, with issues pub-lished on a schedule

N.d.
abbreviation for *no date*

Trans.
abbreviation for *translator*

LO3 The Basics: References

Although sources can come in a variety of forms, the most commonly cited types are periodicals and books. For online postings other than articles and books, APA suggests citing a specific page.

Template for a Periodical Article:

Author's Last Name, Initial(s), Next Author's Last Name, initial(s), & Next Author's Last Name, Initial(s). (year). Article title. *Periodical Title, volume*(issue), pp-pp. doi:00-000000000

Online with doi

Oberg, A. Blades, D., & Thom, J. S. (2007). Untying a dreamcatcher: Coming to understand possibilities for teaching students of aboriginal inheritance. *Educational Studies, 42*(2), 111-139. doi:10.1080/00131940701513185

Online without doi

Cohen J. A. (2008). Treating PTSD and related symptoms in children. *PSTD Research Quarterly, 19*(2), 1-3. Retrieved from http://www.ptsd.va.gov/professional/newsletters/research-quarterly/V19N2.pdf

Print periodical

Benson, P., Karlof, K. L., & Siperstein, G. N. (2008) Maternal involvement in the education of young children with autism spectrum disorders. *Autism: The International Journal of Research and Practice 12*(1), 47-63.

Template for a Book Entry:

Author's Last Name, Initial(s). Book title. Location: Publisher.

Work by one author

Sacks, O. (1995). *An anthropologist on Mars: Seven paradoxical tales.* New York, NY: Alfred A. Knopf.

Chapter in a larger work

Guy, G. R. (2005). Variationist approaches to phonological change. In B. D. Joseph & R. D. Janda (Eds.), *The handbook of historical linguistics* (pp. 369-400). Malden, MA: Blackwell.

Template for a Web Item:

Author's Last Name, Initial(s). (date). *Document title.* Retrieved from URL

Kafka, F. (2005, August 16). *Metamorphosis.* D. Wylie (Trans.). Retrieved from http://www.Gutenberg.org/etext/5200

LO1 MLA Documentation

The MLA system involves two parts: (1) an in-text citation within your paper when you use a source and (2) a matching bibliographic entry at the end of your paper. In the example below, "Edith Kramer" and "(28)" tell the reader that

- the borrowed material came from a source written by Edith Kramer.
- the specific material can be found on page 28 of the source.
- full source details are in the works-cited list under the author's last name.

1. **In-Text Citation in Body of Paper**

> Child psychologist Edith Kramer reflects that "in adult life, art . . . [is] one of the few areas of symbolic living that remain accessible" (28).

2. **Matching Works-Cited Entry at End of Paper**

> Kramer, Edith. *Art as Therapy with Children*. New York: Schocken, 1971. Print.

LO2 The Basics: In-Text Citation

In MLA, in-text citations typically follow these guidelines:

1. Refer to the author (plus the work's title, if helpful) and a page number by using one of these methods:

Last name and page number in parentheses:

> Another reoccurring theme in the art of anorectics is an isolated figure often surrounded by dark colors or stormy weather (Acharya, Wood, and Robinson 11).
>
> Last names only in citation · No comma between names and page number · No "p." for "page"

Name cited in sentence, page number in parentheses:

> Full names in first reference
>
> Psychiatrists Madushree Acharya, Michéle Wood, and Paul Robinson describe the somatic parallel between anorexia and art therapy when they write, "Like the pathological expression of [issues] through the illness, the patient is working through her body; the all important difference is that art therapy is creative and non self-harming" (13).

2. Present and punctuate citations according to these rules:
- Place the parenthetical reference after the source material.
- Within the parentheses, normally give the author's last name only.
- Do not put a comma between the author's last name and the page reference.
- Cite the page number as a numeral, not a word.
- Don't use *p., pp.,* or *page(s)* before the page number(s).
- Place any sentence punctuation after the closed parenthesis.

Glossary Terms

MLA
the Modern Language Association; the professional organization that sets style decisions for English and humanities disciplines

in-text citation
references within the text of a research report, indicating the origin of summarized, paraphrased, or quoted materials

works-cited list
in an MLA paper, a list of all sources cited within the paper, arranged alphabetically by author's last name

LO3 The Basics: Works Cited

While specific types of resources follow variations, here are works-cited templates for the most common entries:

Template for Book:

Author's Last Name, First Name. *Title of Book*. Publication City: Publisher, year of publication. Medium. (Other publication details are integrated as needed.)

Rabin, Murray. *Art Therapy and Eating Disorders*. New York: Columbia UP, 2003. Print.

Template for Periodical Article in an Online Database:

Author's Last Name, First Name. "Title of Article." *Journal Title* volume, issue, and/or date
details: page numbers. *Title of Database*. Medium. Date of access.

Johnson, Karen, and Sarah Parkinson. "There's No Point Raging on Your Own: Using Art
Therapy Groups for People with Eating Disorders." *Group Analysis* 32.1 (Mar. 1999):
87-96. *Academic Search Premier*. Web. 16 Oct. 2010.

Note: If you read the print article, end the citation after the page numbers with "Print" as the medium.

Template for a Web Document:

Author's or Editor's Last Name, First Name (if available). "Title of Page, Posting, or Document." *Title of Web site* (if different from document title). Version or edition used. Publisher or sponsor of site (if known; if not, use N.p.), Date of publication, last update, or
posting (if known; if not, use n.d.). Medium. Date of access.

"Canadian Art Therapy Association: FAQ." Canadian Art Therapy Association, Nov. 2008.
Web. 6 Nov. 2010.

LO4 Format of the Works-Cited Page

The MLA system offers guidelines for the format of the works-cited list. The basics are shown below.

Format for the Works-Cited List

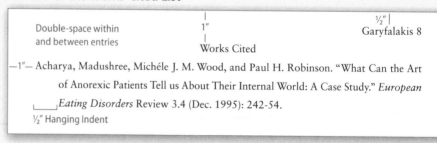

Double-space within
and between entries

1"

½" |
Garyfalakis 8

Works Cited

—1"— Acharya, Madushree, Michéle J. M. Wood, and Paul H. Robinson. "What Can the Art
of Anorexic Patients Tell us About Their Internal World: A Case Study." *European*
Eating Disorders Review 3.4 (Dec. 1995): 242-54.

½" Hanging Indent

LO1 Writing an Application Letter

An application (or cover) letter introduces you to an employer and often highlights information on an accompanying résumé.

Prewrite: Ideas and Organization
- **Research the employer.** What does the company do?
- **Research the position.** What does the job involve?
- **Evaluate your résumé.** Which of your skills and experiences match the job requirements?
- **Identify the contact person(s).** Who will be evaluating your application? What will that person be looking for?

Draft: Ideas, Organization, and Voice

Opening Use a courteous but confident voice.

- Identify the position you seek.
- State your main qualification.

Middle Show how your qualifications fill the reader's needs.

- Give résumé highlights that match the job description.
- Show your knowledge of and interest in the company.

Closing Encourage follow-up contact.

- Request an interview.
- Explain when and where you may be reached.

Revise: Ideas, Organization, Voice, Words, and Sentences
- Is your language clear and business like?
- Do you focus on the reader?

Edit: Conventions and Design
- Is your letter free of errors?
- Is it formatted in a businesslike manner?

LO2 Writing a Recommendation-Request Letter

When applying for a position, you may be asked for references. Be prepared by sending a recommendation-request letter to each desired referral. Include the following in your requests:

Opening Greet the recipient politely.

- Remind the person who you are.
- Explain that you are seeking a recommendation.

Middle Identify the situation.

- Explain why the recipient is suited to judge your abilities.
- Identify the position for which you are applying.
- Briefly tell how your abilities and interests match it.
- Ask for a recommendation.
- Explain where the recommendation should be sent.

Closing Thank the person.

Glossary Terms

application letter
a letter introducing you and your résumé to a possible employer

résumé
a document outlining your training, skills, and experience, plus contact information

recommendation-request letter
a letter asking a trainer, colleague, former employer, or other person to vouch for your abilities

referral
someone to whom other people can be referred for a recommendation about you

Glossary Terms

LO3 Writing a Résumé

The purpose of a résumé is to give readers an easy reference to your skills and abilities. Ideally, your résumé should be revised to suit each position you apply for.

There are two primary résumé formats:

1. Use **chronological** format to feature your employment history—especially if your experience matches the position you seek.
2. Use **functional** format to feature a body of skills that match the position you seek—especially new skills, or if your employment history is short or has gaps.

Sample Chronological Résumé

Contact information leads the résumé.	Pat Colter 3117 Augusta Street Freemont, Oklahoma 73198 (360) 354-5916 p.w.colter@alum.uok-freemont.edu
The desired position is identified.	**Job Objective** Staff writer for *Freemont Daily Clarion*
Special awards, skills, and other highlights are featured.	**Distinctions** Feature of the Year, 2011, for "Global Good: Okies Shape the World Through Microlending" University Honors Scholar, 2011 Marcelle Deluce Award for Outstanding Undergraduate in Journalism, 2010
For a functional résumé, the writer would list experience as "Qualifications and Skills" instead, without dates.	**Employment History** Summer 2011: Intern at *Freemont Daily Clarion* Wrote a weekly human-interest story. Edited local sports stories written by paper's owner. Proofread ad copy. Fall 2010 to Spring 2012: Staff Writer for UOK-Freemont *Voice* Wrote local sports stories at high school and college levels. Averaged one feature weekly and many game summaries. Covered university board and civic government meetings. Averaged two stories per week. Spring 2009: News Reporter, WHLT College Radio Wrote and reported a weekly human-interest program.
Applicable degrees and diplomas are listed.	**Education** 2012: B.A., Journalism, University of Oklahoma-Freemont 2008: Graduate, Writing Program, Freemont School of the Arts